The Journey
of Adulthood

The Journey
of Adulthood

SIXTH EDITION

Barbara R. Bjorklund
FLORIDA ATLANTIC UNIVERSITY

Helen L. Bee

PEARSON
Prentice
Hall

Pearson Education International

Editorial Director: Leah Jewell
Executive Editor: Jeff Marshall
Assistant Editor: LeeAnn Doherty
Supplements Editor: Richard Virginia
Editorial Assistant: Jennifer Puma
Director of Marketing: Brandy Dawson
Senior Marketing Manager: Jeanette Moyer
Assistant Marketing Manager: Billy Grieco
Marketing Assistant: Laura Kennedy
Managing Editor (Production):
    Maureen Richardson
Production Liaison: Randy Pettit
Manufacturing Manager: Nick Sklitsis

Manufacturing Buyer: Sherry Lewis
Cover Design: Jayne Conte
Director, Image Resource Center: Melinda Reo
Manager, Rights and Permissions: Zina Arabia
Manager, Visual Research: Beth Brenzel
Manager, Cover Visual Research and Permissions:
    Karen Sanatar
Composition/Full-Service Project Management:
    Bruce Hobart, Pine Tree Composition, Inc.
Interior Design: L. P. Zeidenstein
Cover Printer: Phoenix Color Corp.
Printer/Binder: The Courier Companies, Inc.

Credits and acknowledgments for material borrowed from other sources and reproduced, with permission, in this textbook appear on appropriate page within text (or on page 409).

Pearson Education LTD. , London
Pearson Education Australia PTY, Limited
Pearson Education Singapore, Pte. Ltd
Pearson Education North Asia Ltd
Pearson Education Canada, Inc.
Pearson Educación de Mexico, S.A. de C.V.
Pearson Education -- Japan
Pearson Education Malaysia, Pte. Ltd
Pearson Education, Upper Saddle River, New Jersey

10 9 8 7 6 5 4 3 2 1
ISBN 13: 978-0-13-506713-0
ISBN 10: 0-13-506713-8

For my twin grandchildren
Aaron Keith Zeman
and
Alese Kristine Zeman
You are my sunshine!
BRB

Brief Contents

Preface   xv

1   Introduction to Adult Development   3

2   Physical Changes   33

3   Health and Health Disorders   69

4   Cognitive Abilities   101

5   Social Roles   130

6   Social Relationships   165

7   Work and Retirement   201

8   Personality   237

9   The Quest for Meaning   267

10   Stress, Coping, and Resistance   297

11   Death and Bereavement   323

12   The Successful Journey   347

Contents

PREFACE   **xv**

I INTRODUCTION TO ADULT DEVELOPMENT   **3**

Basic Concepts in Adult Development   4

Sources of Change   7
Normative Age-Graded Influences *7*   Normative History-Graded
Influences *8*   Nonnormative Life Events *9*

Sources of Stability   11
Genetics *11*   Environment *12*   Interactionist View *12*

A Word About "Age"   13

Setting the Course: Some Guiding Perspectives   14

Developmental Research   16
Methods *17*   Measures *22*   Analyses *23*   Designs *26*

A Final Word   28

Summary   28

Key Terms   30

Suggested Reading   30

2 PHYSICAL CHANGES   **33**

Theories of Primary Aging   34
Oxidative Damage *34*   Genetic Limits *35*   Caloric Restriction *36*
A Word on Theories of Primary Aging *36*

Physical Changes During Adulthood   37
Outward Appearance *37*   The Senses *43*   Bones and Muscles *46*
Cardiovascular and Respiratory Systems *49*   Brain and Nervous System *50*
Immune System *51*   Hormonal System *51*

Changes in Physical Behavior   55
Athletic Abilities *55*   Stamina, Dexterity, and Balance *56*   Sleep *56*
Sexual Activity *56*

Individual Differences in Primary Aging   60
Genetics *61*   Lifestyle *61*   Psychosocial Factors *61*   Economics *61*

Can We "Turn Back the Clock" of Primary Aging?   62

An Overview of the Physical Changes in Adulthood   62

Summary   63

Key Terms   65

Suggested Reading   66

3 HEALTH AND HEALTH DISORDERS   69

Mortality Rates and Causes of Death   70

Morbidity Rates, Illness, and Disabilities   71
Common Health Conditions *71*   Disability *72*   Living Arrangements
for Older Adults *72*   Self-Ratings of Health *73*   Old Age and Disability
in Context *73*

Specific Diseases   74
Cardiovascular Disease *74*   Cancer *75*   Alzheimer's Disease *77*   A Word
About Tobacco Use *80*   Aging and Physical Disease: An Overview *80*

Mental Disorders   81
Anxiety Disorders *82*   Mood Disorders *83*   Impulse Control Disorders *84*
Substance Abuse Disorders *84*   Treatment of Mental Health Disorders *85*

Individual Differences in Health   86
Gender *86*   Socioeconomics, Race, and Ethnicity *89*   Personality and
Behavior Patterns *92*   Genetics *93*   Developmental Origins *94*
The Road to Good Health *95*

Summary   96

Key Terms   97

Suggested Reading   98

4 COGNITIVE ABILITIES   101

Intelligence   102
Age Changes in Overall Intelligence *102*   Components of Intelligence *104*
Reversing Declines in Intellectual Abilities *107*

Memory   107
Memory Systems Components *108*

Real-World Cognition   114
Judgment and Decision Making *114*   Human Factors Research: Assistive
Technology *115*

Individual Differences in Cognitive Change   121
Health *122*   Genetics *123*   Demographics and Sociobiographical
History *124*   Schooling *124*   Intellectual Activity *125*   Physical
Exercise *126*   Subjective Evaluation of Decline *127*   Review of Cognitive
Changes over the Adult Years and a Search for Balance *127*

Summary   129

Key Terms   130

Suggested Reading   130

5 SOCIAL ROLES 133

Social Roles and Transitions 134

Gender Roles and Gender Stereotypes 134

Social Roles in Young Adulthood 137
Leaving (and Returning) Home *137* Becoming a Spouse or Partner *140*
Becoming a Parent *144*

Social Roles in Middle Adulthood 148
The Departure of the Children: The Empty Nest *148* Gender Roles
at Midlife *149* Becoming a Grandparent *149* Caring for an Aging
Parent *151*

Social Roles in Late Adulthood 154
Living Alone *154* Becoming A Care Receiver *154*

Social Roles in Atypical Families 156
Lifelong Singles *156* The Childless *157* Divorced (and Remarried)
Adults *158*

The Effect of Variations in Timing 159

Summary 161

Key Terms 162

Suggested Reading 163

6 SOCIAL RELATIONSHIPS 165

Theories of Social Relationships 165
Attachment Theory *165* The Convoy Model *168* Socioemotional
Selectivity Theory *170* Evolutionary Psychology *170*

Intimate Partnerships in Adulthood 171
Establishing an Intimate Relationship *171* Long-Term Marriages *176*
Good and Bad Marriages *178* Cohabitation and Marriage *179*
Gay and Lesbian Partnerships *182*

Relationships with Other Family Members 184
General Patterns of Family Interaction *184* Parent-Child Relationships
in Adulthood *185* Grandparent-Grandchild Relationships *188*
Relationships with Brothers and Sisters *191*

Friendships in Adulthood 194

Summary 195

Key Terms 197

Suggested Reading 198

7 WORK AND RETIREMENT 201

The Importance of Work in Adulthood 202
Super's Theory of Career Development *202* Gender Differences in Career
Patterns *203*

Selecting a Career   205
Holland's Theory of Career Selection   *205*   The Effects of Gender   *207*
Family Influences   *209*   The Role of Genetics   *211*

Age Trends in Work Experience   211
Job Performance   *212*   Job Training and Retraining   *212*
Job Satisfaction   *213*

Work and Personal Life   213
Work and the Individual   *214*   Work and Marriage   *215*   Work
and Parenthood   *216*   Work and Caregiving for Adult Family
Members   *220*   Household Labor   *220*

Retirement   222
Preparation for Retirement   *222*   Timing of Retirement   *223*   Reasons
for Retirement   *224*   Effects of Retirement   *226*   Nonstandard Exits
from the Labor Force   *230*

A Concluding Note   232

Summary   233

Key Terms   234

Suggested Reading   234

8 PERSONALITY   237

Personality Structures   238
Personality Traits and Factors   *238*   Differential Continuity   *239*   Mean-
Level Change   *240*   Intra-Individual Variability   *241*   Continuity, Change,
and Variability Coexist   *242*   What Do Personality Traits Do?   *243*
Explanations of Continuity and Change   *245*   Genetics   *245*
Environmental Influences   *246*   Evolutionary Influences   *247*
Summing Up Personality Structure   *247*

Theories of Personality Development   248
Psychosocial Development   *248*   Ego Development   *253*   Mature
Adaptation   *256*   Gender Crossover   *258*   Positive Well-Being   *259*

Summary   262

Key Terms   264

Suggested Reading   264

9 THE QUEST FOR MEANING   267

Why a Chapter on the Quest for Meaning?   268

The Study of Age-Related Changes in Meaning Systems   270
Changes in Spirituality   *271*   Changes in Private Beliefs and Practices   *271*
Religion and Health   *273*

Theories of Spiritual Development   275
Development of Moral Reasoning   *276*   Development of Faith   *281*

**Integrating Meaning and Personality:
A Preliminary Theoretical Synthesis   284**
A Synthesizing Model *285*   Stages of Mystical Experience *286*

The Process of Transition   287

Commentary and Conclusions   289

Summary   291

Key Terms   293

Suggested Reading   293

IO Stress, Coping, and Resistance   **297**

Stress, Stressors, and Stress Reactions   298

Types of Stress   300

Effects of Stress   302
Physical Disease *302*   Mental Health Disorders *304*   Individual Differences
In Stress-Related Disorders *305*   Stress-Related Growth *309*

Coping with Stress   310
Types of Coping Behaviors *310*   Social Support *314*   Personality Traits
and Coping *316*

Resilience   317
Reactions to Trauma *317*   Individual Differences in Resilience *318*

Summary   319

Key Terms   320

Suggested Reading   321

II Death and Bereavement   **323**

Achieving an Understanding of Death   324
Meanings of Death *324*   Death Anxiety *325*   Accepting the Reality
of One's Eventual Death *327*

The Process of Death   328
Stages of Death Reactions *328*   The Importance of Farewells *329*
Individual Adaptations to Dying *329*   Choosing Where to Die *332*
Choosing When to Die *335*

After Death Occurs: Rituals and Grieving   336
Ritual Mourning: Funerals and Ceremonies *336*   The Process
of Grieving *337*

Living and Dying: A Final Word   342

Summary   342

Key Terms   344

Suggested Reading   344

12 THE SUCCESSFUL JOURNEY   **347**

Themes of Adult Development   **348**
Young Adulthood: Age 20 to 39 *350*   Middle Adulthood: Age 40 to 64 *352*
Older Adulthood: Age 65 to 74 *355*   Late Adulthood: Age 75 and Older *356*

Variations in Successful Adult Development   **359**
Individual Differences in Quality of Life *360*   Other Measures of Life
Success *362*   A Model of Adult Growth and Development: Trajectories
and Pathways *464*

Summary   **371**

Key Terms   **372**

Suggested Reading   **372**

REFERENCES   **375**

GLOSSARY   **400**

CREDITS   **401**

AUTHOR INDEX   **405**

SUBJECT INDEX   **415**

Preface

An Opening Note from Barbara Bjorklund

Journey of Adulthood is now in its sixth edition and it continues to capture the dynamic process of adult development from young adulthood to the end of life. Its core is made up of research findings from large-scale projects and major theories of adult development, but it also reflects smaller studies of diverse groups, showing the influences of gender, culture, ethnicity, race, and socioeconomic background on this journey. I have balanced new research with classic studies from pioneers in the field of adult development. And I have sweetened this sometimes medicinal taste with a spoonful of honey—a little personal warmth and humor. After all, I am a middle-aged adult who is on this journey along with my husband, looking ahead toward our parents who are in late adulthood and back toward our children who are blazing their own trails.

The first three editions of this book were written by Helen Bee, and although she has retired and was not involved in the more recent editions, I have retained the structure and tone that she set; the comments and stories that use the first person, "I," are mine. I hope there is no confusion.

The first chapter of the book contains the basics for the course—definitions, methods, and basic concepts in the study of adult development. The next seven chapters cover traditional developmental topics, featuring recent research, classic studies, current theories, new directions, and practical applications. The next three chapters cover topics not traditionally found in adult development texts, but which I feel are important to round out a student's experience in this course—the quest for meaning, the inevitability of stress, coping, and resilience in adult life, and the way we face our own deaths and that of our loved ones. The final chapter takes a chronological look at adult development, in contrast to the topical theme in the earlier chapters, and also introduces a model developed by the authors that will "pull the threads together and tie up loose ends."

New in This Edition

The sixth edition of *The Journey of Adulthood* is a complete revision of all chapters. Approximately half of the references are new to this edition as well as 90 percent of the figures and tables. The field of adult development is changing quickly, and this edition of *The Journey of Adulthood* gives a thorough coverage of the changes that have taken place since the previous edition was written four years ago. *The Journey of Adulthood* is about development, and it has developed itself over the past two decades as it has gone through numerous editions. This sixth edition features several types of changes; some reflect changes in the field of adult development and some reflect changes in the world around us, specifically, the academic settings in which this book is used.

One of the most obvious changes is that *The Journey of Adulthood* is now 12 full chapters. In previous editions I had included a short chapter to summarize the content chapters before going on to the final chapter of the book. Due to comments from a number of reviewers, I have omitted the content summary chapter and written one large, overall summary at the end of the book. I have also omitted the separate chapter on theories and instead, included that material in the chapters covering the topics of those theories. Most are found in the chapter on personality. I appreciate the thoughtful comments of many reviewers suggesting that theories belong with the research findings that they explain.

Changes in the Field of Adult Development

The study of adult development is a fairly new field and it expands exponentially from year to year. It began as a field of psychology, but more and more disciplines have found it an important topic for their research interests. This book includes research from the biological and medical sciences, the social sciences, women's studies, economics, education and vocational psychology, clinical psychology, epidemiology, and anthropology, just to name a few. The terminology and methods in these fields have become more and more similar, and many researchers publish in the journals of a variety of fields. There is wonderful collaboration going on and a number of research projects are multidisciplinary. This is an exciting time in developmental science, and this book reflects these trends.

To emphasize these collaborating fields, I have identified each major researcher or theorist with their field of study. As I read through the research journals, it was interesting for me to see what each person's scientific roots were, and I think it will be interesting to beginning students who might be making decisions about their majors or advanced students who might be deciding on careers or graduate school. There are so many opportunities for people interested in adult development, and as professors, we need to remember that we not only teach the content of the courses, but also guide our students in career decisions.

Another change in the field of adult development is that increasingly more research projects reported in major journals are done by international groups of researchers in settings all over the developed world. We no longer are limited to information on adults in the U.S., which may or may not generalize to adults worldwide. We have research being done by Swedish, Japanese, and Egyptian scientists using Swedish, Japanese, and Egyptian participants. When the findings are similar to studies done in the U.S., we can be more confident that the developmental phenomenon being studied is an integral part of the human experience and not something particular to people in the U.S. When the findings are different from studies done in the U.S., we can investigate these differences and find their roots. I have identified these international research teams and the nationalities of their participants. I hope it inspires students to consider "study abroad" programs.

I have also included full names of major researcher and theorists when I discuss their work in detail. Seeing the first and last names make the people more real than conventional citations of "last names, comma, date." Full names show the diversity of scientists—often their gender and their national or ethnic background. It is important for us to realize that this work is being done by a diverse group of people and that students can identify with them and perhaps imagine themselves in similar positions in the future.

One of the most exciting changes in the field of adult development has been its expansion to emphasize younger and younger age groups. When I first began writing in this area, the focus of interest was older adults. The last two editions of this book have featured more and more studies of middle-aged adults, and now young adults have joined the others at center stage. The study of adult development is no longer a study of old age, it is now truly a study of every aspect of adulthood.

Changes in the World Around Us

Since the last edition of this book, there have been many changes in the world around us. As I write this preface, we are mired in a war in Iraq with no end in sight. At home, people who experienced Hurricane Katrina are still recovering over a year after the storm. Single-parent families and dual-earner families in the U.S. (and in many other developed countries) are having a rough time; they receive little cooperation from the government, the workplace, or the community. Many older women, especially those who live alone, are living below the poverty line. The U.S. has the highest rates of mental disorders of any developed country and most of the people reporting these symptoms do not get adequate treatment. Although I try to maintain a positive tone in this book, these aspects of adult life are reality and I have included them in the topics discussed in *The Journey of Adulthood*.

Other changes in the world around us are more positive. Health awareness is increasing at all ages, advances are being made in many areas of disease prevention, detection, and treatment, and a greater percentage of people in developed countries are living into old age. Although there is still no treatment for aging and no sign of a way to increase the existing maximum lifespan, people are increasing the number of healthy years in their lives. Programs such as hospice are making it possible for an increasing number of people to choose to have "a good death" when that time comes. Women are making great strides in professional careers and in their positive adjustment to the empty nest and widowhood. Communication technology has made it easier for families to stay in touch and for older adults to live independently. These are also among the topics selected for this book.

Changes in the Classroom

Courses in adult development are offered in all major colleges and universities in the U.S. and are becoming popular around the world. It is safe to say that graduates in almost all majors will be working in fields that deal with the changes that occur during adulthood. It is also safe to say that students in all majors will be dealing with the topic on a personal level, both their own progress through adulthood and that of their parents. My students at Florida Atlantic University this semester are majoring in psychology, counseling, nursing, criminal justice, pre-medical sciences, pre-law, social work, ocupational therapy, sociology, and education. About one-third speak English as a second language. The majority will be the first in their families to graduate from college. I no longer assume that they have the same academic backgrounds as students a decade ago. For this reason, I include basic definitions of key terms in this book, clear explanations of relevant statistical methods, and basic details of major theories. I meet the readers knowing that the "typical student" is an outdated stereotype, but I meet them with respect for their intelligence and motivation. I firmly believe that it is possible to explain complex ideas clearly and connect with students from a variety of backgrounds and experiences. I do it every week in my lectures and I do it in this book.

Highlights of Changes in This Edition

In Chaper One, I introduce updated definitions and terminology that fit those used in current research articles. Guiding perspectives are clearly stated and explained. I include step-by-step explanations of developmental research, using actual studies from the text as examples.

Chapter 2 features major theories of aging and then takes a look at normal physical aging, system by system. I describe the age-related changes, tell when they begin, what the mechanisms are that underlie them, and what can be done to slow it down (or at least not to speed it up). Latest research on obesity, cosmetic surgery, types of exercise, changes in bone mass density, neuronal plasticity, stem-cell therapy, hormone replacement therapy, and changes in sexual response are discussed. A study of master athletes in Finland shows the gradual slowing down of runners between 30 and 80 years of age.

In Chapter 3, common age-related health disorders are covered, including cardiovascular disease, cancer, and Alzheimer's disease. The causes and risk factors for each are presented with those that can be modified or prevented highlighted. The effects of health disorders are discussed, including disability and residential options for older adults. Mental health disorders, such as anxiety disorders, mood disorders, and substance abuse disorders, are discussed in terms of recent epidemiological studies of the U.S. population, with a focus on treatment. The chapter closes with a discussion of individual differences in health, including gender, socioeconomics, race and ethnicity, personality traits, and genetics. New research on developmental origins of disease is presented, including the link between low birth weight and adult disease, and intergenerational effects in which the grandmother's health affects the children of her female offspring. The chapter closes with a short discussion of what each of us can do to better our chances of a long and healthy life.

Chapter 4 covers changes in cognition over the adult years, beginning with information processing theory and moving on to new information on memory, assistive technology, and drivers' training for older adults. Another new section features web page designs that are user friendly to adults of all ages. Individual differences in cognitive aging include health, physical exercise, and intellectual activity.

In Chaper 5, adulthood is viewed according to social role theory, exploring the sequence of social roles we take on and how we make the transition from one to another. New information includes gender roles in countries with different political structures, longitudinal evidence of the slow transition from dependent child to independent young adult, studies examining marriage versus cohabiting partnerships and their long-term outcomes, and research-based, practical advice on how to make one's marriage successful. This chapter also covers the role of grandfathers raising grandchildren, new qualitative studies on the role of gender in caregiving to aging parents and the role of step-mother. Research evidence is presented on the physical toll of caregiving, including premature cellular aging.

Chapter 6 covers the relationships adults participate in at different stages of life. I begin with attachment theory and its applications in adulthood, a new cross-cultural study of social convoys in the U.S. and Japan, and socioemotional selectivity theory. Social roles transitions, such as mate selection are also explained by concepts of evolutionary psychology. There is a new stage theory of love, based on changes in neurotransmitters and brain activity. A cross-cultural study of long-term marriages shows what happens over the adult years in white, black, and Hispanic couples. Several new studies compare long-term gay and lesbian partnerships with heterosexual marriages, and one study examines relationships of same-sex couples in civil unions in Vermont the first year it was offered. Parent-child relationships in adulthood are covered, including a new study on sibling rivalry among adult children. A study from the Netherlands gives evidence for older parents learning more liberal attitudes from their adult children. Also featured is material on how late-life divorce can affect adult children, how adult children's problems can affect older parents, new research on grandparent-grandchild relationships, and how parental investment theory can extend to grandparents.

Work and retirement are discussed in Chapter 7, beginning with theories of career development and career selection. New research shows strong stability in career choice as early as the middle-school years. A study of twins in Sweden shows a gender difference in the influence of genetics on career choice. New research findings on job burnout are presented as well as new studies of men and women in nontraditional careers. I examine specific guidelines outlining just what policy-makers can do to make families function better when parents work. Gender differences in career patterns lead to gender differences in retirement. Retirement age is increasing in the U.S. and declining in Western Europe. This chapter examines what factors are taken into account when deciding when to retire and what happens when people retire. Another section looks at gender differences in earlier years and how they result in the large proportion of older women in the U.S. living in poverty. I include information on what women can do today to guard against this. New patterns of migration after retirement in the U.S. and Europe are discussed, along with new figures on volunteer workers.

Chapter 8 begins with research on personality structure, covering differential continuity, mean-level change, intra-indivdual variability, and how they can all co-exist. It also includes a section on how personality traits affect relationships, job achievement, and personal health. The second part of the chapter covers theories of personality development that are currently active in the study of adult development— Erikson's theory of psychosocial development, Loevinger's theory of ego development, Vaillant's theory of mature adaptation, and Maslow's theory of positive well-being. Each is presented along with the current research that is being done to further the theories.

The ninth chapter covers the quest for meaning over adulthood. It covers evidence that the quest for meaning, or a sense of spirituality, is a basic human trait. It explains the concept of gerotranscendence and shows how that is manifest in postformal thought. It discusses the decline in religious participation in the U.S. and Europe, but the increase in the proportion of people who seek spiritual understanding. This chapter includes longitudinal evidence of spirituality being influenced by age and gender, and also by cohort. Research is featured showing a link between religiosity and health. Other work is cited showing a genetic predisposition to spirituality, or a "God gene." Kohlberg's theory of moral development is covered, along with the research that it inspired. The study of mystical experiences is discussed along with comparisons of the development of faith, personality, and moral thought.

Chapter 10 begins with a discussion of Selye's theory of general adaptation syndrome and results from a nationwide study on daily stressors in adults' lives. New studies include a longitudinal study of Finnish women showing a link between stress and breast cancer, a longitudinal study of gay men with HIV showing a link beween stress and AIDS onset, and a longitudinal study of American men showing a link between work-related stress and heart disease. New studies are included on post-traumatic stress syndrome in victims of the September 11th terrorist attack and Holocaust survivors, the buffering effect of social support in women combat veterans of the Gulf War, and the positive outcomes of trauma in World War II combat veterans. The chapter ends with new evidence about resilience after trauma and the harm that can be done using a one-size-fits-all approach to recovery.

Chapter 11 discusses how we come to cope with our own eventual death and how we deal with the deaths of others. It begins with a new story of the founding of the hospice movement and continues with age-related differences in death anxiety from researchers in the U.S., Egypt, Kuwait, and Syria. It covers the ways in which people make preparations for death, such as writing living wills, buying life insurance, and becoming potential organ transplant donors. A new study of recently bereaved families compares their ratings of end-of-life care from home health nursing staff, nursing homes, hospitals, and hospices. The Death With Dignity Act in Oregon is discussed in terms of physician-assisted suicide data. A new table presents the diversity found within the U.S. in funeral rites and bereavement rituals, featuring groups such as Latinos, African Americans with roots in the Caribbean, Asian Americans, Native Americans, and many more groups. New research is presented on resilience after the death of a loved one being the most common pattern of response.

The last chapter features a new chronological summary of adult development and ends with a proposed model of development based on the epigenetic landscape concept.

The sixth edition of *The Journey of Adulthood* has not lost sight of the classic studies that are the foundation of our field. They have stood the test of time and are included throughout the text. Each chapter has been substantially rewritten. About 90 percent of the opening stories, Critical Thinking Questions, and Suggested Readings are new. Suggested Readings are arranged in three categories: Reading for Personal Interest, which are popular books for the layperson that deal responsibly with the topic and would be useful to the student on a personal basis; Classic Work, which includes pioneering research done on the chapter topic; and Contemporary Scholarly Work, which are recent review articles or meta-analyses of the topics discussed in the chapter.

Acknowledgements

I am deeply grateful to Helen Bee, for entrusting me, three editions ago, with this book. In turning over *The Journey of Adulthood* to me eight years ago, she presented an opportunity that provided a sharp turn in my own "journey of adulthood," and I have enjoyed the new scenery and new people I have met along the way. Some of them are: Jeff Marshall, Executive Editor; Randy Pettit, Project Liaison; Bruce Hobart, Project Coordinator; Robert Milch, Copy Editor. Thanks also to the many reviewers who offered valuable suggestions. Karen Lynne Barnes, University of Central Oklahoma; Ralph Brockett, University of Tennessee; Gary Creasey, Illinois State University; Jane E. Dwyer, Rivier College; Diane Edwards, Saddleback College; Nancy K. Elwell, Concordia University; Diane K. Feibel, Raymond Walters College–University of Cincinnati; Oney D. Fitzpatrick, Lamar University; Katiapaz Goldfarb, The University of New Mexico; M. James Hannush, Rosemont College; Sara Holland, Texas State University; Fereshteh Oboudiat, St. Joseph's University; Mary Ogles, Metro State College of Denver; Sudha Shreeniwas, University of North Carolina at Greensboro; Donna J. Tyler Thompson, Midland College; Marcia L. Weinstein, Salem State College.

I appreciate the hospitality of the Department of Psychology at the University of Canterbury in Christchurch, New Zealand, where early chapters of this book were written. I also am indebted to my research assistants, Sheryl Spencer and Jessica Wassung, who were not only accurate, diligent, and cheerful, but somehow able to read my mind. Finally, I am ever thankful for the help and support of my husband, David Bjorklund.

Barbara R. Bjorklund
Jupiter Farms, Florida

The Journey
of Adulthood

Chapter 1

Introduction to Adult Development

MY JOURNEY OF adulthood began early, as did that of many women of my generation, when I married shortly after high school and began a family. But unlike many women in my peer group, I spent more time reading than I did having morning coffee with the other moms. I always took a book along to read while the kids had music lessons, baseball practice, and orthodontist appointments. The library was a weekly stop along with the grocery store, and as important to me. By the time my youngest child began kindergarten, I enrolled in college as a freshman—at the age of 29, which was much older than the average at that time. For the next 7 years, my children and I did our homework together at the kitchen table, counted the days to the next holiday break, and posted our grade reports on the refrigerator. Today, as adults, they tell me that they can't remember a time in their childhood when I wasn't in school.

Just before I received my master's degree in developmental psychology, the marriage ended and I spent some time as a single mother. I abandoned plans for a Ph.D. and took a job at the university, teaching psychology courses and doing research on children's memory development. And just as my children began to leave the nest, I married a man whose own journey of adulthood had brought him to fatherhood rather late, making me

Basic Concepts in Adult Development

Sources of Change
Normative Age-Graded Influences
Normative History-Graded Influences
Nonnormative Life Events

Sources of Stability
Genetics
Environment
Interactionist View

A Word about "Age"

Setting the Course: Some Guiding Perspectives

Developmental Research
Methods
Designs
Measures
Analyses

A Final Word

Summary

Key Terms

Suggested Readings

stepmother of a 5-year-old, who quickly became an important part of my life. Not too much later, the grandchildren began to arrive and life settled into a nice routine. It seemed I had done it all—marriage, parenthood, career, single parenthood, stepparenthood, and grandparenthood; my life was full.

Suddenly, my 50th birthday loomed and it seemed to represent so much more to me than turning "just another year older." The half-century mark was quite a shock and caused me to reevaluate my life. I realized that I wasn't ready to ride slowly into the sunset for the next several decades; I needed to get back on track and move forward in my education. The next fall I entered a Ph.D. program in life-span developmental psychology at the University of Georgia. It was an invigorating experience and also very humbling. Instead of being the teacher, I was the student. Instead of supervising the research project, I was the newbie. Instead of being the one giving advice, I was the one who had to ask where the bookstore was, where to park, and how to use the copy machine. But three years later I was awarded a red-and-black hood in a formal graduation ceremony with my children and grandchildren, parents and siblings cheering for me from the audience.

Now I teach part-time at the local university and write college textbooks. My husband and I have moved from our city home to a country home in southeastern Florida, complete with a cypress stand in the front yard and a small pine forest in the back. Our two youngest grandchildren live nearby, and my typical day consists of teaching a university class in the morning and taking my 7-year-old grandson to the library in the afternoon for a book that we can read together at home. We have neighbors nearby with cows and horses, roosters, and even a few emus. So far our own livestock consists only of our 20-year-old cat, but my stepdaughter has been talking about raising miniature goats.

Oh yes, my stepdaughter, who is now 25, decided to move back in with us last fall. She has taken a detour in her own journey of adulthood and enrolled in the dental hygiene program at the community college nearby. So I am a parent again!

Basic Concepts in Adult Development

This book is about adult development, and it follows the tenets of **developmental psychology,** the field of study that deals with the behavior, thoughts, and emotions of individuals as they go through various parts of the life span. The field also includes child development, adolescent development, and **adult development,** which is the particular concern of this book. We are interested in the changes that take place within individuals as they progress from emerging adulthood (when adolescence is ending) to the end of life. Although there are many autobiographies giving first-person accounts of people's lives and many interesting stories about people's experiences in adulthood, this book is based on **empirical research**—scientific studies of observable events that are measured and evaluated objectively. When personal accounts and examples are used (including the opening story about my life), they are chosen to illustrate concepts that have been carefully researched.

Some of you reading this are just beginning the journey of your own adult life; some of you are partway along the road, having traveled through your 20s, 30s, and perhaps 40s, 50s, and beyond. Whatever your age, you are traveling, moving through the years and through the transformations that come along the way. We do not all follow the same itinerary on this journey; you may spend a long time in a location that I do not visit at all; I may make an unscheduled side trip. Or we may visit the same places but experience them very differently. Every journey has **individual differences,** aspects that are unique to the individual. You may not have experienced the trials of single parenthood as I have or the joys of grandparenthood, and I cannot relate to the independence you must feel when living alone or the confusion you experience when your parents divorce. Likewise, there also have to be some **commonalities,** typical aspects of adult life that most all of us can relate to (either now or in the future). Most of us have moved out of our parents' homes (or plan to soon), experienced romantic relationships, entered college with some plans for the future, and either started a family or given some serious thought to parenthood. Without these common goals and experiences, there would be no reason for a book on adult development. My goal for this book is to explore with you both the uniqueness and the common grounds of our adult lives.

Two of the concepts featured in this book are stability and change during the developmental process. **Stability** describes the important parts of our selves that make up a consistent core. It is the constant set of attributes that makes each of us the individuals that we are throughout our lifetimes. In other words, your 40-year-old self will be similar to your 20-year-old self in some ways, as will your 60-year-old self. For example, one of the stable themes of my adult life is a love for books. In fact it goes back to my childhood. Some of my most prized possessions are the books in my library. I always have several books sitting around the house that I am in the process of reading. And last year I started a book club in my new neighborhood that has become a big source of joy for me. Another theme that keeps popping up in my life is children, beginning early on with three younger sisters, then my own children, then my stepdaughter, nieces and nephews, then grandchildren. I have always had a toybox in my living room and sippy cups in the kitchen cabinet. In fact the two themes of books and children often mix. I send books on birthdays for the children on my gift list, and when visiting children spend the night, I have a shelf of children's books in the guestroom, some of them that belonged to their own parents so many years ago. Perhaps you find stability in your life in terms of playing a musical instrument or participating in sports. The genre of books I read may change over the years, and your choice of musical selections or sporting event may be different from time to time, but the core essence of these stable themes remains an integral part of our lives.

● **CRITICAL THINKING**

What are some of the stable themes of your life? How do you think these themes will be expressed 20 years from now?

Change is the opposite force to stability. It is what happens to us over time that makes us different from our younger (and older) selves. An example from my life that illustrates this is travel. As a child I never traveled too far out of my home state of Florida. Almost all of my relatives lived nearby, and those who didn't were more than happy to come and visit us in the warm climate during the winter. In fact, at the age of 35, I had never been on an airplane. But when I married my current husband (and no longer had children living at home), I had the opportunity to travel with him to national conferences and accompany him on international trips as he collaborated with colleagues and worked as a visiting professor around the world. In the last 20 years we have spent extended periods of time in Germany,

Middle adulthood can bring large-scale changes in lifestyle and interests, as illustrated by this photo of author Barbara Bjorklund visiting the site of a Greek temple in Sicily, camera in hand.

Spain, and New Zealand. We have made shorter trips to Japan, China, Italy, Sweden, Norway, Denmark, England, Scotland, Wales, Austria, Switzerland, and Morocco. I am an expert packer, and my office is filled with framed photos I have taken in many exotic locations. To compare myself at 30 and 50, my travel habits would constitute a dramatic change. Other examples of change in the adult developmental process occur when one becomes a parent, switches careers, or decides to move to another part of the country (or to an entirely different country). One way of viewing the journey of adulthood is to consider both the stability and the change that define our lives.

Still another way of looking at this journey is gauging how straight the road is. Some stretches of our lives are **continuous**—slow and gradual, taking us in a predictable direction. My gardening certainly fits this definition. In my earliest apartments I had potted plants, and when we rented our first house, I persuaded the landlord to let me put in a small flower garden. As our yards have grown bigger, so have my garden projects. I enjoy plant fairs, trade plant cuttings with friends, and, of course, read books about gardening. I find it relaxing to spend time "digging in the dirt." I have increased my knowledge and skill over the years. Now that our yard is measured in acres instead of square feet, I'm in heaven. So far I have a butterfly garden in the front yard and I'm working on a vegetable garden in the back. Hopefully I will continue to "develop" as a gardener for many years.

In contrast, our lives also have **stages,** parts of the journey where there seems to be no progress for some time, followed by an abrupt change. Stages are much like driving on a quiet country road for a long time and then getting onto a busy interstate highway (or vice versa). In my adult life I view the years of being home with my young children as a stage which was followed by the abrupt change of the youngest entering school and me starting college. I suddenly went from having minute-to-minute, hands-on parenting duties to the type that involve preparations the night before and then dropping the children off at school in the morning. And I also went from having mostly tasks that involved physical work and concrete thinking skills (how to get crayon marks off the walls) to those that required abstract thinking (Psychology 101). This mother/student stage continued for many years until I reached the single-mother/researcher stage. An interesting question in the study of adulthood is exploring how **typical** these stages of adult life are: Do most adults go through them along their journeys, and if so, do they go through them in the same order and at the same age? Or are they **atypical,** unique to the individual? I think that sending one's youngest child off to school is probably a universal event in a mother's life, signaling the end of one stage and the beginning of another, but I don't think that the transition from full-time mother to full-time student is typical, though it is more common today than it was a generation ago.

A final theme of this book has to do with inner versus outer changes. As we proceed along the journey of adulthood, there are many **outer changes** that are visible and apparent to those we encounter. We enter early adulthood and become more confident in our step and our carriage; we fill out and mature; some of us become pregnant; some begin to lose their hair. In middle age many of us lose and gain weight, increase and decrease in fitness. **Inner changes** are not as apparent to the casual observer. We fall in and out of love, hold our children close and then learn to give them space. We look to our parents for guidance at the beginning of our journeys and then assist them at the end of theirs. And we grow in wisdom and grace. Of course the inner and outer changes are not independent of one another. Outer changes can affect the way we feel about ourselves, and vice versa. They also affect the way others perceive us, and this, in turn, affects our self-perception. Untangling this conceptual ball of yarn is another goal of this book.

Sources of Change

Multiple explanations about what influences adult development are quite common, much to the dismay of students (and textbook authors). In fact, the types of influences that result in change have been classified as (1) normative age-graded influences, (2) normative history-graded influences, and (3) nonnormative life events. In the following section I will describe these various influences and give you some examples so you can see them at work in your own lives.

Normative Age-Graded Influences

When you hear the phrase "sources of change," your first thought is probably of what we call **normative age-graded influences,** those influences that are linked to age and experienced by most adults of every generation as they grow older. There are at least three types of age-graded influences that impinge on the typical adult.

Biology. Some of the changes we see in adults are shared by all of us because we are all members of our species undergoing natural aging processes. This is often represented by the idea of a **biological clock,** ticking away to mark the common changes that occur with time. Many such changes are easy to see, such as hair gradually turning gray or skin becoming wrinklier. Others are not visible directly from the outside but occur inwardly, such as the loss of muscle tissue, which results in a gradual loss of physical strength. The rate at which such physical changes occur varies quite a lot from one person to another, as will be explained more fully in Chapter 2.

Shared Experiences. Another normative influence that is dictated for most of us by our ages can be envisioned by a **social clock** defining the normal sequence of adult-life experiences, such as the timing of marriage, college graduation, and retirement. Even though our society has expanded the choices we have in the timing of these experiences, we still are aware of the "normative" timing of these events. Where we stand in relation to the social clock can affect our own sense of self-worth. The middle-aged man still living at home, the "perpetual student," the older working woman whose friends have retired—all may be doing well in important aspects of their lives, but if those lives are out of sync with what society expects in the way of timing, it may lead to some personal doubts. In contrast, the young adult who is CEO of his own high-tech company, the middle-aged woman who completes law school, and the octogenarian who finishes the Boston Marathon may have reason to celebrate over and above the face value of their accomplishments.

Another effect the social clock can have is **ageism,** a type of discrimination in which opinions are formed and decisions are made about others based solely on the fact that they are in a later period of adulthood. In the United States and many other parts of the world, older adults as a group are perceived by some people to be infirm, cranky, sexless, childlike, senile, and useless. These stereotypes are perpetuated by television sitcoms, commercials, birthday cards, and jokes sent around on the Internet. They are also supported more subtly in the worship of youth that is visible in almost every medium from newspaper ads for cosmetic surgery centers to television programs and films, which seldom feature leading characters who are over 25 (and especially not older women). One of my goals for this book is to give a realistic and respectful look at adults of every age.

Another manifestation of the influence of the social clock in virtually all cultures is the pattern of experiences associated with family life. For example, the vast majority of adults experience parenthood, and once their first child is born they begin a fixed pattern of shared social experiences with other parents that move along with their child's stage of life—infancy, toddlerhood, the school years, adolescence, and preparing to leave home. Each of these periods in the child's life makes a different set of demands on parents—attending childbirth classes, setting preschool playdates, hosting scout meetings, coaching Little League baseball, visiting potential colleges—and this sequence shapes 20 or 30 years of most adults' lives, regardless of their own biological ages.

Obviously, shared developmental changes based on the social clock are much less likely to be universal than those based on the biological clock. But within any given culture, shared age-graded experiences can explain some of the common threads of adult development. Chapter 5 will discuss some of these shared experiences in the form of roles and role transitions in adulthood.

Internal Change Processes. At a deeper level, there may be shared inner changes resulting from the way we respond to the pressures of the biological and social clocks. For example, several theorists have observed that in early adulthood, particularly after the birth of children, parents tend to exaggerate traditional masculine or feminine traits. Then at midlife, after the children are grown and no longer living in the home, many men and women seek to balance their feminine and masculine qualities. Men tend to become more emotionally expressive and warmer than they were during the parenting years, while women become more assertive and independent. In fact, there is some evidence that such a balancing of personality traits occurs in many cultures, as I will describe more fully in Chapters 5. For now my point is simply that this is an example of an internal change that may be linked to the biological and social clocks, but is not caused entirely by one or the other. It is determined by the way we respond to the changes they entail.

Normative History-Graded Influences

Experiences that result from historical events or conditions, known as **normative history-graded influences,** also shape adult development. These influences are helpful for explaining both the similarities found among people within certain groups and also the dissimilarities between people in those same groups. Both are important parts of a course on adult development.

The large social environments in which development takes place are known as **cultures,** and they can vary enormously in the ways they influence the adult life pattern: the expected age of marriage or childbearing, the typical number of children (and wives), the roles of men and women, class structures, religious practices, and laws. I was reminded of this on a recent trip, when a young Chinese mother in Beijing struck up a conversation with me and we began talking about our families. She had a toddler daughter with her who was 2 1/2, just the age of my youngest grandson, I told her. "*Youngest* grandson?" she asked, "How many grandchildren do you have?" I told her I had eight, then realized from her expression of surprise that this was very unusual in China. She explained to me that since 1979 there has been a one-child policy in China. Almost all Chinese parents in urban areas limit their families to one child. She was an only child, her daughter was an only child (and the only grandchild of both sets of grandparents). The typical person in this culture has no siblings, no aunts or uncles, and no cousins. She asked to see pictures of my grandchildren and wanted to know their ages and details about them. We had a very friendly visit, but I could not help but wonder how different my life would be in that culture, and what her life will be like when she is my age.

A **cohort** is a more finely grained concept than a culture because it refers to a group of people who share a common historical experience at the same stage of life. The term is roughly synonymous with generation, but more narrow—a generation refers to about 20 years, whereas a cohort can be a much shorter period. And a generation can refer to a much larger geographic area, while a cohort can be just one country or one region of one country. For example, Cuban Americans who came to the United States in the 1960s to flee Fidel Castro make up an important cohort in south Florida.

One of the most studied cohorts in the social sciences is the group of people who grew up during the Great Depression of the 1930s. This was a time in the United States (and in most of the world) that crops failed, factories closed, the stock market crashed, unemployment skyrocketed, and without unemployment benefits and government social programs, the only help available was from family, neighbors, or churches (none of whom had much to share). Almost no one escaped the effects of this disaster. But what were its effects, and were people affected differently depending on what age they were when the Great Depression hit? That was the thrust of the research on growing up in the Great Depression done by sociologist Glen H. Elder, Jr. (1979). He found that the cohort of people who were teenagers in the depths of the Great Depression showed fewer long-term effects than those who had been in early elementary school at the same time. The younger cohort spent a greater portion of their childhood under conditions of economic hardship. The hardship altered family interaction patterns, educational opportunities, and even the personalities of the children, so that the negative effects could still be detected in adulthood. Those who were teenagers during the Great Depression did not show negative effects in adult life; on the contrary, some of them seemed to have grown from the experience of hardship and showed more independence and initiative in adulthood as a result. Thus two cohorts, rather close in actual age, experienced the same historical event differently because of their ages. The timing of events interacts with the tasks, issues, and age norms, producing unique patterns of influence for each cohort and helping to create common adult-life trajectories for those in the same cohort.

Although the era of the Great Depression is past, this research should remind us that every one of us, as an adult, bears the marks of the events we have lived through and the age-specific ways we reacted to those events. Do you remember the *Challenger* tragedy? The Columbine school massacre? The death of Princess Diana? Certainly everyone remembers the terrorist attacks of September 11th. They all had effects on us, and a different effect depending on our ages. Less dramatic happenings also have an influence on different cohorts, such as the economic conditions of the times, the political and religious climate, the educational system, and the popular culture. As many of these influences as possible need to be considered when researchers are comparing people of different ages in order to find age effects in some characteristic or ability. Table 1.1 shows some of the salient events that occurred in the recent past and the ages of seven different cohorts when these events happened. Find the decade of your birth in the row of dates across the top of the table and then review what age you were when various events happened. If you compare your own cohort with that of your parents (or your children), you will see that the sequence of history may have had different effects on members of the same family.

> ● **CRITICAL THINKING**
>
> Which decade of events in Table 1.1 is the most salient to you? Ask this of people who are younger or older than you. Is there some pattern here?

Nonnormative Life Events

Along with the aspects of yourself that you share with most other adults your age and in your culture, there are **nonnormative life events,** aspects that influence your life that are unique to you, not shared with many others. These can have an important effect on the pathway of your life. Examples of nonnormative life events are having one's spouse die at an early age, inheriting enough money to retire at 40, losing one's sight to macular degeneration, and starting one's own business at 65.

Table 1.1   Selected Events from 1980 to 2005 and the Ages at Which They Were Experienced by Seven Cohorts

Year	Event	1930 cohort	1940 cohort	1950 cohort	1960 cohort	1970 cohort	1980 cohort	1990 cohort
1980	Reagan becomes president	Age 50	Age 40	Age 30	Age 20	Age 10	Infants	Not born yet
1980	John Lennon assassinated							
1981	Charles and Diana marry							
	AIDS identified							
1986	Sally Ride—first woman in space							
1989	Berlin Wall falls							
1989	Students massacred in Tianamen Square							
1990	George H.W. Bush becomes president	Age 60	Age 50	Age 40	Age 30	Age 20	Age 10	Infants
1991	Collapse of USSR							
1991	Operation Desert Storm begins							
1991	Magic Johnson announces he has AIDS							
1992	O. J. Simpson arrested for murder							
1994	Kurt Cobain commits suicide							
1995	Bill Clinton becomes president							
1995	Oklahoma City bombing							
1997	Death of Princess Diana							
1999	Columbine High School massacre							
2000	George W. Bush becomes president	Age 70	Age 60	Age 50	Age 40	Age 30	Age 20	Age 10
2001	Dale Earnhardt killed at Daytona 500							
	World Trade Center/Pentagon attacked by terrorists							
2003	Iraq War begins							
	Saddam Hussein captured by U.S. forces in Tikrit							
2004	Tsunami kills 310,000 in Indonesia and surrounding areas							
	Red Sox win World Series							
2005	Hurricane Katrina hits New Orleans							

Some of these events are nonnormative for anyone at any age, such as losing one's sight and inheriting a large amount of money, but others are nonnormative because of the timing. The death of a spouse is, unfortunately, a normative event in older adulthood, but not so in the earlier years. And starting one's own business may be remarkable in early adulthood, but it is highly nonnormative at the age of 65. As Bernice Neugarten warned us back in 1979, we have to pay attention not only to the event itself, but to the timing. Events

The terrorist attack of September 11, 2001, will surely be a defining event for the cohorts who experienced it.

that are on-time are much easier to cope with (even the death of a spouse) than those that are off-time.

I can speak from experience as one who was off-time in several aspects of my life—becoming a parent early, going to college late, becoming a grandparent early, going to graduate school late. It makes for a good opening chapter of a textbook, but it was not always easy. One problem is the lack of peers—I was always "the older one" or "the younger one," never just one of the group. You don't fit in with your age mates because you are doing something different, but you don't fit in with your fellow students or soccer moms, either, because you are not their age. And if this situation is easy to deal with yourself, sometimes others have problems, such as administrators who don't want to hire beginning professors who are older than they are. So in the best of all possible worlds, it is probably easier to do things "on time" than march to your own drummer—I've just never lived in the best of all possible worlds.

Sources of Stability

In my discussion so far, I have focused on explanations of change. However, some traits and behaviors show patterns of **stability,** having little or no change for significant periods of time. To understand adult development, we must also explore and understand different types of stability. I have divided them according to the classic nature-nurture dichotomy, the biology we are born with and the environment we experience around us.

Genetics

Each of us inherits, at conception, a unique combination of genes. A very large percentage of these genes is identical from one member of the species to the next, which is why our developmental patterns are so much alike—why children all over the world walk at about 12 months, why we go through puberty in our early teens and menopause around 51. But our genetic inheritance is individual as well as collective. The study of **behavior genetics,** or the contributions genes make to individual behavior, has been a particularly active research topic in recent decades. We now know that specific heredity affects a remarkably broad range of behaviors, including cognitive abilities such as IQ, physical characteristics, such as height or body shape or a tendency to fatness or leanness, personality characteristics, and even pathological behavior, such as a tendency toward alcoholism, schizophrenia, or depression (Plomin 2004). The extent to which these traits and tendencies remain in place throughout our lives shows the influence of heredity on stability in development.

In searching for genetic influences on variations in adult behavior, behavior geneticists rely primarily on **twin studies.** These are studies that compare monozygotic twins with dizygotic twins on some behavior. Such studies are based on the fact that *monozygotic twins* develop from the same sperm and ovum and thus share exactly the same genetic patterning, whereas *dizygotic twins* each develop from a separate sperm and ovum, and are therefore no more alike, genetically, than any other pair of siblings. In typical twin studies, measurements of some trait or ability are taken on each twin and then the pairs are compared to see how similar their scores are. If the monozygotic twin pairs are more similar for that trait or ability than the dizygotic twin pairs, then it is taken as evidence that the trait or ability is more influenced by genetics than by environmental factors.

Twin studies are difficult to do because the statistics involved require large numbers of participants, and it is difficult for a researcher to recruit hundreds of pairs of twins. For this reason, several countries that have central databanks of their citizens' birth records and health records have taken the lead in this type of research. The largest databank of twins is in Sweden at the Karolinska Institute in Stockholm. It maintains a database of information on over 140,000 twins. Several studies in this book were based on data from the Swedish Twin Study database, as you will soon find out.

Environment

If our genetic makeup contributes to the parts of our selves that remain relatively stable over time, so does our environment. Although neither our biology nor our upbringing dictates our destiny, both have long-term effects. The lifelong effect of early family experience has been clearly demonstrated by the Grant Study of Harvard Men. Psychiatrist George Valliant (2002), the study's current director, has concluded that those who lived in the warmest, most trusting homes as children are more apt to be living well-adjusted lives in adulthood than those who spent their childhoods in the bleakest homes. Men from the warmest homes are more able, as adults, to express emotions appropriately and openly, to see the world and the people in it as trustworthy, and to have friends with whom they enjoy leisure-time activities. Vaillant's interpretation is that parents who provide basic trust to their children (in this case, their sons), instill a sense of self-worth, good coping skills, the ability to form meaningful relationships, and in general construct a solid foundation for the core values the child will take with him or her throughout adulthood. And what's more, subsequent studies show that these data could predict which men at age 75 would most likely be aging successfully (i.e., are healthy and happy) and which would be aging unsuccessfully (i.e., are sick and sad). Taken together, Vaillant's studies show that at least for extreme situations, early childhood environment can set the course for a lifetime for either emotional openness, trust, and good health or for loneliness, mistrust, and illness. This research led Vaillant to propose a major theory of personality development that will be discussed in Chapter 8.

Interactionist View

Of course there are no simple partitions between genes and environment, and we can't separate their contributions to the stability we experience throughout adulthood. Most developmentalists now subscribe to an **interactionist view** in which one's genetic traits determines how one interacts with the environment and even the environment itself

(Lerner, 2006). For example, a boy with a genetic makeup that promotes avoiding risks will grow up with a certain pattern of interactions with his parents and siblings, and will seek out friends and activities that do not involve high risk. Teachers may view this as stable and sensible, and steer him to a career such as accounting. The result is a young adult with risk-avoiding genes working in a low-risk career environment and enjoying low-risk activities with his friends. He will no doubt marry someone who shares these interests, giving him even more support for this lifestyle. You can imagine the life course of this person, perhaps having one child, living in the same home and working in the same job until retirement. Quiet evenings would be spent at home or at the neighborhood tavern. He would have good health because of regular checkups, exercise, and sensible eating habits. He (and his wife) would use their seatbelts and drive defensively. Vacations would be carefully planned tours of scenic places, and retirement would bring regular golf games with the same friends each week and volunteer work with the foster grandparent program at the local elementary school. Risk avoidance is the theme of this person's life, but can we really say it was caused by his genetic makeup? Or was it the environment? It's the interactionist's chicken-and-egg dilemma.

A Word About "Age"

Most people know that age is just a number. Perhaps ages in childhood give valid information about what to expect in the way of appearance or behavior, but once a child reaches adolescence, many more factors take over. In fact, the further we venture on the journey of adulthood, the more variability there is among people our "own" age. Several types of age have been identified, and they illustrate the many dimensions of adult development.

The number of years that have passed since your birth or the number of candles on your last birthday cake is your **chronological age.** As I mentioned before, this may be important in childhood, when all 7-year-olds look similar and have similar interests and abilities, but in adulthood, this number is seldom relevant, except for young adulthood when driving, purchasing alcohol, and voting are determined by chronological age and in older adulthood when eligibility for Social Security and Medicare are determined by chronological age. However, adult development does not take place because the clocks have struck a certain number of times any more than because the heat from your birthday candles reaches a certain temperature. It may be related, but chronological age does not *cause* developmental changes.

Biological age is a measure of how an adult's physical condition compares with others. "He has the memory of a 50-year-old" and "She runs like a 30 year old" are examples of informal measures of biological age. Of course it depends on the person's chronological age. Having the memory of a 50-year-old means one thing if the person is 70, a much different thing if 30! As you will see in Chapter 2, biological age is used to evaluate aging of the physical systems, such as with bone density scans, in which patients' bones are compared to those of a healthy 20-year-old. Biological age can often be changed by lifestyle changes, as will also be discussed in Chapter 2.

Another type of age is **psychological age,** which is a measure of how an adult's ability to deal effectively with the environment compares to others. A 30-year-old woman who can't pay her electric bill because she couldn't resist buying designer jeans and is often late for work because she oversleeps is functioning like a teenager. Her psychological age is much below her chronological age.

Social age is based on the expected roles a person takes on at a specific point in his or her life. A woman who has her first child at 40 is taking on a role that has a social age

● CRITICAL THINKING

How old are you? What would you estimate your biological age to be? Your social and psychological age? How do they match with your chronological age?

at least a decade younger. A 23-year-old who works full time, goes to school full time, and sends money home to help support her grandmother has a social age much greater than her years. Sometimes biological age, psychological age, and social age are considered in a package as **functional age,** or how well a person is functioning as an adult compared to others. But it seems clear that the question "How old are you?" has a number of answers.

As developmental psychologists we try not to depend solely on chronological age when investigating some aspect of adult behavior. As you will see in the following chapters, many studies use age groups (young adults compared to middle-aged groups), or roles (couples without children compared to couples with children). Often they avoid the chronological age question by comparing the same people before and after they take on a role, such as parenthood or retirement. It is important to keep in mind that development and chronological age do not travel hand in hand, and this becomes more and more apparent the older we get.

Setting the Course: Some Guiding Perspectives

Before any questions about adult development can be asked, we need to determine what platform to stand on—the base from which we set the course of this journey. The next ten chapters in this book cover specific areas of development and include specific theories that guide that research, but two broad approaches are used for all the chapters, and they define the tone of the book.

One major approach of this book is the **life-span developmental psychology approach,** which states that development is lifelong, multidimensional, plastic, contextual, and has multiple causes (Baltes, Reese, & Lipsitt, 1980). Psychologist Paul Baltes and his colleagues introduced these ideas in 1980, and although this approach sounds very ordinary today, it defined a turning point in developmental psychology, which before that time was focused almost exclusively on child development. The major points of the life-span developmental approach are illustrated in Table 1.2, along with some examples of

Development encompasses both gains and losses. Sometimes a health crisis (loss) can result in a healthy new lifestyle (gain).

Table 1.2   Life-Span Developmental Psychology: Concepts, Propositions, and Examples

Concept	Proposition	Example
Life-span development	Human development is a life-long process. No single age is more important than another. At every age, various developmental processes are at work. Not all developmental processes are present at birth.	A 38-year-old single woman makes plans to adopt a child; a 52-year-old bookkeeper becomes less satisfied with her job now that her kids are grown and she has more attention to give to her work; a 75-year-old Civil War buff becomes uninterested in attending re-enactments and begins taking a class in memoir writing. They are all experiencing development.
Multidirectionality	We develop in different directions and at different rates. Developmental processes increase and decrease. At one time of life, we can change in some areas and remain stable in others.	Some intellectual abilities increase with age, and some decline. Young adults show independence when they complete college and start a career, but show dependence at the same time when they remain in their parents' home.
Development as gain and loss	Development is a combination of gains and losses at every age, and we need to learn how to anticipate and adapt to both.	Middle-aged adults whose parents die often report gaining a new feeling of maturity. Young adults add a baby to their family, but may lose some equality in their marriage. Workers start losing speed and precision as they age, but they gain expertise.
Plasticity	Many aspects of development can be modified. Not much is set in stone, but there are limits.	Young people who enter adulthood with behavior problems or substance-abuse problems can overcome them and become responsible, successful adults. Couples with a lot of conflict in their marriages during the childrearing years can be happy once the children are grown. Fathers can stay home with kids and be nurturing and attentive while mothers work outside the home. Older parents can change their values as a result of their young adult children's lifestyles.
Historical embeddedness	Development is influenced by historical and cultural conditions.	People who grew up in the 1970s have more open attitudes toward legalizing drugs than earlier or later cohorts. Those who lived through the Great Depression have different attitudes toward work than members of other cohorts.
Contextualism	Development depends on the interaction of normative age-graded, normative history-graded, and non-normative influences.	Each of us is an individual because of the interaction of influences we share with other adults in general, those we share because of the times we live in, and those that are unique to us.
Multidisciplinary	The study of human development across the lifespan does not belong to psychology alone. It is the territory of many other disciplines, and we can benefit from the contributions of all.	Contributions to the study of development come from the field of psychology, but also from sociology, anthropology, economics, public health, social work, nursing, epidemiology, education, and other disciplines. Each brings a different and valuable point of view.

Source: Adapted from Baltes, 1987.

each, and as you read them over, you will see that this approach opened the door for the study of development at all ages—not just your 12-year-old brother, but also you, your fellow students, your parents, your professor, and even your grandparents.

A second major approach this book takes is the **ecological systems approach to development,** which states that we must consider the developing person within the context of multiple environments. These ideas were introduced by psycholosist Urie Bronfenbrenner in 1979, and they defined another turning point. Up until that time, developmental psychology had mastered laboratory studies of its research participants, but had lost sight of the larger environments, such as the family, the neighborhood, the community, the culture, and the era, in which the behavior under study was taking place. Bronfenbrenner divided the environment into three systems, the *microsystem,* the *exosystem,* and the *macrosystem,* as shown in Figure 1.1. As you will see throughout this book, recent research in most areas of the social sciences has taken this approach, investigating the development of adults in the context of their lives as individuals, as partners in relationships, as parents in families, as workers on job sites, and as members of particular cohorts.

CRITICAL THINKING ●

In Bronfenbrenner's system, what are the specific influences on your development at each level? Does one level have more influence than the others? Do you think this is true of others or unique to you?

Developmental Research

To understand adult development it is important to know a little about the research process, because information today in the social sciences is, for the most part, science-based. I won't attempt to present a whole course on research methods and statistics, but I will cover some of the methods that are used in the studies I describe in the upcoming chapters of this book

All reseach begins with a question. Suppose, for example, that I want to know something about change or stability in personal relationships over the adult years—relationships with a spouse, with other family members, or with friends. Or suppose that I wanted to

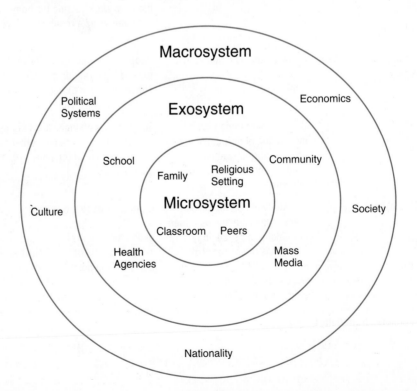

Figure 1.1 Bronfenbrenner's model of the ecological-systems approach to studying development. He suggested that researchers look beyond behavior in laboratory settings and consider how development takes place within multiple environments.

Source: Adapted from Bronfenbrenner, 1979.

study memory over adulthood. Older adults frequently complain that they can't remember things as well as when they were younger. Is this a valid perception? Is there really a loss in memory ability in old age, or earlier? How would I go about designing research to answer such questions? In every instance, there is a set of decisions:

- Should I study groups of people of different ages, or should I study the same group of people over time, or some combination of the two? This is a question dealing with basic research *methods*.
- How will I measure the behavior, thought, or emotion I am studying? How can I best inquire about the quality of marriage—with a questionnaire or in an interview? How do I measure depression—is there a set of questions I can use? These are questions of research *measures*.
- What will I do with the data? Is it enough merely to compare the average number of friends, or the average relationship satisfaction described by subjects in each age group? What else would I want to do to tease out some of the possible explanations? These are questions of research *analysis*.
- What do the results mean? Depending on the research method, measures, and analysis, what is the overall conclusion? What is the answer to the research question I began with? These are questions of research *design*.

Methods

Choosing a research method is perhaps the most crucial decision the researcher makes. This is true in any area of science, but there are special considerations when the topic of study is development. There are essentially three choices: (1) You can choose different groups of subjects at each of a series of ages and compare their responses—in other words, the cross-sectional method; (2) you can study the same subjects over a period of time, observing whether their responses remain the same or change in systematic ways—the longitudinal method; or (3) you can combine the two in any of several ways, collectively called sequential methods.

A **cross-sectional study** in developmental psychology describes a study that is based on data gathered at one time from groups of participants who represent different age groups. Each subject is measured or tested only once, and the results give us information about differences between the groups.

Here is an example of a study using the cross-sectional method. Public health researcher Paul Cleary and his colleagues were interested in knowing whether there were any differences in personal health practices for adults of different ages (Cleary, Zaborski, & Aryanian, 2004). The researchers were part of a large-scale research project known as the Midlife in the United States (MIDUS) National Survey, so they were able to include questions pertaining to personal health in the surveys sent out to 7,000 participants between the ages of 25 and 74. One of the questions was "How much time do you devote to your personal health?" Answers were given as scores on a 10-point scale, with 1 being "very little effort" and 10 being "very much effort." When the results were compiled, the researchers divided them into five groups according to the age of the participants and then by gender, resulting in 10 data points, each giving the average score for one gender at one age group. Figure 1.2 shows the results displayed on a graph. As you can see, the average responses to the question "How much time do you devote to your personal health?" were between 6.8 and 7.8 points. The most obvious result (to me) was that women in every age group responded that they devoted more effort to their health than men, with the biggest difference being in the two groups of people 35 to 44 and 45 to 54 years of age. Men and women were the most similar in the older years of 65 to 74. Women's health efforts increased steadily across

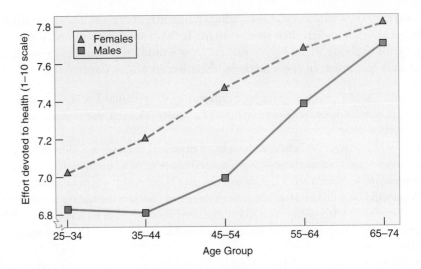

Figure 1.2 Cross-sectional data showing that the amount of effort spent on personal health care increases with age and is greater for women than for men at every age.

Source: Cleary, Zaborski, & Ayanian, 2004.

the adult years, while men's actually declined slightly at 35 to 44 years and then began a sharp increase. Just considering age in general, the figure shows us that the older we get, the more effort we spend on our health. Of course, there are many more findings in the MIDUS study, and I will be discussing them in more detail in later chapters, but for now, this gives you a good example of a cross-sectional research study.

Some cross-sectional studies do not use age groups. Instead they use stages in life, such as comparing young couples without children to couples who have already had their first child to see the effects of parenthood on a marriage. Or comparing young people entering college with those who are graduating to see the effects of education on political views. But all cross-sectional studies are designed to test different people at different points in time—kind of a shortcut for following those people throughout that time period and charting individual changes. The benefit is that it is quicker, easier, and less expensive than following the same people around the whole time. The downside is that it only shows *age differences,* not change. When cross-sectional studies are done with older adults, it is possible that the people in the older groups do not represent the general population as well as those in the younger groups, due to transportation problems, chronic health concerns, and difficulty in recruiting older participants. It is also the case that the older participants are those who have survived into old age and may be healthier and wealthier (and perhaps wiser). But again, the minimal time and effort it takes to conduct cross-sectional studies makes them attractive to most researchers, and many of these problems can be predicted and controlled for.

A **longitudinal study,** by contrast, is one in which a researcher follows a group of people the same age over a period of time, taking measurements of some behavior of interest at regular intervals. In comparison to the cross-sectional study discussed above, a longitudinal study might start with a group of people who are 35 to 44, asking how much effort they devote to their health. Then, 10 years later, the researchers could find the same people, now at the ages of 45 to 54, and ask them the same question again. Finally, another 10 years later, the last data could be gathered when the participants are 55 to 64 years of age. Then comparisons could be made, telling the story of these individuals, at least in regard to *age-related changes* in the time they devoted to their health over their middle years (not just *age-related differences* as are revealed by correlational studies).

An example of a study using the longitudinal method is one done by psychologist Nancy Galambos and her colleagues, who were interested in the development of self-esteem in young adults (Galambos, Barker, & Krahn, 2006). They began the study at the

Year of Testing

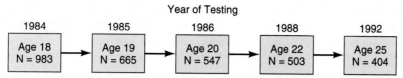

Figure 1.3   Model of a longitudinal study in which 983 students were surveyed in 1984 and then again in 1985, 1986, 1988, and 1992. Note their ages and also the number of students who returned the questionnaires (N).

Source: Data from Galambos, Barker, & Krahn, 2006.

end of the school year in 1984 by giving out questionnaires to 983 high school seniors in a large western Canadian city. Among other things, the questionnaire contained six items from a self-esteem inventory in which participants read such statements, as "On the whole I am satisfied with myself" and "I feel that I have a number of good qualities." They rated each item on a scale of 1 (strongly disagree) to 5 (strongly agree). As Figure 1.3 shows, a year later, when the participants were 19, they received a second questionnaire containing the same questions (and others). Of the 983 original participants, 665 returned the second questionnaire. The third year the process was repeated, and 547 participants, who were now 20 years of age, returned the third questionnaire. Two years later, the researchers sent out a fourth questionnaire and received 503 in return. Finally, in 1992, when the participants were 25 years of age, the final questionnaire was sent out and the return was 404. Although this return was only 45 percent of the original sample size, the response rate is typical of longitudinal studies.

Galambos and her colleagues compiled the data on self-esteem by finding average scores for the group of participants at each age they were surveyed. They also divided the group into male and female subgroups. The results are shown in Figure 1.4. As the graph

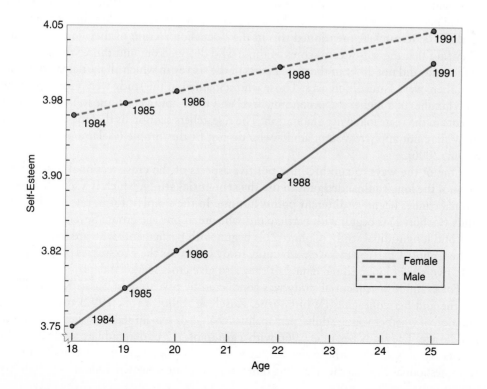

Figure 1.4 Young adults increase in self-esteem between the ages of 18 and 25, according to this longitudinal study. Note the different rates of increase for men and women.

Source: Galambos, Barker, & Krahn, 2006.

shows, the average scores for these young adults ranges between 3.75 and 4.05, and self-esteem for both groups increased between the ages of 18 and 25. There is also a different rate of increase for the males and the females. The males had higher self-esteem at 18, but by 25, their rate was not much higher than that of the females. The females had lower scores at 18, but their rate of increase was greater than that of the males.

The longitudinal method used by Galambos and her colleagues truly demonstrates *change* because the same participants were tested at each age. There were only 404 participants (compared to over 7,000 in the cross-sectional study described above), but the data points on the graph show increases in self-esteem for the same participants over the course of seven years. Another plus for longitudinal studies is that the participants are from the same cohort, which increases the probability that the changes in self-esteem are age related and not the result of some normative history-graded influence on that cohort. However, the minuses of longitudinal studies should be apparent. From the first wave of testing to the published article, the study took 22 years! This method is time-consuming and expensive. In a profession that bases promotion and tenure on annual publication lists, researchers need to balance longitudinal studies with shorter-term work in order not to "perish" due to lack of publications. The most ambitious longitudinal studies I am aware of are done in large European research institutes, such as the Berlin Study of Aging, directed by psychologist Paul Baltes. There are 40 researchers on the staff and hundreds of students and paid researchers. The study began in 1990 by assessing 516 people between 70 and 100 years of age, and it took 14 sessions for each person to receive the initial assessment—a project that took the research staff three years (Baltes & Mayer, 1999). The findings from the Berlin Study of Aging and similar research efforts will be discussed in the upcoming chapters of this book.

Another drawback to longitudinal studies is **attrition,** or participant dropout. The Galambos study began with a fairly general sample of high school students, but as the years went by, each wave of data collection yielded fewer and fewer returns. More than half of the original participants were absent from the last wave of the study. When attrition is present, we need to ask whether those who dropped out might have made a difference in the results. The researchers mentioned this in the discussion section of their journal article. They said that the self-esteem scores of those who dropped out and those who remained in the study did not differ in the earlier parts of the survey in which all participated. However, there were some differences. Those who remained in the study were more apt to be from families of a higher socioeconomic level and more apt to continue to live with their parents in the years following graduation. The researchers caution us that the results of the study may not apply to young adults who do not fit this profile (Galambos, Barker, & Krahn, 2006).

One of the ways to combine the positive aspects of the cross-sectional design with those of the longitudinal design is to use the **sequential study,** which is a series of longitudinal studies begun at different points in time. In the simplest form, one longitudinal study (Cohort 1) is begun with participants who are in one age group. Several years later, a second longitudinal study (Cohort 2) is begun with participants who are the same age as the Cohort 1 participants were when the study began. As the two studies progress, they yield two sets of longitudinal data, but they also give cross-sectional data.

For example, a sequential study was conducted by psychologist Susan Krauss Whitbourne and her colleagues (Whitbourne, Zuschlag, Elliot, et al., 1992) to answer the question of whether young adults' personalities change or remain stable as they moved into middle age. The study began in 1966 with a group of 347 undergraduate students at the University of Rochester whose average age was 20. They were given a personality inventory questionnaire asking them, among other things, to rate statements about their industry (or work ethic) according to how well each described them. In Figure 1.5, this group is shown in the top left box labeled Cohort 1, 1966. In 1977, this group was on average 31 years old, and the researchers sent out questionnaires again, receiving 155 in return, as shown in the box labeled Cohort 1, 1977. Also in 1977 a new group of 20-year-old

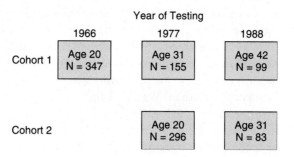

Figure 1.5 Model of a sequential study in which two cohorts were followed beginning at age 20. One cohort was followed for 22 years; one for 11 years. Note ages and number of participants (N).

Source: Adapted from Whitbourne, Zuschlag, Elliot, et al., 1992.

students from the University of Rochester were given the personality inventory questionnaire (Cohort 2, 1977). In 1988 the process was repeated for the participants in Cohort 1, who were now 42 years of age, and Cohort 2, who were now 31 years of age. As you can see, 99 of the original 347 in Cohort 1 returned questionnaires, and 83 of the original 296 in Cohort 2 returned questionnaires.

At this point, there are two longitudinal studies going on, Cohort 1 with data available for the ages of 20, 31, and 42, and Cohort 2 with data available for the ages of 20 and 31. There is also a cross-sectional study going on, with a group of 20-year-olds, a group of 31-year-olds, and a group of 42-year-olds. Figure 1.6 shows how Whitbourne and her colleagues analyzed the results. The top line shows the industry scores for Cohort 1 at ages 20, 31, and 42. The scores increase sharply between 20 and 31, and the increase becomes more gradual from 31 to 42. This definitely shows change in personality traits during adulthood, but does the same hold for other cohorts? The lower line in the figure shows the pattern for Cohort 2, tested at 20 years and 31 years of age. The pattern is different than for Cohort 1. First, the industry scores are much higher at age 20 for Cohort 2 (6.54 for Cohort 1 and 9.19 for Cohort 2), and second, the rate of increase is much slower for Cohort 2. Still, both groups had similar industry scores at the age of 31 (13.58 for Cohort 1 and 14.32 for Cohort 2). The researchers suggest that the 20-year-olds in Cohort 1 were in college during the 1960s, when the work ethic of the establishment was being questioned and rejected, and their low scores on industry were reflections of that

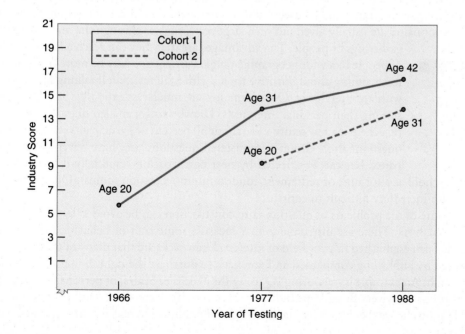

Figure 1.6 Results from sequential study of two cohorts tested at three ages and at three different points in time. Comparing longitudinal results, Cohort 1 shows a sharper increase in industry scores between 20 and 31 years than does Cohort 2; though both have similar scores at age 31. Cross-sectional results suggest that the normative history-graded influences (Vietnam War, Civil Rights issues) lowered the young adults' scores in 1966.

Source: Adapted from Whitbourne, Zuschlag, Elliot, et al., 1992.

era. Once out of school and in the workplace, this group had some catching up to do. Their catching up is represented by the sharp increase in industry scores, which at 31 are very close to the scores of Cohort 2, who were not part of the protest era. Clearly there are non-normative history-graded influences going on here. Perhaps the normative age-graded pattern of change in the personality trait of industry is more like that of Cohort 2, but when history (the Vietnam War, civil rights issues) brings about a large student protest movement, it causes a detour in the journey of adulthood for many in that cohort, although in the case of the personality trait of industry, these college students were able to catch up to speed and be back on track by the time they were 31. We will revisit this study in Chapter 8 when I cover personality development, but for now it serves as a good example of using the sequential method to study development.

Measures

Once the research design is determined, the next major set of decisions has to do with how to measure the behavior of interest. Each method has its own set of advantages and disadvantages, and I will discuss them here briefly.

One of the most common instruments used to gather data is a **personal interview,** that is, having the experimenter ask the participant questions, one on one. Personal interviews can be *structured,* like a multiple-choice test, or *open ended,* like an essay test, or a combination of both. All the major longitudinal studies I have described so far, for example, included extensive interviews. Many sociological studies of adult life also involve structured interviews. Personal interviews have the advantage of allowing the interviewer to clarify questions and ask follow-up questions. Participants feel comfortable talking to a human being and not just writing answers on an impersonal questionnaire. Drawbacks are that the participants might provide responses they feel are socially acceptable to the interviewer, and similarly, the interviewer's feelings toward the participant might cloud the recording or coding of responses, especially with very long interviews. Building rapport between interviewer and participant can be a plus or a minus.

This problem is avoided by using the **survey questionnaire,** a paper-and-pencil form consisting of structured and focused questions that participants can fill out on their own. Questionnaires are usually given out on a large scale, such as through the mail or at large gatherings of people. The advantages are that they can reach a large number of people in a wide geographic range. Participants may be more truthful and forthcoming about sensitive topics with a survey than if talking face-to-face with an interviewer. Questionnaires are much less expensive and time consuming than personal interviews. Drawbacks for mailed questionnaires are that there is a low return rate (about 30 percent of participants return the first questionnaire). Group-administered questionnaires have fewer lost participants, but can be affected by peer participation (especially if given out in high school auditoriums or retirement condominium recreation rooms). Questionnaires are also incredibly difficult to construct.

Some of the problems of questionnaire construction can be avoided by using **standardized tests.** These are instruments that measure some trait or behavior and have already been established in your field of interest. Drawbacks are that many of these tests are owned by publishing companies, and you have to purchase the right to use them in your research. An example is measuring IQ using the Wechsler Scales, or personality using the MMPI or the Myers-Briggs Type Indicator. However, there are also a number of tests available at no change that have been standardized and published in research articles, along with

CRITICAL THINKING

Design a questionnaire for your class asking what their opinion is on the classroom design (the light, seating, room temperature, and so forth).

instructions for administering and scoring them. For example, researchers in a number of studies in this book measure depression in their participants with an instrument known as the CES-D-10, or the Center for Epidemiological Studies Short Depressive Symptoms Scale (Andresen, Malmgren, Carter, et al., 1994). This test is easily retrieved from the Internet after a quick search and is shown in Chapter 3, Figure 3.7. It is a good example of a standardized test that is easily scored and has a good record of **validity** (it measures what is claims to measure) and **reliability** (it does so consistently). How to select a standardized test for your own research? There are reference books that review tests annually, such as the *Mental Measures Yearbook* (Spies & Plake, 2005), but the advice I give students is to read similar studies published by other researchers and use what they use. Selecting a research measure is probably not the best time to be innovative.

These are by no means the only research measures available. As you will see throughout this book, there are many ways to measure human behavior, from complex brain-imaging techniques to 1-item questionnaires ("How would you rate your health? Circle one of the following: Very Good, Good, Average, Poor, Very Poor"). Depending on the research question, either measure could be the best.

Analyses

Once the research method has been chosen and the behavior has been measured, researchers must make another set of decisions about how to analyze the resulting data. Some of the statistical methods now being used are extremely sophisticated and complex. I'll be describing a few of these in later chapters when I discuss specific studies that include them. At this early point, all I want to do is talk about the two most common ways of looking at adult development.

The most common and the simplest way to describe age-related differences is to collect the data (scores, measurement results) for each group, find the means (averages), and determine whether the differences in the means are large enough to be significant, a process known as **comparison of means.** With cross-sectional studies, the means of the age groups are compared. With longitudinal studies, the means of the scores for the same people at different ages are compared. With sequential studies, both comparisons are possible. However, the similarity remains—we are looking for an age-related pattern of change.

If the group of participants is large enough, it is often possible to divide it into smaller groups and look for age differences or continuities in the subgroups, such as women versus men, working class versus middle class, those with young children versus those without young children. If the same pattern appears in all subgroups, we'd be more likely to conclude that this is a significant age-related pattern. However, if the change is different for the subgroups (as is often the case), it opens the door for follow-up questions. For example, in the cross-sectional study I described earlier (Cleary, Zaborski, & Ayanian, 2004), researchers divided the age groups into gender groups also, and they found that different patterns emerged for men and women in the amount of time spent on health-related activities. Not only did the researchers find answers to their questions about age-related change (yes, it increases with age), but they found that it increased more for men and they started out at a disadvantage. That gave the researchers the opportunity to speculate as to why men seem to have so little concern about their health at 25 and do not change in this respect until about 45. In contrast, women have more concern at 24, and they increase in concern their whole lives. Perhaps at 25, women are concerned with childbearing and visit their doctors more often. Perhaps the cultural emphasis on women's appearance causes them to notice subtle signs of aging sooner, while men "coast" for awhile until the signs are more evident. These questions make for good discussion and inspire new research to find answers.

Comparisons of means for different age groups, either cross-sectionally or longitudinally, can give us some insights into possible age changes or developmental patterns, but they cannot tell us whether there has been stability or change within individuals. For this information, a different type of analysis is required: a **correlational analysis.** A correlation is simply a statistic that tells us the extent to which two sets of scores on the same people tend to vary together. Correlations (r) can range from +1.00 to –1.00. A positive correlation shows that high scores on the two dimensions occur together. A negative correlation tells us that high scores on one dimension go with low scores on the other. The closer the correlation is to 1.00 (positive or negative), the stronger the relationship. A correlation of 0.00 indicates no relationship.

CRITICAL THINKING

What would you predict the correlation direction would be for the number of hours students study for an exam and their grades? What about the average speed they drive and the number of infraction points on their driver's licenses?

For example, height and weight are positively correlated: taller people generally weigh more, shorter people less. But the correlation is not perfect (not +1.00) because there are some short, heavy people, and some tall, light people. If you are on a diet, the number of pounds you lose is negatively correlated with the number of calories you eat: high calories go with low weight loss. But this correlation, too, is not a perfect –1.00 (as any of you who have dieted know full well!).

Correlations are also used to reveal patterns of stability or change. For example, researchers interested in personality traits might give personality assessments to participants over a number of years and then correlate the early scores with the later scores for each person. A high positive correlation would show stability for that trait.

Ultimately, however, correlations can tell us only about relationship; they cannot tell us about causality, even though it is often very tempting to make the conceptual leap from a correlation to a cause. Some cases are easy. If I told you that there was a negative correlation between the per capita incidence of television sets in the countries of the world and the infant mortality rates in those countries, you would not be tempted to conclude that the presence of TV *causes* lower infant mortality. You'd look for other kinds of societal characteristics that might explain the link between the two facts such as income level. But if I tell you there is a correlation between the amount of time adults spend with friends and family and the overall life satisfaction those adults report, you would be much more tempted to jump to the conclusion that greater happiness is *caused* by contact with friends and family. And it may be. But the correlation, by itself, doesn't tell us that; it only tells us that there is a relationship. It remains for further research and theorizing to uncover the causal links, if any. Perhaps the greater life satisfaction people have, the more time their friends and family want to spend with them.

One unique way correlational analyses are used in developmental research is to determine the genetic contributions to various behaviors and abilities. I introduced twin studies in an earlier section, and will just explain them in a little more detail here. The typical twin study involves comparing two types of twins, monozygotic and dizygotic, on the behavior you are interested in. For a simple example, let's use height (and twins of the same sex to rule out sex differences). Each twin would be measured and the height recorded. Then two correlations would be computed comparing the twins—one for monozygotic twins and one for dizygotic twins. Which do you think would be more similar in height? Of course the monozygotic twins, because they have the same genes, and height is something that is determined by inheritance to a great extent. But what about other characteristics, like IQ, the tendency toward alcoholism, how religious one is? Those are all characteris-

CRITICAL THINKING

If adopted children were more similar to their adoptive parents on some measure than to their biological parents, what conclusions could you make from that?

tics that have been shown to be influenced by heredity to a significant extent. And the research that revealed this involved correlational analyses.

For example, in a study using data from the Swedish Twin Registry, epidemiologist Erica
Spotts and her colleagues (Spotts, Neiderhiser, Towers, et al., 2004) were interested in
whether marital happiness is influenced by heredity. They gave a test of marital happiness
to over 300 pairs of twins (all women) and their husbands. About half of the women were
monozygotic twins and half were dizygotic twins. When the scores were analyzed, the
monozygotic twin pairs were more alike than the dizygotic twin pairs. As you can see in
Figure 1.7, if one monozygotic twin was happy in her marriage, the other twin tended to
be happy too—and if one was unhappy, there was a good chance that the other was too.
Their marital happiness scores were positively correlated. This was not the case for the dizygotic twins, whose correlations were about half what the monozygotic twins' correlations
were. Comparing the two types of twins' correlations shows the extent of the genetic contribution to marital happiness, because the monozygotic twins share the same genes, while
the dizygotic twins share only half, and as in the case of height, we would not expect them
to be as similar.

In a surprise twist, the researchers also gave the marital happiness questionnaire to the husbands of the twins, who were not related to each other
or to anyone else in the study. As you can see in the figure, the husbands of
the monozygotic twins also were more similar in their marital happiness
scores than the husbands of the dizygotic twins. It seems that the genetic
endowment of the monozygotic twins not only gave the women similar outlooks on marriage, but that the women, in turn, influenced the marital happiness of their husbands.

Another, fairly new way of analyzing data is the **meta-analysis.** This approach combines data from a large number of studies that deal with the same research question. A researcher conducting a meta-analysis selects a research question, such as whether or not
aerobic exercise affects cognitive functioning in older adults. This has been a topic of interest for several decades and is a prominent topic in Chapter 4 of this book. A number
of studies have shown that older adults (and laboratory animals) who participate in vigorous physical activity have better cognitive abilities than their age-mates who are sedentary. However, the studies have used different age groups, different types of physical
activity, and different measures of cognitive ability (not to mention different species).

● **CRITICAL THINKING**

What are some specific ways women can
pass on their level of marital happiness
to their husbands? What about marital
unhappiness?

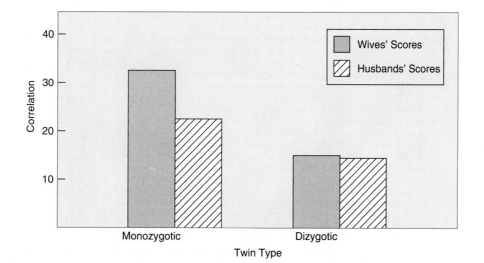

Figure 1.7 Women
who are monozygotic
twins and have the
same genes are more
similar in their marital
happiness than women
who are dizygotic twins
and share only half
their genes. Interest-
ingly, this genetic effect
carried to their hus-
bands (compare striped
columns).

Source: Data from Spotts, Neiderhiser, Towers, et al., 2004.

Psychologists Stanley Colcombe and Arthur Kramer (2003) reviewed this research and conducted a meta-analysis to evaluate the combined results. The first step was an online search to find all the studies of human cognition published in a certain time frame (2000–2001) that had any mention of age, fitness, exercise, and a number of other key words. They narrowed down the 167 articles to 18 (totaling 101 participants) that were longitudinal, supervised (not surveys), dealt with aerobic exercise, had participants assigned randomly to exercise and nonexercise groups, and had participants over the age of 55. They regrouped the data in the studies to fit one overall scheme. Participants' data were divided into three groups: 55–65, 66–70, and 71+. The cognitive tasks that were measured were divided into four types: planning, speed, control, and visuo-spatial. As you can see in Figure 1.8, the researchers found that the participants in the exercise groups performed significantly better on all four types of cognitive tasks than those who were in the nonexercise groups, no matter what age or gender and no matter what type of aerobic exercise was done. These are very impressive results. This meta-analysis tells us that the smaller, individual studies were all tapping into the same big pot—the idea that aerobic exercise is good for the cognitive functioning of people over 55.

Designs

The closing statement researchers are allowed to make depends on what kind of research design has been used, experimental or nonexperimental. If it is experimental, researchers are able to say their findings show that their factor of interest caused the change observed in their subjects. If it is not experimental research, they must limit themselves to saying that their results show a relationship or an association with the change.

The distinctions between experimental and nonexperiental designs could fill a whole book (and there are a number of good ones available), but for now, let me just say that the feature that distinguishes experimental designs from nonexperimental designs is how much control the experimenter has over the way the study is conducted. In the strictest sense of the word, an experimental design has a control group, the participants are selected randomly from the population of interest, they are assigned randomly to groups, there is random assignment of groups to treatment and control conditions, and there is a high degree of control over any outside factors that might affect the outcome. The more of these features that are present, the stronger the case the researcher can make for causality. Table 1.3 shows three types of experimental designs and the presence or absence of these controls.

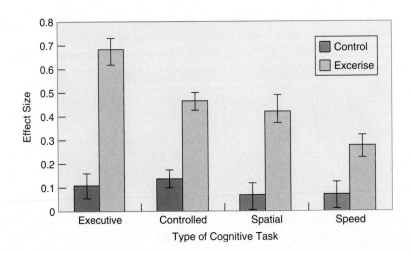

Figure 1.8 Meta-analysis of 18 studies shows that aerobic exercise causes better performance in older adults on four types of cognitive tasks.

Source: Colcombe & Kramer, 2003.

Table 1.3	**Experimental Designs and Their Comparative Features**		
	Pre-Experimental Design	**True Experimental Design**	**Quasi-Experimental Design**
Presence of a control group?	In some cases, but usually not	Always	Often
Random selection of subjects from a population?	No	Yes	No
Random assignment of subjects to groups?	No	Yes	No
Random assignment of treatment to groups?	No	Yes	No
Degree of control over extraneous variables	None	Yes	Some

Source: Salkind, 2003.

Experimental designs include true experiments, pre-experiments, and quasi-experiments, depending on which of the controls listed in the table are present. These experiments are difficult to conduct and are not very useful in answering developmental research questions. One reason is that when comparisons are made between age groups (or between groups of people at different stages of life, such as preretirement versus postretirement), the participants cannot be assigned to groups, they are already in one group or the other. That automatically takes a large amount of control out of the hands of the researcher and opens the door for a number of problems.

Other designs include descriptive research and qualitative research. **Descriptive research** tells the current state of the participants on some measure of interest. The number of people who die of suicide each year at different ages is descriptive research. The rate of births to unmarried women over the past 50 years is descriptive research. And the cross-sectional, longitudinal, and sequential studies discussed earlier are descriptive research. What they have in common is the lack of a high level of experimenter control described earlier in Table 1.2. They are still valuable sources of information on development.

Qualitative research is, quite simply, research without the numbers. It is a very old tradition that has only recently been included in developmental sciences. Although research without numbers may sound very enticing to students who have just completed a statistics course, it is not really a replacement for **quantitative research** (research with the numbers), but a different approach that is used to supplement quantitative research. Qualitative research includes case studies, interviews, participant observations, direct observations, and exploring documents, artifacts, and archival records. If you have ever done genealogy research to find your family history in old records and documents, you have done a form of qualitative research.

An example of qualitative research is a study by sociologists Amy Hequembourg and Sara Brallier (2005) that will be discussed more fully in Chapter 5. They were interested in the role transitions that go on among adult siblings when their elderly parents need care. We have long been aware that daughters are most likely to be the major caregiver of an aging parent, but these researchers found eight brother-sister pairs and interviewed them at length about their roles and feelings about their caregiving responsibilities. They recorded the answers in detail and then spent many months analyzing them. The finished product was a very interesting view of these families. Yes, the sisters did more, but sometimes they were pleased to be in that role. And other times the brothers stepped in and took over. There was evidence of adult sisters and brothers growing closer to each other as they shared the care for their parents. Although it was a study of only 16 participants, it gave more depth than a questionnaire sent out to 5,000. Clearly there is a place in developmental psychology for this type of research, and I am pleased to see it being discussed in research methods books.

Qualitative research is not easy. It needs to be carefully planned, the sources need to be wisely chosen, and questions need to be designed to focus on the topic at hand. If the research involves spending a lot of time with the people being interviewed, the experimenter needs to be able to remain as objective as possible. Data must be recorded precisely and completely. And then the findings need to be organized and written up to share with others.

Qualitative research is an excellent way to begin a new line of research. Epidemiologist David Snowden, the director of the Nun Study of the School Sisters of Notre Dame, started his research by visiting with the elderly nuns in a convent in Minnesota. As a beginning professor, he had no idea of what he wanted to do for a research program, but one day he stumbled onto a room that contained the archives of the convent. Each sister had a file going back to her first days as a nun, often 50 or 60 years before. They had all written essays about their childhoods and why they wanted to be nuns. Snowdon (2001) writes that "for an epidemiologist, this sort of find is equivalent to an archaeologist's discovering an undisturbed tomb or a paleontologist's unearthing a perfectly preserved skeleton" (p. 24). From this beginning, he began the research that became his career. For example, he and his colleagues (Riley, Snowdon, Desrosiers, et al., 2005) found that the more complex the language in the essays the nuns had written as young women, the less likely they were to have Alzheimer's disease in late adulthood. Some of his other research findings are discussed in Chapter 4, but for now, this serves as a good example of qualitative research based on archival records.

A Final Word

On a personal note, I approach the topic of this book both as a developmental psychologist and as an adult. Like many people, I am on this journey of adulthood with my parents, my husband, my friends and family, and my adult children, so my interest is both scientific and personal. I want to understand how it all works and why, both because that is what I have chosen for my career and also because it is what I think about a good deal of the time that I am not at work. My journey through adulthood is no doubt similar to yours, but it is also different in other ways. What I am searching for in this book are the basic rules or processes that account for both the similarities and the differences. I hope you can share with me the sense of adventure in the scientific search as well as in the personal journey.

Summary

1. Developmental psychology includes the study of change and stability over time during childhood, adolescence, and adulthood. The study of adult development covers the time from emerging adulthood to the end of life and is based on empirical research.

2. This book covers individual differences between people and also the commonalities they share. It looks at stability and change, continuity and stages, typical development and atypical development, and the outer and inner changes that occur over the years of adulthood.

3. Sources of change in adulthood are classified into three types: (a) Normative age-graded influences are linked to age and happen to most people as they grow older. They come from both biological and environmental causes, and also from interactions between the two. (b) Normative history-graded influences are factors that only affect some people or groups. These changes include cultural conditions and cohort experiences. One of the best-studied cohorts is the group of people who lived through the Great Depression. (c) Nonnormative life events are unique to the individual and cause developmental changes that are not shared by many.

4. Sources of stability in adulthood include genetics and environmental influences and also the intereactions between the two.

5. The word "age" has many more meanings than how many years one has been alive (chronological age). In various usages it also designates estimates of a person's physical condition compared to others (physical age), the abilities one displays in dealing effectively with the environment (psychological age), and the roles one has taken on (social age). The last three make up a person's functional age. Developmental psychologists seldom depend on chronological age alone in their studies because of these factors. Instead, most use age groups or stages in life.

6. This book will approach the topic of adult development using the tenets of life-span developmental psychology, a set of ideas introduced by Baltes in 1980 that encouraged psychologists to study development at many ages and to view development in a broader scope than they had before.

7. A second approach this book will take is based on the ecological systems view introduced by Bronfenbrenner in 1979. This set of ideas inspired psychologists to consider the whole person, not just the isolated behavior of a participant in a laboratory experiment.

8. The first step in doing developmental research is to select a research method. There are three possibilities: (1) cross-sectional studies gather data on a group of people representing different age groups, (2) longitudinal studies follow the same people over a long period of time, gathering data at several points along the way, and (3) sequential studies combine the preceding methods by conducting two longitudinal studies during different time periods, thereby making it possible to do both longitudinal and cross-sectional comparisons. There are pros and cons to each method.

9. After a method is chosen, a researcher needs to choose an appropriate measure. Some of the most common ones in developmental research are personal interviews, survey questionnaires, and standardized tests.

10. The next step in developmental research is selecting analyses. Most research uses either comparison of means, which involves computing the means of the measurement scores for each group and testing them statistically to see if they are significantly different, or correlational analysis, in which the researcher compares scores for several measurements for the participants to see if there is a relationship between the characteristics being measured. Correlations are used to show both change and stability. They are also used to demonstrate heritability by comparing scores of monozygotic twins with scores of dizygotic twins.

11. The meta-analysis is a relatively new way to analyze research data. It combines data from a number of previously published studies that focus on the same research question. This is done by combining the data and re-analyzing it as a larger, more powerful study.

12. The final step in developmental research involves stating conclusions, and this depends on whether the research design was experimental or not. If the design was experimental,

it is possible to conclude that the results of the study were caused by the factor of interest. Experimental designs include true experiments, pre-experiments, and quasi-experiments, and they differ in the amount of control the experimenter has over the conditions of the study and the outside factors that might also cause similar results. Experimental designs are not often used in developmental research.

13. Research designs that are not experimental provide valuable knowledge about development even though researchers cannot conclude that their factor of interest caused the results. These designs include descriptive research and qualitative research.

Key Terms

developmental psychology, 4

adult development, 4

empirical research, 4

individual differences, 4

commonalities, 5

stability, 5

change, 5

continuous, 6

stages, 6

typical, 6

atypical, 6

outer changes, 6

inner changes, 6

normative age-graded influences, 7

biological clock, 7

social clock, 7

ageism, 7

normative history-graded influences, 8

cultures, 8

cohort, 8

nonnormative life events, 9

stability, 11

behavior genetics, 11

twin studies, 12

interactionist view, 12

chronological age, 13

biological age, 13

psychological age, 13

social age, 13

functional age, 14

life-span developmental psychology approach, 14

ecological systems approach, 16

cross-sectional study, 17

longitudinal study, 18

attrition, 20

sequential study, 20

personal interview, 22

survey questionnaire, 22

standardized tests, 22

validity, 23

reliability, 23

comparison of means, 23

correlational analysis, 24

meta-analysis, 25

experimental designs, 27

descriptive research, 27

qualitative research, 27

quantitative research, 27

Suggested Reading

Reading for Personal Interest

Segal, N. L. (1999). *Entwined lives: Twins and what they tell us about human behavior.* New York: Dutton.

Psychologist Nancy Segal is a twin researcher, in several senses of the word. She does research on twins and is a twin herself. This book is a clear explanation of twin studies and also fun to read because she uses informal stories about her research subjects and her own experience as a twin.

Snowdon, D, (2003). *Aging with grace: What the Nun Study teaches us about leading longer, healthier, more meaningful lives.* New York: Bantam Books.

Epidemiologist David Snowdon tells the story of his ongoing research project of 678 Roman Catholic nuns and how they are aging. His inquisitiveness and their enthusiasm shine through in this book and provide a good picture of successful aging.

Terkel, S. (1995). *Coming of age: The story of our century by those who've lived it.* New York: St. Martin's Griffin.

Studs Terkel's talent is teaching us about an era by telling the stories of individuals who experienced it. In this book he brings us the stories of people who were alive in 1900 and who personally experienced most of the 20th century. It tells about their thoughts of families, jobs, war, aging, and the end of life. This book is an enjoyable way to learn 20th-century history and perhaps understand our older family members a little better.

Classic Work

Elder, Glen. H., Jr. (1974). *Children of the Great Depression.* Chicago: University of Chicago Press.

Classic study by sociologist Elder of people who had been children of different ages during the Great Depression in the United States, showing how their development trajectories were changed by how they experienced these years.

Neugarten, B.L. (1979). Time, age and the life cycle. *American Journal of Psychiatry, 136,* 887–894.

Sociologist Bernice Neugarten was the first to write about the biological and social clocks and how they influence our lives.

Vaillant, G. E. (1977). *Adaptation to life.* Boston, MA: Little Brown.

Psychiatrist George Vaillant writes about the Grant longitudinal study of Harvard men from college years through age 55.

Contemporary Scholarly Work

O'Rand, A. M. (2006). Stratification and the life course: Life course capital, life course risks, and social inequality. In R. H. Binstock & L. K. George (Eds.), *Handbook of aging and the social sciences* (pp. 145–162). San Diego: Academic Press.

A sociologist's view of early factors that have effects on later adult development such as childhood experiences, parents' influences, education, health, and delinquency. This handbook chapter is a good discussion of the effects of non-normative life events.

Salkind, N. (2005). *Exploring research* (6th Ed.) Upper Saddle Brook, NJ: Prentice-Hall.

If you want a good review of research methods, this clearly written and well-organized book fills the bill.

Walker, A. (2006). Aging and politics: An international perspective. In R. H. Binstock & L. K. George (Eds.), *Handbook of aging and the social sciences* (pp. 339–359). San Diego: Academic Press.

We all know that the distribution of age groups is changing in the U.S. and all over the world, but what is that doing to the political landscape? Do current cohorts of adults have different political agendas? This is a fascinating review of how this demographic change is affecting government policy at every level.

Chapter 2

Physical Changes

Theories of Primary Aging
   Oxidative Damage
   Genetic Limits
   Caloric Restriction
   A Word on Theories of Primary Aging

Physical Changes During Adulthood
   Outward Appearance
   The Senses
   Bones and Muscles
   Cardiovascular and Respiratory Systems
   Brain and Nervous System
   Immune System
   Hormonal System

Changes in Physical Behavior
   Athletic Abilities
   Stamina, Dexterity, and Balance
   Sleep
   Sexual Activity

Individual Differences in Primary Aging
   Genetics
   Lifestyle
   Psychosocial Factors
   Economics

Can We "Turn Back the Clock" of Primary Aging?

An Overview of Physical Changes in Adulthood

Summary

Key Terms

Suggested Reading

ONE OF OUR favorite family stories comes from an experience my sister Patty had with our 82-year-old mother during a visit to a neurologist's office. Patty is a registered nurse and the expert in the family when it comes to our parents' healthcare. She usually accompanies Mom and Dad to their doctors' appointments and then communicates the information from the doctor to the rest of us in the family. Mom had been having problems for a while finding her way around. She didn't drive anymore, but she could not recognize familiar landmarks or give people directions to familiar places. So we scheduled a battery of neurological tests over the course of a few days and then a meeting with a neurologist. As Patty and my mother sat in the office, the doctor explained to them that Mom was having problems with spatial functions and that it was due to changes in certain parts of the frontal cortex that were not unusual in people her age. My sister, always the nurse, asked what the diagnosis was. The doctor explained that it was atrophy of the prefrontal cortex. "But what is the diagnosis?" she asked again, perhaps wondering if it was early stages of Alzheimer's disease or some other form of dementia. As the doctor attempted to reword his answer yet again, my mother spoke up, "I have an 82-year-old brain," she said, "that's what he is trying to say!"

Since that time it has become a family joke. When someone asked my brother-in-law why he was suddenly wearing glasses for reading, his answer was, "I have 45-year-old eyes, that's why." And when my father takes the elevator instead of walking a flight of stairs, he defends it by blaming his "86-year-old lungs."

The concept my family is expressing is known as **primary aging,** the gradual, shared, inevitable changes that will happen to most of us. The term **secondary aging,** which will be covered in the next chapter, refers to the more sudden changes that happen to some individuals and not others and are often the result of disease, poor health habits, and environmental influences. I will begin this chapter with some of the theories of primary aging and then describe the changes most adults experience with age in the major systems of the body. Then I will discuss the effects of primary aging in complex behaviors like sleep and sexual activity. Finally, I will cover some of the individual differences that are found in primary aging patterns and answer the age-old question, "Can we turn back the clock?"

Theories of Primary Aging

Why do we age? This has been the subject of speculation for centuries, but the technology necessary to evaluate it is fairly new. As a result, the biology of aging is a relatively young field with a plethora of data but no grand theories on which a significant number of scientists agree (Austad, 2001). Instead, there are a hundred or more fledgling theories that have been offered by various biologists. As behavior geneticists Gerald McClearn and Debra Heller (2000) suggest, "The scientific pessimist might lament the absence of a compelling unified theory; the scientific optimist will revel in the richness of the empirical data and the diversity of the current theoretical propositions" (p. 1). I have selected a few of the more recent theories to describe here, along with support and criticism for each.

Oxidative Damage

One theory of primary aging is based on random damage that takes place on the cellular level. This process involves the release of **free radicals,** molecules or atoms that possess an unpaired electron and are by-products of normal body metabolism as well as a response to diet, sunlight, x-rays, and air pollution. These molecules enter into many potentially damaging chemical reactions, most of which the healthy body can resist or repair. But with age the resistance and repair functions decline, the oxidative damage increases, and the result is primary aging.

A number of vitamins and minerals, such as Vitamins C and E, have been identified as **antioxidants,** substances having properties that protect against oxidative damage. Many nutritional supplements are on the market containing large doses of these substances. However, there is little evidence that they can delay primary aging in humans, and large doses of some supplements can be harmful. Most people in developed countries have adequate supplies of these nutrients in their diets, and no benefit has been shown for larger doses.

Better advice comes from neuroscientist James A. Joseph and his colleagues (Joseph, Shukitt-Hale, Denisova, et al.,1999), who fed aging rats diets consisting of only one food item—either blueberries, strawberries, or spinach. After 8 weeks, the results were improved memory and motor coordination accompanied by decreased signs of oxidative stress. Blueberries worked best—the human equivalent of one cup per day. When components of the whole foods were analyzed, there was no single "magic substance" that could be made into a supplement and sold in health food stores. Instead, the benefits come from a blend of multiple components found in the food. Joseph and his colleagues concluded that primary aging is related to oxidative stress and inflammation, and that changes in memory and motor abilities in old age can be prevented or reversed by nutritional changes. A list of foods that are rich in antioxidants is shown in Table 2.1.

Table 2.1	Foods Rich in Antioxidants	
Fruits	**Vegetables**
• Blueberries	• Alfalfa sprouts
• Cherries	• Beets
• Kiwis	• Broccoli
• Pink grapefruit	• Brussel sprouts
• Oranges	• Corn
• Plums	• Eggplant
• Prunes	• Kale
• Raisins	• Onions
• Raspberries	• Red bell peppers
• Red grapes	• Spinach
• Strawberries	

Source: Brown (2004).

Genetic Limits

The theory of genetic limits centers on the observation that every species has a characteristic maximum life span. Something between 110 and 120 years appears to be the effective maximum life span for humans, while for turtles it is far longer, and for chickens (or dogs, or cats, or cows, or most other mammals) it is far shorter. Such observations led cellular biologist Leonard Hayflick (1977, 1994) to propose that there is a genetic program setting the upper age limit of each species. Hayflick showed that when human embryo cells (such as cells from the skin) are placed in nutrient solutions and observed over a period of time, the cells divide only about 50 times, after which they stop dividing and enter a state known as **replicative senescence** (Hornsby, 2001). Furthermore, cells from the embryos of longer-lived creatures such as the Galápagos tortoise double perhaps 100 times, while chicken embryo cells double only about 25 times. The number of divisions a species will undergo before reaching replicative senescence is known as its **Hayflick limit,** and there is a correlation between that number and the species's longevity. According to the genetic limits theory, aging results when we approach the Hayflick limit for the human species, exhausting the ability of our cells to replicate themselves (Olshansky, Hayflick & Carnes, 2002).

The mechanism behind the genetic limits theory of aging comes from the discovery that chromosomes in many human body cells (and those of some other species, too) have, at their tips, lengths of repeating DNA called **telomeres.** Telomeres appear to serve as a timekeeping mechanism for the cells. On average, the telomeres in the skin and blood cells of an adult are much shorter than those of an infant; the telomeres in an older adult's cells are even shorter. And once the telomeres are used up, the cell stops dividing.

In a recent study, cellular biologist Elizabeth Blackburn and her colleagues (Epel, Blackburn, Lin, et al., 2004) examined the telomere lengths in the chromosomes of a group of women who were living under highly stressed conditions and compared them to a group of low-stressed women as controls. The high-stressed women were all mothers and primary caregivers of a child with a chronic illness; the low-stress controls were mothers of a healthy child (or several healthy children). The telomeres in the blood samples of the high-stressed women were significantly shorter than those of the control women. In fact, researchers estimated that the stress of caring for a chronically ill child shortened a woman's telomeres to the length of a low-stressed woman who was 10 years older. This research is important because it gives a very compelling picture of how stress can affect primary aging at the cellular level.

Other studies following this research line have focused on human cells that are not constrained by Hayflick limits—stem cells. Not only do they have the ability to divide an unlimited number of times, they also have the ability to form into various types of cells to correct deficits in organs. Human embryos are the most promising source of stem cells, but federal funding for this type of research in the United States was restricted by the Bush administration because of its concern that life begins once conception takes place. However, California and Massachusetts have begun funding this type of research on the state level, and research on embryonic stem cells continues in other countries in the hopes of ensuring maximum longevity for more people (Binstock, Fishman, & Johnson, 2006).

Caloric Restriction

One of the most promising explanations of why we age is that aging is connected with our diets—not so much what we eat, but how many calories we metabolize per day. This idea was first suggested 60 years ago when researchers studied the effects of **caloric restriction (CR)** on lab rats by feeding them diets drastically reduced in calories (50 to 70 percent of normal diets), but containing all the necessary nutrients. Animals put on these diets shortly after weaning stayed youthful longer, suffered fewer late-life diseases, and lived significantly longer than their normally fed counterparts (McCay, Crowell, & Maynard, 1935). More recent studies have supported these findings, showing that animals on CR, compared to controls, have increases in DNA repair activity, growth hormone production, immune system function, and cardiac function. They show lower incidence of cancer, autoimmune disease, cataracts, and hypertension. The females show a delay in the age-related loss of fertility, and both male and female animals show an increase in sex hormone production. Animal studies have also suggested that CR may reduce damage in humans with Alzheimer's disease (Patel, Gordon, Connor, et al., 2005) and Parkinson's disease (Mattson, 2003).

Would CR increase human longevity? One problem is that to receive maximum benefits, we would have to reduce our caloric intake by 30 percent. People eating a 2,200-calorie diet would need to cut back to 1,540 calories—difficult enough for a few months, but close to impossible as a lifetime regimen. As several of my students have commented, "It may increase life expectancy, but do you really call that living?" The solution may be found in the discovery of a *CR mimetic*—a substance that would give the same health and longevity for humans that CR does for animals without reducing our normal food intake. Several possible candidates have been found, but none have been tested on humans. Work continues to find a substance that will be safe and, as the researchers say, "will enable people to have their cake—a longer, healthier life—and eat it too" (Lane, Ingram, & Roth, 2004, p. 41).

CRITICAL THINKING ●

What would a daily meal plan be for someone on a diet of 1,540 calories per day?

A Word on Theories of Primary Aging

I should caution you again not to expect that any single theory will be proven to be the one and only correct answer to the question of why we age. In fact, the "separate" theories presented here are beginning to cross boundaries and merge. For example, researchers who suggest that CR may reduce the neuronal damage of Alzheimer's disease and Parkinson's disease explain that the mechanism for this is that CR protects against oxidative stress in the DNA of neurons, an explanation that blends the dietary intake theory and the oxidative stress theory. And the study of high-stressed women with prematurely shortened telomeres also reports that these women had more free radical damage to their cells than the controls—a finding that combines genetic limits and oxidative stress.

What can I say? This is clearly a good example of the process of scientific investigation. It is not so much a competition over which theory is right, but different researchers approaching the same question, "Why do we age?" with their own methods and theories, converging on similar answers that bring us closer to the truth.

Physical Changes During Adulthood

Other chapters in this book cover changes in thinking abilities, personality, spirituality, and disease patterns during adulthood. This one deals with the physical aspect of adult development, beginning with outward appearance and working through the senses, various systems of the body, and ending with changes in hormonal functions.

Outward Appearance

When I discuss primary aging in my classes, a few students always comment that they would welcome the chance to live to 100 or beyond, "as long as I don't *look* that old." Perhaps not everyone shares that opinion, but most of us are concerned about our outward appearance and how it will change as we navigate the years of adulthood. Many of the most obvious signs of aging belong in this category, and we see them in our parents and grandparents, our friends, and sometimes in the mirror. I have selected two categories for this section—weight and body composition, skin and hair. These are concerns for adults of all ages, including textbook authors.

Weight and Body Composition. Changes in weight follows a pattern over adulthood, first rising into the 30s and 40s, staying level into the 50s and 60s, then declining by the 70s, following the shape on a graph of an inverted U. Figure 2.1 shows the weight curve for men and women in the MIDUS (Midlife in the United States) survey (Rossi, 2004).

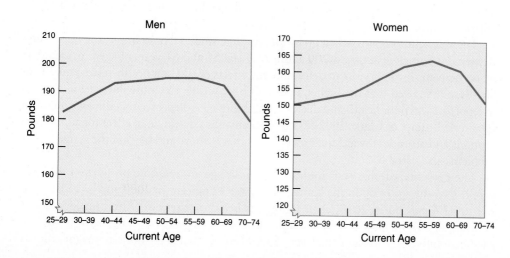

Figure 2.1 Both men and women gain weight in young adulthood and middle adulthood, losing in the late 50s, but in slightly different patterns.

Source: Adapted from Rossi (2004).

Most of the weight loss in later life is due to muscle and bone tissue being lost and replaced with fat, which weighs less. This midlife weight gain is accompanied by changes in body shape; fat slowly leaves the face and lower parts of the arms and legs, only to reappear in the upper arms, thighs, belly and buttocks. The MIDUS study also showed that hip and waist measurements of men and women increase steadily into the 60s, and then decline. A hopeful note is that this "middle-age spread" is not inevitable. Exercise and diet can go a long way toward prevention and correction (Littman, Kristal, & White, 2005). Unfortunately, this is also the age when exercise and diet are more of an effort and our lifestyles are slowing down.

Beyond the concern of appearances, increased weight has serious health consequences, as will be discussed in the next chapter, and is becoming increasingly prevalent among adults throughout the developed countries of the world. How do you stand in the body composition evaluation? Table 2.2 shows how to find your **body mass index (BMI)** by finding your height (in inches) in the far left column and moving across that row to find your weight. The number at the top of the column is your BMI. According to the U.S.

CRITICAL THINKING ●

Where do some of the people on the "Ten Most Beautiful" lists rank on the BMI scale?

Department of Health and Human Services (2004b), BMIs less than 19 are considered *underweight*, 19 to 24 are considered *normal weight*, 25 to 29 are *overweight*, and 30 and above are *obese*. This is not a perfect system, because some healthy, very muscular people would be assigned the "overweight" label based on their height and weight, but the BMI is used by most health organizations and medical researchers around the world to evaluate body composition.

Over two-thirds of adults in the United States are in the overweight BMI range, and over one-third are in the obese range. The proportions of people in the overweight range have remained fairly constant over the last four decades, but those in the obese range have increased steadily, as can be seen in Figure 2.2. The health risks linked to obesity include increased risk of cardiovascular disease, diabetes, knee replacement surgery, hyptertension, pancreatitis, chronic fatigue, insomnia, death from cancer (Patterson, Frank, Kristal, et al., 2004), depression (Roberts, Deleger, Strawbridge, et al., 2004), and reduced life expectancy from all causes (Fontaine, Redden, Wang, et al., 2003).

Not only does obesity lead to shorter lives and poorer health outcomes, it also can affect the accuracy of how individuals rate their health. Regardless of their actual health, when compared to nonobese individuals, people who are obese rate their health as lower and, as a result, limit their physical activity and social functioning (Yan, Daviglus, Liu, et al., 2004). Obese people visit physicians more often, take more medication, and use hospital emergency facilities more often than normal-weight individuals (Guallar-Castillón, López, Lozano, et al., 2002).

These conclusions are backed up by longitudinal studies. For example, the Health and Retirement Survey of almost 8,000 adults between 51 and 61 years of age provided data on participants for four years to determine the effects of BMI on health-related quality of life. Results showed that the higher a person's BMI rating, the more likely he or she was to report having poor health and decreased mobility regardless of actual disease condition (Damush, Stump, & Clark, 2002). Clearly obesity has a detrimental effect for adults' perceptions and attitudes toward their own health that is above and beyond the actual health problems associated with it.

The epidemic of obesity is found in all adult age groups. The proportion of obese people over the age of 60 in the United States was 32 percent in 2000 and is predicted to rise to 37.4 percent in 2010, challenging our healthcare system (Arterburn, Crane, & Sullivan, 2004). In addition, middle-aged people who were obese in the early 1970s had Medicare bills 30 years later that were $3,000 more than their normal-weight cohorts

Table 2.2 Body Mass Index (BMI) Table

To use this table, find the appropriate height in the left-hand column. Move across row to a given weight. The number at the top of the column is the BMI at that height and weight.

BMI Height (Inches)	19	20	21	22	23	24	25	26	27	28	29	30	31	32	33	34	35	36	37	38	39	40
																						Weight (Pounds)
58	91	96	100	105	110	115	119	124	129	134	138	143	148	153	158	162	167	172	177	181	186	191
59	94	99	104	109	114	119	124	128	133	138	143	148	153	158	163	168	173	178	183	188	193	198
60	97	102	107	112	118	123	128	133	138	143	148	153	158	163	168	174	179	184	189	194	199	204
61	100	106	111	116	122	127	132	137	143	148	153	158	164	169	174	180	185	190	195	201	206	211
62	104	109	115	120	126	131	136	142	147	153	158	164	169	175	180	186	191	196	202	207	213	218
63	107	113	118	124	130	135	141	146	152	158	163	169	175	180	186	191	197	203	208	214	220	225
64	110	116	122	128	134	140	145	151	157	163	169	174	180	186	192	197	204	209	215	221	227	232
65	114	120	126	132	138	144	150	156	162	168	174	180	186	192	198	204	210	216	222	228	234	240
66	118	124	130	136	142	148	155	161	167	173	179	186	192	198	204	210	216	223	229	235	241	247
67	121	127	134	140	146	153	159	166	172	178	185	191	198	204	211	217	223	230	236	242	249	255
68	125	131	138	144	151	158	164	171	177	184	190	197	203	210	216	223	230	236	243	249	256	262
69	128	135	142	149	155	162	169	176	182	189	196	203	209	216	223	230	236	243	250	257	263	270
70	132	139	146	153	160	167	174	181	188	195	202	209	216	222	229	236	243	250	257	264	271	278
71	136	143	150	157	165	172	179	186	193	200	208	215	222	229	236	243	250	257	265	272	279	286
72	140	147	154	162	169	177	184	191	199	206	213	221	228	235	242	250	258	265	272	279	287	294
73	144	151	159	166	174	182	189	197	204	212	219	227	235	242	250	257	265	272	280	288	295	302
74	148	155	163	171	179	186	194	202	210	218	225	233	241	249	256	264	272	280	287	295	303	311
75	152	160	168	176	184	192	200	208	216	224	232	240	248	256	264	272	279	287	295	303	311	319
76	156	164	172	180	189	197	205	213	221	230	238	246	254	263	271	279	287	295	304	312	320	328

Source: U.S. Department of Health and Human Services (2004b).

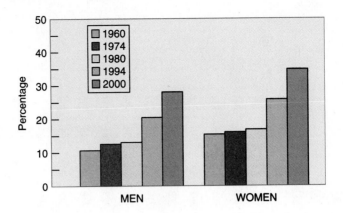

Figure 2.2 Five surveys spanning 40 years show that the prevalence of obesity for men and women in the U.S. has increased dramatically in the past two decades.

Source: Adapted from U.S. Department of Health and Human Services (2004b).

(Daviglus, Liu, Yan, et al. 2004). Young adults are part of the problem also; in a survey of 738 college students aged 19 to 27 years, 21.6 percent were overweight and 16.2 percent were obese. Over two-thirds of the students reported that they ate fewer than five servings of fruit and vegetables per day, had less that 20 grams of fiber in their daily diets, and had physical exercise less than three days a week—counter to recommendations for maintenance of healthy weight and body composition (Huang, Harris, Lee, et al., 2003).

Although twin studies show that heredity contributes to adult weight and body composition (Schousboe, Willemsen, Kyvik, et al., 2003), the major risk factor for obesity seems to be living in a culture with unhealthy diets and lifestyles. Studies of immigrants to the United States show that they often begin life here at healthy weights and body compositions, but after 15 years of living in the culture of their new country, their obesity rates approach those of native-born Americans. Figure 2.3 shows the proportion of Hispanic immigrants with BMI ratings in the obese range based on how long they have been in the United States. As you can see, a little over 9 percent are obese when entering the United States, and almost 15 percent have weights in the obese range when they have been in the United States for 15 years or more. In contrast, the overall rate of obesity in the United States is about 33 percent (Kaplan, Huguet, Newsom, et al., 2004).

The message to adults of all ages (and national origins) is that eating a healthier diet (less fat, more fruits and vegetables, more fiber, smaller portions, fewer calories) and adopting a more active lifestyle (more physical activity, less sitting in front of the TV), has an effect on weight and body composition, and therefore on physical health, perception of health, quality of life, mobility, and longevity.

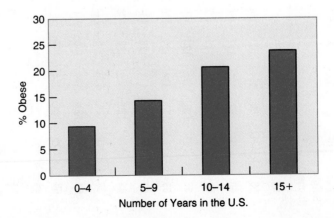

Figure 2.3 The prevalence of obesity among Hispanic immigrants increases the longer they live in the U.S.

Source: Kaplan, Huguet, Newsom, et al. (2004).

Skin and Hair. Wrinkles of the skin, which become particularly evident beginning at 40 or 50, result in part from the redistribution of body fat. It also occurs because of a loss of elasticity in the skin, part of a pervasive loss of elasticity that affects muscles, tendons, blood vessels, and internal organs as well as skin. The loss of elasticity is especially noticeable in skin that has been continually exposed to the sun, such as the skin of the face and hands.

From a quick trip down the beauty aisle of a drugstore or a look at the annual earnings of a cosmetic company, you would get the impression that many miracle cures are available for aging skin. However, the only effective products available over the counter are those that will cover up the wrinkles and age spots. One product available by prescription seems to be effective in reversing skin damage due to exposure to the sun. Several well-designed lab studies have shown that applying Retin-A (tretinoin) to the skin for several months not only changed the appearance of damaged skin but also reversed some of the underlying changes that had occurred (Rosenfeld, 2005).

Skin damage that is too severe to be remedied by prescription creams can be treated by more extreme techniques, such as chemical peels or microdermabrasion, in which the outer layers of the skin are removed by chemicals or abrasion. As you might expect, these minimally invasive medical procedures are more expensive than skin creams and carry more risks. Nevertheless, many people have been pleased with the results and find that when they look younger, they feel younger. Table 2.3 shows the top procedures performed by plastic surgeons, along with the average surgeon's fee in the United States and the percentage of patients having these procedures in each of four age groups. As you can see, the

Table 2.3	Procedures Performed Most Frequently by Plastic Surgeons in the U.S. in 2004, Average Surgeon's Fee, and Proportion of Patients in Four Age Groups that Undergo Each Procedure						
Procedure		**Number of Procedures Performed in 2004**	**Percent of Patients in Each Age Group**				
Minimally Invasive Procedures	**Average Surgeon's Fee**		**19–34 Years**	**35–50 Years**	**51–64 Years**	**65+ Years**	
Botox	$ 376	2,992,607	10	55	28	7	
Chemical peel	$ 607	1,090,523	8	40	38	4	
Microdermabrasion	$ 173	858,867	7	58	25	2	
Laser hair removal	$ 428	573,970	36	44	8	6	
Sclerotherapy (for varicose veins & spider veins)	$ 322	544,898	13	45	33	8	
Cosmetic Surgery Procedures							
Liposuction	$2223	324,891	28	51	18	2	
Nose reshaping	$3332	305,475	37	32	11	3	
Breast augmentation	$3373	264,041	50	42	6	1	
Eyelid surgery	$2523	233,334	5	33	48	14	
Facelift	$4822	114,279	1	22	59	18	

Source: American Society of Plastic Surgeons (2005).

35- to 50-year-old age group makes up the largest segment for these procedures (American Society of Plastic Surgeons, 2005).

There are two minimally invasive procedures that are increasing in popularity for both men and women. One is injections of Botox, a diluted preparation of a neurotoxin that paralyzes the muscles under the skin and eliminates creases and frown lines. This is now the most frequent procedure done by plastic surgeons for both men and women. The second procedure (not among the top five yet) involves filling in the soft tissue areas of the face with collagen, a protein found naturally in the body and lost with age, producing wrinkles and sagging skin. Recently, a new substance, hyaluronic acid, has been approved for injection under the skin and has become almost as popular as collagen. Known in the United States as Restylane, this natural substance that is found in connective tissues throughout the body cushions, lubricates, and keeps the skin plump. Botox and collagen have to be reinjected every few months; Restylane lasts somewhat longer—6 to 9 months. All these substances need to be injected by qualified medical professional and carry slight risks. And needless to say, all are expensive (the average price for Restylane treatment is $439) and not covered by most health care insurance plans (Rosenfeld, 2005).

Cosmetic surgery procedures that tighten the skin and get rid of sags and wrinkles are becoming more and more popular with both men and women, with men making up 13 percent of cosmetic surgery patients in 2004. Table 2.3 also shows the proportion of patients having these procedures in each age group. Breast augmentation and nose reshaping are done mostly on 19- to 34-year-olds, while liposuction is favored by those 35 to 50. Eyelid surgery and facelifts are done mostly on the 51- to 64-year-old group (American Society of Plastic Surgeons, 2005).

CRITICAL THINKING ●

In an average evening of TV viewing, how many commercials are for products that claim to restore youth or conceal the signs of aging?

Hair loss is a common characteristic of aging for men and, to a lesser extent, women. Some men begin to lose hair in young adulthood, but virtually all adults experience thinning of hair beginning in the 50s or 60s. Graying of hair differs widely among ethnic groups and among individuals within any one group. Asians, collectively, gray much later than Caucasians, for example.

Primary aging means changes in hair color and skin texture for almost everyone.

Men and women have used chemical and natural dyes to conceal gray hair throughout history, and it is still a widespread practice today. Other old solutions in new boxes are wigs and hairpieces, and hair replacement "systems." In addition, new drugs have become available that slow down or reverse hair loss, some over the counter for men and women, such as Rogaine (monoxidil), and others by prescription for men only, such as Propecia (finasteride). The most extreme solution to hair loss is hair transplant, a surgical procedure in which small plugs of hair and skin are transplanted from a high-hair-growth area of the body to the hairless part of the scalp. Over 43,000 men in the United States had hair transplants in 2004, a 50 percent increase from the previous year (American Society of Plastic Surgeons, 2005). Again, none of these anti-aging measures actually turns back the clock, but when they are done by experienced professionals and the patients have realistic expectations, they can give a good morale boost for those who need one.

The Senses

A second series of body changes noted by many adults as they age affects the senses of vision, hearing, taste, and smell. Vision is by far the most researched, followed by hearing, with taste and smell trailing far behind.

Vision. This is the last sense to develop in infants and the first to show signs of decline in middle age. It is also the sensory system that has the most complex structure and function and, as you might guess, has the most to go wrong. A diagram of the parts of the eye is shown in Figure 2.4. During normal aging, the lens of the eye gradually thickens and yellows, and the pupils lose their ability to open in response to reduced light. The result is that the older we get, the less light gets to our retinas, the site of visual receptor cells. In fact by 60, our retinas are getting only 30 percent of the light they did in our 20s (Woodruff-Pak, 1997). One of the changes we experience as a result is a gradual loss of visual acuity, the ability to perceive detail in a visual pattern. To test this yourself, try reading a small-print book both indoors where you usually study and then outdoors in the full sunlight. If you are like most of adults, you will notice that the clarity of the print is better in the bright sunlight.

Around the age of 45, the lens of the eye, which has been accumulating layers of cells since childhood and gradually losing elasticity, shows a sharp decrease in its ability to accommodate, or change shape to focus on near objects or small print. This loss further reduces overall visual acuity in middle-aged and older adults. Most people with reduced visual acuity or loss of near vision, a condition known as presbyopia, can function quite well with prescription glasses or contact lenses.

This is an area where the evidence of the large baby boom generation is very obvious. The growing number of people requiring reading glasses (or "readers") has made a large market for these visual aids. But the new look makes it clear that these are not your grandmother's reading glasses. Bright-colored frames and designer cases are featured in many stores, as well as ads encouraging middle-aged customers to buy several pairs to keep around the house or to match their outfits. Publishing companies have also been quick to tap this market, releasing larger-sized books with larger print (and larger prices).

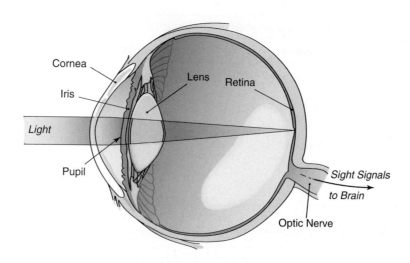

Figure 2.4 Cross-section view of the human eye.

Another visual change that takes place throughout adulthood is a gradual loss of **dark adaptation,** the ability of the pupil to adjust to changes in the amount of available light. This begins around 30, but most people experience a marked decline after the age of 60. This causes minor inconveniences, such as difficulty reading menus in dimly lit restaurants or finding seats in darkened movie theaters. It also causes more dangerous situations, such as problems seeing road signs at night or recovering from the sudden glare of oncoming headlights. This is one of the reasons older people prefer attending matinee performances, making "early-bird" dinner reservations, and taking daytime classes at the university instead of participating in nighttime activities.

Two more conditions of aging in the visual system may or may not be part of normal aging, but they are so common that I will include them here. The first is **cataracts,** gradual clouding of the lens of the eye, so that images are no longer transmitted sharply to the retina. Cataracts are the most common eye disorder found in adulthood. The bad news is that more that 50 percent of adults over 60 experience this visual problem; the good news is that they are usually quickly and safely corrected with outpatient surgery under local anesthetic. This surgery involves removing the cloudy part of the lens and implanting an artificial lens that can even be designed to correct for visual acuity. Cataract surgery has become the most common surgical procedure in the United States; over 1 million are done each year, but many people do not have access to this treatment. In spite of the ease and success of surgery, cararacts remain the cause of about one-half of the vision loss in the United States (Gohdes, Appathurai, Larsen, et al., 2005). Risk factors for cataracts are shown in Table 2.4.

A second common condition of the visual system is glaucoma, a buildup of pressure inside the eye that ultimately can destroy the optic nerve and lead to blindness. Glaucoma is the second leading cause of blindness for all people in the United States and the first leading cause of blindness for African Americans. Glaucoma is easily treated with eye drops, laser treatment, or surgery, but first it has to be detected. What are the warning signs of glaucoma? Like other hypertension problems, there are few. It is estimated that 2 million people in the United States currently have glaucoma, but half are not aware that they have it. Glaucoma can be detected as part of a routine eye examination, and it is recommended that people over 40 be screened yearly (Friedman, Wolfs, O'Colmain, et al., 2004). Risk factors for glaucoma are also shown in Table 2.4.

Table 2.4	**Risk Factors for Age-Related Visual Conditions**	
Cataracts	**Glaucoma**	**Age-Related Macular Degeneration**
increased age	increased age	increased age
family history	family history	European ancestry
female gender	African American ancestry	
hypertension*	diabetes*	
diabetes*		
UV exposure*		

*Can be controlled or prevented.

Source: Adapted from Gohdes, Appathurai, Larsen, et al. (2005); Friedman, Wolfs, O'Colmain, et al., (2004).

A third common condition of the visual system is age-related **macular degeneration,** a disorder that affects the retina, causing central vision loss. The cause of this disorder is not clear, but the prevalence is; about half of vision loss in the United States is caused by age-related macular degeneration. Vitamin therapy and laser treatment have shown hopeful results for some types of this disorder, and rehabilitative interventions have helped people with low vision to function independently and increase their quality of life (Gohdes, Appathurai, Larsen, et al., 2005). Risk factors for age-related macular degeneration are also included in Table 2.4.

The overall result of declining visual ability over middle and late adulthood can be limiting in many ways. Often older adults give up driving, which means they are no longer able to do their shopping and banking and no longer as able to visit friends, participate in leisure activities, attend religious services, or go to doctors' offices on their own. There is also a loss of status for some older adults when they must stop driving (Wahl & Tesch-Römer, 2001). Decreased vision is also associated with many other problems in older adults, such as falls, hip fractures, family stress, and depression. Because so many causes of vision loss are age-related, the growing number of older people in the developed world is a good predictor of the number of people who will experience this disability. The U.S. Center for Disease Control predicts that the prevalence of blindness will double by the year 2020. The implications for public health officials are to support early intervention, diagnosis, and treatment (Gohdes, Appathurai, Larsen, et al., 2005).

Hearing. Most adults in their 30s begin to experience some hearing loss, mainly of higher tones. There is also shortening of the *loudness scale*—that is, there is confusion between loud tones that are not being heard as well as before and softer tones that are still being heard accurately. Without the loud-soft discrimination, it is difficult to perceive which sounds are coming from nearby and which are from across a noisy room—which words are coming from your dinner partner and which from the waitress two tables over. This condition is known as **sensorineural hearing loss,** and is caused by damage to the tiny hairs inside the **cochlea,** a small shell-shaped structure in the inner ear. This mechanism is responsible for picking up sound vibrations and turning them into nerve impulses that will be transmitted to the hearing centers of the brain.

Understandably, any degree of hearing loss can interfere with social interactions, especially conversations with softer, higher-voiced women and children and the enjoyment of music, television, and telephone conversations. Mild to moderate hearing loss interferes more with formal social interactions, such as asking directions from a stranger on the street or consulting with a medical specialist, than with intimate social interactions, such as talking with a spouse across the breakfast table or visiting in the home of old friends. In contrast, severe hearing loss creates tremendous difficulties in close relationships (Wahl & Tesch-Römer, 2001).

By age 65, about a third of adults have some significant hearing impairment, and the figures rise sharply with age. Men are more likely than women to suffer significant hearing loss. The best prevention of hearing loss is to limit exposure to loud noise, both on the job and in leisure activities. Once hearing loss becomes a problem, hearing aids are available that feature digital technology, directional microphones, feedback control devices, and even specific programs for listening to music or listening to conversation. These devices amplify and direct sound to better its chance of being picked up by the impaired hearing system. When sensorineural hearing loss is severe, doctors may recommend **cochlear implants,** a surgical procedure that allows sound waves to bypass the hair cells and go directly to the acoustic nerve.

> **CRITICAL THINKING**
>
> What are some specific ways that severe hearing loss might cause problems in close relationships?

Taste and Smell. Taste and smell depend on three mechanisms that interact to enable us to enjoy the food we eat and the fragrances in our environment. They also provide survival information that keeps us from eating food that is spoiled and warns us of dangerous substances such as smoke or gas leaks. These mechanisms consist of smell, taste, and common chemical sense. Smell takes place in the **olfactory membrane,** a specialized part of the nasal membrane. It consists of millions of receptors and thousands of different kinds of cells. This variety lets us distinguish between an endless number of odors.

About three-quarters of the "taste" we perceive in food comes from these odor receptors (Doty, 2001). In addition, we experience taste through the **taste buds,** which are receptor cells found on the tongue, mouth, and throat. Saliva dissolves food and the molecules that are released stimulate the receptors. Taste buds specialize; they respond to either sweet or salty tastes (at the front of the tongue), sour tastes (on the sides of the tongue), or bitter tastes (at the back of the tongue). Irritating properties of food and odors are sensed by receptors on the moist surfaces of the mouth, nose, throat, and eyes. These convey the spiciness of chili peppers and the coolness of mint. All three types of receptors take information to different parts of the brain where the total experience is integrated and translated into messages, such as knowing you are having a pleasurable dining experience or that the milk in your refrigerator has outlived its expiration date (Fukunaga, Uematsu, & Sugimoto, 2005).

The ability to taste and smell declines over the adult years, beginning about 30 years of age and becoming more noticeable around 65 or 70. Over 2 million people in the United States have disorders of taste or smell, and most of them are older adults. This happens for several reasons. First, less saliva is produced in older people, reducing the release of molecules in food to be sensed by the taste buds. Second, there are fewer taste buds—about half as many at 70 years of age as at 20; those that detect sweet and salty flavors decline more rapidly, making us salt our food and sweeten our coffee or tea to a greater extent than in earlier years. There is also a decrease in the number of odor receptors in the nose as we age (Rosenfeld, 2005).

CRITICAL THINKING

What are some of the health and safety implications of older adults' decline in ability to detect tastes and smells?

The risk factors for loss of taste and smell are older age, belonging to the male gender, smoking, living in urban areas, and working in industries such as paper and chemical manufacturing. Older adults with a sudden loss of taste and smell should see a doctor to rule out causes that can be treated or controlled, such as viral infections, allergies, nasal polyps, diabetes, vitamin deficiencies, and complications from medications.

Bones and Muscles

The major change involved in primary aging of the bones is calcium loss, which causes bones to become less dense and more brittle. Peak bone mass is reached around the age of 30, followed by a gradual decline for both men and women, but the overall effect of this bone loss is greater for women for several reasons. First, women's bones are smaller and contain less calcium—in other words, even if the decline is equal, women have started out at a disadvantage. Second, the decline is not equal; as can be seen in Figure 2.5, women's bone loss rate shows a marked acceleration between the ages of 50 and 65, resulting in a significant increase in the risk of fractures earlier than in men. This severe loss of bone mass, or **osteoporosis,** is a major public health problem that currently affects 44 million people in the United States, 68 percent of whom are women. There is controversy over whether osteoporosis is a disease or not because it is so predictable and because the process is not distinguishable from normal aging of the bones except in degree of severity. I have chosen to include it in this chapter, but it's a judgment call.

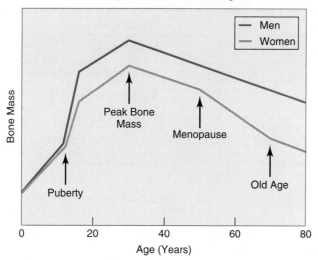

Changes in Bone Mass with Age

Figure 2.5 The greatest bone mass is found around age 30 for both men and women, with the later decline being faster for women after age 50 (menopause).
Source: MRC Human Nutrition Research (2006).

Osteoporosis is based on a measure of **bone mass density (BMD),** which is easily determined with a test called a DXA scan (dual-energy x-ray absorptiometry scan) of the hips and spine. The results are compared to those of a young healthy person. If the BMD is between 1 and 2.5 standard deviations lower, the condition is considered **osteopenia,** or moderate bone loss. (One standard deviation is a change of 10–12 percent). Half of all women over 50 have osteopenia and are at moderate risk of fracture; almost all women over 80 show signs of osteopenia. BMD measures that are more than 2.5 standard deviations below normal define osteoporosis. Osteoporosis affects 20 percent of women over 50 and half of all women over 80. The biggest problem caused by osteoporosis is the increased risk of injury after a fall. Diminished eyesight and a decreased sense of balance result in a greater number of falls as we get older. When brittle bones are entered into the equation, falls can result in serious injury, disability, loss of independent living, and even death. In fact, more women in the United States suffer from hip fracture than from cancers of the breast, endometrium, and ovary combined (Goldman & Hatch, 2000).

Physicians have been warned that the expected increase in the number of older adults in the population will increase the number of cases of osteoporosis and related bone fractures. Worldwide, more than 2 million aging men and women per year are expected to experience osteoporosis-related fractures resulting in medical costs of over $17 billion, and these numbers will increase. By 2025, the number of fractures is predicted to reach 3 million a year with a cost of $25 billion. New strategies to prevent osteoporosis focus on promoting bone health throughout life, starting with childhood, through proper diet containing required amounts of calcium and Vitamin D. Healthy bones also require a regimen of exercise of the weight-bearing muscles, including high-impact exercise such as running and jumping (Kuehn, 2005).

Measuring bone mass density is becoming more and more a part of routine examinations by gynecologists, internists, and family physicians. Plans are underway to include osteoporosis screening as part of annual dental checkups. Treatment of bone loss consists of Vitamin D, estrogen, and drugs that increase the effect of estrogen and restore lost bone integrity, such as Fosomax (bisophosphonates). Recently more emphasis is being placed on *patient adherence* to treatment for bone loss. Patients are being urged to refill their prescriptions before they run out of medication and to follow the instructions carefully to

Table 2.5	Risk Factors for Osteoporosis and Osteoarthritis
Osteoporosis	**Osteoarthritis**
increased age	increased age
family history	female gender (after 50)
female gender	family history
European ancestry	history of joint injury*
history of earlier bone fracture	history of repeated joint stress*
history of anorexia nervosa	overweight BMI*
sedentary lifestyle*	
smoking*	
more than moderate alcohol consumption*	
underweight BMI*	

*Can be changed or prevented.
Source: Adapted from Goldman & Hatch (2000); Kuehn (2005); National Institutes of Arthritis & Musculo-skeletal Disease (2005).

ensure that the drug is being absorbed well into the system and to avoid unpleasant side effects. New medication-delivery systems are available that allow patients to take only one pill a month. The major risk factors for osteoporosis are given in Table 2.5.

Over the adult years, bones also change at the joints. **Osteoarthritis** is a condition that occurs when the soft cartilage that covers the ends of the bones wears away with use and age. This allows the bones to rub together and causes pain, swelling, and loss of motion at the joint. According to the National Institutes of Health (2002) 20 million people in the United States have osteoarthritis, most of them over the age of 65. In older adults this condition is more prevalent in females; in middle-aged adults it is more apt to appear in males, probably because of work and sports injuries.

Osteoarthritis can lead to depression, anxiety, feelings of helplessness, lifestyle limitations, job limitations, and loss of independence. However, most people with this condition find that the pain and stiffness of osteoarthritis can be relieved with anti-inflammatory and pain-relief medication, and also an appropriate balance of rest and exercise to preserve range of motion. Other people with osteoarthritis report that they have found help through alternative and complementary medical treatment, such as acupuncture, massage therapy, vitamins, and nutritional supplements. Others have injections of *hyaluranic acid,* which is a natural component of cartilage and joint fluid. Studies are currently being done on all of these treatments (National Institutes of Health, 2002).

When people with osteoarthritis cannot find relief from these treatments, there is the surgical option of joint replacement. In recent years, over 150,000 hip joints and over 300,000 knee joints have been replaced annually in the United States with high success rates, the vast majority due to osteoarthritis (Bren, 2004). Risk factors for osteoarthritis are also shown in Table 2.5.

With age, most adults experience a gradual decrease in muscle mass and strength. The reason for this is that the number of muscle fibers decrease, probably as a result of reduced levels of growth hormones and testosterone. Another normal, age-related change is that muscles slowly lose their ability to contract as quickly as they did at younger ages. In addition, older people do not regain muscle mass as quickly as younger people after periods of inactivity, such as when recovering from illness or injury. All this being said, most older people have adequate muscle strength to attend to the tasks they need to do, and many stay at high levels of functioning as master athletes. However, even the best will notice some decline as they age (Beers, 2004).

Two types of exercise help rebuild muscle mass and strength. *Resistance training* involves contracting muscles by lifting or pushing and holding the contraction for up to 6 seconds. Resistance exercises can build muscle mass which in turn causes the body to burn more calories. Strengthening the leg muscles can help improve balance. The second type of exercise that is recommended is *stretching*, which lengthens muscles and increases flexibility. Stretches should be held for 5 seconds when beginning, but up to 30 seconds with increased practice. Many adults have found that exercising in a swimming pool has a lot of benefits. Water provides additional resistance and assists with balance, and classes in public pools give the added benefit of social interaction.

Cardiovascular and Respiratory Systems

The cardiovascular system includes the heart and its blood vessels, and you may be glad to hear that the heart of an older person functions about as well as a younger person's unless there is some disease present. However, the difference arises when the cardiovascular system is challenged, as happens when a person exercises heavily. Then the older heart is slow to respond to the challenge and cannot increase its function as much as a younger heart.

Another age-related change is that the walls of the arteries become thicker and less supple, so do not adjust to changes in blood flow as well as younger arteries. This loss of elasticity often causes higher blood pressure in older people than in younger ones. Figure 2.6 shows the proportion of people of different ages in the Midlife in the United States (MIDUS) study who are being treated for high blood pressure. As you can see, the proportion increases with age for both men and women (Cleary, Zaborski, & Ayanian, 2004).

The respiratory system is made up of the lungs and muscles involved in breathing. This system weakens slightly with age, but in healthy people who don't smoke, the respiratory function is good enough to support daily activities. As with the cardiovascular system, the difference is noticed when the system is challenged, as it is with vigorous exercise or at high altitudes (Beers, 2004).

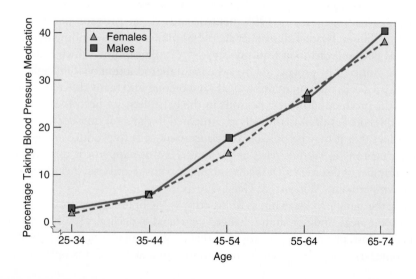

Figure 2.6 The proportion of men and women taking blood pressure medication increases sharply with age from the late 30s to the mid-70s.

Source: Cleary, Zaborski, & Ayanian (2004).

One good piece of news is that regular exercise can reduce some of these effects of aging. Exercise can make the heart stronger and lowers blood pressure; well-toned muscles can aid in circulation and breathing. Aerobic exercise, which includes brisk walking, running, and bicycling, is recommended for the cardiovascular and respiratory systems. However, the amount of exercise people do on a regular basis also declines with age. Researchers with the MIDUS survey found that moderate exercise for men remains relatively stable from the 20s to the 70s, but vigorous exercise declines for both men and women beginning in the 50s, as does moderate exercise for women (Cleary, Zaborski, & Ayanian, 2003).

Brain and Nervous System

Many people believe that old age means deterioration of the brain, and research in the past seemed to support this, but recent technologies have shown that loss of **neurons,** or brain cells, in primary aging is much less severe than once thought. It is confined to certain parts of the brain and sometimes is related to an improvement in function instead of a loss. Neuronal loss varies considerably from person to person. In addition, there are some neurons in the brain that appear in duplicate, a feature called **redundancy,** so that neuron loss may not always result in loss of function (Beers, 2004).

New evidence shows that the nervous system is characterized by lifelong **plasticity**, meaning that neurons are capable of making changes with age. Examples of this plasticity are the growth of new projections, known as **dendrites,** to make new connections with other neurons, changing response rates and thresholds, and taking over the function of nearby neurons that have been damaged. Brain change also involves changes in the number of receptors on neurons (Beers, 2004).

Another example of plasticity in the brain is **pruning,** the ability to shut down neurons that are not needed in order to "fine-tune" the system and improve functioning of the remaining neurons. Most pruning takes place in early infancy, but there is also evidence that some neuron loss in old age may reflect this process (Woodruff-Pak, 1997). So, although there is a loss in the total number of neurons with age, not all of the loss translates into functional decline.

Aside from neuronal loss and plasticity, the role of **neurogenesis,** or growth of new neurons in adulthood, has been investigated. Scientists in the past concluded that mature neurons did not divide and replicate themselves, but a new line of research has given a different view of neurogenesis. In 1998, neuroscientist Peter Eriksson and his colleagues, (Eriksson, Perfilieva, Bjork-Eriksson, et al., 1998) published their finding that the human brain forms new neurons in at least one site—the hippocampus, which is important for forming memories. The process involves the natural production of **stem cells,** immature undifferentiated cells that can multiply easily and mature into many different kinds of cells. Although the production of new neurons in the brain has not been found in other sections and does not result in many cells as compared to the total number in the brain, scientists believe that it may be possible to induce stem cells to produce a large number of functional neurons in various parts of the brain. If this happens, it may be possible to treat any number of disorders that involve neuronal damage and loss, including Alzheimer's disease (Kempermann, Wiskott, & Gage, 2004).

Clearly the aging process is not as destructive to the brain as was once thought. There is gain in some areas, and not all the changes are related to decline. However, the sum total of the neuron loss, pruning, and regrowth is that the brain may function less well with age. Older people take somewhat longer to react to stimuli than younger people and may show a reduction in certain mental abilities, such as short-term memory and the ability to re-call words. As you will learn in Chapter 4, many of these changes of primary aging are apparent only in laboratory tests and may not be noticeable to healthy people in their day-to-day lives.

Immune System

The immune system protects the body in two ways: The **B cells,** produced in the bone marrow, make proteins called **antibodies,** which react to foreign organisms (such as viruses and other infectious agents), and the **T cells,** produced in the thymus gland, reject and consume harmful or foreign cells, such as bacteria and transplanted organs. B cells show abnormalities with age, and these have been implicated in the increase of autoimmune disorders in older adults. With age, T cells show reduced ability to fight new infection. It is difficult to establish that the aging body's decreasing ability to defend itself from disease is a process of primary aging. It is possible, instead, that the immune system becomes weakened in older adulthood as chronic diseases become more prevalent and exercise and nutrition decline.

Taking vitamin supplements to boost immune function is a topic of controversy. On one side are the scientists who believe that there are no remedies available today that can stop primary aging or even slow it down; on the other side are commercial interests that profit from the sale of these products and claim that they will do wonders. In between are the facts that about one-third of elderly adults have vitamin deficiencies because of poor nutrition and lack of exposure to sunlight (Chandra, 1997). My personal conclusion is that that unless your physician tells you otherwise, young and middle-aged adults with relatively healthy diets and lifestyles don't need to worry about vitamin supplements. For older adults, especially those with appetite loss or who don't get outdoors much, a daily multiple vitamin may help and can't hurt—except for the cost (Rosenfeld, 2005).

Hormonal System

Both men and women experience changes in their neuroendocrine systems over the course of adult life, beginning about age 30. Growth hormone decreases with age, reducing muscle mass, as discussed earlier in this chapter. *Aldosterone* production decreases, leaving some older adults prone to dehydration and heat stroke when summer temperatures soar. Insulin production decreases, allowing the level of sugar in the blood to rise higher after a meal and take longer to return to normal. However, as with many other aspects of primary aging, most of these changes are not noticeable until late adulthood (Beers, 2004). One change in the neuroendocrine system that is more obvious (and sometimes problematic) to some is the reduction of hormones that results in the loss of reproductive ability, a time of life known as the **climacteric.** The climacteric takes place gradually for men over middle and late adulthood, and more abruptly for women around the late 40s and early 50s.

The Climacteric in Men. Research on healthy adults suggests that the quantity of viable sperm produced begins to decline in a man's 40s, but the decline is not rapid, and there are documented cases of men in their 80s fathering children. The testes shrink gradually, and after about age 60, the volume of seminal fluid begins to decline. These changes are associated in part with testicular failure and the resulting gradual decline in **testosterone,** the major male hormone, beginning in early adulthood and extending into old age (Rhoden and Morgentaler, 2004). Declining hormone levels in men are also associated with decreases in muscle mass, bone density, sexual desire, appetite, red blood cells, and cognitive functions, and with increases in body fat and depressive symptoms (Almeida, Waterreus, Spry, et al., 2004).

CRITICAL THINKING ●

Before you read on, what have you heard about menopause? Do you think men undergo a similar period of change in midlife? What picture do the media give us of this part of adulthood?

Just how large the decline in testosterone may be is not yet clear. One complication in the research is that there are large individual differences in hormone levels among men, and testosterone levels are also influenced by injury, obesity, alcohol intake, and both physical and psychological stress (Gould, Petty, & Jacobs, 2000). At the very least, it appears that the hormone changes that are part of the climacteric in men are more complex than first supposed.

The Climacteric in Women. During middle adulthood, women's menstrual periods become irregular, then further apart, and then stop all together. **Menopause** is defined as occurring 12 months after the final menstrual period. *Premenopause* is the time when women are still menstruating, but irregularly. *Perimenopause* is the time immediately prior to menopause, including the 12 months after a woman has her final menstrual period. *Postmenopause* is simply the time after menopause, extending until the end of the woman's life. The main cause of menopause is ovarian failure, leading to a drop in a key female hormone, **estrogen,** although there are complex changes in other hormones as well, such as **progesterone,** which is an important factor in the menstrual cycle, triggering the sloughing off of the material accumulated in the uterus.

General knowledge about menopause ranges from old wives' tales that portray menopausal women as neurotic old hags to claims of pharmaceutical companies that their products will make women forever young and immune to age-related diseases. Fortunately, several large-scale longitudinal studies have recently contributed accurate, scientific-based information on the timing of menopause and the changes that most women experience during this process. Two of the best are the Massachusetts Women's Health Study (MWHS), a 5-year study of 2,170 women (McKinley, 1996), and the Study of Women's Health Across the Nation (SWAN), a 10-year multicultural study of 3,306 women (Santoro, 2004). From these studies we know that the average age of menopause for women in the United States is 51.3 years, ranging from 47 to 55 years of age. Although the age of menarche (first menstrual period) has become younger and younger in the developed countries in the last generation due to better nutrition and health care, the age of menopause has been stable for thousands of years. Considering that women today can expect to live well into their 70s, most will spend about one-third of their lives in the postmenopause years.

As with men, this series of hormone changes is accompanied by changes in more than reproductive ability. There is some loss of tissue in the genitals and the breasts, and breast tissue becomes less dense and firm. The ovaries and uterus become smaller, the vagina becomes shorter and smaller in diameter with thinner and less elastic walls, and there is less lubrication produced in response to sexual stimulation.

The most frequently reported and most distressing physical symptom that comes with the menopausal transition is the **hot flash,** a sudden sensation of heat spreading over the body, especially the chest, face, and head. It is usually accompanied by flushing, sweating, chills, and often palpitations and anxiety. The duration of hot flashes averages about 4 minutes. They are first experienced in the late perimenopausal stage and continue for an average of two years into the postmenopausal stage. Women who reported hot flashes in the two studies cited earlier were also apt to report other symptoms related to menopause, such as headaches, backaches, swelling, shortness of breath, breast sensitivity, weight gain, irritability, fatigue, tension, nervousness, depression, lack of motivation, and insomnia. However, the majority of women (68 percent) who reported hot flashes in the Massachusetts Women's Health Study said that they were not bothered by them. Thirty-two percent consulted their doctors for treatment because the hot flashes were frequent and severe or caused insomnia.

What about women's psychological functioning around the time of menopause? It has long been believed by some that menopause can bring irrational behavior and volatile mood changes. Early studies comparing the psychological functioning of groups of women who were premenopausal with groups of women who were postmenopausal failed to show differences in rates of such clinical disorders as major depression, anxiety disorder, and schizophrenia. However, more recently several studies that divided women into pre-, peri-, and postmenopausal status have shown that women in the perimenopausal stage are more apt to have depressive symptoms and anxiety, especially those women who also report hot flashes (Luff, Khine, Schmidt, et al., 2005). Hormone therapy relieves both hot flashes and depressive symptoms in these patients, suggesting that they are caused by age-related hormonal changes (Soares, Steiner, & Prouty, 2005). Women with a history of schizophrenia are at risk of relapse at perimenopause, and there is a higher incidence of new-onset schizophrenia at this time than at premenopause or postmenopause (Kulkarni, 2005).

However, I must remind you that even though these studies show significant differences in these disorders at perimenopause, the absolute number of women who experience them is very small, and, unlike major depression, depressive symptoms are not severe and do not last for long. These findings are serious enough for mental health professionals to take note, but certainly not evidence for keeping the old wives' tales alive.

Hormone Replacement. If aging of the various neuroendocrine systems in men and women is due to a decline in hormone production, why not replace the lost hormones and reverse the process? This is not a new or novel suggestion, and it has been the impetus behind many failed "fountain-of-youth" therapies throughout history, including the injection of pulverized sheep testicles into patients in the 1890s and testicle transplants from human cadavers in the 1920s (Hayflick, 1994). Needless to say, none of these measures restored youth, but more recent attempts to replace diminished hormone supplies in aging adults have met with more success. Although none reverse the aging process, they do slow it down somewhat.

The most-used hormone replacement regimen is a combination of estrogen and progestin prescribed for women at menopause. This **hormone replacement therapy (HRT)** provides menopausal and postmenopausal women with the hormones once produced by their ovaries and sharply reduces the symptoms of the climacteric. Estrogen pills and injections have been available since the 1940s but were not widely used until the 1960s. Since then, their use has risen and fallen, depending on the perceived risks and benefits.

During the late 1990s, reports were released showing that women on HRT had lower incidence of colorectal cancer, coronary heart disease, bone fractures, Alzheimer's disease, and other types of cognitive loss. In 1997, HRT use was at an all-time high. Although the research findings were valid, the studies were almost all based on quasi-experimental designs— women who had chosen to take HRT had better health than those who did not choose to take HRT (refer back to Chapter 1 for a review of research designs). Considering that the women in the HRT group were probably in a higher economic group, had higher educational levels, and were more vigilant about their overall health care than the women in the group that did not take HRT, these findings initiated a group of longitudinal experimental design studies in which women were randomly assigned to HRT and placebo groups. As the results of these studies came in, the causal connection between HRT and good health became less and less convincing. Now the results of longitudinal studies are becoming available, but they are mixed, depending on the age HRT is begun, the type of estrogen used, and women's individual health histories. Today women are counseled to talk to their physicians about the menopause symptoms they are experiencing in order to decide what is the best course of treatment. HRT should not be considered a preventative measure against heart disease, Alzheimer's disease, and osteoporosis. New drugs are available that have some of the protective benefits of HRT without the risks (Cheung, 2005).

Although controversial, testosterone replacement therapy is popular among aging men in the form of injections, skin patches, and gels. The controversy arises over whether testosterone in older men is protective or harmful. On the protective side, studies have shown that low testosterone levels are associated with cardiovascular disease (Rhoden & Morgentaler, 2004) and Alzheimer's disease (Moffat, Zonderman, Metter, et al., 2004). However, short-term studies of whether testosterone replacement will prevent these diseases have not been conclusive, and long-term studies have not been done.

On the harmful side, testosterone is associated with prostate cancer; the standard treatment for this condition is "chemical castration," a drug that suppresses testosterone throughout the body. Whether testosterone replacement therapy in older men would increase the risk of prostate cancer has been researched for decades, and there is no compelling evidence that testosterone causes this type of cancer. It is possible that prostate cancer becomes more prevalent at the same age that testosterone levels begin to decline (Rhoden & Morgentaler, 2004). And what about sexual dysfuntion that occurs at the same time testosterone levels drop? Most men who report sexual dysfunction have adequate levels of testosterone, suggesting that their problems are not caused by hormones but by other health problems, such as heart disease, diabetes, and neurological disorders (Gould, Petty, & Jacobs, 2000). Sexual dysfunction for both men and women will be discussed later in this chapter.

Age-related declines for both sexes have been documented in two other hormones, **DHEA** (dehydroepiandrosterone) and **hGH** (human growth hormone). Not only do these hormones decline naturally with age, but animal studies have shown that replacing these hormones reverses aging and provides protection against disease. What about humans? The findings are mixed. Human studies with DHEA replacement have shown "remarkable" increases in self-reported physical and psychological well-being. They have also shown increased lean body mass in both sexes and increased muscle strength in men (Lamberts, van den Beld, & van der Lely, 1997). A double-blind placebo-controlled study of men and women from 60 to 79 years of age has shown beneficial effects for the women only, including bone growth, improvement in skin condition, and increased libido (Baulieu, Thomas, Legrain, et al., 2000). However, although DHEA is currently available in health food stores and over the Internet, it has not been approved for use as an anti-aging product, and the scientific verdict on its effectiveness and safety is still not in.

Treatment that replaces hGH in humans has been successful for children who do not attain normal height and with adults who suffer from diseases that affect pituitary function. The U.S. Food and Drug Administration (FDA) has not approved hGH replacement therapy for healthy aging adults. Nevertheless, anti-aging clinics thrive, administering hGH injections to thousands of patients who have been promised increased muscle mass, renewed sex drive, youthful bodies, and sharper minds. Products that contain hGH (or claim to) are easily available over the Internet and account for millions of dollars of sales each year, most from aging adults. Some of these products contain doses so small that they would have no effect; others are provided in delivery systems that are inappropriate, such as nasal sprays that don't allow the large hGH molecule to pass into the blood stream and pills that result in the hGH being destroyed in the stomach by digestive enzymes. Medical school professor Thomas Perls

CRITICAL THINKING

If the hGH sold on the Internet is worthless, why are there so many Web sites and so many repeat customers?

considers the sale and administration of hGH as an anti-aging remedy to be "perhaps the most blatant and organized form of quackery today" (Perls, 2004, p. 684). At best, explains Perls, the products are useless; at worst they are dangerous.

Changes in Physical Behavior

The changes in various body systems discussed so far form the foundation for age-related changes in more complex behaviors and day-to-day activities. These changes include a gradual slowing of peak performance, the decline of stamina, dexterity, and balance, changes in sleep habits, and the changes that occur in sexual functioning for both men and women.

Athletic Abilities

For most of us, the most pervasive change is a quite distinct (and accurate) feeling of becoming slower and slower as we get older. This is not an illusion, and it is not restricted to the last years of adulthood. The process of slowing begins much earlier, although it may be detected only by those who are operating at peak physical capacity, such as athletes. In any sport, the top performers are in their teens or 20s, especially in any sport involving speed. Swimmers often peak in their teens; short-distance runners in their early 20s; baseball players at about 27. As endurance becomes more involved in performance, such as for longer-distance running, the peak performance age rises, but the top performers are still in their 20s.

> ● **CRITICAL THINKING**
>
> Based on what you have learned so far, what would you guess the peak ages would be for gymnasts, golfers, and marathon runners?

Cross-sectional comparisons of athletic performance in **masters events**, defined as competitions for those age 30 or 35 and older, show the same kind of pattern: a steady drop in speed with increasing age. You can see one example in Figure 2.7, which shows the average times for the 100-meter sprint for master runners in the European Veteran Athletics Championship held in Jyvaskylä, Finland (Korhonen, Mero, & Suominen, 2003). As you can see, for both men and women, the time it takes to run the 100-meter sprint increases in a steady, gradual curve. For men, the time goes from 11 seconds at age 40 to about 18 seconds at 85; women go from 13 seconds at age 35 to 22 seconds at 85. Longitudinal studies show a less steep decline, but there is absolutely no doubt about the basic shape of the curve. We slow down as we get older.

A slowdown in athletic ability begins in the 20s, although it is only noticeable for those who are top performers.

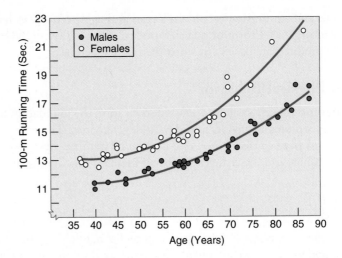

Figure 2.7 Running time on 100-meter sprint for men and women master athletes increases with age.

Source: Korhonen, Mero, & Suominen (2003).

Stamina, Dexterity, and Balance

In addition to loss of speed, all the physical changes associated with aging combine to produce a reduction in stamina, dexterity, and balance. The loss of **stamina,** which is the ability to sustain moderate or strenuous activity over a period of time, clearly arises in large part from the changes in the cardiovascular and respiratory systems, as well as from changes in muscles. **Dexterity,** the ability to use the hands or body in a skillful way, is lost primarily as a result of arthritic changes in the joints.

Another significant change, one with clear practical ramifications, is a gradual loss of **balance,** the ability to adapt body position to change. Older adults are likely to have greater difficulty handling uneven sidewalks or snowy streets, or adapting the body to a swaying bus. All of these situations require flexibility and muscle strength, both of which decline in old age. A comparison between younger and older adults performing a walking task shows an age-related increase in **gait stability**—the length of time both feet are on the floor at once—which causes a corresponding decline in balance (Cromwell & Newton, 2004). One result of the less steady balance is a greater incidence of falls among the elderly. As mentioned before, declining eyesight and brittle bones combine with the decline in balance to produce a serious health risk for older adults.

Sleep

Another consequence of the changes in the neurological system is an increased likelihood of **insomnia,** or the inability to have normal sleep patterns. As we age we tend to go to sleep earlier in the evening and wake up earlier in the morning. It takes longer to fall asleep and we spend fewer hours in slow-wave sleep, the deeper, refreshing, restorative stage of sleep. These age-related changes in sleep patterns are more profound for men than for women. Breathing disturbances during sleep also become more common, and sleep is interrupted more often during the night. Since repeated awakenings in the night and less slow-wave sleep mean that older adults are often not getting enough restful sleep at night, daytime napping becomes much more frequent. The need for daytime naps, in turn, can have a major impact on the rhythm and pattern of a person's daily life (Feinsilver, 2003).

Some of the sleep problems among older people are due to health problems and medications, factors that are part of secondary aging. But some of the difficulties in sleep seem to be due to primary aging. Psychologist Donald Bliwise (1997) investigated sleep patterns in a longitudinal study of over 200 adults and found that the sleep of the older adult seems to be intrinsically lighter, making other factors, such as pain, coughing, urge to urinate, and hot flashes, more likely to cause sleep disruption. Sleep problems in older adults are also caused by psychological factors, such as depression and anxiety. For example, bereavement can cause sleep disturbance in older adults for as long as 2 years after the death of a loved one (Beers, 2004).

Pharmaceutical remedies for sleep problems range from hypnotics to antidepressants, but most recent recommendations involve lifestyle changes, such as limiting the time spent in bed, increasing the time spent outdoors in daylight, and increasing physical exercise, especially in the mornings (Tworoger, Yasui, Vitiello, et al., 2003).

Remedies for insomnia include increased physical exercise and time spent outdoors.

Sexual Activity

As a result of changes in various systems of the body, sexual behavior shows the effects of primary aging. The key indicator used in research is the number of times per month people of different ages have intercourse. A number of early studies have shown that among people in their 20s with regular partners, the number is high—as much as 10 times or more per month, dropping to about 3 times per month for people in their 60s, and this is found in both cross-sectional and longitudinal studies. For example, over 1,000 men in the Massachusetts Male Aging Study were asked this question the year the study began and then again 9 years later. The participants, who ranged in age from 40 to 60 at the beginning of the study, reported having intercourse an average of 6.5 times per month. Nine years later the average was 4.7 times, a significant overall decline with age (Araujo, Mohr, and McKinlay, 2004). A similar decline with age is found for women, too. For example, in a survey of U.S. women, respondents who were 35 to 44 years of age reported having intercourse an average of 5.8 times per month; 45 to 54 years of age reported 5.0 time per month, and those 55 to 59 years of age reported 3.5 times per month (Lauman, Gagnon, Michael, et al., 1994).

However, one problem with this research question is that it reduces a very complex human interaction into a simple frequency count. Few studies tell us about the quality of the sexual relations people have at different ages or about types of sexual expression that don't involve intercourse. One alternative, which I will report below, is to ask questions about sexual dysfunction and report how many different things go wrong with age, but I would welcome some research done in the tone of positive aging that tells about things that go right, about adaptations people make to their declining frequency counts, and perhaps about an increase in the quality of sexual relations when long-term partners are comfortable with each other and have more time to relax and enjoy intimacy.

Whether an adult is sexually active or not depends on a number of factors. First it is necessary to have the physical ability to participate in some form of sexual behavior; second is the need for the desire to do so; third is the availability of a willing and desirable

● CRITICAL THINKING

How would you design a study to determine whether the drop in sexual activity with age is a function of age or of length of partnership?

partner; and fourth is access to a private place where sexual activity can take place comfortably. Let's look at these factors in more detail.

Physical Ability. Changes involved with primary aging can translate into changes in sexual response for both men and women. Studies of the physiological components of the sexual responses of younger men and women (aged 20 to 40) compared to older men and women (aged 50 to 78) show that there are differences in all four stages of sexual response (Medina, 1996). These changes, which are described in Table 2.6, show that sexual responses of older men and women are a little slower and a little less intense and, at least for women, can be painful. Although most of the changes result in less sexual activity with age, some of the changes, such as an end to concerns about pregnancy and no longer having children living in the home, can have the opposite result (Fraser, Maticka-Tyndale, & Smylie, 2004).

One of the most common sexual problems is **erectile dysfunction (ED),** which is defined as the inability for a man to have an erection adequate for satisfactory sexual performance. This problem occurs in an estimated 30 million men in the United States, half of them over 65. Thus, erectile dysfunction is associated with age, occurring in 5 percent of men between 40 and 65, and in 25 percent of men over 65 (Schover, Fouladi, Warneke, et al., 2004). Although erectile dysfunction occurs for many reasons (heart disease, diabetes, excessive alcohol consumption, medication, smoking), the underlying mechanism seems to be similar in most cases—a shortage of **cyclic GMP,** a substance that is released by the brain during sexual arousal. Part of the job of cyclic GMP is to close down the veins of the penis that normally drain away blood so that the blood supply increases and the tissues become engorged and erect. When cyclic GMP is in short supply, regardless of the reason, the result is erectile dysfunction. In the last decade, drugs have been developed that

Table 2.6	Sexual Response in Older Adults (50–78 Years of Age) Compared to Younger Adults (20–40 Years of Age)	
Phase	**Women**	**Men**
Excitement	Vaginal lubrication takes 1–5 minutes (compared to 15–30 seconds in younger women).	Erection after stimulation takes 10 seconds to several minutes (compared to 3–5 seconds in younger men).
Plateau	Vagina does not expand as much, the minor labia do not redden as much due to increased blood flow, and the clitoris does not elevate and flatten against the body as much (compared to the response of younger women).	Pressure for ejaculation is not felt as quickly (compared to younger men).
Orgasm	Vagina contracts and expands in 4 to 5 smooth, rhythmic waves occurring at 0.8-second intervals (compared to 8 to 10 waves occurring at 0.8-second intervals in younger women). Uterus contracts and is sometimes more painful (compared to younger women).	Urethra contracts in 1 to 2 waves at 0.8 second intervals (compared to 3 to 4 times at 0.8-second intervals for younger men), and the semen can travel 3 to 5 inches after expulsion (compared to 12 to 24 inches younger men).
Resolution	Return to prearousal state is more rapid (compared to younger women).	Return to prearousal stages and takes only a few seconds (compared to stages in younger men which take from minutes to hours).

Source: Medina (1996).

magnify the effects of cyclic GMP, making erections possible if even a small amount of the substance is present. One of these drugs, Viagra (sildenafil citrate), was approved in 1997, and during the first 2 weeks it was available to pharmacies, it was prescribed to a record number (36,000) of patients (Handy, 1998). In the last few years, new drugs have become available for ED that are time released to give men a wider window of opportunity in the timing of their sexual activity (Schover, Fouladi, Warneke, et al. 2004).

As mentioned before, one of the effects of menopause for some women is vaginal dryness and the reduced ability to lubricate when sexually aroused. This is often alleviated by estrogen treatment, either pills, patches, or creams, or the use of an artificial lubricant. However as will be discussed later in this section, sexual behavior involves more than erectile functioning and vaginal lubrication; there is also desire, general health and well-being, sexual satisfaction, and ability to achieve an orgasm. There is also relationship quality and the sexual functioning of one's partner. So far there is no "little blue pill" that will correct problems in all these areas.

In addition, secondary aging has a profound effect on sexual activity, not only the diseases that directly affect sexual function (diabetes, heart disease, prostate disease), but also those that have indirect effects (arthritis, stroke, dementia) as well as some medications. Couples who are not able to participate in intercourse as they get older often find other ways to have sexual relations or intimate physical contact, and those for whom intercourse is awkward or painful often develop new sexual strategies to overcome the limitations.

Desire. Lack of desire to participate in sexual activity is common at all ages of adulthood and in both men and women. For example, young adults report loss of desire when career pressures and parental responsibilities are at a peak. Older adults report loss of desire because they believe that sex is only for the young or those with youthful bodies. Although the lack of desire increases with age in men (Araujo, Mohr, & McKinlay, 2004; Bacon, Mittleman, Kawachi, et al., 2003) and in women (Tomic, Gallicchio, Whiteman, et al., 2006; Fraser, Maticka-Tyndale, & Smylie, 2004), clinicians report that it is by far the most common female sexual disorder.

Researchers who are searching for a "Viagra for women" have focused on the lack of desire rather than on the arousal phase that was targeted for men. The likely candidate is testosterone, which is associated with sexual desire in both men and women, and a number of products are being tested for women, such as testosterone patches, sprays, and gels. Although no product has been approved by the U.S. Food and Drug Administration (FDA), as of this writing, U.S. doctors have been treating women with testosterone preparations that have been approved only for men, a practice called "off-label use." Research results have been positive, but the FDA is not convinced of the safety of the products and has called for long-term testing with larger numbers of women. This has been controversial because similar long-term safety trials were not required before the FDA approved Viagra (Eserink, 2005).

My reactions are mixed. As a woman I oppose federal authorities using different standards to evaluate remedies for women than for men, but on the other hand, I do have serious reservations about tampering with anyone's hormones. And I think that comparing the ingredients used in Viagra with testosterone is like comparing apples and oranges. Hopefully the next edition of this textbook will bring better news for women.

It should be noted that there are safe and proven remedies for female sexual dysfunction that have been helpful to many couples, such as reducing alcohol consumption and stress, increasing exercise and quality time together as a couple, and consulting a professional sex therapist. (Interestingly, in placebo control trials of one testosterone product, researchers reported that before the women knew whether they had been using the product with the active ingredient or the placebo, 36 percent of the women in the placebo group said they were so pleased with the results of their treatment that they would want to continue it if it were available. To me this shows that there is a big component of "mind over matter" in human sexuality.)

Sexual Partner. The major factor cited in many studies of age-related declines in the frequency of sexual relations is the availability of a partner. With age, social losses (death of a spouse, divorce, separation) overtake social gains (marriage, remarriage, new social contacts), and older adults find themselves less likely to have an available partner even if they are willing and able to have a sexual relationship. This is especially true of women. Due to the their greater longevity, the practice in our culture of women marrying older men, and the age-old double standard that does not condone casual sex for women, women are much more apt to find themselves without a sexual partner in later years.

Another barrier to older adults finding a sexual partner can be their adult children, who resent or otherwise discourage their widowed or divorced parents from forming new romantic partnerships. Some adult children worry about losing their inheritance to new spouses or taking care of additional aging family members, and others simply refuse to acknowledge their parents' sexuality in late adulthood (Alexander & Allison, 1995).

Privacy. For the 5 percent of older adults who are in nursing homes and for those who live with their adult children, privacy is a major stumbling block to sexual relations, even if they have the desire, the ability, and a willing partner. Nursing homes and other residential facilities for older adults can be problematic for sexually active residents, married or single. Courses in gerontology for nursing home directors and staff often include information on sexuality in older adults and how to structure the environment to be conducive to their activities (McConnell & Murphy, 1997). Homophobic attitudes make it very difficult for older gay and lesbian adults to establish or maintain relationships in nursing homes or the homes of their adult children. For many the answer has been gay and lesbian retirement homes and assisted living centers (Clunis, Fredriksen-Goldsen, Freeman, et al., 2005).

Other Forms of Sensual Activity. Not all types of sensual pleasure entail all of these requirements. Erotic dreams and sexual fantasies can be sources of arousal and pleasure for older adults who lack partners or the physical capability to have intercourse. In a survey of healthy people between 80 and 102 years of age, 88 percent of the men and 72 percent of the women reported fantasizing about sex (Crooks & Baur, 1990). Masturbation is practiced by many older adults who have no sexual partners. According to one study, almost 50 percent of healthy women over the age of 60 reported that they practiced masturbation (Kaiser, Wilson, & Morley, 1997). Another study showed that 17 percent of men over the age of 65 report masturbating several times a week (Janus & Janus, 1993). Together these findings clearly indicate that sexuality is an integral part of most adults' lives throughout the life span, whether in partnered intercourse or other forms of sensual activity.

Individual Differences in Primary Aging

As I discussed in Chapter 1, there is often a big difference between group means and individual measurements in research findings. The accounts of primary aging in this chapter so far have followed the practice, for example, of reporting the *average* scores for 40-year-old men or the *mean* scores for 75-year-old women. But we can look around us and see that there is a lot of diversity among people of the same ages. In fact, the older we get, the more differences there are between us and our age-mates. If you have had the opportunity to attend a high school reunion, you will know what I mean. Seniors in high school are very similar, and they look and behave in much the same manner, but at 28, differences are already apparent. Some have not changed much from their 18-year-old appearance, and others have begun to show changes in body shape and thinning of hair. By the time you reach your 30th reunion, the differences will be even more dramatic. What factors are involved in this diversity? And, more specifically, what factors might pertain to the aging process for *me?*

Genetics

Twin studies and other family studies show that longevity is moderately heritable (McClearn, Vogler, & Hofer, 2001), but this may be due to the absence of genetic predispositions for certain diseases and not the presence of "longevity genes," as you will see in the next chapter. You are probably aware of the diseases with genetic patterns if you have had a physical exam lately. Most physicians now ask you about the disease history of your parents, your grandparents, and even your aunts and uncles. In particular, they are likely to ask you about the family patterns of heart disease, cancer (particularly breast cancer), Alzheimer's disease, glaucoma, and osteoporosis, each of which is known to follow hereditary patterns.

Lifestyle

Another possibility is that our lifestyles affect the rate, or even the pattern, of primary aging. One factor that appears to be highly significant is exercise. My interest in this particular aspect of aging stems in part, I am sure, from my own decision to begin doing aerobic exercise regularly. As a result of doing the last revision of this book, I took my own advice and added weight training to that routine. I am far from perfect in following a strict schedule, and I can't claim to really enjoy it (yet), but I do it and I'm glad. And it seems that I am not alone in the midlife decision to become more active. The gym I belong to has a large number of happy, healthy-looking men and women of all ages who work out regularly. In fact, the name of the low-impact aerobics class I attend was recently changed from "20-20-20" to "Silver Foxes"!

   Another lifestyle factor that affects primary aging is obesity. Recent findings have shown that obesity not only shortens life but also makes the years one lives be filled with inactivity, social isolation, chronic health conditions, and depressive symptoms. Eating a healthy diet not only reduces weight, but also makes it unnecessary to worry about nutritional supplements and anti-aging potions.

Psychosocial Factors

Another significant contributor to successful aging is attitudes, beliefs, and adaptability. The Harvard College men and inner-city men studied from the 1940s to the present by psychiatrist George Vaillant and his colleagues (Vaillant & Mukamal, 2001) show that successful aging can be predicted by psychosocial factors much earlier in life. For example, perseverance at age 20 and seeking education predicted better health and more positive outlook at age 65. In the middle years, absence of depression, a stable marriage, humor, altruism, and good friends were strong predictors of future health and happiness. Although some of these factors are beyond one's own control, the results of the study show that psychosocial factors in early and middle adulthood can have profound and long-lasting effects on our health and well-being in the later years.

> ● **CRITICAL THINKING**
>
> Why might a good sense of humor in middle age predict health and well-being in the older years?

Economics

Good health in all stages of adulthood is a key factor in the enjoyment of life, and it is not distributed equally within a community or around the world. As you can tell from this chapter, good health in late life is highly dependent on our earlier years, especially our ability to afford preventive health care and good nutrition, and to live in a safe environment. Economics is also important to health in the later years. In general, for most indicators of primary aging discussed in this chapter, non-Hispanic black adults have a greater incidence of these conditions than non-Hispanic white adults (with the exception of osteoporosis), and Hispanic adults of any race are in between. For example, a survey of Medicare beneficiaries showed that twice as many non-Hispanic black recipients (10 percent) as non-Hispanic white persons (5 percent) reported having delays in obtaining adequate health care due to costs, with Hispanic recipients in between at 7 percent (Wallace, Villa, Enriquez-Haass, et al., 2000). The same is probably true of the lower incidence of age-related conditions among people having higher versus lower education levels, higher and lower incomes, and living in developed countries versus developing countries. When positive outcome depends on good nutrition, preventive medical exams, environmental safety, lower stress, and time for exercise and leisure activities, it is clear that economic conditions are major factors in primary aging in the United States and throughout the world.

Can We "Turn Back the Clock" of Primary Aging?

At the beginning of the 21st century, amid all the claims for anti-aging procedures and products, 51 of the leading scientists in the field of aging from around the world wrote a position paper titled *The Truth About Human Aging* (Olshansky, Hayflick, Carnes, 2002). In general, their answer to the question of whether it was possible to actually stop primary aging or turn back the clock was no. They stated that today's biomedical advances can manage degenerative diseases related to primary aging, but not modify the aging process. Lifestyle changes can help people lead longer and healthier lives, but will not affect the aging process. Medical interventions for age-related diseases will increase life expectancy, but not slow down aging. Diets high in antioxidant foods can prevent age-related disease and increase life expectancy, but antioxidant supplements have not been shown to affect these diseases or primary aging. Caloric restriction has not been tested in humans, but it is possible that future research could identify a mimetic that would slow aging. In summary, all our efforts may lessen our chances of age-related diseases, but the underlying process of primary aging cannot be modified at this time.

The scientists warn us not to spend our money on products that claim to slow, stop, or reverse aging. They urge us to support responsible research in genetic engineering, stem cell research, geriatric medicine, and therapeutic pharmaceuticals, because they believe that these endeavors will eventually result in a way to slow the rate of aging, postpone age-related disease, and extend the period of healthy life.

An Overview of the Physical Changes in Adulthood

I have reviewed the myriad details of primary aging in Table 2.7, showing the physical characteristics of adults at different ages. When you look at the information this way, you can see that adults are clearly at their physical peak in the years from 20 to 40. In the years of midlife, from 40 to 65, the rate of physical change varies widely from one person

Table 2.7	Review Table of Physical Changes in Adulthood		
20–40 Years	**40–65 Years**	**65–75 Years**	**75+ Years**
Weight and girth begin to increase around 30.	Weight continues to increase until 50s, remains stable until 60; girth continues to increase.	Weight and girth begin to decrease in 70s	Weight and girth remain stable.
Facial features remain youthful for most; some men begin hair loss.	Skin begins to wrinkle and lose elasticity. Thinning of hair for men and women, more extreme for men.	Wrinkles and loss of skin elasticity increase.	Wrinkles and loss of skin elasticity increase.
Beginning of vision and hearing losses, declines in taste and smell, but not generally noticeable.	Near vision loss in 40s; dark adaptation becomes apparent in 60s; cataracts begin in 40s. Slight losses in taste and smell. Hearing loss is more noticeable.	Vision loss continues. Cataracts common. Loss of taste and smell becomes noticeable, especially sweet and salty tastes.	Visual and hearing losses continue.
Peak bone mass reached at 30.	Bone mass begins to decline gradually for men and more sharply for women, especially after menopause.	Bone mass continues to decline. Risk for fractures increases, especially for women.	Bone mass continues to decline. Risk for fractures increases sharply, especially for women.
Some neuronal loss, but not noticeable.	Neuronal loss continues, especially in brain centers related to memory.	Neuronal loss continues, some slowing of reaction time and cognitive processes apparent.	Neuronal loss continues and cognitive processes show definite decline.
Production of major hormones begins to decline, but not noticeable.	Hormones continue to decline, fertility declines gradually for men; sharply for women after menopause.	Hormones continue to decline.	Continued low levels of major hormones.
Sexual responses begin slow decline.	Sexual responses become slower, less intense.	Sexual responses continue to decline, though lack of partner is top reason for not having sexual relations.	Sexual responses continue to decline, though many continue to enjoy sexual relations throughout adulthood.

to the next, some experiencing a loss of physical function quite early, others much later. From age 65 to 75, the loss of some abilities continues, along with significant increases in chronic diseases—both trends that accelerate in late adulthood. But here, too, there are wide individual differences in the rate of change and effective compensations. Many adults maintain perfectly adequate (or even excellent) physical functioning well into their 80s. In the oldest group, however, all these changes accelerate, and compensations become more and more difficult to maintain.

Summary

1.   The oxidative damage theory of primary aging says that we age as a result of damage from free radicals that are released during normal cell metabolism. The genetic limits theory says that we age because our cells are programmed to stop dividing

once we have reached a certain age. The caloric restriction theory says that our longevity is controlled by the number of calories we metabolize in our lifetime. Each theory has research supporting it, and many of the findings seem to support more than one theory.

2. Weight increases gradually, starting toward the end of young adulthood, remains stable in middle adulthood, and then begins to decline in later adulthood. This is accompanied by a gradual increase in hip and waist measurements for both men and women, leveling off in later adulthood.

3. Obesity is on the rise in adults of all ages in the United States and other developed countries. Aside from the diseases related to obesity, it also affects self-perceptions of health, ability to exercise, and social interactions. The main cause is eating an unhealthy diet and leading a sedentary lifestyle.

4. Skin begins to wrinkle toward the end of young adulthood and become more noticeable in the middle years. "Remedies" sold over the counter for aging skin only cover the signs of aging. An increasing number of men and women are having cosmetic surgery and other medical treatments to change their appearance, especially in middle age.

5. Vision begins to decline in early adulthood, but is not noticeable until middle age. Around 45, near vision is lost more suddenly, but can be corrected with reading glasses or contact lenses. The incidence of cataracts, glaucoma, and macular degeneration increases beginning in middle age. Hearing loss begins in the 30s, but is not noticeable until middle age, when adults have problems hearing higher and softer tones. Taste and smell begin to decline in the 30s, and this becomes more noticeable in the late years of middle age.

6. Bone mass density peaks around 30 and then begins to decline for both men and women. The decline is gradual for men and sharp for women at menopause. Women are at greater risk for osteoporosis and fractures. Osteoarthritis is a common condition in older adults and can lead to decreased activity and depressive symptoms.

7. Muscle mass and strength decline slowly and do not affect the daily activities of most adults. Resistance training and stretching exercises can help slow down the decline. Changes in the heart and respiratory system are gradual and do not affect the daily activities of most adults, but heavy exercise brings slower responses in the later years. Aerobic exercise can help.

8. The brain loses neurons with age, but not at the high rate once believed. However, the nervous system is capable of making adjustments to the losses, and there is evidence that new neurons can be created in parts of the adult brain.

9. The immune system does not function as well in later adulthood as it did in earlier years, partly due to the greater prevalence of chronic diseases and susceptibility to stress. Vitamin supplements may help in later adulthood.

10. There is a gradual decline in hormone production and reproductive ability in both men and women from early adulthood into middle age, with a sharp decrease for women at menopause. Hormone replacement is possible, but should be approached with caution and in consultation with a medical professional.

11.   Sleep becomes lighter as we age, and insomnia is more common. Sleep patterns change to earlier bedtimes and earlier awakenings. Lifestyle changes can help and should be tried before medication.

12.   Sexual activity is a complex set of behaviors determined by physical ability, desire, availability of a partner, and privacy. New medication is available to help with physical ability in men, but other factors can cause sexual activity to decline with age. Many couples remain sexually active throughout their lives.

13.   Primary aging is affected by many individual differences. Genes spare some people from predispositions to certain conditions, such as glaucoma and osteoporosis. Lifestyle factors, such as exercise and healthy diet, promote slower decline. Economic factors affect health practices and also the quality of medical treatment.

14.   Most experts agree that there is as yet no way to "turn back the clock" of primary aging. We should avoid products and therapies that make this claim and support responsible research that may make this a possibility in the future.

Key Terms

primary aging, 34

secondary aging, 34

free radicals, 34

antioxidants, 34

replicative senescence, 35

Hayflick limit, 35

telomeres, 35

caloric restriction (CR), 36

body mass index (BMI), 38

lens, 43

pupil, 43

retina, 43

visual acuity, 43

accommodate, 43

presbyopia, 43

dark adaptation, 44

cataracts, 44

glaucoma, 44

macular degeneration, 45

sensorineural hearing loss, 45

cochlea, 45

cochlear implants, 45

olfactory membrane, 46

taste buds, 46

osteoporosis, 46

bone mass density (BMD), 47

osteopenia, 47

osteoarthritis, 48

neurons, 50

redundancy, 50

plasticity, 50

dendrites, 50

pruning, 50

neurogenesis, 50

stem cells, 50

B cells, 51

antibodies, 51

T cells, 51

climacteric, 51

testosterone, 51

menopause, 52

estrogen, 52

progesterone, 52

hot flash, 52

hormone replacement therapy (HRT), 53

DHEA, 54

hGH (human growth hormone), 54

masters events, 55

stamina, 56

dexterity, 56

balance, 56

gait stability, 56

insomnia, 56

erectile dysfunction (ED), 58

cyclic GMP, 58

Suggested Reading

Reading for Personal Interest

Austad, S. N. (1997). *Why we age: What science is discovering about the body's journey through life.* New York: Wiley.

Biologist Steve Austad wrote this book to tell the nonbiologist about a new view of aging by giving a clear (and sometimes funny) account of the history, theories, experiments, and personalities of the people involved in the field of aging research. The book dismisses a lot of popular myths and misinformation about aging, leaving the facts well organized and easy to understand.

Nelson, M. E. (2006). *Strong women, strong bones.* New York: Perigee Trade.

Miriam Nelson is a medical researcher at Tufts University and was involved in the studies cited in this book on the benefit of weight training for older men and women. This book spells out a 30-minute, 2-day-a-week program that brings many health benefits to women of all ages, but especially those who are 40 and over. This is a good example of translating medical research into a responsible self-help book.

Olshansky, S. J., & Carnes, B. A. (2001). *The quest for immortality: Science at the frontiers of aging.* New York: Norton.

Two of the leading researchers in the science of aging present a small book in a conversational tone about the historical quest we humans have had for life extension. It covers a lot of the relevant theory and research findings in everyday language. Highly recommended for nonscientists who are interested in the topic of aging.

Classic Work

Harman, D. (1956). Aging: A theory based on free-radical and radiation chemistry. *Journal of Gerontology, 2,* 298–300.

This is the article in which the free-radical theory of aging was first introduced.

Hayflick, L. (1965). The limited in vitro lifetime of human diploid cell strains. *Experimental Cell Research, 37,* 614–636.

This is biologist Leonard Hayflick's early publication indicating that human cells grown in the lab have a limit to the number of times they replicate.

McCay, C., Crowell, M., & Maynard, L. (1935). The effect of retarded growth upon the length of life and upon ultimate size. *Journal of Nutrition, 10,* 63–79.

One of the first studies to suggest that slowing growth might increase longevity.

Contemporary Scholarly Work

Newell, K. M., Vaillancourt, D. E., & Sosnoff, J. J. (2006). Aging, complexity, and motor performance. In J. E. Birren & K. W. Schaie (Eds.), *Handbook of the psychology of aging* (pp. 163–182). San Diego: Academic Press.

Good review of how posture, locomotion, and dexterity change with age.

Perls, T. T. (2004). Anti-aging quackery: Human growth hormone and tricks of the trade: More dangerous than ever. *Journal of Gerontology: Biological Sciences, 59A,* B682–B691.

Medical professor Thomas Perls warns against the use of human growth hormone to prevent aging, giving specific facts about it's effects, the legal issues, and the methods used by internet salespeople to provide useless products.

Schieber, F. (2006). Vision and aging. In J. E. Birren & K. W. Schaie (Eds.), *Handbook of the psychology of aging* (pp. 129–161). San Diego: Academic Press.

Experimental psychologist Frank Schieber presents a thorough and up-to-date review of how the visual system changes with age.

Wise, P. M. (2006). Aging of the female reproductive system. In E. J. Masaro & S. N. Austad (Eds.), *Handbook of the biology of aging,* (pp. 570–590). San Diego: Academic Press.

Biophysiologist Phyllis Wise gives a detailed review of the hormonal and behavioral changes in the female reproduction system over the course of adulthood.

Chapter 3

Health
and Health
Disorders

Mortality Rates and Causes of Death

Morbidity Rates, Illness, and Disability
Common Health Conditions
Disability
Living Arrangements for Older Adults
Self-Ratings of Health
Old Age and Disability in Context

Specific Diseases
Cardiovascular Disease
Cancer
Alzheimer's Disease
A Word About Tobacco Use
Aging and Physical Disease: An Overview

Mental Disorders
Anxiety Disorders
Mood Disorders
Impulse Control Disorders
Substance Abuse Disorders
Treatment of Mental Health Disorders

Individual Differences in Health
Gender
Socioeconomics, Race, and Ethnicity
Personality and Behavior Patterns
Genetics
Developmental Origins
The Road to Good Health

Summary

Key Terms

Suggested Reading

EVERY YEAR THERE is a race run in our town, and probably in yours too, called the "Race for the Cure," and it is intended to raise awareness (and money) for breast cancer prevention, detection, treatment, and research. The term "race" is fairly loose—ours is in January, and many women go in groups to enjoy a brisk walk in the Florida sun along the waterway, talking with each other and greeting friends they see along the route. A good number of men participate too, and lots of kids on skateboards, rollerblades, and in strollers. But the theme of the day is on everyone's minds—this form of cancer will strike (or has struck) one of every nine women in the United States. Women who are breast cancer survivors are given hot-pink T-shirts; the others get white ones. The splashes of pink among the white say more than a textbook full of medical statistics. *A whole lot of women have had breast cancer and survived to walk in the sun.*

This chapter is about health and disease. I wish it were more about health and less about disease, but in truth, disease is part of adult life, and the longer we live the greater the chance we will have one disease or another. Many diseases, like breast cancer, have greater detection rates and survival rates all the time. Some, like lung cancer, can be prevented to a great extent through lifestyle changes. And others, like Alzheimer's disease, are more difficult to prevent or to treat at present. I will start this chapter with some general statistics about disease patterns and then cover the most prevalent physical and mental health disorders. Finally, I will review the research on individual differences in health and disease.

Mortality Rates and Causes of Death

Figure 3.1 shows the mortality rate, or the probability of dying in any one year, for American men and women in various age ranges. You can see that fewer than one-tenth of 1 percent of adults aged 15 to 24 die in any given year, while over 15 percent of adults over 85 die each year (National Center for Health Statistics, 2004). The fact that older people are more likely to die is surely no great surprise (although you may be comforted to see how flat the curve is into the 60s).

There are also different causes of death for people at different ages. Table 3.1 gives the major causes of death of people in the United States by age. Three of the top five causes of death of very young adults (aged 15 to 24) aren't even diseases; they are accidents, homicides, and suicides. By young adulthood (25 to 44) accidents are still in first place, but cancer and heart disease are second and third. Middle-aged adults (aged 45 to 64) have cancer and heart disease in first and second place, and for older adults (aged 65 and over) these two diseases are reversed in first and second place, and Alzheimer's disease makes its first appearance in the top five causes of death (Hoyert, Kung, & Smith, 2005).

According to the World Health Organization, adults in the developing countries of the world also succumb most often to heart disease, stroke, and lower respiratory infections, but HIV/AIDS is the fourth most prevalent cause of death in these countries. Found in the top ten causes are other infectious diseases such as diarrheas, tuberculosis, and malaria, which are now very uncommon in the developed countries of the world, where they have been considered preventable or treatable for over half a century (Mathers, Stein, Fat, et al., 2002).

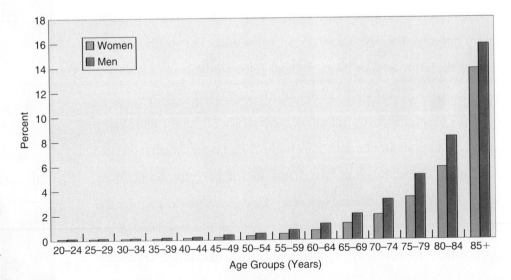

Figure 3.1 The mortality rate in the U.S. increases with age and is lower for women than men at every age.

Source: National Center for Health Statistics, 2004.

Rank	15–24 Years	25–44 Years	45–64 Years	65+ Years
1	Accidents	Accidents	Cancer	Heart disease
2	Homicide	Cancer	Heart disease	Cancer
3	Suicide	Heart disease	Accidents	Stroke
4	Cancer	Suicide	Diabetes	Lower respiratory disease
5	Heart disease	Homicide	Stroke	Alzheimer's disease

Table 3.1 Major Causes of Death in U.S. by Age Group

Source: Data from Hoyert, Kung, & Smith (2005).

Morbidity Rates, Illness, and Disabilities

Not all diseases lead to disability, and not all disability is caused by disease. There are conditions such as hearing loss and arthritis that are not technically diseases, but instead part of normal aging for a large number of otherwise healthy people. I have combined these diseases, illnesses, and other disorders in this discussion and call them "conditions."

CRITICAL THINKING

Before you read on, which age group would you predict has the highest rate of acute short-term health problems such as colds and flu, college students or their grandparents?

Common Health Conditions

You might assume that an age-related pattern would emerge for the **morbidity rate,** or illness rate, with older adults suffering from more of all types of health conditions. But that is not the case. Younger adults are actually about twice as likely as are those over 65 to suffer from short-term health problems, which physicians call **acute conditions,** including colds, flu, infections, or short-term intestinal upsets. It is only the rates of **chronic conditions,** longer-lasting disorders such as heart disease, arthritis, or high blood pressure, that show an age-related increase. Older adults are two to three times more likely to suffer from such disorders than adults in their 20s and 30s.

As you can see in Figure 3.2, the most common health disorders for adults 65 and older are arthritis, high blood pressure, and heart disease, all problems with low rates among

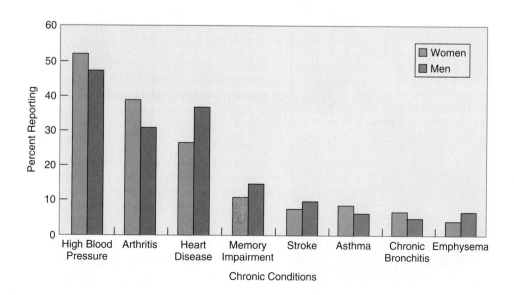

Figure 3.2 Rates of chronic conditions for U.S men and women 65 and older are higher than for younger adults and there are substantial gender differences, but half report no chronic conditions at all.

Source: Federal Interagency Forum on Aging Related Statistics (2004).

younger adults. At the same time, in my usual search for a balanced view of aging, it is important to point out that almost half of adults 65 years of age and older have no chronic health conditions at all.

Disability

Psychologists, epidemiologists, gerontologists, and even lawyers who deal with guardianship cases all define disability as the extent to which an individual is unable to perform two groups of activities: (1) basic self-care activities, such as bathing, dressing, getting around inside the home, shifting from a bed to a chair, using the toilet, and eating, collectively called **ADLs (activities of daily living),** and (2) more complex everyday tasks, such as preparing meals, shopping for personal items, doing light housework, doing laundry, using transportation, handling finances, using the telephone, and taking medications, referred to as **IADLs (instrumental activities of daily living).** About 13 percent of adults 65 and older report having problems with at least one ADL, and about 20 percent report problems with at least one IADL. The incidence of disability is lower for those in their 60s and 70s than those in their 80s (Vierck, 2004). As you can imagine, older adults spend much of their time on these activities, and their ability to perform them is a key indicator of their quality of life.

Having a chronic illness or health condition does not directly translate into being disabled. It is quite possible to have one or more chronic conditions without experiencing significant disability. One person may have high blood pressure that is controlled with medication and exercise; another adult may have arthritis that responds well to medication and places no limitation on major activities. For most adults, the crucial issue is not whether they have a chronic condition but whether that condition has an impact on their daily life, requiring restriction in daily activities or reducing their ability to care for themselves or participate in a full life.

The vast majority of older adults live in their own homes even when they need special equipment or in-home assistance. Not only do they prefer aging in place, it is also the best arrangement for their overall well-being.

Living Arrangements for Older Adults

In spite of the proportion of people 65 and over who report having chronic illnesses (about 50 percent) or needing assistance with daily living (about 20 percent), only about 5 percent live in nursing homes or skilled care facilities. About 81 percent of women and 90 percent of men aged 65 or older are **community dwelling,** which means that they live in their own homes either with their spouses or alone. (More women live alone due to their greater number in this age group.) Clearly, many older adults have found ways to compensate for their disabilities, find in-home help with the care they require, or take care of each other so they can remain in their homes during their later years. This concept is known as **aging in place,** and 40 years of research has shown that this is the living arrangement the vast majority of older people want for their last years, and also what is best for them. For example, people who live in their own homes cope better with widowhood (Swensen, 1998), loss of mobility (Krothe, 1997), and sub-optimal housing (Crystal & Beck, 1992) than those who have alternative living arrangements. It seems clear that with age, we increasingly feel that there is no place like home.

With this in mind, healthcare planners have turned their attention away from making institutional care more attractive and focused instead on ways to modify older people's homes to fit their needs. Part of the home modification process for older adults involves basic safety measures, such as installing adequate lighting, removing small rugs, and marking edges of stair steps. More complex measures involve installing devices for the specific limitations of the residents, such as wheelchairs, outdoor ramps, and accessible shower stalls. The third set of items to help the older adult age in place involves the use of appliances and other devices designed to help older people age in place. This will be discussed in more detail in the section on human factor research in Chapter 4.

For those whose health is poor, especially those with many disabilities, one of the possible outcomes is a **nursing home** or other skilled care facility. As I mentioned above, only about 5 percent of the U.S. population 65 and older lives in nursing homes at any given time, most of them 85 years of age or older (National Center for Health Statistics, 2004). Men are likely to spend less time in nursing homes than women, and married people are likely to spend less time than single people, especially single women with no children, few social contacts, and significant disability. Nursing home care is nearly always the choice of last resort for either the elders themselves or their families. Yet the economics of care and the burden of caring for a disabled elder are such that institutional placement is sometimes the only reasonable choice. I will discuss this point more fully in Chapter 5.

In the last decade there have been some compromises between aging in place and nursing home care. Older adults who are still independent but do not want the responsibilities of cooking, housekeeping, or driving often move into **congregate living facilities,** where they live in their own apartments but have their meals in a community dining room. Housekeeping, transportation, and other services are available as needed. The next level of care comprises **assisted-living facilities,** where people are able to function with limited assistance, for example, needing help with bathing or medication.

Self-Ratings of Health

Another way we might measure adults' health, other than evaluating activities of daily living, would be quite simply to ask them to rate their own health on some simple scale. We know that such self-ratings have some validity, because meta-analyses show a strong positive correlation between self-ratings of health and more objective measures of physical and mental health (Pinquart & Sorensen, 2001). Epidemiologists Margaret Lethbridge-Çejku and Jackline Vickerie (2005) included self-ratings of health as part of the U.S. National Health Interview Survey. Not surprisingly, when asked about their health, young adults were far more likely than older adults to rate themselves as being in better health. However, as you can see in Figure 3.3, more than a third of adults over the age of 75 rated themselves as being in excellent or very good health, and two-thirds of the adults in this age group said their health was good or better. This does not mean, of course, that an 85-year-old who describes himself or herself as being in "excellent" health has the same physical functioning as a 25-year-old who chooses the same description.

Old Age and Disability in Context

It is important for me to put the information on overall rates of disease and disabilities into some kind of context so that you do not take away from this section the impression that

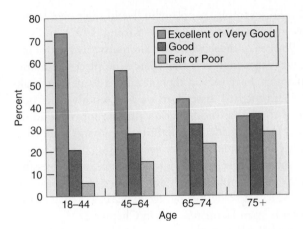

Figure 3.3 Percentage of people at four ages answering the question "How do you rate your own health?" Even in the oldest group, almost one-third respond, "Excellent or Very Good."

Source: Data from Lethbridge-Çejku & Vickerie (2005).

all older adults suffer from severe disabilities. Let me reemphasize some basics: Half of people in the United States 65 and over have no chronic illness of any kind; roughly three-fourths of all adults over 65 are able to perform all the tasks necessary for daily life without assistance. Furthermore, the incidence of disability is declining among older adults in the United States. Ninety-five percent of Americans 65 and over are community dwelling. Although this increases with age, about 80 percent of those over 85 are aging in place.

I would also be remiss if I did not mention that adults younger than 65 can also have their activities of daily living limited by a chronic illness. About 5 percent of young adults (18 to 44 years of age) and 12 percent of middle-aged adults (45 to 64) report needing assistance with IADLs, compared to 20 percent of adults 65 or older (National Center for Health Statistics, 2004).

Specific Diseases

I have discussed the major causes of death and disability for adults. This section covers three diseases in detail, chosen because they are among the most prevalent causes of death and disability for adults, and because they are the focus of very active research programs around the world. The following sections on cardiovascular disease, cancer, and Alzheimer's disease give a good picture of how health affects our lives (and also how our lives affect our health).

Cardiovascular Disease

The leading cause of death for adults in the United States and all over the world is **cardiovascular disease.** This is a disorder of the heart and blood vessels that covers a number of physical deteriorations; the key change is in the coronary arteries, which slowly develop a dangerous accumulation of **plaques,** or fat-laden deposits. This process is known as **atherosclerosis,** and it is not a normal part of aging. It is a disease, and not all older adults have it. Atherosclerosis is caused by inflammation, which normally is part of the protective processes of the immune system. But instead of protecting us, this type of inflammation forms plaques in the artery walls and sometimes causes the plaques to rupture and form blood clots that block the arteries, leading to heart attack or stroke (Libby, 2004).

The death rate from cardiovascular disease has been dropping rapidly in the past two decades in the United States and most other industrialized countries. Yet it remains the leading cause of death and disability among both men and women in the United States and throughout the developed world (Mathers, Stein, Fat, et al., 2002). Some people are at greater risk of contracting cardiovascular disease than others. Risks factors are listed in Table 3.2. As you will notice, some of these factors are under our control, such as sedentary lifestyle, and others are not, such as being older than 50.

Another point I want to make about these risk factors is that they are cumulative. Each one you have increases the probability you will have cardiovascular disease (and each one you quit will lower your chances). A good illustration of the cumulative effects of

CRITICAL THINKING

What are some of the reasons that the rate of cardiovascular disease is declining in the United States?

Table 3.2	**Risk Factors for Cardiovascular Disease**

- Smoking or exposure to environmental tobacco smoke*
- Obesity*
- Sedentary lifestyle*
- Diabetes*
- High cholesterol or abnormal blood lipids*
- High blood pressure*
- Being male
- Being older than 50
- Family history of cardiovascular disease

*Can be modified or prevented.
Source: Adapted from Torpy (2003).

risk factors comes from cardiologist Gerald Berenson and epidemiologist Sathanur Srinivasan, and their colleagues in the Bogalusa Heart Study, an ongoing longitudinal study of over 16,000 black and white residents of a semirural district of Louisiana (Berensen & Srinivasan, 2005). This study, which began in 1972, has followed some of its participants from birth to age 40, concentrating on health and lifestyle factors that may contribute to heart disease. Researchers evaluated a group of 30- to 48-year-olds to determine how many risk factors they had for cardiovascular disease. Then, using ultrasound imagery, they measured the thickness of their artery walls. The results clearly showed that the more risk factors that were present in the participants, the thicker their artery walls. This study demonstrated that risk factors are more than just statistics—they translate directly into visible symptoms of cardiovascular disease.

I feel I should emphasize something here: *Coronary heart disease is the number-one killer of women throughout the developed world.* The numbers can be misleading, because the average age that men have heart attacks and die from heart disease is younger than the average age for women. Comparing heart disease rates can give the impression that cardiovascular disease is a men's health problem. However, the facts show that it can be even more deadly for women. Research shows that women are almost twice as apt to die than men in the year following their first heart attack. Women are more likely than men to have a painless progression of early heart disease, and when they experience symptoms, it is not the crushing pain on the left side of the chest that men commonly have. Instead, women's symptoms include nausea, fatigue, dizziness, pain in one or both arms, neck or jaw pain, and shortness of breath. When these early warning signs are not noticed or are misinterpreted, the first heart attack for women is often severe and fatal (Parmet, 2004).

Many believe that breast cancer is the biggest health enemy for women. The truth is that breast cancer isn't even the top cause of cancer death for women anymore (it has been surpassed by lung cancer). A woman has a 3 percent chance of dying of breast cancer compared to a 50 percent chance of dying from cardiovascular disease. (Torpy, 2002).

Cancer

The second leading cause of death for men and women in the United States is cancer, a disease in which abnormal cells undergo rapidly accelerated, uncontrolled division and often move into adjacent normal tissues. It can then spread through the bloodstream or lymph vessels to more distant tissues in the body, including the brain. Cancer can take root in any part of the body.

Beginning in 1990, the incidence and death rate from cancer began to decline significantly in the United States for the first time since national recordkeeping began, and this has continued at about 1 percent per year (Edwards, Brown, Wingo, et al., 2005). Nevertheless, cancer remains the second leading cause of death for adults in the United States, with lung cancer being the leading cause of cancer death for both men and women.

The incidence of cancer increases with age; a 70-year-old is about 100 times more likely to have cancer than a 19-year-old. Another change with age is in the type of cancer one is likely to have. Breast cancer is the most frequent cause of cancer death for women under 55, while leukemia is most frequent for young adult men, and lung cancer is most frequent for middle-aged men. Once men and women reach 55, lung cancer remains the top cancer killer and stays there through the rest of the life span (Gibbs, 2004).

The cause of cancer is currently a topic of active debate. It was long believed that cancer began with a series of random mutations that made the tumor-suppressing genes in a cell turn off and the tumor-stimulating genes turn on. Once this occurred, the mutated cell would divide and replicate itself excessively, resulting in cancer. Recently it has been possible to study the genetic makeup of human cancer cells, and we have learned that things are much more complex. For example, the cells within a tumor do not have identical genes, as we would expect if they came from a single mutated cell. Also, not all cancer cells have mutations in both the tumor-stimulating and tumor-suppressing genes. These and other findings have resulted in several new hypotheses for the cause of cancer and new avenues of research (Gibbs, 2004).

The decline in cancer deaths in the last decade is due to advances in treatment, early detection, and prevention. A growing number of people have made lifestyle changes in order to reduce their risks of cancer. The risk factors are shown in Table 3.3.

Early detection of cancer includes having mammograms, pap smears, prostate exams, colonoscopies, and routine skin examinations, depending on age and sex. The numbers have increased for these screening procedures each year, and the survival rates for the types of cancers they detect have also increased. Still, cancer screening rates are not consistent for all groups. For example, mammograms are recommended for *all* women 40 and over,

Table 3.3	Risk Factors for Cancer

- Tobacco use (cigarettes, cigars, chewing tobacco, snuff)*
- Unhealthy diet (low in fruits and vegetables)*
- Sedentary lifestyle*
- Obesity*
- Excessive alcohol use*
- Unprotected exposure to strong sunlight*
- Chemical and radiation exposure in the workplace*
- Sexually transmitted diseases*
- Being older than 50
- Family history of cancer

*Can be modified or prevented.
Source: Adapted from Torpy (2004).

but the typical woman undergoing a mammogram is non-Hispanic white, educated, born in the United States, and with medical insurance coverage. The hopeful news is that the number of women in other groups having mammograms increases each year (Edwards, Brown, Wingo, et al., 2005).

Alzheimer's Disease

The fifth leading cause of death for people 65 and over is **Alzheimer's disease,** a progressive, incurable deterioration of key areas of the brain. Unlike cardiovascular disease and cancer, which can occur throughout adulthood, Alzheimer's disease is truly a disease of old age, with 90 percent of the cases developing after the age of 65. Once considered a rare disorder, Alzheimer's disease has become a major public health problem in the United States and throughout the world, primarily because of the greater proportion of older people in our population. Alzheimer's disease afflicts 1 out of 10 Americans over 65 and about a third of those over 80—some 4 million people (Schmiedeskamp, 2004). If you are like 20 million other people in the United States, you are acutely aware of this disease because you have a family member with Alzheimer's disease and are experiencing its effects firsthand.

Alzheimer's disease is the most prevalent type of **dementia,** a category of conditions that involve global deterioration in intellectual abilities and physical function. It involves significant impairment of memory, judgment, social functioning, and control of emotions. Other types of dementia can be caused by multiple small strokes, Parkinson's disease, multiple blows to the head (as among boxers), a single head trauma, advanced stages of AIDS, depression, drug intoxication, hypothyroidism, some kinds of tumors, vitamin B_{12} deficiency, anemia, and alcohol abuse. I don't expect you to memorize this list, but I do want you to realize that a loss of cognitive functioning in an older person is not necessarily Alzheimer's disease; sometimes it is a condition that can be treated and has a more favorable outcome.

There is no cure at this time for Alzheimer's disease, but progress is being made in several areas. There have been advances in diagnosing the disease and predicting its course. Until the 1990s, Alzheimer's disease could only be diagnosed with certainty after death when an autopsy could be conducted, but recently, clinicians have developed a behavioral assessment battery that is sometimes combined with neuroimaging techniques. As many as a dozen cognitive abilities are measured, and patients must show significant decline on all of them before a diagnosis of Alzheimer's disease is made. This cognitive battery is a very accurate diagnostic tool when used by a skilled professional, with or without the neuroimaging. Ninety percent of the people who are diagnosed with Alzheimer's disease using this test later have the diagnosis confirmed at autopsy (Ingram, 2003). Other research has made it possible to predict the probable course of the illness for individual patients, making it possible for them and their families to have some control over their lives by making plans for the future (Stern, Tang, Albert, et al., 1997).

Genetic researchers are making advances in identifying the causes of Alzheimer's disease, the first step toward a cure. It has been known since the early part of the 20th century that many of the people who die of dementia have specific abnormalities in the brain tissue. One of these abnormalities, first identified by neuropathologist Alois Alzheimer in 1907, is called senile plaque. These are small, circular deposits of a dense protein, beta-amyloid; another abnormality is neurofibrillary tangles, or webs of degenerating neurons, as illustrated in Figure 3.4. However, it was only recently that researchers identified some of the genes that mutated and caused the buildup of senile plaques in the brain (Launer, 2005). I say "some of the genes" because it is now thought that a number of different genes can cause Alzheimer's disease.

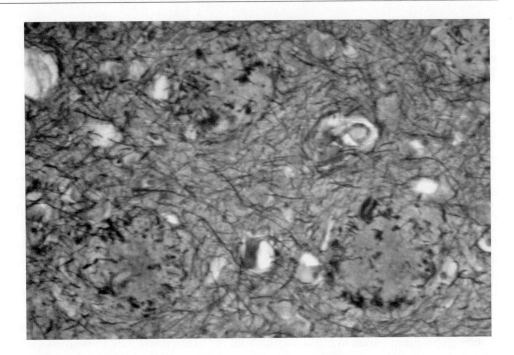

Figure 3.4 This photo shows a sample of brain tissue from a patient diagnosed with Alzheimer's disease. You can see the dense deposits of plaque and tangled, fragmented dedrites.

Source: Scheibel (1992).

Ironically, we know the most about the type of Alzheimer's disease that affects the fewest people—early-onset Alzheimer's, the type that occurs in the 50s and 60s, involves rapid deterioration, and accounts for only about 10 percent of the cases. Genetic testing is available for people who have a high incidence of early-onset Alzheimer's disease in their families.

The causes of late-onset Alzheimer's disease are less clear, although it accounts for 90 percent of cases. Psychologist Margaret Gatz and her colleagues (Gatz, Fratiglioni, Johansson, et al., 2005) have conducted studies comparing over 1,500 monozygotic and dizygotic twins who were 65 years of age or older to show that there is a genetic component for late-onset Alzheimer's disease. They found that if one member of a monozygotic twin pair has the disease, there is a 59 percent chance that the other twin will develop it; the rate for dizygotic twins is only about 30 percent. Further, if one monozygotic twin develops Alzheimer's disease, the second will develop it in a shorter time than two dizygotic twins. Figure 3.5 shows the ages that pairs of monozygotic twin in this study were diagnosed with Alzheimer's disease. The tops of the dark-colored bars tell the ages when the first twin of each pair was diagnosed; the tops of lighter bars tell the ages when the second twin of each pair was diagnosed. The shorter the lighter bars, the closer together the diagnoses. The average time between the monozygotic twins' diagnoses was three years—significantly less than for dizygotic twins. As explained in Chapter 1, this method is based on the reasoning that because monozygotic twins share the same genes and dizygotic twins share only half of their genes, these probabilities indicate a moderate influence of genetics on the incidence of Alzheimer's disease.

As mentioned earlier, the greatest risk factor for Alzheimer's disease is age. Other risk factors are shown in Table 3.4. Some of the risk factors should seem familiar to you by now because they are the same factors that put us at risk for cardiovascular disease. In fact, people with cardiovascular disease are more apt to get Alzheimer's disease than people with healthy hearts. It has been suggested that both diseases are caused by inflammation (Launer, 2005).

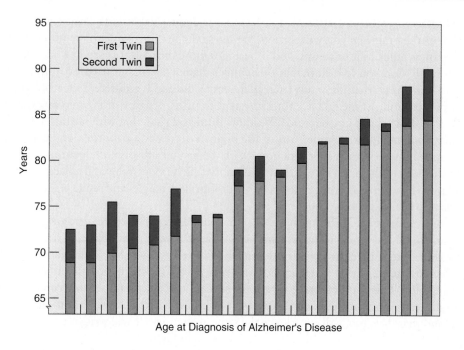

Figure 3.5 The age of diagnosis for 18 monozygotic pairs of twins who both contracted Alzheimer's disease is, on average, 3 years apart, significantly closer than the age of diagnosis for dizygotic twins.

Source: Gatz, Fratiglioni, Johansson, et al. (2005).

Recently researchers have been looking for signs in early or middle adulthood that predict Alzheimer's disease in later adulthood. For example, results from the Honolulu Asia Aging Study showed that increased levels of inflammation in middle adulthood were associated with diabetes, stroke, and high blood pressure in midlife, but also, years later, with Alzheimer's disease (Schmidt, Schmidt, Curb, et al., 2002). And findings from the Nun Study, a group of 678 members of the School Sisters of Notre Dame, have shown that lower levels of linguistic ability at 22 years of age were associated with greater incidence of Alzheimer's disease some 60 years later (Riley, Snowdon, Desrosiers, et al., 2005).

Other ideas for preventing Alzheimer's disease are based on less rigorous science. Correlational studies have shown that older people who participate in more intellectual activities, such as playing chess, doing Suduko number puzzles and crossword puzzles, and reading for pleasure, are less likely to develop Alzheimer's disease. Of course this may be true, but there is also a chance that the inverse is true—people who will develop Alzheimer's disease may not do these things because of early deficits (Gatz, 2005). Still, it can't hurt to pursue mentally stimulating activities throughout life—and it might help.

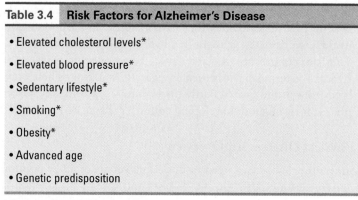

Table 3.4	Risk Factors for Alzheimer's Disease

- Elevated cholesterol levels*
- Elevated blood pressure*
- Sedentary lifestyle*
- Smoking*
- Obesity*
- Advanced age
- Genetic predisposition

*Can be modified or prevented.
Source: Adapted from Launer (2005).

I want to end this section with a few words about Alzheimer's disease and normal aging of the brain. As you will see in Chapter 4, the memory of an older adult is not as sharp or as quick as it once was, and it becomes more difficult to learn new information. This might lead you to believe that Alzheimer's disease is just an extreme form of normal aging, but this is definitely not true. Alzheimer's disease is a different creature entirely. For comparison, let me go back for a moment to primary aging of the nervous system, a subject I wrote about in Chapter 2. We know from autopsies that with normal aging there is some neuronal loss in some parts of the brain, a decrease in dendrites, and evidence of a change in neurotransmitter function. With Alzheimer's disease, the neuronal loss is in specific parts of the brain involved with memory (the hippocampus and adjacent regions), and there is evidence of a large number of neurofibrillary tangles and senile plaques in these parts as well (Andreasen, 2001).

It is important to distinguish between primary aging and secondary aging in mental processes. All too often, primary caregivers of older people with dementia do not recognize that there is a medical problem, even when their loved one has severe dementia. One of the most frequently cited reasons is that they believed that their family member was "just getting old." This is unfortunate for the 10 percent of dementia cases that can be treated and disheartening for the younger caregivers who believe that these conditions are normal and that they, too, will experience the same as they age. (I will write more about caregivers of family members with Alzheimer's disease in Chapter 5.)

A Word About Tobacco Use

If you only do one thing to ensure that you live a long and healthy life, your best bet would be not to smoke (or to quit if you do). Tobacco use is the number-one preventable cause of disease and premature death in the United States. It directly kills over 440,000 people per year and indirectly kills another 38,000 through second-hand smoke. Over 80 percent of lung cancer cases are caused by tobacco, likewise 30 percent of other types of cancer, including cancer of the mouth, tongue, larynx, stomach, pancreas, bladder, and kidney (American Cancer Society, 2005).

Some good news is that a smaller proportion of people in the United States are smoking today and those who are smoking are smoking less. The bad news is that smoking rates now decrease with age, meaning more young adults smoke than older adults. It is no longer the wealthy, sophisticated people who smoke, but those with less education and income (American Cancer Society, 2005).

Around the world, smoking is an even bigger problem than it is in the United States. According to the World Health Organization, tobacco use is responsible for 10 percent of all adult deaths in developing countries. As smoking rates in the United States have declined over the past three decades, they have increased in the poorest countries of the world. Unfortunately, it seems that in the minds of many citizens of developing countries, cultural progress and national development involve adopting stereotypical Western behaviors such as cigarette smoking. These outdated stereotypes are communicated partly through tobacco company advertising that is prevalent throughout developing countries (Essen & Leeder, 2004).

CRITICAL THINKING

What reasons would tobacco companies have for advertising so heavily in poor countries?

Aging and Physical Disease: An Overview

Before I go on to other subjects, I need to underline yet again a key point about what I have said so far concerning both specific diseases and disease in general: Although the risk of having some disease increases with age, no one of these specific diseases is an inevitable part of aging. It may be common to develop some atherosclerosis as you get older, but it is not a normal part of aging; Alzheimer's disease increases in frequency in the later years of life, but dementia (of any type) is not a normal part of aging in the same sense that puberty is a normal part of physical development in childhood, or that menopause is part of normal aging for middle-aged women.

Of course, the physiological changes in the immune system, the neurological system, and the cardiovascular system that do appear to be part of primary aging obviously contribute to the increased vulnerability to disease as we get older. But that does not explain why one person gets cancer, another heart disease, and another remains essentially disease-free into old age.

Mental Disorders

The diagnosis and treatment of mental disorders is a fairly new topic of scientific investigation. Before Freud's time, mental disorders were more the realm of religion or philosophy, and once they became accepted as treatable health conditions, each school of therapists had its own classification system and treatment plan. It was not until 1980 that a standardized system of symptoms and diagnoses was agreed upon by mental health professionals in the United States in the form of the *Diagnostic and Statistical Manual,* 3rd edition, or *DSM-III* (American Psychiatric Association, 1980). This advance was important for therapists and their patients, but it also made it possible for epidemiologists to compile data and answer questions about our country's mental health. Since that time several large-scale surveys have been conducted, giving us answers about the state of the nation's mental health and what changes have occurred over the past few years.

One of the most recent studies of this type, the National Comorbidity Survey, conducted by sociologist Ronald Kessler and his colleagues, consists of data from face-to-face interviews with over 9,000 randomly selected adults in the United States. This study replicates a similar study done 10 years before, and the results have been compared to see what changes have occurred during that time. They have also been compared to related studies done in other countries. Findings from this survey tell us that about 46 percent of people in the United States experience some sort of mental illness during their lifetimes—disorders either of mood, anxiety, substance abuse, or impulse control. Furthermore, within a 12-month period, 26 percent experience some sort of mental health disorder. The good news is that these numbers are the same as were found in a similar study done 10 years before, so mental illness has not increased. The bad news is that these numbers are the highest in any developed country (Kessler, Berglund, Demler, et al., 2005). The four categories of disorders included in this study are shown in Table 3.5, along with examples of the disorders and findings from the study. (Less common disorders, such as schizophrenia and autism, were not included because they are not amenable to a household survey.)

Table 3.5 shows the median age of onset for each of the four groups of disorders. **Onset** refers to first occurrence, and as you can see, unlike most physical disorders, mental disorders generally have their onsets in adolescence and early adulthood. As a result, they involve more years of chronic illness and disability, and cause more premature deaths than chronic physical disorders. Further complicating the duration of these disorders is the recent finding that the median time it takes for a person with a mental disorder to seek treatment can range from 8 years for some types of mood disorders to 23 years for some types of anxiety disorders. A significant proportion of people never seek treatment (Wang, Berglund, Olfson, et al., 2005).

The National Comorbidity Survey also provides data on the **prevalence** of mental disorders, which is the percentage of people experiencing a certain disorder for a given period, such as in their lifetimes or during the last 12 months. As you can see in Table 3.5,

Table 3.5	Mental Health in the U.S: Survey Results				
DSM Classification	Examples	Lifetime Prevalence (1)	12-month Prevalence (2)	Median Age of Onset (3)	% Male/ % Female
Anxiety Disorders	Phobias, post-traumatic stress disorder, obsessive-compulsive disorder	28.8%	18.1%	11 years	38% male/ 62% female
Mood Disorders	Depression, bipolar disorder	20.8%	9.5%	30 years	40% male/ 60% female
Impulse Control Disorders	Conduct disorder, intermittent explosive disorder, ADHD	24.8%	8.9%	11 years	59% male/ 41% female
Substance Abuse Disorders	Alcohol and drug abuse or dependence	14.6%	3.8%	20 years	71% male/ 29% female
Any Disorder Above		46.4%	26.2%	14 years	48% male/ 52% female

(1) Percent who have had this type of disorder at least once in their lifetimes.

(2) Percent who have had this type of disorder in the last 12 months.

(3) Age at which 50% of the cases had appeared.

Source: Data from Kessler, Berglund, Demler, et al. (2005), Table 2, p. 595 & Table 3, p. 596; Kessler, Chiu, Demler, et al. (2005), Table 1, p. 619; Wang, Berglund, Olfson, et al. (2005), p. 605.

the lifetime prevalence for various types of mental health disorders ranges from 14.6 percent (substance abuse disorders) to 28.8 percent (anxiety disorders). Forty-eight percent of people reporting a mental health disorder in this study were men; 52 percent were women, mirroring the gender distribution in the United States. Across the adult years, the 12-month prevalence of most mental disorders increases from young adulthood to middle adulthood and then declines, with the lowest rates being for adults who are 60 years of age and older (Kessler, Berglund, Demler, et al., 2005).

Participants in this study were rated as to the severity of their symptoms. The results showed that 22 percent were serious, 37 percent were moderate, and 40 percent were mild. More than 40 percent of the respondents classified as having one of the four types of mental disorders listed above were **comorbid,** meaning that they had more than one disorder, and not surprisingly the more disorders they reported, the greater the severity of their symptoms (Kessler, Chiu, Demler, et al., 2005).

Below is a discussion of the four types of disorders included in this study and some information about the treatment that adults in the United States seek out for their mental health disorders.

Anxiety Disorders

Anxiety disorders are the leading type of mental health disorder for adults in the United States. Disorders of this type involve feelings of fear, threat, and dread when no obvious danger is present. During a 12-month period, approximately 18 percent of American adults report experiencing an anxiety disorder (Kessler, Chiu, Demler, et al., 2005). The most common anxiety disorders are **phobias,** which are fears and avoidance out of proportion to the danger presented; **post-traumatic stress syndrome,** which is an emotional reaction experienced repeatedly to a traumatic event that happened in the past (and will be discussed in more detail in Chapter 10); and **obsessive-compulsive disorder,** which involves guilt and anxiety over certain thoughts or impulses. Although many adults experience anxiety disorders, these usually begin in childhood. Half the people who have anxiety disorders experience the first one before the age of 11; three-quarters of the people who have anxiety disorders have already experienced one before the age of 21. More women than men experience anxiety disorders (Kessler, Berglund, Demler, et al., 2005).

Mood Disorders

Mood disorders are the second most common type of mental health disorder for adults in the United States. These involve a loss in the sense of control over emotions, resulting in feelings of distress. A fifth of us will experience

In the past year, about one in five adults in the United States reported symptoms of anxiety disorder that took them out of the flow of everyday life.

some sort of mood disorder over the course of our lifetimes, including major depression and bipolar disorder. More women than men experience mood disorders. **Major depression** is typified by a long-term, pervasive sense of sadness and hopelessness. In the National Comorbidity Survey, major depression was the most prevalent disorder for adults in the United States, affecting over 16 percent of respondents during their lifetimes. The rates of major depression are high all over the world and increasing; it was the fourth leading cause of disease-related disability in the world in 1990 and will become the second leading cause by 2020 (Bloom, 2005). The World Health Organization reports that for women, major depression is the leading cause of disease-related disability in the developed nations of the world (World Health Organization, 2001).

The question of whether more older adults than younger adults suffer from depression seems like an easy one, but it is not. First, we need to define what we mean by "depression." The National Comorbidity Survey discussed above and other research studies use the guidelines set out by the *DSM-IV* to define major depression (see Table 3.6). When this strict definition is used, the onset is most often in early adulthood, around the age of 30, with three-quarters of people who will ever have major depression already experiencing it by the age of 43. When age groups are compared, rates of major depression are significantly lower for older adults than young and middle-aged adults. In fact, when major depression occurs for the first time in an older person, it is often related to a disease such as Alzheimer's disease (van Reekum, Binns, Clarke, et al., 2005) or cardiovascular disease (Bjerkeset, Nordahl, Mykletun, et al., 2005).

In comparison, when it comes to **depressive symptoms,** the results are quite different. Studies in this area are done using symptoms checklists, such as the Center for Epidemiologic Studies Short Depression Scale (CES-D 10), shown in Table 3.7. As you can see, the symptoms are not as severe and are not required to be as long-lasting as with major depression. When this criteria is used in research, older adults exhibit higher rates of depression than those in the middle years (Kessler, Mickelson, Walters, et al., 2004). Depressive symptoms include more indicators related to chronic health

CRITICAL THINKING

Not everyone with a mental health disorder seeks treatment. Is there one type of disorder for which you think people would be more likely to seek treatment than others? Why?

Table 3.6	Diagnosis for Major Depression

Five of the following items must be present during the same 12-week period, including one of the two items marked with an asterisk:

1. Depressed mood for most of the day.*

2. Loss of interest or pleasure in all, or almost all, activities.*

3. Significant weight change when not dieting (loss or gain).

4. Significant change in sleep habits (insomnia or hypersomnia).

5. Psychomotor agitation or retardation almost daily.

6. Fatigue or loss of energy almost daily.

7. Feelings of worthlessness or excessive or inappropriate guilt almost daily.

8. Diminished ability to think or concentrate, or indecisiveness almost daily.

9. Frequent thoughts of death or suicide without a specific plan, or a suicide attempt, or a specific plan for committing suicide.

Source: Adapted from American Psychiatric Association (2000).

problems or the deaths of friends or relatives, both of which are more common in older adults.

In summary, major depression and other mood disorders are generally mental health problems of young adults. Older adults may exhibit a number of depressive symptoms, but these may be the result of the health problems, bereavement, and loss of social contacts that occur more often at that stage of life. Chronic depression that begins in older adulthood is often related to disease.

Impulse Control Disorders

The category of **impulse control disorders** is defined as those disorders that affect a person's judgment or ability to control strong and often harmful impulses. It includes disorders of conduct, oppositional-defiant behavior, intermittent explosive disorder, and attention-deficit/hyperactivity disorder. More men experience impulse control disorders than women. All of these disorders, with the exception of intermittent explosive disorder, are usually considered childhood disorders, but recent studies have shown that over 4 percent of adults report experiencing symptoms of attention deficit/hyperactivity disorder in the past 12 months, just half the rate that is reported in childhood. This suggests that about half of the children with this disorder will continue to experience it in adulthood (Kessler, Chiu, Demler, et al., 2005).

Substance Abuse Disorders

The category of **substance abuse disorders** involves abuse or dependence on drugs or alcohol, and as you can see back in Table 3.5, about 15 percent of adults in the United States experience one of these disorders during their lives, with half reporting onset before age 20 and half after age 20. Three-quarters of the people who will ever experience one of these disorders will do so by the age of 27. Substance abuse disorders are more common in men than in women. The most common disorder in this category is alcohol abuse, which is experienced by about 13 percent of people in the United States, the second most

Table 3.7	Test for Depressive Symptoms: Center for Epidemiologic Studies Short Depression Scale (CES-D 10)

Instructions: Below is a list of some of the ways you may have felt or behaved. Please indicate how often you have felt this way during the past week by checking the appropriate box for each question.

Item	Rarely or none of the time (less than 1 day)	Some or a little of the time (1–2 days)	Occasionally or a moderate amount of the time (3–4 days)	All of the time (5–7 days)
1. I was bothered by things that usually don't bother me.	❑	❑	❑	❑
2. I had trouble keeping my mind on what I was doing.	❑	❑	❑	❑
3. I felt depressed.	❑	❑	❑	❑
4. I felt that everything I did was an effort.	❑	❑	❑	❑
5. I felt hopeful about the future.*	❑	❑	❑	❑
6. I felt fearful.	❑	❑	❑	❑
7. My sleep was restless.	❑	❑	❑	❑
8. I was happy.*	❑	❑	❑	❑
9. I felt lonely.	❑	❑	❑	❑
10. I could not "get going."	❑	❑	❑	❑
Score for each check in column	3	2	1	0
*reverse for items 5 & 8	*0	*1	*2	*3

A score of 10 or more is considered depressed.
Source: Radloff (1977); Andresen, Malmgren, & Carter (1994).

common disorder after major depressive disorder (about 17 percent). Adults over the age of 45 were less likely than people under 30 to report ever having a drug-use disorder, which researchers concluded was a cohort effect (Kessler, Berglund, Demler, et al., 2005).

Treatment of Mental Health Disorders

Only about 40 percent of adults with mental health disorders seek some sort of treatment. Considering all the recent advances in psychopharmacology and psychotherapy, this shows that the optimistic picture of "curing" mental illness is not a reality for the majority of people who suffer from these disorders. To make matters worse, only about a third of those who seek help actually get treatment that is judged adequate by professional guidelines (Wang, Lane, Olfson, et al., 2005).

CRITICAL THINKING ●

Take a minute to go back to the list in Table 3.7. How many items sound like false stereotypes of aging?

Another third of the people who seek treatment for mental health disorders go to **complementary and alternative medicine providers,** such as chiropractors, acupuncturists, herbalists, or spiritualists, none of whose methods have been supported by scientific data. Still, patients report that these complementary and alternative medicine providers listen to them and include them in treatment decisions. It is important for mainstream mental health professionals to adopt some of this "bedside manner" and use it to make their conventional treatment more attractive (Wang, Lane, Olfson, et al., 2005).

Another problem is that a significant number of people who receive medication and/or therapy from medical professionals do not have apparent disorders (Wang, Lane, Olfson, et al. 2005). I can't help but think of the many magazine ads and TV commercials for antidepressants and antianxiety medication that make these disorders seem no more serious than bad hair days, ending with the message to ask your physician about this product. It seems that with mental health care, the right treatment is just not getting to the right people.

One group that is conspicuously absent in seeking any type of care for mental health disorders is people over 60. Part of the problem is a cohort effect. Many people in that age group are the tail-end of the Greatest Generation—those who were self-sufficient, thrifty, and kept their problems to themselves. Another reason older adults with mental health disorders may not seek treatment is that many of the symptoms, especially those of mood disorders and anxiety disorders, are similar to false stereotypes of aging—losing interest in things that once brought you pleasure, feeling hopeless and helpless, suffering from vague aches and pains, being afraid of the neighborhood around you. When older people buy into these false stereotypes of aging, they don't view their symptoms as disorders and don't seek treatment. This is further complicated when their family members think the same way and don't urge their older relatives to get help.

In summary, it seems that the public relations aspects of mental health do not interface well with the advances in pharmaceuticals and therapy. We need more education about what is a mental disorder and what is not, more information about proven treatment and where to find it, better treatment for people who do seek it, and more people-friendly professionals providing proven, conventional therapies. Let's hope that the next decade's wave of studies shows some progress in this area.

Individual Differences in Health

So far in this chapter I have covered age-linked patterns for various physical diseases and mental health conditions. However, as you no doubt realize, this is not a matter of "one rule fits all." Within these age patterns are a variety of individual differences caused by factors such as gender, socioeconomic, racial and ethnic differences, personality differences, and even genetic variation. The following is a discussion of some of these factors.

Gender

One fact apparent already in several of the tables and figures in this chapter is that women and men have different patterns of health problems. Men have shorter life expectancies than women and higher rates of heart disease, hypertension, substance abuse, death by suicide, death by accident, and overall cancer rates. Women live longer than men, but when they die, they do so from basically the same diseases that men do. They just develop them later in life. Women have more chronic health conditions and more disability than men, specifically more major depression, anxiety disorders, arthritis, asthma, migraine headaches, thyroid disease, gall bladder problems, and urinary and bladder problems, among others

(Cleary, Zaborski, & Ayanian, 2004). Women are more likely to spend their later years in nursing homes, because they outlive their spouses. In fact many of these gender differences are due simply to the fact that women live longer and are older, on average, than men.

One interesting study that demonstrated this gender difference examined data on twins. Biobehavioral researcher Carol Hancock Gold and her colleagues (Gold, Malmberg, McClearn, et al., 2002) identified 605 pairs of Swedish twins born between 1906 and 1915 who were unlike-sex twins (male-female twins). The practice of using twins reduced the differences in background characteristics and also the differences in survival rates (since both twins had survived to old age). They found that the female twins had more total health problems and non-life-threatening health problems than their brothers, but the male twins had more life-threatening health problems, including more life-threatening cardiovascular disease. Interestingly, there was no difference in their self-rated health.

Where might such gender differences come from? The explanations are partly biological, partly environmental. Most investigators agree that the differences in longevity and in later onset of major disease are primarily biological: Women have a genetic endowment that gives them protection in early adulthood against many fatal diseases, such as cardiovascular disease. Why this discrepancy? Most theorists believe that it is because women's overall health during the childbearing and early parenting years has been more important to the survival of the species than men's. Once menopause sets in, there is more equality in disease rates. There are also gender differences in exposure to hazardous environments (such as dangerous chemicals and noisy workplaces), although that difference is probably smaller in more recent cohorts as women have moved more into traditionally male occupations, and as workplaces have become safer for both genders. Gender relates to other factors too, such as health awareness and amount of effort spent on health care, which are higher for women than men throughout adulthood (Cleary, Zaborski, & Ayanian, 2004). Perhaps one reason women live longer is because of this vigilance (and also why men with wives live longer than men without them).

There are robust gender differences for specific mental health disorders; women have higher rates of major depression and most anxiety disorders, while men have higher rates of substance abuse disorders and impulse control disorders. Women's heightened vulnerability to disorders that affect emotional functioning is thought to be due, in part, to estrogen levels—the same hormones that provide protection from some physical diseases (Chrousos, Torpy, & Gold, 1998). Testosterone, on the other hand, seems to protect most men against depression by blunting the effect of stress and negative emotions. This sex difference has been demonstrated by studies of autonomic reactions to stress that show females responding to distressing photos with higher heart rates and skin conductivity than males. Similar studies using brain imaging have shown women responding to photos of people with fearful facial expressions with more widespread activity in brain areas that generate fear responses than men. Women also respond to stressful situations with more brain activity in areas linked to depression and anxiety than men. It has been suggested that women's fast and extreme reaction to stress is an evolutionary adaptation that helped our ancestral mothers protect their young. In today's world, however, this reactivity seems to be one of the factors that produces higher rates of mood disorder and anxiety disorder in women. In contrast, men's hormones make them more likely to react to stress through drug and alcohol use and loss of impulse control (Holden, 2005).

There is some reason to suspect that women's mental health is also affected by gender inequality, specifically the level of employment opportunities, economic autonomy, and reproductive rights available in their communities. Because these vary by state, psychiatric epidemiologist Ying-Yeh Chen and colleagues (Chen, Subramanian, Acevedo-Garcia,

CRITICAL THINKING

Men have higher rates of impulse control disorders. Could you make an argument that it was an adaptive mechanism for our ancestral fathers?

et al., 2005) were able to evaluate the levels of these indicators of equality in each of the states of the United States. *Employment opportunities* for a state were evaluated by women's median earnings, male versus female earning ratios, women's labor force participation, and proportion of women in professional and managerial occupations. *Economic autonomy* was based on the percentage of women with health insurance, women's educational attainment, women's business ownership, and percentage of women living above the poverty level. *Reproductive rights* were based on the state's legislative support and funding of abortion rights and access to contraception. The states that ranked in the top five (1–5) and the bottom five (46–50) for these measures of gender equality are shown in Table 3.8. The researchers then examined data from the National Maternal Infant Health Survey to compare the levels of depressive symptoms for women in the top-ranked states with those for women in the bottom-ranked states. The results showed that women in states with high levels of gender equality reported fewer depressive symptoms than women in states with low levels of gender equality. The authors concluded that lack of gender equality appears to contribute to women's depressive symptoms and may help explain the higher rates of depression among women.

> **CRITICAL THINKING** ●
>
> Can you suggest some other statewide indicators of gender equality? How do you think your state ranks?

There are even greater gender differences in the prevalence of anxiety disorders and mood disorders in developing countries. To cite one example, this was illustrated in a study that compared the rates of mental health disorders in a developed country (Great Britain) with those in a developing country (Chile). After surveying over 10,000 people, the researchers found that the women in both countries had higher rates of mood disorders and anxiety disorders than the men, but the differences were significantly greater in Chile (Rojas, Araya & Lewis, 2005).

One important factor that has to be considered in regard to health differences between genders is the relative lack of knowledge the medical community has about women's health. Until the late 1980s, almost all large-scale health studies were conducted with male participants and the results were generalized to women. The 1990s brought the start

Table 3.8	Women's Equality Indices: Top Five and Bottom Five States		
Rank	**Employment and Earnings**	**Economic Autonomy**	**Reproductive Rights**
Top Five States			
1	Alaska	Maryland	Hawaii
2	Connecticut	Colorado	New York
3	Maryland	Connecticut	Oregon
4	Massachusetts	Vermont	Connecticut
5	California	Massachusetts	Iowa
Bottom Five States			
46	Arkansas	Kentucky	Kansas
47	Mississippi	Louisiana	Mississippi
48	Louisiana	West Virginia	Nebraska
49	Alabama	Arkansas	North Dakota
50	West Virginia	Mississippi	Kentucky

Source: Data from Chen, Subramanian, Acevedo-Garcia, et al. (2005).

of a number of longitudinal studies of women's health, such as the Women's Health Initiative (WHI), the Study of Women's Health Across the Nation (SWAN), and the Nun Study of the School Sisters of Notre Dame, but they are still young in terms of longitudinal studies and often arrive at confusing recommendations. We are still catching up in knowledge about cardiovascular disease in women, whether estrogen replacement therapy is healthy or harmful, and how women react to drugs that have been tested only on men. Recent practices now require all federally funded clinical research to include women in sufficient numbers to analyze gender differences in responses to drugs or other treatments (Simon, 2005).

Socioeconomics, Race, and Ethnicity

Given everything I have said so far, you will not be a bit surprised to learn that there are significant differences in the health patterns across adulthood for different economic groups or for various racial and ethnic groups. In addition to differences in life expectancy, which I've already mentioned, there are differences in the probability of chronic disease or disability. And there are differences between racial and ethnic groups in risks for specific diseases.

Socioeconomic Level. The clearest data I know that show socioeconomic differences in health and disability over adulthood come from two large surveys of over 59,000 people in the United States analyzed by sociologist James House and his colleagues (House, Kessler, & Herzog, 1990; House, Kessler, Herzog, et al., 1992). They looked at reports of chronic conditions and disability as a function of socioeconomic level and age. The results were extremely clear. All socioeconomic groups showed an increase with age in chronic conditions and limitations, but the increase is much earlier and steeper for the lower socioeconomic levels. People with good incomes and higher education also tend to have better mental health (Kessler, Chiu, Demler, et al., 2005), and when they have problems are more apt to seek treatment early (Wang, Lane, Olfson, et al., 2005).

Other research tells us that the same socioeconomic differences exist for specific diseases, such as arthritis, hypertension, and some kinds of cancer (Adler, Boyce, Chesney, et al., 1994), major depression (Cutrona, Russell, Brown, et al, 2005), and Alzheimer's disease (Evans, Hebert, Beckett, et al., 1997; Nielson, Lolk, Andersen, et al., 1999). Similar socioeconomic differences in physical and mental health, rate of disability, and longevity have been found in many other industrialized counties, such as Sweden (Thorslund & Lundberg, 1994) and Finland (Pirkola, Isometsä, Suvisaari, et al., 2005), and they occur within ethnic groups in the United States as well in the general population. That is, among non-Hispanic black adults and Asian American adults, the better-educated and those with higher incomes have longer life expectancies and better health (Guralnik & Simonsick, 1993).

A substantial portion of such social class differences in health can be accounted for by variations in health habits. People with lower incomes and less education are more likely to smoke and to lead sedentary lifestyles (American Cancer Society, 2005). In addition, adults with lower incomes are less able to afford medical care when they are ill, not to mention tests and screening that could lead to early detection of illnesses (Alaimo, Briefel, Frongillo, et al., 1998). Another candidate is poor nutrition. The cumulative effect of medical neglect and undernutrition in the early years is likely to be higher rates of both disease and disability in later years as well as shorter life expectancy (Deeg, Kardaun, & Fozard, 1996).

One study that dramatically underscores the connection between economic well-being and health was done by sociologist Colleen Heflin and her colleagues (Heflin,

Siefert, & Williams, 2005), who investigated the connection between major depression in women and **food insufficiency,** defined as not having enough for your family to eat. She interviewed 753 women who were welfare recipients in Michigan, gathering data on their economic conditions, stressful life events, experiences of domestic violence and discrimination, and whether their household "sometimes" or "often" did not have enough food to eat. Results showed that food insufficiency was strongly associated with major depression in these women, even when the other factors were considered. The authors concluded that although this is a sad statement for our country, it is also a factor for major depression that could be easily modified, lowering rates of disability in these women and the resulting disruption of families and impaired child development.

Racial and Ethnic Groups. Before I start this section I need to warn you that this topic is not as simple as it seems. There is little agreement on how to divide up people in the United States into racial and ethnic groups, how to define members of the groups, and what to do with those who don't quite fit into a group (or those who fit into more than one group). The following information is based on the groups identified by the most recent U.S. census, but I acknowledge that there are other widely used classification systems and terminology.

The ethnic group within the U.S. population that seems to have the best health picture is Asian Americans and Pacific Islanders. They have the lowest rates of cardiovascular disease, hypertension, arthritis, and serious psychological distress. They are, understandably, the most likely to rate their health as "excellent." Women in this group have the lowest death rate from cancer of any other subgroup in the United States (National Center for Health Statistics, 2004). Why the good health? The traditional diets of these groups are healthier than the typical diet in the United States, and the smoking rate is low (Edwards, Brown, & Wingo, 2005). However, as with other immigrant groups, the longer they live in the United States, the higher the risk of disease due to their adopted lifestyle (Reed & Yano, 1997).

Non-Hispanic white adults have the longest overall life expectancy of any group in the United States, with women living longer than men. They have the highest rates of anxiety disorders, mood disorders, and substance abuse disorders (Kessler, Berglund, Demler, et al., 2005), but they are more apt to seek treatment for mental disorders, especially if they are under 60 and have good incomes (Wang, Lane, Olfson, et al., 2005).

In many respects, Hispanic Americans have a rather good health picture, although they are not always included as a separate group in government statistics, but are classified as either "black" or "white." Members of this group who have reached 65 years of age actually have a longer life expectancy than non-Hispanic whites, in part due to a significantly lower rate of major types of cancer and heart disease among both men and women (Markides & Black, 1996). They also have lower risk of anxiety disorders and mood disorders than non-Hispanic whites (Kessler, Berglund, Demler, et al., 2005). People in this group who were born in other countries and came to the United States as immigrants tend to be in better health than Hispanic Americans who were born in the United States (Stephens, Franks, & Townsend, 1994), a situation known as the "healthy immigrant effect." Unfortunately, this benefit seems to disappear after immigrants become accustomed to the U.S. culture, as I mentioned in Chapter 2 when I wrote about obesity rates among immigrant groups.

Hispanic Americans have the highest rate of diabetes among the major subgroups in the United States, and this high rate is found mostly in Mexican Americans. (Interestingly, the same high rate of diabetes is found in Native Americans, who share genes with Mexican Americans. In contrast, Cuban Americans do not have this high rate of diabetes and do not share genes with Mexican Americans, although they are classified with them as Hispanic (Rogers, 1991). Go figure!

Adults classified as non-Hispanic blacks in the United States have shorter life expectancies than white adults, especially black males. The top ten causes of death for this group are similar to the other groups in the United States, except that it is the only group to include homicide (number 6) and HIV/AIDS (number 7), which each account for about 4 percent of deaths. Non-Hispanic black adults have the highest rates of hypertension and stroke, and the second highest rates of diabetes, after Native Americans and Alaskan Natives (National Center for Health Statistics, 2004). Meta-analyses have shown that a number of these differences can be explained almost completely by economic factors, such as living in neighborhoods that are more dangerous and more distant from medical facilities, and being restricted to jobs that are more hazardous (Smith & Kington, 1997). Non-Hispanic blacks have lower rates of osteoporosis than other groups, and a resulting lower rate of disability from bone fractures. Women in this group are less likely to commit suicide than any other subgroup, but more likely to be obese. Non-Hispanic black men and women have lower risks of mood disorders, anxiety disorders, and substance abuse disorders than non-Hispanic white adults (Kessler, Berglund, Demler, et al., 2005).

American Indians and Alaskan Natives have the lowest life expectancy of any group in the United States. They have the highest rates of diabetes, hypertension, tuberculosis, arthritis, alcoholism, smoking, and serious psychological distress, all potentially disabling. Of all racial/ethnic groups in the United States, members of this one are the least likely to rate their health as "excellent." The two leading causes of death for this group are similar to other groups (heart disease and cancer), but the third most common cause of death is accidents (National Center for Health Statistics, 2004). These high rates of disease and premature death are due in large part to economic conditions, but sociohistorical factors are at work too. The only hopeful thing I can offer is that some progress is being made. For example the rates of breast cancer for women in this group have recently declined (Edwards, Brown, Wingo, et al., 2005), but reviewing the health data for this group of U.S. citizens, descendants of the original inhabitants of this country, is disturbing.

Racial Discrimination in Healthcare. Research evidence suggests that racial discrimination in the healthcare system contributes to black adults receiving lower levels of health care than adults in other groups.

Medical researchers Eric Schneider and his colleagues (Schneider, Zaslavsky, & Epstein, 2002) examined medical records for over 300,000 Medicare managed-care patients who were over 65 years of age. Because all the patients were enrolled in the same medical plan, differences between black and white patients could not be explained by lack of access to health care. The research controlled for patients' income level, education, and quality of the clinic visited for health care. Still, as shown in Figure 3.6, there were significant differences in the procedures the black and white patients received. For example, compared to white patients with similar conditions, black patients with diabetes were less likely to receive eye examinations, black patients with heart attacks were less likely to receive beta-blockers, and black patients hospitalized for mental disorders were less likely to receive follow-up care.

A more recent study showed that older black patients who were diagnosed with major depression were less likely to receive antidepressant medication and psychotherapy than older white patients with the same diagnosis (Strothers, Rust, Minor, et al., 2005). The

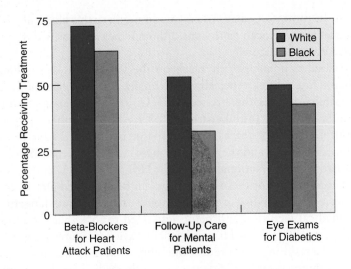

Figure 3.6 Black and white patients enrolled in Medicare do not receive the same medical treatment, even when income level, education, and quality of clinic visited are taken into consideration.

Source: Schneider, Zaslavsky, & Epstein (2002).

researchers suggested that the racial disparity might be explained by biases among doctors and cultural differences that promote a tendency for some older black adults to shun health care measures or distrust white doctors.

Personality and Behavior Patterns

The idea that one's personality contributes to one's physical health is the basis of the fairly new fields of health psychology and behavioral medicine, but the idea itself is very old, dating back at least to Hippocrates in ancient Greece. The first empirical demonstration of this relationship was provided by cardiologists Meyer Friedman and Ray Rosenman (1959), when they identified a behavior pattern that predicted risk for coronary heart disease. Since then, this area of research has become well accepted. Specific stable patterns of thinking, feeling, and behaving are indeed associated with increased risk of illness and premature death (Smith & Gallo, 2001).

Individuals classified as having a **type A behavior pattern** are achievement-striving, competitive, and involved in their jobs to excess; they feel extreme urgency with time-related matters and are easily provoked to hostility. People who do not fit this description are referred to as type B. Although the issue has been debated actively for over four decades, it seems clear that when careful measures are made, people who fit the type A behavior pattern are at greater risk of coronary heart disease than those with type B behavior (Smith & Gallo, 2001).

A great deal of research has been done to determine how this effect takes place, and generally researchers have found both a direct link (type A behavior affects physical health through such mechanisms as increasing stress reactions and lowering immune function) and an indirect link (type A behavior causes the person to create and seek out stressful situations that, in turn, elicit more type A behavior, which leads to physical responses). In other words, people who have this personality style are apt to create other situations that call for similar responses. People who are always racing against the clock to get to important appointments will place themselves in traffic situations that bring forth additional type A responses, thus further increasing the risk for physical problems.

Another personality component, **hostility,** which is defined as a negative cognitive set against others, has also been associated with cardiovascular disease and premature death from other causes (Miller, Smith, Turner, et al., 1996). Again there are several pathways suggested in addition to the direct one of hostility affecting physical responses. People who are high in hostility no doubt have hostile relationships with others, such as in their marriages, and these hostile interactions add more health risk (and subtract the protective effect of social support). Hostile people also are known to engage in more high-risk behavior, such as smoking and excessive alcohol use, which could increase the chance of negative health outcome (Siegler, 1994).

People who are high in **optimism,** that is, who have a positive outlook on life, believe that good things are going to happen to them, and cope with life's problems by taking steps to find direct solutions (instead of hoping that someone will rescue them or placing blame on others), are less apt to suffer from serious physical illness and less likely to die prematurely (Seligman, 1991).

One recent finding that concerns positive emotion and health is from epidemiologist David Snowdon. The Nun Study, the ongoing longitudinal study of 678 Catholic nuns from the School Sisters of Notre Dame, has given us a good picture of aging for women who live in the same sheltered environment and practice good health habits. In one particular report (Danner, Snowdon, & Friesen, 2001), autobiographical essays of 180 nuns were examined to determine how positive their outlooks were. The tone of these essays, written when the women were in their early 20s, were then compared to the women's longevity 60 years later. The more positive the essays were, the greater the longevity of the women who wrote them.

If you are like me, you are probably wondering whether anything can be done to change people who are type A, hostile, or pessimistic, since personality is considered an enduring component of the individual. Many of the researchers cited in this section are cautious about using the term "personality" for this very reason; instead, they use other terms, such as "behavior patterns." But whatever terms are used, the question remains: Is it possible to recognize these unhealthy traits in oneself and make some modifications? Preliminary studies show that this is possible to some extent. For example, one group of researchers managed to reduce hostility in men with heart disease and show some short-term improvement (Gidron, Davidson, & Bata, 1999). Others are investigating how these coping mechanisms develop in childhood, with the possibility of early educational interventions (Russek & Schwartz, 1997). I will discuss this more in Chapter 10.

> ● **CRITICAL THINKING**
>
> If negative behavior patterns such as hostility have both direct and indirect effects on health, how about positive behavior patterns? What would the direct and indirect effects be?

Genetics

One's **genotype,** the personal complement of genes that each of us possesses, has a big influence on our health. Most of you are probably aware of the diseases that are determined by a single gene, such as hemophilia and Huntington's disease. There are other diseases that are linked to a combination of genes, such as Alzheimer's disease, as discussed earlier. These gene combinations seem to influence disease by making some individuals more susceptible than others to environmental factors, such as tobacco smoke leading to lung cancer, head injury leading to Alzheimer's disease, or fatty diets leading to cardiovascular disease.

Researchers are now investigating how one's genes can affect one's individual responses to different treatments for diseases. For example, a number of genes have been identified that determine which of several drugs would be most successful in treating leukemia patients. Progress is also being made in identifying genes relating to drug responses for cancer, asthma, and cardiovascular disease treatment (Couzin, 2005). These findings may someday lead to the practice of personalized medicine, in which your own DNA sequence becomes part of your medical history and is used in making decisions about what screening tests you should have to prevent disease and, if a disease is present, which treatment is best suited for you.

Developmental Origins

Several researchers have presented evidence suggesting that some diseases of adulthood are determined partly by environmental events earlier in life. Epidemiologist David Barker and his colleagues introduced this idea almost three decades ago when they examined birth and death records for over 5,000 men born within a 20-year period in the same area of England. They found that the men with the lowest weights at birth had the highest likelihood of dying from strokes (Barker, Winter, Osmond, et al., 1989). Since that time, research with humans and other species has given rise to the **developmental origins hypothesis** of adult health and disease, which states that growth during the fetal period, infancy, and the early years of childhood is a significant factor in adult health (Barker, 2004).

Environmental factors present in early development that have been studied include maternal nutrition, season of birth, and smoking. The resulting adult health outcomes include hypertension, diabetes, osteoporosis, and mood disorders (Gluckman & Hanson, 2004). Figure 3.7 shows data from almost 23,000 men indicating that those with lower birthweights were at higher risk for hypertension and diabetes in adulthood.

Furthermore, evidence has been found that if a woman suffers malnutrition during pregnancy, her child is likely to be born at a low birth weight. And if that child is a daughter, *her* children's birth weight and subsequent health could be affected by the malnutrition experienced during the grandmother's pregnancy, even if the daughter did not experience malnutrition herself (Gluckman & Hanson, 2004). The explanation for this is that the ova is formed during the prenatal period. Malnutrition of the pregnant woman affects her developing fetus, and if the fetus is female, the malnutrition would affect the development of her ova. Not only can we trace our health status back to our childhood and prenatal experiences, we can go back to our *mothers'* prenatal months when half our genetic material was being formed, an influence referred to as **intergenerational effects.**

One more connection between early environment and adult health is the relationship between childhood infectious disease and cardiovascular disease, cancer, and diabetes mellitus. One study demonstrating this connection was done by economic historians Tommy Bengtsson and Martin Lindström (2003), who examined 18th-century medical records in four parishes in Sweden for a period of 128 years. They found that the people who had the fewest infectious diseases in infancy were the ones who had the greatest longevity. Even when periods of food shortage during that century

Figure 3.7 Data from more than 22,000 men over the age of 40, showing the relationship between birth weight and risk for two diseases in adulthood, hypertension and diabetes. The lower the birth weight, the greater the risk.

Source: Adapted from Gluckman & Hanson (2004).

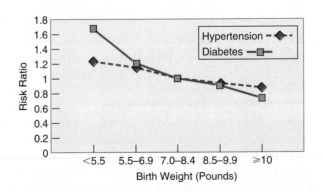

were considered, infant infections remained the strongest factor in determining adult longevity. It is suggested that the link between early childhood infections and early death in adulthood is inflammation (Finch & Crimmins, 2004), which, as mentioned earlier in this chapter, is implicated in a number of major diseases in adulthood, such as heart disease, cancer, and Alzheimer's disease.

For those of us in developed countries, the incidence of childhood infectious disease is low, and some researchers suggest that the increase in our life spans during the 20th century was due to this fact. However, in developing countries, diseases like tuberculosis, diarrheal illnesses, and malaria are still prevalent. Epidemiologists believe that once these childhood diseases are controlled, there will be a corresponding drop in the rates of life-limiting adult diseases that involve inflammation and a resulting increase in longevity (Finch & Crimmins, 2004).

The Road to Good Health

I have reviewed the changes in health through adulthood in Table 3.9, but I want to end with a reminder that the health disorders and diseases discussed in this chapter don't happen to everyone, and don't happen at random. Many can be prevented; others can be detected early and treated successfully, or at least controlled. The best advice is still to eat healthy, exercise, get regular checkups, know your family health history, and seek scientifically proven treatment early for whatever disorders occur. Live a balanced life with time for supportive relationships and activities that reduce stress. Don't smoke; if

> ### CRITICAL THINKING
>
> Do you know your family's health history? Does it contain health conditions that may be inherited? What could you do to reduce your risk for these conditions?

Table 3.9	Review of Health and Illness Over the Adult Years		
Age 20–39	**Age 40–64**	**Age 65–74**	**Age 75+**
Lowest death rate; top causes of death are accidents, homicide, and suicide.	Low death rate; top causes of death are cancer and heart disease.	Death rate begins to increase; top causes of death are heart disease and cancer.	Higher death rate; top causes of death are heart disease, cancer, and stroke.
Acute illnesses most common.	Acute illness and chronic conditions at moderate risk.	Chronic conditions present, but most report having none. Almost all are aging in place.	Chronic conditions and disability more common. 80% are aging in place. One-third report their health as "excellent" or "very good."
Negligible incidence of dementia.	Early-onset Alzheimer's can begin, but accounts for only 10% of all cases.	Alzheimer's present in 5–10%; other dementias present but can be treated.	33% have Alzheimer's disease.
Highest rates of onset for major depression around 30. Moderate rates of depressive symptoms.	Lower rates of major depression. Lower rates of depressive symptoms.	Very low rates of onset for major depression. Higher rates of depressive symptoms. Low rates of seeking treatment for mental health disorders.	Major depression symptoms, often due to Alzheimer's disease. Higher rates of depressive symptoms, probably due to chronic health problems and bereavement. Low rates of seeking treatment for mental health disorders.

you do smoke, quit. Practice safe sex. Wear your seatbelts and safety helmets. With all the medical advances I have read about in preparation for this chapter, I have seen no evidence for magic potions or pills that provide a shortcut to good health and long life. People who try to convince you otherwise are, in the words of medical professor Thomas T. Perls, "quacks" (Perls, 1994, p. 690).

Summary

1. Mortality rates increase with age, especially after 60. Causes of death are different for different ages, with accidents, homicides, and suicides leading the list for younger adults, heart disease and cancer for older adults.

2. Older adults have a greater incidence of chronic conditions such as arthritis, high blood pressure, and cardiovascular disease. Still, about half of adults 65 and older report having no chronic disease at all.

3. Rates of disability also increase with age, although over 80 percent of adults 65 and over report needing no assistance with tasks of daily living.

4. About 81 percent of women 65 and older and 90 percent of men this age are community dwelling. Only 5 percent are in nursing homes, and most of them are in their 80s.

5. Disability is not just found in older adults; about 5 percent of young adults and about 12 percent of middle-aged adults need assistance with independent activities of daily living.

6. Cardiovascular disease is the top cause of death among adults throughout the world. It involves the blocking of coronary arteries by plaques in the artery walls and can lead to heart attack. Some risk factors are under our control, such as smoking and leading a sedentary lifestyle. Others are not under our control, such as family history and age. Women get cardiovascular disease at the same rate as men, only later in life and with different symptoms.

7. The second leading cause of death for adults in the United States is cancer, which involves rapid division of abnormal cells invading nearby tissue or spreading to other parts of the body. The incidence of cancer increases with age. Risk factors for cancer that are under our control are smoking, obesity, and unprotected exposure to bright sunlight. Factors that are not under our control are age and family history.

8. The fifth leading cause of death among older adults is Alzheimer's disease, caused by progressive deterioration of certain parts of the brain. The result is loss of cognitive ability and physical function. Alzheimer's disease is seldom seen before 50, and 90 percent of the cases occur after 65. Many of the risk factors for Alzheimer's disease are the same as for cardiovascular disease, and both may be linked to inflammation earlier in life. Some of the risk factors that can be modified are smoking, sedentary lifestyles, and obesity. Those that can't are age and genetic predisposition.

9. The rate of mental health disorders in U.S. adults has remained stable in the past decade but is higher than in any other developed country. The most common types are anxiety disorders (phobias, PTSD, and obsessive-compulsive disorder) and mood disorders (major depression and bipolar disorder). The onset of most mental health disorders is in adolescence and early adulthood. Major depression is more apt to affect young and middle-aged adults than older adults, who are more apt to report depressive symptoms.

10. The majority of people who have experienced mental health disorders in the past 12 months have not sought treatment, and a third who did, received inadequate treatment. Those who did not seek treatment are more likely to be older adults than younger or middle-aged adults.

11. Men and women have different patterns of both physical and mental health problems. Men have shorter life expectancies and higher rates of life-threatening physical diseases and more mental disorders involving alcohol and substance abuse and impulse control disorders. Women have more chronic diseases and higher rates of major depression and anxiety disorders. This difference is partly biological and partly sociocultural.

12. People in lower socioeconomic groups have lower levels of physical and mental health than higher socioeconomic groups and decline in physical health more quickly. This difference is due to health habits and the effects of stress.

13. Asian Americans and Pacific Islanders have the best health picture of any group in the United States, due in part to their traditional lifestyles, which include healthy diets and low smoking rates. The lowest level of health in the United States is found in Native American and Alaskan Native groups.

14. Another factor that can affect health is behavior patterns (type A, hostility, pessimism) that lead to cardiovascular disease and early death. Low birth weight and early childhood infections have been linked to such adult health problems as diabetes and mood disorders.

15. Many physical and mental health disorders can be prevented through healthy lifestyles. Others can be detected early and treated successfully. There are no shortcuts to good health and no magic pills.

Key Terms

mortality rate, 70

morbidity rate, 71

acute conditions, 71

chronic conditions, 71

ADLs (activities of daily living), 72

IADLs (instrumental activities of daily living), 72

community dwelling, 72

aging in place, 72

nursing home, 73

congregate living facilities, 73

assisted-living facilities, 73

cardiovascular disease, 74

plaques, 74

atherosclerosis, 74

cancer, 75

Alzheimer's disease, 77

dementia, 77

onset, 81

prevalence, 81

comorbid, 82

anxiety disorders, 82

phobias, 82

post-traumatic stress syndrome, 82

obsessive-compulsive disorder, 82

mood disorders, 83

major depression, 83

depressive symptoms, 83

impulse control disorders, 84

substance abuse disorders, 84

complementary and alternative medicine providers, 86

food insufficiency, 90

type A behavior pattern, 92

hostility, 92

optimism, 93

genotype, 93

developmental origins hypothesis, 94

intergenerational effects, 94

Suggested Reading

Reading for Personal Interest

Costa, J. K. (2004). *Learning to speak Alzheimer's: A ground-breaking approach for everyone dealing with the disease.* Boston: Houghton Mifflin

If you are one of the 4 million people in the U.S. with a family member who has Alzheimer's disease, this book gives a guide of how to adjust to the different stages of the disease and how to relate to the patients' own reality to give them dignity and personhood. The author's husband died of this disease and she includes many useful ideas for caregiving.

Hamer, D., & Copeland, P. (1998). *Living with our genes: Why they matter more than you think.* New York: Doubleday.

Hamer is one of the world's leading behavioral geneticists. In this book he and co-author Copeland explain how our genes affect many health-related behaviors such as depression and anxiety, addiction, and eating habits. This book is informative, clearly written, and fun. The chapter on sex, which explains the genetics of the "Venus and Mars distinction," alone is worth the price of the book.

Wilde, C. (2003). Hidden causes of heart attack and stroke: Inflammation, cardiology's new frontier. Studio City, CA: Abion.

This book offers a thorough discussion about the role of inflammation in health problems. It's a good resource for adults of any age who want to be proactive about their health.

Classic Work

Friedman, M., & Rosenman, R. H. (1959). Association of a specific overt behavior pattern with increases in blood cholesterol, blood clotting time, incidence of arcus senilis and clinical coronary artery disease. *Journal of the American Medical Association, 169,* 1286–1296.

This paper was the first time "type A" was introduced to the scientific world. The authors described an "action-emotion complex" that consisted of striving for achievement, being overly involved in one's job, being extremely competitive and hostile, and experiencing urgency in time-related matters. Friedman and Rosenman showed that this type of behavior pattern was related to certain physical symptoms of coronary heart disease.

Scheier, M. F., & Carver, C. S. (1987). Dispositional optimism and physical well-being: The influence of generalized outcome expectancies on health. *Journal of Personality, 55,* 169–210.

This was one of the first reviews of research suggesting that people's optimism (or outcome expectancies) were related to their physical well-being. Possible explanations offered were that optimistic people had a trait (hardiness) that buffered them against the harmful effects of stress.

Peterson, C., & Seligman, M. (1987). Explanatory style and illness. *Journal of Personality, 55,* 237–265.

These two scientists first suggested that a person's way of explaining the world (optimism or pessimism) has an effect on her or his physical health. It came out at the same time and in the same journal as Scheier and Carver's (above) classic paper on dispositional optimism, showing that great minds think alike. They take slightly different approaches, but the result is the same. The four writers are now credited for this productive line of research.

Contemporary Scholarly Work

American Psychiatric Association (2000). *Diagnostic and statistical manual of mental disorders DSM-IV-TR* (Text Revision). Washington, DC: American Psychiatric Association.

This is the authority on diagnosing mental disorders. The APA revises this manual about every 6 years, and it includes the most recent descriptions of various mental disorders—the symptoms, prevalence, and variations, plus the all-important diagnosis numbers. If you are planning a career in clinical psychology, medicine, mental health counseling, or any related field, this is a must for your bookshelf. If you are just interested in psychology and mental disorders, you might enjoy owning it also.

Knight, B. G., Kaskie, B., Shurgot, G. R., et al. (2006). Improving the mental health of older adults. In J. E. Birren & K. W. Schaie (Eds.), *Handbook of the psychology of aging* (pp. 407–424). San Diego: Academic Press.

Psychotherapists Bob Knight and his colleagues review the most common mental disorders of older adults and discuss the available interventions.

Mathews, K. A. (2005). Psychological perspectives on the development of coronary heart disease. *American Psychologist, 60,* 783–796.

Karen Mathews received the Award for Distinguished Scientific Applications of Psychology from the American Psychological Association in 2005 for her work in health psychology. This article reflects her overview of the work that has been done to date on linking psychological factors with heart disease and suggesting what needs to be done.

Whitfield, K. E., & McClearn, G. (2005). Genes, environment, and race: Quantitative genetic approaches. *American Psychologist, 60,* 104–114.

The authors, behavioral geneticists, explain the basic concepts of genes and race and argue that an understanding of both is necessary to understand racial disparities in health.

Chapter 4

Cognitive Abilities

Intelligence
Age Changes in Overall
Intelligence
Components of Intelligence
Reversing Declines
in Intellectual Abilities

Memory
Memory Systems Components

Real-World Cognition
Judgment and Decision Making
Human Factors Research:
Assistive Technology

**Individual Differences in
Cognitive Change**
Health
Genetics
Demographics and
Sociobiographical History
Schooling
Intellectual Activity
Physical Exercise
Subjective Evaluation of Decline

**Review of Cognitive Changes
over the Adult Years
and a Search for Balance**

Summary

Key Terms

Suggested Reading

MY PARENTS TOOK me out to a steakhouse for my 53rd birthday, and when I had trouble getting catsup to pour out of a new bottle onto my fries, Dad showed me a trick he had learned from a catsup salesman—you tap the neck of the bottle sharply against your outstretched index finger and the catsup comes out easily. Then he and Mom reminisced about their friend Don Iverson, the catsup salesman. He lived in Savannah, Georgia, and they had last visited him on the way home from their honeymoon. Don's wife had made a standing rib roast for dinner with peach cobbler for dessert. What a great time they had, eating and playing cards and talking until early morning. What was Don's wife's name? Neither could remember. They talked back and forth a little, trying to come up with the name of the catsup salesman's wife they had not seen in 55 years but finally agreed in desperation: "We just can't remember anything anymore!"

It's true that my parents were growing old—they were 77 and 80 at the time of that birthday dinner—but remembering the catsup salesman's name, the city he lived in, and even what his wife had served for dinner that evening over 50 years before is impressive at any age. Yet one of the most popular stereotypes of aging is cognitive loss, and it is a stereotype that even older adults hold about themselves. The same lost car keys or forgotten phone number that at 30 or 40 is a normal slipup is viewed as a symptom of early senility at 70 or 80. But what is typical of cognitive aging and what is myth? One of the busiest fields of aging research has some surprising answers.

Intelligence

When we think of evaluating age changes in cognitive processes, most of us think immediately of IQ scores. Does IQ change as we get older? If so, is there a sudden drop at a certain age, or is the change gradual? Are some types of intelligence affected more than others? These types of questions have long been the basis of cognitive aging studies, but before I review their findings, let me say a few words about the concept of intelligence and about IQ tests, the tools we use to measure that concept.

Defining **intelligence** is one of the slipperier tasks in psychology. The typical definition goes something like this: "the aggregate or global capacity of the individual to act purposefully, to think rationally and to deal effectively with his environment" (Wechsler, 1939, p. 3). In other words, intelligence is a visible indicator of the efficiency of various cognitive processes that work together behind the scenes to process information in various ways. The field of psychology that studies the measurement of human abilities such as intelligence is **psychometrics.**

Many psychologists assume that there is a central, general intellectual capacity, often called *g,* which influences the way we approach a great number of different tasks (Spearman, 1904; Jensen, 1998). The score on an intelligence test is intended to describe this general capacity, known as the **IQ (intelligence quotient).** As you may know from previous courses, the average IQ score is normally set at 100, with scores above 100 reflecting above-average performance and scores below 100 reflecting below-average performance.

In addition to *g,* some psychologists who study intelligence are interested in the specific components of intellectual capacity. On standard IQ tests, these capacities are measured by the various subtests that make up the total IQ score. For example, the Wechsler Adult Intelligence Scale (WAIS) is made up of subtests that measure verbal abilities and performance abilities. The scores of each of these subtests are combined to produce a **verbal IQ** and a **performance IQ,** which in turn are combined to produce a single **full-scale IQ.** Verbal IQ can be compared with performance IQ, and subtests can be grouped in a variety of other ways, depending on the researchers' interests.

Age Changes in Overall Intelligence

Now let's get to some of the research findings on age changes in intelligence. Do IQ scores decline with age or stay constant? Most of the early information on consistency or change in adult intelligence came from cross-sectional studies (1920s to 1950s), which seemed to show that declines in IQ began in early adulthood and continued steadily thereafter. This depressing conclusion was widely reported and widely believed, along with the popular finding (now outdated) that the adult brain loses 100,000 neurons each day. But beginning around the 1960s, evidence from longitudinal studies began changing this, showing that adult intelligence was stable until at least age 50 (which was as far as the studies extended at that point in time).

In the decades since then, we have learned a lot more about adult intelligence. Researchers of cognitive aging have developed new designs that do away with some of the confounds of traditional methods and have extended longitudinal studies to include people in their 60s, 70s, 80s, and beyond. Although results continue to show some cognitive decline with age, the news is much more optimistic. There are aspects of adult thought processes that function at very high levels into very old age. When decline occurs, it is often much less extreme than once thought, and we often compensate so that it is not noticeable. Moreover, there are precautions we can take that will increase our chances of staying bright and high functioning throughout our lives.

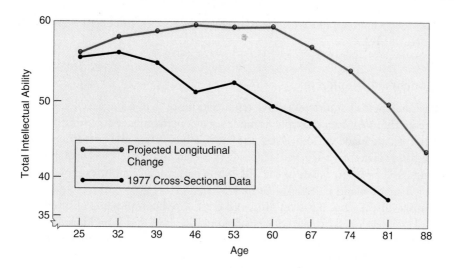

Figure 4.1 Age changes in total IQ based on cross-sectional data (lower line) and longitudinal data (upper line). Depending on cross-sectional data in the past led to erroneous conclusions that cognitive performance begins to decline around 40 and that the decline is very fast.

Source: Data from Schaie (1983).

Figure 4.1 shows the contrast between longitudinal and cross-sectional analyses of IQ scores in the Seattle Longitudinal Study. This study used a sequential design that allowed for both longitudinal and cross-sectional comparisons. The numbers are not traditional IQ scores with a mean of 100. Instead they have been calculated to show the change in scores for each participant over the course of the study, with the beginning score set at 50, and a standard deviation of 10. Thus two-thirds of all adults should fall between scores of 40 and 60 (one standard deviation on either side of the mean), and about 95 percent should fall between 30 and 70 (Schaie, 1994).

When you compare the longitudinal and cross-sectional data, you can see that they yield very different answers to the question, "What happens to IQ over the course of adulthood?" The cross-sectional evidence, of which the lower curve is highly typical, shows a beginning decline in IQ starting somewhere between ages 32 and 39. The longitudinal information suggests a rise in IQ through middle adulthood. Only in the period from 67 to 74 do the total IQ scores in the samples drop below those seen at age 25.

The obvious explanation for the difference between the cross-sectional and longitudinal comparisons is that there are cohort effects at work here. As years of education, good health, and the cognitive complexities of life have increased over the past century, the average scores for each successive cohort have gone up. In fact, researchers have found that average verbal IQ scores for groups of older adults are increasing by over four and a half points each decade (Uttl & Van Alstine, 2003). As a result, cross-sectional studies comparing people born decades apart may show lower IQ scores for older people, but they are not accurate predictors of what the future holds in store for young people today.

One more statistical note: I have been talking about standard deviations, and you probably know some long definition of this term. But in plain English, just how much intelligence are we talking about here? One standard deviation in IQ is 15 points. In Figure 4.1, the difference between the point on the vertical axis labeled 50 and the point labeled 40 is only 15 IQ points. If the subjects in this study began at age 25 with an average IQ of 100, they increased to about 113 or so, stayed there until about 60 years of age, and then began to decline. But they were 70 when they crossed the 100 IQ line again on the way down and still hadn't declined to the 85 IQ line by age 88.

To summarize, there is good support for the optimistic view that general intellectual ability remains fairly stable through most of adulthood. But now let's dissect intelligence

● CRITICAL THINKING

If these cross-sectional studies measured the height of participants who were 20, 40, 60, and 80 years of age, what would you predict the results would show? How might you explain the results?

a little and see what happens with age to some of the specific intellectual abilities that are components of IQ.

Components of Intelligence

As mentioned before, standardized IQ tests yield more than a single score. The full-scale IQ score on the WAIS, for example, is made up of a performance score and a verbal score, which in turn are made up of five subtests each. When verbal and performance scores are separated and viewed over age, verbal abilities generally show increases or stability through the adult age span up to as late as the 70s, while performance abilities show much earlier decline (Busse & Maddox, 1985; Denney, 1982).

A similar distinction, between fluid and crystallized components of intelligence, was proposed and developed by psychologists Raymond Cattell and John Horn (Cattell, 1963; Horn & Cattell, 1966) and is now widely used by researchers studying adult cognition. **Crystallized intelligence** is heavily dependent on education and experience. It consists of the set of skills and bits of knowledge that we each learn as part of growing up in a given culture, such as verbal comprehension, vocabulary, the ability to evaluate experience, the ability to reason about real-life problems, and technical skills learned for a job and other aspects of life (balancing a checkbook, making change, finding the salad dressing in the grocery store). On standardized tests, crystallized abilities are usually measured by vocabulary and by verbal comprehension (e.g., reading a paragraph and then answering questions about it).

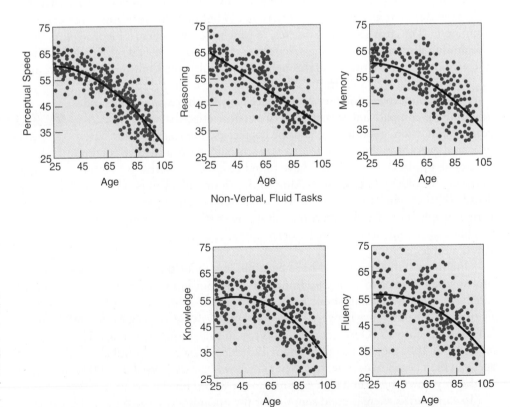

Figure 4.2 Adults in the Berlin Study of Aging show earlier declines on tests of nonverbal, fluid tasks (upper row) than on tests of verbal, crystallized tasks (lower row).

Source: Lindenberger & Baltes (1997).

In contrast, **fluid intelligence** is a more basic set of abilities "requiring adaptation to new situations and for which prior education or learning provide relatively little advantage" (Berg & Sternberg, 2003, p. 105). A common measure of this is a letter series test. You may be given a series of letters like A C F J O and have to figure out what letter should go next. This demands abstract reasoning rather than reasoning about known or everyday events. Most tests of memory are also part of fluid intelligence, as are many tests measuring response speed or abstract kinds of mathematics. Horn and his colleagues concluded that crystallized abilities generally continue to rise or show stability over adulthood and well into the 70s, while fluid abilities begin to decline earlier (Horn & Donaldson, 1980; Horn & Hofer, 1992). Just how much earlier the decline is for fluid abilities has been debated; cross-sectional studies show that it begins around 35 or 40 years of age, longitudinal studies show that it begins in the 60s (Sternberg, Grigorenko, & Oh, 2001).

Whatever labels we apply to these two broad categories of intellectual ability, and whatever tasks researchers use to evaluate them in people of different ages, the results are similar. Nonverbal, fluid abilities, such as those shown in the upper row of the graphs of Figure 4.2, show earlier, steeper declines than verbal, crystalized abilities, such as those shown in the lower row (Lindenberger & Baltes, 1997).

Similar findings come from the Seattle Longitudinal Study data discussed earlier. Instead of Wechsler subtests this study measured primary mental abilities (Thurstone, 1938): *verbal meaning, spatial orientation, inductive reasoning, number,* and *word fluency.* Figure 4.3 shows the longitudinal gradients for the five factors. As you can see, there is a modest gain in all abilities from age 25 to 32, but then declines begin in word fluency and number abilities, both of which are fluid abilities. (But also notice that neither goes below the starting point until around age 53.) Around age 46, two abilities stop increasing—verbal meaning and spatial orientation—although neither crosses below its starting point until

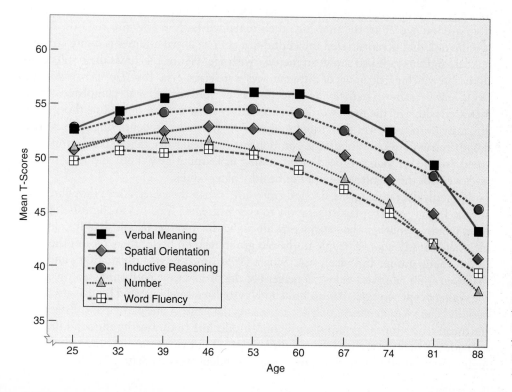

Figure 4.3 K. W. Schaie combined data from several segments of the Seattle Longitudinal Study to estimate age changes in five primary mental abilities from 25 to 88 years of age. These data show that substantial cognitive changes occur only late in life and tend to occur for fluid abilities (number and word fluency) sooner than crystallized abilities (verbal meaning, spatial orientation, and inductive reasoning).

Source: Schaie (1994).

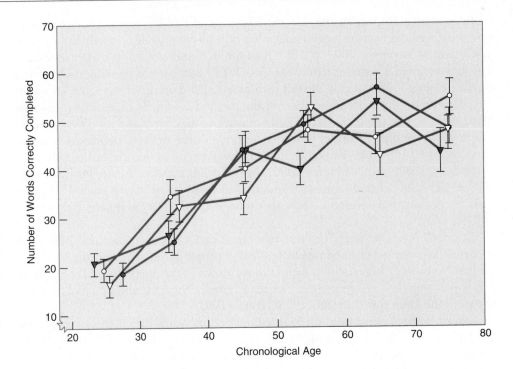

Figure 4.4 The number of words correctly completed in the *New York Times* crossword puzzle increases with age for over 800 adults in four different studies. Each line represents the results of a different study.
Source: Salthouse (2004).

much later (at 74 for verbal meaning and around 65 for spatial orientation). The last to start declining is inductive reasoning, at 53, crossing below its starting point around 65 years of age (Schaie, 1994).

Performance on specific tasks of crystallized memory ability has been shown to increase with age, such as asking participants to select which one of five words is a synonym for a target word. Psychologist Timothy Salthouse (2004) found that this ability increased from around age 20 to the mid-50s, then remained fairly stable into the 80s. Another specific task that demonstrated the endurance of crystallized abilities is doing crossword puzzles, and this skill also shows an increase with age. Figure 4.4 shows the results of four studies in which participants of different ages were given *New York Times* crossword puzzles to solve. As shown in the figure, the number of words participants completed correctly increased with age; the most words were solved by those in their 60s, while those in their 20s and 30s solved fewer than those in their 70s. The tasks of identifying synonyms and doing crossword puzzles represent components of intelligence that depend more on accrued knowledge than on speed of processing or learning new skills, and they fit hand-in-glove with the cognitive abilities of healthy older adults.

Not only does intelligence decline more slowly than the experts once thought, but we are also finding out that few rules apply to everyone when it comes to cognitive aging. In other words, even when the mean scores are higher for younger people than for older people, there are still a lot of people in the old group who do better than a lot of the people in the young group, and vice versa. Schaie (1996) measured this variability and found that even at 80 years and older, 53 percent of the people were performing comparably to the young people on tests of both fluid and crystallized intelligence. This can also be seen back in Figure 4.2, in which each dot represents the score of one participant. Even though the mean scores for the group show significant decline (indicated by the solid lines), the individual scores show a lot of variability; there are individuals at the oldest ages scoring higher than individuals at the youngest ages (Lindenberger & Baltes, 1997).

Reversing Declines in Intellectual Abilities

Beginning in the 1970s, when it became apparent that intelligence did not drop off drastically with age, researchers began asking if anything could be done to reverse the moderate decline in IQ shown in longitudinal studies. The answer was yes. Different studies showed that physical exercise brought about significant improvement in intellectual performance (Powell, 1974), as did training subjects in the components specific to the task being tested (Labouvie-Vief & Gonda, 1976) and training in nonspecific aspects of the test, such as willingness to guess when one is not sure of the correct answer (Birkhill & Schaie, 1975).

Schaie and his colleague (Schaie & Willis, 1986) included a training study in one wave of their ongoing longitudinal project to determine whether training was effective for people who were already showing a decline or just for those who had not yet begun to decline. Participants, aged 64 to 94, received 5 hours of training. About half of the participants had shown a decline over the last 14 years, and about half had not. Some received training on spatial orientation, and some on inductive reasoning, both abilities that tend to decline with age and are considered more resistant to intervention. When the results of the training were examined for those who had declined, it was found that about half had gained significantly and 40 percent had returned to their former level of performance. Of those who had not yet shown declines, one-third increased their abilities above their previous levels.

Seven years later, the same researchers retested about half of these subjects and compared them to other participants in the study who were the same age and had not received training. The scores of the group that received training had declined from their previous levels, but they performed better than the controls, even though it had been 7 years since their training. These participants were then given an additional 5 hours of training, which again raised their test scores significantly, but not to the level of 7 years earlier (Willis & Schaie, 1994). Similar results have been found for memory training in a visuomotor task over a 2-year period (Smith, Walton, Loveland, et al., 2005), and a perceptual-motor task over a 5-year period (Rodrigue, Kennedy, & Raz, 2005).

● **CRITICAL THINKING**

What games can you think of that might be beneficial to older adults' spatial orientation? What games might boost inductive reasoning?

Memory

Memory is defined as the ability to retain or store information and retrieve it when needed. Although IQ is the most familiar concept in cognition for most adults, memory is clearly the topic that causes the most concern. As illustrated in my story about the catsup salesman at the beginning of this chapter, older adults often incorrectly interpret minor memory lapses as signs of serious mental failure and at the same time do not give themselves credit for the many accurate and important memory tasks they perform each day. Most adults over the age of 65 report that they have noticed a recent decline in their memory abilities, and most express concern over it, associating it with illness, loss of independence, and their own mortality (Wilson, Bennett, & Swartzendruber, 1997). For some older people, the effect goes beyond normal concern. Clinical psychologists have reported an increase in the number of patients who show pathological levels of anxiety that their failing memory is symptomatic of Alzheimer's disease (Centofanti, 1998). So this is an important topic on several levels—for professionals who work with older clients, for young and middle-aged adults who have older parents, and for older adults themselves; it is important to know about the age-related change in memory ability, its causes, and what, if anything, can be done to prevent, reverse, or compensate for it.

Memory Systems Components

As fruitful as the psychometric approach has been for viewing overall changes in mental abilities through the adult years, the **information-processing perspective** has given us a closer look at the "processes, representations, and strategies that individuals use to perform intellectual tasks" (Berg & Sternberg, 2003). This field relies strongly on the model proposed by psychologists Richard Atkinson and Richard Shiffrin (1968). The model consists of three memory storage areas. The **sensory store** refers to the initial step as information is picked up by the senses and processed briefly by the perceptual system; the **short-term store** is the second step, as information is held for 30 seconds or so and either discarded or encoded for storage in the **long-term store,** where it can remain for years. Almost 25 years later, psychologists Daniel Schacter and Endel Tulving (1996) proposed a similar model but suggested that the components were distinct memory systems rather than steps in a single process. I have combined the two models in the following discussion to take advantage of the familiarity of one and the added dimensions of the other. And I have provided Table 4.1 to show the two models and compare their components and the effects of age on each component.

Sensory Store. The sensory store is actually a collection of channels that transmit sensory and perceptual information to specialized parts of the brain that analyze, integrate, and briefly hold selected bits for further processing. The sensory memory system has not been the focus of much direct research, but it is implicated in the recent findings that the decline in cognitive abilities found in some older adults is better explained by their hearing and visual abilities than by their chronological ages (Lindenberger & Baltes, 1997). If these higher-order cognitive processes are being compromised by hearing and visual deficits, the memory system that is involved is surely the sensory system. If the ears and eyes of older adults are not functioning up to speed, the result would certainly throw a monkey wrench into the process of analyzing, integrating, and briefly holding incoming information. In fact, sensory memory might very well be working perfectly, but without accurate raw material, and if so, that would be why the resulting information products are defective.

Table 4.1	**Two Models of Memory Systems with Age Changes**	
Three Successive Stages of Memory (Atkinson & Shiffrin, 1968)	**Five Major Systems of Memory (Schacter & Tulving, 1996)**	**Changes with Age**
Sensory Store	Perceptual representation system	Decline in sensory systems (hearing and vision) leads to deficits at all memory levels
Short-Term Store	Primary memory/working memory	Small, gradual changes in primary memory throughout the adult years; substantial decline in working memory.
Long-Term Store	Episodic memory	Declines with age; can be compensated for somewhat with environmental support
	Semantic memory	Mostly stable until the 70s, then gradual decline. Retrieval of specific words and names begins decline in middle adulthood.
	Procedural memory	Little change with age.

This is exactly the situation researchers produced in a study with young adults who had normal hearing ability and normal sensory memory systems. They played a recorded list of words to the participants and then asked them, some time later, to recall as many words as they could. On a second trial they distorted the sounds of the word list to resemble the hearing of an older adult. They asked for the young participants' recall again and compared it to that of a control group of older adults. The first trial (with the normal tape) showed a distinct advantage for the young adults, but the second trial (with the distorted tape) showed that the young adults' recall had declined to the level of the older control group (Spinks, Gilmore, & Thomas, 1996). The message is that if information is blocked from accurately entering an information-processing system, the result is poor memory performance, even when other parts of the system are functioning well.

Short-Term Store. The short-term memory system is where we hold information "in mind," either to passively store it for immediate recall (holding a phone number someone has told you until you can find your cell phone to call it) or to more actively perform mental operations on it. The passive end of the continuum is called **primary memory;** the active end is called **working memory** (Baddeley, 1986). Primary memory refers to the amount of information we can hold in memory while performing some type of operation on it; working memory refers to the ability to perform the operations. Researchers have found that primary memory, as measured by tests of digit span, shows only small declines with age through the 70s and 80s (Gregoire & Van der Linden, 1997) and remains relatively stable through the mid-90s (Bäckman, Small, Wahlin, et al., 2000). In contrast, tests of working memory show substantial decline with age (Berg & Sternberg, 2003).

This split between primary memory and working memory was demonstrated by psychologist Denise Park and her colleagues (Park, Hedden, Lautenschlager, et al., 2002). They gave a variety of memory tasks to participants in seven age groups, ranging from the 20s to the 80s. The results for the primary memory tasks are shown in the upper panel of Figure 4.5. The tests included watching the experimenter point to a sequence of colored blocks and then repeating the sequence or listening to a sequence of digits and then repeating the sequence. As you can see, the decline in scores over this age range was moderate. Compare the results in the top panel to those in the lower panel of Figure 4.5, which shows the same participants' scores for tests of working memory. These test involved storing information in memory while performing some computation on it. For example, in the reading-span test, participants listened to a sentence ("After dinner the chef prepared dessert"). They were asked to answer a multiple-choice question about the sentence ("What did the chef prepare? a. fish, b. dessert, c. salad") and remember the last word of the sentence (dessert) until a number of sentences had been presented. The trajectory for these tasks, as you can see, shows a much steeper decline with age than for the primary memory tasks.

We also have some longitudinal data to consider on the subject of age-related change in working-memory abilities. Psychologist David Hultsch and his colleagues (Hultsch, Hertzog, Dixon, et al., 1998) gave various memory tests to a group of 297 older Canadian adults who were participants in the Victoria Longitudinal Study. The average age of one group of participants was 65 when they were first tested, and the average age of the other group was 75. Three years later, both the younger group (now 68) and the older group (now 78) showed significant declines in verbal working memory, and the older group had a significantly greater decline than the younger group.

What is the reason for this decline in working memory? One theory is that older people don't have the mental energy, or attentional resources, that younger people do (Craik

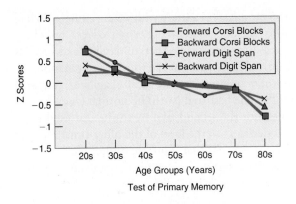

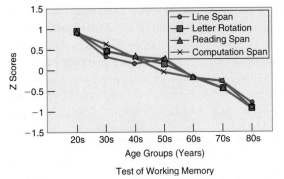

Figure 4.5 Scores for primary memory tasks (upper panel) show slower decline with age over the course of adulthood than do scores on working-memory tasks (lower panel).

Source: Park, Lautenschlager, Hedden, et al. (2002).

& Byrd, 1982). A related idea is that older people are not as able to use the strategies required by working-memory tasks (Brébion, Smith, & Ehrlich, 1997). Another explanation offered is a decline in processing speed (Salthouse, 1996). A fourth hypothesis is that older adults are less able to inhibit irrelevant and confusing information (Hasher & Zacks, 1988). And a fifth idea is that older adults are not as able to engage in the reflective processes required for successful working-memory processes (Johnson, Reeder, Raye, et al., 2002). All of these ideas are represented in current memory research, so it will be interesting to see what unfolds.

Long-Term Store. The long-term memory system deals with both our store of facts and our ability to recall events that happened to us in the past. The store of facts is known as **semantic memory;** the ability to recall recent events is known as **episodic memory.** When you appear on the TV program *Jeopardy* and come up with the correct name of the 15th president of the United States, you are using your semantic memory. When you come home and tell your friends and family about your trip to Los Angeles and the whole game-show experience, you are using your episodic memory. (And when I write here that the 15th U.S. president was James Buchanan, I am using *The World Almanac Book of Facts,* an external memory store I keep next to my desk.)

When older people say, "My memory isn't as sharp as it used to be," they are talking about their episodic memory. In information-processing terms, it would be expressed this way: "My storage and retrieval processes don't seem to be working as efficiently as they once did." Episodic memory is typically studied in the lab using recall paradigms. People of different ages are presented with a list of words, either a written list or a list read by the experimenter. Later (anywhere between a few seconds and several days) they are instructed to recall as many of the words as they can. The typical findings are that older adults do not recall as many of the words as younger adults, and that this decline, though relatively slow, is continuous over the adult years; it begins early, perhaps as early as the late teens and early 20s, and is continuous into at least the mid-90s (Salthouse, 1998).

When the older adults are given some type of environmental support, such as strategy instructions at encoding or cues at retrieval (or both), their recall performances increase and approach the levels of the younger adults' recall ability. For example, researchers have found declines in older adults' recall abilities but not their recognition abilities over a 16-year period (Zelinski & Burnight, 1997). Because episodic memory is important in many aspects of everyday life, such as grocery shopping and medication adherence, it has

If your memory was like a refrigerator, encoding would be like putting the groceries away in the right drawers and compartments. What analogies could you make about storage and retrieval? How would you explain forgetting the name of an old friend in "refrigerator terms"?

been a popular topic for human factors research, as I will discuss a little later in this chapter.

What about semantic memory? We know that IQ subtests that deal with vocabulary and general knowledge show very little, if any, decline with age (Salthouse, 1991), so it seems that semantic memory is fairly stable before age 75. In addition, studies of middle-aged adults (aged 35 to 50) show no age changes on semantic memory tasks (Bäckman & Nilsson, 1996). Studies of participants in the Berlin Aging Study between ages 70 and 103 show a gradual but systematic decline in the performance of tasks that tap this store of facts and word meanings (Lindenberger & Baltes, 1994).

The one exception to the rule of semantic memory remaining quite stable over the years is the case of **word-finding failures**—that feeling many middle-aged and older adults get when they know the word they want to use

Procedural memory includes skills that are handed down in a culture from generation to generation

but just can't locate it at the moment. This would certainly be a task that taps semantic memory (Burke, MacKay, Worthley, et al., 1991). And the related memory phenomenon of **name-finding failures**—the failure to come up with "the name of that blonde guy who stars in *Lost*"—also begins to increase in middle age (Maylor, 1990). Psychologist Fergus Craik (2000) explains these exceptions by suggesting that specificity is the key to whether a long-term memory system component is stable or declines with age—tasks that require a specific word or name as an answer are more difficult and show a decline with age, whereas other tasks that require a more general answer are easier and remain stable up to late adulthood. In the example given earlier of the *Jeopardy* game experience, "James Buchanan" is a very specific item of information, and failure to recall it could not be compensated for by the use of other words. However the story about the trip to L.A. is more general information, and even if some specific items could not be recalled (for example, the name of the host of *Jeopardy*), the story could still be told using "the game-show host" or "the star of the show" instead of "Alex Trebek." Using Craik's explanation, the reason semantic memory is so stable with age is that it is usually general rather than specific. And the reason there are age-related changes in episodic memory is the specificity.

Another component of the long-term store is **procedural memory.** This is the memory system responsible for skill learning and retention (Tulving, 1985). The skills that depend on this system include cognitive skills such as playing bridge and solving crossword puzzles, school skills such as reading and doing long division, and even motor skills such as driving and tying one's shoelaces. Once learned, these skills involve well-learned, automatic mental processes. We don't have to remind ourselves how to use a can opener or how to ride a bike, and the fact that these skills are independent of conscious memory seems to protect them from the effects of aging and brain damage. Relatively few direct studies of age-related changes in procedural memory have been conducted, but general findings are that there is little change with age over adulthood, except for tasks that require speeded performance (Dixon, de Frias, & Maitland, 2001). Further evidence on the durability of procedural memory is found in studies of individuals suffering from various types of

● **CRITICAL THINKING**

What's in your procedural memory? What contents would you have in common with other students in your class, and what contents would be unique?

amnesia. Although this symptom is defined by loss of memory ability in many areas, procedural memory abilities often remain at normal levels (Schacter, 1997).

Reversing Declines in Memory Abilities. If some types of memory ability decline with age, what happens if older adults are taught special strategies to compensate for their processing problems? This is the idea behind a good many memory-training studies. For example, older adults have been successfully trained to remember names of people they have just met by using internal memory aids such as mental imagery to form associations between the people's faces and their names (Yesavage, Lapp, & Sheikh, 1989). In other studies, older adults have been given training on encoding, attention, and relaxation strategies in order to improve word recall (Stigsdotter & Bäckman, 1989, 1993). And participants in the Berlin Aging Study learned to use the method of loci to improve their recall performances by associating words on the recall list with landmark buildings along a familiar route in their city (Kliegl, Smith, & Baltes, 1990).

To answer the question about the efficacy of training, yes, training improves declining memory function, but no, it doesn't do away with the decline completely. In none of these studies did the performance of older adults reach the level of young adults, but all brought significant improvement over the subjects' earlier performance or over a control group of older adults who received no training.

CRITICAL THINKING ●

How many external memory aids do you use in a typical day? (You might start with class notes.)

Other memory researchers have focused on training older adults to use external memory aids, such as making lists, writing notes, placing items-to-be-remembered in obvious places, and using voice mail, timers, and handheld audio recorders. In one such study, psychologists Orah Burack and Margie Lachman (1996) randomly assigned young and old adults to two groups—list-making and non-list-making—and gave them word recall and recognition tests. As expected, in the standard recall condition (non-list-makers), the older adults performed less well than the younger adults, but for the list-makers, there were no significant differences between the old and young groups. In addition, the older list-makers performed better than the older non-list-makers.

In an interesting twist, the authors of this study added a condition in which some of the list-making subjects were told ahead of time that they would be able to refer to their lists during the recall test but then were not allowed to use them. These subjects benefited as much from making the lists and not using them as the subjects who made the lists and did, suggesting that the activity of list making improves memory even when the list is not available at recall. (If you have ever made a grocery list and left it at home, you will realize that the act of making the list is almost as good as having it with you.)

Studies such as these show that training on both internal and external memory aids can benefit older adults whose memories are not as sharp as they were in younger years. They may not bring back 100 percent of earlier abilities, but intervention and improvement are possible.

Memory in Context. Studies of age changes in memory using the information-processing approach are one of the most widely researched topics in the field of aging and have yielded valuable insights into this aspect of adult development. However, their dependence on laboratory tasks may not tell the complete story of how thinking changes with age. Typical tasks in memory experiments "are relatively stripped down in terms of familiarity or meaningfulness," and little attention is paid to individual characteristics of the participants (Hess, 2005, p. 383).

A number of researchers have adopted an approach to adult cognition known as the **contextual perspective.** Its proponents believe that the information-processing approach fails to consider that cognitive processes across adulthood take place in wider contexts than a laboratory task and appear in a different light when age-related contexts are considered.

The contextual perspective considers the **adaptive nature of cognition,** the idea that as we age our lives change, and that successful aging depends on how we adapt our cognitive styles to fit those changes. For example, younger adults tend to be involved in education or job training and thus are more apt to focus their cognitive abilities on acquisition of specific facts and skills, often for the benefit of authority figures. In contrast, older adults are often involved in transmitting their knowledge to the younger generation and thus may focus their cognitive abilities on extracting the emotional meaning from information and integrating it with their existing knowledge. Traditional lab tasks that investigate age differences are more similar to the typical cognitive activities of young people (Hess, 2005).

This difference was demonstrated in a study by psychologist Cynthia Adams and her colleagues (Adams, Smith, Pasupathi, et al., 2002) in which women in two age groups were given a story to remember and retell either to the experimenter or to a young child. The younger group's average age was 20; the older group's was 68. Those who had been instructed to retell the story to an experimenter resembled a typical laboratory experiment and the results were not surprising; younger women recalled more of the story than older women. However, for those who were instructed to retell the story to a young child, older women recalled as much of the story as younger women. In addition the older women were more apt to adjust the complexity of the story to fit the young listener. Adams and her colleagues concluded that older people can recall stories as well as younger people when the goals are adjusted to fit the context of their lives—when they are given a task appropriate for a grandmother's goals rather than those of a young student.

The relative importance of emotional content also differs by age, as demonstrated by psychologists Helene Fung and Laura Carstensen (2003). People in four age groups, ranging from 20 to 83, were shown advertisements featuring different types of appeals—emotional, knowledge-related, or neutral. As illustrated in Figure 4.6, those in the older groups remembered more information from the emotional advertisements than the other two types, and those in the younger group remembered more information from the knowledge-related advertisements. Carstensen suggests that younger people are interested in processing information to acquire knowledge; in contrast, older people are interested in processing information to enhance positive emotions. Unfortunately, most laboratory studies of memory are devoid of emotional content, thus favoring younger participants.

Another factor that is not considered in traditional lab studies is the role of negative stereotypes of aging and memory ability. When members of a group are aware of a negative stereotype that is widely held about their group, they can experience anxiety when they are put in a position that might confirm the stereotype. This contextual factor is known as **stereotype threat,** and one example is the negative stereotype of older adults as forgetful. As I mentioned in the beginning of this section, age-related memory loss is a very touchy topic for many adults, and some researchers argue that older adults' cognitive abilities are compromised just by the fact of being in a memory study. In fact when the "memory" part of the study is

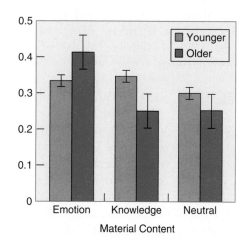

Figure 4.6 Older participants remember more information than younger participants when material has emotional appeal; younger participants remember more when material has knowledge appeal.

Source: Fung & Carstensen (2003).

deemphasized, older adults perform better (Hess, Hinson, & Statham, 2004). In a study of older adults who were around the age of 78, researchers found that their memory ability declined as more words describing negative stereotypes were added to the test materials. When asked about concerns about their own memory abilities, those who expressed more concerns were the ones whose recall was affected the most by the stereotypes (Hess, Auman, Colcombe, et al., 2003). Negative stereotypes affect memory performance for older adults, and the size of the effect is related to the amount of concern they express about their own memories.

Real-World Cognition

The following section covers a slightly different type of cognitive research. Instead of documenting age differences in cognitive abilities or demonstrating how different memory components change (or do not change) with age, the goal of research on real-world cognition is to explore how real adults think as they go about their daily activities. I will start with how they make judgments and decisions, and then cover what aspects of daily life they have problems with, such as taking medication correctly and driving, and what technology is available to assist them.

Judgment and Decision Making

Making judgments and making decisions are complex cognitive skills that require the coordinated interplay of various types and levels of thinking. These abilities were important for the survival of the earliest humans and are also important today. Although the study of judgment and decision making is an established area of cognitive psychology, it has only recently been applied to adulthood and aging. We are all aware that the types of judgments and decisions people are required to make change with age, but the question asked in the following section is whether the quality of the judgments and decisions changes—that is, whether there are age-related changes in the underlying cognitive processes (Sanfey & Hastie, 2000).

One type of judgment or decision that adults are frequently required to make across the life span is choice, or choosing among a set of alternatives that have multiple attributes. Which university should you attend when you have been accepted by three, all having different tuition, distance from home, prestige, and amount offered you in scholarships? Or which of two treatments to choose for your illness, when each has different risks, side effects, costs, and probabilities of success?

Many studies of this skill are done in labs using a matrix of attributes known as a choice board. Figure 4.7 shows a car-buying dilemma. Key factors in a decision include comparing total price, number of passengers each car will hold, fuel efficiency, and manufacturers' rebates offered for each car. The categories are visible, but the attributes are on cards, placed face down on the matrix. (Some labs use computer screens.) Participants are told to look at whatever information they need and take the time necessary to make the decision. The cards that the participant turns over, the pattern in which they are turned, and the time each card is studied are all recorded. When the choice-making processes of younger and older adults are compared, we learn something about age differences in this type of judgment and decision making.

Using a choice-board technique, researchers investigated how young adults (mean age 23) and older adults (mean age 68) chose which of six cars to buy after having an opportunity to compare them on nine features. A later study compared the apartment-rental

CRITICAL THINKING ●

Think of an important decision you have made recently. What would your matrix board look like?

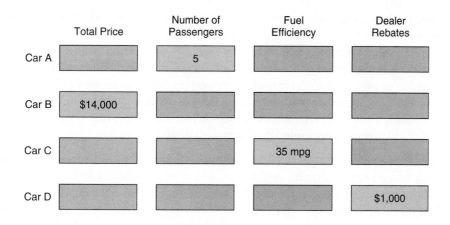

Figure 4.7 Example of a choice board used in studies of decision making. This one includes four factors for each of four car choices.

choices of the two groups when five apartments were shown on the choice board with 12 features available for each apartment (Johnson, 1993). Another group examined decision-making processes of 20-year-olds versus people in their 60s and 70s as they made complex financial decisions (Hershey & Wilson, 1997). In a study of medical-treatment choice, young women, middle-aged women, and older women were compared on their decision-making processes in a simulated situation involving breast cancer treatment (Meyer, Russo, & Talbot, 1995). Although these studies ran the gamut on decision topics, they all had similar results. Basically, older people utilized less information and took less time than younger people to make their choices. Regardless, there was essentially no difference between the choices made by the two groups.

One possible explanation is that older people recognize their cognitive limitations and make decisions based on less complex thought processes. However, the fact that their decisions are the same as those of the younger people in these studies suggests an alternative explanation. This hypothesis is that older people are experts on making such choices as which apartment to rent, which car to buy, which medical treatment to undergo. By the time most adults reach the older stage of life, they have gone through these thought processes many times, and they approach them much like a chess master approaching a chess board, using deductive reasoning and tapping their long-term store of experiences. This explanation is supported by the accounts given by some of the subjects when asked to "think aloud" while making choices (Johnson, 1993).

These studies affirm that when adults of any age are evaluated in the context of their current lifestyles, interests, and areas of expertise, they show much better cognitive capabilities than on traditional, "one-size-fits-all" laboratory tests.

Human Factors Research: Assistive Technology

Human factors research is a hybrid field that combines psychology with engineering to uncover real-world problems people have and locate or create devices that will solve them (Charness, Park, & Sabel, 2001). Studies in the United States and Germany have shown that older adults spend most of their time on seven activities, the instrumental activities of daily living (IADLs) discussed in Chapter 3: managing one's medications, finances, transportation, shopping, household maintenance, meals, and telephoning. These activities take up more and more time as physical and cognitive abilities decline. How to remain independent in the face of changing abilities is the major problem that older adults face every day.

Recent studies of the disability rates of older people in the United States show that during the 1990s, fewer people reported having difficulty with activities of daily living (ADLs) and fewer reported needing help with ADLs. However, there were indications that one of the reasons for this decline in difficulties and need for help from others was due to an increase in the use of **assistive technology,** mechanical and electronic devices designed to help with the activities of daily living (Freedman, Crimmins, Schoeni, et al., 2004). Whether due to increased costs for healthcare workers or the increased availability of devices, there is good evidence that more and more older people are benefiting from assistive technology. There are several areas in which this technology is being applied to improve the lives of older adults and adults of all ages with disabilities.

Medical Instructions. As we get older, most of us have more chronic health problems and as a result take more prescription medication than younger adults. Figure 4.8 shows that the number of prescriptions increases with age, and that the number of prescriptions for people of all ages has increased over the last few decades, probably because of advances in medical treatment. As you can see, almost half the people over 65 take three or more prescribed drugs on a regular basis, and another 30 percent take one or two prescribed drugs. In fact, only about 15 percent of people in this age group take no prescribed drugs (U.S. Centers for Disease Control and Prevention, 2004). When you combine the large number of prescription drugs with the findings on age-related memory losses, it can lead to serious problems.

In a series of studies, psychologist Denise Park and her colleagues (Park & Jones, 1997; Park & Mayhorn, 1996), tackled the role of cognition in *medication adherence,* taking medication at the times and conditions prescribed by one's physician. The patient's cognitive functioning includes understanding the physician's instructions, reading and comprehending the labels on prescription bottles, organizing the medication instructions into a daily plan that might include multiple doses and instructions for other medication, remembering the plan, and remembering to actually take the medication. Older people are more likely to have problems on many of these aspects.

One preliminary factor in the use of electronic assistive devices to help remember medication is whether older people would like to have them. Remember, we are dealing with community-dwelling adults who generally make their own decisions and, if like my

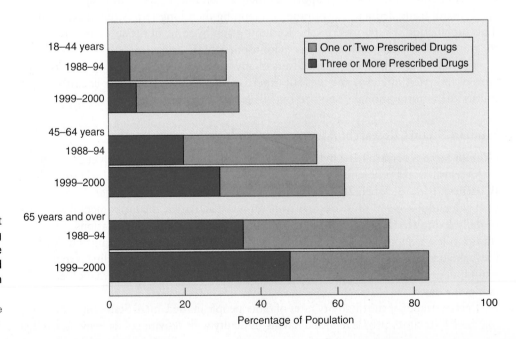

Figure 4.8 The percent of U.S. adults reporting prescription drug use increases by age and has also increased in the last two decades.

Source: U.S. Centers for Disease Control and Prevention (2004).

parents, are not easily persuaded by others. However, in a study of 100 such elders ranging in age from 65 to 91 years, researchers found that 58 percent stated that they would indeed use such a device if one was available and affordable. Their idea of affordable was $26 to $50. Five percent of the participants already used electronic devices to remind them of their medication regimen, but others relied on low-tech memory devices such as calendars, post-it notes, and boxes with compartments labeled for the days of the week. Some used elaborate procedures for keeping track of which pills they had taken each day. For example, one person reported:

> I keep bottles with 10 pills in them. I write down the number taken and the time and date (for a 10-day period). Then I set an alarm to remind me to take the next dose. Each time I count the remaining pills (Cohen-Mansfield, Creedon, Malone, et al., 2005, p. 13).

Some of the high-tech external aids that have been designed to help older adults use their medication effectively include caps for prescription containers that contain microchips programmed to beep when it's time to take the medication (Hertzog, Park, Morrell, et al., 2000) and digital wristwatches that store medical information and alert the owner with beeps and instructions (Bakker, 1999). Other ideas are medication dispensers that not only signal when a dose is due, but also dispense it in the proper amount (Liu & Park, 2003).

In related work, researchers investigated the success rate of young and old adults who were using a blood glucose meter to monitor their insulin treatment for diabetes. The instructions were provided by the manufacturer on a videotape and resulted in the younger adults being only 75 percent accurate in their use of the meter and the older adults being only 25 percent accurate. By revising the videotape to provide better-structured information that fostered understanding of the basic task requirements, researchers were able to increase the accuracy to 90 percent for both the young and old adults (Mykityshyn, Fisk, & Rogers, 2002). It seems that older people are at a distinct disadvantage when trying to understand poorly designed instructions, but with better designed instructions, they comprehend as well as younger adults.

Driving. The topic of older adults and driving brings forth a variety of opinions, most very emotional. Some young adults believe that there should be upper age limits on drivers' licenses or at least mandatory testing once a driver reaches a certain age. Older adults view their cars as a lifeline to the outside world. They fear they will lose their independence if they are not allowed to drive. And this is not such an irrational fear in many areas of the United States, where public transportation is unreliable, unsafe, or nonexistent. Legislators in many states realize that supporting such measures would put them in disfavor with a large number of older citizens, who are more apt to be voters than younger citizens. Middle-aged adults worry about their elderly parents' driving abilities and anguish over when and how they will convince Mom or Dad to give up the car keys.

Everyone seems to have an opinion on this topic, but what are the facts about older drivers? First, there are a lot of drivers in this category; in 2003, there were over 20 million licensed drivers 70 years of age or older in the United States. Another way of describing this is that 10 percent of all licensed drivers are in this age group. Older drivers comprise 5 percent of all traffic injuries, 12 percent of all traffic fatalities, and 16 percent of all pedestrian fatalities. However, these numbers don't give us an accurate picture of older adults' driving records because older adults don't drive as much as younger adults. When the U.S. Department of Transportation examined the accident rates for different age groups, adjusting for the number of miles driven per year, the results gave a clearer picture of the situation. As you can see in Figure 4.9, the youngest and the oldest drivers are

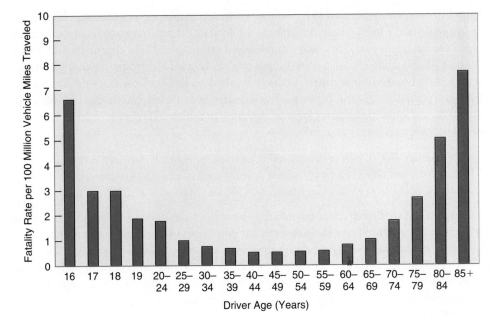

Figure 4.9 When the number of miles traveled is considered, drivers under 25 years of age and those over 70 are more apt to be killed in auto accidents than drivers between those ages.

Source: National Highway Traffic Safety Administration (1999).

the ones most apt to be killed in auto crashes. The fatality rate for drivers 70 years of age and older is nine times that of drivers from 25 to 69 (National Center for Statistics and Analysis, 2001).

Several caveats are necessary here: First, the vast majority of older drivers are never involved in auto crashes. They are experienced drivers, and compared to younger drivers, they take fewer risks, are more likely to use seat belts, and are less likely to drink and drive. Second, these numbers represent people who have died as a result of an auto crash, not necessarily those who caused the accident. It also stands to reason that an older person who is involved in a crash may be more apt to die as a result than a younger person in the same situation. But keeping all this in mind, it is still clear that driving is more hazardous for older drivers (and for very young drivers) than for middle-aged drivers, and that there are better solutions to this problem than simply legislating older drivers off the roads.

Several studies have examined the driving records of older adults to determine what factors predict risk for crashes. Health, medication, mobility, and sensory abilities are the most obvious candidates, and this is exactly what psychologist Richard Sims and his colleagues (Sims, McGwin, Allman, et al., 2000) looked at in a study of 174 Alabama drivers who were over the age of 55. After gathering data on these aspects of their participants' lives, they followed them for 5 years to see who would be involved in auto crashes and what factors would predict this risk. Of the factors they examined, one of the best predictors was the **useful field of view (UFOV),** the area of the visual field that can be processed in one glance. Older drivers who had a reduction in their useful field view of 40 percent or more were twice as likely to be involved in an auto crash as those with normal visual fields.

Earlier in this chapter I discussed the basic information-processing system, and you will probably recall that the first component of this system is sensory memory, where information is collected from the various senses and either sent along for further processing or allowed to fade away, virtually unnoticed. Obviously, the amount of information being picked up by the visual system is important for information processing in sensory memory and subsequent memory systems. The ability to visually process a large area of the environment at once is important for many tasks, including driving. In fact, the useful field of view has been shown to be a better predictor of driving ability than visual acuity, the standard vision test that is given to drivers (Hoffman, Atchley, McDowd, et al., 2005).

Recent research has shown that the useful field of view is not a constant perceptual ability; it decreases in lab studies when the individual is attending to other activities, such as performing verbal or spatial tasks. Psychologists Paul Atchley and Jeff Dressel (2004) showed that young, healthy college students displayed a reduction in their useful field of view when participating in a spoken word-selection task. The time it took them to react to stimuli in the periphery of their visual fields was four times what it took when attending to the visual task alone. And their accuracy in detecting stimuli was significantly reduced when the word task was added. Although this was a test done in the lab and not on the road, it has serious implications for drivers of all ages who multi-task behind the wheel. And for older drivers who may already have reduced visual-field abilities, the message is even stronger. Driving is a very demanding and complex cognitive activity and should not be combined with competing tasks, such as talking on cell phones, especially for older drivers who may have reduced functional visual fields. Talking on cell phones while driving has been banned in Australia, Brazil, France, Germany, India, Italy, Japan, the Netherlands, Russia, Sweden, and the U.K. In the United States, as of this writing, it has only been banned in Connecticut, the District of Columbia, New Jersey, and New York. Some cities have enacted bans, and other states have partial bans, such as for teenage drivers or school bus drivers.

● **CRITICAL THINKING**

What is the law in your area pertaining to cell phone use and driving? Do you agree or disagree? Why?

After this somber message, there is some bright news; it is possible to train people to have larger useful fields of view (Ball, 1997; Owsley, Ball, McGwin, et al., 1998). One demonstration of this was done by psychologist Daniel Roenker and his colleagues (Roenker, Cissell, Ball, et al., 2003), who worked with 70 older drivers whose average age was 72 years and who had reduced useful fields of view. The participants were given one of two training methods, speed-of-processing training or driving simulator training.

The speed-of-processing training involved a touch-screen computer on which targets appeared for various durations in the periphery of the visual field. Participants were required to respond to the targets as soon as they were detected. The participants were trained individually, and the difficulty of the task was increased until the participant reached a proficiency criterion. The average time for proficiency was 4.5 hours of training.

Those in the driving-simulator condition had a review of general rules of the road followed by films that covered crash avoidance, managing intersections, and scanning the road ahead. This was followed by an in-car demonstration that reviewed driving skills. The total training time for this group was 5 hours.

Two weeks later, all the participants in both groups were tested on a detailed road test measuring an impressive 455 items that comprised safe driving. The driving skills of both groups had improved, but in different ways. The speed-of-processing group made fewer dangerous maneuvers than they had at baseline, such as ignoring traffic signals at intersections and misgauging the space between cars when making turns across an intersection, two behaviors that contribute substantially to car crashes. They also had improved their reaction time an average of 277 milliseconds. (In real-life terms, this translates into being able to stop 22 feet sooner when going 55 miles an hour—not a trivial improvement.) The driving-simulator group did not improve on reaction time, but did improve on the specific skills on which they were trained, such as turning into the correct lane and signaling, which did not happen with the speed-of-processing group.

Eighteen months later, the participants were tested again, and the improvements for the speed-of-processing group, for the most part, were still present. Roenker and his colleagues suggest that the training in speed of processing serves to increase the useful field of view for older drivers, and that this increase translates to improvement in driving ability, specifically in the speed with which drivers process and act upon complex visual information. They recommend that this training be implemented for older adults who may be at risk for driving problems.

Another part of driving that many older adults report as problematic is navigating and wayfinding. They feel competent when operating the car, which is a highly practiced, automatized skill, but when finding their way on unfamiliar roads or following maps or other directions, they make errors because they are attending to the effortful task of wayfinding and their driving ability worsens. New automotive technology that may be helpful includes electronic navigating devices that provide real-time assistance and directions. However, it is important for older drivers to be trained to use them comfortably and not have them become additional distractions while driving (Liu & Park, 2003).

Other human factors researchers are working on ways to make traffic signs more salient to older drivers, improving lane markings on highways so that they are more visible at night to older drivers, putting up signs to serve as cues for upcoming road signs, designing refresher courses for older drivers, improving features of automobiles, and recommending specific types of physical therapy to aid in greater flexibility and strength while driving (Rogers & Fisk, 2000).

Personal Computers and the Internet. A fairly new dilemma faced by older adults is learning to use personal computers and the Internet (Charness, 2001). Although this may not sound like a major concern, consider the many parts of our everyday lives that are enhanced by the use of personal computers, from communicating by e-mail, to paying bills, to ordering merchandise via the Internet, to participating in political campaigns. A few moments of thought should bring forth the realization that being able to use personal computers and the Internet could be a solution to many problems that the elderly experience—for example, limited access to shopping and banking, social isolation, lack of transportation, difficulty hearing telephone conversations. The popular idea that older people are resistant to computer use has not proven to be true. Although older adults' use of personal computers and the Internet is rising faster than any other age group, they are still lagging behind their younger counterparts.

A number of studies have examined the use of personal computers by adults of different ages and found, generally, that adults of all ages are capable of using personal computers and the Internet for a variety of tasks, although older adults may require more training and may not be able to use a computer at the same speed that younger adults would. When older adults are given access to computers and age-appropriate instructions, most are capable and enthusiastic users. Community centers and nursing homes that have installed computers report that elderly residents who use them show increased feelings of accomplishment, self-confidence, autonomy, competency, self-esteem, and mastery.

Assistive technology is available that helps level the playing field for older people who want to use personal computers. Among other things, there are oversize keyboards that make it easier for those with arthritic fingers to type, peel-and-stick labels for the keys that make the letters and symbols easier to read for diminished eyesight, and software that increases the size and visibility of the cursor and magnifies the screen.

Web page design has been a topic of interest for human factors researchers who are interested in optimizing older adults' ability to use the Internet (Morrell, Dailey, & Rousseau, 2003). Many of their research findings have been incorporated into the design of the National Institutes of Health Web site for seniors, *www.NIHSeniorHealth.org*. I have reproduced one page in Figure 4.10. As you can see, the Web site is easy to read and to navigate. The text is set in Helvetica typeface, which is easier for older adults to read than a "busier" serif typeface (Ellis & Kurniawan, 2000). The print size is 12 to 14 points,

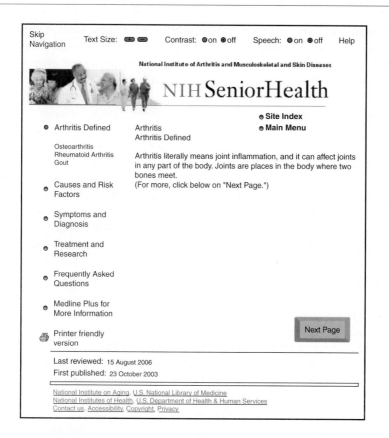

Figure 4.10 National Institute on Aging Web site designed to be easy to use by older adults. It utilizes easily read, solid black letters in upper and lower case, left-justified text, solid white background, and clear instructions in active (not passive) voice. The buttons are large and change colors when clicked on. Each page fills one screen, so scrolling is not necessary.

Source: National Institute on Aging (2006).

which is preferred by older people over smaller sizes, and the letters are a mix of upper- and lowercase, not all uppercase, which are harder to read (Hartley, 1994).

The text is left-justified, the background is solid white, and the lettering is black. Headlines are black, dark blue, or deep purple. No "wallpaper" backgrounds are used. Yellow, light blue, or green are not used close together. All these features of the text have been shown to be user friendly to older adults (Echt, 2002). The writing style is clear and uses the active voice because it is more understandable (Park, 1992). Topics are discussed clearly and simply. All sections are well labeled and well organized. Photos, illustrations, animation, and videos are embedded in the segment of the text that they help explain (Morrell & Dailey, 2001).

The Web site is easy to navigate, and the navigation buttons are consistent and clearly labeled (Holt & Morrell, 2002). All the pages have identical layouts, and the navigation buttons are in the same place on each page (Hartley & Harris, 2001). Buttons and icons are large and change colors when activated (Jones, 1995). No pull-down menus are used because they are difficult for people with arthritis and compromised motor skills (Rogers & Fisk, 2000). Plus, minimal scrolling is needed because each page fits on one screen (Morrell & Dailey, 2001).

After reading this literature and navigating the NIH Web site, I am convinced that all Web page designers, regardless of the age of their target audience, should take notice!

Individual Differences in Cognitive Change

If cognitive decline with age were the rule, we would all fade away together in a predictable pattern, showing little variation in change from our agemates. As you have surely observed in your family or your community, this is not the case; chronological age is only

● **CRITICAL THINKING**

How user-friendly are other Web sites to older adults? How would your favorite Web sites measure up using the design features discussed here?

part of the story. Your grandmother and her best friend, Lillian, may be only a few years apart and may have had similar cognitive abilities in early and middle adulthood, but now, in their early 70s, Grandma may be an honor student at the community college and know the names of all 56 people in her condo, while Lillian needs help balancing her checkbook and making a grocery list. What factors might predict this difference in cognitive change?

Health

As is well known, poor health can affect cognition, but it is important to keep in mind that this is true for people of any age. The reason health is a topic for discussion here is that older adults are more apt to experience health problems that interfere with cognition. Another word of caution is necessary; most of these factors are known only to be predictive of or related to cognitive change—whether they are causes has not been well established.

Vision and Hearing. My first candidate for markers of cognitive change would be vision and hearing difficulties. We know from Chapter 2 that about 23 percent of people in their 70s have hearing impairment and most have some visual disability. The prevalence of decline in these two sensory systems is further illustrated by psychologists Ulman Lindenberger and Paul Baltes (1994; Baltes & Lindenberger, 1997), who tested the vision and hearing abilities of 156 participants, aged 70 to 103, from the Berlin Study of Aging. Tests of cognitive abilities had shown the expected decline with age, but when the vision and auditory evaluations for the participants were added to the equation, the researchers found that these deficits explained 93 percent of the variance in IQ measures.

Does this mean that vision and hearing loss are responsible for declines in cognitive ability? Not really; it only shows a relationship between sensory abilities and cognitive abilities. The explanation suggested is a common-cause hypothesis, meaning that the declines in intellectual abilities and the corresponding declines in sensory abilities are most likely caused by some other factor that underlies them all (Lindenberger & Baltes, 1994; Salthouse, Hancock, Meinz, et al., 1996), The general term for this common factor is "brain aging," and we do not know with certainty what specific mechanisms are involved. However, the best guess at the moment is age-related changes in the white matter of the brain, thought to be caused by loss of myelin, the protective coating on neurons that assist signal transmission, and gradual decline in the function of dopamine, which is a neurotransmitter in some circuits of the brain (Bäckman, Small, & Wahlin, 2001).

Chronic Disease. Some 85 percent of people over 65 have one or more chronic diseases. The major diseases contributing to cognitive decline are Alzheimer's disease and other dementias, but others have been implicated also, such as obesity combined with high blood pressure (Waldstein & Katzel, 2006), deficiencies of vitamin B_{12} and folic acid, thyroid disease (Bäckman, Small, & Wahlin, 2001), clinical depression (Kinderman & Brown, 1997), and subclinical depression (Bäckman, Hill, & Forsell, 1996). Cardiovascular disease accounts for a large proportion of cognitive decline, and it predicts performance on tests of episodic memory and visuospatial skills even when age, education, gender, drug use, and mood are controlled for (Fahlander, Wahlin, Fastbom, et al., 2000).

As I have already mentioned, studies of cognitive change in older adults are hampered by health confounds before they are diagnosed. A similar situation occurs with *terminal decline,* the drop in cognitive functioning in the months before death, regardless of age or diagnosable disease (Berg, 1996; Small & Bäckman, 1999). In longitudinal studies it is possible, although difficult, to keep track of participants for a number of years after the data are gathered in order to control for the effects of undiagnosed chronic disease in earlier stages of the study.

Cortisol levels in the blood, which are related to stress, are implicated in verbal-recall ability (Greendale, Kritz-Silverstein, Seeman, et al., 2000). Cortisol levels have also been related to the volume of the hippocampus, a brain structure involved in memory (Lupien, DeLeon, DeSanti, et al., 1998). Again, older individuals are more likely to experience the effects of stress than younger people, and this may be one of the factors contributing to lower scores on tests of cognitive abilities (Hess, 2005).

Medication. Related to health itself is another cause of cognitive decline in later adulthood—the medication people take for their chronic conditions. Many drugs have side effects that affect cognitive processes in people of all ages, and some drugs affect older people more strongly because of slower metabolic processes. Often these side effects are mistaken for signs of normal aging, such as bodily aches and pains, sleep disturbances, and feelings of sadness and loss. Other drug-related problems that can contribute to cognitive decline in older people are overmedication and harmful drug interactions. Many older people see a number of different doctors, and it is important for each to know what drugs are being prescribed by the others.

Genetics

A factor that undoubtedly underlies many of the health-related differences in cognitive aging is genetics. The strength of genetic influence on a behavior is measured by *heritability scores.* Studies comparing the traits and abilities of pairs of individuals with varying degrees of family relationship have demonstrated that cognitive abilities are among the most heritable of behavioral traits. Meta-analyses of studies involving over 10,000 pairs of twins show that about 50 percent of the variance in individual IQ scores can be explained by genetic differences among individuals (Plomin, 1990). Furthermore, researchers report that for general cognitive ability, heritability increases with age, starting as low as 20 percent in infancy and increasing to 40 percent in childhood, 50 percent in adolescence, and 60 percent in adulthood (McGue, Bouchard, Iacono, et al., 1993).

To find out about the heritability ratings of cognitive abilities in older adulthood, health geneticist Gerald McClearn and his colleagues (McClearn, Johansson, Berg, et al., 1997) conducted a study of Swedish twin pairs who were 80 years of age or older. In this study, 110 identical twin pairs and 130 same-sexed fraternal twin pairs were given tests of overall cognitive ability as well as tests of specific components of cognition. As the graph in Figure 4.11 shows, identical twin pairs, who have the same genes, had scores on the tests that were significantly more similar to each other than did fraternal twin pairs, who share only about half their genes. Since we know that genes are implicated in many diseases and impairments (such as vision, hearing, and chronic diseases), these findings of a genetic contribution to cognitive decline should come as no surprise.

Another interesting result of this study is the variation in heritability for the different cognitive abilities, ranging from 32 percent to 62 percent. Taken together, these findings show not only that cognitive ability is influenced by genetics, but that different types of cognition are influenced to different extents.

As a final word on this subject, I must point out that even if approximately 60 percent of the individual differences in general cognitive ability in older adults can be explained by genetics, 40 percent must be considered environmental in origin. In Figure 4.11, you should note that none of the bars reaches the 100 percent level. This means that even identical twins with identical genes are not identical in cognitive abilities.

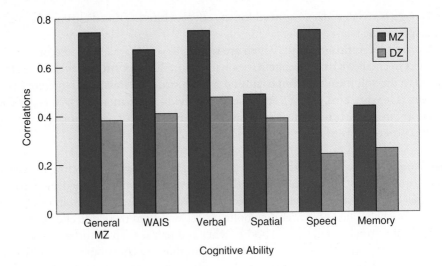

Figure 4.11 Correlations on tests for a number of cognitive abilities are higher for monozygotic twin pairs (who share the same genes) than for dizygotic twin pairs (who share about 50 percent of their genes), demonstrating significant and separate genetic contributions for those abilities.

Source: McClearn, Johansson, Berg, et al. (1997).

Demographics and Sociobiographical History

Women have a slight advantage over men in several cognitive areas (episodic memory, verbal tasks, and maintaining brain weight), and these gender differences continue into very old age (Bäckman, Small, & Wahlin, 2000). Military service is another factor that predicts levels of cognitive ability in later adulthood. Researchers followed a group of 208 veterans for over 11 years and found that their cognitive abilities declined less than those of a civilian control group, even after education was taken into account, suggesting that military training or service might have some long-term effect on cognitive well-being (McLay & Lyketsos, 2000).

CRITICAL THINKING

Can you think of an alternative explanation for the findings that veterans show less decline in cognitive abilities than the civilian population?

Another set of factors is what Baltes calls **sociobiographical history,** the level of professional prestige, social position, and income experienced throughout one's life. It was once thought that people who had led privileged lives in these respects would be less likely to decline in cognitive abilities as they grew older, but most of the research evidence shows otherwise; the *rate* of decline is the same, regardless of what blessings people have received or earned in their lifetime (Christensen & Henderson, 1991; Salthouse, Babcock, Skovronek, et al., 1990; Lindenberger & Baltes, 1997). The only difference is that the more privileged individuals usually attain higher levels of cognitive ability, so that even if the rate of decline is equal, their cognitive scores are still higher at every age (Smith & Baltes, 1999).

Schooling

Formal education predicts the rate of cognitive decline with age. All other things being equal, people with fewer years of formal schooling will show more cognitive decline as years go by than will their same-aged peers with more years of formal education. This evidence comes from the repeated finding that better-educated adults not only perform some intellectual tasks at higher levels but maintain their intellectual skill longer in old age, a pattern found in studies in both the United States (Compton, Bachman, Brand, et al., 2000; Schaie, 1996) and in Europe (Cullum, Huppert, McGee, et al., 2000; Laursen, 1997)

There are several possible explanations of the correlation between schooling and maintenance of intellectual skill. One possibility is that better-educated people remain more intellectually active throughout their adult years. It may thus be the intellectual activity ("exercise" in the sense in which I have been using the term) that helps to maintain the mental skills. Another possibility is that it may not be education *per se* that is involved here, but underlying intellectual ability, leading both to more years of education and to better maintenance of intellectual skill in old age. A related explanation is that some tests used to measure cognitive ability may actually be measuring educational level instead (Ardila, Ostrosky-Solis, Roselli, et al., 2000). Studies with illiterate, nonschooled adults (Manly, Jacobs, Sano, et al., 1999) have shown that some types of cognitive tests reflect lack of literacy and schooling (comprehension and verbal abstraction), whereas others reflect true cognitive decline (delayed recall and nonverbal abstraction).

Intellectual Activity

Adults who read books, take classes, travel, attend cultural events, and participate in clubs or other groups seem to fare better intellectually over time (Wilson, Bennett, Beckett, et al., 1999; Schaie, 1994). It is the more isolated and inactive adults (whatever their level of education) who show the most decline in IQ. Longitudinal studies have shown that demanding job environments (Schooler, Caplan, & Oates, 1998) and life with spouses who have high levels of cognitive functioning (Gruber-Baldini, Schaie, & Willis, 1995) help to ward off cognitive decline. In contrast, widows who had not worked outside the home showed the greatest risk of cognitive decline in the Seattle Longitudinal Study (Schaie, 1996).

A number of studies have shown that cognitive processes are preserved in later adulthood for people who exercise those processes regularly through such activities as playing chess (Charness, 1981) or bridge (Clarkson-Smith & Hartley, 1990), doing crossword puzzles (Salthouse, 2004), or playing the game of Go (Masunaga & Horn, 2001). The sets of highly exercised skills required for such activities are known as *expertise,* and studies have shown that older people who have expertise in specific areas retain their cognitive abilities in those areas to a greater extent than agemates who do not share this expertise.

Older people who exercise cognitive skills, like these chess players, retain those skills well into late adulthood.

However, before you rush out and join a chess club. I must warn you that most of these studies are correlational, which means that other factors may be contributing to the retention of cognitive ability, much like the studies of people who do physical exercise. They might be in better health to begin with or receive more social stimulation and support at the gym or bridge club.

Physical Exercise

The case for a causal link between physical exercise and intellectual skill is a bit stronger, although still not robust. The fundamental argument, of course, is that exercise helps to maintain cardiovascular (and possibly neural) fitness, which we know is linked to mental maintenance. And researchers who compare mental performance scores for highly physically active and sedentary older adults consistently find that the more active people have higher scores.

Aerobic exercise has been targeted specifically because of its role in promoting cell growth in the hippocampus and other brain structures involved in memory. Most of these studies are correlational, so we face the problem of determining whether the memory changes are caused by the aerobic exercise or by other factors, such as higher education level, better health, or more social support. Nonetheless, a meta-analysis of studies that randomly assigned participants to exercise and nonexercise conditions found that exercise has positive effects on cognitive functioning. In fact, the greatest effects were on tasks such as inhibition and working memory, which are directly relevant to normative age differences in memory performance (Colcombe & Kramer, 2003).

In a follow-up study, the researchers used MRIs to assess the effects of exercise on brains structures. They found that the biggest difference was in the cortical areas most affected by aging. Although the subjects in this study had not been randomly assigned to exercise and nonexercise groups, the combination of studies provides reasonable support for exercise having an impact on age-related memory performance. Clearly the extent to which an individual exercises (or doesn't) should be considered when assessing memory abilities in later adulthood (Colcombe, Erikson, Raz, et al., 2003).

A longitudinal study by psychologist Robert Rogers and his colleagues points us in the same direction (Rogers, Meyer, & Mortel, 1990). They followed a group of 85 men from age 65 to age 69. All were in good health at the beginning of the study, and all were highly educated. During the 4 years of the study, some of these men chose to continue working, some retired but remained physically active, and some retired and adopted a sedentary lifestyle. When these three groups were compared at the end of the study on a battery of cognitive tests, the inactive group performed significantly worse than the two active groups.

Of course (as many of you will have figured out yourselves), there is a difficulty built into these studies and many others like them, despite the researchers' care in matching the active and inactive groups for education and health. These groups are self-selected rather than randomly assigned. The active group chose to be active, and it remains possible that adults who are already functioning at higher intellectual levels are simply more likely to choose to maintain their physical fitness. A better test would be an experiment in which healthy, sedentary adults are randomly assigned to exercise or nonexercise groups and then tested over a period of time. Results from such experimental studies of exercise are highly mixed. Some find that the exercise group improves or maintains mental test scores better than the nonexercise control group (Hawkins, Kramer, & Capaldi, 1992; Hill, Storandt, & Malley, 1993) while others do not (Buchner, Beresford, Larson, et al., 1992; Emery & Gatz, 1990; Madden, Blementhal, Allen, et al., 1989). There is some indication that physical exercise is more likely to have positive effects on mental performance when the exercise program lasts for a longer period of time, such as a year or more, although there are not many data to rely on here.

This is by no means an exhaustive review of the research in this very active field. I simply wanted to give some examples of work that supports the argument of those who take the contextual perspective of cognitive aging. Sure, no one argues with the evidence that cognitive abilities decline with age, but there is active debate about how much the decline is and in which areas of cognition. There are also some lessons in the research on individual differences about steps that might be taken to delay or slow down the inevitable decline. Certainly it seems that we would increase the probability of maintaining our cognitive abilities as we grow older if we engage in physical and cognitively challenging activities throughout adulthood. It also would help to find ways to minimize stress in our lives or develop better coping abilities.

Subjective Evaluation of Decline

One factor that is not implicated in cognitive decline is our own opinion of our cognitive abilities. There is a very strong relationship between age and subjective reports of cognitive decline—the older the group is, the more reports there are of intellectual failure. However, when reports of cognitive decline are compared with actual tests of intellectual functioning, there is virtually no relationship. In a very thorough investigation of this phenomenon, researchers questioned almost 2,000 people in the Netherlands ranging in age from 24 to 86. They asked about various components of cognitive functioning (such as memory, mental speed, decision making) and how they rated themselves compared to their agemates, compared to themselves 5 to 10 years ago, and compared to themselves at 25 years of age. Results showed that participants' perceptions of cognitive decline began about age 50 and increased with age, covering all the cognitive domains included in the questionnaire. However, when participants' actual cognitive abilities were measured, there was no relationship between their abilities and their subjective assessments (Ponds, van Boxtel, & Jolles, 2000). This suggests that adults believe that cognitive decline begins around 50 and begin to interpret their cognitive failures and mistakes as due to aging, whereas the same lapses at earlier ages would have been attributed to other causes, such as having too much on their mind or not getting enough sleep the night before. (This should bring you back to the beginning of the chapter and the story of my parents and the catsup salesman.)

CRITICAL THINKING

Have you forgotten anything recently or become confused with instructions of some kind? How did you explain these cognitive failings? If you were 20 years older, would the explanations be different?

Review of Cognitive Changes over the Adult Years and a Search for Balance

The changes in cognitive abilities due to age are reviewed in Table 4.2. There is no doubt that people become slower and less accurate with age on many types of cognitive tasks, and this is the case even for the healthiest among us. But what is the best way to view these overall changes? Psychologist Roger Dixon takes the position that we should look at cognitive change in terms of both losses and gains (Dixon, 2000).

Dixon points out that there are gains in terms of abilities that continue to grow throughout adulthood, such as new stages of understanding (Sinnott, 1996) and increases in wisdom (Baltes & Smith, 1990; Baltes & Staudinger, 1993). There are also gains in terms of doing better than expected. For example, although Schaie (1994) found a general trend of decline in cognitive abilities with advanced age, not all abilities follow that trend. In fact, 90 percent of all the participants in his study maintained at least two intellectual abilities over the 7-year time period they were studied. Dixon (2000) also points

Table 4.2   Review of Cognitive Changes over the Adult Years

Age 20–40	Age 40–65	Age 65–75	Age 75+
Peak performance on Full Scale IQ tests.	Full Scale IQ scores remain stable until around 60, then begin gradual decline.	Full Scale IQ scores continue gradual decline	Full Scale IQ scores begin to decline more rapidly around 80.
Crystallized and fluid intelligence scores are high and stable.	Crystallized abilities remain stable or increase; fluid abilities begin slight decline.	Crystallized abilities remain stable or increase; fluid abilities continue to decline.	Crystallized abilities begin to show some decline; fluid abilities continue to decline and are always lower than crystallized abilities. There is considerable individual variation, and training can be effective.
Primary memory and working memory are stable; episodic memory begins slow but continuous decline; semantic memory is stable; procedural memory is stable.	Primary memory remains stable; working memory begins gradual decline. Episodic memory continues slow decline; semantic memory remains stable; procedural memory remains stable.	Primary memory remains stable; working memory continues gradual decline; episodic memory continues slow decline, semantic memory remains stable (except for word-finding and name-finding errors), procedural memory remains stable (except for speeded tasks); concern about memory ability increases.	Primary memory remains stable until at least mid-90s; working memory begins to decline more rapidly; episodic memory continues slow decline until at least mid-90s; semantic memory begins to show gradual decline; procedural memory remains stable (except for speeded tasks); training can somewhat improve memory skills.
Memory in context of gathering knowledge is high. Good practical judgments are made by examining all the information available.	Memory in context of gathering knowledge begins to decline, and emotion becomes more important.	Memory in context of emotion increases, as well as passing down information to the next generation.	Emotional content and generativity continue to be major contexts for memory.
Real-life cognition is good, but increases through these years. Good decisions are made after much examination of fact. Cognitive systems are equal to the activities of daily living for most adults.	Real-life cognition remains high. Good decisions are made more quickly than in younger years due to expertise. Cognitive systems are still able to support daily life activities.	Increase in number of prescriptions plus declines in memory bring need for assistive technology for many. Driving ability begins to decline, calling for many to adjust their evening schedules and have UFOV tests. Driver training may be valuable. This is a good time to learn to use a PC and the Internet for shopping, banking, social contacts.	Declining health and memory abilities bring need for clear instructions for self-care and assistive technology for many. Driving ability declines sharply, calling for many to restrict driving to familiar areas and undergo tests of vision, hearing, and reaction time. Driver training may be valuable. PC use continues to be useful if started in earlier years.

to compensation as a gain in the later years, when we find new ways of performing old tasks, find improvements in one skill as the result of losses in another, and learn to use our partners or others around us as collaborators. This viewpoint may be overly rosy, but there is a good deal of truth in it. The process of cognitive aging is not entirely a story of losses, and this gives us a nice balance with which to end the chapter.

Summary

1. Early studies of IQ scores for people of different ages showed that intelligence began to decline in the early 30s and continued sharply downward. Later, longitudinal studies showed that the decline didn't start until people reached their 60s and the decline was moderate. The difference is primarily due to cohort effects.

2. Scores of fluid intelligence abilities (nonverbal) decline starting in the 60s. Crystallized intelligence abilities (verbal) remain stable well into the 70s or 80s.

3. Declines in intellectual abilities can be reversed using specific training for various abilities, physical exercise, and general test-taking training. This training has long-term effects.

4. Memory is most often studied using an information-processing perspective that divides the memory function into three storage areas: sensory store, short-term store, and long-term store.

5. Age-related changes in the sensory store are usually a function of changes in the visual and hearing systems. The short-term store has one component that remains relatively stable through adulthood (primary memory—holding information "in mind") and one that declines in later years (working memory—performing operations on information held "in mind"). The long-term store includes episodic memory—information about recent events, and semantic memory—general factual information. Episodic memory declines with age, and semantic memory is stable until the 70s except for the recall of specific words or names. Another compenent, procedural memory—how to perform familiar tasks—is relatively unaffected by age or injury.

6. Memory loss can be partially compensated for by external aids (lists, calendars) and training (mental imagery, method of loci).

7. Some researchers, using the contextual perspective, show that older people do better on memory tests if the tasks better fit the cognitive styles they have adapted to fit their lifestyles, such as using information with emotional content, proposing a task that involves transmitting knowledge to the next generation, or avoiding stereotype threat.

8. In real-world cognition, older people are able to make good decisions and judgments in less time and using less information than younger people, probably drawing on their greater store of experience.

9. Human factors research provides practical solutions to the problems of aging, including the loss of cognitive abilities. Examples of this assistive technology are medicine boxes and timers to help people take their medication as prescribed and medical instructions that are easier to understand.

10. The number of older drivers on the road is increasing. Although they are more experienced, more apt to use seatbelts, and less apt to drive while intoxicated than younger drivers, they are involved in more traffic fatalities. Because driving is essential to daily life in many areas, researchers have identified the useful field of view as a critical factor in safe driving. It is possible to train older adults to increase this visual ability. It is also possible to reduce distractions (such as cell phone use) that decrease the useful field of view.

11.   More and more older adults are using personal computers and the Internet. Human factors researchers have devised assistive technology to make these more user-friendly, such as age-appropriate instructions, large-print screens, and better-designed Web sites that interface well with the cognitive abilities of older users.

12.   Not everyone ages in cognitive abilities at the same rate. Some of the individual differences are in the area of health, including vision and hearing, chronic disease, and medication. Genes play a role, as does one's education and income history. Mental and physical exercise can lead to better cognitive abilities in later years.

13.   Older people's subjective evaluations of their cognitive abilities are based more on their stereotypes of aging than on any actual decline.

Key Terms

intelligence, 102

psychometrics, 102

g, 102

IQ (intelligence quotient), 102

verbal IQ, 102

performance IQ, 102

full-scale IQ, 102

crystallized intelligence, 104

fluid intelligence, 104

memory, 107

information-processing perspective, 108

sensory store, 108

short-term store, 108

long-term store, 108

primary memory, 109

working memory, 109

semantic memory, 110

episodic memory, 110

word-finding failures, 111

name-finding failures, 111

procedural memory, 111

contextual perspective, 112

adaptive nature of cognition, 113

stereotype threats, 113

human factors research, 115

assistive technology, 116

useful field of view (UFOV), 118

sociobiographical history, 124

Suggested Reading

Reading for Personal Interest

Andreason, N. C. (2005). *The creating brain: The neuroscience of genius*. Washington, DC: Dana Press.

Where does creativity come from? How does it differ from high levels of intelligence or skill? What goes on in the brain during creative processes? Is it some state of altered consciousness? Neuropsychiatrist Nancy Andreason explores all these topics in this book.

Einstein, G. O., & McDaniel, M. A. (2004). *Memory fitness: A guide for successful aging*. New Haven, CT: Yale University Press.

The authors are professors who teach courses on memory and who also do research on the topic. In this book they write about memory in general and how to improve yours. They talk about training, mnemonic techniques, and even

nutrition. It's good advice based on sound scientific evidence.

Legato, M. J. (2005). *Why men never remember and women never forget*. New York: Rodale Books.

Marianne Legato, who is a physician, cites differences in men and women's thinking and tells about the physiological reasons underlying them. She covers issues ranging from infidelity, child rearing, depression, addiction, and aging, explaining ways men and women can understand their differences and better and communicate with each other.

Classic Work

Atkinson, R. C., & Shiffrin, R. M. (1968). Human memory: A proposed system and its control processes. In K. W. Spence & J. T. Spence (Eds.), *The psychology of learning and motivation* (Vol. 2, pp. 89–195). New York: Academic Press.

This proposal of one of the earliest information-processing models, is still in use today with some modification.

Horn, J. L., & Cattell, R. B. (1966). Refinement and test of the theory of fluid and crystallized intelligence. *Journal of Educational Psychology, 57,* 253–270.

This paper justified the bifurcation of general intelligence into two distinct types of abilities. Although other cognitive psychologists have had other terminology and definitions for similar theories, this is the one that caught on and is still in use today.

Contemporary Scholarly Work

Dixon, R. A., De Frias, C. M., & Maitland, S. B. (2001). Memory in midlife. In M. E. Lachman (Ed.), *Handbook of midlife development* (pp. 248–277). New York: Wiley.

Sternberg, R. J., Grigorenko, E. L., & Oh, S. (2001). The development of intelligence at midlife. In M. Lachman (Ed.), *Handbook of midlife development.* New York: Wiley.

These two handbook chapters contain comprehensive reviews of research findings on intelligence and memory during the middle years, an area that has been relatively ignored until recently.

Hoyer, W. J., & Verhaeghen, P. (2004). Memory aging. In J. E. Birren & K. W. Schaie (Eds.), *Handbook of the psychology of aging* (pp. 209–232). San Diego: Academic Press.

This article details the changes in various memory systems over adulthood and reviews research on training techniques and the effects of enrichment on memory.

Scialfa, C. T. & Fernie, G. R. (2004). Adaptive technology. In J. E. Birren & K. W. Schaie (Eds.), *Handbook of the psychology of aging* (pp. 425–441). San Diego: Academic Press.

The authors review recent research on how technology is used to assist with communication, health, and transportation.

Chapter 5

Social Roles

Social Roles and Transitions

Gender Roles and Gender Stereotypes

Social Roles in Young Adulthood
Leaving (and Returning) Home
Becoming a Spouse or Partner
Becoming a Parent

Social Roles in Middle Adulthood
The Departure of the Children: The Empty Nest
Gender Roles at Midlife
Becoming a Grandparent
Caring for an Aging Parent

Social Roles in Late Adulthood
Living Alone
Becoming a Care Receiver

Social Roles in Atypical Families
Lifelong Singles
The Childless
Divorced (and Remarried) Adults

The Effect of Variations in Timing

Summary

Key Terms

Suggested Reading

I TEACH DEVELOPMENTAL psychology courses at a university in south Florida, and I enjoy the role of professor. I am fortunate to be at a satellite campus of a larger school, so I am able to get to know the students, and many of them recognize me around campus and stop to talk to me about the courses they are planning to take, the graduate schools they are applying to, or some point we covered in class. It is especially enjoyable for me because the other part of my career, writing this textbook, is very isolated. For that job I have an office at home where I interact during the day with my research assistant (via e-mail) and my cat. Together, the two professional roles provide a pleasing balance.

Interestingly, my husband is a professor on the main campus of the same university, and I find myself on "his" campus from time to time. The difference in my roles from one campus to the other is striking. On "my" campus I am asked about my classes, my book, or some bit of academic intrigue; on my husband's campus, I'm asked about the family or our latest vacation. Clearly, I have the role of professor on one campus and the role of wife on the other.

However, being viewed as a professor is not my most prestigious role. Two afternoons a week I pick up my 4-year-old grandson at his preschool. When I walk into the classroom, I first hear whispering around the play tables, "Shayne, Shayne, your grandma's here!" Then Shayne will look up, break into a big grin, run over to me and hug my knees, saying "Grandma!

Grandma!" I'm sure that not even the president of our university gets tributes like that on a regular basis.

In addition to all these roles, I am a wife, a mother, a daughter, a sister, an aunt, and a stepmother. Many of these roles, such as textbook author and grandmother, are fairly new, and many of the old ones, such as daughter and mother, have the same titles but the content has changed over the years. Reflecting on the changing roles in my life gives me a good measure of my progress on the journey of adulthood.

This chapter is about the roles we occupy in adulthood, with an emphasis on the adjustments we make as they change over time. I will begin with a short discussion of social roles and transitions, and then will go on to the roles that are typical in young adulthood, middle adulthood, and older adulthood. Sprinkled among these is a discussion of gender roles and how they change within our other roles. Finally I will talk about those who don't fit the broad categories—the lifelong singles, the childless, and the divorced and remarried. And I want to emphasize, as you may know already, that the transitions from one role to another are often as challenging as the roles themselves.

Social Roles and Transitions

The term **social roles** refers to the expected behaviors and attitudes that come with one's position in society. One way adult development is studied is by examining the succession of social roles that adults typically occupy over the years. Until recently, adulthood was described in terms of the *number* of roles an individual occupies at different stages of life. The theory was that people acquired a large number of roles in the early years of adulthood and then began shedding them in the later years. In fact, "successful aging" was once measured by how many roles an older person had relinquished and how willingly they had been relinquished (Cumming & Henry, 1961). Recently this viewpoint has changed to one of **role transitions.** This new emphasis acknowledges that, with few exceptions, roles are neither gained nor lost, they change as the life circumstances of the individual change (Ferraro, 2001). The young adult makes the transition from full-time student to young professional; the middle-aged adult moves from being the parent of a dependent teenager to the parent of an independent adult; and the older adult may lose some roles as friends and family members die, but the remaining roles increase in richness and the satisfaction they provide (Neugarten, 1996). Studying role transitions involves finding out how people adjust when they change from one role to another and how the transition affects their other roles.

> **CRITICAL THINKING**
>
> What role transitions have you experienced in the last few years? What kind of adaptations did they require?

In the past chapters I have talked about patterns of change over adulthood in health and physical functioning—changes that are analogous to the hours on a **biological clock.** In this chapter I will talk about patterns of change over adulthood in social roles—comparable to the hours of a **social clock.** To understand the social role structure of adult life, we need to look at the age-linked social clock and at the varying gender roles within each period of adult life. I will explore the personal relationships within these social and gender roles in Chapter 7 and then return to the description of adult roles patterns in Chapter 8, where the topic of work roles will be the central focus. Here let me begin with a brief look at what we know about gender roles and stereotypes before looking at age changes in social roles.

Gender Roles and Gender Stereotypes

It is useful to distinguish between gender roles and gender stereotypes. **Gender roles** describe what men and women actually do in a given culture during a given historical era; **gender stereotypes** refers to sets of shared beliefs or generalizations about what men and women in a society have in common, often extending to what members of each gender *ought* to do and how they *should* behave. Although gender stereotypes can be useful, they also can be inaccurate, and they are particularly harmful when they are used to judge how well an individual man or woman is measuring up to some standard of behavior.

Gender stereotypes are surprisingly consistent across cultures. The most comprehensive evidence comes from psychologists John Williams and Deborah Best (1990), who have investigated gender stereotypes in 25 countries. In each country, college students were given a list of 300 adjectives (translated into the local language where necessary), and asked whether the word was more frequently associated with men, with women, or neither. The results showed a striking degree of agreement across cultures. In 23 countries, a vast majority of the people agreed that male stereotype is centered around a set of qualities often labeled **instrumental qualities,** such as being competitive, adventurous, and physically strong, while the female stereotype centered around qualities of affiliation and expressiveness, often referred to as **communal qualities** such as being sympathetic, nurturing, and intuitive (Turner & Turner, 1994).

● **CRITICAL THINKING**

Is the concept of expecting communal behavior from females and instrumental behavior from men becoming outdated? Why or why not?

If gender roles are what men and women actually do in a particular culture, what are the origins of these roles? How do boys and girls learn to be men and women? The classic answer comes from **learning-schema theory,** which states that children are taught to view the world and themselves through gender-polarized lenses that make artificial or exaggerated distinctions between what is masculine and what is feminine. As adults, they direct their own behavior to fit these distinctions (Bem 1981, 1993). A similar explanation comes from **social role theory,** stating that gender roles are the result of young children observing the division of labor within their culture, thus learning what society expects of them as men and women, and then following these expectations (Eagly, 1987, 1995).

Both of these theories of origins of gender roles deal with **proximal causes,** factors that are present in the immediate environment. Other theories explain the origins of gender roles using **distal causes,** factors that were present in the past. For example, **evolutionary psychology** traces the origins of gender roles to solutions our primitive ancestors evolved in response to problems they faced millions of years ago. It explains that females and males are genetically predisposed to behave in different ways. The genes for these behaviors are present in us today because throughout human history they have allowed men and women in our species to survive and to select mates who help them produce and protect children who, in turn, pass the genes along to the next generation (Geary, 2005).

The debate between exponents of these theories has been going on for several years (Eagly & Wood, 1999; Friedman, Bleske, & Sheyd, 2000; Kleyman, 2000; Ellis & Ketelaar, 2000), but recently all sides seem to have broadened their ideas and drawn closer, adopting a viewpoint that considers both proximal and distal causes. This **biosocial perspective** considers that a bias for masculine roles and feminine roles evolved over the course of human evolution, based on biological differences (distal causes), and interacts with current social and cultural influences (proximal causes) to produce gender roles that reflect the individual's biology, developmental experiences, and social position (Wood & Eagly, 2002).

An interesting demonstration of this perspective on gender roles was based on the question: What happens when social and economic situations change suddenly within a culture? If gender roles are truly based on interactions between biological and social influences, a change in the social environment should bring changes in gender roles and gender stereotypes. This was the question psychologist Alice Eagly and her colleagues investigated (Diekman, Eagly, Mladinic, et al., 2005) by comparing the prevailing gender stereotypes held by young adults in the United States with those in Chile and Brazil to determine whether actual changes in the roles of men and women influence gender stereotypes. The United States was chosen for this study because the roles of men and women have changed *asymmetrically*—women have moved into the workplace in large numbers and taken on traditionally masculine roles, but men have not taken on feminine roles to the same extent. Chile and Brazil were chosen because their political history involved a transfer from authoritarian military rule to democracy in the late 1980s, giving both men and women more self-determination and independence. Although women in these countries lag behind women in the United States in filling jobs that were traditionally held by males, the changes for both men and women in the past 20 years have been more drastic in these countries than in the United States. The authors predicted that this *symmetrical* change, essentially the same for men and women, would produce a different pattern in gender role stereotypes.

Eagly and her colleagues gave young adults in the three countries a list of characteristics and asked them to rate how well each would apply to the average person in their country. (The attributes are listed in Table 5.1.) To add another dimension to the mix, the participants each reported on three "average persons" in their culture—one who was an adult in 1950, one who is currently an adult, and one who would be an adult in 2050.

Table 5.1	Examples of Gender-Role Stereotypes
Communal (Feminine Stereotype)	**Instrumental (Masculine Stereotype)**
Affectionate	Competitive
Sympathetic	Daring
Gentle	Adventurous
Sensitive	Aggressive
Supportive	Courageous
Kind	Dominant
Nurturing	Unexcitable
Warm	Stands up under pressure
Imaginative	Good with numbers
Intuitive	Analytical
Artistic	Good at problem solving
Creative	Quantitatively skilled
Expressive	Good at reasoning
Tasteful	Mathematical
Cute	Rugged
Gorgeous	Muscular
Beautiful	Physically strong
Pretty	Burly
Petite	Physically vigorous
Sexy	Brawny

Source: Adapted from Diekman, Eagly, Mladinic, et al. (2005).

Results showed, as expected, that both men and women in the South American countries were viewed as increasing in instrumental, stereotypical male attributes from 1950 to 2050, reflecting the societal changes that these young adults had been witness to in their lifetimes. However, for the U.S. sample, only the women were viewed as increasing in these instrumental attributes, reflecting the fact that women have made big gains in expanding their roles in the United States, while men's roles have remained near the same high level of determination and independence.

My conclusion from this is that although gender roles are part of our evolutionary legacy, they are moderated by conditions we experience during our lifetimes, and these changes are reflected in the gender stereotypes of our contemporary culture. It also shows me that gender roles (and stereotypes) are dynamic; they change as our culture changes. Our job is to examine the stereotypes we hold in our minds (and hearts) to make sure they reflect current conditions for men and women, not try to make men and women reflect stereotypes that may be out of date.

> **CRITICAL THINKING**
>
> What would you predict would be the results of a similar study using retired adults in Chile, Brazil, and the United States as participants instead of young adults?

Social Roles in Young Adulthood

Anyone who has been through the years of young adulthood and anyone who is currently in that process would surely agree that there are more changes in social roles at this time than in any other period of life. This period during which young people take on the social roles of early adulthood is known as the **transition to adulthood.**

The content of social roles and the pattern of role transitions open to young adults in the United States have become more flexible and diverse over the years and less directed by any cultural or institutional structure. Young people leave high school and have a wealth of possibilities open to them and an ever-extending period of time to move into the roles of adulthood (Shanahan, 2000). The sequence in which young people move into their adult roles varies enormously too. Some people complete high school, go to college or enter some type of career training, establish themselves economically, and move out of the parental home. Others complete high school, move out of their parents' home, take a series of entry-level jobs around the country for a few years, and then move back with their parents, ready to begin college. A few marry immediately after high school, but many leave the parental home to enter cohabiting relationships as they make the transition to adulthood. So there are clearly a variety of options open to young people as they navigate entry into the roles of adulthood.

> **CRITICAL THINKING**
>
> What role transition made you feel that you were finally an adult? If you haven't reached this point, what role transition do you anticipate will do this in the future?

The lack of ironclad rules and expectations has benefits; young people are not necessarily pushed into roles that may not be right for them, such as spending four years studying for a career for which they are ill-fitted or rushing into an early marriage with someone who is not a good match. Research suggests that this long period of transition also serves to correct problem trajectories begun in childhood and provides a discontinuity or turning point toward successful adulthood (Schulenberg, Sameroff, & Cicchetti, 2004). Studies have shown that a number of young people entering adulthood with less than optimal mental health outlooks, including antisocial behavior and substance abuse, are able to turn their lives around during the extended transition to adulthood, often after assuming the role of partner in a good relationship, college student, or member of the military (Elder, 2001).

Leaving (and Returning) Home

The leaving-home process for young adults has a lot of variability today, both in the timing and the destination, and this is demonstrated well in my own family. One of my children moved out immediately after high school into a cohabiting relationship. Another

Many households today include young adults who have not moved out of their parents' homes (or who have moved out and returned).

went away to college and came home each summer for nine years. And my husband's daughter, who never lived with us on a permanent basis during childhood, has moved in and out of our "empty nest" several times during her early adult years as she attended college and was "between apartments." In fact as I write this, she is back again while her own place undergoes extensive repairs for hurricane damage. We now refer to our guest room as "Heidi's room."

What is the most accurate picture of the moving-out process for young people? As seen in Figure 5.1, the most recent U.S census shows that almost 55 percent of young men and 46 percent of young women in the United States aged 18 to 24 were living in their parents' homes at the time of the interview. The proportion dropped to about 14 percent of men and 7 percent of women for those aged 24 to 35 (Fields, 2003b). The percentages

Figure 5.1 More young men than women live in their parents' homes, though the proportion for both decreases with age.
Source: Data from Fields (2003b).

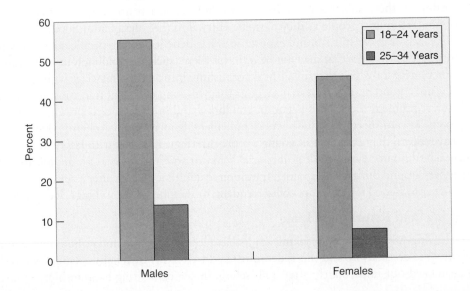

have increased significantly in the last five years. Although this gives us an account of where people lived on one particular day, it also raises a lot of questions: Why were they living at home? Did they always live there, or did they move out and then come back? Why are males more likely to live with their parents than females? How do the young people feel about living at home, and how do their parents feel about it? These questions are a little harder to answer.

The average age young people leave their family home is currently around 20. The reasons for staying in the parental home until later are many: today's jobs require more years of education, more young people borrow money to go to college, the high cost of housing makes it difficult for entry-level workers to have their own place, more young people attend community colleges or satellite campuses of larger universities near their parental home, parents are more affluent and better able to support their adult children, parents have larger homes and fewer children to support, young adults are not drafted into military service as in generations past, couples are marrying later, adult children of recent immigrants from certain countries are traditionally expected to remain in the family home until marriage.

There are more men living at home than women because when couples marry and leave home, the new husband is usually older than the new wife; in other words, he has remained in the family home until a later age than she has. Another reason (according to my students) is that some parents are less restrictive of sons who live at home than of daughters, and also expect less from their sons in terms of doing their own laundry and cleaning up after themselves.

Many young adults leave their parents' home and then return. In a number of countries surveyed, the incidence of these "boomerang kids" has doubled in the last few decades. In the United States, it is estimated that about half of all young people who move out of their parents' homes for at least 4 months will return again. The younger they are when they move out, the more likely they are to return. The reasons young people return to the family home are similar to the reasons for not leaving in the first place, and often are precipitated by some misfortune, such as losing a job, filing bankruptcy, or getting a divorce. (Sometimes it is the parents' misfortunes, such as poor health or financial reversals, that cause the adult child to return home.)

The various patterns of attaining adult status were the topic of a study by psychiatric epidemiologist Patricia Cohen and her colleagues (Cohen, Kasen, Chen, et al., 2003), who interviewed 240 men and women at least 27 years of age or older. Questionnaires and extensive interviews covered each month of the participants' life from the age of 17 to 27 years, some 120 months. One of the areas included was the transition out of the parental home and into an independent living arrangement either alone or with a committed partner. Each month was rated with a TL (transition level) score, with 0 being totally childlike and 99 being totally adultlike. Figure 5.2 shows two depictions of the results.

The left panel of Figure 5.2 shows that, as a whole, the group increased from a TL score of around 27 to 69, or about 4 points per year. This shows that on average, the young adults in the study made steady and gradual progress out of their parents' homes and into their own places of residence between 17 and 27 years of age. The females began their leave-taking process earlier and made the transition to adult living arrangements more quickly, but the men sped up their processes in the mid-20s.

The right panel of Figure 5.2 shows a different view of the same data. Ten percent of the men were selected, and their TL scores were plotted to show individual trajectories—the human story behind the averages. As you can see, few if any participants represent the average trajectory. Three had essentially flat lines, meaning they started out living with their parents and being dependent at age 17 and stayed in that arrangement through the age

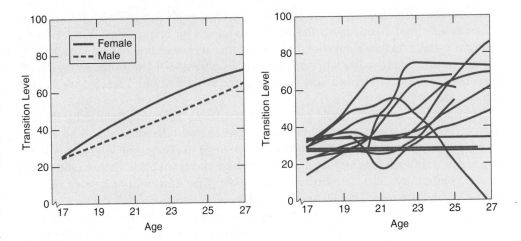

Figure 5.2 (Left panel) The transition level (TL) for moving out of the parental home for 240 young men and women shows a gradual average increase over age from 17 to 27, with young women going through the transition sooner. (Right panel) The transition levels for individuals show no clear patterns and much variability.

Source: Cohen, Kasen, Chen, et al. (2003).

of 27. One individual started out on the road to independence, but shortly after the age of 21, started a steep decline and was totally childlike at 27. The remaining nine men showed increased independence over the years, but not on the smooth path suggested by the graph of the averages.

What all this tells us is that the process of moving from childhood to independent adult status has become more complex than it used to be, with more intermediate steps, more backtracking and second chances, and more options for the individual young adult (and their parents).

Becoming a Spouse or Partner

Marriage remains the traditional form of partnering in the United States and around the world, but the proportion of people who marry is decreasing. In the United States, the percentage of single women who entered first marriages has dropped almost by half in the last three decades. Figure 5.3 shows that in 1970 about 77 percent of single women over age 15 became married women, while in 2004, the number was just under 40 percent. This is an indicator of several trends in the United States and other developed countries. Couples are marrying at later ages than in the past few decades, and are more frequently choosing to live together without marrying.

According to the most recent figures from the U.S. Census Bureau, the average age of marriage has increased by almost 4 years for men in the last three decades and almost 5

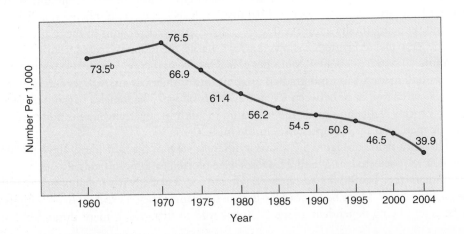

Figure 5.3 The percentage of marriages in the U.S. has declined sharply in the last 30 years.

Source: National Marriage Project, Rutgers University (2005).

years for women (Kreider, 2005). When people marry later, the result is an overall decline in number of marriages each year and fewer married people in the adult population. Why do young people today delay marriage? Some of the answers are that couples want to enjoy a higher standard of living in their marriages than couples in the past, and there is not as much pressure as in the past for a couple to marry in order to have a sexual relationship (or even children).

Another reason young adults are marrying at later ages is the increased rate of **cohabitation,** or living together without marriage, which has increased dramatically in the United States since the 1960s. Today a young adult's first living arrangement with a romantic partner is more apt to be a cohabiting relationship than a marriage. Currently there are more than 11 million people living in unmarried, heterosexual relationships in the United States (Fields & Casper, 2001). For the first time in history, most of the couples who get married today are already living together in a cohabiting relationship (Stanley, Whitton, & Markman, 2004). But this does not mean that cohabitation is just a step on the way to marriage; it is predicted in the United States that for every 100 couples in their first cohabiting experience, about 58 will be married 3 years from now and 39 will no longer be together. The remaining three will still be cohabiting (Bramlett & Masher, 2002).

Most of the people who cohabit in the United States are white, but African Americans have the greatest percentage of people in cohabitation relationships; Hispanic Americans are less likely to cohabit than whites or African Americans. Worldwide, cohabitation rates vary a lot. Sociologists Patrick Heuveline and Jeffrey M. Timberlake (2004) examined data from over 68,000 women who were part of the United Nations Family and Fertility Survey to determine the prevalence of cohabitation. Figure 5.4 shows the percentage of women under 45 years of age in 17 countries who have experienced at least one cohabitation relationship, ranging from a high of 89 percent in France to a low of 4 percent in Poland. These numbers reflect differences in the economy, religion, partnership laws and benefits, and availability of affordable housing in each country, among other things.

The percentages of people who cohabit in each country don't tell the whole story; there are different types of cohabitation. Heuveline and Timberlake also evaluated the cohabitation patterns for each country based on how long the cohabitation relationship lasted and whether it ended in marriage or not. Cohabitation relationships that fit the "prelude to marriage" pattern are those that most often end in marriage, regardless of the

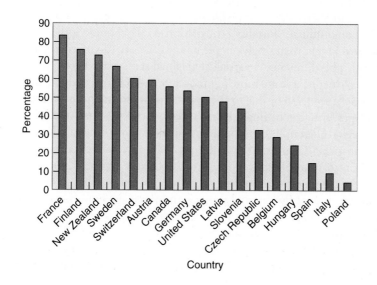

Figure 5.4 The percentage of women who have cohabited by the age of 45 for 17 countries shows that the prevalence of this living arrangement depends on the economy, partnership laws and benefits, availability of affordable housing, and religion of each country, among other things.

Source: Heuveline & Timberlake (2004).

CRITICAL THINKING ●

Do you agree with Heuveline & Timberlake's conclusions that cohabitation in the United States is an alternative to being single instead of an alternative to being married? Why or why not?

ration of the relationship. The researchers found this pattern in five countries: Finland, Slovenia, Austria, Belgium, and Switzerland. Cohabitation relationships that fit the "alternative to marriage" pattern are those that last a long time and do not result in marriage. The countries that fit that pattern were France, Canada, and Sweden. And cohabitation relationships that do not last long and do not result in marriage fit a pattern the researchers termed "alternative to single." These include New Zealand and the United States.

As stated before, marriages occur at later ages for today's generation of young adults. Although the divorce rate is higher than in the past, there is a trend for couples married in the last three decades to stay married longer than their earlier counterparts. Of course most of these data refer to people in their first marriages and may not be representative of the general population (including me). About 21 percent of married people are in a second (or third) marriage, many of which will be long and happy unions. Of all currently married people (regardless of their marital track records), one-third will celebrate their 25th anniversaries together, and almost 6 percent will be together on their 50th anniversaries (Kreider, 2005).

Gender Roles in Early Partnerships. Whether a young person cohabits first or moves directly into a marriage, it is clear that the acquisition of this new role brings profound changes to many aspects of the person's life. One of the major changes is in gender roles. Men and women have more **egalitarian roles,** or equal roles, at the beginning of a marriage or partnership, before children are born, than at any time until late adulthood. But this does not mean that traditional gender roles have no impact at this time of life—they clearly do. For example, household tasks tend to be divided along traditional gender lines, with women doing more of the cooking and cleaning, and men more of the yard work, household repairs, and auto maintenance. And even in this relatively egalitarian period of early marriage, wives still perform more total hours of household work than their husbands, even when both are employed (Winstead, Derlaga, & Rose, 1997).

Marital Status and Health. One of the cornerstones of the field of health psychology is that social relationships enhance health. Since marriage is the most important relationship for most people, researchers have compared the health and longevity of married people and single people. They have found that in a wide variety of mental and physical conditions, the health of married people, both male and female, is reliably and significantly better than the health of unmarried people. This result is consistent with studies done in a large number of cultures across the world (Diener, Gohm, Suh, et al., 2000). Furthermore, in the National Longitudinal Mortality Study (Johnson, Backlund, Sorlie, et al., 2000), married people lived longer than single people in any category (divorced, separated, widowed, never married). This difference is partially explained statistically by an effect called **marital selection**—healthier people are more apt to marry and stay married; but a substantial portion of the benefit seems to be due to the **marital protection** effect—married people have more advantages in terms of financial resources, social support, and healthier lifestyles (Robles & Kiecolt-Glaser, 2003), as will be discussed more fully in Chapter 10.

Health statistician Charlotte Schoenborn (2004) reviewed data from the U.S. Center for Disease Control and Prevention on the marital status and health of 127,000 people in the United States. Figure 5.5 shows the proportion of people who reported being in poor or fair health for each of five marital statuses and three age groups. Married people of all age groups were least likely to report that their health was "poor or fair," followed by those living with a partner, the divorced and separated, the widowed, and last, the never-married.

Of course it is difficult to separate people these days simply into categories of married and single. Some "single" people may be recently widowed after many years of marriage,

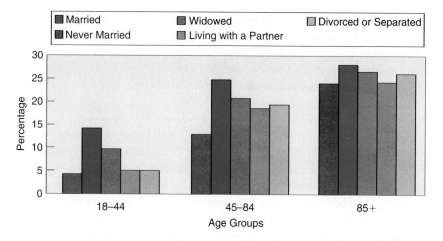

Figure 5.5 "How is your health?" Those who answered that it was "poor or fair" tended to be divorced, separated, or widowed at all ages. Married people were least apt to respond "poor or fair" across the adult years health.

Source: Schoenborn (2004).

and some "married" people may be in the second year of a third marriage. Our marital histories are not all-or-nothing statuses. Sociologists Hilke Brockman and Thomas Klein (2004) took this into account in their study of over 12,000 German adults, applying a life-course analysis to the effects marriage has on mortality. They found that married people, indeed, lived longer on average than single people. They also found that getting married for the first time signaled a possible decline in one's health; the first two years of the transition to marriage brought an increase in mortality risk for both men and women, as does any marital transition (divorce, separation, widowhood). However, after the first two years, the situation improves; for the subsequent seven years, both men and women enjoy a significant increase in health. After that, health rates for men continue to increase significantly, and rates for women increase somewhat. The authors concur with previous researchers that marriage is good for your health, but caution us to consider the "marital biographies" of individuals rather than simply their current marital status.

Another caution relevant to this topic is that *marital stability* (staying married) is not necessarily the same as *marital happiness.* You have, no doubt, known couples who have long but unhappy marriages, and it will not surprise you to know that when researchers divide married people into "happy" and "unhappy" groups, those who are unhappily married report more depressive symptoms than people who are not married at all (Fincham & Beach, 1999). Other studies have found that the happily married enjoy better physical health than their unhappily married friends. For example, Alzheimer's patients who had spouses who were neither critical nor overly involved in their caregiving exhibited fewer negative symptoms of the disease (Vitaliano, Young, Russo, et al., 1993). Parkinson's disease patients with high scores on a standardized test of marriage adjustment exhibited fewer symptoms when interacting with their spouses than those who scored lower (Greene & Griffith, 1998). And in a 4-year longitudinal study of 364 husbands and wives, those who reported happier marriages were also apt to report less overall illness (based on 56 symptoms or diseases) than those who reported unhappy marriages (Wickrama, Lorenz, & Conger, 1997). Finally, it may comfort you to know that people who report being happily married have less periodontal disease and fewer cavities in their teeth than those who report being unhappily married (Marcenes & Sheiman, 1996).

Taken together, these studies provide compelling evidence for a strong link between marital happiness and health, both mental and physical (and dental). Health psychologists Janice Kiecolt-Glaser and Tamara Newton (2001) reviewed these studies and others, and identified some key components of marital discord, particularly verbal conflict, that are implicated in differential health outcomes. Couples whose discussions include conflict,

CRITICAL THINKING

How would you design a study to determine whether people celebrating their 50th anniversaries in your community had high levels of marital happiness or just high levels of marital stability?

especially conflict with hostility expressed, show higher heart rates, blood pressure, muscular reactivity, and changes in endocrine and immune functions than do those who have discussions without conflict. Not only do we know that unhappy marriages and poor health go hand in hand, but we have some firm evidence now of the physical-emotional mechanisms involved. Unhappiness can be hazardous to your health!

Gender Differences in the Effect of Marriage on Health. Although the marriage/health connection holds true for both men and women, it is stronger for men. For example, being married gives women a 50 percent decrease in mortality over unmarried women, whereas being married gives men a 250 percent increase in mortality over their unmarried compatriots (Ross, Mirowsky, & Goldsteen, 1990). One of the reasons suggested is that women tend to be promoters of good health practices. They are more apt than men to eat nutritious meals, exercise regularly, have routine checkups, and avoid unhealthy practices such as smoking, drinking to excess, and using harmful drugs. For this reason, when men take on the role of husband, they are apt to adopt a healthier lifestyle too (Umberson, 1992).

But before you conclude that women somehow lose out when they marry, I will remind you that we are talking about *percentage increase* in mortality. Married men increase their longevity by a larger percentage than married women, but their wives have greater longevity to begin with. The best we can say is that marriage helps men live a lot longer than single men and helps women live longer than single women. So women are not losing anything when they marry—they just don't gain as much as men do.

Becoming a Parent

One of the major transitions that most adults experience in the years of early adulthood is becoming a parent. Roughly 85 percent of adults in the United States will eventually become parents, most often in their 20s or 30s. For most, the arrival of the first child brings deep satisfaction, an enhanced feeling of self-worth, and perhaps (as in my case) a sense of being an adult for the first time. It also involves a profound role transition, often accompanied by considerable changes in many aspects of one's former life.

Just as young adults are leaving their parents' homes and marrying at later ages, they are also delaying the transition to parenthood. The average age at which women gave birth for the first time has increased 3.5 years over the past three decades. The trend toward later childbearing is evident in most developed countries, as you can see in Figure 5.6, which shows average age increases for women's first births that range from 4.2 years older in Iceland to 1.6 years older in the Slovak Republic.

The overall trends seem very clear, but as usual with such sweeping generalizations, there are many exceptions. First, the pattern of delayed birth in the United States is more apt to be true of non-Hispanic white women and Asian and Pacific Islander women than of any other ethnic/racial group (Hamilton, Ventura, Martin, et al., 2005). Second, the delays in leaving the parental home, marrying, and becoming a parent does not mean that young adults are going through these role transitions in this sequence. There is a dramatic increase in the United States in the number of couples making the transition to parenthood before marriage. The rate of births to unmarried women in the United States has increased from 5 percent to 35 percent in the last four decades. Over a third of all children born in this country today are born to unmarried parents (National Marriage Project, 2005).

A closer look at these data on the transition to parenthood gives a surprising (to me) picture. The birth rates to unmarried women under 20 are down in the last three decades, as is the percentage of unintended pregnancies (Ventura & Bachrach, 2000). The rate of

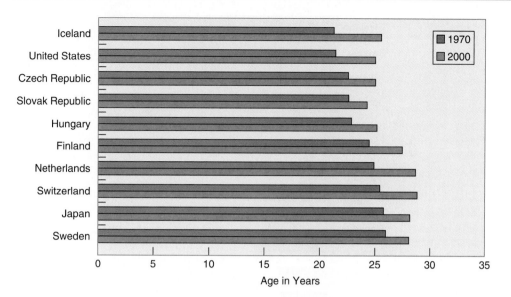

Figure 5.6 The age at which women are giving birth to their first child has increased in the last 30 years in most developed countries.

Source: Data from Mathews & Hamilton (2002).

contraception use is up in the past two decades for women of all ages and all racial/ethnic groups (U.S. Centers for Disease Control & Prevention, 2004). The stereotype of unwed mothers being very young and pregnant by accident is quite inaccurate. My interpretation of these numbers is that more couples are intentionally entering parenthood before they enter marriage, and they are doing it at later ages. These changes have occurred in other developed countries. For example, Figure 5.7 shows the increases in births to unmarried women for 16 developed countries for 1980 and 1998; the United States ranks close to the middle in this group (Ventura & Bachrach, 2000).

The stereotype of unmarried mothers being abandoned by the child's father and raising the child alone is faulty also. Although the percentage of women who are pregnant when they marry has decreased, some 40 percent of unmarried women who gave birth last year were cohabiting with the child's father. And even when the father is not present in the home, often the mother has a cohabiting partner who, although unrelated to the children, presumably takes on some of the parental responsibilities. According to the U.S. Census, 23 percent of children in the United States live with a single mother (never married, divorced, or widowed), but about one in 10 of these children (11 percent) have their mother's intimate partner living in the home with them. The situation is different for children living with a single father. Some 11 percent of all children live with a single father, but one-third of them (33 percent) also have the father's partner living in the home. The proportions vary significantly by racial/ethnic group (Fields, 2003b). Recent research suggests that the mere presence of two parents in the household is quite different for children's well-being than living in a home with married parents, as I will discuss more in Chapter 6.

Gender Roles among Couples with Children. After marriage, gender roles seem to move slightly in the direction of traditionalism. The effect of the birth of the first child is to accentuate this shift markedly. Anthropologist David Gutmann (1975) refers to this process as the **parental imperative** and argues that the pattern is wired in, or genetically programmed. He suggests that because human children are so vulnerable, parents must meet both the emotional and the physical needs of the child, and doing this is very difficult for one person. The woman bears the child and nurses it, so it is natural, Gutmann suggests, for the division of role responsibility to fall along the traditional lines.

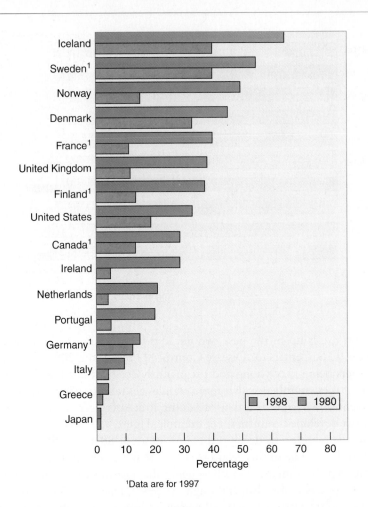

Figure 5.7 The percentage of births to unmarried women increased in many countries in recent decades.
Source: Ventura & Bachrach (2000).

[1]Data are for 1997

Gutmann based his ideas partly on his investigations of gender role changes among adults in other cultures, including the Navaho, the Mayan, and the Druze. However, there have been similar and more recent findings in the United States. For example, one study showed that after the birth of a first child, a woman assumes more responsibility for both child care and household tasks than either partner had predicted before the child was born (Cowan, Cowan, & Herning, 1991). However, other studies show that men with working wives are doing more child care now then they used to. When surveyed, 30 percent of fathers in dual-earner families report that they take on more child care responsibilities than their wives (Bond, Galinsky, & Swanberg, 1998). This may reflect the fact that when young adults have grown up in dual-earner families, they have different ideas of parenting roles than their peers who grew up with stay-at-home mothers. But if you include all forms of housework—child care, cooking, cleaning, running errands, and so on—most wives still do more than most husbands, even when both work full-time (Goldberg & Perry-Jenkins, 2004).

Given my own belief in egalitarian gender roles (a belief I am sure is quite clear from what I have already written!), it is easy for me to give the impression that an uneven division of household tasks is invariably a source of strain or difficulty. So let me offer a bit of balance here. Whether a wife, or a couple, finds a traditional division of labor to be a problem or not depends very much on their attitudes about gender roles in general. For example, one study suggests that middle-class dual-earner couples, many of whom hold relatively egalitarian views, experience higher levels of overall conflict when the wife thinks the husband is not doing his equal share of housework. But in working-class couples, many of whom hold more traditional views of gender roles, the lowest levels of marital conflict occurred when the division of labor was most traditional, with the wife doing the greater bulk of the housework (Perry-Jenkins & Folk, 1994). A recent study shows that working-class mothers feel more distress when they find themselves having less child care responsibility after their babies are born than they had anticipated when interviewed during pregnancy (Goldberg & Perry-Jenkins, 2004). Findings like this remind us that what is important for the functioning of a marriage is the relationship between what each spouse believes should be the division of labor and what is actually occurring. When the belief and the reality match reasonably well, the relationship benefits; when there is a poor match, there are more likely to be problems in the marriage. I will discuss the effects work has on family (and vice versa) in Chapter 7.

Parents who grew up in dual-earner families are more apt to share household tasks equally than those who grew up in single-earner families.

Parenthood and Marital Happiness. Unlike the transition to marriage, which seems to be accompanied by an increase in happiness, the new role of parent seems to bring a decrease in happiness and marital satisfaction. The general finding is of a curvilinear relationship between marital satisfaction and family stage, with the highest satisfaction being before the birth of the first child and after all the children have left home.

The decline in new parents' marital happiness is not new. Almost 50 years ago social scientists identified this transition as one of the most difficult adjustments in the family cycle (Lemasters, 1957). A good number of studies over the years have traced the cascade toward divorce for many couples from the point at which they become parents (Feldman, 1971; Belsky, Spanier, & Rovine, 1983; Cowan & Cowan, 1995; Belsky & Kelly, 1994; Crawford & Huston, 1993). However, not all new parents show this decline, and certainly not all new parents end up unhappy and divorced. What makes the difference, and is there a way to predict which newlywed couples will make it through the transition to parenthood and which will falter along the way?

One study that has identified some important factors in the transition to parenthood was done by psychologist John Gottman and his colleagues (Shapiro, Gottman, & Carrère, 2000). The study was unique in that it began with newlyweds and then followed them for the next 6 to 7 years. The researchers found that the wives who became mothers during the course of the study had higher marital happiness scores as newlyweds than the wives who remained childless. They also had steeper rates of decline in marital happiness, sometimes continuing for several years after the birth of their child. Husbands who became fathers showed no difference from husbands who remained childless.

Gottman then divided the couples who had become parents into two groups—those in which the wife had declined in marital happiness and those in which the wife had stayed the same or increased in marital happiness. Looking back over the initial interview these couples had participated in as newlyweds, several differences were found that could predict whether the wives would decline in happiness or not. First, if the husband expressed fondness for and admiration of his wife during the interview, and awareness of his wife and their relationship, the wife would show stability or even increase in marital happiness as they made the transition to parenthood. However, if the husband had expressed negativity toward his wife or disappointment in the marriage, the wife's marital happiness would decline as they became parents. The wife had a hand in this also—her happiness was predicted by the awareness she expressed of her husband and their relationship. Gottman explains these predictors as components of the *marital friendship* that makes difficult times, such as the transition to parenthood, easier to get through. It seems that the fondness and admiration the spouses express for each other serves as the glue that holds the marriage together and a buffer that protects the relationship. If new parents are aware of the state of their relationship and the difficult time their respective spouses are having during this role transition, they will feel more satisfaction and happiness in their marriage. I will have more to say about marriage relationships in Chapter 6.

To wrap up this section, let me reiterate that young adulthood is the time that the greatest number of social role transitions take place and also a time of extremely complex and demanding adjustments. Adapting to these changes is not simple, even when they are done gradually through entering semi-independent states such as living in the parental home longer, moving into a cohabiting relationship instead of marrying, and delaying parenthood. All I can say is that it is a good thing that this time of life usually coincides with peaks in mental and physical well-being. My message for young adults is that it gets easier and it gets better. And my message to those who are past this time of life is to think back and offer a little help (or at least a few words of encouragement) to the young adults in their lives who are navigating these important transitions.

Social Roles in Middle Adulthood

During the middle years, existing roles are redefined and renegotiated. This time of life brings stable levels of physical health and increases in self-reported quality of life (Fleeson, 2004). Between the ages of 40 and 65, the parenting role becomes less demanding as children become more self-sufficient. Women's childbearing years end during this time, and most men and women become grandparents, a role that is, for most, less demanding than parenthood and more pleasurable. Marriages and partnerships become happier (or people end troublesome ones and either find more agreeable partners or opt to live alone). Relationships with one's parents slowly change as they grow older and begin to need assistance in parts of their daily lives. The work role is still demanding early in middle adulthood, but most adults have settled into their careers and are usually competent in their jobs. Many experience a role transition from junior worker to senior worker and mentor, taking the time to help younger colleagues learn the ropes of the workplace. This is not to say that the biological and social clocks have stopped, just that they are ticking less loudly than in early adulthood.

The Departure of the Children: The Empty Nest

Women now in their 40s and 50s in the United States had their last child, on average, when they were 26. If we assume that the last child will leave home when he or she is 25 or 26, the women in this current middle-aged cohort will be in their early 50s when the last child leaves. Because men marry at slightly older ages, the average middle-aged man today will be 55 or 56 when his last child departs for independent living.

This stage is sometimes called "postparental," as if the role of parent stopped when the last child walked out the door, suitcase in hand. Clearly, it does not. Adults who have reared children go on being parents the rest of their lives. They often continue to give advice, provide financial assistance and instrumental help, baby-sit with grandchildren, and provide a center for the extended family. But on a day-to-day basis, the role of parent clearly changes, becoming far less demanding and less time-consuming.

Folklore would have it that this empty-nest stage is a particularly sad and stressful period, especially for women. Research shows, to the contrary, that the results of this role transition are more positive than negative (Hareven, 2001). Marriages are happier than they have been since before the children were born, and many couples report experiencing this phase of their marriage as a second honeymoon (Carstensen, Graff, Levenson, et al., 1996). Women who have fewer day-to-day family responsibilities often take the opportunity to restructure their lives, moving to a new career, seeking out new interests, or returning to college for the degree they postponed when the children came along. Journalist Gail Sheehy (2006) recently traveled around the United States interviewing women in this age group and found them to be assured, alluring, and open to sex, love, new dreams, and spirituality. Surely these findings are not consistent with the pessimistic view of this time of life that many hold.

When children are "launched" into independence, their parents often find new interests together and renew their preparenting closeness.

Gender Roles at Midlife

A big topic of interest in the study of midlife is that of changes in gender roles. Anthropologist David Gutmann, who believes that men and women become more traditionally gendered as they enter the transition to parenthood, suggests, a **crossover of gender roles** occurs at midlife. Women take on more and more of the traditionally masculine qualities or role responsibilities, becoming more assertive, while men become more passive (Gutmann, 1975, 1987).

There appears to be a kernel of truth in Gutmann's view of these changes, but more systematic studies suggest that it is better to describe the change as an **expansion of gender roles** rather than a crossing-over. There are signs of decreased gender-typical behavior in middle age, at least among some groups (Helson & Wink, 1992). Perhaps because the children are gone from home, there is less pressure toward traditional role divisions, and both men and women at midlife can begin to express previously unexpressed parts of themselves. For some men, this means an increased expression of compassion or nurturance; for some women, it means increased assertiveness or autonomy.

Becoming a Grandparent

For today's adults, one of the central roles of middle adulthood is that of grandparent. In fact, it is among the top three most important roles claimed by both middle-aged men and women (Reitzes & Mutran, 2002). About three-fourths of adults in the United States become grandparents before they are 65, and over half of women experience this event before the age of 54 (Marks, 1996).

CRITICAL THINKING

What is your opinion on the empty-nest syndrome? Have you observed this in your parents or perhaps in yourself? Did this time of life bring an increase in life satisfaction? A decrease?

With longevity increasing, it has been predicted that men and women today may spend close to half of their lives in the role of grandparent (Silverstein & Marenco, 2001). Today's grandparents are filling roles that are much different from the roles their own grandparents filled. Not only are they younger, healthier, and more affluent, they also have busy, complex lives with multiple roles that include working grandmothers, step-grandfathers, graduate-student grandmothers, and dating grandfathers. It is not easy to define the role of grandparent because it depends on all these factors plus the distance between the grandparents' and grandchildren's homes, the relationship between the parents and grandparents, the number of grandchildren, the health and income of everyone concerned, and many other factors. Considering the myriad changes in the lives of middle-aged adults in the last two generations, most of us are unable to use our own grandparents as models for today's grandparenting role. As a result, most families construct their own grandparent/grandchild roles.

However, there are some broad generalizations I can talk about. There are gender differences; grandmothers, especially maternal grandmothers, have broader and more intimate roles than grandfathers. Grandmothers have more contact with their grandchildren, especially their granddaughters, and play a more affectionate role (Silverstein, Giarrusso, & Bengtson, 1998). The relationships between grandparents and their grandchildren will be discussed more in Chapter 6.

To be fair, I should include evidence of the less-than-fun side of grandparenting. There can be problems, and the most frequent stem from disagreements over childrearing between the grandparents and parents of the grandchildren (Somary & Stricker, 1998). Some grandparents have trouble making the transition from full-time parent to the more egalitarian role of parent to an adult child who has children of his or her own. (And some adult children have problems in their role transitions, too.)

Grandparents Raising Grandchildren. Recently a substantial number of grandparents have moved into the role of parenting their grandchildren, often referred to as **surrogate parenting.** This role does not entail living with the grandchild's parents and helping out, but consists of reassuming the parenting role for the grandchildren in one's own home when the parents are either absent or not able (or willing) to fulfill their roles as parents. Although this situation is not unusual in African American families, it has become increasingly common among white and Hispanic families as well. According to the U.S. Census Bureau, almost 6 million grandparents are living with at least one grandchild who is 18 years of age or younger. While this includes three-generation households, some 42 percent of these grandparents are responsible for the basic needs of the grandchildren, and more than half of them are grandparents 65 and older (Gist & Hetzel, 2004). Looking at the situation from the children's side, 6.3 percent of all children in the United States who are under 18 live in grandparent-headed households, and this has increased by almost a third since the 1990 census (Simmons & Dye, 2003). The reasons for this trend are varied—adult children become parents too early, suffer from mental and physical illnesses, are addicted to drugs or in prison, or have died as the result of illness or lifestyle.

One study that examined the role of grandparents as surrogate parents was done by social work researchers Roberta Sands and Robin Goldberg-Glen (2000). They interviewed 129 grandparents who were in the role of surrogate parent for at least one grandchild, asking about the sources of stress in their lives. Results showed that regardless of the grandparents' age, race, or number of grandchildren living in the home, the major sources of stress came from problems with the grandchildren's parents (they weren't involved in supporting their children either with attention and emotional support or with financial support, and they added to the grandparents' stress with their own financial and personal problems) and problems with the grandchildren's learning (they had attention-deficit hyperactivity disorder or were discipline problems at school).

Although most research involves grandmothers, social work researchers Stacey Kolomer and Philip McCallion (2005) interviewed 33 grandfathers who were caregivers for their grandchildren and compared them to a group of grandmothers. They found that the grandfathers were more apt to be raising the grandchildren with the help of their spouse, more likely to be working full-time outside the home, more apt to be white, and had lower depression levels than the grandmothers. Their big concerns were the loss of freedom that their family situation brought and also concerns for their own health, worrying about what would happen to the family if their health failed.

Grandparents who take on the role of surrogate parent have difficulty getting any financial help. In most states, if unrelated people take in children whose parents cannot take care of them, they are eligible for foster-parent funds, but grandparents and other relatives are not. It is also difficult for grandparents to collect child support from their grandchildren's fathers (or mothers), even when the court has ordered it as part of a divorce settlement. They are in a legal limbo unless the parents agree to relinquish their parental rights, and without legal guardianship, grandparents have difficulty getting medical treatment for their grandchildren and information from the schools. With more and more middle-aged people taking on the role of surrogate parents to their grandchildren (and more and more people being grandparents in general), one hopes that this situation will soon change.

Caring for an Aging Parent

For most of today's middle-aged adults, an important role is that of being the adult child of an aging parent. Over a fourth of middle-aged adults report that their mothers and fathers are living, and only 10 percent of middle-aged adults report that both parents are in good health (Marks, Bumpass, and Jun, 2004). Figure 5.8 illustrates these data along with the proportion of middle-aged men and women who report having various combinations of parents in various states of health. As you can see, over a third of middle-aged adults in this survey report having at least one parent who is not in good health. Although the major caregiver of an older adult is most commonly his or her spouse, the task is usually taken on by the adult children when the spouse is not available due to divorce, poor health, or death.

Gender and Caregiving. Daughters and daughters-in-law are usually the adult children who take on the care of a parent in poor health. This has been explained in various ways, mostly based on the traditional gender role of women as kin-keepers, or the idea that women have more flexible work schedules, or are "closer" to the parent (both geographically and emotionally), plus the fact that elderly mothers, with whom daughters are presumably closer, are more prevalent than elderly fathers, with whom sons are presumably closer (Brody, Litvin, Albert, et al., 1994).

But although valid to some extent, this picture is too simple for my liking. The question "Who provides the care?" seldom has a one-word answer. Most situations require several paragraphs. In my own family, my three sisters provide most of the care for our elderly parents because they live nearby and I'm across the state. However, it depends on what is going on in their lives. My parents also have a home healthcare worker who visits on a daily basis. I pitch in when I am in town. Our husbands have their roles too—one manages a rental property my parents own, and another makes sure my father gets out several times a week to have lunch "in town" or walk around the hardware store. And then there is the staff at the senior residence where my parents live, who provide meals and laundry service. My parents are also able to help each other out; my father jokes that he is able to push

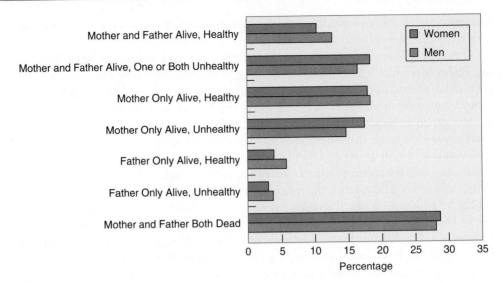

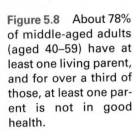

Figure 5.8 About 78% of middle-aged adults (aged 40–59) have at least one living parent, and for over a third of those, at least one parent is not in good health.

Source: Data from Marks, Bumpass, & Jun (2004).

my mother's wheelchair and she is able to remember where they are going. If it takes a village to raise a child, it takes at least a small community to care for elderly parents.

Gender roles in parental caregiving were examined in a study by sociologists Amy Hequembourg and Sara Brallier (2005), who interviewed sister-brother pairs who were caregivers for their elderly parents. The sisters in all eight pairs were the "coordinators" for the care of their parents, even though seven of the eight sisters worked full-time. They had taken on the traditional women's role of knowing what the parent needed, making plans to take care of those needs, telling the brother what needed to be done, and planning for future needs. The brothers fell into two groups. Four of them had the traditional male role of "helper." They waited until the sister told them of their parents' needs and assigned them a specific task, not surprisingly traditional male tasks such as car repairs, lawn maintenance, and household repairs. If the sister did not do this, they believed that everything was fine and their parents didn't need anything.

One helper brother, who was asked who did the most for his mother, replied this way:

> Oh, Tricia does. She'll come down and spend the whole weekend . . . I'll call my mother and ask her, "What are you doing this weekend?" She says, "Oh, Tricia is coming down." I say, "All right. If you need something, call me" (Hequembourg & Brallier, 2005, p. 61).

The other four brothers in the study had assumed the role of co-providers. Although their sisters were also the supervisors of the parents' care, they took more direct responsibility and provided a range of care for their parents that crossed traditional gender lines, such as providing emotional support, administering medication, and bathing. The co-provider brothers had more flexible work schedules. One was a clergyman who described how he was able to care for his mother with Alzheimer's disease:

> . . . because in the morning a lot of people have to be in to work at eight thirty or so. Whereas . . . nobody expects me until ten, and so that automatically gave me a little piece of time in the morning . . . And of course . . . you go home in the afternoon, but then you come back for two or three hours in the evening. And so it wouldn't be unusual to say, "Well, I'll knock off at four thirty today and I'll check on Mom now because it's going to be a real late meeting tonight" (Hequembourg & Brallier, 2005, pp. 62–63).

Co-provider brothers were more apt to think about the future needs of their parents and consider that their caregiving was actually giving help to their parents; helper brothers were more apt to view their caregiving as giving help to their sisters.

The Impact of Caregiving. In the past 15 years, there have been a great number of studies exploring the effect of parent care on the lives of the caregivers. In most of these studies, the recipient of care has been diagnosed with some form of dementia, most often Alzheimer's disease. Because such people gradually lose their ability to perform the simplest of daily functions, they require a steadily increasing amount of care, and the demands on the caregiver can be very large indeed, up to and including constant supervision. When the middle-aged caregiver is also holding down a job, caring for a spouse, and assisting grown children and grandchildren, the impact can be substantial.

The cumulative evidence indicates that caregivers of elderly parents report having more depressive symptoms, take more antidepressant and antianxiety medication, and report lower marital satisfaction than is true for matched comparison groups of similar age and social class (Rose-Rego, Strauss, & Smyth, 1998; Martire & Schulz, 2001; Sherwood, Given, Given, et al., 2005). They are less likely to exercise or follow a nutritious diet, get adequate sleep, take time to rest when ill, or remember to take their medication than similar people who are not caregivers. The results are increased weight (Vitaliano, Young, Russo, et al., 1996), compromised immune function (Kiecolt-Glaser, Glaser, Gravenstein, et al., 1996), and lower levels of overall physical health (Schulz, O'Brien, Bookwala, et al., 1995). Collectively, these effects on mental and physical health go by the name of **caregiver burden.**

Added to the caregiver burden for some middle-aged adults are the competing demands from their still-dependent (or almost independent) adult children, a situation that is known as the **generational squeeze** (or being part of the "sandwich generation"). As you may be able to tell from my comments throughout this book, I can relate personally to this concept. Being fortunate enough to have a busy career, two adult children, a semi-adult stepdaughter, eight grandchildren, two parents in their 80s, and two parents-in-law in their 70s, some days I feel as though my picture should appear next to this term in the dictionary!

Although some minimize this quandary by pointing out that only one-fourth of people between 35 and 54 have full-time jobs, dependent children at home, and parents with limited health (Putney & Bengtson, 2001), I argue that when you consider that each adult who cares for an elderly parent usually has a spouse who is involved, the numbers add up quickly. I would also argue that it is not necessary to have a full-time job, dependent children, *and* parents who need assistance to feel the generational squeeze.

A number of studies have examined the role of caregiver to one's elderly parent in relationship to other roles. Two theories have been suggested for the effect of multiple roles. The **role strain theory** (Goode, 1960; Brody, 1981) argues that there is a limit to the number of roles a person can take on; having multiple roles can exacerbate stress and lead to a decline in physical and psychological well-being. The **role enhancement theory** (Thoits, 1983) argues the opposite; multiple roles are beneficial because some roles serve as buffers against stress from other roles. In one study, gerontologists Mary Ann Stephens and Aloen Townsend (1997) interviewed 296 women who were primary caregivers to disabled parents or parents-in-law and were married, had jobs, and had children still living in the home. The results showed that women caregivers with multiple roles experienced more negative effects of caregiving if they had stress in any of their other roles. They experienced a buffering effect from their role as an employee if they felt their job was rewarding. Caregivers are less apt to report having depressive symptoms if they have adequate social support from friends and other family members (Li, Seltzer, & Greenberg, 1997) and instrumental support from paid helpers and community services (Bass, Noelker, & Rechlin, 1996). Women who care for their parents do better if they have a satisfying marriage, rewarding job, and children (Stephens & Townsend, 1997). Clearly, the effect of multiple roles isn't a simple one of just having too many items on one's list of things to do. It also depends on what the roles are, what social support is forthcoming, and whether or not one perceives them as rewarding.

Social Roles in Late Adulthood

In late adulthood, we make transitions into simplified forms of former roles—we move into smaller homes or retirement communities, we leave our full-time jobs and spend our time on part-time work, volunteer work, or caregiving for spouse, relatives, or friends, we take pride in the development of our grandchildren and great-grandchildren, we watch our children mature, and we enjoy their success and happiness. Some roles are not of our choosing—the role of living alone, usually as widow or widower, and the role of care receiver, but they are also part of the journey of adulthood for many older adults.

At one time, late adulthood was considered a time of role loss. Even when the concept of role transition became popular, the results of these transitions for older adults were often considered to be stress, grief, and a sense of loss. More recently, studies have shown that there are no typical ways that adults react to role transitions in late adulthood. Different people experience these transitions in different ways, and even the same person may experience extreme disruption in his or her life during these transitions only to recover and takes on new roles with gusto (Ferraro, 2001). So instead of viewing late adulthood as a time of loss, researchers are busily investigating the wide range of outcomes possible and the personal factors that might predict the outcomes for different individuals.

Living Alone

One of the new challenges that comes to many adults in their later years, most frequently to women, is that of learning to live alone, a change brought about by losing the role of spouse due to widowhood or sometimes divorce. I will talk about the experience and adjustment to the death of a spouse in Chapter 10, but here I want to take up the topic of living alone in late adulthood for whatever reason. Figure 5.9 shows the living arrangements for people 65 years of age and older in the United States. As you can see, almost 20 percent of men and 40 percent of women fall into this group. Such a choice is less common among people of Hispanic and Asian origins than among non-Hispanic white and black adults. Hispanic Americans and Asian Americans have higher proportions of older adults living with relatives other than spouses.

In Japan, only 7 percent of older adults live alone; 60 percent live with a child (Silver, 1998). In the United States and in other Western countries in which there is adequate financial support for older citizens, the great majority of older adults live alone by choice, not because there is no other alternative. Even when their health declines, most older adults in the United States will persist in living alone as long as possible. In contrast, most elderly people in Japan report that they prefer to live with their adult children, regardless of their health status (Silver, 1998).

Becoming a Care Receiver

One role that few older adults plan to fill is that of care receiver. After spending many years of one's life as an independent adult and caregiver to their children, their own parents, and sometimes their grandchildren, many adults find themselves on the other end of the caregiving process. Although it sounds like a long-overdue reward, most older adults in West-

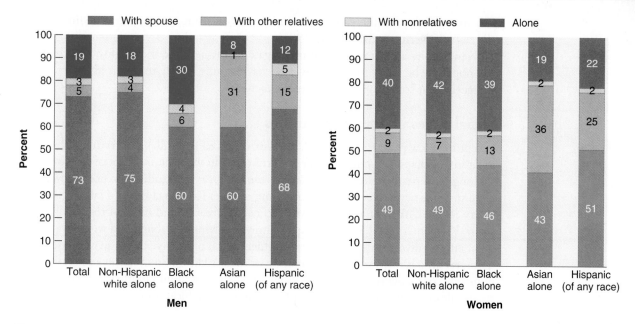

Figure 5.9 Living arrangements of older adults in the U.S. vary widely depending on gender and racial/ethnic group.

Source: Federal Interagency Forum on Aging Related Statistics (2004).

ern countries feel that losing one's independence in addition to having to be cared for by family members is simply adding insult to injury.

In a slight departure from the earlier interest in caregiving, some researchers have been studying the effects this situation has on the care recipient (Newsom & Schulz, 1998). Receiving care from family members in late adulthood has a number of advantages, the most obvious being that it allows one to remain independent and decreases the amount of paid help that is necessary. Less obvious benefits are that it gives the opportunity to become closer to family members in the time remaining, time for mending fences and deepening feelings for each other (Martire & Schulz, 2001). Studies have shown that older adults who have help available if they need it feel that staying healthy is under their own control rather than caused by external and uncontrollable factors (McAvay, Seeman, & Rodin, 1996). These feelings of self-efficacy have proved to be important in maintaining health and functional ability (Bandura, 1997). Furthermore, older adults who are cared for by family members in some activities of daily living are more apt to take better care of themselves in the other activities they are still able to handle (Norburn, Bernard, Konrad, et al., 1995).

Being the recipient of care by family members also has its negative effects. We are familiar with cases of elder abuse or incidents of intentional criticism or hostility directed at older adults by family caregivers (Pillemer & Suitor, 1992), but even well-intentioned caregiving can have negative effects on the recipient. In a study of caregiving spouses of older stroke patients, the most unhelpful "caregivers" were critical of the patients' attempts at recovery, overestimated or underestimated their abilities, and did not provide the type of assistance needed (Clark & Stephens, 1996).

These failed attempts at caregiving lead to an increase in depressive symptoms for the patient and an erosion of feelings of control (Krause, 1995). Other studies show that older adults who are recipients of excessive caregiving may lose confidence in their own ability to function and as a result become even more disabled (Seeman, Bruce, & McAvay, 1996). Caregiving in the form of providing more help than is actually needed to older arthritis patients can result in increased pain and inactivity (Romano, Turner, Friedman, et al., 1992; Turk, Kerns, & Rosenberg, 1992).

New studies are being done to investigate this issue more thoroughly, and the result will hopefully be a way to fit caregiving behavior more closely to the needs of those who are receiving it so it can have its intended benefits.

Social Roles in Atypical Families

Except for a few paragraphs on unmarried or widowed individuals, everything I have said so far in this chapter describes the life patterns of adults who adopt the social roles of spouse (or long-term partner) and parent. But of course a great many adults do not follow such a pattern. Some never marry, and an increasing number have no children. Half of those who marry in the United States today will eventually divorce, and most of them will marry again (Kreider, 2002). The "traditional" family involving a husband and wife, several children, and no divorce (the pattern upon which much of family sociology was based until quite recently) is not a valid representation of today's family. So in fairness to families like mine (and probably yours) I cannot leave this chapter without talking about those whose social role experience in adulthood differs from this mythical "norm."

Lifelong Singles

Men and women are staying single longer in the United States and other developed countries, so it is difficult to determine whether the rate of lifelong singles is increasing, decreasing, or staying the same. Just by definition, it is difficult to know the number of *lifelong* singles until they reach the end of their lives. However we can get a good estimate by examining data from the U. S. Census. Figure 5.10 shows the proportion of men and women in different age groups who reported in 2003 that they had never married. Although the rate keeps declining through young adulthood and middle age, by age 65, a little over 4 percent of the population qualify as lifelong singles (Fields, 2003a). This is about half the rate that it was in the United States 30 years ago, and about half the rate of lifelong singles in many European countries (Newtson & Keith, 1997).

The health of the older lifelong single adult has been the topic of a number of studies. Although married people report higher levels of well-being than widowed, divorced, separated, and lifelong single people, the lifelong single group is a close second and gaining

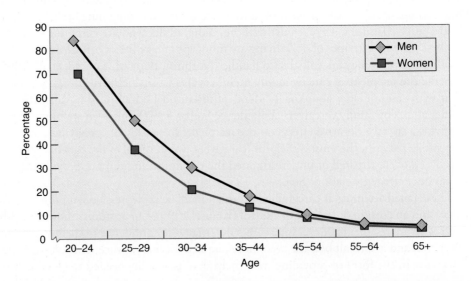

Figure 5.10 The percentage of never-married men and women decreases with age, and by the age of 65, more than 95% have married at least once.

Source: Data from Fields (2003a).

each decade (Marks, 1996). Of the large group of older single adults (divorced, separated, widowed, and lifelong single), the lifelong singles have the best health and fewest disabilities. Furthermore, they report the most satisfaction with being single (Newtson & Keith, 1997). This certainly dispels the myth of fading spinsters and frail elderly bachelors!

An important challenge for the single adult is to create a supportive network, especially to find a confidant with whom life's problems may be discussed. In an investigation of causes and remedies of loneliness in a group of German elders, developmental psychologist Martin Piquart (2003) found that those who had never been married reported being less lonely when they had close relationships with siblings and friends. Interestingly, widowed and divorced people the same age did not report that their ties with sibling and friends were important in alleviating loneliness. Their loneliness depended on whether their adult children were close to them or not. Piquart concluded that people who have been married depend on the social support of their spouse and children, while those who have always been single have cultivated close relationships with siblings and friends.

The Childless

CRITICAL THINKING

What do you think are some of the reasons for the increase in voluntary childlessness in the United States and around the world?

Despite all the current news about advances in infertility treatment, late-life pregnancies, and women choosing to have children without the benefit of marriage (or even a partner in their lives), the rate of childlessness is increasing dramatically for U.S. women. (And we assume the same is true for men, although most statistics report only women's fertility rates.) According to the most recent census figures, about 19 percent of women today over the age of 44 have no children (Dye, 2005). This is almost double the proportion of childless women in the 1970s (10 percent). These data are shown in Figure 5.11. The increase in childlessness has also occurred in other developed countries.

In the past, women who arrived at their mid-40s without children were a source of comment, usually sympathetic. It was thought that either they were physically unable to have children or had forgone motherhood to devote themselves to their careers or their elderly parents. Those who seemed happily childless were either considered selfish or else warned that they would be sorry in their later years with no children or grandchildren in their lives (Woollett & Marshall, 2001). Today, childlessness has become a choice, and a valid choice in the minds of many people, and sometimes the source of envy by friends who are parents.

One real decrement for childless people is that life in our society seems to be shaped by family milestones. Without children, the rhythm of the family timetable is simply not there to structure the adult's life experiences (Somers, 1993). For better or for worse, there

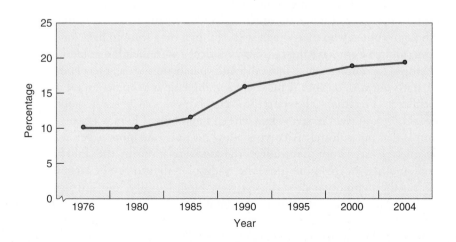

Figure 5.11 The percentage of women over 40 in the U.S. who are childless has almost doubled in the past 30 years.

Source: Data from Dye (2005).

is no change in relationship or roles when the first child is born, no celebration when the first child starts school, no bar mitzvahs or first dates or leaving home—no empty nests because the nest has never been full (or, perhaps, has always been full).

For women without children, another major difference is in the role of worker. Without children to care for, there is far less barrier to a woman's pursuit of a full-time career. Whether women who have made a commitment to a career choose not to have children or whether those who do not have children subsequently make a stronger career commitment is not completely clear. Some of both may well occur. What is clear is that childless women are more likely to work throughout their adult lives, to have somewhat higher-level jobs, and to earn more money.

One final interesting tidbit: We might expect that childless adults would lack adequate emotional support in later life, when aid from children appears to become so significant. Surprisingly, the research shows quite a different pattern. Several studies show that among postretirement adults, happiness or life satisfaction, loneliness or self-esteem, is unrelated to the amount of contact the adult has with children or grandchildren. At this life stage, childless adults appear to be as happy as those with extended families, although this is more often true of those who are childless by choice than for those who are childless by circumstance (Connidis & McMullin, 1993), and more true for childless women than childless men (Zhang & Hayward, 2001). I think it is safe to say that the picture of adults without children is not one of persisting sadness or regret.

Divorced (and Remarried) Adults

About one-third of today's young adults who marry will divorce before they reach their 10th anniversary, and most will remarry, with an average unmarried interval of 3.5 years. The rate of remarriage is highest among white men (about 75 percent) and lowest among African American women (about 32 percent). Remarriage rates are also linked to age: the younger you are when you divorce and the fewer children you have, the greater the likelihood that you will remarry. And among all who remarry, more than half will divorce a second time. About a third of these will remarry once again (Kreider, 2005).

Nonetheless, it is clear that divorce brings with it a larger and more complex set of roles to fill. The single parent must often fill a larger share of the adult family roles: breadwinner, emotional supporter, housekeeper, child caregiver, activities director, chauffeur, and the rest. With remarriage, more new roles emerge. One becomes a spouse again and frequently a stepparent. About 90 percent of men and women in a second marriage have at least one child from a previous relationship. If the new spouse's children are young, one might easily go from being a childless adult to having children in the home on a daily basis. This is especially true for men because children most often have their primary residence with their mothers.

Although women who marry men with children may seem to have an easier role because the children don't have their primary residence with their father (and her), in many ways, being a stepmother can be more difficult than being a stepfather. The role of a stepmother starts out with one of the most threatening false stereotypes found in legends and classic children's literature—the evil stepmother. I doubt if there is a stepmother alive who has not said, "I don't want to seem like a wicked stepmother!" I know I have. Another complication is that our cultural stereotypes allow for only one mother per child, so a stepmother must be careful not to intrude in the special relationship the child has with his or her "real" mother. At the same time, the traditional division of household tasks often means that the stepmother does the extra cooking, laundry, and nurturing when the stepchildren visit. This ambiguity in role content is no doubt also present in the stepchild's reaction to the stepmother. I doubt if there is a stepchild alive who has not said to his or her stepmother, "But you aren't my *real* mother."

Although the role of stepmother is hardly new, researchers have only recently begun to study its dynamics. In one of the first studies I am aware of, researchers surveyed 265 step-mothers about the contents of their roles. They found that most of these women defined their roles as being either motherlike or a supportive adult (Orchard & Salberg, 1999). More recently, family studies researchers Shannon Weaver and Marilyn Coleman (2005) inter-viewed 11 stepmothers in depth and found that the women described one of three dis-tinct roles. The first role is "mothering, but not mother," in which women describe serving as a responsible and caring adult, a friend, a provider of emotional support, or a mentor. One stepmother explained it this way:

> I guess when they were with us I was basically in a mothering role. I made sure that I did the things that a mother would do in a family . . . I have a lot of the feelings that a mother would have and maybe some boundaries that a mother doesn't have because you're their dad's wife. You're the stepmother; you're not really their mother. And that might be different if [my husband] had custody or if . . . their real mother wasn't living . . . I think the role evolved into whatever it is because they had a mother that they lived with that was a good mom. They didn't want a replacement for their mom, and I didn't want to be a replacement cause that's not what they needed. I don't know. It's kind of a different role (Weaver & Coleman, 2005, p. 487)

The second is an "other-focused" role in which the women described serving as a liaison or buffer between the stepchild and the biological parents. This role was described by one stepmother this way:

> What I've done a lot of times is try to take some of the pressure off of [my husband] of having to deal with his ex-wife so much by being the one that picked [my stepdaughter] up at her mom's . . . I don't have the kind of feelings that he has for her. (Weaver & Coleman, 2005, p. 488)

The third role is that of "outsider," in which the stepmother has no direct role with the stepchildren. This is how one of the women in the study described it:

> My role is to kind of be laid back and let [my stepson] spend time with his dad and visit with his grandparents or to entertain myself or just hang out (Weaver & Coleman, 2005, p. 486.)

Weaver and Coleman conclude their study by calling for more study of the role of step-mother and how it relates to women's well-being. It is surely one area where the feelings involved in caring for a child who belongs to one's spouse are often in conflict with the expectations of the spouse, the child's biological mother, the stepchildren themselves, the extended family, and the culture. For a role that is so prevalent in today's families and shows no sign of decreasing in the near future, it seems like a much-needed line of research.

And before we end this section on divorce and remarriage, let's not forget the eco-nomics of it all. Divorce means that a one-family income needs to be stretched to support two families, a fact that lowers the standard of living for all family members. During the year following the divorce, women who are divorced have an in-come 30 percent lower than women who are not divorced, and five years later they still have an income 12 percent lower (Smock, Manning, & Gupta, 1999). Many of the detrimental effects of divorce for women and children can be traced to the economic loss rather than the divorce itself.

CRITICAL THINKING

What are some of the reasons that di-vorce has a larger economic impact on women than on men?

The Effect of Variations in Timing

Social timing refers to the roles we occupy, how long we occupy them, and the order in which we occupy them. It also depends on the culture we live in and what expectations our society has for role transitions (Elder, 1995). For example, to become a parent at 15 may be expected in some societies and may even happen frequently in our society, but it is considered "off-time" by mainstream U.S. norms. Similarly, a 45-year-old man who does not want to get involved in marriage or parenthood because he values his independence is similarly considered off-time. Both these behaviors would be acceptable, or "on-time," at other ages. The extent that one's roles are on-time or off-time is hypothesized to be of prime importance to one's social development and well-being (McAdams, 2001).

The concept of a social clock becoming important in adulthood was first proposed by sociologist Bernice Neugarten and her colleagues (Neugarten, Moore, & Lowe, 1965). They viewed this as an important distinction between children and adults in that adults were capable of viewing their lives both in the past and in the future, comparing their past selves with their present selves and anticipating their future selves. It also allows us to compare our own life cycles with those of others. Neugarten believed that we form a mental representation of the "normal, expectable life cycle" and use this to evaluate our own lives and the lives of others.

Young adults who continue living at home with their parents, not having a serious romantic relationship or a job with career potential, are no doubt aware of their off-time development. Middle-aged adults are likewise aware that the time has come to either reach their career goals or disengage. Likewise, older adults fare better when they are able to make age-appropriate role transitions in their lives (such as accepting care from their children). Psychologist Jette Heckhausen (2001) theorizes that the stronger the correlation a person's social role sequence has with developmental norms, the less stress he or she will have in life.

To my thinking, the idea of a social clock adds another dimension to the roles we move into during adulthood. It's not only important to assume the expected roles and fulfill them well, but also to assume them at the right time and in the right order. This is not always within our control, as exemplified by the 27-year-old woman who becomes a widow when her husband dies in an auto accident, or the 75-year-old grandmother who is raising her school-aged grandchildren (and her 77-year-old husband who goes back to

CRITICAL THINKING ●

Think of the roles you currently occupy. Which ones are on-time, and which are off-time?

Table 5.2	Review of Social Roles Throughout Adulthood	
Age 20–39	**Age 40–65**	**Age 65+**
Transition to roles of independent adult takes place slowly.	Roles become more intense as children get older, jobs become more important, and community involvement takes on leadership responsibilities.	Roles have less content as children become more independent and retirement arrives. Roles of volunteer worker and great-grandparent become important.
Maximum gender-role differentiation, especially after the transition to parenthood.	Gender roles remain strong while children are in the home.	Gender roles expand to allow for more freedom, but do not "cross over."
Roles with parents involve assistance and advice from them.	Roles with parents are more equal than at other times of life.	Roles with parents involve assistance and advice to them, caregiving.
Role of spouse is optional, either by remaining single or cohabiting. Marriages often end in divorce.	Role of spouse is central, though divorce and remarriage may occur.	Role of spouse for many has changed to role of widower, or role of remarried widower.
Transition to parent role.	Role with children is central.	Role with children remains central, adjustments need to be made if children become caregivers.

work to support them). However, it is accurate to predict that people who are off-time with the social clock of their culture are more apt to have difficulty in their roles and less apt to report high levels of life satisfaction (Hurwicz, Dunham, Boyd-Davis, et al., 1992).

As in earlier chapters, I have pulled together the various patterns of change with age in a review table (Table 5.2) so that you can begin to build up a composite picture of the qualities and experiences of adults in different age groups. The key point to be reemphasized is the one with which I began this chapter: Despite all the variations in timing and sequence, the basic shape of the pattern of role transitions seems to be similar for most adults. We move into more roles in early adulthood, renegotiate and make transitions into different roles in middle adulthood, and make still more transitions in late adulthood. Some of the roles are ruled by the biological clock and some by the social clock, but there is a similar basic itinerary for most adults.

Summary

1. Despite many variations today in the timing and sequence of roles, adulthood is still largely structured by the patterns of roles adults take on and the roles transitions they experience.

2. Gender roles are fairly diverse and describe what people really do within their roles as men and women; gender stereotypes are shared beliefs about what men and women have in common. The stereotypes for women usually center around communal qualities (being nurturing and intuitive); the stereotypes for men usually center around instrumental qualities (being adventurous and competitive).

3. Learning-schema theory states that gender roles are based on distorted views that exaggerate gender differences. Social role theory states that gender roles are based on observations of male and female behavior. Evolutionary psychology states that gender roles are based on inherited traits men and women have that were critical to survival and reproduction for our primitive ancestors. The biosocial perspective states that gender roles are an interaction of hereditary biases and current social and cultural influences.

4. The transition to adulthood is a change in roles from dependent child to semi-independent adult. It can include moving out of the parental home, entering college or military service, entering into a marriage or cohabitation relationship, becoming financially independent, and becoming a parent. These roles are not taken on in a single typical sequence, and many young adults move in and out of them several times before viewing themselves as totally adult.

5. Adults are marrying at later ages and a greater percentage are cohabiting before marriage, and this is true in developed countries throughout the world. However, marriage remains the preferred form of committed relationship, and over 90 percent of adults in the United States marry at some point in their lives.

6. Although gender roles are egalitarian within early committed relationships, men and women divide household tasks along gender stereotypical lines, and women do more hours of housework even when both work full-time. Married men and women are healthier than single men and women, and the benefit of marriage is far greater for men than for women.

7. Adults are delaying the transition to parenthood in the United States and other developed countries. The percentage of children born to unmarried parents has increased, with over one-third of all births in the United States being to unmarried

parents. However, almost half of these were born to parents who were cohabiting at the time of the birth.

8. When men and women become parents, their gender roles become more traditional. The amount of childcare and housework that fathers do is increasing, but mothers still do more, even when they have full-time jobs.

9. In the middle years of adulthood, the role of parent changes from a day-to-day role to a more distant one as children move out of the house and start their own families, but the role of parent does not end. Most parents find this transition to be positive and use the new freedom to restructure their own lives.

10. Middle age is the time of life when most people become grandparents. This role can take many forms. For a growing number of grandparents, it means stepping in as surrogate parents, which usually involves regaining former roles of day-to-day parenting and returning to work to support a new generation.

11. Another role in the middle years is that of caregiver for aging parents. About a third of middle-aged men and women have at least one parent in poor health who requires care. Although women are often the first-line caregivers, many family members help out. When the burden of caregiving is extreme and long lasting, it can lead to depression, marital problems, and physical illnesses.

12. Social role transitions in late life include learning to live alone, more common for women than for men, and becoming the receiver of care, which can be a difficult transition.

13. Not everyone fits the discussion above. Some people never marry (about 4 percent in the United States). Those who have close relationships with friends and relatives report being as happy and fulfilled as their married peers with children, and they have better health than those who are divorced, separated, or widowed. A growing number of adults over 40 (about 20 percent) have no children. Among retired people, childless adults are as happy as those with children.

14. About one-third of couples marrying today will divorce within 10 years. Most will remarry, causing a number of role transitions, such as ex-spouse, stepmother, and stepfather.

15. Although we have a lot of flexibility today in the timing of social roles, life is still easier when the roles are moved through on-time instead of off-time.

Key Terms

social roles, 134

role transitions, 134

biological clock, 134

social clock, 134

gender roles, 134

gender stereotypes, 134

instrumental qualities, 135

communal qualities, 135

learning-schema theory, 135

social role theory, 135

proximal causes, 135

distal causes, 135

evolutionary psychology, 135

biosocial perspective, 135

transition to adulthood, 137

cohabitation, 141

egalitarian roles, 142

marital selection, 142

marital protection, 142

parental imperative, 145

crossover of gender roles, 149

expansion of gender roles, 149

surrogate parenting, 150

caregiver burden, 153

generational squeeze, 153

role strain theory, 153

role enhancement theory, 153

social timing, 159

Suggested Reading

Reading for Personal Interest

Fisher, H. (2004). *Why we love: The nature of chemistry and romantic love.* New York: Henry Holt.

Helen Fisher is an anthropologist who uses a knowledge of chemistry and neuroimaging to explain what happens when people fall in love.

Hetherington, M. & Kelly, J. (2003). *For better or for worse: Divorce reconsidered.* New York: W. W. Norton.

Psychologist Mavis Hetherington is one of the leading experts on family life and the adjustments required on all parts by divorce. In this book she tells about some of the 1,400 families she has studied over the past 30 years and gives excellent practical advice, based on her research, of what parents can do to adjust to divorce and to help their children through this difficult time

Morris, V. (2004). *How to care for aging parents.* New York: Workman.

As the cover of this book says, "If you think you need this book, you do." Journalist Virginia Morris is a familiar guest on TV shows and this book provides a wealth of solid and compassionate information on caregiving whether you are providing legal and financial advice to your parents or involved in hands-on, day-to-day care.

Rienstra, D., (2002). *Great with child: Reflections on faith, fullness, and becoming a mother.* New York: Tarvher/Putnam.

This book is a highly personal account on how the experience of pregnancy and childbirth changes a woman's life. Debra Rienstra is a professor of English and her husband is a minister. She tells her story with quotes from Shakespeare, the *Bhagavad Gita,* Milton's *Paradise Lost,* the *Better Homes and Gardens* parenting book of the 1950s, the Bible, and feminist poet Lucille Clifton, among others. But best of all she tells a very intimate story about pregnancy and childbirth and attachment and marriage. If you are considering the role of mother or have already stepped into it, this book will probably echo some of your own thoughts and emotions and add others that will further enrich your experience.

Townsend, N. (2002). *The package deal: Marriage, work, & fatherhood in men's lives.* Temple University Press.

Anthropologist Nicholas Townsend has studied a group of men who graduated 30 years ago from a high school in northern California. This book tells about how they feel about fatherhood and the importance of home, intergenerational support, and home ownership. It shows that women are not alone in trying to "have it all," work, marriage, and children.

Classic Work

Eagly, A. H. (1987). Sex differences in social behavior: A social role interpretation. Hillsdale, NJ: Erlbaum.

Social psychologist Alice Eagly suggested her social role theory of gender differences in this article.

Gutmann, D. (1975). Parenthood: A key to the comparative study of the life cycle. In N. Datan & L. H. Ginsberg (Eds.), *Life-span developmental psychology: Normative life crises* (pp. 167–184). New York: Academic Press.

Anthropologist David Gutmann collected data about parenthood practices from a number of cultures to show that there are many similarities, specifically that when young adults become parents they adopt more traditional gender roles than they had as nonparents. His interpretation is a genetic one—that these behaviors are preprogrammed in order to ensure the best chances of the survival of the children.

Contemporary Scholarly Work

Campbell, L., & Ellis, B. J. (2005). Commitment, love, and mate retention. In D. M. Buss (Ed.), *The handbook of evolutionary psychology* (pp. 419–446). Hoboken, NJ: John Wiley & Sons.

This chapter is an explanation of intimate relationships from the viewpoint of evolutionary psychology.

Hamon, R. R., Ingoldsby, B. B. (Eds.) (2003). *Mate selection across cultures.* Thousand Oaks, CA: Sage.

This book contains chapters written by various authors who have researched how people of different cultures select spouses (or have spouses selected for them). Countries included are India, Japan, China, Spain, the Netherlands, Egypt, Israel, Turkey, Ghana, Kenya, Trinidad and Tobago, the Bahamas, and the U.S. It gives a good picture of the global diversity in this relationship process, but also some of the similarities.

Hunter, A. G., & Taylor, R. J. (1998). Grandparenting in African-American families. In M. E. Szinovacz (Ed.), *Handbook on grandparenthood* (pp. 70–86). Westport, CT: Greenwood Press.

Hunter and Taylor cover the topic of grandparenthood in African-American families, discussing the personal meaning grandparenthood has for the individual, the expectations the community holds for grandparents, the social support grandparents give (and receive), and how all these have changed over the past century.

Chapter 6

Social Relationships

THERE ARE NOT many developmental psychology jokes, but this is one a student in my human development class told me many years ago:

A child psychologist was sitting in his office writing a textbook when he heard an annoying sound, "Squeak, squeak, squeak." He looked outside and saw a little child on a tricycle riding across his newly surfaced driveway. He ran outside and yelled angrily at the boy to get off his property and take his tricycle with him. A neighbor observed this and said to him, "How can you call yourself a developmental psychologist and write books on child development when you are so intolerant of little children?" The psychologist replied, "Because, madam, I like children in the abstract, not in the concrete."

Besides it's being a very bad pun, I also like this joke because it helps me keep my priorities straight. I do most of my writing in my office at home, and while I am writing this chapter on relationships, I have a lot of "relating" going on around me, especially of the family variety. It is summer, and two of my grandsons are visiting from Virginia this week. Next week their two sisters will arrive to replace them. Two local grandsons near their age are in and out of the house as well. We have a rule that Grandma works in the mornings, so we'll do fun things in the afternoons, but there are still issues that demand my attention, like whose turn it is to use the raft in the pool and whether they can have leftover pizza for breakfast. When I am

Theories of Social Relationships
Attachment Theory
The Convoy Model
Socioemotional Selectivity
   Theory
Evolutionary Psychology

Intimate Partnerships in Adulthood
Establishing an Intimate
   Relationship
Long-Term Marriages
"Good" and "Bad" Marriages
Cohabitation and Marriage
Gay and Lesbian Partnerships

Relationships with Other Family Members
General Patterns of Family
   Interaction
Parent-Child Relationships in
   Adulthood
Grandparent-Grandchild
   Relationships
Relationships with Brothers
   and Sisters

Friendships in Adulthood

Summary

Key Terms

Suggested Reading

tempted to say, "Please leave me alone so I can write this section on grandparent-grandchild relationships," I remember the joke about the developmental psychologist and laugh.

If I sound a little authoritarian in this chapter on relationships, it is because I am living it as I write—not in the abstract, but smack dab in the concrete.

This chapter deals with **social relationships**—dynamic, recurrent patterns of interactions with other individuals and how they change over the course of adulthood. In Chapter 5, I described the changes that occur within individuals as their social roles change during the years of adulthood; in this chapter I will discuss changes in the give-and-take interactions between people and how such changes affect them (and the people they give to and take from).

If you think about your own social relationships—with your parents, your friends, your spouse or partner, your co-workers—it's clear immediately that these relationships are not all the same, either in intensity or in quality. And if you think back a few years, it should also be clear that each of your relationships has changed somewhat over time. This is the dynamic quality of social interactions—each give and take changes each participant, which, in turn, changes the relationship. The topic is highly personal and complex. A fairly new field, it is difficult to study scientifically, but I think you will find it interesting and important on several levels.

I plan to start this chapter with a discussion of some current theories about the development of relationships, then cover what we know about specific relationships within partnerships, families, and friendships.

Theories of Social Relationships

The study of social relationship development in early childhood is a prominent topic of research and theory, but only recently has attention been focused on social relationships in adulthood. As you will see, attachment theory has extended an early childhood theory into adulthood. Evolutionary psychology deals primarily with the young adult years and intimate partnerships. Socioemotional selectivity theory addresses older adulthood, and the convoy model seem to cross the life span.

Attachment Theory

One of the oldest and best-known theories of social relationships is **attachment theory.** The concept of **attachment** is most commonly used to describe the strong affectional bond formed by an infant to his or her major caregiver. Psychiatrist John Bowlby (1969) and developmental psychologist Mary Ainsworth (Ainsworth, Blehar, Waters, et al., 1978), two of the major theoretical figures in this area, have both made a clear distinction between the attachment itself, which is an invisible, underlying bond, and **attachment behaviors,** which are the ways an underlying attachment is expressed by the person. Since we cannot see the attachment bond, we have to infer it from the attachment behavior. In infants, we see it in their crying when their favored person leaves the room, in their clinging to the favored person when they are frightened, in their use of the favored person as a safe base for exploring some new situation. The three key underlying features are (1) association of the attachment figure with feelings of security, (2) an increased likelihood of attachment behavior when the child is under stress or threat, and (3) attempts to avoid, or to end, any separation from the attachment figure (Weiss, 1982).

In adults, of course, many of these specific attachment behaviors are no longer seen. Most adults do not burst into tears if their special person leaves the room; adults maintain contact in a much wider variety of ways than what we see in young children, including the use of phone calls, e-mail, and imagery. But if we allow for these changes in the attachment behavior, it does appear that the concept of attachment is a useful way to think about many adult relationships.

First of all, we appear to form strong new attachments in adulthood, particularly to a spouse or partner, and we usually maintain our attachment to our parents as well. As one attachment theorist puts it, "In all these instances individuals display need for ready access to the attachment figure, desire for proximity to the attachment figure in situations of stress, heightened comfort and diminished anxiety when in the company of the attachment figure, and a marked increase in discomfort and anxiety on discovering the attachment figure to be inexplicably inaccessible" (Weiss, 1982, p. 173).

Attachment theorists suggest that very young children can be classified according to their attachment behavior as exhibiting either *secure, anxious,* or *avoidant* attachment. More precisely, they propose that each child creates an **internal working model** of attachment relationships, which are a set of beliefs and assumptions about the nature of all relationships, such as whether others will respond if you need them and whether others are trustworthy. Based on early childhood experiences, this internal working model has components of security or insecurity.

Developmental psychologist Mary Main and her colleagues (Main & Hesse, 1990; Main, Kaplan, & Cassidy, 1985) extended this theory to adulthood, suggesting that each adult also has a basic internal working model of attachment, based on, but not necessarily identical to, the internal model created by the child in the early years of life. Main devised the Adult Attachment Inventory (AAI), a way to measure adult attachment using an interview in which the subject was asked to talk about his or her childhood experiences and current relationship with his or her parents. Based on an analysis of this interview, Main identified three types of adult attachment, as shown in Table 6.1.

Longitudinal research shows that an infant's attachment classification tends to remain stable into young adulthood (Waters, Merrick, Albersheim, et al., 1995), and other studies show that adults' attachment classifications correspond to their children's classifications on infancy attachment measures (van IJzendoorn, 1995). Adult attachment is also related to the care middle-aged adults give to their elderly parents (Cicirelli, 1998). Considered together, this evidence points to attachment as being a relatively enduring mental representation that is established in the early years and continues into adulthood, enabling the adult to establish a similar relationship with his or her own children.

> ● **CRITICAL THINKING**
>
> Where were you on September 11, 2001? Were there attachment figures you needed to contact? What were your emotions before and after you were in touch with them?

Table 6.1	**Types of Adult Attachment**
Secure/Autonomous/Balanced	These adults value attachment relations and view those relationships as having been influential in their current personalities. The subjects speak freely and coherently about their early experiences and have thought about what motivated their parents' behavior.
Dismissing or Detached	These adults minimize the importance or the effects of their early experience. They may idealize their parents but have poor recall of their childhood, often denying negative experiences and emotions or calling them normal or typical. Their emphasis is on their own personal strengths.
Preoccupied or Enmeshed	These adults often talk about inconsistent or role-reversed parenting. They may be confused about their experiences or about what was expected of them. As adults, those in this group are still caught up in their family and in their relationships, still struggling either with anger or with the desire to please.

Source: Main & Hesse (1990); Main, Kaplan, & Cassidy (1985).

Over the last two decades, attachment theory has been useful in explaining adult relationships outside the family, such as romantic relationships, as will be discussed later in this chapter.

The Convoy Model

Another approach to relationships in adulthood comes from developmental psychologist Toni Antonucci and her colleagues (Kahn & Antonucci, 1980; Antonucci, 1990), who use the term **convoy** to describe the ever-changing network of social relationships that surrounds each of us throughout our adult lives. "Convoy relationships serve to both shape and protect individuals, sharing with them life experiences, challenges, successes, and disappointments" (Antonucci, Akiyama, & Takahashi, 2004, p. 353.). These relationships affect how the individual experiences the world. They are reciprocal and developmental; as the individual changes and develops through time, the nature of the relationships and interactions is also likely to change

CRITICAL THINKING

Who is in the inner circle of your convoy? What about the middle and outer circles? What changes would you predict 10 years from now?

In her research using the convoy model, Antonucci (1986) developed a mapping technique. She asked respondents to report on three levels of relationships and write the names of the people within three concentric circles. The inner circle is for names of people who are so close and important to the respondent that he or she could hardly imagine life without them. The middle circle is for people who are also close, but not as close as those in the inner circle. And the outer circle is for names of people who are part of the respondent's personal network but not as close as the other two groups. The convoy map is useful for comparing age differences in both the size and the contents of social networks.

For example, in a recent study, the social convoys of men and women of different ages from the United States and Japan were examined (Antonucci, Akiyama, & Takahashi, 2004) to investigate differences and similarities in the number of people in their social networks and also the particular people they named in each circle. Figure 6.1 show the composition of these, showing age-related changes in social networks. Names written higher in the circles were given more frequently than those lower. As you can see, in young adulthood (20–39 years), the closest circle for both groups contained mother, spouse, son, and daughter. The Japanese social networks included the father; the U.S. networks did not.

The 40- to 59-year-old groups continued to name spouse, daughter, son, and mother, but the mother was named less frequently than the spouse and the daughter for both groups, showing perhaps that the relationships with the daughters grew more important as the daughters became adults.

At 60 to 69 years, the mother had left the central circle (no doubt due to death); the sister has joined the closest group for the U.S. respondents (probably because people in the United States have more siblings), and the son was mentioned more frequently than the daughter for the Japanese respondents. At 70 to 79 years the spouse was not named as frequently as the son (in Japan) and the daughter (in the United States), probably due to death of the spouse. The sister remained in the U.S. group, but did not appear in the Japanese group. For the oldest group (80–93 years), daughters were named more than sons (and spouses), and grandsons entered the picture for the Japanese participants.

Antonucci and her colleagues suggest some reasons for the age differences in the two cultures' convoy contents. Their major emphasis, however, is on how similar the Japanese and U.S. groups were in both number of convoy members and convoy contents, and how similar the convoys were for the male and female participants. These similarites

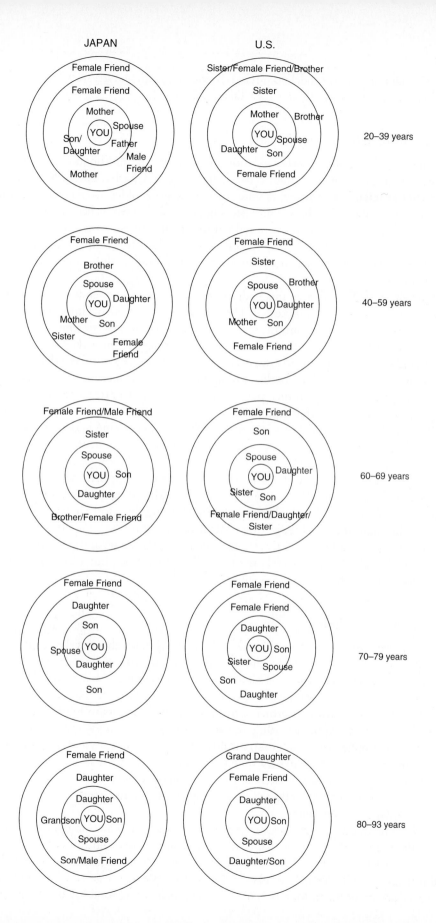

Figure 6.1 Social convoys of U.S. men and women were compared to those of Japanese men and women for five different age groups. Although there were some cultural differences and gender differences, the greatest differences for both groups were the content of the social convoys over the course of adulthood.

Source: Adapted from Antonucci, Akiyama, & Takahashi (2004).

indicate that the convoy model no doubt taps into some universal aspect of human social relationships (Antonucci, Akiyama, & Takahashi, 2004).

Socioemotional Selectivity Theory

Yet another explanation of social relationship changes in adulthood comes from psychologist Laura Carstensen (1995; Carstensen, Fung, & Charles, 2003). Known as **socioemotional selectivity theory,** it states that as we grow older, we tend to prefer more meaningful social relationships. This results in our social networks becoming smaller but more selective as we devote our limited emotional and physical resources to a smaller group of relationships that are deeply satisfying emotionally. In other words, the quantity of social relationships declines with age, but the overall quality remains the same (or even better).

Carstensen explains that younger adults perceive time as open-ended, measuring it by how long they have been on this earth. They are motivated to pursue information, knowledge, and relationships. In contrast, older adults perceive time as constrained, measuring it in terms of how long they have left on this earth. They are motivated to pursue emotional satisfaction, deepening existing relationships and weeding out those that are not satisfying. Research findings have backed this up by showing distinct age differences in social relationships and also the topics people are most likely to attend to and remember (Carstensen, Mickels, & Mather, 2006).

In a study of adults aged 18 to 94, no age differences were found in the number of close relationships reported (Fung, Carstensen, & Lang, 2001). However, older people reported fewer peripheral social relationships than younger people. When younger people had a larger proportion of close social relationships compared to peripheral ones, they reported lower levels of happiness. This was not true for the older people. This is a good demonstration of the socioemotional selectivity theory, showing that closer relationships are important throughout adult life, but peripheral relationships become effortful with age because energy is limited and activities of daily life take up more and more time. Having more close friends than peripheral ones is satisfying in old age, but a correlate of unhappiness for younger adults.

Evolutionary Psychology

The final theory to be discussed is based on the growing belief that social relationships had an important role in human evolution, perhaps the central role in the design of the human mind (Buss & Kenrick, 1998). This is based on the premise that our early ancestors banded together in small social groups as an important survival strategy (Caporeal, 1997). Social relationships provided protection from predators, access to food, and insulation from the cold. Simply put, according to **evolutionary psychology,** individuals who carried genes for cooperativeness, group loyalty, adherence to norms, and promotion of social inclusion were more apt to survive in the primal environment and pass on these genes to their descendants (and ultimately to us). These genes continue to affect our social and cognitive behavior and are reflected in the ways we form and maintain social relationships in today's environment.

According to this theory, today's members of our species have biological systems that foster the formation and maintenance of social relationships, and this is manifested in a universal "need to belong." This need drives us to engage in frequent and pleasurable social interactions with a small number of familiar people who care about us and depend on us to care about them. Members of all human societies respond to distress and protest

Our species' ability to form social bonds and be loyal and cooperative within our "tribe" may be due to genetic inheritance from our primitive ancestors, who found these abilities crucial to survival in their environment.

when they are separated from their social group or when a close relationship ends. (Baumeister & Leary, 1995). The need to belong is observed in all human societies and in many other primate social species (de Waal, 1996).

You have no doubt noticed that these theories have a lot of similarities. In fact the proponents of convoy theory are now writing about attachment as the "glue" that holds the convoys together, and writing about socioemotional selectivity as evidence that the convoy model applies to later adulthood. Evolutionary psychologists are referring to attachment as an evolved mechanism to ensure the survival of infants. It seems pretty clear that the theories have more similarities than differences. There has been an active movement in the social sciences to pursue a multidisciplinary approach to this important topic (Berscheid, 1999). I think you will see even more evidence of this convergence as I use these theories to discuss specific types of relationships, beginning with intimate partnerships.

Intimate Partnerships in Adulthood

One social relationship that almost all adults experience is the intimate partnership. Most of the research on this topic involves married couples, but I will also discuss cohabiting relationships, both with heterosexual and same-sex partners. And I will also include some of the first research findings on gay and lesbian couples in civil unions. Although it seems like a variety of topics, I think you will find that romantic partners in committed relationships, whatever the nature of the relationship, have more similarities with each other than differences.

Establishing an Intimate Relationship

The process of choosing a life partner and formalizing the relationship is found in every known culture; 90 percent of people in the world will marry at some point in their lives (Campbell & Ellis, 2005). How such partnerships are arrived at has been the interest of researchers for some time, and in recent studies this process has been referred to as **mate selection.** The majority of people in the world select their own mates and do it on the basis of a combination of subjective feelings that include "euphoria, intense focused attention on a preferred individual, obsessive thinking about him or her, emotional dependency on and craving for emotional union with this beloved, and increased energy" (Aron, Fisher, Mashek, et al., 2005, p. 327). Anthropologist Helen L. Fisher (2000; 2004), suggests that mate selection depends on three distinct emotional systems: lust, attraction, and attachment. Each of these systems has its own neurological wiring. The *lust system* causes men and women to experience sexual desire and seek out sexual opportunities. The *attraction system* directs men and women to attend to specific potential mates and to desire an emotional relationship with them. The *attachment system* drives men and women to be close to the target of attraction (and lust) and to feel comfortable, secure, and emotionally dependent with that person. Fisher's theory of relationship formation seems like a good one to me, and it makes a good model for viewing the components of the process of partnership formation.

Lust. This system should be familiar to all psychology majors, not because of their torrid personal lives but because it was the cornerstone of Freud's classic psychoanalytic theory. Freud believed that **libido,** or sexual desire, was the foundation of all intimate relationships, and that one's experience of such relationships depends on how much sexual desire one feels for the other person, whether one is consciously aware of it or not (Jones, 1981). Lust is certainly part of romantic love, but it can also operate independently. Most adults are familiar with feelings of lust toward someone they have no romantic involvement with and also the inverse—not feeling sexual desire toward someone they do have a romantic involvement with. The lust system is powered by androgens in both men and women. Some evidence suggests that the hormones responsible for attachment may decrease the levels of androgen, causing sexual desire to decline as attachment increases. Using an automobile analogy, lust could be viewed as the accelerator of romantic love.

Attraction. If lust is the accelerator in Fisher's theory, then attraction is the steering wheel, determining where the lust will be directed. The experience of attraction is also known as romantic love, obsessive love, passion (Sternberg 1986), passionate love (Hatfield, 1988), and limerance, which is described as thinking of the other person all the time, even when you are trying to think of other things, and feeling exquisite pleasure when the other person seems to return your feelings (Tennov, 1979). Mate-attraction behavior is observed in every known human culture (Jankowiak & Fischer, 1992) and in all mammals and birds (Fisher, 2000). The attraction system is associated with increased levels of dopamine and norepinephrine and decreased levels of serotonin, all neurotransmitters in the brain.

In a study of brain activity, young men and women who reported being in love for 1 to 7 months were shown a photo of their loved one and asked to think about a pleasurable event that had occurred when they were together (Aron, Fisher, Mashek, et al., 2005). As a control, they were shown a photo of a neutral person in their lives and asked to think about pleasurable events with that person. Results showed that viewing a photo of their loved one and thinking about a pleasant interaction with him or her activated regions of the brain that are rich in dopamine receptors, regions that are associated with the motivation to acquire a reward. These regions were not activated when the participants turned their attention and thoughts to a neutral person. Furthermore, the length of time a person had been in love caused different activation patterns; the more recent the relationship, the stronger the activation. The authors emphasize that the patterns of brain activation for new romantic love are different from those associated with the sex drive (or lust system, as Fisher calls it), indicating that they are distinct systems.

The topic of what attracts one person to another, or two people to each other, was traditionally explained by **filter theory,** which states that we begin with a large pool of potential mates and gradually filter out those who do not fit our specifications (Cate & Lloyd, 1992). An alternative explanation was **exchange theory,** which says that we all have certain assets to offer in a relationship, and we try to make the best deal we can. For example, a woman with domestic skills might be willing to exchange them for a man who has a good income. Or an older man with a well-known family name and good income might exchange them for a young woman with good physical features (Schoen & Wooldredge, 1989).

Evolutionary psychologists have a somewhat different explanation of mate selection, although their conclusions are similar. Their explanation is based on our ancient ancestors' need to increase their chances of reproducing and of providing for their children until they were old enough to fend for themselves. Men, who needed someone to bear and feed their children, looked for fertility—young women with healthy features, especially those related to childbearing, such as large breasts and optimal hip-to-waist measurement ratios. Women, who needed someone to care for their needs during pregnancy and to protect them and their infants during the first few years after birth, looked for men with status and resources.

These preferences in mate selection have been demonstrated in studies across cultures. For example, psychologist Todd Shackelford and his colleagues examined data from over 9,000 young adults living in 37 different cultures around the world and found sex differences on three out of four universal dimensions of mate preference for long-term relationships. As predicted by evolutionary psychology, women value social status and financial resources more than men do, and also dependability, stability, and intelligence. Men value good looks, health, and a desire for home and children more than women do (Shackelford, Schmitt, & Buss, 2005).

In another study, these preferences were demonstrated across time in data from college students that spanned a period of 57 years (Buss, Shackelford, Kirkpatrick, et al., 2001). Groups of young men and women were surveyed in 1939, 1956, 1967, 1977, 1984–85, and 1996 and asked to rate how important various characteristics were to them in selecting a partner for a long-term relationship. The top-10 characteristics for the most recent group are shown in Table 6.2. To the right of each characteristic is the rank order it was given by the 1939 cohort.

The results of this study showed that the biggest gender difference in mate preference is that men across all five decades place more importance on women who are physically attractive (good looks), and women place greater importance on men who will be good providers for their families (desire for home and children, ambition, industriousness). This finding supports the main tenets of evolutionary psychology, but other aspects of the study also support some of the refinements of modern evolutionary science—the idea that culture and evolution are integrated. For example, chastity as a characteristic for a potential mate was in 10th place for the 1939 college students, but fell to 16th for men and 17th for women in the most recent cohort. Buss suggests that this reflects the advances in reliable birth control devices and the sexual revolution of the 1960s.

> **● CRITICAL THINKING**
>
> In Table 6.2, the desire for a home and children ranks higher for women than for men. How would you explain this gender difference?

Attachment. Fisher's attachment system has some similarity to its namesake, Bowlby's attachment theory, discussed earlier in this chapter. Although Bowlby initially formulated his theory to explain parent-infant relationships, he believed that attachment was a lifelong process and that the quality of relationship one had with parents was the base for later attachments, including romantic partnerships. Recent attachment theorists have suggested

Table 6.2	Rank Order of Preferences for Long-Term Relationship Characteristics for Young Men and Women in 1996 (and 1939)		
Men's Mate Preferences Top Ten Characteristics in 1996 (Rank Order in 1939)		**Women's Mate Preferences Top Ten Characteristics in 1996 (Rank Order in 1939)**	
1	Mutual attraction, love (4)	1	Mutual Attraction, love (5)
2	Dependable character (1)	2	Dependable character (2)
3	Emotional stability, maturity (2)	3	Emotional stability, maturity (1)
4	Pleasing disposition (3)	4	Pleasing disposition (4)
5	Education, intelligence (11)	5	Education, intelligence (9)
6	Good health (5)	6	Desire for home, children (7)
7	Sociability (12)	7	Ambition, industriousness (3)
8	Good looks (14)	8	Sociability (11)
9	Desire for home, children (6)	9	Good health (6)
10	Ambition, industriousness (9)	10	Similar educational background (12)

Source: Adapted from Buss, Shackelford, Kirkpatrick, et al. (2001).

that attachment between romantic partners is a mechanism that evolved to keep parents together long enough to raise their children. Men and women who are able to feel secure together and lonely when apart are more apt to be committed to each other and to the task of raising their child safely into adulthood. Interestingly, the hormone oxytocin plays a central role in mother-infant attachment and also in women's romantic attachment to a mate (Campbell & Ellis, 2005).

Another link between early childhood attachment relationships with one's parents and adult attachment relationships with one's intimate partners is the topic of a large portion of adult attachment research. As mentioned before, extensions of Bowlby's attachment theory have been used to suggest that adult romantic relationship styles are reflections of the attachment bond the adults had with their parents in childhood (Bartholomew, 1990; Hazan & Shaver, 1987). In one demonstration, psychologists Cindy Hazan and Phillip Shaver (1991) gave adults a questionnaire with three descriptions and asked them to select the one that best characterized the way they felt about romantic relationships. The three descriptions paralleled Ainsworth's three types of attachment in infants. Initial findings were that the proportion of adults selecting each style are similar to the proportion of infants classified in each style (approximately 55 percent secure, 20 percent anxious, and 25 percent avoidant), which suggests that these styles in young-adult romantic relationships reflect internal working models of attachment established in early childhood. Later research by others (Feeney & Noller, 1996; Mikulincer & Orbach, 1995) confirmed these percentages, and a study by Shaver and colleagues shows that the proportions are similar in people who range in age from 15 to 54 years (Michelson, Kessler, & Shaver, 1997). It has also been shown that attachment styles are relatively stable over time—at least for several years (Feeney & Noller, 1996).

Subsequent research showed that adults who classified themselves as secure reported higher levels of satisfaction with their relationships than those who classified themselves in the anxious and avoidant categories (Brennan & Shaver, 1995). People showing anxious attachment were more obsessed with their relationships than were secure or avoidant people and reported more frequent partners and more frequent breakups (Kirkpatrick & Davis, 1994). Participants showing avoidant attachment tended to react to stress in a relationship by withdrawing from their partners (Simpson, Rholes, & Nelligan, 1992). And what are securely attached people like as relationship partners? "Secure adults communicate their feelings more accurately and sensitively than insecure adults, perceptively notice their partners' needs and feelings, respond more empathically, and express more optimism about the relationship" (Koski & Shaver, 1997, p. 44).

An extension of Hazan and Shaver's model has been proposed that has four categories of attachment styles based on a person's model of the self and others (Bartholomew & Horowitz, 1991). Based on self-reported ratings of how well different statements describe their own attitudes toward relationships, people are classified as *secure* (having a positive model of both self and others), *dismissing* (having a positive model of self and a negative model of others), *preoccupied* (negative model of self and positive model of others), or *fearful* (negative model of both self and others). The descriptions used in this study are shown in Table 6.3, along with the attachment classifications that correspond to each. Using this relationship questionnaire with young adults, the researchers found that almost half rated themselves as secure, while the other half were equally distributed among the remaining three categories.

It is still not clear what role infant attachment plays in adult romantic relationships. The research on this question is correlational, and the fact that the same proportion of people fall into similar categories in adulthood as in childhood is not definitive proof that early attachment bonds continue into adulthood and influence romantic relationships. It is argued that there are fundamental differences between the two relationships: Infants are dependent on parents, and there is an inequality in the relationship. The parent anticipates and then fulfills the infant's needs, while the infant, by contrast, is clueless. In romantic relationships, there is more of an equality, with both members giving and receiving care and engaging in mutual intimacy as autonomous individuals (Bell & Richard, 2000). Another point of view holds that the adult form of attachment is found in concern for the next generation and not in romantic relationships (McAdams, 2000).

> ● **CRITICAL THINKING**
>
> Which romantic attachment style best describes you? Do you see a correspondence between your adult attachment type and the relationship you had with your parents as a young child?

Table 6.3	**Adult Romantic Attachment Styles**
Attachment Type	**Description**
Secure	"It is relatively easy for me to become emotionally close to others. I am comfortable depending on others and having others depend on me. I don't worry about being alone or having others not accept me."
Preoccupied	"I want to be completely emotionally intimate with others, but I often find that others are reluctant to get as close as I would like. I am uncomfortable being without close relationships, but I sometimes worry that others don't value me as much as I value them."
Fearful	"I am somewhat uncomfortable getting close to others. I want emotionally close relationships, but I find it difficult to trust others completely or to depend on them. I sometimes worry that I will be hurt if I allow myself to become too close to others."
Dismissing	"I am comfortable without close emotional relationships. It is very important to me to feel independent and self-sufficient, and I prefer not to depend on others or have others depend on me."

Source: Adapted from Bartholomew & Horowitz (1991).

On the other hand, one study provides support for the argument that early attachment is the precursor of later romantic relationships. It is part of a longitudinal study conducted by sociologist Rand Conger and his colleagues (Conger, Cui, Bryant, et al., 2000), in which 193 young adults in their early 20s were interviewed along with their romantic partners. Information about their relationship quality was compared to information about their family life when they were in 7th grade to determine which aspects of family life were most related to successful romantic relationships (those that were warm, supportive, low in hostility). Surprisingly, the parents' relationship was not a significant factor. It didn't matter what kind of relationship the parents had with each other while the child was growing up. What mattered most was the relationship between the young person and his or her parents during that time. So the jury is still out on this issue, and it continues to be a popular topic of research and theory.

Long-Term Marriages

The preceding discussion has covered different thinking on how partners select each other, but what happens after that? As you well know, not all couples who marry or otherwise commit to a partnership end up living happily ever. Some do, but others drift into empty relationships, some divorce, and some live together in a constant war zone. What makes the difference? This is both an academic question and a practical one. Almost all of us wind up in partnerships of one kind or another, and it's safe to say that almost all of us want them to be happy and long-lasting. We know a good deal about what goes wrong with marriages, thanks to studies of couples in therapy, but we don't know a lot about what goes right. However, several longitudinal studies have looked into this very topic—and one has considered racial/ethnic factors in long-term, committed relationships.

In a 10-year longitudinal study of marriages, the Denver Family Project, psychologist Howard Markman and colleagues (Lindahl, Clements, & Markman, 1998; Lindahl, Malik, & Bradbury, 1997) studied couples from before marriage until well past their 10th anniversaries. For this group, marital satisfaction declined during the first 3 years but then leveled off and remained stable during the remainder of the first decade. Even though there were significant drops in marital satisfaction, most respondents expressed little distress about their relationships.

About 20 percent of the couples in the Denver Family Project divorced during the 10 years they were being studied. When Markman compared the data collected before marriage from the divorce group to the data from the nondivorce group, some interesting differences emerged. Women in the divorce group had been younger at the time of marriage than those in the nondivorce group and showed a lack of problem-solving skills. Men in the divorce group had expressed more negativity about the relationship than those in the nondivorce group. And both men and women in the divorce group had shown greater inability to acknowledge and accept the thoughts and feelings their partner expressed about the relationship.

The Denver Family Project also offered the participating couples marriage counseling, some of which was successful and some not. When the two types of outcomes were compared, several factors stood out that predicted poor chances of restoring the marriage: if the husband made comments to the wife that were insulting, hostile, and destructive; if the wife was unable (or unwilling) to contribute to solving their problems; and if both spouses were insensitive to the emotional needs of the other. In other words, partners who are willing to listen and pay attention to each other, respond to each other's needs, and make attempts to find solutions to their problems have greater chances of successful marriages.

One criticism of studies of long-term marriages are that the samples consist largely of white middle-class couples. In fact, in a meta-analysis of longitudinal studies of marriages, researchers found that 75 percent of the samples were white and middle-class (Karney & Bradbury, 1995). Since these participants don't begin to represent the general population of the United States, much less the rest of the world, this is a problem. However, one study has addressed this in a straightforward way. Researchers in social work Richard Mackey and Bernard O'Brien (1999) selected a sample of 60 long-term married couples. The group included white, African American, and Mexican American couples who were diverse in religion, education, income, age (40 to 70 years), and number of children (1 to more than 5). What the couples did have in common was that all had been married for at least 20 years and had experienced no extensive marriage problems.

Each spouse was interviewed about aspects of their marriage during three time periods—the beginning (before children), the child-rearing years, and the empty-nest years (after the children had left home). The results are shown in Figure 6.2. Panel 1 in the upper left shows the couples' *overall marital satisfaction* at each point in time. The decline during the child-rearing years for women is very dramatic, going from 63 percent in the beginning years to 50 percent in the child-rearing years. Men's overall satisfaction

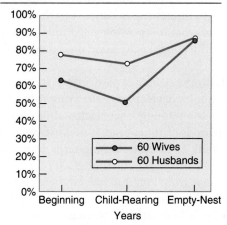

Panel 1. *Percentage of respondents reporting marital satisfaction over the years.*

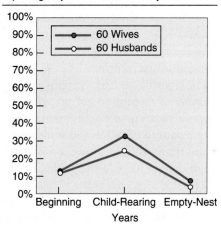

Panel 2. *Percentage of wives and husbands reporting major conflicts over the years.*

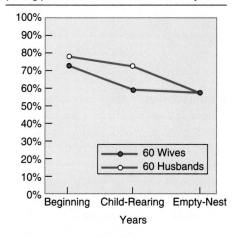

Panel 3. *Percentage of wives and husbands reporting positive sexual relations over the years.*

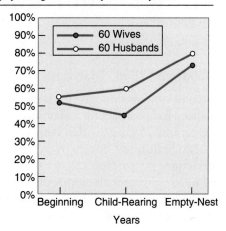

Panel 4. *Percentage of respondents reporting psychological intimacy over the years.*

Figure 6.2 A diverse group of long-time married couples recalled the quality of their relationships across the years on four variables.
Source: Adapted from Mackey & O'Brien (1999).

declined less (78 percent to 73 percent) during the child-rearing years, and large percentages of both spouses reported overall satisfaction in the empty-nest years (85 percent for wives and 87 percent for husbands).

Panel 2 in the upper right of Figure 6.2 shows the pattern of *major conflicts,* defined as those that disrupted the relationship and caused emotional distance, diminished communication, and feelings of unhappiness. As you can see, couples reported low rates of major conflict in the beginning years, significantly more in the child-rearing years (especially for wives), and the lowest levels in the empty-nest years.

The graph in Panel 3, shown in the lower left of Figure 6.2 shows the percentages of couples reporting *positive sexual relations,* defined as being satisfied with both the quality and the frequency of their sexual relations. In the beginning years, approximately three-quarters of the husbands and wives reported positive sexual relations, but this declined during the next two time periods. The empty-nest years found about 55 percent of both husbands and wives reporting positive sexual relations.

CRITICAL THINKING

Looking over the four panels in Figure 6.2, compare the wives' reports of their relationship during the child-rearing years with the husbands'. What explanation could you offer about why the wives seemed to have more difficulty during those years than the husbands?

The percentage of couples reporting *psychological intimacy* is shown in Panel 4, which you can see in the lower right of Figure 6.2. This is defined as comfort and closeness in sharing personal thoughts and feelings with their spouses. As you can see, the wives show the familiar curvilinear pattern of higher scores at the beginning and empty-nest time periods and lower scores in the child-rearing time period, with husbands showing a slight increase in the child-rearing years. This finding is interesting in contrast to the pattern for sexual relations in the preceding panel. It seems that it is possible for couples to grow in the ability to share their personal thoughts and feelings at the same time they are declining in sexual relations.

The study has several strengths along with its diverse sample of participants. It taps into a number of dimensions of the relationships couples develop over the years instead of using one measure of overall marital satisfaction. Interestingly, these factors didn't follow a single pattern of progress through the three periods of time. Studies that use only one general relationship measure to evaluate something as complex as long-term marriages, are not doing justice to their subject matter.

The study also has some weaknesses. It was not truly longitudinal; all the data were collected at once and depended on the participants' memories about earlier times in their marriages. And I am not too comfortable with the "all-or-nothing" scoring. For example, people were classified as either positive or negative about their satisfaction with their sexual relations—much too simple an answer for so complicated a question. However, all that being said, Mackey and O'Brien's study remains a relatively elegant study of diverse long-term marriages.

"Good" and "Bad" Marriages

A second window through which we can look at intimate partnerships is a comparison of good and bad or successful and unsuccessful marriages. It is important for men and women to enter into marriage with a sense of commitment, good problem-solving skills, maturity, and healthy self-esteem. However, the most central factor seems to be the pattern of interactions the partners create together. The most consistent difference between happy and unhappy couples is simply the relative proportion of "nice" or "nasty" everyday encounters. Psychologist John Gottman and his colleagues (Gottman & Notarius, 2000) have shown very clearly that couples who will eventually divorce can be identified years ahead of time by looking at the pattern of positive and negative exchanges. In fact, Gottman claims that he is able to observe a couple's interactions for an hour and predict with 95 percent accuracy whether they will still be together in 15 years (Carrére & Gottman, 1999). When negative items like the ones Gottman singled out as the "Four Horsemen of the Apocalypse"—*criticism, contempt, defensiveness,* and*stonewalling*— exceed the positive by too much, divorce becomes far more likely (Gottman, Katz, & Hooven, 1997). "One can think of each partner in a marriage as having a built-in meter that measures the totality of accumulated negativity in this interaction" (Gottman,1994a, p. 333). He proposes that once the level of the meter rises above some threshold, the partner's perception of the marriage "flips" from positive to negative. The accumulation of negativity may be gradual, but the feeling, the perception, switches rapidly, and the person then considers separation or divorce.

But Gottman (1994b) is not proposing that all good marriages are alike and that all bad marriages are the same. His research suggests that there are three quite different types of stable or enduring marriages.

- *Validating marriages.* In these marriages, disagreements rarely escalate. The partners listen, say, "Mmm-hmm" or "I see" a lot, and express mutual respect even when they disagree.
- *Volatile marriages.* These couples squabble a lot, disagree, and don't listen to each other very well when they argue. But they also laugh and show more affection than the average couple. They approach all their interactions with more passion, but the balance of positive and negative is in favor of positive.
- *Avoidant marriages.* Gottman also calls these couples "conflict minimizers." They don't try to persuade each other, they simply agree to disagree, without apparent rancor.

There are also two distinct types of unsuccessful marriages, each having its own trajectory toward divorce (Gottman & Levenson, 2002):

- *Hostile negative marriages.* These couples show high levels of anger toward each other, with the wife expressing disappointment and negative emotions directed at her husband. This behavior in the first few years of marriage predicts that the couple is likely to divorce early, around seven years after they married.
- *Emotionally unexpressive marriages.* These couples show extreme lack of emotion, either positive or negative, when they interact. There is little affection, humor, anger, or facial expressions. Their physiological measures show high levels of skin conductivity, an indicator of suppressing emotional expression. Couples who display this behavior in the first few years of marriage are likely to divorce at midlife, probably after years of distance and isolation.

> **● CRITICAL THINKING**
>
> Gottman does not believe that anger is necessarily a bad thing in marriages. Think of a situation that would cause anger between spouses. Tell how the situation might be handled by a couple in a volatile marriage and how the same situation might be handled by a couple in a hostile negative marriage.

Fortunately, negative patterns in marriage can be changed. Therapists who work with couples have found that marital satisfaction can be increased significantly by teaching couples how to understand each other better, increase affection, attend to each other and influence each other more, practice healthy conflict resolution, and create shared meaning within their relationship. It is possible for couples whose relationships have grown distant or hostile to acquire new skills or relearn earlier patterns of interaction (Gottman & Silver, 1999). Some of Gottman's principles for successful marriages are shown in Table 6.4.

Cohabitation and Marriage

In Chapter 5 I discussed the role transition from single adult to cohabiting partner and how this transition is becoming increasingly common in the United States and other de-

Table 6.4	**Principles for a Successful Marriage**

Get to know your spouse's inner world. Who are your partner's best friends, what are your partner's life's dreams, basic philosophy of life, hopes in life, major sources of stress recently, favorite music? Have you shared yours with your partner?

Nurture fondness and admiration for your partner. What first attracted you to each other? What are your partner's achievements and sources of pride? Be glad to see each other when you meet at the end of the day and when you wake up in the morning. Let each other know that you love and care for each other. Make time for romance and sex.

Turn toward each other, not away. Let your partner into your life by discussing the happenings of your day and listening to theirs. Keep in touch during the day. Participate in each other's free-time activities. Do shopping or errands together. Talk together, watch TV together, travel together. Make being together a priority, not just a convenience.

Let your partner influence you. Value your partner's opinion and seek it often. Let your partner know that you listen to their advice and take it seriously. Ask for help when solving problems. Be willing to discuss small issues in your relationship.

Know the difference between solvable problems and perpetual problems. Work on the solvable ones, and learn to respect your partner's viewpoint on the perpetual ones.

Create shared meaning. Make small rituals of mealtimes, weekends, holidays. Enjoy the symbols of your relationship, such as wedding photos and gifts you have given each other. Reminisce together. Tell (and retell) stories about how you first met, how you selected the name of your first child, what you did on your first vacation together.

Source: Gottman & Silver (1999).

veloped countries. I would like to add a note about the relationships that are formed between cohabiting couples and what effect they have on subsequent marriages.

About 58 percent of cohabiting couples in the United States today will end up married to each other (Bramlett & Masher, 2002). What is the effect of cohabitation on subsequent marriage? One popular notion is that cohabitation is a trial run for marriage, and that couples who marry after living together will be more successful because they "know what they are getting into," and "have all the problems ironed out." One survey showed that 61 percent of young adults believed this (Johnson, Stanley, Glenn, et al., 2002). However, research shows that when married couples have lived together before marriage, the divorce rates are higher than for couples who followed the more traditional route of moving in together after marriage (Kieran, 2002). They also have lower marital satisfaction (Stanley, Whitton, & Markman, 2004) and poorer communication patterns (Cohan & Kleinbaum, 2002).

CRITICAL THINKING ●

Before you read on, what are your thoughts about cohabitation? Do you believe it is helpful for a couple to live together so that they can get all their problems worked out before marriage? Do you think couples who cohabit before marriage have better marriages than those who move in together after marriage?

Why would this be true? Some argue that there is a selection effect—those who are more mature and have stronger relationships follow the traditional path to marriage, while those with doubts and troubled relationships opt for cohabitation first (Woods & Emery, 2002). Others believe that the experience of cohabiting changes the couple's attitudes about marriage (Magdol, Moffitt, Caspi, et al., 1998). However, a study by psychologist Howard Markman and his colleagues (Kline, Stanley, Markman, et al., 2004) showed that there are two distinct types of cohabitation relationships that lead to marriage; one in which the couple becomes engaged before moving in together, and then gets married,

Couples whose marriages have become distant or hostile can make changes in their patterns of inter-action that lead to greater understanding, affection, and shared meaning.

and the other in which the couple becomes engaged after moving in together, and then marries. The former tends to lead to marriages as successful as couples who did not co-habit before marriage; the latter tends to lead to less successful marriages. Why? The au-thors conclude that couples who become engaged before moving in together are ready to make a formal commitment to each other and that their relationships are more similar to those of couples who marry before living together than to those of couples who cohabit without that commitment.

Given the recent increase in births to cohabiting couples, researchers have also begun to look into such matters as the differences between cohabiting families and married fam-ilies and the effect of the parents' marital status on the children. In one such study, de-velopmental psychologists Stacey Rosenkrantz Aronson and Aletha Huston (2004) compared mother-infant relationships in three types of families: single-mother families, two-parent cohabiting families, and two-parent married families. They found that the mother-infant relationships were better in the two-parent married families than the other groups, with single-mother families and two-parent cohabiting families showing the same low level of mother-infant attachment. A closer look revealed that selection effects ac-counted for most of the differences. Single mothers and cohabiting mothers were similar in that they were younger and less educated. Surprisingly, such factors as family income, the time the mother spent with the infant, and the social support the mother received from friends and family did not make a difference in the mother-child relationship. The re-searchers concluded that there are problems involved with being a single mother with no partner in the home, but the problem is *not* simply the absence of the child's father; the problems are within the parents themselves and their relationship. Individual factors of the mothers (and no doubt the fathers) who choose to marry contribute to better mother-infant relationships than the factors of those who choose to remain single or to cohabit. The authors warn us against believing that family problems can be solved simply by adding the father's presence to the single-mother family.

My interpretation of these findings is that marriage has become an optional relationship for parents-to-be, and as a result it means *more* than it ever did before. A generation ago marriage was a "piece of paper" to many, required for young adults to have a sexual relationship, live together, or have children. Today marriage represents taking a relationship to a new level of commitment. Sadly, for many the choice to become parents doesn't carry the same weight. This is not to say that marriages today are going to last longer or be happier in the long run, but it seems that when couples are willing to commit to marriage, (or even become engaged, as discussed in the previous study) they are more mature and better able to establish solid relationships with each other and with their new child.

Gay and Lesbian Partnerships

Long-lasting, committed relationships between same-sex partners are very common today, and it is possible for gay and lesbian partners to be married or enter into other public, legal partnerships in Europe, Canada, and some parts of the United States. However, these relationships are still openly condemned by some political and religious leaders and a number of people who feel that they threaten our society. For this reason, it is difficult to know with any certainty how same-sex partnerships are like opposite-sex partnerships and how they are different. It is even difficult to know the number of these partnerships and how successful they are. However, despite the difficulties and stress faced by gay and lesbian people, many manage to live in long-lasting, committed partnerships (Patterson, 2000).

We know that about 4 to 6 percent of adults in the world can be characterized as exclusively or typically homosexual (Gonsiorek, 1991). We also know that a little over 10 percent of the 5.5 million people who are cohabiting in the United States today are same-sex couples (Simmons & O'Connell, 2003). Around half of all gay men and about three-quarters of lesbian women are in committed relationships. Many of these relationships are ongoing, long-term partnerships. About 25 percent of gay couples and about 20 percent of lesbian couples have been together for 10 years or more. Among lesbians, monogamy within a long-term relationship is about as common as in heterosexual relationships (marriage or

Long-term committed relationships are common among gay and lesbian couples, with much the same sources of happiness and problems as heterosexual marriages.

cohabitation), but monogamy is much less commonly a feature of gay male relationships. In one large national study, for example, most lesbian couples preferred and experienced monogamous relationships, while most gay couples did not (Bryant & Demian, 1994).

In a longitudinal study of gay and lesbian couples, psychologist Lawrence Kurdek (1998) questioned 66 gay male couples and 51 lesbian couples over a period of 5 years. Kurdek asked both partners to fill out questionnaires telling about their current relationship and their thoughts about what an ideal relationship would be by rating a set of statements on a scale from 1 to 9, depending on how much they agreed with each one. The statements were about doing things together as a couple, acting independently, and dealing with each other as equal partners. Over the 5-year period, both the gay and lesbian couples reported that they did fewer things together as a couple, which is similar to findings for heterosexual couples. Kurdek explains that the need for togetherness decreases over time as a sense of trust and security intensify.

Couples also reported each year on their degree of commitment to each other, and this was used as a measure of relationship quality. What were the predictors that relationship quality would change from one year to the next? For both gay and lesbian couples, problems over treating each other as equal partners predicted that the couple's commitment would be lower the next year. Lower commitment was also predicted when partners rated independence over doing things together as a couple. In other words, this suggests that in gay and lesbian relationships, perceived equality needs to remain stable, and togetherness needs to be more important than autonomy for the quality of the relationship to be maintained over time.

In a comparison of gay, lesbian, and married heterosexual couples in long-term relationships, Kurdek (2004) collected measures of psychological adjustment, personality traits, relationships styles, conflict-resolution techniques, and social support. The major differences between the groups of couples was found in three areas: relationship style (gay and lesbian couples had more autonomy and equality), conflict resolution (gay and lesbian couples were better at resolving conflicts), and social support (heterosexual married couples had more social support from their families).

In July of 2000, the state of Vermont began to offer civil unions to same-sex couples, becoming the first state in the United States to grant the same legal benefits, civil rights, and protection as married couples who lived in the state. Psychologist Esther D. Rothblum and her colleagues (Solomon, Rothblum, & Balsam, 2004; Todosijevic, Rothblum, & Soloman, 2005) contacted all 2,475 gay and lesbian couples who had entered into these unions the first year that it became legal. Almost half were willing to participate by filling out questionnaires about their relationships, providing names of same-sex couples in their social circle who did not have civil unions, and providing the names of their married heterosexual siblings and their spouses.

How do gay men and lesbians in civil unions differ from those who were not in such unions? The gay men in civil unions were closer to their family of origin than those who were not in civil unions, and the lesbians in civil unions were more open about their sexual orientation. How do gay men and lesbians in civil unions differ from their married heterosexual siblings? The gay and lesbian couples had not been in their relationships as long and had less traditional division of labor and childcare roles than did the heterosexual couples. What factors are important in relationship satisfaction for gays and lesbians in civil unions? Like other couples, similarity in age and emotional outlook were important, but unlike other couples, similarity in income and education did not make a difference. What are sources of stress for gays and lesbians in civil unions? For the men, worries about HIV/AIDS, violence, and harassment were significantly higher, whereas for lesbians stress was more likely to be caused by friends' and family members' reaction to their sexuality.

The fear of violence reported by the participants was not groundless, as demonstrated in a related study of another group of gay, lesbian, and bisexual adults (Balsam, Rothblum, & Beauchaine, 2005). It showed that in comparison with their heterosexual siblings, these adults reported experiencing more violence over their lifetimes—more childhood psychological and physical abuse by parents, more childhood sexual abuse, more partner psychological and physical victimization in adulthood, and more sexual-assault experiences in adulthood. Clearly studies of same-sex partnerships need to address discrimination, victimization, health concerns, and lack of social support, topics that are not present in the same degree in heterosexual relationships (Green, 2004).

Although these studies by no means present a complete picture of gay and lesbian partnerships, they feature creative, solid research that gives valuable information about this topic. Perhaps the most important finding is that homosexual relationships are far more like heterosexual relationships than different. Although long-term committed relationships are probably less common in the gay and lesbian community, such commitments, when made, involve love and strong attachment. Many last a lifetime. Since same-sex relationships by definition involve two people who have both been socialized toward the same gender role, there are some differences in the dynamics of the relationships. But the human urge to form one close, intimate, central attachment is as evident in gay relationships as it is in heterosexual relationships.

Relationships with Other Family Members

Defining "family" is not an easy task. Each time I find a definition, I realize that it doesn't apply to my particular family group, or to the family that lives next door to me. It's not that we are so unusual, but that family is a hard concept to pin down into a definition that includes all the people we consider family. We have biological relatives, adopted relatives, and step- and half-relatives. Some of us have close friends who function as family members. Then there is the situation of ex-family members, and who knows what will happen when surrogate mothers and sperm-donor fathers are considered! However, I do like the solution suggested by gerontologist Rosemary Blieszner (2000), who writes that when it comes to researching family relationships, "It is not possible to identify family members via external observation. Rather, individuals must specify the members of their own families" (p. 92). Presumably, like beauty, family is in the eye of the beholder.

My guess is that your version of "family" may be complicated too. Unfortunately, research on family relationships in adulthood has not yet caught up to this complexity. Most attention has been directed to parent-child relationships, with less emphasis on sibling relationships or grandparent-grandchild links. There is essentially no information available on relationships between stepsiblings or in-laws (let alone former in-laws). In the future I hope we will see explorations of a broader array of "family" connections and their effects on adult development.

General Patterns of Family Interaction

When my youngest child moved out of the house at 18, I admit that I experienced a few moments of panic. Would he ever come back to see us? Why? He had a comfortable apartment, he was a good cook, he knew how to do his own laundry, he had a good job. But Sunday rolled around and there he was sitting at the dining room table with my husband and me, his grandparents, his sister and her husband, and his 2-year-old nephew. And he has been there almost every Sunday since, for almost 20 years, first bringing his girlfriend (who later became his wife), then his children, and sometimes his wife's parents. Now I realize why. Because we are family, and once a week we touch base, catch up on the news, and recharge our batteries for the coming week.

During the 1970s and 1980s, social scientists grappled with the idea that **nuclear families** (parents and their children) in the United States were in danger of being isolated from their **extended families** (grandparents, aunts and uncles, cousins). The reason for their concern was that young families had become more mobile than ever before, moving across the country to seek out job opportunities that were not available in their hometowns. But closer examination showed that although the mobility was a fact of family life, the isolation was not. Families had begun using communication technology—cell phones, text messaging, e-mail, picture phones, digital cameras—to keep in touch with each other and to keep their family relationships strong (Williams & Nussbaum, 2001).

Sociologist Vernon Bengtson has theorized that the quality of any family relationship can be evaluated on six dimensions. This **intergenerational solidarity theory** states that family relationships depend on:

- *Associational solidarity*—the frequency and patterns of interaction in various types of activities.
- *Affectional solidarity*—the type and degree of positive sentiment held about family members, and the degree of reciprocity of these sentiments.
- *Consensual solidarity*—the degree of agreement on values, attitudes, and beliefs among family members.
- *Functional solidarity*—the degree to which family members exchange services or assistance.
- *Normative solidarity*—the perception and enactment of norms of family solidarity.
- *Intergenerational family structure*—the number, type, and geographic proximity of family members (Bengtson & Schrader, 1982, p. 116).

According to this theory, family members can be very close if they have frequent interactions, feel a great deal of affection toward each other, share basic attitudes and opinions, help each other when help is needed, agree with the basic beliefs of the family unit, and have the means to interact with each other (either living close together or having access to communication technology). To the extent that any of these factors is not present, the relationships will be less close.

Parent-Child Relationships in Adulthood

Most adults live near their parents, have frequent contact with them, report feeling emotional closeness, and share similar opinions. Sixty percent of adults report that they have at least weekly contact with their parents, and 20 percent have daily contact (Lawton, Silverstein, & Bengtson, 1994). Most older adults with children have at least one child who lives within 10 miles of their home (Lin & Rogerson, 1995).

One big question in the study of parent-child relationships in adulthood is "What happens to the attachment bond from childhood?" Does it end, leaving independent adult children ready to form new and different relationships with their parents? Or does it continue, with adjustments made for the adult status of the child? Bowlby (1969) claimed that attachment diminished during adolescence and then disappeared, except in times of illness or extreme distress, being transferred to romantic partners. One attachment theorist puts it this way: "If children are eventually to form their own households, their bonds of attachment to the parents must become attenuated and eventually end. Otherwise, independent living would be emotionally troubling. The relinquishing of attachment to parents appears to be of central importance among the individuation-achieving processes of late adolescence and early adulthood" (Weiss, 1986, p. 100).

Developmental psychologist Victor Cicirelli (1991) has a different interpretation of attachment theory. He believes that parent-child attachment does not decline in adolescence, but changes slightly in form. Instead of physical proximity being the key, communication becomes important. Most independent adults of every age, regardless of where they live, carry on imaginary conversations with their parents and, if possible, communicate with them in person, through letters, telephone calls, and e-mail. Cicirelli believes that attachment can survive into adulthood because adults are capable of substituting symbols of parents (memories, photos, family heirlooms) for their physical presence and of supplementing this symbolic relationship with occasional visits, phone calls, and other communication.

I must agree with Cicirelli on this issue, as I believe anyone would who enjoys relationships as either the adult child of older parents or the parent of adult children (or both). The viewpoints of Bowlby and Weiss, as discussed above, which hold that parent-child attachment disappears in adulthood and is somehow transformed into romantic relationships, never rang true to me, even as a college student, and now that I have adult children, it seems even less viable. The fact that most adults do not interact with their parents on a day-to-day basis as they did in the early years isn't proof to me that the bond is gone. In fact, the whole idea of internal mental representations seems to be a compelling argument that adults can maintain this attachment bond and still be independent, mentally healthy adults.

According to Bengston's theory of intergenerational solidarity, affection is an important component in family relationships. Mutual expressions of affection between family members are often seen as a measure of how close the relationship is and how it is progressing. The inverse is true as well: the absence of expressions of affection in a relationship can signal deterioration, as discussed in the section on "good" and "bad" marriages. The parent-child relationship in adulthood also involves expressions of affection, and how these expressions are perceived by the parents and the adult children can be important.

For example, young children often perceive their parents' affection as a finite resource, and when they observe their parents expressing affection to their siblings, they fear that there won't be enough left for themselves. This implicit belief is thought to fade away as the child becomes more cognitively mature and realizes that a parent's love is not a concrete, tangible commodity and that the old saying is true, that "parents' hearts expand to hold all of their children." However, a recent study by communication researchers Kory Floyd and Mark T. Morman (2005) shows that remnants of this belief are found in young adulthood.

In a study of 115 fathers (average age 51) and their sons (average age 23), the researchers asked participants to rate how much affection the fathers expressed for the sons through either verbal statements (such as saying "I love you"), direct nonverbal gestures (such as hugging or kissing), or supportive behaviors (doing favors for them). They also asked how many sisters and brothers the sons had. Results showed that the more siblings the sons had, the less affection of all types they reported receiving from their fathers. In contrast, the fathers' reports of affection expressed toward their sons were not affected by the number of children in the family. Does this show that parental love is spread too thin when one has several children? Not really. What it more likely shows is that there can be real differences between perceptions of relationship quality depending on which generation you belong to and the makeup of your family.

Another important component of intergenerational solidarity, according to Bengtson, is consensual solidarity, agreeing on values, attitudes, and beliefs. It is presumed that children will learn these lessons from their parents, but there is also evidence that parents' values, attitudes, and beliefs can be broadened by their adult children. A longitudinal study of older adults in the Netherlands demonstrated that the lifestyles and experiences the adult children introduce to their parents have an effect on the parents' attitudes in late adulthood. Sociologists Ann-Rist Poortman and Theo van Tilburg (2005) surveyed 1,700 men and women who had been born between 1903 and 1937, asking them about their beliefs concerning gender equality and moral issues. They also asked questions about unconventional life experiences of their parents (whether their mothers had been employed outside the home or had been divorced) and their children (whether they had cohabited or divorced, whether their daughters worked or their sons did not work). Older people whose children had cohabited or divorced tended to be more progressive in their beliefs about gender role equality and their moral attitudes toward voluntary childlessness, abortion, and euthanasia than those whose adult children had not had those experiences. Interestingly, the older adults were not influenced by how unconventional their parents had been, or else they were no longer under the influence of childhood experiences that had occurred 70 or 80 years earlier.

The authors of this study suggest that parents of adult children who are demonstrating unconventional behavior, such as cohabiting or divorcing, face the decision to either change their attitudes or risk distancing themselves from their child. In a larger sense, the authors suggest, the influence young adults have on their parents in this respect is an important mechanism of social change whereby younger members of society, who are more apt to be influenced by cultural change, can pass their attitudes on to the older members of the society, thus bringing greater progress to the overall group.

The Effects of Late-Life Divorce. Divorce among older people is increasing. We are familiar with the effects of divorce on young children, but what happens to adults when their parents divorce? The popular concept is that children suffer less from parental divorce the older they are, but some researchers argue that this is not true; adult children are as affected emotionally by parental divorces as young children (Cooney, Hutchinson, & Leather, 1995). After divorce, adult children typically have less contact and less close relationships with their fathers, although one recent study showed that for many sons, this estrangement was only the initial reaction, and eventually they gained new respect for their fathers and went on to enjoy close relationships again (Pryor, 1999).

> **CRITICAL THINKING**
>
> Why would relationships with fathers be affected more than those with mothers after parents divorce?

A parental divorce can bring financial problems if adult children are in college or still dependent on their family for support. And even when older parents have not been providers for their adult children, their divorce disrupts the traditions and symbols that were until then the center of the extended family. The family home is often sold as a result of the parents' divorce, holidays are split between "Mom's house" and "Dad's house." The roles the parents filled have changed, and if either parent remarries, there are changes brought by new family members. Adult daughters often become confidants for the mother after the divorce and acquire the role of social director for the father (reminding him of family birthdays, conveying family news, making sure he has a place to go for Thanksgiving dinner).

One additional effect of having divorced parents is that unmarried older parents need more assistance sooner than married ones. For example, my parents have been happily married for over 60 years, and even though they have some limitations, they are able to help each other out. My father can't hear the doorbell, and my mother has problems walking, but when visitors come, my mother hears the doorbell and tells my father; he goes to the door and greets the guests. They manage to live in their own apartment in a senior residence with daily visits from a home-care helper and family. I compare my situation with that of friends who have divorced parents. Several friends have two aging parents to care for in two separate households. I'm sure the situation will become more common as the divorce-prone baby boomers get older. It is clear that the effects of divorce on children don't end when they reach adulthood.

Problem Children in Adulthood. Unfortunately, not all children outgrow their childhood problems, and others acquire problems in adulthood. What effect does this have on older parents? Is there an age that parents can quit feeling responsible for their children's problems? Apparently not, at least not for most parents. A major cause of late-life distress for older adults is the problems their adult children are having. Children's problems are a primary cause for depressive symptoms in older adults, and the greater the problem, the greater the parents' depression (Dunham, 1995). Parents feel helpless and guilty because they have not been able to solve their children's problems. Examples of problems that affect parents are children's divorces, financial crises, and drug or alcohol problems. For unknown reasons, fathers are more susceptible to the effects of problem children than mothers at this age (Williams & Nussbaum, 2001).

Grandparent-Grandchild Relationships

As I said in Chapter 5, a large majority of people have the role of grandparent, and an even larger number have the role of grandchild. For most children, their relationship with their grandparents is second only to that with their parents. Due to the structure of contemporary families and the increasing longevity of older adults, the grandparent-grandchild relationship can be a long-term one, commonly extending into the grandchild's adult years. And due to a decrease in the number of children in families and the increase in the health of middle-aged people, grandparents are able to enjoy closer, more active relationships with their grandchildren than in past generations. I know I am probably "preaching to the choir" here, because, like me, you are probably part of a grandparent-grandchild dyad and are living the facts expressed above. Unfortunately, social scientists have seemed not to notice this change; very little research is available on this topic, and what has been done is lacking in depth, methodological sophistication, and theoretical foundation (Brown & Roodin, 2003).

To be fair, the grandparent-grandchild relationship is difficult to study because of the many variables—grandparents' ages, number of grandparents, grandchildren's ages, number of grandchildren, gender of grandparent and grandchild, just to name a few. However, considering the growing numbers and importance of this relationship, I expect that this will soon become an active area of research.

Here is what we know about how grandparents and grandchildren relate to each other: the age of the grandchild makes a difference in the way the grandchild views the relationship with the grandparents and, as a result, in the relationship itself. A study of adolescent grandchildren in Belgium found that young adolescents valued the emotional support, mentoring, and reassurance their grandparents gave, while older adolescents mentioned emotional dependency less often and links to the family's past more often (Van Ranst, Verschueren, & Marcoen, 1995). In a longitudinal study of grandparents' and grandchildren's affection over time, results fell into a curvilinear pattern which was high in childhood, low in adolescence, and then moderately high in adulthood (Silverstein & Long, 1998).

In addition, the age of the grandparents makes a difference in their relationship with their grandchildren. Not surprisingly, young grandparents take a more active role in the lives of their grandchildren (Aldous, 1995). Older grandfathers find more meaning in their relationships with grandchildren than younger grandfathers (Baranowski, 1987), and younger grandmothers offer more direct instrumental and social support to their grandchildren when the parents divorce (Johnson, 1985).

Gender matters in grandparenthood also. As with other relationships, women are the kinkeepers in this one too. Grandmothers are closer to grandchildren than grandfathers, especially maternal grandmothers, making the grandmother's relationship with her daughter's daughter especially close (Hyde & Gibbs, 1993). Grandparents relate differently to male grandchildren than female grandchildren; they have more social interaction with granddaughters and more instrumental interactions with grandsons (Kennedy, 1992).

In a study several years ago, college students were asked to rank their grandparents according to the time they spent with them, the resources they shared with them, and the emotional closeness they felt to them. For all three categories, students ranked their mother's mother the highest, followed by their mother's father, their father's mother, and their father's father (DeKay, 2000). The results are shown in Figure 6.3. The same pattern has been found in many similar studies, and I don't think anyone would find it very surprising—in fact I would have responded the same way about my grandparents at that age. However, psychologists W. Todd DeKay and Todd Shackelford (2000) explained these data using an evolutionary psychology perspective. They argue that the grandparents' rankings reflect the relative confidence each grandparent has that the grandchild is truly his or her biological descendant and as a result will carry their genes into a new generation.

Considering that the rate of error in parentage (charmingly known as the *cuckold rate,* from an old English word for a man whose wife has been unfaithful) is about 10 to 15 percent in modern cultures (Cerda-Flores, Barton, Marty-Gonzales, et al., 1999), a good number of grandparents stand to invest time, resources, and emotional attachment in grandchildren who are not biological relatives. The reasoning goes like this: A mother is sure her child is her biological descendant; a father is not so sure. Taking this a step further, a mother's mother (or maternal grandmother) is also sure that the grandchild is her biological relative and thus carries her genes. The mother's father is not so sure; the child is surely his daughter's child, but is his daughter truly his child? He can't be sure, so he invests less than his wife in the relationship. The paternal grandmother knows that the child's father is her biological son, but she is not so sure about the grandchild being her son's biological child. Chances are that if she has a daughter, she will invest more in grandchildren from that branch of the family. Finally, the paternal grandfather has a lot of doubts. Is his son truly his biological

● **CRITICAL THINKING**

Using an evolutionary psychology perspective, would you be closer to nieces and nephews who are your sisters' children or those who are your brothers' children? Why?

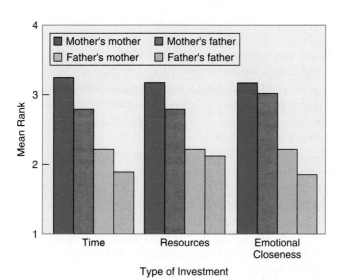

Figure 6.3 Students rated their grandparents on a scale from 1 to 4 based on emotional closeness, time spent together, and resources they provided (gifts, money). Maternal grandmothers were highest ranked, followed by maternal grandfathers, paternal grandmothers, and paternal grandfathers.
Source: Adapted from DeKay (2000).

descendant? And if he is, is the grandson the child of his son? According to DeKay and Shackelford, this explains the low investment on the part of the paternal grandfathers.

Perhaps you are wondering why the rating for maternal grandfather is higher than the rating for paternal grandmother, since they seem to have equal doubts about their grandchild's relatedness to them. The reason is that not all generations have the same incidence of marital infidelity (Laumann, Gagnon, Michael, et al., 1994). It has been estimated that the grandparents' generation had a lower incidence of infidelity (12 percent) compared to the parents' generation (20 percent), so the doubt the paternal grandmother has about her grandchild's relatedness (did her daughter-in-law cheat on her son?) is more probable than the maternal grandfather's doubts (did his wife cheat on him?).

Of course I can generate other reasons to explain why the mother's parents invest more in the relationship with their grandchildren. Perhaps young couples settle closer to the wife's parents than the husband's parents and it is due to proximity. Perhaps the mother, as kinkeeper, is more attuned to promoting the relationship between her children and her parents than her husband is with his parents. Perhaps the younger family is more similar to the maternal grandparents in traditions, social practices, and family customs, since the wife usually promotes these things. Or perhaps we somehow base our emotional relationships on the probability that some grandchildren carry our genes and others may not.

Another factor that is important for grandparenting in the United States is racial/ethnic group. African American grandparents view their relationships with their grandchildren as more central to the family than do white grandparents. They believe they have a responsibility for caregiving and providing security, cohesion, and structure within the family. They have higher status within the family and carry more authority than white grandparents, especially grandmothers. When African American grandparents serve as surrogate parents for their grandchildren (see Chapter 5), they are often able to draw upon their own experiences of being raised by grandparents and to receive social support from friends who are in the same situation. This may be one reason why African American grandparents who have taken on this role report significantly less caregiver burden than those in other groups (Pruchno, 1999).

Hispanic grandparents in the United States have different relationships with their grandchildren than non-Hispanic grandparents. The families are typically large and include several generations living close together, reporting strong feelings of emotional closeness, but the grandparent-grandchild relationship does not include high levels of exchange and support. This seems to be due, in part, to language differences within the family. It is not unusual for grandparents to speak only Spanish and grandchildren to speak (or prefer to speak) only English, causing a gap between the generations that is hard to bridge (Brown & Roodin, 2003).

Now that grandparents' relationships with adult grandchildren are becoming more common, research interest has followed. Grandparents report that these relationships provide important emotional meaning to their lives (Silverstein & Long, 1998), and adult grandchildren describe their relationships with grandparents as significant, meaningful, close, and enduring (Hodgson, 1992).

In a study that interviewed both grandparents and adult grandchildren, sociologist Candace Kemp (2005) found that adult grandchildren and their grandparents view their relationships as a safety net—a potential source of support which provides security even though it may never be tapped into. Both generations reported that they "just knew" that if they needed help, the other would be there for them. Actual help was common also, with grandparents providing college tuition and funds to help adult grandchildren buy homes; grandchildren helping with transportation and household chores. Adult grandchildren represent the future to their grandparents and give them a feeling of accomplishment; grandparents represent the past to their grandchildren, holding the keys to personal history and identity. It seems clear that adult grandchildren and their grandparents are able to build on their early years and develop unique relationships together in adulthood.

Relationships with Brothers and Sisters

The great majority of adults have at least one living sibling, and this relationship in adulthood is becoming the topic of increased research interest as the baby boomers get older. (One benchmark of this generation is that they have more siblings than children.) Descriptions of sibling relationships in everyday conversation range from exceptional closeness, to mutual apathy, to enduring rivalry. While rivalry and apathy certainly both exist, moderate emotional closeness is the most common pattern. It is really quite unusual for a person to lose contact completely with a sibling in adulthood.

Sibling relationships are important in early adulthood in that they can help compensate for poor relationships with parents. Psychologist Avidan Milevsky (2005) surveyed over 200 men and women between the ages of 19 and 33, asking questions about their relationships with their siblings, their parents, and their peers. They were also given questions to measure their loneliness, depression, self-esteem, and life satisfaction. Those who had low support from their parents had significantly higher well-being scores if they were compensated with high levels of social support from their siblings. Figure 6.4 shows the well-being scores for the participants who had low parental support. Those with high sibling support scored significantly lower on the depression and loneliness measures and significantly higher on the self-esteem and life-satisfaction measures than participants who had low sibling support.

There is also evidence that sibling relationships become even more significant in later adulthood. Sociologist Deborah Gold (1996) interviewed a group of older adults about their relationships with their sisters and brothers over the years they had been adults. The respondents were 65 years of age or older, had at least one living sibling, had been married at some point in their lives, had children, and were living independently in the community.

Gold asked about how various life events during adulthood might have contributed to the change in closeness between the sibling pairs. Figure 6.5 shows life events from early, middle, and late adulthood along with the magnitude and direction of change in

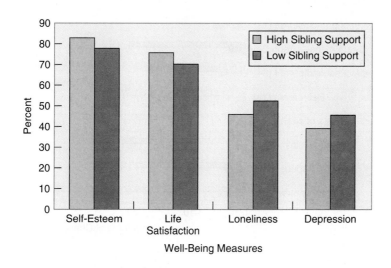

Figure 6.4 Young adults with low levels of parental support report significantly better scores on measures of well-being when they have high levels of support from their siblings
Source: Data from Milevsky (2005).

closeness. As you can see, events in early adulthood, especially marriage and having children, seem to cause distancing between siblings. As one male respondent said about his relationship with his brother:

> We had been close during our teen years, but the challenges of growing up—of becoming adults—interrupted our closeness. Instead of worrying just about ourselves and each other, we each had a job, a wife, and a family to worry about. We weren't close any more, that's true, but we didn't hate each other either—we were running as fast as we could to keep up with things (Gold, 1996, p. 240).

Beginning in middle adulthood, life events are characterized as bringing siblings closer together, especially the death of their second parent. A woman who was the oldest of three sisters said,

> When Mom finally died after a long and difficult illness, I thought it was up to me to try to stay close to my sisters. I was surprised—and pleased—when I realized that we all naturally looked to each other (Gold, 1996, p. 238).

Late adulthood also brings life events conducive to increased closeness between siblings. Retirement brings more free time to spend together and can reunite siblings whose jobs required them to live far apart. Loss of spouse or illness brings siblings to help "fill in the blanks." Finally, some siblings end up being the only surviving members of their family of origin and the only ones to share the memories. One woman respondent talked about her relationship with her sister, her last remaining sibling of nine:

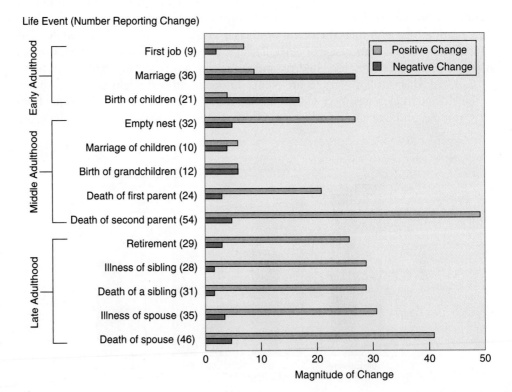

Figure 6.5 Siblings report on what life events triggered changes in their relationships with each other, how large the changes were, and whether they were positive or negative changes. Negative changes occur earlier in adulthood and positive changes later, especially on the death of their second parent.

Source: Data from Gold (1996).

We call every other day . . . sometimes every day. There is no one else left. We are the family survivors, and that has made us very close (Gold, 1996, p. 241).

To be fair, 18 percent of the respondents reported becoming more emotionally distant from their siblings with time. Some went through the typical distancing in early adulthood and never got back together; others had anticipated that life events would bring renewed closeness and were disappointed that they did not, especially when they had anticipated more help during bad times such as widowhood or illness.

What type of sibling relationships are the closest? If you are a woman who is lucky enough to have a sister (I have three!), it will be no surprise to you that two sisters are the closest, followed by a brother-and-sister pair and then by two brothers. Also, people who are single and those who have no children tend to have stronger relationships with their siblings (Campbell, Connidis, Davies,1999).

Research shows that among elderly men and women, those who described themselves as close to a sister had the lowest levels of depression. Those with poor relationships with their sister(s) had the highest levels of depression, while the quality of relationships with brothers was unrelated to depression (Cicirelli, 1989). Similarly, research shows that among recently widowed women, those who had a sister nearby adjusted far better to widowhood than did those lacking sisterly support. The availability of brothers had no such beneficial effect, and neither did contact with children (O'Bryant,1988). Once again, it is women—mothers, wives, sisters—who are the kinkeepers and who provide the nurturance and emotional support.

Friendships in Adulthood

Developmental psychologist Dorothy Field (1999) defines **friendship** as "a voluntary social relationship carried out within a social context" (p. 325). She goes on to stress the discretionary aspect of friendship—unlike other relationships, it depends not on proximity or blood ties or institutionalized norms, but on personal reasons that vary from individual to individual. As vague as the concept of friendship may be, it is still an important one, and although most of the developmental attention has been focused on friendships in childhood and adolescence, there have been a number of studies in the last decade or so that examine this topic in adulthood.

For example, in one study, 53 three-generation families of women, some of them Anglos, some of them Hispanic Americans, were interviewed about their close relationships. Results showed that for both the Anglo and the Hispanic women, friends became less central with age and family became more so (Levitt, Weber, & Guacci, 1993).

We also have a small piece of longitudinal data from the Berkeley Intergenerational Studies, which followed 50 participants from adolescence through middle adulthood. The researchers asked about relationships with best friends over the years. Analyses showed that the frequency of interaction with a best friend dropped between age 17 and age 50, while closeness rose slightly (Carstensen,1992).

Looking at attachment styles in friendship patterns, psychologist Jeffrey Webster (1997) recruited a group of 76 healthy older adults (mean age 68 years) through an ad in a Canadian newspaper directed at community-dwelling adults over the age of 50. Webster assessed the attachment styles of these participants and compared them with those of the young adults in the Bartholomew and Horowitz (1991) study discussed earlier in this chapter. As illustrated in Figure 6.6, the largest proportion of the older adults (52 percent) gave responses that assigned them to the dismissive category, compared to only 18 percent of

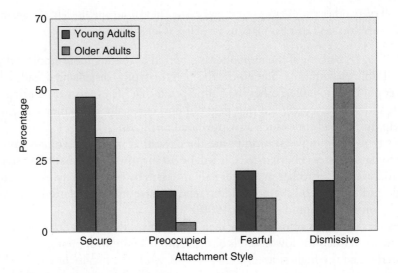

Figure 6.6 More young adults show secure attachment styles, while more older adults show dismissive attachment styles, possibly a coping skill adopted to deal with the losses common in the later years.

Source: Data from Webster (1997).

the younger group. In contrast, only a third of the older group (33 percent) were classified as secure, compared to almost half of the younger group (47 percent).

Webster suggested that the large proportion of dismissive-relationship styles, which reflect a positive model of the self and a negative model of others, could be a coping skill that older people adopt as a reaction to the death of a spouse or other separation from loved ones. Over half of this sample were either widowed, divorced, or separated, and Webster's view that belief in one's own independence rather than the need for a partner is an adaptive move in late adulthood is a good one, especially when boosted by subsequent findings that the dismissive and secure participants scored higher than the preoccupied or fearful ones on a test of overall happiness. Another explanation is that this study shows the socioemotional selection process at work (Carstensen, 1995). Older people may be content with the existing relationships in their lives and not motivated to add new social relationships, even those that might involve potential new partners.

Other researchers have studied gender differences in friendship patterns. One finding is that women's friendships are based on *talk*—personal, disclosive, and emotionally rich. They give support and share feelings through their conversations and, in doing so, forge bonds that are both deep and complex (Johnson, 1996). Men's friendships are marked by *doing*—playing sports, watching sports, and helping each other with tasks such as home repairs. Men's friendships are deep and caring, but this is not expressed directly. Instead they back-slap, make jokes about each other, and throw "affectionate" punches. When men do talk to each other, it revolves around sports, work, politics, and other impersonal topics, not the intimacy-building talk that women use to develop friendships.

One of my all-time favorite quotations, from an interview with a 38-year-old male executive, clearly illustrates the difference in self-disclosure:

> I have three close friends I have known since we were boys and they live here in the city. There are some things I wouldn't tell them. For example, I wouldn't tell them much about my work because we have always been highly competitive. I certainly wouldn't tell them about my feelings of any uncertainties with life or various things I do. And I wouldn't talk about any problems I have with my wife or in fact anything about my marriage and sex life. But other than that I would tell them anything. [After a brief pause he laughed and said:] That doesn't leave a hell of a lot, does it? (Bell, 1981, pp. 81–82).

Table 6.5	Review of Changes in Relationships over Adulthood		
Age 20–40	**Age 40–65**	**Age 65–75**	**Age 75+**
Intimate romantic relationships are formed, possibly based on early attachment to parents. Partners are selected based on strong feelings of lust and attraction, but cultural conditions have an effect also. Marriages are high in positive sexual relations and low in conflict.	Marriages decline somewhat in satisfaction and positive sexual relations during parenting years, increase in conflict. Divorce rate is lower than in earlier years.	Marriages are highest in satisfaction and psychological intimacy, lowest in conflict and positive sexual relations in the empty nest years. Divorce rate is low, although many start new relationships after death of spouse.	Those with living spouses express high satisfaction with marriages, although there is evidence of changes in attachment styles for some to dismissive, perhaps to guard emotions against inevitable losses.
Social convoys include mothers, spouses, friends, siblings, and children.	Social convoys more often include sons and daughters in closer circles, less often include mothers.	Social convoys more often include female friends and daughters, less often include spouses.	Social convoys include fewer people, grandchildren appear as important relationships.
Family relations are strong even if physical distances between members are far. Young adult children continue to learn from their parents and parents change their attitudes based on their children's lifestyles. Siblings provide support for each other when parents do not.	Siblings are more distant during the parenting years.	Siblings regain some closeness, especially when parents die and when sisters are involved.	Siblings are very close, especially sisters, widowed siblings, and siblings who never married or have no children.
Relationship problems come from romantic partnership breakups, divorce, infertility, and parents' divorces.	Relationship problems come from parenting issues with adolescent children, divorce, parents' divorce.	Relationship problems come from death of spouse, adult children's financial and marital problems, grandchildren's problems, parents' declining health.	Relationship problems come from death of spouse, children's financial and marital problems, grandchildren's problems.

As in previous chapters, I have included a review table of changes that occur in major types of relationships over the adult years (see Table 6.5).

Summary

1. Attachment theory was originally formulated to explain the relationship between infants and their parents. Subsequent hypotheses suggested that the attachments formed in infancy were relatively permanent and were reflected in other relationships later in life.

2. Other theories of social relationships include the convoy model, which considers the group of significant people who travel with us in our lives at different points

in time. Socioemotional theory states that as people grow older, they prefer to have a few close, emotional relationships instead of many more casual relationships. Another explanation of the importance of social relationships is provided by evolutionary psychology, stating that the tendency to bond together with similar people is a genetic mechanism passed down from our primitive ancestors because it contributed to their survival and reproductive success.

3. Almost all adults experience relationships with intimate partners, and the formalization of intimate partnerships is found in all cultures. Most people of the world select their own partners. Some social scientists hypothesize that establishing an intimate partnership is a process that includes the lust system, the attraction system, and the attachment system, each involving a separate neurotransmitter system and pattern of brain activity.

4. The relationship with an intimate partner is typically the most central relationship in adulthood. The process of partner selection is influenced initially by perceived similarity and by propinquity, as well as by internal models of attachment. In addition, according to evolutionary psychology, people seem to be attracted to others based on physical signs of good health and potential reproductive success.

5. Attachment theory has also been used to explain success in creating romantic relationships. People who are classified as secure in their attachment will also have longer-lasting, happier romantic relationships than those who are in other, less secure categories.

6. Long-term marriages show that overall satisfaction is high in early adulthood, declines in the child-rearing years, and is highest in the postparental years. Negativity is implicated in "bad" marriages, with criticism, contempt, defensiveness, and stonewalling serving as the Four Horsemen of the Apocalypse that bring marital problems and ultimate divorce.

7. Couples who cohabit before marriage have higher divorce rates and lower levels of marital happiness than couples who marry without cohabitating. However, when couples commit to marry and then cohabitate as an engaged couple, they have marriages as happy and long-lasting as couples who marry without cohabiting.

8. Most gay and lesbian adults in the United States are in committed relationships, and around 20 percent of the couples have been together 10 years or more. Recently gay and lesbian couples have been able to marry in some countries and some parts of the United States, and others have participated in commitment ceremonies to formalize their intimate partnership. Those who opt for civil unions are more open about their sexual orientations and closer to their parents and siblings.

9. Interactions with adults and their parents occur at high and relatively constant levels throughout adulthood. Most adults have at least weekly contact with their parents. Some studies show increased closeness with siblings in middle and late adulthood.

10. Late-life divorces are increasing, and a new issue for young and middle-aged adults is dealing with their parents' divorce. The problem has proved to be a serious one

for many due to the loss of the family home and holiday traditions, the addition of stepparents and adult stepsiblings, and the need to care for elderly divorced parents.

9. The problems of one's children are always cause for concern, even when the children are adults. Major causes of distress for older parents are children's divorces, financial problems, and drug or alcohol problems.

10. For the present generation, grandparents play more of a companion role than the family-authoritarian or family-burden roles prevalent in the past. However, the role is very broad and depends on many factors, such as the age of the grandparent and grandchild, the distance between homes, and the relationship of the grandparents and the children's parents. There is a gender difference, with grandmothers both enjoying the role more than grandfathers and also being more influential to their grandchildren. Maternal grandparents are usually closer than paternal grandparents, especially if parents divorce. African American grandparents, especially grandmothers, have a more central role in the family than white grandparents.

11. The relationship with maternal grandmothers is considered closest by their grandchildren, followed by maternal grandfather, paternal grandmother, and paternal grandfather. This is interpreted by evolutionary psychology as reflecting the probability that the grandchildren are truly biological descendants of the grandparent.

12. Although relatively constant over the life span, relationships with siblings appear to be strongest in late adulthood. Changes in sibling relationships seem to be related to life events, with events occurring later in life (death of parents, retirement) making siblings closer than events occurring in early adulthood.

13. Friendships are important in young adulthood and middle age, with significant gender differences. Family relationships take precedence in the later years. Older people's attachment styles are more apt to be dismissive than secure, and some suggest that this is a defensive measure against loss of relationships. Others suggest that it illustrates the idea that older people are content with their few close relationships and are not interested in starting more casual ones.

Key Terms

social relationships, 166

attachment theory, 166

attachment, 166

attachment behaviors, 166

internal working model, 167

convoy, 168

socioemotional selectivity theory, 170

evolutionary psychology, 170

mate selection, 172

libido, 172

filter theory, 173

exchange theory, 173

nuclear families, 185

extended families, 185

intergenerational solidarity, 185

friendship, 193

Suggested Reading

Reading for Personal Interest

Bernstein, R. (2005). *Families of value: Personal profiles of pioneering lesbian and gay parents.* New York: Marlowe.

Attorney Robert Bernstein is the former national president of PFLAG (Parents, Friends, and Family of Lesbians and Gays). This book gives the stories of eight families that are headed by gay or lesbian couples who demonstrate love and courage as the first generation to live honestly and openly together.

Coontz, S. (2005). *Marriage: A history.* New York: Viking.

Historian Stephanie Coontz traces the institution of marriage back into history to show the change from economic and social foundations to emotional ones.

Gottman, J. M., & Silver, N. (1999). *The seven principles for making marriage work.* New York: Three Rivers Press.

Gottman has spent his career studying couples in his marriage lab and he has written many research articles on what makes marriages work and what predicts divorce. This is his book for the general public that gives down-to-earth advice about making marriages successful.

Classic Work

Levinson, D. J. (1978). *The seasons of a man's life.* New York: Knopf.

Psychologist Daniel Levinson studied 40 men over the period from young adulthood through middle age and concluded that there are stages (or seasons) that most men experience and that they are defined by relationships with others, a spouse, children, social groups, and co-workers. This was pioneering work in the field of adult development and inspired studies of many other groups.

Bowlby, J. (1969). *Attachment and loss: Vol. 1. Attachment.* New York: Basic Books.

This is the first of three books by psychoanalyst John Bowlby that were the foundation for attachment theory. They have very strong Freudian tones and reflect Bowlby's experiences during World War II working with children's evacuation and resettlement in war zones.

Hazan, C., & Shaver, P. (1987). Romantic love conceptualized as an attachment process. *Journal of Personality and Social Psychology, 52,* 511–524.

These two social psychology researchers were the first to extend attachment theory to romantic relationships in adulthood.

Contemporary Scholarly work

Antonucci, T. C., Akiyama, H., & Merline, A. (2001). Dynamics of social relationships in midlife. In M. E. Lachman (Ed.), *Handbook of midlife development* (pp. 571–598). New York: Wiley.

Toni Antonucci and her colleagues remind us that there are positive aspects of being in the "sandwich generation," such as receiving social support from both older parents and the younger generations.

Hareven, T. K. (2001). Historical perspectives on aging and family relations. In R. H. Binstock & L. K. George (Eds.), *Handbook or aging and the social sciences* (pp. 141–159). San Diego: Academic Press.

Family historian Tamara Hareven present a comprehensive review of life-span development and how it has changed since the 19th century. She skillfully takes demographic facts and tells what the effects were in terms of people's family relationships.

Hendrick, S. S., & Hendrick, C., (2000). Romantic love. In C. H. Hendrick & S. S. Hendrick (Eds.), *Close relationships: A sourcebook* (pp. 203–215). Thousand Oaks, CA: Sage.

Psychologists Susan Hendrick and Clyde Hendrick offer a good review of the scientific classifications of love and the research that has been done on this popular topic. (In fact, the whole volume is excellent.)

Krause, N. (2006). Social relationships in late life. In R. H. Binstock & L. K. George (Eds.), *Handbook or aging and the social sciences* (pp. 182–200). San Diego: Academic Press.

It is well-known that social relationships are important in adulthood, but what about in late life? This chapter contains a review of the research on this topic and tells how social relationships differ at this stage in life and how they are different for different cohorts. It also reviews evidence of the social support/health connection.

Orbuch, T. L., Veroff, J., & Hunter, A. G. (1999). Black couples, white couples: The early years of marriage. In E. M. Hetherington (Ed.), *Coping with divorce, single parenting, and remarriage: A risk and resiliency perspective* (pp. 23–43). Mahwah, NJ: Erlbaum.

The authors of this article review the results of a longitudinal study being conducted at the University of Michigan (Early Years of Marriage Project), comparing the results of black couples and white couples and considering the different sociohistorical factors that impinge on their lives and relationships.

Chapter 7

Work
and Retirement

THE REVEREND WILLIAM Augustus Johnson is a working man. He is 93 years old and lives in a retirement home, confined to a wheelchair ever since his left foot was amputated, but he works at his church every day, where he serves as pastor emeritus. He spends about 5 hours calling church members, writing letters, and reading church literature—trying to keep up with the times. "Things are moving so swiftly these days, I have to stay up nights to catch up with them" (Terkel, 1995, p. 209). He also writes a sermon each week, although his church has several other pastors. He wants to be ready on Sunday in case he is needed.

How did Reverend Johnson choose his career? He didn't. Like many Baptist ministers, the career chose him. He was "called" one day when he was 25 years old. "I wanted to be a lawyer like Perry Mason," he explained. But instead he heard a voice asking him to preach. At first he said no. "I'd just started to learn to dance and was enjoying it. But I was a Christian and a deacon in the church and I woke up to the fact that you don't tell God 'no' " (Terkel, pp. 211–212). That was the beginning of a career spanning almost seven decades and three generations of parishioners.

Retirement? "I'd just like to go in one Sunday morning and say, 'Beloved, this is my last sermon. May the Lord be with you.' Go out, get my hat, and be taken home. I can't see the pressure of seeing people I knew as babies, grown men now, saying to me 'Pastor, why did you leave us?' None of that" (Terkel, 1995, p. 214).

The Importance of Work in Adulthood
Super's Theory of Career Development
Gender Differences in Career Patterns

Selecting a Career
Holland's Theory of Career Selection
The Effects of Gender
Family Influences
The Role of Genetics

Age Trends in Work Experience
Job Performance
Job Training and Retraining
Job Satisfaction

Work and Personal Life
Work and the Individual
Work and Marriage
Work and Parenthood
Work and Caregiving for Adult Family Members
Household Labor

Retirement
Preparation for Retirement
Timing of Retirement
Reasons for Retirement
Effects of Retirement
Nonstandard Exits from the Workforce
A Concluding Note

Summary

Key Terms

Suggested Reading

And what about a legacy? Reverend Johnson sums it up: "I just want to be remembered as someone who cried with you when your baby was sick, who went to the cemetery with you. I was there. I don't send somebody else unless I just can't make it in the snow with this one leg" (Terkel, 1995, p. 214).

Although not many of us can identify fully with the Reverend Johnson, I think there is some common ground we can recognize in his attitude toward work. Most of us have made changes in our initial career paths; we strive to do our jobs well, feel gratified when our efforts are recognized, and hope that our work has made some difference in the world. Even if your "job" at the moment is being a student, we all have a basic need to be good at what we do and to think of it as important. This chapter is about work—its importance in our lives, how we choose careers, how careers are affected by age, how we incorporate career and personal life, and how we plan for and adjust to retirement.

The Importance of Work in Adulthood

For most us, our jobs occupy a hefty portion of our time, our thoughts, and our emotions. They determine in large part where we live, how well we live, and with whom we spend time—even after working hours. On another level, our jobs provide a good deal of our identity and self-esteem. The role of worker is not a static one; over the years changes take place in the economy, technology, workforce composition, and social climate. Individuals change too; we go from intern to full-fledged professional as a result of attaining a degree. We go from full-time paid worker to full-time unpaid parent as the result of new parenthood. We go from work to retirement as a function of age. We go from retirement to part-time work when we find that the days are too long or the expenses of retirement are higher than we thought. These various work situations over the years of adulthood can be summed up in the term **career,** the patterns and sequences of occupations or related roles held by people across their working lives and into retirement.

I start this chapter with a discussion of two major theories, one on the centrality of careers to adult life, and one on how we select careers. Then I go on to cover how patterns of work are different for men and women, and how the work experience changes with age. Then I will cover the interaction of work and personal life. Finally, I will discuss retirement, which, it may surprise you to find out, is not simply the opposite of work.

Super's Theory of Career Development

Vocational psychologist Donald Super was the author of the best-known theory in the field of vocational psychology—the **life-span/life-space theory,** based on the concept that individuals develop careers in stages, and that career decisions are not isolated from other aspects of their lives. Although this theory was first proposed some 45 years ago (Super, 1957), it has been continuously revised and updated to keep pace with changes in workers and the workplace (Super, Starishevsky, Matlin, et al., 1963; Super, Savickas, & Super, 1996).

Not only is Super's theory influential to researchers and other theoreticians, it is also useful in applied settings for vocational counselors in high schools and colleges, and for human resource officials in businesses (Hartung & Niles, 2000). Super created a number of career-development tests to assess individuals' career adjustment, interests, and values. If you have ever taken the Adult Career Concerns Inventory (ACCI), the Career Development Inventory (CDI), or the Work Values Inventory (WVI), you have had your career trajectory evaluated according to Super's theory.

Table 7.1	Super's Five Stages of Career Development	
Stage	**Approximate Age**	**Tasks and Issues to be Faced**
Growth	4–14	Identify with significant others and develop self-concepts. Spontaneously learn about the world. Develop work-related attitudes, such as orientation toward the future, establishing control over life, developing sense of conviction and purpose, attaining attitudes and competencies for work.
Exploration	15–24	Crystallize career preference. Specify and implement an occupational choice.
Establishment	25–44	Stabilize in a job. Consolidate job. Advance in a job.
Maintenance	45–65	Hold achieved job. Update and innovate tasks. Perhaps reevaluate and renew.
Disengagement	65+	Decelerate workloads and productivity. Plan for and implement retirement. Shift energy to other aspects of life.

Source: Adapted from Hartung & Niles (2000); Super, Savickas, & Super (1996).

The first component of Super's theory, the *life span,* is divided into five distinct career stages, each with specific developmental tasks and issues to resolve. The five stages are displayed in Table 7.1, along with approximate ages for each. These stages are the major developmental pathway of the life span, according to Super, and our task is to make our way through them. However, we also cycle back through some of the stages at various times in our careers when we change jobs or leave the workplace to go back to school or to retire.

Super acknowledged that the work role is not the only role people have in their lives and thus cannot be considered in isolation from other roles. In fact, he goes so far as to say that the work role is best perceived in terms of its importance relative to other roles an individual plays (Super, 1990). The second component of his theory, the *life space,* deals with these roles. Researchers and vocational counselors (not to mention individuals who are evaluating their own career paths) need to also consider the relative importance of school, work, home, family, community, and leisure. Their importance is measured by tests assessing role salience—the degree of one's participation, commitment, and value expectation in the roles in each of these five areas.

> **CRITICAL THINKING**
>
> Which of Super's five stages best describes you today? Which do you think will describe you 10 years from now?

Gender Differences in Career Patterns

The first big distinction in career patterns is between men's and women's work lives. Although women are now represented in all major areas of work, gender is still a big factor in almost all aspects of careers. Men and women may perform their jobs equally well, but they are not the same, and knowing a person's gender predicts a lot about their career pattern. There are three major differences in the career paths of men and women.

First, *more men work full-time than women.* This is illustrated by Figure 7.1, which shows the number of men and women in the United States who hold full-time jobs. As you can see, fewer women hold full-time jobs than men, but the difference is becoming smaller each year—about 74 percent of men and about 62 percent of women in recent years (U.S. Bureau of Labor Statistics, 2005).

Why do more men work full-time than women? It's partly because of demographics; older people aren't as apt to work full-time as younger people, and there are more women

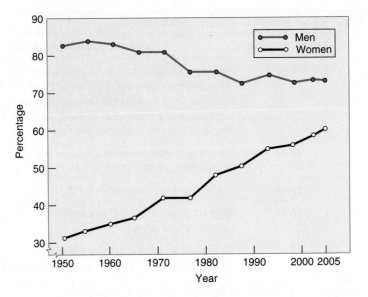

Figure 7.1 A greater number of men than women hold full-time jobs, but the gap is closing because of a steady increase in the percentage of women who work outside the home.

Source: U.S Bureau of Labor Statistics (2005).

in this age group than men. Another reason is a combination of biological and social factors—it is difficult for couples to have children when both spouses are working full-time, and the wife is usually the spouse to quit her job or reduce her work schedule when a child is born or while children are young.

This leads us to a second gender difference; *women move in and out of full-time jobs more freqently than men do* (O'Rand & Henretta, 1999). Men start their work careers with full-time jobs and usually keep working full-time until they retire. If their career is interrupted, it is usually due to being laid off and unable to find another job. Women, on the other hand, are more apt to start working full-time, leave the workforce when a child is born, go back to part-time work when the child is a few years old, perhaps stop again for a second child, and then go back to full-time work when the children are older. Women are also more apt to leave their own jobs when their spouses are transferred to another location, a situation that often leads to a period of unemployment for the women until they find a new job.

The third gender difference is, *women are more apt to work in part-time jobs than men.* This type of nonstandard work schedule is almost exclusively filled by women in the United States and worldwide. In the United States, 25 percent of women who work hold part-time jobs and only 10 percent of men (U.S. Bureau of Labor Statistics, 2005). In Europe, about half of all working women are part-time employees (ranging from 8 percent in Greece to 66 percent in the Netherlands). This type of work schedule may seem ideal for women who want to combine work and family, but the downside is that most of these jobs in the United States are in the service sector and feature lower wages and few benefits (O'Rand & Henretta, 1999).

One of the major impacts of the two genders having different career paths is that women's career discontinuities result in lower salaries (Eliason, 1995) and lack of job advancement (Melamed, 1995). Thanks to these (and other) factors, women earn less money than men even when they work full-time. According to the U.S Bureau of Labor Statistics (2005), women's salaries average 80 percent of men's. Nevertheless, many college women who have been interviewed about their career plans express admiration for women who interrupt their careers to have children and care for them (Bridges & Etaugh, 1995), and the majority state that they plan to do the same (Schroeder, Blood, & Maluso, 1992). A recent study of high school girls in the United Kingdom showed that most of these adolescents had formed career plans that would accommodate time out of the workforce because they perceived societal pressures against combining work and motherhood (Marks & Houston, 2002).

Having jobs with lower salaries, fewer benefits, and less chance for advancement, combined with moving from full-time to part-time to unpaid leaves of absence, has an obvious effect on women's career paths and financial security (and of course their family's security), but it also has a delayed effect which I will cover later in this chapter when I write about women and retirement. But first let us look at the beginnings of a career path and the process of choosing a career.

Selecting a Career

Selecting a career is not simply one big decision. As Super's theory suggests, careers develop over many years, and the path is not a linear one. The National Longitudinal Survey of Youth shows that between the ages of 18 and 38, the average number of jobs men and women have in the United States is just over 10 (U.S. Bureau of Labor Statistics, 2003). Teenagers work in jobs of convenience that fit their school schedules. College students work weekends and at seasonal jobs during summer breaks. Adults find that their jobs have been outsourced or moved to a different area of the country, so they retrain for a different job. Careers can often follow a mazelike path, but there are some central features. The work we like to do and the work we do best are aspects of our selves that do not change much over our lifetimes.

Holland's Theory of Career Selection

Vocational psychologist John Holland (1958, 1997) has been the major voice in the area of career selection for several decades. His basic argument is that people seek work environments that fit their **vocational interests,** which are defined as personal attitudes, competencies, and values (Hartung & Niles, 2000). Holland believes that there are six basic vocational interests: social, investigative, realistic, enterprising, artistic, and conventional, sometimes abbreviated as SIREAC types. These interests are displayed in Figure 7.2, along with the traits for each type and the preferred work environments.

A number of tests can be used to determine a person's vocational interest type according to Holland's theory, some given by vocational counselors, some given over the Internet for about $10. These tests all ask you to tell whether you like, dislike, or are indifferent to a long list of school subjects, activities, amusements, situations, types of people, and jobs. Your answers are converted into six scores, one for each type. The top three scores define your vocational interest type. For example, if you score highest on social (S), investigative (I), and artistic (A) factors, your vocational type would be identified as "SIA." This would help you (or your career planner), to steer you toward a career that would be a good fit with your vocational interests.

Holland's theory has been extremely well researched over the years since it was introduced in the 1950s, and the findings have generally supported Holland's contention that vocational interest types affect career choices (Helms, 1996; Holland, 1996). Some critics of Holland's theory argue that finding a job that fits one's vocational interests may lead to greater job satisfaction, but does not predict that one will achieve in the job or stay with it over the long term (Schwartz, 1992). There is also the obvious weak point that the theory is based on college-bound high school students or college students, so it may not be applicable to older workers.

From a related point of view, other researchers are investigating the developmental path of vocational interests—when they are formed and whether they undergo changes with

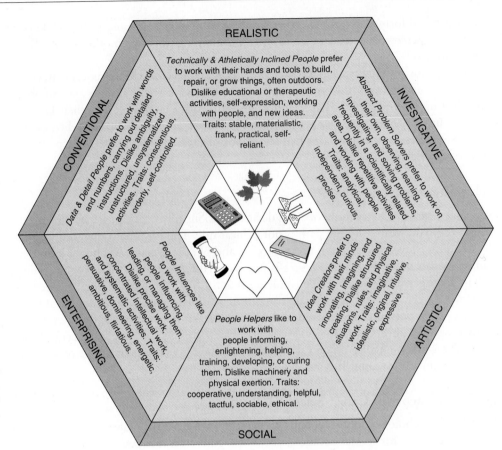

Figure 7.2 Holland's six basic types of people based on vocational interests (attitudes, abilities, and values). He believed that people were better adjusted and did better work when their jobs matched their vocational interests.

Source: Holland (1992).

age. For example, psychologist K. S. Douglas Low and his colleagues (Low, Yoon, Roberts, et al., 2005) performed a meta-analysis on data from 66 longitudinal studies on vocational interests, with participants ranging from 12 to 40 years of age, to find out how stable vocational interests are over adolescence and early adulthood. As you can see in Figure 7.3, the correlations between participants' early vocational interests, as measured in the longitudinal studies, ranged from 0.55 to 0.70, showing moderate to high levels of stability.

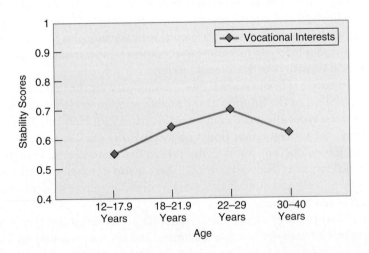

Figure 7.3 Vocational interests remain stable from early adolescence to middle age.

Source: Data from Low, Yoon, Roberts, et al. (2005).

The same study shows that there is a sharp increase in stability between 12 and 18, and a more gradual increase in stability between 18 and 30, followed by a sharp decline between 30 and 40. This indicates that the age at which most people consolidate their vocational interests is between 12 and 18, far younger than was commonly believed by school personnel and vocational counselors. The researchers suggest that vocational counseling should begin in elementary school, and that as soon as children enter school they should be exposed to a wide range of vocational activities, especially those designed to counter gender and racial stereotypes in career choices.

Other developmental work is focused on the reciprocal effects of vocational interests and careers. The thinking is that if the work we do is such a big part of ourselves, the work environment must have some reciprocal influence on our personalities. This is the notion of "niche-seeking," the idea that we select environments to fit our personalities, and that the environments, in turn, influence the further development of our personalities (Scarr, 1992; Van Manen & Whitbourne,1997).

The Effects of Gender

Gender is one of the major factors in career choice. Although this becomes less and less true each year, there is still a stereotype of "his and her" jobs, a social phenomenon known as **occupational gender segregation.** This doesn't mean that young men and women are routinely told in so many words that they should take certain jobs, but there is unspoken pressure from many directions to conform to what they see around them (Cejka & Eagly, 1999). This process works against women in several ways. There are more "his jobs," than "her jobs," and the traditional male jobs are typically higher in both status and income than the traditional women's jobs. Most of the jobs held predominantly by women are pink-collar jobs, such as secretarial and clerical jobs, retail sales positions, and service jobs.

● **CRITICAL THINKING**

Did you have vocational interests in childhood? How stable have they been? Do they match what you are interested in today?

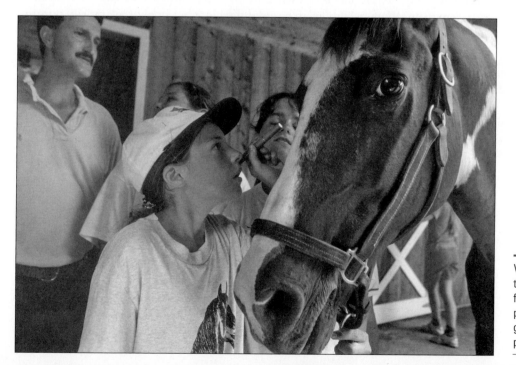

Vocational interests seem to be established well before adulthood, and young people benefit from early guidance and exposure to possible careers.

They are low in status and pay, offer few benefits, and give little chance for advancement. Another category of jobs that are traditionally held by women is in professions like teaching and nursing. These require college degrees, but do not have the income or chances for advancement that male-dominated professions have. The result of this occupational segregation is that many young women (and girls) are given the silent message that they have the choice of either being in a good career with high pay, benefits, and advancement, or being feminine—that is, following one of the "female" career paths that they see around them.

In a longitudinal study, psychologist Karen O'Brien and her colleagues (O'Brien, Friedman, Tipton, et al., 2000) questioned over 200 young women about their career plans when they graduated from high school and then again five years later. Over that time period, the women's career plans had changed. They now wanted to go into careers that were more traditional and less prestigious—careers that underutilized their competencies. Although 90 percent of the young women had not married at the time of the second interview, the researchers suggest that they had begun anticipating the problems of integrating career with family, and had modified their career plans accordingly.

Should we interpret this to mean that young women today are giving up their best career dreams and settling for less in anticipation of their future families? Perhaps, but I can think of some other explanations that should be considered before we accept this view. One is that 17- and 18-year-olds are extremely idealistic and think they can do anything. Perhaps this study shows that five years worth of maturity brought more realistic goals. I would like to see the same study done with young men. I wouldn't be surprised to find a reduction in career aspirations for them also. O'Brien and her colleagues add another question mark: What might be happening in the colleges to change these women's ideas about career? Ninety-seven percent of the sample had attended college in the five-year period between interviews. Did they meet with sexual discrimination or other pressures in their classes or from their advisers? We know from a survey of medical students that almost a third of the women had been influenced in their choices of specialties because of gender discrimination and sexual harassment encountered in medical school (Stratton, McLaughlin, Witte, et al., 2005).

One topic of interest here is women who work in nontraditional jobs. What can we learn from them? Women enrolled in nontraditional trade school programs and pursuing nontraditional majors in college report being supported and influenced by their fathers and brothers more often than those in traditional programs (Whitson & Keller, 2004). Similarly, when women who worked in the trades as plumbers, electricians, or carpenters were asked why they had chosen their careers, some reported having role models who encouraged them. Others felt they had a natural ability for this type of work and were independent enough not to be discouraged by other people's opinions. Not surprisingly, many of the women had very a strong sense of self; they were confident, self-assured, and comfortable with their career choices. Other studies of women in nontraditional jobs find that they have higher levels of job satisfaction than women in more traditional jobs (O'Farrell 1995), but they experience more stress than their male co-workers and or women in traditional jobs (Gerdes, 1995).

CRITICAL THINKING ●

What do you think are some of the reasons why women in nontraditional jobs express higher levels of job satisfaction than women in traditional jobs?

Those of us who are involved in higher education, whether as professors or students, should not be surprised to hear that more women than men are currently enrolled in colleges and universities, and that they are majoring in areas traditionally considered "men's work." Figure 7.4 shows the increase in the percentage of women graduating in dentistry, medicine, and law over the last three decades. These increases aren't being fueled by women in general, but by specific groups; for example, the increase in dentistry and medical degrees is disproportionately fueled by Asian American women, and the increase in law degrees by African American women (Costello & Stone, 2001).

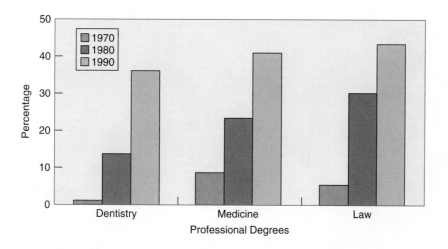

Figure 7.4 The proportion of women awarded degrees in dentistry, medicine, and law has increased dramatically in the past three decades.

Source: Data from Costello & Stone (2001).

Men who work in nontraditional occupations have been the focus of at least one study. Business and management researcher Ruth Simpson (2005) interviewed 40 men in the United Kingdom who worked as elementary school teachers, flight attendants, librarians, and nurses. She found that they entered their careers in three distinctive ways: one group was *seekers*—men who actively chose the traditionally female occupation; another was *finders,* who didn't seek the occupation but found it while making career decisions; and the third was *settlers,* who started in traditionally male jobs, then became dissatisfied and actively sought the nontraditional occupation. Over half of the men reported feeling discomfort in their roles and used various means to deal with this. Some gave incomplete or skewed information when asked about their work ("I am a teacher" instead of "I am an elementary school teacher," or "I am in tourism" instead of "I am a flight attendant"). Others played up the masculine side of their job, such as emphasizing the sports coaching they did as an elementary school teacher.

As I said before, this gap in "his and hers" jobs is getting smaller and smaller. It will be a few years before the gender distribution we see in the classroom is translated into change in the workplace, but at least we are heading in the right direction. And in my never-ending search for balance, I need to mention that young women are not the only ones limited by gender stereotypes in careers. For every young woman who has the ability and desire to be a carpenter or an auto mechanic, there may be a young man who has the ability and desire to be an elementary school teacher or a dental assistant but is discouraged by the unspoken "rules." Although men who cross the gender segregation lines in jobs seem to have their own sort of difficulties compared to women who take nontraditional jobs, either way it is still an unnecessary stumbling block for young people on the journey of adulthood.

Family Influences

Families affect occupational choice in at least two ways. First, families can have a profound effect on educational attainment. Middle-class parents are far more likely than working-class parents to encourage their children to attend college and to provide financial support for such further education. This is not just an ability difference in disguise. Even when you compare groups of high school students who are matched in terms of grades or test scores, it is still true that the students from middle-class families are more likely to go on to further education and better-paying, higher-prestige jobs. And young

When parents actively support higher education, their children achieve more in their future careers.

people from working-class families that put a strong emphasis on academic and professional achievement are also likely to move up to middle-class jobs (Gustafson & Magnusson, 1991).

Most of the young women today who are facing career choices have grown up with a working mother. Studies show that these young women have different ideas about gender and job selection than their peers who had homemaker mothers. For example, across many ethnic groups, young women with working mothers face their own futures with better self-esteem, higher educational goals, and aspirations toward more prestigious careers (Beal, 1994). Some of this difference certainly comes from having a resident role model, but there are other differences in these families than the simple fact that the mothers work outside the home. Women who work have different attitudes, personalities, and behaviors that impact on their children (and so do their husbands). Families with working mothers have different child-rearing practices and different division of chores. The result is often more responsibility and independence for the children, especially the daughters.

Another area in which the family influences the careers of adolescents and young adults is the marital status of the parents. A number of studies have shown that single parents do not provide the same level of encouragement and financial support as married parents to children preparing for careers. And this is true even when the income of the parents is considered. Young people living in stepfamilies do not fare much better, unless the parent and step-parent have had biological children together (Aquilino, 2005). This fact seems to turn the whole household into a "reconstituted family," and all the children benefit (Ganong & Coleman, 1998).

Why should divorced parents be less supportive of their children? One reason is that noncustodial parents may not have the same contact with and closeness to their children as they would if they lived together. Another reason is that support after high school is not required in most states, and many divorced parents feel that if they contribute to their child's college expenses, it will lessen the obligation the custodial ex-spouse might feel. This is not a surprising finding considering that divorced couples have probably never had a good history of cooperating with each other and working toward common goals, but as a result, young adults with divorced parents are less likely to receive financial support from their parents when they are beginning to develop their careers.

The Role of Genetics

There is evidence that career choice is also influenced by genetics. If you consider that various cognitive strengths and physical abilities are inherited, it should come as no surprise that people end up in occupations that showcase these traits. Looking at a family tree, it is not uncommon to find generations of people in the same occupation. My grandfather and two of his brothers were plumbers, and my father's generation produced even more (including my father). But was this because there is a "plumbing gene" in our family, or because tradition called for fathers to train their sons in their trade and pass down the family business? Genetic epidemiologist Paul Lichtenstein and his colleagues (Lichtenstein, Hershberger, & Pedersen,1995), offer some insight into this question. They gathered occupational histories of 118 pairs of monozygotic twins and 180 pairs of dizygotic twins who ranged in age from 26 to 87 years and were part of the Swedish Twin Registry. The researchers evaluated the participants' career histories and assigned each twin a score based on occupational status, using a standard Swedish socioeconomic scale. The five categories were (1) unskilled and semiskilled worker, (2) skilled worker, (3) assistant nonmanual employee, (4) intermediate nonmanual employee, (5) employed and self-employed professionals, higher civil servants, and executives. For the males, the monozygotic twins' occupational status scores correlated significantly higher than the scores for the dizygotic twins. In other words, if one identical twin was a level 2 on the socioeconomic scale (skilled worker), there was a significantly greater chance that his twin would also be a level 2 than if they were fraternal twins, indicating a genetic influence for occupational status.

> ● **CRITICAL THINKING**
>
> In the study of Swedish twins described here, the researchers also had a group of farmers in their sample, but removed them because there were too few to analyze. If there had been enough, which type of twin pairs do you think would be more apt to both be farmers, monozygotic or dizygotic? Why?

In contrast, the women twins did not show this genetic effect, but rather showed a stronger environmental effect. Considering that this sample had a mean age of almost 60, a sizable number of these women belonged to a cohort in which women were restricted to certain jobs or worked with their husbands in a family business. Neither of these situations would reflect an inherited genetic ability or interest. And to back this up, when the women's data were analyzed by age groups, the younger women were more apt to show the male pattern of genetic influence than were the older women. This supports earlier predictions that in countries that have social welfare programs to promote equal access to higher education, there would be an increase in the magnitude of genetic effects with time—thus younger women who had more opportunity to obtain education and job training compatible with their talents, interests, and competencies would show stronger genetic effects in the careers they developed (Heath, Berg, Eaves, et al., 1985).

Age Trends in Work Experience

Actual work performance is one area where older people hold their own, and the same is true for job satisfaction. When skill sets of older workers become obsolete, retraining is possible with the right methods. How can we reconcile these findings with the information in earlier chapters about age-related decline in cognitive and physical abilities? This is an interesting dilemma, and one that has some *very* real implications for the near future. As sociologist John C. Henretta (2001) reminds us, with all the hoopla about baby boomers reaching retirement age in the near future, we seem to forget that before they retire, they will spend a good amount of time being older members of the workforce. What can we anticipate from this "graying of the workplace"?

Job Performance

Most research concludes that performance on the job does not appear to change with age; that older workers are as good as younger workers by most measures (Clancy & Hoyer, 1994; Warr, 1994). This is a little surprising, because we also know from previous chapters that lab studies typically show age-related declines in abilities that are central to many jobs, such as reaction time, sensory abilities, physical strength and dexterity, and cognitive flexibility. Psychologists Timothy Salthouse and Todd Maurer (1996) reviewed this paradox in the research literature and suggested several explanations. One idea is that we consider job performance as made up of two factors: general ability and **job expertise,** or job experience. General ability may decline with age, but job expertise increases, perhaps enough to compensate for the decline, an **ability/expertise tradeoff.**

An example of the ability/expertise trade-off is demonstrated in a classic study of typing ability among women who ranged in age from 19 to 72 years (Salthouse, 1984). Two tasks were used, one that measured reaction time (ability) and one that measured typing speed (experience). Not surprisingly, speed of reaction decreased with age; older women took more time to react to visual stimuli. However, typing speed was the same regardless of age. How did this happen? Researchers explained that the older women relied on their increased job experience to compensate for their decreased general ability. As they typed one word, they read the next few words and were ready to type those words sooner than their younger colleagues who processed the words one at a time.

A similar effect was demonstrated in a study of musicians. When asked to play a complex piano passage, older professional pianists who maintained high levels of deliberate practice performed as well as young professional pianists; however, for amateur pianists, the younger ones performed significantly better than the older ones (Krampe & Ericsson,1996). Other studies have shown the benefit of expertise in airline pilots performing simulated flight exercises (Hardy & Parasuraman, 1997), and for clinical psychologists and college professors applying wisdom-related knowledge (Smith, Staudinger, & Baltes, 1994).

These findings of stable job performance across age groups is substantial support for the idea that crystallized abilities and highly practiced abilities can compensate for age-related declines in other abilities. They explain why older workers may not show declines in job performance when the demands remain stable over time (Czaja, 2001).

Job Training and Retraining

Although the topic of age differences in job training has not been well investigated, I expect to see a lot of research interest in that area soon. To revisit Super's theory of career development for a moment, recall the stages he outlined: growth, exploration, establishment, maintenance, and disengagement (review Table 7.1), and recall also his notion that people may go back through some of these stages from time to time during their careers, a process he calls **career recycling.** As career paths become more flexible, this recycling process has become more common, especially for the stages of exploration and establishment. As things change in the workplace (new technology, downsizing, automation) and in workers' lives (young children start school, older children complete college, job-related stress builds up), individuals explore career options and often decide to retrain. For example, if you are in a college classroom at the moment, there is a good chance you are a **nontraditional student,** one who is over the age of 25. If you are not in this category, there is an excellent chance that the person next to you is, no doubt engaged in career recycling.

Almost half the college students in the United States now are considered nontraditional (Luzzo, 2000). Most of them have been in the workforce or have been working in the home raising their children and are now back for retraining in order to take the next step in their careers (Peterson & González, 2000). Add to them the workers who are being retrained by their companies and the workers picking up new skill sets with a do-it-yourself format, and the total is a considerable proportion of adults of all ages who are learning new job skills. The participation rate for on-the-job training of workers 45 to 61 years of age is 20 percent (O'Rand & Henretta, 1999). This is impressive when you consider that the rate of workers of any age taking on-the-job training at any time during their career is only 10 percent. Studies of job-related tasks, such as computer training, show that older adults are capable of learning the new skill sets as well as younger workers, but they take longer, need more help, and make more errors on posttests (Kelley & Charness, 1995).

The little we know about older adults and job training (or retraining) seems optimistic, but some questions remain. Does instruction need to be modified to reach adults of all ages? Are some methods better for some age groups? Do people work better with age-mates, or does a mixed-age group bring better results? We need to learn more about job training and retraining with older adults to answer these questions.

Job Satisfaction

Studies show that older workers are more satisfied with their jobs than younger workers (Clark, Oswald, & Warr, 1996), and this might be a partial explanation of why job performance does not decline as workers get older (Schooler, Caplan, & Oates, 1998). Why would work satisfaction rise with age? In part, this pattern seems to be explained by time-in-job rather than age itself. Older workers have typically been in their job longer, which usually means that they have reached a level with more intrinsically challenging or interesting jobs, better pay, more job security, and more authority. This is an important point to keep in mind, because as people change jobs more often, as women move in and out of the labor market, many people will not accumulate large amounts of time-in-job and so may not experience the rise in satisfaction that is normally correlated with age. Similarly, if women move into the job market for the first time in their 30s or 40s, they may experience the peak of job satisfaction in their 50s rather than in their 40s. (This may be why women who don't begin to work outside the home until after their children are older often work past traditional retirement age, as I will discuss a little later in this chapter.)

Still, time-in-job cannot account for all of what we see. There are also "young" jobs and "old" jobs. Young people are much more likely to hold physically difficult, dirty, or less complex and less interesting jobs. In addition, there is undoubtedly some selective attrition operating here. Workers who really dislike some line of work tend not to stay in it long enough to be dissatisfied older workers. Older workers in any given occupation are thus likely to be people who choose to stay in that line of work because it gives them a good match to their personality or their interests.

Older workers may also have a more realistic attitude toward work. As my friend explained to her 16-year-old son, who was complaining about how much he disliked his summer job bagging groceries, "That's why they call it 'work' and not 'entertainment,' and that's why they pay you to do it and not charge admission." I'm sure that none of the retirees who work at the supermarket in the same job would need that explanation spelled out for them. Whether this is a cohort effect (the older generation had to work harder because times were rough when they were young) or an effect of increased wisdom, the lower expectations of older workers lead to higher job satisfaction.

Work and Personal Life

Freud said that the defining features of life were work and love, and nowhere does this ring more true than in the intersection almost everyone experiences as we merge our jobs and personal lives. There is a bidirectional effect between work and the individual, work and committed relationships, and work and family. We may be more aware of the effects our personal lives have on our work, but our jobs also have profound effects on our personal lives. I will start with work and the individual, then discuss work and various relationships—marriage, children, older family members who need care. And I will even cover household labor, a frequent topic of discussion in many homes.

Work and the Individual

Although older people are more satisfied with their jobs than younger people, workers of any age can experience the effects of heavy workplace demands. One example is **job burnout,** a combination of exhaustion, depersonalization, and reduced effectiveness on the job. This is especially common among workers whose jobs involve expressing emotion or being empathetic, such as nurses and social workers. Burnout has commonalities with depression, but the symptoms of burnout are specific to the job environment, whereas depression is more pervasive. Techniques used to relieve job burnout include a combination of helping the individual with coping strategies and making changes within the organization (Maslach, Schaufeli, & Leiter, 2001).

Not everyone in a difficult job responds to it with adverse reactions. For example, single workers are more apt to experience burnout, especially single men, suggesting that social support could be a protective factor. Several personality traits have been identified that relate to job stress and burnout: *low levels of hardiness*—being uninvolved in daily activities and resistant to change, *external locus of control*—attributing events to chance or powerful others instead of to one's own abilities and efforts, and *avoidant coping style*—dealing with stress in a passive and defensive way (Semmer, 1996). These coping mechanisms will be discussed in more detail in Chapter 10.

CRITICAL THINKING ●

What kinds of jobs would you predict have the highest rates of job burnout?

A related issue is **unemployment,** the state of being without a paid job when you are willing to work. In 2004, 6.1 percent of the population of the United States over 16 was unemployed. Unemployment is not distributed at random through the population. The rate is twice as high for black men than white men and twice as high for black women than white women (U.S. Bureau of Labor Statistics, 2005). It is also higher for people who live alone—whether widowed, divorced, separated, or lifelong single—than for married people living with their spouses. Being unemployed has obvious effects on financial well-being, but it also has been implicated in poor physical health, anxiety, depression, alcoholism, and suicide (Nelson, Quick, & Simmons, 2001).

Although unemployment may occur for several reasons (relocation, recent graduation from college), most of the research on this topic concerns **job loss**—paid employment being taken away from an individual. Job loss can be the result of a business closing, jobs being outsourced overseas, or a slowdown in the market for some product or service, and unfortunately is common in the United States in spite of a robust economy. For example, in 2003, there were over 5,000 mass layoffs leading to over a million workers experiencing job loss (McKee-Ryan, Song, Wanberg, et al., 2005). A larger proportion of these laid-off workers were older adults. Although employers are prohibited by law in the United States from making lay-off decisions based on age, they can decide based on seniority, salary, or poor health, all of which are related to age. As discussed earlier in this chapter, job performance does not decline with age; nevertheless, older workers are more likely to be laid off than younger workers, are less likely to be reemployed, and, if reemployed, are more likely to take a pay cut in their new jobs than younger workers (Hipple, 1999).

Job loss and the subsequent period of unemployment are strongly related to mental health problems and a decline in many areas of well-being, and the negative effects increase the longer the person has been unemployed. Surprisingly, women who have experienced job loss have higher rates of mental health problems and lower levels of life satisfaction than men in the same situation (McKee-Ryan, Song, Wanberg, et al., 2005). This could be because women are more apt to suffer from depression, or it could reflect the fact that job loss represents a larger financial problem for women than for men.

Not surprisingly, it is not only the actual job loss that causes problems but also the threat of job loss. Sociologist Leon Grunberg and his colleagues (Grunberg, Moore, & Greenberg, 2001) found that workers who are exposed to layoffs among friends or coworkers experience significantly lower job security, higher levels of depression, and more symptoms of poor health than workers who have not been exposed to layoffs.

The Workers Adjustment and Retraining Notification Act of 1988 (known as WARN) requires employers to give employees 60 days notification before large-scale layoffs. This act was passed by Congress in hopes of alleviating stress among workers who might be laid off abruptly. However, the effect of WARN has been that employers often send warnings to a large number of workers because they are unsure of how many they will be laying off 60 days later. Thus some workers receive warnings and then are not laid off. What happens as a result of those 60 days of uncertainty? In the study of workers exposed to layoffs cited above, 13 percent of the participants had received such a warning but had not been laid off. Compared to those who had only been exposed to layoffs through friends and coworkers, the warned group had a significantly lower sense of job security and more symptoms of depression and poor health, even though they had retained their jobs (Grunberg, Moore, & Greenberg, 2001).

Losing one's job is difficult for anyone, but there are some age differences. It is difficult for a young person just leaving school to be unemployed because it interferes with establishing a career and an identity as an adult (McKee-Ryan, Song, Wanberg, et al., 2005). It is difficult for older workers because of the problems they have finding a new job and adjusting to new work conditions. A good number of older people take early retirement after losing their jobs because they have little hope of getting new ones. However, being laid off is worst for middle-aged adults. Usually they have reached a middle or high level in the company structure and have problems finding a job with comparable pay and prestige, but they are also too young to retire with a pension or benefits. Those who have strong social support from family and friends, who can frame the situation so that they don't feel the job loss is their fault, and who have good individual coping skills, will usually have the best outcome (Aiken, 1998).

Work and Marriage

There is ample evidence that work has an influence on relationship commitment—that is, having a job, being out of school, having a good income, and being settled in a career are often prerequisites for entering into marriage or a committed partnership. However, it also seems that the partnership, in turn, has an effect on the work life of each partner. A number of studies show that married men earn higher wages than unmarried men, even when education and work experience are held constant (Gray, 1997), and the same is true for women's incomes (Waldfogel, 1997). This effect seems to hold for indicators other than income; for example, married men earn higher performance ratings on the job than unmarried men (Korenman & Neumark, 1991), they are absent from work less often (Keller, 1983), and they are more likely to participate in on-the-job training programs (Lynch, 1992) than unmarried men.

Sociologist Elizabeth Gorman (2000) investigated the differences in attitude toward work between married and never-married adults. She found that married men and women are significantly more interested in the income potential of a job than single individuals. In addition, married men and women are less satisfied with their current incomes than single individuals. Gorman believes that the attitudes expressed by the married participants in her study lead to more productive behaviors in the workplace and higher evaluations of job success, whether it be measured by income, promotions, or number of days on the job per year.

Women's work and marital stability are related, but there is disagreement on how to explain the findings. For example, the more hours a married woman works outside the home, the greater chance that her marriage will end in divorce (Greenstein, 1995). It is not clear whether the hours worked contribute to the marriage problems or whether the marriage problems stem from other causes and the women are working more hours as a result of the discord. It could be the case that marriage problems are followed by an increase in income for wives in anticipation of divorce or to increase bargaining power in the marriage.

CRITICAL THINKING

Some parents of young children choose to work different shifts to eliminate the need for daycare. If you had friends considering this path, what advice would you give them?

Couple's work schedules have a more clear-cut effect on relationship stability than just number of hours worked. Sociologist Harriet B. Presser (2000) has looked at the timing of work for both husbands and wives, specifically the nonstandard work schedules, or **shift work,** including evening shifts, night shifts, and rotating shifts. A preliminary look at labor statistics shows that shift work is becoming more and more common in the United States. If both spouses have jobs, there is a one-in-four chance that one of them will be a shift worker, and if they have children, the likelihood goes up to one in three. Usually these irregular schedules are not the choice of the workers but are determined by the employers. What do irregular work schedules do to marriages? When children are present, having one spouse who works a fixed night schedule (half the hours worked are between midnight and 8:00 A.M.), significantly increases the chance of divorce or separation. If it is the husband who works the night shift, the chance of divorce or separation is over six times higher than for husbands who work days, and if it is the wife who works the night shift, it is almost three times higher. Rotating shifts for wives (but not for husbands) double the chances of marital dissolution. Presser suggests that night shifts bring lack of sleep, stress from being out of sync with other family members, and loss of intimacy and social life together. Surprisingly, working evening shifts (half the hours worked are between 4:00 P.M. and midnight) for either the wife or husband had no effect on marital stability.

"Career choice" for many women means leaving their paid jobs for a number of years when they have young children and are working full-time as caregivers for their families.

Work and Parenthood

In the United States, approximately 64 percent of married couples with children are considered "dual-career" families, meaning that both parents are employed. In addition, there are a large number of single parents who are even more apt to combine family and careers. However, as discussed earlier in this chapter, it is more typical for men to remain in the labor force and for women to move in and out of

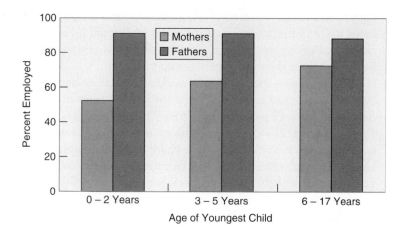

Figure 7.5 The proportion of parents who work increases for mothers as a function of their children's ages, but remains stable for fathers.

Source: Data from U.S. Bureau of Labor Statistics (2005).

employment due to family obligations. If the proportion of working parents is examined by gender, this fact is clearly illustrated in Figure 7.5. Almost all fathers are employed; the proportion of mothers employed depends on the age of the children. As a result, the number of years women spend in the workplace during their careers depends on the number of children they have; the more children a woman has, the less time she is apt to spend in the workplace (Kaufman & Uhlenberg, 2000).

Early studies showed that being a parent did not reduce the working hours of men, and it was concluded that parenthood did not have an effect on men's careers (Hyde, Essex, & Horton, 1993; Presser, 1995). More recently, researchers have argued that it is not accurate to measure the effects of parenthood on men's and women's careers using the same ruler. Some point out that men's role in the family has traditionally been one of provider, and that men respond to parenthood with a greater commitment to their careers (Kaufman & Uhlenberg, 2000). For example, one study found that when husbands become new fathers, they increase their work by 2 weeks per year (Nock, 1998). We saw in the last section that men who are married are more motivated to work hard and increase their incomes, so it stands to reason that these men would be even more motivated when they become fathers. This is supported in a study by sociologists Gayle Kaufman and Peter Uhlenberg (2000), who examined data from the National Survey of Families consisting of almost 4,000 married men and women under 50 living in the United States. An interesting dichotomy appeared; men were more likely to be employed if they were fathers and to work more hours the more children they had. Women, on the other hand, were *less* likely to work if they had children, and they worked *fewer* hours the more children they had.

Similar findings come from a study by economists Robert Lerman and Elaine Sorensen (2000), who analyzed data gathered over 13 years as part of the National Longitudinal Survey of Youth. Their group of interest was unwed fathers, men who had various degrees of contact with their children. The researchers were interested in determining what factors predict change in the pattern of contact between the fathers and their children. One of the strongest predictors of increased contact was higher income, but the timing of the effect was a surprise: Fathers who increased contact with their children during one year of the study showed a subsequent increase in the number of hours worked and the amount of income earned during the following years. It seems that once a father becomes more involved in his children's lives, he starts working more hours and making more money, not vice versa.

To summarize, parenthood has an effect on the careers of men and women. Parents are different workers than nonparents. Mothers are more apt to change their career

CRITICAL THINKING ●

Before you read on, what have you heard about children of working mothers? Have you heard that daycare has negative effects on children's behavior and later academic success? Do you think it is best for women to stay home with their preschoolers unless they absolutely need the income?

pattern to accommodate their role as mother, and men are more apt to become more committed to their careers as traditional breadwinners for their children. But does work have an effect on the parenting roles of men and women? That is the topic I will take up next.

The increase of mothers in the workforce has been one of the biggest social changes in the United States over the last two generations. The numbers have gone from 47 percent in 1975 to 72 percent in 2004 (U.S. Bureau of Labor Statistics, 2005), and with this increase came dire warnings about the negative effects it would have on the children. Early concerns about neglected children haven't materialized; the fact that a mother has a job outside the home, in and of itself, has no effect on her children's well-being. Instead, factors such as home environment, quality of daycare, parents' marital status, and the stability of mother's employment determine the outcome for her children (Gottfried, 2005). To the contrary, a mother in the workforce can be a benefit to her children if she has good support at home and at work; when mothers are willingly in the workforce, their children have increased academic achievement and fewer behavior problems than children whose mothers are not in the labor force—or who are there unwillingly (Belsky, 2001). When children of working mothers grow up, they have more egalitarian attitudes (Riggio & Desrocher, 2005). The daughters of working mothers consider more options when choosing careers, and the sons are more apt to share in the household work when they marry (Gupta, 2006).

One effect of maternal employment is that fathers' involvement in the lives of their children increases. Fathers spend more time with their children than their fathers spent with them, and 30 percent of fathers reported that their childcare responsibilities are equal to those of their wives or more (Bond, Swanberg, & Galinsky, 1998). Children with two working parents now spend an average of one hour more a day with their parents than children did 25 years ago (Bond, Thompson, Galinsky, et al., 2002).

Other research has focused less on whether parents (especially mothers) work and more on what kind of work they do. For example, studies have shown that the complexity of the work mothers do on the job is related to the extent they provide an enriched home

The fact that a mother works outside the home has no negative effect on the well-being of her child and can have long-term positive effects.

environment for their children. The more a mother's job offers the opportunity for her to focus on complex tasks with minimal supervision, the more she is apt to provide cognitive stimulation, emotional support, and safety for her children. And this is true regardless of her educational level (Menaghan & Parcel, 1995).

In my usual search for balance, I don't want to paint too rosy a picture of the world of dual-earner families. First, the U.S. workplace is not friendly to families. The rules were set in 1938, and although there have been adjustments, they still reflect the family structure of that time (Halpern, 2005). For example, the United States is one of only five countries in the world that does not offer paid maternity leave to its workers; the others are Australia, Papua New Guinea, and the African countries of Lesotho and Swaziland (United Nations Statistics Division, 2005). Another example is that it is legal in the United States for employers to pay part-time employees (most of whom are women) less per hour than full-time employees doing the same job, and to deny them medical benefits, sick leave days, and paid vacation days. Taking unpaid time off to care for a new baby or an aging parent, working part-time at greatly reduced pay while children are young, forgoing promotions because the new job would interfere with family responsibilities, all these are trade-offs parents frequently must make.

The American Psychological Association (2004) recently reviewed the situation faced by U.S. parents in the workforce and made recommendations for policy-makers, employers, schools, and communities. Some of these ideas are for policy-makers to consider programs that provide paid family and medical leave and to support job training and parent training for young fathers (Halpern, 2005). Other recommendations are shown in Table 7.2.

The picture at home is not totally rosy, either. As I mentioned before, about a third of fathers in dual-earner families report doing an equal share of the household work or more, but that still leaves two-thirds of dual-earner families in which the mother works outside the home and then returns home to work the "second shift." This is true even when the spouses work the same number of hours and when the wife makes more money than the husband

● **CRITICAL THINKING**

According to the APA, an important step schools can take to help families is to "align school and work calendars." Would this apply to your college or university also? Do students with children miss classes when holiday schedules are different or the children's schools have early-release days?

Table 7.2	Recommendations for Family and Work Intersection

For Employers

Recognize that "family friendly" is good business.

Establish flexible workplace policies.

Address stress, health, and work.

For Public Policy Makers

Be aware of work, education, wages, and poverty connections.

Support job and parent training.

Consider state and other government programs that provide paid family and medical leave.

Explore options that provide or supplement health insurance for the working poor to eliminate health disparities.

Make small business loans available to family businesses.

For Schools and Communities

Advocate for universal quality early childhood programs near public transportation.

Support after-school programs.

Align school and work calendars.

Arrange multiple services at sites and at times when people need them.

Acknowledge the positive outcomes working mothers provide.

Acknowledge the positive outcomes involved working fathers provide.

Lessen parental work stress.

Recognize the benefits of combining work and family roles.

Source: American Psychological Association (2004).

(For a copy of the full report, go to http://www.apa.org/work-family/fullreport.pdf)

(Bond, Thompson, Galinsky, et al., 2002). And then there is the case of single parents, who do it all. So in spite of the news that progress is being made for dual-earner families, there remains a lot to be done on a number of fronts.

Work and Caregiving for Adult Family Members

Caring for children is not the only family responsibility that many men and women need to combine with their careers. An increasing number of working adults have caregiving responsibilities for adult family members—parents or parents-in-law who are frail or ill, spouses with dementia or other chronic disabilities, or adult children or siblings who are disabled and can't care for themselves. A recent survey by the National Alliance for Caregiving and AARP (2004) showed that 21 percent of adults in the United States provide care for at least one adult family member. And a fifth of these provide more than 40 hours of care per week. The proportion of men involved in caregiving is increasing steadily—the most recent figures showed that about 40 percent of caregivers are men, although women contribute more hours of caregiving per week and do more hands-on caregiving tasks. Almost 60 percent of caregivers combine their caregiving with their career. Figure 7.6 shows the extent to which these individuals have had to make adjustments in their work lives to compensate for their caregiving responsibilities. As you can see, one-fourth of them have had to leave the workforce by either taking a leave of absence, opting for early retirement, or just giving up work entirely.

I discussed the role of caregiver in Chapter 5. The role becomes even more demanding when it is combined with one's career. A group of family-caregiver advocates has reviewed the state of family caregiving in the United States and has come up with a set of principles for change, including more family-friendly policies in the workplace for caregivers, such as offering flextime, work-at-home options, job-sharing, counseling, and dependent-care accounts (Feinberg, Horvath, Hunt, et al., 2003).

Household Labor

Housework, unpaid family work, housekeeping, domestic engineering, family chores—whatever you want to call **household labor**—few people enjoy doing it, but we all need it done. The topic of who does the meal preparation and cleanup, the grocery shopping, the laundry, and the housecleaning is a common one in discussions between parents and children, and between spouses. In the past decade, household labor has become the topic of over 200 research articles and books. Why should serious scholars be interested in house-

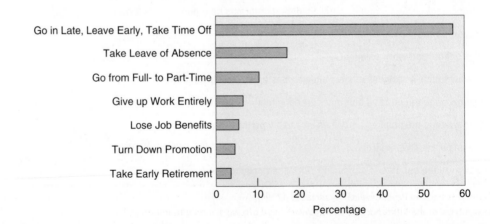

Figure 7.6 Proportion of caregivers/workers who made adjustments in their careers due to their caregiving responsibilities.

Source: National Alliance for Caregiving and AARP (2004).

hold labor? One reason is that it is embedded in complex patterns of social relations. According to sociologist Scott Coltrane, household labor is "related to gender, household structure, family interaction, and the operation of both formal and informal market economies" (Coltrane, 2000, p. 1208).

What has this research told us? First, that as a group we spend about as many hours doing unpaid family work as we spend doing paid job-related work (Robinson & Godbey, 1997). Second, women do more of this work than men, and even when others help out, whether paid domestic help or family members, women are responsible for their instruction and supervision. When a man contributes to the unpaid family work, it is often seen as an optional activity that helps out his wife in "her" duties rather than assuming the responsibility himself (Coltrane, 2000).

As women move through adulthood from single person to wife to mother, the amount of housework they do increases, while men's decreases as they proceed along the same developmental path. Interestingly, the time spent in paid work is distributed in the opposite direction—it *increases* for men and *decreases* for women as new roles are added. The result of this is that when you add together the paid and unpaid work, men and women are about equal at every stage of family development. But it seems that women don't always view this as a good trade—unpaid work is trivialized and minimized, considered mindless drudgery that anyone can do. Because it does not bring money into the home, the woman who spends her time on housework while her husband spends his time in paid work has less power and status in the relationship. Some women in these unbalanced situations perceive this as unfair and become depressed and dissatisfied with their marriages.

In the United States, women do two to three times as much housework as men (Bianchi, Milkie, Sayer, et al., 2000); women are more apt to adjust their work and home schedules to accommodate family (Sanchez & Thomson, 1997); and employed wives have less leisure time and more stress than employed husbands (Milkie & Peltola, 1999). In spite of all this, the majority of men and women consider their division of labor to be "fair" (Coltrane, 2000).

Most of the research supports a *gender-division model* of housework; in other words, in most cases, housework is done by women. However there are other perspectives that have been considered, such as the *time-availability model,* meaning that the housework is usually done by the person who has the most time available to do it, and the *relative-resource model,* which says that the housework is usually done by the person who has brought the least resources into the family (income, education, social status, age). All three have received some empirical support (Bianchi, Milkie, Sayer, et al., 2000), but many questions are raised about how to separate gender from resources and time.

Other factors make a difference in the division of household labor. Women who work more hours, do shift work, or have jobs with more prestige do less housework and their husbands do more. What determines whether or not a family hires someone to do the housework? It's the wife's income, not the husband's (Cohen, 1998). And education has an interesting effect; the more education a woman has, the less housework she does, but the more education a man has, the *more* housework he does (Orbuch & Eyster, 1997). Young couples (who are apt to have more egalitarian views and more education) share housework more equitably than older couples, although some studies have shown that retired men help more with housework than they did before retirement (Piña & Bengtson, 1995). Men who were raised by working mothers are more apt to help with housework, but only if their fathers were also present in the home, suggesting that the fathers served as role models for sharing household labor (Gupta, 2006).

CRITICAL THINKING

If you live with others, who does the household labor? Is it distributed according to gender, time availability, or relative resources?

Single women and cohabiting women do less housework than married women, single and cohabiting men do more than married men, and women in first marriages do more housework than those in second marriages (Nock, 1998).

Race and ethnicity are factors in housework division, with black men doing more housework than white men, but still half as much as black women (Orbuch & Eyster, 1997). Latino families generally follow the same patterns as Anglo families with one exception: both Latino men and women are less apt to view the housework division as unfair to the wives (DeMaris & Longmore, 1996).

Clearly the division of household labor is an issue with myriad levels of complexity, but this short review should give you an idea of some of the factors that feed into the decisions about who does what around the house.

Retirement

The concept of **retirement,** or the career stage of leaving the workforce to pursue other interests, such as part-time work, volunteer work, or leisure interests, is relatively new. My grandfather was the first person in his family to retire. He was the eldest son, and his father (as well as his grandfather) had been farmers who continued working until they died. Even if they had worked in salaried jobs, there was no social security until 1935 (and then it was called "old age survivors' insurance"). My grandfather worked for the city water department, and when he turned 65 in 1949, he was given a gold watch and a picture of himself shaking hands with the mayor. He began collecting social security, and several years later, so did my grandmother, who had never worked outside the home. Workers my grandfather's age were pioneers; they had no role models for retirement and may have felt a little sheepish about leaving the job while they were still able-bodied and had all their wits about them. It is hard to imagine today how much our retirement behavior and expectations have changed since that time.

Today retirement is quite different. Many people spend 20 years or more in this stage, and many look forward to it. They spend their time doing a variety of things; they travel, take classes at the university, and become political activists. Another difference today is that retirement is seldom an all-or-nothing state. People retire from one career after 20 years and then begin a second one or take a part-time job. Others collect a pension at 65 and continue working full-time. And some, like Reverend Johnson in the opening of this chapter, stay with the same company, but take positions with a lighter load. It is really difficult to divide adults into "retired" and "working" categories. Keeping all this in mind, I will jump in with both feet and write about when, how, and why people retire—and also where.

Preparation for Retirement

Retirement is not something that suddenly happens to us on some random date. Barring an unexpected illness, disability, or job layoff, the vast majority of adults who retire do so after some period of planning and expectation. Many adults prepare for retirement beginning perhaps as early as 15 or 20 years ahead. They talk with their spouses, with relatives and friends, read articles, do some financial planning, and think about where they will live. These activities seem to increase fairly steadily as the expected retirement date draws closer. However, another good chunk of people (about 20 percent) within 10 years of retirement report that they "hardly ever" think about retirement and don't discuss it with anyone (Ekerdt, Kosloski, & DeViney, 2000).

There is a gender difference in preparing for retirement. Women are not as likely to plan for retirement as men are. Women are less likely than men to participate in employer-sponsored pension plans and are more likely to cash out accumulated pension assets when they change jobs. This gender difference remains in force even when men and women in similar jobs are compared. Women are twice as likely to have no retirement income except social security. Many depend on their husbands to "take care of things," but not even those who are recently divorced or widowed make the effort to prepare for retirement that their male co-workers do (Hardy & Shuey, 2000). This lack of planning translates into large gender differences in retirement income, as will be discussed later in this chapter.

● **CRITICAL THINKING**

Before you read on, what age do you consider to be "retirement age"? At what age will you be eligible for full social security benefits? (If you haven't checked recently, you might be surprised.)

Timing of Retirement

Just as planning varies, so does the actual timing of retirement. We tend to think of 65 as "retirement age" because that is the current age at which people in the United States are able to start receiving full social security benefits and be enrolled in Medicare. However, the average age of retirement is actually 62, and that has been the case since 1985 (Clark, Burkhauser, Moon, et al., 2004). Still, there is a lot of variability from this average.

Figure 7.7 shows the proportions of adults of various ages who are in the **labor force** and officially working at paid jobs. These data extend back to 1984 and forward to 2014. If you examine the figure you will see that a little over 80 percent of adults between the ages of 25 and 55 years of age are currently in the labor force. Likewise, a little over 60 percent of those from 55 to 64 years of age are working, a little over 20 percent of those 65 to 74 years of age, and a little over 5 percent of those over 75 are in the labor force. Looking back to 1984 and forward to 2014, you can see that although the younger group has remained stable, the older three groups have increased in labor force participation and are expected to continue this increase into the next decade. This number has remained about the same for the past two decades and is expected to stay the same for at least another decade (U.S. Bureau of Labor Statistics, 2005).

One reason for the increase in older workers is that each year the group of people reaching retirement age are healthier, on average, than the group before, so more of them are able to work if they choose to. Also, mandatory retirement was ended for most jobs in the United States in 1986, making it possible for older workers to continue in their jobs if they so desired. The number of physically demanding jobs has declined from 20 percent in 1950 to 7.5 percent in the 1990s, making it easier for older adults to do the work required in many jobs. In addition, as of 2000, there is no longer a penalty for people 65

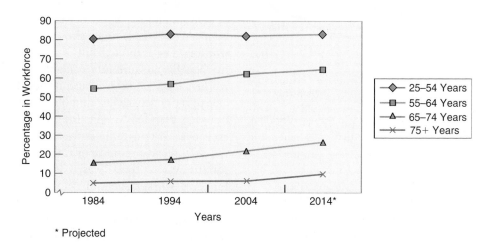

* Projected

Figure 7.7 The proportion of U.S. adults in the workforce has increased slightly for older age groups over the last two decades; this trend is expected to continue into 2014.

Source: U.S. Bureau of Labor Statistics (2005).

and older who collect social security and continue to work (Clark, Burkhauser, Moon, et al., 2004). Other reasons have been discussed in earlier parts of this book; grandparents are becoming increasingly responsible for the support of their grandchildren, which often means re-entering the workforce after retirement or staying in it when they reach retirement age (see Chapter 5). Women make up larger parts of the older groups, and their workforce participation has increased steadily, as will be discussed more in the next section.

This picture of an abundance of older workers in the labor force is not found in other developed countries. Figure 7.8 shows the proportion of adults between 55 and 64 who are part of the labor force in Germany, France, and Italy, compared to the United States. As you can see, the numbers are lower for those three countries and have declined since 1980 in France and Italy, while they are higher and have increased for the United States. One reason for this is that higher taxes in the European countries take away the incentive for continuing in the work force once retirement age is reached. Another reason is that, over the years, strong labor unions in the European countries have won generous retirement benefits for workers, and early retirement incentives have been used as a way to increase jobs for younger workers (Alesina, Glaeser, & Sacerdote, 2005).

Many European countries are concerned that the increasing elderly population will outpace the reduced labor force and the state pension funds will be depleted. Some are slowly increasing the age at which full benefits will be paid for retirees. Although the situation is not as grave in the United States, with its higher level of participation in the workforce, the age at which full benefits will be paid retirees is slowly increasing here also, from 65 to 67 in the future, reducing some of the financial incentive for retirement (Clark, Burkhauser, Moon, et al., 2004).

Reasons for Retirement

As was discussed in earlier sections of this chapter, retirement is not always a voluntary decision. A good number of older workers find themselves unemployed due to layoffs, mergers, or bankruptcies, and have difficulty finding another job at the same level and salary. A viable option for some of these individuals is to retire early. However, for most people, the decision of when to retire is more complex and depends on the interaction of a number of factors.

Finances. Economists and other social scientists have found that the biggest determinant in the decision to retire is the value a worker receives from staying on the job compared to the value he or she would receive from retiring. **Work-related value** is not only the worker's salary, but also the increase in pension and social security benefits to be received later if he or she continues working. For example, "full" social security benefits are currently available when workers reach 65 years of age; if they decide to retire between 62 and 65, they receive less than full benefits for the rest of their lives. If they retire between 65 and 70, they receive more than full benefits for the rest of their lives. Clearly, the longer a worker stays on the job, the higher the social security benefits will be. Some private pension plans work the same way. In addition, there are other val-

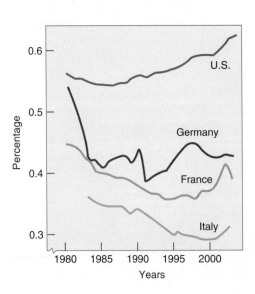

Figure 7.8 The proportion of adults 55 to 64 in the labor force in Germany, Italy, and France is low and has declined in the last few decades compared to that in the U.S.

Source: Adapted from Alesina, Glaeser, & Sacerdote (2005).

ues related to staying on the job, such as health insurance coverage for the worker and his or her family and other incentives the employer might offer for continued employment (Clark, Burkhauser, Moon, et al., 2004).

Workers weigh this package of value for staying on the job with the **retirement-related value.** In this package is personal wealth—how much is in savings, investments, home equity, and other assets. It also includes how much the worker would receive in social security and pension benefits, as well as what might be earned from other work, such as a part-time job or consulting work (Howard, 1998). Health insurance coverage is also part of this package. Medicare, the national medical coverage for workers, is not available until a person reaches 65, but some employers continue health insurance for retirees. Making these decisions is even more complex in many instances because the status of a spouse must be added to the equation.

For most people, evaluating the "stay on the job" package with the "retire now" package requires the advice of a financial expert (and perhaps a fortune teller). Yet in a national survey of over 3,000 adults in the United States, fewer than 40 percent had discussed retirement with a financial adviser (National Council on the Aging, 2002). The same survey reported that among people who were retired, over 70 percent said that financial considerations were the most important factor in their decision to retire.

Health. Another important factor in the timing of retirement is health. Again, this is not a simple matter. Health can affect the decision to retire in two ways. Increased medical expenses and the need for health care insurance can increase the chances that workers will stay on the job—and this involves not only the individual worker's health, but also that of his or her spouse and other family members (Clark, Burkhauser, Moon, et al., 2004). The second effect is that poor health can make working difficult and lead to a lower salary or transfer to a lower-paying position, making retirement more attractive. This is especially common in physically demanding jobs (Uccello, 1998). Alternatively, the poor health of a spouse or family member can lead to increased caregiving responsibilities and subsequent retirement. As mentioned earlier in this chapter (Fig. 7.6), about 3 percent of people who tried to combine caregiving and careers solved the problem by taking early retirement (National Alliance for Caregiving and AARP, 2004).

Family. Children and grandchildren play a role in deciding when to retire. With parenthood coming later and retirement opportunities coming earlier, having children still in the home might be a reason to remain in the workforce. And even if the children are out of the home, parents may want to provide college tuition and other types of support (Genevay, 2000). In addition, as observed back in Chapter 5, an increasing number of grandparents are raising grandchildren, often without much financial help from the parents or the state. The consequence is that many grandfathers (and some grandmothers) delay retirement to support another generation of their families.

Family is one of the most-mentioned reasons women cite for retiring. Many decide to retire because their husband has retired, but this companionable-sounding statistic can be misleading. Many of these wives report that they feel pressured by their husbands to retire before they are ready to leave their jobs (Szinovacz & DeViney, 2000). If a woman has worked during her child-rearing years, she is more apt to retire earlier; if she has only begun to work after her children were grown, she is more apt to retire later (Henretta, O'Rand, & Chan, 1993).

Career Commitment. The reasons for retiring cannot all be evaluated with dollar amounts. Some people just enjoy working and are not eager to retire. This factor is career commitment: those who are self-employed and highly committed to their careers retire later than those who work for others or are less committed. Workers who have lower standards for their work output, less identification with the company, and more dissatisfaction with their jobs and supervisors are more apt to retire early, compared to those who do not share these attitudes (Howard, 1998).

Leisure-Time Interests. Another nonfinancial reason to retire is that life outside the workplace is calling. Workers who have hobbies, recreation interests, and active social lives are apt to retire earlier than those who do not. In addition, those who enjoy travel and doing home-improvement projects are more eager to retire (Howard, 1998).

Effects of Retirement

Once an adult has retired, what happens? Does life change totally? Does health decline? The striking fact is, that for most adults, retirement itself has remarkably few effects on income, health, activity, or attitudes.

Changes in Income. Adults in the United States who are 65 and older have a variety of income sources, the major one being social security, which makes up 39 percent of the average income for retirees. Figure 7.9 shows the proportion of income that comes from various sources. *Earnings* are from jobs they hold. *Pensions* are from private companies, state, local, or federal government, the military, or personal retirement accounts such as 401Ks. *Asset income* is interest from savings, dividends from stock, and income from rental property.

However, this doesn't tell us how the incomes of retired adults compare to their pre-retirement incomes. We know that income typically drops when retirement begins, but this may not have a negative effect on the retiree's lifestyle. Many own their homes free-and-clear and thus no longer have to make mortgage payments, their children are launched, they are eligible for Medicare and thus have potentially lower payments for health care, and they are entitled to many special senior-citizen benefits. When you include all these factors in the calculation, you find that many retirees have fewer expenses after they re-

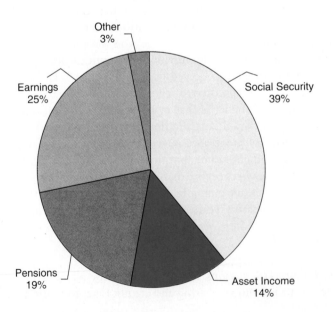

Figure 7.9 Sources of income for U.S. population aged 65 and over.

Source: Data from Federal Interagency Forum on Aging Related Statistics (2004).

tire. In the United States, incomes for some older adults actually increase after retirement, because the combination of social security and other government benefits is greater than the salaries they earned in their working years.

This upbeat report on the economic status of American elderly is possible primarily because of improvements in social security benefits in the United States over the past several decades. Indeed, the financial position of America's elderly has improved more than that of any other age group in recent years. As you can see in Figure 7.10, the percentage of people 65 and over who were living in poverty in 1966 was 28.5 percent; in 2002, the most recent year for which we have data, the number was 10.6 percent (Proctor & Dalaker, 2003).

But just as the figures on the drop in income with retirement are misleadingly pessimistic, the figures on the rate of poverty for retired persons are misleadingly optimistic. While the number living below the official poverty line (which was $9,800 a year in 2006 for a person living alone) has indeed dropped, there are still a large percentage in the category referred to as the "near poor," those whose incomes are between the poverty threshold and 25 percent above the poverty threshold (or $12,250 a year in 2006). In fact, this group is made up predominantly of older adults. And because these older adults are ineligible for many special programs designed to provide support for the poor, they are in many ways the worst off financially of any subset of the elderly (Costello, Wight, & Stone, 2003).

Like other social ills, poverty in old age is not equally distributed across ethnic groups or gender. Older women are about twice as likely to be poor as older men, and black and Hispanic elders are considerably more likely to be poor than white elderly adults. Combining these two factors, we find that the group most likely to be poor is African American women who are 65 and older and living alone, among whom 43 percent live below the poverty line and 54 percent are in the "twilight zone" of having incomes 25 percent above the poverty line. Finally, because women live longer than men, which means there are many more older women than men, we find that roughly two-thirds of all the elderly poor are women (Costello, Wight, & Stone, 2003).

This **feminization of poverty,** in which we find a larger proportion of women than men among the poor, especially among older adults, has many causes. An obvious one is that so many older women are widowed. In the United States, the social security rules are such that when a woman becomes a widow, she is entitled to either her own social security benefits or 100 percent of her husband's social security benefits, whichever is higher. That may seem like a good deal, but in fact it results in a substantial drop in household income. When the husband was still alive, both spouses received pension support; after he dies, there is only one pension check, and the widow's total income will be somewhere

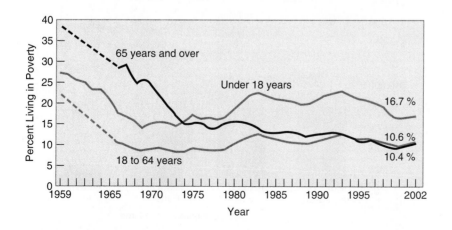

Figure 7.10 Poverty rates have declined in the last 50 years, and the biggest decline has been for people 65 and older.

Source: Proctor & Dalaker (2003).

Women have even more need than men to plan for retirement; at retirement age they have typically worked fewer years at lower salaries and have more years to live then their male counterparts.

between half and two-thirds the previous household income, even though many of her expenses, such as housing and taxes, stay the same. This drops a great many women into poverty (Gonyea & Hooyman, 2005).

It is too simple to attribute older women's greater likelihood of poverty simply to widowhood or living alone. The gendering of poverty in old age flows from a whole string of gender differences that women have experienced over their lifetimes and which come home to roost in their later years. Current cohorts of older women were much less likely to work, less likely to be involved in private pension plans if they did work, and more likely to work at lower wages than their male peers, all of which affects their incomes at retirement. Add to this the facts I've already presented about women moving in and out of the labor force to raise children or to care for elderly family members. The result is that a lower proportion of retired women than men have incomes from earnings (13 percent vs. 23 percent) and from pensions (30 percent vs. 44 percent). This leads to gender differences in personal income, as illustrated in Figure 7.11, which shows the median income

Figure 7.11 Women who are 65 and older have a lower median income from all sources than men in the same age group.

Source: Costello, Wight, & Stone (2003).

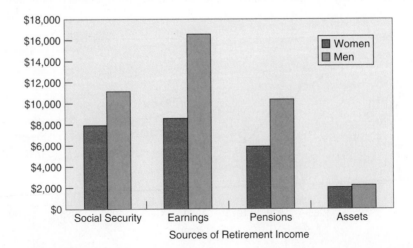

for women and men 65 and over from various sources, given that they have any income from those sources. As you can see, women have much lower incomes than men for social security, earnings, and pensions, but are about equal with earnings from assets.

Some consolation is that married women this age share their husbands' greater personal income, but almost half of women who enter retirement are widowed, divorced, or never married, making this "sharing" a moot point for them. Another consolation for younger women is that these figures represent a cohort of women whose roles did not necessarily include working outside the home or being involved in financial decisions. Hopefully, coming cohorts of women will reach retirement age with a more equitable distribution of personal income. It would be nice if we had a state-supported family-leave policy and other financial help for women who are the kinkeepers for so many, but the outlook is not optimistic. Women who choose to limit their income and career opportunities for family reasons, whether childcare or caregiving for adult family members, need to look ahead and make adjustments in their financial plans so that they will be compensated fairly in their later years. Perhaps the feminization of poverty will be ancient history when young adults of today reach retirement age.

Many of the statistics I've given you are quite discouraging and give a very negative impression of the financial status of the elderly. But let us not lose sight of two bits of information I gave you at the beginning of this section: on average, the effective income of older adults declines only slightly at the time of retirement, and the elderly in the United States are better off financially now than ever in the past.

Changes in Residence. Another effect of retirement for many adults is an increase in choices about where to live. When you are no longer tied to your job, you can choose to live nearer to one of your children or move south for sunnier weather. How many people this age move? The U.S. Census Bureau tells us that between 1995 and 2000, about 3 million people 65 years of age or older took part in **domestic migration,** moving their residences from one county to another or to a different state within the United States (He & Schachter, 2003). Although this is only 8 to 9 percent of the population in this age group, it still represents a major decision and a life-changing event for this group of older adults.

Among those who engaged in domestic migration, 26 percent made a move to another state in another region of the country. The states losing the most older adults to domestic migration were New York, Illinois, and California; the top destinations were Florida, Arizona, and Nevada. Most of the domestic migration can be explained by weather; older people are moving where the climate is warmer. In Europe, the same holds true; people of retirement age migrate to the south, and with travel restrictions between the European Union countries being relaxed, there has been a large increase in northern Europeans moving to southern Europe, especially people from Great Britain moving to Spain, Portugal, Greece, and Malta (Longino & Bradley, 2006).

Sociologist Charles Longino (2001) refers to the act of moving toward warmer weather and outdoor activities as an *amenity move.* In contrast, older retirees who move usually are going "back home," closer to their children and familiar surroundings, a process known as a *kinship move* and undertaken by about 18 percent of those who earlier made amenity moves. Finally, for some, there is a move that doesn't show up on these graphs because it is usually to an assisted-living facility or some type of nursing home within the community. In Longino's terms, this is called an *institutional move.*

One large group that doesn't show up in the census figures are those who take part in **seasonal migration,** or "the snowbirds" as we in south Florida affectionately call them. These are retired people like my in-laws, who enjoy the warm winters of the south and southwest but don't want to make a complete break from home. They split the difference by spending winters in the sunshine and the summers in their home states. These seasonal migrants tend to be white, healthy, educated, in their 70s, and married. Almost all are homeowners back north, and surprisingly, over 80 percent own their winter residences also. About two-thirds of the snowbirds in Florida have made the annual migration for at least 10 years (Smith & House, 2005).

What happens when snowbirds get older? They stay "back home" year-round. Only about 20 percent relocate permanently to their vacation homes; most shorten their visits as their health declines and then reluctantly end their seasonal stays when they can no longer make the move, or when one of them dies.

The topic of retirement migration has become very popular recently as the economies of states such as Florida and Arizona are enriched by new residents who bring income with them but don't take away jobs or add children to the school system. Many areas are now actively attracting retirees in hopes of boosting their economies. Another related topic of research interest is how these new residents, who are more apt to vote than younger residents, affect the political climate of their adopted communities.

Nonstandard Exits from the Labor Force

The majority of people who decide to retire leave the workforce never to return again, but there are some exceptions. Some leave and then return to their former jobs, some retire and take jobs that are less strenuous or require fewer hours, some work as volunteers. The following section tells about some of these "nontraditional exits" from the labor force.

Shunning Retirement. We all hear about middle-aged people who claim to enjoy work so much that they plan to keep working when they reach retirement age, even if they have comfortable pensions. If you are like me, you might be skeptical about these forecasts, but one longitudinal study showed that these predictions have some validity; men who made this claim in their 50s were more likely to be working in their 70s and 80s (Parnes & Sommers, 1994). In fact, if you recall from Figure 7.8, about 32 percent of men and 23 percent of women over 65 are still in the workforce (U.S. Bureau of Labor Statistics 2005). These "retirement shunners" are often highly educated individuals in professions like academia, where their personal lives blend into their professional lives, and they are highly motivated and involved in their work. Many have wives who are in similar professions and share their dedication to work. Another group that continues working as long as possible is at the other end of the spectrum—lower-income workers who have little education and low wages. Often they have no retirement pensions except social security, so simply cannot afford to retire.

Returning to the Workforce. A small number of workers retire and then reenter the labor market at some point after their retirement, either in a different job or in a similar job with a different company. My grandfather, whom I used as an example of retirement earlier in this chapter, did just this. A few years after receiving his gold watch, he returned to work and established a family plumbing business with my father. He worked with my dad for 8 years, teaching him the ropes of the trade, and then retired again. The practice of going back to work after retirement is done by 25 percent of the men and 20 percent of the women who retire (O'Rand & Henretta, 1999). Again, the reasons are myriad—need for income, loneliness, need to feel useful, restlessness. A few even make another attempt at retirement and then go back to work for a third time!

Gradual Retirement. Another nontraditional exit from the labor force is to retire and take a **bridge job,** which can be a part-time job or a less stressful full-time job. This is done by about 45 percent of retired men, especially those who retire at early ages from jobs such as police work, the military, and other government jobs. Often the job is related to their careers—for instance, police officers who take jobs as security guards or as police officers in small towns. Others take their knowledge and expertise into the classroom and become teachers. Some enjoy the social interaction that comes with being supermarket baggers or discount store greeters. A few workers use this opportunity to do some kind of work that they always wanted to do but was not feasible during their full-time working years. My father-in-law, for example, retired from his job with the police force in a small New England town and started a lawn service in his neighborhood. He had always enjoyed doing yard work, but with a large family to support it was never a career option. Now retired and in his late 70s, he spends several days a week during spring and summer on "his lawns" in Massachusetts. When fall comes he rakes the leaves one last time and then heads for Florida until it's time to go back north for the spring fertilizer sale.

Volunteer Work. If you have visited a hospital, a school, or a museum lately, you have no doubt had contact with a retired person who donates his or her time to your community. About 45 percent of retired women and 35 percent of retired men in the United States contribute their time to various community services, a higher rate of volunteerism than in any other age group. To give you an idea of the contribution these people make, volunteers with the National Senior Services Corps (which includes the Foster Grandparents Program, the Retired and Senior Volunteer Program—RSVP, and the Senior Companion Program) logged 171 million hours in 2003–2004, contributed by 634,000 persons 60 and older. They tutored, counseled, cared for, and mentored children; provided social support and instrumental support for the frail and elderly; staffed community projects such as blood drives and health-awareness seminars (National Senior Services Corps, 2004). And who knows what benefits the volunteer work brought to the volunteers themselves in terms of better health, increased social support, and decreased depression?

Phased Retirement. Phased moves from full-time work to permanent retirement are usually designed by the employer and offered as an option for senior employees. This practice is more common in Japan and some European countries than in the United States. In Japan, where companies set mandatory retirement ages, workers reaching that age are given a lump-sum retirement settlement and the option of (1) exiting the workforce completely, (2) joining a family business or starting their own business, or (3) taking a part-time job with the same company at lower wages (Usui, 1998).

The benefits of this retirement plan for workers are obvious. They have their retirement cake and eat it too. They have the lump-sum payment, but are not shut out of the workforce. They can still feel the pride and social support that come from having a job, plus more free time and a part-time salary. The employers have top-level workers at reduced salaries who can be placed in whatever section of the company that needs the help, often serving as mentors or trouble-shooters. And there is the overall benefit of keeping valued seniors in the workplace while still freeing up full-time jobs for younger workers (Kalleberg, 1998).

The closest thing we have to this is something called **phased retirement,** a situation in which an older person is working for an employer part-time as a transition to retirement. In these situations, the worker may be receiving some retirement benefits while still employed. However, there are all sorts of tax problems involved, and workers usually have to officially retire and be hired back in the new capacity, thus risking the loss of employee benefits (Purcell, 2000). Surveys show that workers would favor phased retirement

Table 7.3	Review of Changes in Careers over Adulthood	
Age 20–40	**Age 40–65**	**Age 65+**
Vocational interests, which have been stable since pre-teen years, are acted upon in selections of first jobs, college majors, or vocational training. Changes are made until a good job–vocational interest fit is reached and career is established.	Middle-aged adults usually remain in the same career but change employers as they advance. Some workers retrain for new jobs due to layoffs in the early 40s and early 50s. In late 50s and early 60s, they tend to take early retirement if laid off.	A growing number of workers continue their careers well past traditional retirement age. Some leave their major jobs and take bridge jobs that are less stressful or involve fewer hours. Others lend their skills and expertise as volunteer workers.
Men tend to move into the full-time labor force and remain until retirement. Women move in and out of the full-time labor force as they have children and care for them.	The departure of children from home leads women to start new careers or take on new responsibilities in existing fields.	Some workers this age retire and then return to work again, sometimes several times, depending on their health and expenses.
Job performance increases with experience and, for men, as family obligations increase.	Job performance remains high despite declines in physical and cognitive abilities, probably due to expertise.	Job performance remains high for experts and those who maintain a high level of practice.
Job-family intersection is most difficult during this time as most couples combine careers, marriages, and children.	Job-family intersection is easier, but now can include caregiving for elderly parents or surrogate parenting of grandchildren.	Family responsibilities seldom interfere with work, although some older workers leave work to become caregivers for their spouses.
Little thought of retirement.	Preparation for retirement begins in the 40s and early 50s, especially for men.	People this age are eligible for Social Security and Medicare, but the average senior depends on other sources for 60% of his or her income. Women have less retirement income than men their age from every source.
Residential moves at this age are usually related to career moves (or spouses' career moves).	Some early-retired people make amenity moves to areas with warm weather and leisure activities. Others become "snowbirds."	Some who are in good health continue to live in "retirement" areas or commute in the winter. Those in declining health move to be closer to family.

if it meant they could collect pension benefits while remaining on the payroll in a reduced capacity, so this may become easier for U.S. companies in the near future.

A Concluding Note

I have reviewed changes in careers over the years of adulthood in Table 7.3, and I would like to conclude this chapter with some words of wisdom. When retired men and women were surveyed about which stage of their lives had been the best, 75 percent of those who had done extensive planning for their retirement years responded with "the best is now." Only 45 percent of those who had not done much planning rated their current stage as best (Quick & Moen, 1998). Considering all we have covered on this topic, it seems clear to me that (to paraphrase an old joke) the three most important factors for successful retirement are planning, planning, and planning.

Summary

1. For most adults, career is a lifelong pattern of full-time and part-time work, time out for family responsibilities and retraining, and ultimately retirement pursuits. It occupies a central part of our time, thoughts, personal identity, and self-esteem.

2. The major theory in the field of vocational psychology for decades has been the life-space/life-span theory of Donald Super. His model shows the stages of career and the tasks that must be done at each stage. It takes into account that career must be integrated with other roles in life.

3. There are gender differences in the typical career paths of men and women. Women are less apt to work full-time, more apt to move in and out of the labor force, and more apt to work part-time than men. The result for women is lower income, less chance for advancement, fewer benefits during the work years, and less retirement income than men.

4. The best-known theory of career selection is that of John L. Holland, who suggests that people are happiest in job environments that fit their vocational interests. Holland devised tests to evaluate people on five types of vocational interests.

5. Gender is a big factor in career selection. Both men and women tend to select careers that are stereotypically defined as gender-appropriate. Unfortunately, the "female" jobs usually pay less and have fewer benefits and chance of advancement than the "male" jobs. Studies of men and women who have chosen nontraditional jobs are giving some useful insight into the career-selection process. Other factors are family influences and genetics.

6. Although physical, sensory, and cognitive declines accompany age, measures of actual job performance show no age-related declines. One explanation is that the experience of older adults compensates for decline in abilities.

7. Older workers express more satisfaction in their work lives than younger workers. There are many explanations for this, including attrition, cohort effects, and types of jobs each age group has.

8. Job stress can have negative effects on the individual, including burnout, but not having a job can be even worse. Unemployment is a serious life crisis for most adults, and even more serious for middle-aged workers than for those of other ages. Even the possibility of job loss can cause stressful reactions.

9. Marriage seems to increase work performance and goals for both men and women. Work conditions can affect marriage stability. Divorce rates are related to situations in which one partner works a night shift or the wife works a rotating shift.

10. Men are apt to work more hours the more children they have. Women are apt to work fewer hours the more children they have. Whether a mother works outside the home does not influence the well-being of her children one way or another. More important factors are the home environment, day-care quality, the parents' marriage, and the stability of the mother's employment. The workplace could be changed in a number of ways to fit the realities of today's families.

11. About one-fifth of all workers are also caregivers for a frail or disabled adult family member. The workplace could also be changed in a number of ways to fit this reality.

12. Women do more household labor than men, even when both work full-time.

13. There are many factors that influence the decision to retire. Among them are finances, health, family, career commitment, and leisure-time interests.

14. For most people, retirement brings slightly lower incomes but also lower expenses. For some, retirement brings a change of residence to another part of the country, or the beginning of a pattern of seasonal migration to warmer parts of the country.

15. Nontraditional ways to leave the labor force include shunning retirement, taking a less stressful job, working part-time, and working as a volunteer.

Key Terms

career, 202

life-span/life-space theory, 202

vocational interests, 205

occupational gender segregation, 207

job expertise, 212

ability/expertise tradeoff, 212

career recycling, 212

nontraditional student, 212

job burnout, 214

unemployment, 214

job loss, 214

shift work, 216

household labor, 220

retirement, 222

labor force, 223

work-related value, 224

retirement-related value, 225

feminization of poverty, 227

domestic migration, 229

seasonal migration, 229

bridge job, 230

phased retirement, 231

Suggested Reading

Reading for Personal Interest

Bolles, D. (2005). *What color is your parachute? A practical manual for job-hunters and career-changers.* Berkeley, CA: Ten Speed Press.

The cover of the newest edition of this book proclaims that it is "the best selling job-hunting book in the world," and that is true. It has sold 8 million copies over the last 30 years. No matter your age or your college major, this book is for you. The Library of Congress recently included it in the top 25 books that have changed people's lives, along with *War and Peace* and *On Walden Pond.* It is continually updated and gives adults a way to evaluate their abilities, their career situations, and their options. I have given at least a dozen copies of this book to relatives who graduate from high school, college, or are just thinking about a career change.

Crittenden, A. (2001). *The price of motherhood: Why the most important job in the world is still the least valued.* New York: Metropolitan.

The author is an economics journalist and mother whose work has been nominated for a Pulitzer Prize. In this book she draws together research in economics, developmental psychology, sociology, history, and law, along with interviews of hundreds of women, to show that the job of motherhood is both revered by our society and exploited. She skillfully sets up the problem and then presents innovative solutions. Whether you are male or female, if you have a family or plan ever to have a family, you should read this book and add Crittendon's insights to your decision-making toolbox.

Terkel, S. (1995). *Coming of age: The story of our century by those who've lived it.* New York: St. Martin's Press

Studs Terkel is a Pulitzer Prize–winning journalist who has made a career of interviewing everyday people and teaching us history through their words. This book is a collection of interviews with people who were born at the beginning of the 20th century, and although it covers many important aspects of their lives, the centrality of work shines brightly through. For those of us whose careers are still a work in progress, it is interesting to visit these individuals who can view their careers from a different perspective.

Classic Work

Super, D. E. (1957). *The psychology of careers.* New York: Harper & Row.

Early formulation of Super's life-span/life-space theory.

Holland, J. L. (1973). *Making vocational choices: A theory of careers.* Englewood Cliffs, NJ: Prentice-Hall.

The original publication of Holland's career theory.

Contemporary Scholarly Work

Hardy, M. (2006). Older workers. In R. H. Binstock & L. K. George (Eds.), *Handbook of aging and the social sciences* (pp. 201–218). San Diego: Academic Press.

Sociologist Melissa Hardy reviews age discrimination and policies regarding older workers in the United States and other countries.

Moen, P. (2001). The gendered life course. In R. H. Binstock & L. K. George (Eds.), *Handbook of aging and the social sciences* (5th ed., pp.179–196). San Diego: Academic Press.

This chapter contrasts the life choices made by both men and women, but is especially salient for women because of the long-term consequences of some of their career decisions. It should be a real eye-opener for women of any age (and their boyfriends, husbands, and sons).

Monk, A. (1997). The transition to retirement. In J. I. Kosberg & L. W. Kaye (Eds.), *Elderly men: Special problems and professional challenges* (pp. 144–158). New York: Springer.

Covers the special issues men face as they make the transition from full-time worker to full-time retiree. The author, a professor of social work, considers older men the "forgotten minority," and this chapter addresses their gender-related experiences.

Purcell, P. J. (October 2000). Older workers: Employment and retirement trends. *Bureau of Labor Statistics, Monthly Labor Review.*

This author, a specialist in social legislation at the U.S. Library of Congress, is very well informed about older workers and retirement. He explains technical matters very clearly. If you need more detail than I provided in this chapter, I highly recommend this article.

Chapter 8

Personality

Personality Structures
  Personality Traits and Factors
  Differential Continuity
  Mean-Level Change
  Intra-Individual Variability
  Continuity, Change,
    and Variability Coexist
  What Do Personality Traits Do?

**Explanations of Continuity
and Change**
  Genetics
  Environmental Influences
  Evolutionary Influences
  Summing Up Personality
    Structure

**Theories of Personality
Development**
  Psychosocial Development
  Ego Development
  Mature Adaptation
  Gender Crossover
  Positive Well-Being

Summary

Key Terms

Suggested Reading

GROWING UP IN a large extended family is like having instant access to longitudinal information about a variety of human behaviors. One may not have observed all the "participants" through all the stages of their lives, but there are always older relatives to provide the missing "data." For example, as children my sister Rose and I always enjoyed spending time with our grandmother's older sister, Aunt May. She was a retired teacher, had no children, and had never married, but her home was designed for children's visits. She had a chess board, a Scrabble game, and a set of dominoes tucked under her sofa. There was a huge porch swing, an endless supply of homebaked cookies, and a workroom devoted to pottery complete with a potter's wheel and kiln.

After one particularly fun-filled visit to her house, we commented to our mother that Aunt May was probably so patient and so much fun in her old age because she regretted not having children herself, but our mother laughed and said, "Oh no, Aunt May has always been good with children and a lot of fun. Age doesn't change a person's basic qualities. She was having 'mud and cookie' parties when I was your age and she was in her 40s. And your grandmother said May was like a second mother to her—always watching out for the younger kids in the family and making up games to amuse them."

Although our mother was not a research psychologist, she was voicing the basic concept of personality stability within an individual over the life

237

span. I think most of us have our own theories about personality and age, some based on personal experience within our own families and some based on stereotypes. This chapter delves into this complex topic and should sort things out a bit, sometimes supporting our personal theories and sometimes replacing them with others.

Personality Structures

Personality consists of a relatively enduring set of characteristics that define our individuality and affect our interactions with the environment and other people. The study of personality psychology encompasses a large range of interesting topics—traits, motivations, emotions, the self, coping strategies, and the like. In fact, before you took your first psychology course, this is probably what you thought the field was all about. It is one of the oldest specialties in psychology and has been a very active forum in the study of adult development. The main question is: What happens to personality as we go through adulthood and into old age? There appear to be only two possible answers to this question: Either personality is continuous or it changes. However, research over four decades has shown that the answer is not so simple. A better answer is, "It depends." First, it depends on which type of continuity or change is being studied. Then, it depends on which personality factor we are interested in. And furthermore, it depends on the age of the adults being studied, their life experiences, genetic makeup, and the way the data are gathered (Alea, Diehl, & Bluck, 2004). So if you like mental roller-coaster rides, hang on!

My plan of attack for this topic is to cover research based on trait theory that argues generally for personality stability across most of the adult years. Then, I will tackle some recent research based on traditional developmental theories that argues for a good deal of change in personality over adulthood. I will add a section on positive psychology and, finally, try to tie it all together. Coping strategies deserve more than a brief mention and are covered in their own section in Chapter 10.

Personality Traits and Factors

The early formulations of personality come from names that are familiar to you, such as Freud, Jung, and Erikson, developmental theorists whose ideas were based on the premise that many aspects of adult life, including personality, are dynamic and evolving throughout the life span in predictable ways. Many of these theories were based on specific changes at specific ages brought about by resolution of tension between competing forces in life. (I will discuss these theories in more detail later in this chapter along with some current research based on their concepts of personality.) About 20 years ago, a new generation of personality psychologists began arguing that it wasn't enough to have a popular theory that was enthusiastically endorsed; it was also important for a personality theory to be empirically tested and validated (McCrae & Costa, 1990). Therefore, it was necessary to define personality more precisely. One of the biggest problems was deciding just what the "enduring characteristics" were that should be studied empirically. What are the basic **personality traits,** or patterns of thoughts, feelings, and behaviors exhibited by our human species?

A good example of a personality trait is how a person typically behaves in social situations. Some people are retiring and some are outgoing. If you think of several people you know well and consider how they usually act around other people, you can probably arrange them along a continuum from most outgoing to most retiring. The continuum from outgoing to retiring is a personality trait, and the position each of your friends occupies along that dimension illustrates how they rate on this trait. I use the term "typ-

CRITICAL THINKING

Think of what your closet looks like today. Where would that put you on the "orderly-messy" continuum? Does this reflect a trait for you or a state?

ically" here so as not to confuse personality traits with **personality states,** which are more short-term characteristics of a person. If you go to a party after an argument with your best friend, your usual outgoing *trait* may be eclipsed by your withdrawn *state,* but your trait is still outgoing.

Personality traits were not new to psychology in 1990. To the contrary, there were too many of them: "Thousands of words, hundreds of published scales, and dozens of trait systems competed for the researcher's or reviewer's attention. How could one make any generalization about the influence of age on personality traits when there appear to be an unlimited number of traits?" (Costa & McCrae, 1997, p. 271). The solution was to narrow down the great number of personality traits into a small number of **personality factors,** groups of traits that occur together in individuals. For example, if people who score high in modesty also score high in compliance, (and those who score low in one also score low in the other), it stands to reason that tests that evaluate modesty and compliance are probably tapping into the same well. The basic question was: How many different wells (or factors) are there?

Personality psychologists Robert McCrae and Paul Costa (1987) started with two dimensions that had been long agreed upon, Neuroticism (N) and Extraversion (E). By using a procedure called factor analysis, they found evidence for three more factors: Openness (O), Agreeableness (A), and Conscientiousness (C). The result of this work was the **Five-Factor Model (FFM)** of personality (also known as the "Big Five Model," although to my knowledge, neither Costa nor McCrae has ever used this term). Since that time, they have devised and revised a test instrument, the latest version of which is called the Revised NEO Personality Inventory. This inventory has been translated into many languages and been administered with similar results to people representing a large number of backgrounds. Basically, researchers have found that no matter what the ages of the individuals tested or what their gender or cultural background, people's personality traits fell into patterns around these five factors, or personality structures. These five factors are shown in Table 8.1 along with the traits that are clustered within them.

The five-factor model is not the only factor analysis model of personality, and the NEO Personality Inventory is not the only test used to evaluate personality traits. There are also the familiar Minnesota Multiphasic Personality Inventory (MMPI), the California Psychological Inventory (CPI; Gough, 1957/1987), the Sixteen Personality Factor Questionnaire (16PF; Cattell, Eber, & Tatsuoka, 1970), and others. Currently, the five-factor model is the standard, and when other tests are used, their factors are often converted to the terminology of the NEO Personality Inventory. But regardless of the test used, researchers had defined a limited set of personality factors and traits that fell within them to begin scientific research on the question of what happens to personality over the course of adulthood.

Differential Continuity

Now that the history and methodology have been covered, what does the study of personality factors tell us about personality continuity and change? One way of conceptualizing what happens to personality over adulthood is to investigate **differential continuity,** which refers to the stability of individuals' rank order within a group over time. In other words, do the most extraverted participants at Time 1 (for example, age 20) remain among the most extraverted participants at Time 2 (for example, age 50)? And do the lowest-ranked participants still score in the lowest ranks of Extraversion 30 years later? This type of question is usually answered by correlating the ranking

CRITICAL THINKING

In your high school class, the guy who drove too fast and always left studying until the last possible moment would probably have ranked the highest of your group in "excitement seeking." If he maintained that top ranking in your group, what behavior might you expect of him at your 20-year class reunion? And if your class decided to retire together to a condo in Florida at 62, what behavior would you anticipate from him at that age?

Table 8.1	Five Factors of Personality and the Traits They Include	
Neuroticism (N)	**Conscientiousness (C)**	
Anxiety	Competence	
Angry hostility	Order	
Depression	Dutifulness	
Self-consciousness	Achievement striving	
Impulsivity	Self-discipline	
Vulnerability	Deliberation	
Extraversion (E)	**Agreeableness (A)**	
Warmth	Trust	
Gregariousness	Straightforwardness	
Assertiveness	Altruism	
Activity	Compliance	
Excitement seeking	Modesty	
Positive emotions	Tender-mindedness	
	Openness (O)	
	Fantasy	
	Aesthetics	
	Feelings	
	Actions	
	Ideas	
	Values	

Source: Costa & McCrae (1992).

order for the group of participants at Time 1 with their rankings at Time 2. If the correlation coefficient is positive and sufficiently high, it means the group generally stays in the same rank order, and that the personality factor (in this case, Extraversion), is considered moderately stable. More interestingly, comparisons can be made between intervals in young adulthood (for example, age 20 to age 30) and then again in older adulthood (for example, age 50 to age 60), assessing whether this personality factor is more stable at one time of life than another.

Using this method, we know that personality traits remain moderately stable throughout adulthood, and that their stability increases with age (we get "stabler and stabler"). This is even true when the time period from childhood to early adulthood is included, which has long been thought to be a time of life-changing roles and identity decisions. Figure 8.1 shows the rank-order correlations from childhood to late adulthood, reflecting data from 152 studies of personality (Roberts & DelVecchio, 2000). As you can see, there is an increase in rank-order stability from age 6 to age 73. Other things we know about rank-order stability are that these patterns don't differ much from one personality factor to another, show no gender differences, and are very similar no matter what type of assessment method is used (Caspi, Roberts, & Shiner 2005).

In summary, personality traits are surprisingly stable during childhood and throughout adulthood, increasing steadily until about 50 and then leveling off. Even in the oldest groups, there is a correlation coefficient of around 0.70, which means that total stability has not been reached (as it would if the coefficient were 1.00), showing that there are still some changes taking place in rank order.

Mean-Level Change

The concept of **mean-level change** refers to changes in a group's average scores over time. If your first-year college class was tested on some personality measure (for example, Conscientiousness), and then tested again in your senior year, would the averages of the group change significantly? And if so, why? Mean-level change is attributed to maturation (such as menopause for women at midlife) or cultural processes shared by a population (such as the normative changes of finishing school, starting a career, and leaving the parental home).

In a cross-sectional study of participants from five different cultures, those over 30 showed higher mean-level scores for Agreeableness and Conscientiousness, and those under 30 showed higher scores for Extraversion, Openness, and Neuroticism (McCrae, Costa, Pedroso de Lima, et al., 1999). In a similar study, researchers divided Extraversion into two components, Social Dominance and Social Vitality. Then, in a review of three cross-sectional studies and three longitudinal studies, they showed that Social Dominance increases with age between 20 and 80, whereas Social Vitality decreases (Helson & Kwan, 2000).

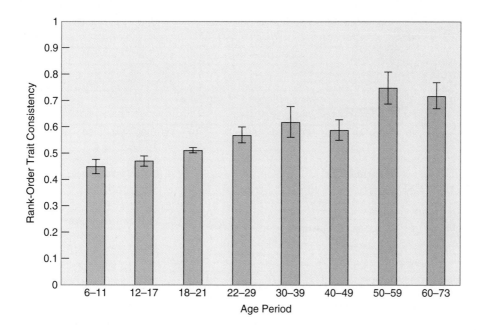

Figure 8.1 Rank-order correlations show that differential consistency remains high from childhood through late adulthood and increases through middle adulthood.

Source: Roberts & DelVecchio (2000).

In a meta-analysis of 92 studies, researchers found that personality factors not only changed, but showed distinct patterns of change. These patterns of change are shown in Figure 8.2. For example, Conscientiousness, Emotional Stability, and Social Dominance (one component of Extraversion) showed significant increases, especially in young adulthood. Participants increased in Openness and Social Vitality (a second component of extraversion) in adolescence, but then decreased in old age. Agreeableness did not increase much from adolescence to middle age, but did increase at 60 and 70 (Roberts, Walton, & Viechtbauer, 2006).

Evidence for mean-level change in older adults is similar; personality trait scores from a group of 74- to 84-year-old participants were compared to an older group of participants 85 to 92 years of age, and researchers reported that the older group showed higher scores for Agreeableness. Furthermore, 14 years later, the "younger" group had shown an increase in these traits which brought them up to the level of the original "older" group (Field & Millsap, 1991).

The message from these studies is that personality does change predictably with age, and continues to change at least to the age of 92. We become more and more agreeable, more conscientious, more emotionally stable (or less neurotic), and more socially dominant. We become more open and socially vital in young adulthood, but then decline in old age. These patterns seem to be independent of gender and cultural influences.

Intra-Individual Variability

Another way to chart the progress of personality traits over adulthood is to look at **intra-individual variability,** or in other words, find out whether the personality traits of an individual remain stable over the years or change. This is done by giving personality tests to individuals at several points in time and then correlating each person's scores from Time 1 with the scores for Time 2, and so on. This is not the same as differential stability, because you are correlating the actual scores, not the rank order. One of the few studies of this type was an examination of self-confidence measures in women over a 30-year period. Researchers found several patterns of increase and decline during those years (Jones & Meredith, 1996). Another study of intra-individual variability correlated five-factor

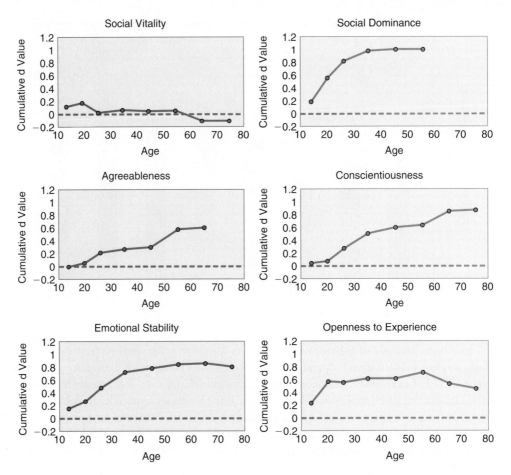

Figure 8.2 Cumulative change for six personality-trait domains across the life course show distinct patterns.
Source: Roberts, Walton, & Viechtbauer (2006).

scores for men between the ages of 43 and 91, finding that most showed declines in Neuroticism and no changes in Extraversion with age. However, this was not true for all the participants, and many showed different patterns of individual variability even in very late adulthood (Mroczek & Spiro, 2003).

Continuity, Change, and Variability Coexist

How do human personality structures within a group show differential continuity, mean-level change, and intra-individual variability over time? It's quite possible to understand if you consider it in terms of something more familiar, such as exam scores. For example, I generally give three exams in my class on psychology of women. The class shows *differential continuity* because those who are the top students on the first exam are usually the top students on the second and third exams too, while those at the bottom of the grading scale remain in that rank order. However, there is also considerable *mean-level change.* The average score for the first exam is always significantly lower than the later exams. Some students don't take the subject matter seriously and are shocked to see questions about genetics, d-scores, and research findings. Others explain that they need to take one exam in a class before they know what to study for the next ones. Whatever the reason, almost everyone improves on the second exam, showing mean-level change for the class alongside differential continuity. And there is also *intra-individual variability.* Although most students follow the patterns described thus far, there are exceptions each semester. A student can start off strong with a top grade on the first exam, then get inundated with work as the semester goes on, floundering on the later exams as a result of trying to burn the candle at both ends. Another can start out strong, get frazzled at midterm, and then buckle down to pull up the grade on the final. The result is differential continuity, mean-level change, and intra-individual variability, all in the same class. And the same is true for personality traits across adulthood.

What Do Personality Traits Do?

Researchers have identified five major personality factors and a large number of traits associated with one factor or another, and they have explained the patterns of stability and change across adulthood, but recently work has been done on just what personality traits do other than define our uniqueness. Three developmental areas have been identified that are shaped by personality: cultivating relationships, striving and achieving, and maintaining and promoting health (Caspi, Roberts, & Shiner, 2004).

Personality and Relationships. Personality traits are important in the development of intimate relationships in adulthood. Neuroticism and Agreeableness in particular are strong predictors of relationship outcome. The higher a person is in Neuroticism and the lower in Agreeableness, the more apt he or she is to be in conflicted, dissatisfying, and abusive relationships, and the more quickly the relationships will dissolve (Karney & Bradbury, 1995). In a longitudinal study that followed the relationships of adolescents into adulthood, researchers found that high levels of Neuroticism predicted that the individual would repeat the same negative experiences from relationship to relationship (Ehrensaft, Moffitt, & Caspi, 2004).

> ● **CRITICAL THINKING**
>
> In Table 8.1, look over the traits listed under the personality factor Neuroticism. How might high levels of each contribute to the demise of romantic relationships? What relationship effects might the traits in the Agreeableness factor have?

The influence of personality on intimate relationships happens in at least three ways. First, personality helps determine with whom we choose to have a relationship, often someone with a similar personality. For example, a person who is high in Neuroticism would tend to seek a relationship with a person who shares that trait. Second, personality helps determine how we behave toward our partners and how we react to our partner's behavior. A person high in Neuroticism who is in a relationship with a similar person will express negative behavior toward the partner and will meet the partner's negative behavior with further escalation of negativity. And third, personality evokes certain behaviors from one's partners. For example, people high in Neuroticism and low in Agreeableness express behaviors that are known to be destructive to relationships: criticism, contempt, defensiveness, and stonewalling, which you may recall from Chapter 6 as the "Four Horseman of the Apocalypse" in marriages (Gottman, 1994a).

Research in this area is currently limited to intimate partnerships, but personality could be useful in exploring relationship dynamics between parents and children, friends, employers and employees, and within groups.

Personality and Job Achievement. The personality traits that make up the factor of Conscientiousness are the most important predictors of a number of work-related markers of achievement, such as occupational attainment and job performance (Judge, Higgins, Thoreson, et al., 1999). If you look back at Table 8.1, you will see why. The traits included in this factor include competence, order, dutifulness, and self-discipline. In fact, if you look around your classroom, you will probably see a lot of Conscientiousness being displayed because it also predicts academic achievement. These traits are integral to completing work effectively, paying attention, striving toward high standards, and inhibiting impulsive thoughts and behavior.

The traits involved in Conscientiousness could affect job achievement in several ways. First, people choose niches (jobs) that fit their personality traits. We feel comfortable doing things we are good at and get pleasure from. Second, people who display these behaviors are singled out by others to be given jobs and promotions. Third are selection processes; people who are not conscientious leave high-achievement jobs (or are asked to leave). And fourth is the obvious fact that people who are high in Conscientiousness actually do the job better (Caspi, Roberts, & Shiner, 2004).

Researchers have shown that all five of the personality factors predict good job performance if the job is a good match for the personality (Judge, Higgins, Thoreson, et al., 1999). This finding should remind you of John Holland's theory of career selection discussed in Chapter 7.

Personality and Health. The most dramatic finding about personality is that it is closely related to health and longevity. People who have high levels of Conscientiousness and low levels of Neuroticism live longer (Danner, Snowdon, & Friesen, 2001). Other studies show that people low in Agreeableness (having high levels of anger and hostility) are at risk for heart disease (Miller, Smith, Turner, et al., 1996).

This link between personality traits and health can take place in a number of ways. First, personality can directly affect the functioning of the body, as seems to be the case with the link between hostility and heart disease. The physiological reactions summoned by hostility act directly as pathogens to cause disease. Second, personality can lead to behaviors that either promote health or undermine health. People who are high in Agreeableness are more likely to have close relationships with supportive people, a factor known to be a buffer against stress-related diseases. People high in Neuroticism are more likely to smoke and indulge in other high-risk health behaviors, while those high in Conscientiousness are more likely to have regular checkups and watch their diets (Caspi, Roberts, & Shiner, 2004). And fourth, personality may be linked with the type of coping behaviors there are in one's repertoire and which one chooses to use when confronted with stress (Scheier & Carver, 1993). This connection with personality and stress is also discussed in Chapter 10.

In a meta-analysis of 194 studies, psychologist Brent Roberts and his colleagues (Roberts, Walton, & Bogg, 2005) correlated scores on Conscientiousness-related traits (review Table 8.1) and nine different health behaviors, such as drug use, risky driving, and risky sex practices. Conscientiousness was significantly correlated to each of them, meaning that knowing a person's score on Conscientiousness would allow you to predict his or her likelihood of engaging in these health behaviors. The results are shown in Figure 8.3.

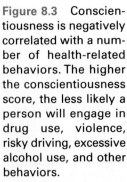

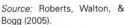
CRITICAL THINKING

If you gave personality tests to the people at your gym and the people across the street at the ice cream shop, which group do you think would have the highest scores on Conscientiousness? In what setting might you find a group that was exceptionally high in Extraversion? Openness? Agreeableness? Neuroticism?

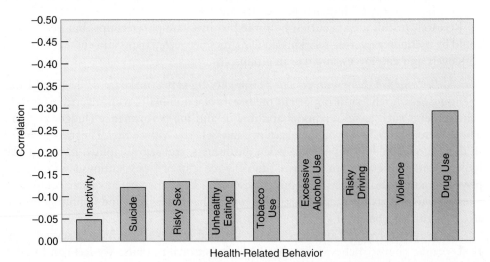

Figure 8.3 Conscientiousness is negatively correlated with a number of health-related behaviors. The higher the conscientiousness score, the less likely a person will engage in drug use, violence, risky driving, excessive alcohol use, and other behaviors.

Source: Roberts, Walton, & Bogg (2005).

As you can see, drug use, violence, risky driving, and excessive alcohol use show the largest correlations. The lower one's Conscientiousness score, the more likely one is to engage in those behaviors. Other behaviors shown in Figure 8.3 had smaller correlations, but were still significantly predicted by Conscientiousness. As the authors state, "People who are not conscientious have quite a number of ways to experience premature mortality. They can die through car accidents, through acquisition of AIDS via risky sexual practices, through violent activities such as fights and suicides, and through drug overdoses. People can still suffer from an attenuated life span in middle age through not eating well, not exercising, and smoking tobacco, which all lead to heart disease and cancer" (Roberts, Walton, & Bogg, 2005, p. 161).

Explanations of Continuity and Change

We know that there is evidence of both continuity and change in various personality traits, but what is less clear is why. What factors influence these features of personality? The explanations may sound familiar by now—genes and environment. There is also an explanation from evolutionary psychology that uses the interaction of both.

Genetics

To what extent do our genes determine our personalities? The short answer is "quite a lot." In fact, about 40 to 60 percent of the variance in personality types is heritable. Furthermore, the five major factors are influenced by genetics to about the same extent, and there seem to be few gender differences.

Studies comparing the personality scores of monozygotic twins and dizygotic twins illustrate the extent of this genetic influence. Psychologist Rainer Riemann and his colleagues (Riemann, Angleitner, & Strelau, 1997) compiled personality data for nearly 1,000 pairs of adult twins in Germany and Poland to investigate the heritability of the five-factor model of personality. Each participant completed a self-report questionnaire, and then the twins' scores were correlated with their co-twins' scores. As you can see in Figure 8.4, the identical-twin pairs, who shared the same genetic makeup, had significantly

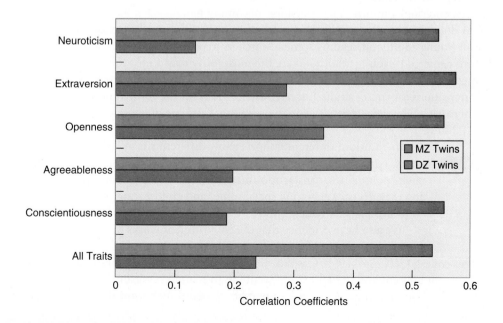

Figure 8.4 Monozygotic twins' scores for five personality factors show higher correlations than scores for dizygotic twins, showing that there is a genetic influence for personality structures.

Source: Adapted from Riemann, Angleitner, & Strelau (1997).

CRITICAL THINKING ●

Which related pairs would you predict to have the most similar personality scores, grandparents and grandchildren or first cousins? Or would it be the same? Why?

higher correlations than the fraternal-twin pairs, who shared only about 50 percent of their genes, suggesting that all five of these personality trait structures are moderately influenced by genetics.

In an interesting twist, Riemann and his colleagues also gave questionnaires to two friends of each twin and asked them to respond about the twin's personality, providing an objective rating to compare with the self-reports. The two friends agreed with each other substantially (the correlation coefficient was 0.63), and the means of their scores agreed with the twins' self-reports moderately (the correlation coefficient was 0.55), all adding evidence to the heritability of personality traits.

We have a number of studies reporting the heritability of the five major personality factors, but not much is known about the genetic contribution to the smaller, lower-level traits that make up the five factors. Limited research with children has shown that some of these primary traits of personality are affected more by environment. For example, altruism and prosocial behavior (components of Agreeableness) have been found to be more an effect of siblings' shared environment than their genetic makeup (Krueger, Hicks, & McGue, 2001). In addition, we don't have much knowledge about whether the influence of genes on personality changes with age. A limited number of studies show that Extraversion and Neuroticism appear to be stable over the adult life span. Most studies on changes in heritability involve children and adolescents (Caspi, Roberts, & Shiner, 2004).

Environmental Influences

As important as genetic influences are on personality, the environment has an affect also, both directly and in combination with genetic factors. Although individuals' personality measures tend to remain stable in rank-order positions through adulthood, there is room for some change (as shown back in Figure 8.1), even in the later years, presumably due to environmental influences. Longitudinal studies of twins show that personality change is more influenced by genetics in childhood than in adulthood, meaning that environmental influences are more prominent in adulthood (Plomin & Nesselrode, 1997).

Changes in mean-level measures of personality are common and tend to occur mostly in young adulthood, a time that is very dense in role transitions (leaving home, starting careers, entering committed partnerships, becoming parents). For example, measures of social dominance, conscientiousness, and emotional stability all increase in mean level during young adulthood, leading some researchers to believe that "life experiences and life lessons centered in young adulthood are the most likely reasons for the patterns of development we see" (Roberts, Walton, & Viechtbauer, 2006, p. 18). All cultures support these role transitions for young adults and have expectations for the content of these roles. This might explain why these traits develop universally at this time of life (Helson, Kwan, John, et al., 2002).

CRITICAL THINKING ●

What types of childrearing practices would tend to raise the Conscientiousness scores of children?

In addition, different cohorts show different mean levels of personality traits. For example, more recent cohorts show higher scores on measures of social dominance, conscientiousness, and emotional stability, perhaps showing the effects of changing social values and childrearing practices (Roberts, Walton, & Viechtbauer, 2006).

We also have evidence that the environment works in combination with genetic factors to maintain differential stability. Psychologist Avshalom Caspi and his colleagues (Caspi, 1998; Caspi & Roberts, 1999), suggest that individuals' genetic endowment and environmental factors combine to maintain personality traits over the years of adulthood, a concept known as **person-environment transactions.** This point of view has become increasingly popular in developmental psychology, especially in studies of personality development in childhood, and is similar to the concepts of niche fitting (Super & Harkness, 1994) and goodness of fit (Wachs, 1994).

Person-environment transactions can be conscious or unconscious and happen in a variety of ways. *Reactive transactions* take place when we react to, or interpret, an experience in a way that is consistent with our own personality or self-concept. If a friend calls you two days after your birthday to congratulate you and have a nice long chat, you can either interpret it as meaning that you are not important enough to be called on your birthday or that you are so important that your friend waited two days until there was time for a long talk. Either reaction would tend to perpetuate your established way of thinking about yourself.

Evocative transactions are those in which we behave in a way that elicits reactions from others that confirm our own personality or self-concept. People who have low self-esteem often reject compliments or overtures of friendship and, as a result, end up even more convinced that they are not valued by others.

Proactive transactions occur when we select roles and environments that best fit our personalities and self-concept. If you are not high on extraversion, you will probably not make career decisions that put you into a job that involves working directly with people. Not only will you be happier in a more solitary work environment, but this choice will also serve to maintain your introverted traits.

Finally, *manipulative transactions* are those strategies in which we attempt to change our current environments by causing change in the people around us. An example is an extraverted manager who is transferred into a quiet office and proceeds to motivate his coworkers to be more outgoing. To the extent that this maneuver is successful, the manager is creating an environment that serves to reinforce his or her own personality traits.

Evolutionary Influences

If personality structure has substantial genetic components and is similar in all cultures, it probably evolved over generations along with our other human traits. Evolutionary psychologist David Buss (1997) argues that personality traits are based on the most important features of the social groups our early ancestors lived in. It was important for our species to have indicators of who was good company (Extraversion), who was kind and supportive (Agreeableness), who put in sustained effort (Conscientiousness), who was emotionally undependable (Neuroticism), and who had good ideas (Openness). According to Buss, these differences (and the ability to perceive them in others) have been important to the survival of our species.

Summing Up Personality Structure

In this section I have covered research based on personality structures, mainly the five-factor model that was defined by Costa and McCrae in the 1990s. Using the NEO Personality Inventory, researchers are able to assign scores to each factor, giving each participant in the study a numerical personality profile. These studies are usually done as self-reports and with very large groups of people. Once the scores are computed, the patterns can be analyzed to find out how personality changes over time, whether there are cultural differences, and the like. It is quick and easy, and it is empirical. We have learned a lot about human personality from these studies—I'd venture to say that we have probably learned more *scientifically supported facts* about personality in the last two decades using this type of research than we learned in the past century from personality theories that were never tested empirically. However, numerical scores lack the depth and richness that we know reside within ourselves and the people we know well. To try and tap into these dimensions of personality, I will now make a 180-degree turn and discuss theories of personality development.

Theories of Personality Development

Another approach to changes in personality across adulthood is to conduct research based on some of the early theories of personality development, most of which had their roots in Freudian psychoanalytic theory. Full explanations of these theories comprise a whole course in itself, and I'm sure you are familiar with the basic concepts from your other classes, so I will only briefly describe them before going on to the current research findings. Although these researchers use different terminology and research methods, many of their findings fit well with the trait theory findings, as I will explain in a summary at the end.

Psychosocial Development

The most influential theory of personality development is that of psychoanalyst Erik Erikson, who proposed that psychosocial development continues over the entire life span and results from the interaction of our inner instincts and drives with outer cultural and social demands (Erikson, 1950, 1959, 1982). For Erikson, a key concept is the gradual, stepwise emergence of a sense of identity. To develop a complete, stable personality, the person must move through and successfully resolve eight crises or dilemmas over the course of a lifetime. Each stage, or dilemma, emerges as the person is challenged by new relationships, tasks, or demands. As you can see in Table 8.2, each stage is defined by a pair of opposing possibilities, such as trust versus mistrust, or integrity versus despair. Erikson also talked about the potential strengths to be gained from a healthy resolution of each dilemma, which are also listed in the table. A healthy resolution, according to Erikson, is finding a balance between the two possibilities.

There are four dilemmas that describe adulthood, beginning with Stage V, *identity versus role confusion,* which is the central task of adolescence and those in the early 20s. In achieving **identity,** the young person must develop a specific ideology, a set of personal values and goals. In part, this is a shift from the here-and-now orientation of the child to a future orientation; teenagers must not only consider what or who they are but what or who they will be. Erikson believed that the teenager or young adult must develop several linked identities: an occupational identity (what work will I do?), a gender or gender-role identity (how do I go about being a man or a woman?), and political and religious identities (what do I believe in?). If these identities are not developed, the young person suffers from a sense of confusion, a sense of not knowing what or who one is.

Stage VI, *intimacy versus isolation,* builds on the newly forged identity of adolescence. **Intimacy** is the ability to fuse your identity with somebody else's without fear that you're going to lose something yourself (Evans, 1969). Many young people, Erikson thought, make the mistake of thinking they will find their identity in a relationship, but in his view, it is only those who have already formed (or are well on the way to forming) a clear identity who can successfully enter the fusion of identities that he calls intimacy. For those whose identities are weak or unformed, relationships will remain shallow and the young person will experience a sense of isolation or loneliness.

The next stage of personality development, Stage VII, is *generativity versus self-absorption and stagnation.* **Generativity** is concerned with establishing and guiding the next generation. It encompasses procreation, productivity, and creativity. The bearing and rearing of children is clearly a key element in Erikson's view of generativity, but it is not the

Table 8.2 Erikson's Stages of Psychosocial Development

Approximate Age (Years)	Stage	Potential Strength to Be Gained	Description
0–1	I. Basic trust versus mistrust	Hope	The infant must form a first, loving, trusting relationship with the caregiver or risk a persisting sense of mistrust.
2–3	II. Autonomy versus shame and doubt	Will	The child's energies are directed toward the development of key physical skills, including walking, grasping, and sphincter control. The child learns control but may develop shame if not handled properly.
4–5	III. Initiative versus guilt	Purpose	The child continues to become more assertive and take more initiative, but may be too forceful and injure others or objects, which leads to guilt.
6–12	IV. Industry versus inferiority	Competence	The school-aged child must deal with the demands to learn new, complex skills or risk a sense of inferiority.
13–18	V. Identity versus role confusion	Fidelity	The teenager (or young adult) must achieve a sense of identity—both who he or she is and what he or she will be—in several areas, including occupation, gender role, politics, and religion.
19–25	VI. Intimacy versus isolation	Love	The young adult must risk the immersion of self in a sense of "we," creating one or more truly intimate relationships, or suffer feelings of isolation.
25–65	VII. Generativity versus self-absorption and stagnation	Care	In early and middle adulthood, each adult must find some way to satisfy the need to be generative, to support the next generation or turn outward from the self toward others.
65+	VIII. Ego integrity versus despair	Wisdom	If all previous stages have been dealt with reasonably well, the culmination is an acceptance of one-self as one is.

Source: Adapted from Erikson (1950, 1959, 1982).

only element. Serving as a mentor for younger colleagues, doing charitable work in society, and the like, are also expressions of generativity. Adults who do not find some avenue for successful expression of generativity may become self-absorbed or experience a sense of stagnation. The strength that can emerge from this stage, according to Erikson, is care, which implies both taking care of and caring for or about others or society.

Erikson's final proposed stage, or Stage VIII, is *ego integrity versus despair*. **Ego integrity** is achieved when people look back over their lives and decide whether they find meaning and integration in their life review or meaninglessness and unproductivity. If they see that they have resolved well the conflicts that arose in each previous stage, they are able to reap the fruit of a well-lived life, which Erikson labels "wisdom."

Erikson was a good thinker. He had a combination of formal training in psychoanalysis and informal training in a variety of arenas—as an art student, in his work with Native American tribes, in his studies of the lives of a diverse group of individuals such as Mahatma Ghandi, Martin Luther, and Adolf Hitler. His theory makes sense intuitively—it fits the way we think about our own lives and those of others. But how does it hold up under scientific scrutiny? A number of researchers have found ways to test Erikson's theory, with mixed results.

In many work settings, middle-aged people demonstrate generativity by serving as mentors for their younger colleagues.

Psychologist Susan Krauss Whitbourne and her colleagues devised a test instrument, the Inventory of Psychosocial Development (IPD), that provides numerical scores for Erikson's psychosocial stages (Walaskay, Whitbourne, & Nehrke, 1983–84). In a sequential study of men and women, they found that scores for Stage V (identity versus role confusion), increased significantly when participants were between the ages of 20 and 31, but remained stable between the ages of 31 and 42. The mean scores for this group are depicted in Figure 8.5 by the solid line marked Cohort 1. This supports Erikson's views that ado-

Figure 8.5 Mean scores for Erikson's stage V (Identity) for two cohorts. Scores for both cohorts increase between ages 20 and 31, but not for older ages.

Source: Adapted from Whitbourne, Zuschlag, Elliot, et al. (1992).

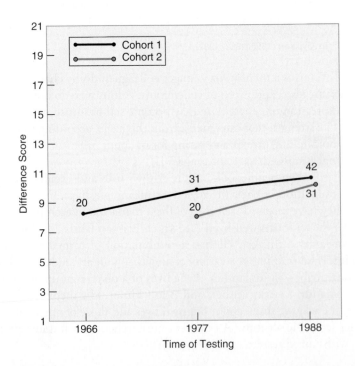

lescence and early adulthood is a time to question and explore alternative possibilities for adult identity. Eleven years later, the researchers repeated the testing on a new group of 20- to 31-year-olds and found the same results, depicted by the dotted line labeled Cohort 2, showing that this was probably not an effect of one particular cohort (Whitbourne, Zuschlag, Elliot, et al., 1992).

Similar results were found for scores on stage VI (intimacy versus isolation), another developmental task that takes place in young adulthood. Cohort 1 of the study increased in intimacy measures between the ages of 20 and 31, but maintained stability between 31 and 42. Cohort 2, eleven years later, showed the same increase between 20 and 31. These results are shown in Figure 8.6.

Erikson's stage VII (generativity versus stagnation) is the stage that has been studied the most. For example, psychologists Kennon Sheldon and Tim Kasser (2001) measured the personality development of a group of adults by asking them to list their current goals, or some of the things they are typically trying to do in their everyday lives that they may or may not be successful at. These goals were then coded according to which Eriksonian stage they best typified. Strivings that involved giving to others or making one's mark on the world were coded as stage VII (generativity vs. stagnation). Results showed that older persons were more concerned with generativity than identity, supporting Erikson's belief that this is a major task in later years.

Interestingly, Sheldon and Kasser also found that adults of all ages reported having intimacy goals, or in other words, listed personal goals that increased the quality of relationships. The researchers interpreted these findings as supporting Erikson's assumptions of lifelong development and the order in which the stages present themselves to individuals across the life span, but the lack of reduction of intimacy goals with age "raises the possibility that once mature psychosocial themes become salient within a person's life, they tend to remain important rather than fade away, to be replaced by new themes" (Sheldon & Kasser, 2001, p. 495). Considering the importance that close connections with others have throughout life, it stands to

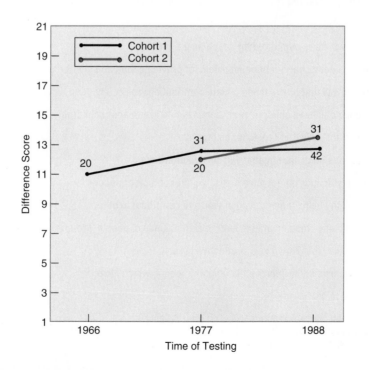

Figure 8.6 Mean scores for Erikson's stage VI (Intimacy) for two cohorts. Scores for both cohorts increase between ages 20 and 31, but not for older ages.

Source: Adapted from Whitbourne, Zuschlag, Elliot, et al. (1992).

reason that once an individual develops the ability to form intimate bonds, it will remain a priority in his or her list of goals.

Another test instrument that measures generativity is the Loyola Generativity Scale (LGS), which consists of 20 statements that participants rate according to how well each applies to them personally (Jackson & Paunonen, 1980). These statements are given in Table 8.3 and reflect an overall orientation or attitude regarding generativity in one's life and social world. Psychologist Dan McAdams and his colleagues (McAdams, de St. Aubin, & Logan, 1993; McAdams, Hart, & Maruna, 1998) gave the LGS, along with several other generativity measures, to 152 men and women who made up a stratified random sample of citizens living in Evanston, Illinois. The participants represented three age groups of adults: young (22 to 27), midlife (37 to 42), and old (67 to 72). Results showed that adults in the midlife group, as predicted by Erikson's theory, scored higher on generativity than both the younger and the older group (see Figure 8.7).

Interestingly, male participants who were not fathers scored significantly lower on generativity than fathers and women in general. The researchers speculate that fatherhood may

CRITICAL THINKING ●

How could you design a study, using the Loyola Generativity Scale, to show that professors have higher levels of generativity than people the same age in other occupations? What do you think the results would be?

Table 8.3   Loyola Generativity Scale

How well do each of the following statements apply to you? (Rate each item on a scale from 0 to 3, where 0 = never applies to me, and 3 = applies to me very often)

1. I try to pass along the knowledge I have gained through my experiences.

2. I do not feel that other people need me.

3. I think I would like the work of a teacher.

4. I feel as though I have made a difference to many people.

5. I do not volunteer to work for a charity.

6. I have made and created things that have had an impact on other people.

7. I try to be creative in most things that I do.

8. I think that I will be remembered for a long time after I die.

9. I believe that society cannot be responsible for providing food and shelter for all homeless people.

10. Others would say that I have made unique contributions to society.

11. If I were unable to have children of my own, I would like to adopt children.

12. I have important skills that I try to teach others.

13. I feel that I have done nothing that will survive after I die.

14. In general, my actions do not have a positive effect on other people.

15. I feel as though I have done nothing of worth to contribute to others.

16. I have made many commitments to many different kinds of people, groups, and activities in my life.

17. Other people say that I am a very productive person.

18. I have a responsibility to improve the neighborhood in which I live.

19. People come to me for advice.

20. I feel as though my contributions will exist after I die.

Source: Jackson & Paunonen (1980).

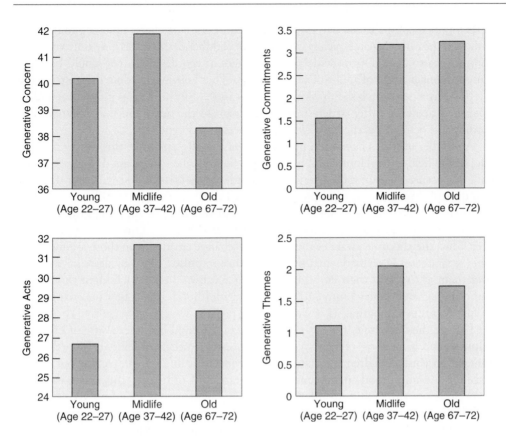

Figure 8.7 Adults in the middle-aged group (37–42 years) score higher on four measures of generativity than either younger or older adults.

Source: McAdams, Hart, & Maruna (1998).

have a dramatic impact on men's generativity, increasing their concern for the next generation. (To be fair, one could also argue that experiencing an increase in generativity inspires men to become fathers.)

Another study examined correlates of generativity within the community in a sample of adults ranging in age from 35 to 65 years, half of whom were African American and half white. High generativity scores were related to wider networks of friends, more social support, and greater feelings of satisfaction with social relationships for both groups. For white adults, generativity was related to church attendance, and for black adults, political involvement (Cole & Stewart, 1996). In another study of middle-aged adults, generativity was associated with high levels of life satisfaction, happiness, self-esteem, goal stability, good health, and sense of coherence in life (McAdams & Azarow, 1996).

In summary, empirical studies have shown that there is some basis for Erikson's adult stages of psychosocial development. Although the ages do not always match Erikson's "optimal ages" for a stage, there is ample evidence that young adulthood is a time of emphasis on identity concerns. Midlife seems to be a time of forming generativity goals. Intimacy is important in young adulthood, as Erikson stated, but is also a concern at other ages. However, Erikson's theory held that stages are never "over," but are just replaced by new dilemmas, so it is not surprising that so important an aspect of life as intimacy is a concern throughout adulthood.

Ego Development

A second theory with Freudian roots comes from psychologist Jane Loevinger (1976), who suggested a number of stagelike levels of ego development. Like Erikson, Loevinger believed that each level was built on the level that preceded it, but unlike Erikson's theory, a person must complete the developmental tasks in one stage before moving to the next. Although the early stage is typically completed in childhood, the stages have only very loose connections to ages. Thus a wide range of stages of ego development would be represented among a group of adults of any given age. What Loevinger is describing, in essence, is a pathway along which she thinks we all must move. But the rate of movement and the final stage achieved differ widely from one person to the next, and that difference, according to Loevinger, is the basis of different personality types.

A number of stages have been presented over the 30 years or so this theory has been part of the field of developmental psychology. Some earlier stages are difficult to gather data on because they are most likely to be found in very young children. Later stages are also difficult because so few people have reached them. Loevinger (1997) presented the information shown in Table 8.4 as the seven stages that are best supported by her data.

The earliest stage that can be measured is the *impulsive stage.* This occurs in small children when they become aware of themselves as separate entities from those around them. This separateness is verified when they experience impulses, but they don't have control over them at first and their emotional range is narrow. "In small children this stage is charming; when it persists into adolescence and adulthood, it is at best maladaptive and in some cases psychopathic" (Loevinger, 1997, p. 203).

During the next stage, the *self-protective stage,* the child becomes aware of his or her impulses and gains some control over them in order to secure at least an immediate advantage. In young children it is natural to be egocentric and self-protective, but in adolescence and adulthood, this becomes exploitation of others. In this stage, there is a preoccupation with taking advantage of others and of others taking advantage of oneself, and this is often expressed in hostile humor. Unlike in the impulsive stage, adults in the self-protective stage are capable of very adaptive behavior and can be very successful.

People in Loevinger's next stage, the *conformist stage,* are able to identify themselves with their reference group, whether it is family, peer group, or work group. They think in terms of stereotypes and are rather limited emotionally to standard clichés—they report being happy, sad, mad, glad, and so on.

The *self-aware stage* is characterized by awareness that there are allowable exceptions to the simple rules the conformists live by. People are aware that they don't always live up to the group's professed standards (and neither do other members of their group). They

Table 8.4	**Loevinger's Stages of Ego Development**		
	Characteristics		
Level	**Impulse Control**	**Interpersonal Mode**	**Conscious Preoccupation**
Impulsive	Impulsive	Egocentric, dependent	Bodily feelings
Self-protective	Opportunistic	Manipulative, wary	"Trouble," control
Conformist	Respect for rules	Cooperative, loyal	Appearances, behavior
Self-aware	Exceptions allowable	Helpful, self-aware	Feelings, problems, adjustments
Conscientious	Self-evaluated standards, self-critical	Intense, responsible	Motives, traits, achievement
Individualistic	Tolerant	Mutual	Individuality, development, roles
Autonomous	Coping with conflict	Interdependent	Self-fulfillment, psychological causation

Source: Loevinger (1997).

realize that they have an existence that is separate from their group, and this can be the basis of some loneliness and self-consciousness. It may not surprise you to know that this stage is the one most common in late adolescents and young adults.

At the *conscientious stage,* people have formed their own ideals and standards instead of just seeking the approval of their group. They express their inner life using rich and varied words to describe their thoughts and emotions. They have long-term goals and may even be overly conscientious. This stage may seem similar to Erikson's stage of identity versus role confusion, but Loevinger argues that it can occur well past adolescence and continue far into adulthood.

The next stage is called the *individualistic stage,* and this is the time people take a broad view of life as a whole. They think in terms of psychological causes and are able to consider their own developmental processes.

People in the *autonomous stage* begin to see the multifaceted nature of the world, not just the good and the bad. Life is complex and situations don't have simple answers or even one best answer. There is a lessening of the burden taken on at the conscientious stage and a respect for the autonomy of others, even one's own children. And there is the ability to see one's own life in the context of wider social concerns.

Although not included in Table 8.4, Loevinger's theory includes a stage known as the integrated stage. It is not treated in most discussions of her theory because it is seldom seen in the general population. This stage includes further development of the abilities found in the prior two stages (individualistic and autonomous), plus an integration of the vital concerns of one's own life with those of the wider society. This sounds very similar to Maslow's stage of self-actualization, which will be discussed later in this chapter and also in Chapter 9.

Loevinger's theory deals with the integration of new perspectives on the self and others, and the stages, or levels, are measured by the Washington University sentence-completion test of ego development (Hy & Loevinger, 1996). In this test, participants are asked to complete 18 sentence stems, such as "My mother and I . . . ," "A man's job . . . ," and "Rules are . . ." Each response is scored according to guidelines, and then a total score is computed that corresponds to a particular stage or level of ego development.

The sentence-completion test is used to assess the ego development of adults across the life span. For example, young adults' ego development stage was found to be a reflection of problems experienced in childhood and adolescence. Those who had a history of externalizing disorders (attention problems or aggressive behavior) were below the conformist level at age 22, indicating that they had not reached a stage that involves respect for rules. Those who had a history of internalizing disorders (anxiety or depression) had not advanced beyond the conformist level at age 22, indicating that although they had respect for rules, they had not reached the self-aware level (Krettenauer, Urlich, Hofmann, et al., 2003).

Psychologists Jack Bauer and Dan McAdams (2004) interviewed middle-aged adults who had been through either a career change or a change in religion, asking questions about personal growth. They also computed their ego development stage according to the Washington University sentence-completion test described above. Participants who were at higher levels of ego development on the sentence-completion test were more apt to describe their personal growth in both career change and religion change in terms of *integrative themes* (having new perspectives on the self and others). These adults described their personal growth as increased self-awareness, better understanding of relationships, and a higher level of moral reasoning—all themes that reflect more complex thinking about one's life and meaningful relationships.

Researchers in adult education Janet Truluck and Bradley Courtenay (2002) gave older adults (55 to 85 years of age) the Washington University sentence-completion test to

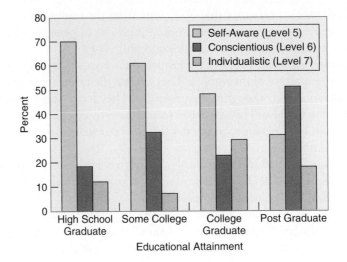

Figure 8.8 In older adults, higher education is related to higher levels of ego development.

Source: Adapted from Truluck & Courtenay (2002).

assess their ego development. There were no gender differences or age effects, but as shown in Figure 8.8, educational level was positively related to ego development. The proportion of people who scored in level 5 (self-aware) was higher for those with only a high school education and declined for people with some college, for college graduates, and then for those with a postgraduate education. The proportion of those in levels 6 and 7 (conscientiousness and individualistic) generally increased with educational attainment. Although some researchers have found that educational level is related to ego development in earlier adulthood (Labouvie-Vief & Diehl, 1998), these findings of lifelong effects of education on ego development are interesting, especially considering that the older participants' education had been attained decades earlier.

CRITICAL THINKING

The simplest explanation of how college education contributes to ego development is that people learn important lessons in college and remember them all their lives. What is another explanation?

Mature Adaptation

A theory that seems to be a cross between Erikson's and Loevinger's theories is that of psychiatrist George Vaillant (1977, 1993). He begins by accepting Erikson's stages as the basic framework of development, but inserts an additional stage between Erikson's stages of intimacy and generativity at some time around the age of 30. Vaillant calls this stage *career consolidation,* the stage when young adults are intent on establishing their own competence, mastering a craft, or acquiring higher status or a positive reputation.

Like Loevinger, Vaillant describes a direction in which personality growth or development may occur, but he does not assume that everyone moves the same distance in this direction. In particular, Vaillant is interested in *mature adaptation,* potential progressive change in the ways adults adapt psychologically to the trials and tribulations they face. The major form of adaptation he discusses is the **defense mechanism,** Freud's term for a set of normal, unconscious strategies used for dealing with anxiety. Everyone has some anxiety, so everyone uses defense mechanisms of some kind. All of them involve some type of self-deception or distortion of reality. We forget things that make us uncomfortable or remember them in a way that is not so unpleasant; we give ourselves reasons for doing something we know we shouldn't do; we project our unacceptable feelings onto others rather than acknowledge them in ourselves. What Vaillant has added to Freud's concept is the notion that some defense mechanisms are more mature than others. In general, mature defenses involve less distortion of reality. They reflect more graceful, less uncomfortable ways of coping with difficulties. Vaillant's central thesis is that an adult's defense mechanisms must mature if he or she is to be able to cope effectively with the slings and arrows of normal life.

Vaillant arranged defense mechanisms into six levels, with the first level as the most mature. The six levels, along with examples of each, are shown in Table 8.5. Vaillant believed that people use defense mechanisms from several levels at any point in their lives, and at times of stress, may regress to lower levels. However, in the course of life maturation, adults add more and more adaptive defense mechanisms to their psychological toolboxes and use fewer and fewer of the less mature defense mechanisms. So instead of this being a stage theory with discreet steps of development, Vaillant considered his theory as more of a slope, with those who use more mature defense mechanisms having more integrated personalities and being more successful in their lives (Vaillant, 2002).

Vaillant based many of his ideas on data from the Harvard Men's Study, a longitudinal study that began with 268 men of the 1922 graduating class of Harvard College, and followed them throughout their lives (Heath, 1945). Although Vaillant was not born when the study began, he joined the research group in its 30th year and is still gathering data on the surviving participants. (Interestingly, his father, who died when Vaillant was 13, was an original participant in the study.)

Vaillant's theory was based on data from numerous interviews, personality tests, and other measurements that were given to the men in the Harvard study over the years. When personality factors research began to take center stage in the study of personality, he and his colleagues adapted the concept of the five-factor model to fit the longitudinal study of Harvard men. By reviewing early interviews and test results, the researchers were able to assign scores for the five major personality factors to the men at age 22, some 45 years earlier. Then they gave the five-factor personality inventory (NEO-PI) to the 163 surviving participants and compared the early scores with the later scores. The results showed low

Table 8.5	Vaillant's Six Levels of Defense Mechanisms	
Level	**Defense Mechanism**	**Example**
I. High Adaptive Level	Altruism	Dealing with stress over health by participating in a race to raise funds for researching a disease.
II. Mental Inhibition Level	Repression	Dealing with stress over childlessness by expelling thought and wishes from conscious awareness.
III. Minor Image Distorting Level	Omnipotence	Dealing with stress over military assignment by glorifying one's special training and high-tech equipment.
IV. Disavowal Level	Denial	Dealing with stress over marital problems by refusing to acknowledge that a hurtful incident, apparent to others, occurred.
V. Major Image Distorting	Autistic fantasy	Dealing with stress over potential layoff by daydreaming about an ideal job instead of taking action to find a new one.
VI. Action Level	Help-rejecting complaining	Dealing with stress over money problems by complaining, but then rejecting offers of help and advice.

Source: Adapted from American Psychiatric Association (2000).

but significant intra-individual stability for three factors, Neuroticism, Extraversion, and Openness, in spite of the cards stacked against the study, such as the very long interval between tests, different tests, and Time 1 being at such a young age (Soldz & Vaillant, 1999).

In addition to looking at individual stability over a 45-year interval, Soldz and Vaillant also investigated other details of these men's lives to see if their early personality traits were related to actual events and outcomes over the life course. Some of the results were that Extraversion at the age of 22 predicted maximum income during one's working years; the higher a participant scored on this trait, the more money he made. Openness at 22 predicted creative accomplishments during the men's lifetimes, and early Conscientiousness scores predicted good adult adjustment and low levels of depression, smoking, and alcohol abuse. (Recall earlier in this chapter that Conscientiousness is also related to good health.)

Gender Crossover

Psychoanalyst Carl Jung (1933) believed that the second half of life was characterized by exploring and acknowledging the parts of oneself that had been hidden during the first half of life. Men allowed the softer, more nurturant parts of their personalities to emerge, while women became more independent and planful. Influenced by Jung's psychoanalytic thought about aging, anthropologist David Gutmann (1987) believed that adult gender differences in personality begin in young adulthood when both men and women accentuate their own gender characteristics and suppress the opposite-gender characteristics in order to attract mates and reproduce. After the parenting years are over and these roles are not paramount in their lives, according to this theory, they are able to relax the suppression and allow some of the "other-gender" characteristics to emerge.

Gutmann referred to this relaxation of gender roles at midlife as **gender crossover,** as discussed in the section on gender roles in Chapter 5. He believed that aging does not represent a loss at this time but, rather, a gain in personal freedom and new roles within the "tribe." Gutmann also found support for his ideas in his experiences among the Mayan, Navajo, and Druze societies showing that men move from active mastery, which involves making changes in external circumstances, to accommodative mastery, which is making changes in one's inner self; and that women move from accommodative to active mastery.

Psychologist Ravenna Helson and her colleagues (Helson, Pals, & Solomon, 1997) reviewed data from three longitudinal studies of different cohorts of college students. They found support for Gutmann's theory in the responses of the young women participants, most of whom expressed interest in marriage and family. The difference in cohorts was that the earlier cohorts (who were young adults in the 1930s and 1940s) were concerned about choosing between a career and a family, and the more recent ones (who were young adults in the 1980s) were concerned about combining both a career and a family. The males in the study seldom expressed those concerns.

Helson explored the reasons for change and ruled out the narrow interpretation of stereotypical gender traits as important for parenting; the dramatic increase in women's competence, independence, and self-confidence was independent of whether the women were mothers or had remained childless. Furthermore, it depended on what opportunities were available for women at the time they were going through these age-related changes.

There seems to be evidence of men and women's personalities blending in middle and late adulthood, but this does not constitute a true "crossover," in which women become more masculine than men and men become more feminine than women. What the research findings show is best described as an increased openness to the expression of previously unexpressed parts of the self. The cause for this blending does not strictly seem to be parenthood, because it is not limited to those who have had children. The change seems to be stronger for women than for men. Helson suggests that we are viewing a complex biosocial phenomenon that involves hormones, social roles, historical changes, and economic climate. However, it is strong enough to show up in these studies and in similar studies in other cultures, so it seems to be a worthwhile research topic for the future.

Positive Well-Being

Another approach that has its roots in psychoanalytic theory comes from psychologist Abraham Maslow (1968/1998), who traced his theoretical roots to Freud and offered some highly original insights. As a humanistic psychologist, Maslow's most central concern was with the development of motives or needs, which he divided into two main groups: deficiency motives and being motives. *Deficiency motives* involve instincts or drives to correct imbalance or to maintain physical or emotional homeostasis, such as getting enough to eat, satisfying thirst, or obtaining enough love and respect from others. Deficiency motives are found in all animals. *Being motives* in contrast, are distinctly human. Maslow argued that humans have unique desires to discover and understand, to give love to others, and to push for the optimum fulfillment of their inner potentials.

In general, Maslow believed that the satisfaction of deficiency motives prevents or cures illness, and re-creates homeostasis (inner balance). In contrast, the satisfaction of being motives produces positive health. The distinction is like the "difference between fending off threat or attack, and positive triumph and achievement" (Maslow, 1968/1998, p. 32). But being motives are quite fragile and do not typically emerge until well into adulthood, and then only under supportive circumstances. Maslow's well-known needs hierarchy (shown in Figure 8.9) reflects this aspect of his thinking. The lowest four levels all describe different deficiency needs, while only the highest level, the need for **self-actualization,** is a being motive. Further, Maslow proposed that these five levels emerged sequentially in development and tend to dominate the system from the bottom up. That is, if you are starving, the physiological needs dominate. If you are being physically battered, the safety needs dominate. The need for self-actualization emerges only when all four types of deficiency needs are largely satisfied.

Instead of studying people with mental health problems, Maslow sought to understand the personalities and characteristics of those few adults who seemed to have risen to the top of the needs hierarchy and achieved significant levels of self-understanding and expression, people such as Eleanor Roosevelt, Albert Schweitzer, and Albert Einstein. Some of the key characteristics of self-actualized people, as Maslow saw them, are having an accurate perception of reality, being involved in deep personal relationships, being creative, and having a good-natured sense of humor. He described self-actualized individuals as having **peak experiences**—feelings of perfection and momentary separation from the self when one feels in unity with the universe.

Maslow and other humanistic psychologists such as Carl Rogers had their major influence in clinical

Figure 8.9 Maslow's hierarchy of needs proposes that lower needs dominate the individual's motivations and that higher needs become prominent only late in life and when the lower needs are satisfied.

Source: Maslow (1968/1998).

psychology and self-help movements. In some of the later adaptations and applications of these ideas by others, the need for self-actualization has become more self-centered and less centered on the collective well-being of humankind than Maslow had envisioned. One reason is that Maslow's theory had little empirical testing; it was not stated very scientifically, and there were no means developed for assessing the dominance of the various motives he proposed. For some reason this theory did not attract the attention of research psychologists who might have picked up the ball and advanced it further down the field. However, there is something about Maslow's theory that is appealing to us; it fits our gut-level feeling of what life is all about. We can experience its truth in our lives almost every day. When we feel endangered by terrorist attacks, we are not too interested in whether we will be graduating next year with two gold braids on our shoulders or just one.

Recently, there has been a renewed interest in humanistic psychology and new attempts to use it as a basis for empirical studies. Foremost among this movement has been the appeal by psychologists Martin Seligman and Mihaly Csikszentmihalyi (2000) for a new focus that turns away from a disease model of human behavior that is fixated on curing or preventing negative conditions such as mental illness, crime, failure, victimization, abuse, brain damage, negative effects of stress, and poverty. Instead, they offered the following focus on **positive psychology:**

> The field of positive psychology at the subjective level is about valued subjective experiences: well-being, contentment, and satisfaction (in the past); hope and optimism (for the future); and flow and happiness (in the present). At the individual level, it is about positive individual traits: the capacity for love and vocation, courage, interpersonal skill, aesthetic sensibility, perseverance, forgiveness, originality, future mindedness, spirituality, high talent, and wisdom. At the group level, it is about the civic virtues and the institutions that move individuals toward better citizenship: responsibility, nurturance, altruism, civility, moderation, tolerance, and work ethic. (Seligman & Csikszentmihalyi, 2000, p. 5)

One aspect of this movement is a personality theory that has some components of Maslow's theory of self-actualization. This new theory, formulated by psychologists Richard Ryan and Edward Deci (2000), is known as **self-determination theory.** It holds that personality is based on individuals' evolved inner resources for growth and integration. Ryan and Deci believe that the need for personal growth and personality development is an essential part of human nature. The extent to which we succeed in this endeavor is the basis of our personalities, much as in Loevinger's theory described earlier in this chapter. Ryan and Deci have identified three basic needs that must be satisfied across the life span in order for an individual to experience what they call *eudaimonia*—a sense of integrity and well-being similar to Maslow's concept of self-actualization. These basic needs are for competence, autonomy, and relatedness. They theorize that individuals cannot thrive without satisfying all three of these needs—and thus an environment that fosters competence and autonomy but not relatedness, for example, will result in a compromised sense of well-being.

Competence, according to Ryan and Deci's theory, is the feeling of effectiveness as one interacts with one's environment. It's not necessary to be the best, but in terms of the U.S. Army slogan, it's important to "be all that you can be." It's feeling challenged and seeing the results of your efforts. This can be difficult during late adulthood, but the authors caution that competence doesn't mean being better than before; sometimes it means modifying the environment, selecting which activities to perform, and redirecting extra resources to doing those activities well—a strategy they refer to as "having a choice over challenges."

The need of *autonomy* means that we need to feel that our actions are being done by our own volition. We are making decisions to act, and our actions reflect our true inner selves and not someone else's rules or guidelines. It means that a person is acting due to internal controls and not external ones. This is not always easy for independent adults, but it is much more difficult at other stages of life, such as childhood, adolescence, and the later years of adulthood when people are dependent on others to a greater degree. However, Ryan and LaGuardia (2000) believe that dependence does not rule out autonomy. In fact, they found that dependent patients in nursing homes that allow them to make many of their own decisions are both physically and psychologically healthier than patients in homes that allow less autonomy.

Relatedness, in self-determination theory, refers to the feeling of being connected to, cared about, and belonging with significant others in one's life. It's the feeling that others are standing behind you with love and affection. Like the other basic needs, this one changes with age. In the later years, the quality of contact with friends and family members takes precedence over the quantity of contact. Kasser and Ryan (1999) found that the quality of relatedness and social support felt by nursing-home residents along with the sense of autonomy (and the support they felt for being autonomous) predicted positive outcomes, such as lower incidence of depression, higher satisfaction with life, and higher self-esteem.

Ryan and Deci, and others, have tested their theory with empirical research over the past decade using a test instrument called the General Causality Orientations Scale (Deci & Ryan 1985), which measures self-determination on competence, autonomy, and relatedness by presenting vignettes of typical achievement or social situations (such as applying for a job or interacting with a friend). Each vignette is followed by three statements representing each of the three basic needs. Participants are asked to rate on a scale of 1 to 7 how likely it would be for them to respond the same way to the situation depicted in the vignette. This test yields three independent scores that evaluate the participants'

> **CRITICAL THINKING**
>
> What does your college or university do to foster feelings of autonomy, relatedness, and competence in its students? Are these measures successful? Can you suggest any other measures that could be taken to promote a sense of eudaimonia in students?

Feelings of competence, independence, and relatedness lead to a sense of overall well-being in any stage of life.

self-determination on the three needs. This test (and others) has been used with participants at all ages of the life span along with measures of well-being, health, achievement in school, life satisfaction, and so forth. Results have shown that all three factors are necessary for personal well-being. For example, researchers found that competence without autonomy did not lead to higher levels of personality development. No matter how well a person performed a task, if he or she was promised rewards for doing it well, or if performance was influenced by threats, deadlines, directives, or goals imposed by others, the feelings of competence alone did not suffice. Instead, high levels of performance influenced by choice, acknowledgment of feelings, and opportunities for self-direction resulted in feelings of both competence and autonomy. When these two needs are fulfilled in a person who also feels a strong sense of relatedness to others, such as family members, professors, supervisors, or co-workers, the person is able to advance toward his or her developmental goals.

Summary

1.   Early ideas about adult personality were based on grand theories of development that were popular and enthusiastically endorsed but not empirically tested and validated.

2.   One of the first methods of testing and validating ideas about personality was the trait structure approach, in which a small number of trait structures were identified through factor analysis. The most prominent of these models is Costa and McCrae's five-factor model, which identifies Neuroticism, Extraversion, Openness to experience, Agreeableness, and Conscientiousness as the basic factors of human personality.

3.   Differential continuity has been found for the major five factors of personality through childhood and adulthood. People tend to keep their rank orders within groups regardless of gender. The level of stability increases with age through the 70s, but never becomes totally stable, showing that personality can change throughout life.

4.   What happens to personality traits as people get older? We become more agreeable and conscientious, less neurotic and open. This seems to be true regardless of culture and gender.

5.   Personality trait structures can be stable in some ways (differential continuity) and change in others (mean-level changes). The former is relative to others in your age group, the latter is your group in comparison to a different age group. You can be the most conscientious person in your age group throughout your life, but the average level of scores for that trait may increase as you (and your agemates) get older.

6.   Personality traits are related to the development of intimate relationships, career success, and health in adulthood. People who are high in agreeableness and low in neuroticism have relationships that last longer and are more satisfying that those who are lower in these traits. Those who have high levels of conscientiousness are more apt to do their jobs well and advance quickly in their careers than those who are lower in these traits. High levels of conscientiousness and low levels of neuroticism predict better health and longevity.

7.   The five major personality structures have a significant genetic component, but there are mixed findings about the primary factors. The genetic influence is found to be greater in childhood than in adulthood, when environmental influences are stronger.

8.   People work together with their environments to keep their personality stable by the way they interpret events, the way they act toward others that elicits responses

compatible with their personalities, the way they select situations that fit and re-inforce their personalities, and the way they make changes in surroundings that are incompatible with their personalities.

9. Evolutionary psychologists argue that personality traits give us important survival cues about the people in our environment, and as a result, have been selected for throughout our evolutionary history.

10. Erikson's theory of psychosocial development states that personality development takes place in distinct stages over the life span. Each stage represents a conflict the individual must try to resolve. Each resolution attempt brings the potential for a new strength gained. Four stages take place in adulthood as individuals attempt to establish identities, form intimate partnerships, tend to the next generation, and find meaning at the end of their lives. Although Erikson's theory was not data based or scientifically tested before it was presented, recent research has shown that establishing an identity is a concern for younger adults but not for middle-aged adults, and that this is true for intimacy also. Other studies have shown that middle-aged adults are more concerned with generativity goals than younger adults.

11. Loevinger's theory of ego development parted with Erikson on the concept of stages. She believed that adults make their way along the incline from one stage to the other, but don't have to complete the whole progression. Personality depends on which stage a person ultimately attains. The stages represent movement toward interdependence, values, attitudes toward rules, and evaluations of the self. Recent research has shown that Loevinger's test of ego development predicts how people will describe personal outcomes of life events, and that ego development increases with education (but not with age).

12. Vaillant's theory of mature adaptation is based on levels of defense mechanisms—normal, unconscious strategies we use for dealing with anxiety. He posed six levels, beginning with the most mature and proceeding on to those that involve more and more self-deception, suggesting that we use several levels, but the ones we use the most determine the maturity of our adaptations. Recent research has incorporated trait-theory tests with more traditional personality evaluations on a group of older Harvard men who have been studied longitudinally since they were undergraduates. Vaillant has found stability in Neuroticism, Extraversion, and Openness over a 45-year period; some factors at the age of 22 predicted later outcomes in health and career.

13. Gutmann's theory of gender crossover explains that young adults strive to display accentuated gender traits in order to attract mates and raise children. After the parenting years are over, they are able to express the hidden sides of their personalities by displaying the gender traits of the opposite sex. Studies show that there is a tendency for both men and women to incorporate characteristics of the other gender, but it's more of a blending than a true crossover, and it seems to be independent of being a parent.

14. Maslow's theory of self-actualization consists of stages of a sort, in the form of a needs hierarchy, with the most-pressing biological needs coming first; once they are satisfied, the individual turns his or her attention to higher-level needs. The highest is self-actualization, which Maslow believed was seldom achieved. A recent reformulation of this theory is found in self-determination theory, which states our basic needs as being competence, autonomy, and relatedness. Research based on this idea has shown that fulfilling all three needs is necessary for high scores on a number of indicators of well-being, such as career success, good health, and life satisfaction.

Key Terms

personality, 238

personality traits, 238

personality factors, 239

personality states, 239

Five-Factor Model, 239

differential continuity, 239

mean-level change, 240

intra-individual variability, 241

person-environment
    transactions, 246

identity, 248

intimacy, 248

generativity, 248

ego integrity, 249

defense mechanism, 256

gender crossover, 258

self-actualization, 259

peak experiences, 259

positive psychology, 260

self-determination theory, 260

Suggested Reading

Reading for Personal Interest

Erikson, E. H. (1993). *Gandhi's truth: On the origins of militant nonviolence.* New York: Norton.

Erikson's Pulitzer Prize–winning biography of Mahatma Gandhi, national leader in India and originator of militant nonviolence. Erikson also wrote a biography of Martin Luther (*Young Man Luther: A Study in Psychoanalysis and History*) and wrote about his own relationship with Huey Newton, a militant Black Panther leader in the 1960s (*In Search of Common Ground*).

Erikson, E. H. (1989/1994). *Vital involvement in old age.* New York: Norton.

Erikson gives the final version of his eight-stage theory and then writes about the late-life work he did with people in their 80s who had been studied longitudinally for over 50 years. A remarkably detailed and intimate picture of aging that will motivate the individual to strive toward vital involvement in life. It speaks to us as members of the larger society about what we can do to enhance the lives of our elders.

Gutmann, D. (1997). *The human elder in nature, culture, and society.* Boulder, CO: Westview.

The story of Gutmann's cross-cultural research, incorporating many of his findings in a very readable way that would be valuable to thoughtful people considering their own parenting and postparenting years or those of their parents.

Seligman, M. E. P. (2004). *Authentic happiness: Using the new positive psychology to realilze your potential for lasting fulfullment.* New York: Free Press.

Psychologist Martin Seligman believes that psychology has spent too much time studying sources of unhappiness, and as president of the APA, he challenged the field to start thinking about sources of happiness. In this book, he discusses some of that new research, but he also tells us how to increase our happiness on a personal level. He has tests, Web sites, and homework activities that help readers identify their personality strengths and the best pathways to authentic happiness.

Classic Work

Erikson, E. H. (1985/1994). *The life cycle completed: A review.* New York: Norton.

Erikson, E. H. (1980/1994). *Identity and the life cycle.* New York: Norton.

Psychoanalyst Erik Erikson wrote several books explaining his theory of psychosocial development using examples from his own life as well as from other cultures.

Gutmann, D. (1987/1994). *Reclaimed powers: The new psychology of men and women in late life.* New York Basic Books.

Anthropologist David Gutmann spells out his ideas about changes in gender roles over the years of adulthood. He draws on his vast knowledge of roles in other cultures, such as the Navajo, the Maya, and the Druze.

Loevinger, J. (1976). *Ego development.* San Francisco: Jossey-Bass.

Psychologist Jane Loevinger explains her theory of ego development.

Maslow, A. (1998). *Toward a psychology of being* (3rd ed.). New York, Wiley.

This book describes Maslow's ideas of self-actualization and the hierarchy of needs in a simple, straightforward style.

McCrae, R.R., & Costa, P.T. (1987). Validation of the five-factor model of personality across instruments and observers. *Journal of Personality and Social Psychology,* 52, 81–90.

An early discussion of the five-factor model of personality.

Vaillant, G. E. (1977). *Adaptation to life: How the best and brightest come of age.* Boston: Little, Brown.

The 40-year report on the Grant study of Harvard men. These 268 men were followed through their careers and into retirement, and psychiatrist George Vaillant used the results to formulate a personality theory of mature adaptation. An interesting and very readable account of the study results.

Contemporary Scholarly Writing

Hulbert, K. D., & Schuster, D. T. (Eds.). (1993). *Women's lives through time: Educated American women of the twentieth century.* San Francisco: Jossey-Bass.

The papers in this book describe a longitudinal study of American college women, varying from the class of 1930 up to groups graduating in the 1970s. The emphasis is on the impact of women's role changes in the 20th century on their choices and early adult life patterns. Not all these studies pertain to personality, so some of the book will be more relevant to other chapters of this text.

Mroczek, D. K., Spiro, A., III, & Griffin, P. W. (2006). Personality and aging. In J. E. Birren & K. W. Schaie (Eds.), *Handbook of the psychology of aging* (pp. 363–377). San Diego: Academic Press.

A review of recent research in the field of personality and aging.

Chapter 9

The Quest
for Meaning

Why a Chapter on the Quest for Meaning?

The Study of Age-Related Changes in Meaning Systems
Changes in Spirituality
Changes in Private Beliefs and Practices
Religion and Health

Theories of Spiritual Development
Development of Moral Reasoning
Development of Faith

Integrating Meaning and Personality: A Preliminary Theoretical Synthesis
A Synthesizing Model
Stages of Mystical Experience

The Process of Transition

Commentary and Conclusions

Summary

Key Terms

Suggested Reading

TENKAI, AS DESCRIBED by geneticist Dean Hamer (2004), is a man with a spiritual smile, a smile that says he is at peace with the world and with himself. He lives in a Buddhist monastery in Japan, although his background is typically American. Tenkai's search for meaning began when he was a 24-year-old high school teacher and, after breaking up with his girlfriend, began to ask himself questions about the meaning of life. What is the purpose of life? Why am I here? This mental quest turned into a journey that took him all over the world, including a stint in a spiritual retreat in Austria, an ashram in India, a monastery in Nepal, and finally to Japan. He found his answers in Zen Buddhism, a religion that teaches self-enlightenment through meditation. He explains that he did not find meaning by changing his thinking, but by changing his perception, his sense of the way things are. In other words he changed his consciousness.

Sister Anne Baker's search for meaning began 60 years earlier than Tenkai's and was much quicker. The 6th-grader was sitting at her desk in school, thinking about her dreams of becoming a country music singer, when a light switch flipped on and she knew that the purpose for her life was to become a Catholic nun. She never had a doubt after that. She found meaning in the traditions of her church. She has taught math to high school students for 45 years and has gone from an 18-year-old woman in a white Dominican habit to a 78-year-old woman in a flowered dress and short gray hair. She finds meaning in daily prayers, teaching, and such activities as leading the recycling program for her school and picketing along the highway with Mothers Against Drunk Driving (Marion, 2006).

Although not many of us have gone to the extremes of Tenkai or shared the epiphany experience of Sister Anne Baker, it's safe to say that we can all identify with parts of their stories. Spirituality is a common characteristic of our species. Burial sites that date back 30,000 years reveal bodies buried with food, pots, and weapons, seemingly provisions for the afterlife. And today, in the midst of nanotechnology and biomedical advances, 82 percent of people in the United States responded to a recent poll that they believe in God (Harris Poll, 2005b). This sense of the spiritual, also known as the **quest for meaning,** is the self's search for ultimate knowledge of life through an individualized understanding of the sacred (Wink & Dillon, 2002). Whether through the practice of traditional religion or a personal quest to find self-enlightenment, the search for meaning is an integral part of the human experience.

Recently geneticists claim to have discovered the "God gene," a segment of DNA that is responsible for spirituality in our species. Geneticist Dean Hamer (2004) explains that spirituality is one of our basic human instincts, that the predilection to be spiritual (or to seek meaning) is present to one extent or another in each person from birth, and it interacts with the environment to produce culturally specific attitudes and behaviors. Although it may seem strange to apply scientific testing to spirituality, the geneticists are saying the same thing as the anthropologists who found the ancient burial sites: The quest for meaning is a common characteristic of our species. This chapter addresses that quest and how it unfolds over the adult years.

Why a Chapter on the Quest for Meaning?

In Chapter 8, I talked about age-related changes in personality and the progression toward self-actualization, which are certainly aspects of inner growth in adulthood. But there is another aspect to inner development—perhaps more speculative, but certainly no less vital to most of us—that touches on questions of meaning. As we move through adulthood, do we interpret our experiences differently? Do we attach different meanings, understand our world in new ways? Do we become wiser, or less worldly, or more spiritual?

Certainly, a link between advancing age and increasing wisdom has been part of the folk tradition in virtually every culture in the world, as evidenced by fairy tales, myths, and religious teachings (Campbell, 1949/1990). Adult development, according to these sources, brings an increased storehouse of worldly knowledge and experience. It also brings a different perspective on life, a different set of values, and a different worldview, a process often described as **self-transcendence,** or coming to know oneself as part of a larger whole that exists beyond the physical body and personal history. What I am interested in knowing is whether this process is part of—or potentially part of—the normal process of adult development.

You may well think that the answers to such questions lie in the province of religion or philosophy, not psychology. Despite the increasing number of psychologists over the years interested in the psychology of religion, in wisdom, and in adults' ideas about life, you are not likely to find a chapter on this subject in any other textbook on adult development. So perhaps my first task here is to explain to you why I think this is important. Why talk about meaning? There are three reasons.

- *It is the meaning we attach to experience that matters rather than the experience itself.* Most fundamentally, psychologists have come to understand that individual experiences do not affect us in some uniform, automatic way; rather, it is the way we interpret an experience, the meaning we give it, that is really critical. There are certain basic assumptions individuals make about the world and their place in it, about themselves and their capacities that affect their interpretations of experiences. Such a system of meanings is sometimes referred to as an *internal working model* that determines how we experience the world. I've touched on other aspects of the same point in earlier chapters. For example, in Chapter 6, I covered attachment theory and explained how we form internal working models of the attachment relationships we had with our parents, and how these models influence the way we approach relationships with other people. If my internal model includes the assumption that "people are basically helpful and trustworthy," that assumption is clearly going to affect not only the experiences I will seek out, but my interpretation of my experiences. The objective experiences each of us has are thus filtered through various internal working models before they convey meaning to us. I would argue that the ultimate consequence of any given experience is largely (if not wholly) determined by the meaning we attach and not the experience itself. To the extent that this is true, then, it is obviously important for us to try to understand the meaning systems that adults create.

> ● **CRITICAL THINKING**
>
> How might the exact same experience, such as the eruption of a volcano, be interpreted very differently by people who have differing meaning systems? What other examples can you think of?

- *The quest for meaning is a basic human characteristic.* A second reason for exploring this rather slippery area of adult development is that the quest for meaning is a central theme in the lives of most adults. This is echoed in the writings of many clinicians and theorists. Psychoanalyst Erich Fromm (1956) listed the need for meaning as one of the five central existential needs of human beings. Psychiatrist Viktor Frankl (1984) argues that the "will to meaning" is a basic human motive. Theologian and psychologist James Fowler has made a similar point: "One characteristic all human beings have in common is that we can't live without some sense that life is meaningful" (1981, p. 58). Thus, not only do we interpret our experiences and in this way "make meaning," but it may also be true that the need or motive to create meaningfulness is a vital one in our lives.

- *Most cultures support the tradition that spirituality and wisdom increase with age.* There has always been anecdotal evidence of **gerotranscendence,** the idea that meaning systems increase in quality as we age, beginning with myths and fairy tales about wise elders (Tornstam, 1996). Early theorists in psychology explained the development of meaning as a growth process. For example, psychoanalyst Carl Jung (1964) proposed that young adulthood was a time of turning outward, a time to establish relationships, start families, and concentrate on careers. But at midlife, when adults become aware of their own mortality, they turn inward and strive to expand their sense of self. In this way, the outward focus of the first half of life is balanced by the inward focus of the second half, completing the process of self-realization. Similarly, psychologist Klaus Riegel (1973) proposed that cognitive development extends to **postformal stages** that appear in midlife when adults are able to go beyond the linear and logical ways of thinking described in Piaget's formal operations stage. In this postformal stage, adults are able to view the world in a way that adds feelings and context to the logic and reason proposed by Piaget, and use their cognitive abilities in a quest for meaning (Sinnott, 1994).

Other theorists view the development of meaning systems as a response to the constraints and adversities of aging. In this point of view, age brings physical limitations and loss, and many people respond to this by concentrating on the unconstrained spiritual aspects of the self and disengaging from the parts of life that are troublesome (Atchley, 1997). Related to this explanation is the idea that higher levels of spirituality are responses to adversity, and that those who experience difficult social conditions in life tend to be more spiritual than those who do not (McFadden, 1999).

The second half of life brings a change from outward to inward concerns and from physical to spiritual values.

No matter whether changes in meaning systems over age are a function of normal development or the result of adversity, it is generally agreed that the development of meaning systems in adulthood is a real phenomenon and worthy of scientific attention.

The Study of Age-Related Changes in Meaning Systems

Assuming that I have persuaded you that this subject is worth exploring, we now come to the equally sticky/tricky question of method. How do we explore something so apparently fuzzy? An obvious idea is to look at **religiosity,** the outward signs of spirituality, such as participation in religious services or being a member of a religious organization. Quantitative studies of such matters attempt to answer questions like: Do adults attend religious services more (or less) as they get older? Is there some kind of age-linked pattern? One body of research is based on this line of reasoning, and I'll look at the evidence it presents in a moment. However, there are other approaches that also have to be discussed.

Some theologians and psychologists believe that we need to dig deeper than observable behavior and use a measure of personal, individualized spirituality to answer questions about age-related changes in meaning systems. We all know of people who go through the motions of religiosity but cannot be described as spiritual. Some researchers use questionnaires asking about personal beliefs, and others use personal interviews, asking essay-type questions that give more depth but are more difficult to analyze. These studies are very fruitful because they have shown that personal beliefs about the quest for meaning are not necessarily related to religiosity (Roof, 1999).

Yet another approach is to use a qualitative method, such as reviewing case studies drawn from biographies or autobiographies, personal reports by well-known adults (politicians, saints, philosophers, mystics) about the steps and processes of their own inner development. Collections of such data have been analyzed, perhaps most impressively by William James (a distinguished early American psychologist) in his book *The Varieties of Religious Experience* (1902/1958), and by theologian and philosopher Evelyn Underhill in her book *Mysticism* (1911/1961). Of course, personal reports do not fit with our usual notion of "scientific evidence." The participants being studied are not representative of the general population, and the "data" may not be objectively gathered. Still, information from such sources makes a valuable contribution to theories of age-related changes in meaning systems. They tell us something about what may be possible, or about the qualities, meaning systems, or capacities of a few extraordinary adults who appear to have explored the depths of the human spirit. Yet even if we accept such descriptions as valid reports of inner processes, it is a very large leap to apply the described steps or processes to the experiences of ordinary folks. I am going to take that leap in this chapter. You will have to judge for yourself whether it is justified.

I need to make one further preparatory point: It is surely obvious (but nonetheless worth stating explicitly) that I bring my own meaning system to this discussion. Of course, that statement is true about the entire book (or anyone else's book). I approach this subject with a strong hypothesis that there are "higher" levels of human potential than most of us have yet reached, whether they are expressed in Maslow's terms as self-actualization, in Loevinger's concept of the integrated personality, or in any other terms that express advanced progress in the quest for meaning. When I describe the various models of the development of meaning systems, I am inevitably filtering the theories and the evidence through this hypothesis. There is no way I can avoid this, any more than you can avoid filtering this chapter through your own assumptions, your own meaning system. Keep it in mind as you read further.

I will begin with some empirical research on the search for meaning in adulthood and then add some discussion of the development of moral thinking, which is a manifestation of spirituality. And finally, I will discuss some qualitative work, some case studies of the quest for meaning by prominent writers and historical figures. Then I will try to tie together the evidence I have presented into a meaningful whole or at least a framework that will guide your thinking on this important topic.

Changes in Spirituality

Let us begin with the empirical research on spirituality. There has been a surge of research on religious practices and other aspects of spirituality in the last decade or so. Figure 9.1 shows the increase in articles published on these topics during two time periods—1975 to 1989, and 1990 to 2004. As you can see, there has been a large increase, from 36 articles during the first 15-year period to 229 during the more recent 15-year period (Koenig, 2006). And one of the most-studied topics within this area has been whether spirituality increases with age.

Although overall attendance and membership in religious organizations have dropped in the United States over the last 50 years, cross-sectional data show that attendance at religious services is higher for adults 65 years of age and older than for younger adults (Idler, Musick, Ellison, et al., 2003). The few longitudinal studies on this topic show a decline in religious participation in very late life, but it is related to declining health and functional ability (Benjamins, Musick, Gold, et al., 2003). In general, the consensus seems to be that there is an increase in religiosity over the life course, with a short period of health-related dropoff at the end of life (Idler, 2006). In addition, there are some definite gender and racial/ethnic differences in religiosity. Women attend religious services at higher rates than men for all ages and in all religions and countries studied (Miller & Stark, 2002). African Americans and Mexican Americans, and especially the women in these groups, have higher levels of religious participation than other groups in the United States (Taylor, Chatters & Levin, 2004). Religious participation is higher in the United States than in most European countries.

> ● **CRITICAL THINKING**
>
> What explanations could you suggest for women attending religious services more frequently than men? How does this fit with other gender differences you have studied in this book?

Changes in Private Beliefs and Practices

When it comes to religious beliefs and private religious activities such as engaging in prayers, meditating, or

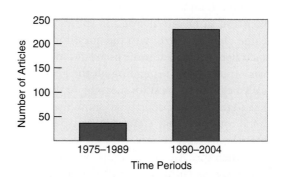

Figure 9.1 The number of research articles published on the topic of religious practices and spirituality have increased 600-fold in the past decade or so.

Source: Data from Koenig, 2006.

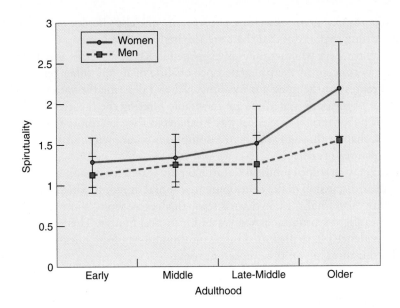

Figure 9.2 Spirituality increases with age, but there are different patterns for the two genders. Both genders are stable in their spirituality until middle adulthood. Women begin an increase in middle adulthood and this continues into late adulthood. In comparison, men don't begin an increase until late-middle adulthood.

Source: Wink & Dillon, 2002.

reading sacred texts, cross-sectional studies show that older adults also participate in private religious behavior more than younger people (Idler, Musick, Ellison, et al., 2003). And a longitudinal study that showed a dropoff in attendance at religious services in very late adulthood showed stable or even increased levels of private religious practices at the same time (Idler, Kasl, & Hays, 2001). The conclusion from these studies is that there is an increase in religious beliefs and private religious activities over adulthood, with a period of stability at the end of life (Idler, 2006).

In a longitudinal study that spanned 40 years, psychologist Paul Wink and sociologist Michele Dillon (2002) analyzed data from the Institute for Human Development longitudinal study to evaluate participants on their level of spirituality over the course of the study. There were over 200 men and women in the study, and most were interviewed four times between the ages of 31 and 78. In addition, the participants represented two cohorts, the younger born in 1927 and the older in 1920. The results are shown in Figure 9.2. As you can see, there was an increase in spirituality for women from middle to late-middle to older adulthood, and an increase for men from late-middle to older adulthood.

When the younger and older cohorts were compared, Wink and Dillon found different patterns of spiritual development, as shown in Figure 9.3. The younger cohort increased significantly throughout their adult lives, while the older cohort, although significantly more spiritual in early adulthood, only increased in the last stage, between late-middle and older adulthood. Wink and Dillon concluded that there is a tendency for men and women to increase in spirituality between the mid-50s and mid-70s. They become more involved with the quest for meaning as they become increasingly aware that their lives will end at some point in the future. The years from early to middle adulthood were more varied depending on the gender and the cohort being studied. Women typically begin their quest for meaning in their 40s (but not before). In addition, people born less than a decade apart may show the same general increase in spirituality over adulthood, but they may show different patterns of spirituality. Wink and Dillon speculate that the younger cohort, who showed greater spirituality in their 30s, were living in the 60s when the "Age of Aquarius" was in its prime, and they were at an age that was more responsive to cultural changes than the older cohort, who were in their 40s at the time.

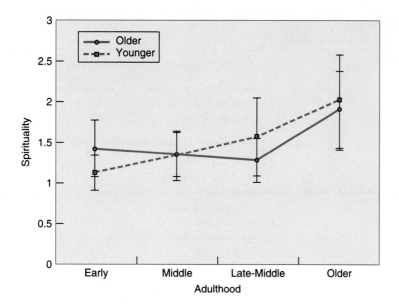

Figure 9.3 The age-related increase in spirituality is different for two cohorts born seven years apart. The older cohort (born in 1920) did not show an increase in spirituality until late-middle adulthood. In comparison, the younger cohort (born in 1927) showed an increase in spirituality throughout adulthood, from early adulthood until late adulthood.

Source: Wink & Dillon, 2002.

So to answer the question of whether there is an increase in spirituality during adulthood, the answer is yes, but the timing depends on age, gender, and also the cultural conditions that prevail when adults are at certain critical ages.

Psychologist Padmaprabha Dalby (2006) performed a meta-analysis on recent studies of changes in spirituality over the adult years and found an age-related increase in certain aspects of spirituality, such as integrity, humanistic concern, positive relationships with others, concern for the younger generations, relationship with a higher power, self-trancendence, and acceptance of death. However, these increases seemed to be responses to the adversities of later adulthood, such as poor health, disability, one's own impending death, and the loss of loved ones, rather than related to age itself. This has been suggested as an alternative to the idea that an accumulation of general life experience brings forth self-transcendence, but as Dalby points out, there are no studies comparing people of the same ages who differ in health and other measures of adversity.

> ● **CRITICAL THINKING**
>
> How might you design an experiment to determine whether older people are more spiritual because of their age or because of the adversity they have faced? What do you hypothesize about the results?

Religion and Health

In the past several years, a large number of studies in a variety of scientific fields, including psychology, epidemiology, and medicine, have explored the relationship of religion and health. In general, there have been consistent and robust findings that people who attend religious services live longer than people who do not, and that this result is stronger for women than for men (Tartaro, Lueken, & Gunn, 2005). What is it about attending religious services that affects health? A number of mechanisms have been suggested, including the fact that most religions promote healthy behavior, provide social support, teach coping skills, and promote positive emotions (McCullough, Hoyt, Larson, et al., 2000).

In one study of the effect of religious participation and spirituality on physiological stress reactions, psychologist Jessica Tartaro and her colleagues (Tartaro, Lueken, & Gunn, 2005) found that participants who scored high on a test of religiosity and spirituality showed lower levels of cortisol responses to lab-induced stress. The researchers gave the

---

Table 9.1   Sample Items from the Brief Multidimensional Measure of Religiousness/Spirituality (BMMRS)

I find strength and comfort in my religion

many times a day.
every day.
most days.
some days.
once in awhile.
never or almost never.

I am spiritually touched by the beauty of creation

many times a day.
every day.
most days.
some days.
once in awhile.
never or almost never.

I feel a deep sense of responsibility for reducing pain and suffering in the world.

Strongly agree
Agree
Disagree
Strongly disagree

I have forgiven those who hurt me.

Always or almost always
Often
Seldom
Never

How often do you go to religious services?

More than once a week   Once or twice a month
Every week or more often   Once or twice a year
Every month or so   Never

How often do you pray privately in places other than at church or synagogue?

More than once a day
Once a day
A few times a week
Once a week
A few times a month
Once a month
Never

I think about how my life is part of a larger spiritual force

a great deal.
quite a bit.
somewhat.
not at all.

I try hard to carry my religious beliefs over into all my other dealings in life.

Strongly agree
Agree
Disagree
Strongly disagree

Source: Adapted from the Fetzer Institute, 1999.

---

test to 60 undergraduate students who represented a variety of religious affiliations, including 22 percent who had their "own beliefs." Sample questions from this test are shown in Table 9.1. Later the students' cortisol levels were measured before and after performing two computer tasks that had been shown to induce physiological indicators of stress reactivity. As I will explain in Chapter 10, cortisol is a hormone released as part of the stress response and is related to decreases in immune system response. Results are shown in Figure 9.4. For the question, "To what extent do you consider yourself a religious person?" those who responded, "Not at all," showed significantly higher cortisol response levels than those who responded that they were "slightly," "moderately," or "very" religious. When responses to the specific religious or spiritual practices were examined, two areas were found to be associated with the cortisol response—forgiveness and frequency of prayer. The researchers concluded that religious practices and spiritual beliefs, especially forgiveness and prayer, may serve to protect individuals from the damaging effects of stress. Forgiveness is also linked with positive health outcomes in earlier studies (McCullough, Hoyt, Larson, et al., 2000), and so is prayer (Pargament, 1997).

Other studies show that religiousness/spirituality is related to lower cortisol levels in long-term AIDS survivors (Ironson, Solomon, Balbin, et al., 2002) and lower blood pres-

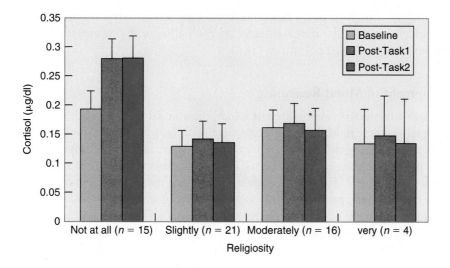

Figure 9.4 Young adults who described themselves as "not being religious at all" had greater stress reactivity than those who described themselves as being "slightly," "moderately," or "very" religious.

Source: Tartaro, Luecken, & Gunn, 2005.

sure in older adults (Koenig, George, Hays, et al., 1998). Meditation has been linked to both lower cortisol levels and lower blood pressure levels (Seeman, Dubin, & Seeman, 2003). In an example that will be discussed further in Chapter 10, it has been demonstrated that people who possess the personality trait of *hardiness,* who are committed to finding meaning in their lives, are more resilient to the effects of stress than those who have lower levels of this trait. They have confidence that they will be able to cope with whatever situations life hands them and will find meaning in the process (Maddi, 2005). Although the religion and health link seems indisputable, questions still remain about spirituality that is not expressed in religious-service attendance. I would also like to see more on the different effects religion seems to have on men versus women. And, of course, most of these studies are cross-sectional or conducted with participants who are college students. They tell us little about possible changes in the role of religion in adults' lives as they age, or about other changes in meaning systems that may be taking place. To explore this, we need to look at some broader theory and case studies.

Theories of Spiritual Development

For several reasons, I want to start this exploration with a look at psychologist Lawrence Kohlberg's theory of the development of **moral reasoning**—reasoning about what is right and wrong and how to judge the rightness or wrongness of an act. Although the questions Kohlberg addressed touch on only a corner of the subject I am examining, his basic theoretical model is the foundation of much of the current thinking about adults' evolving worldviews

Participating in religious services is related to better coping skills, less severe stress reactions, better health, and longer lives, especially for women.

or meaning systems. Kohlberg's theory has been tested extensively with empirical research and is widely accepted by developmental psychologists, so it provides a relatively non-controversial jumping-off point.

Development of Moral Reasoning

Faced with a conflict between different values, on what basis does a child or an adult decide what is morally right or wrong, fair or just? Kohlberg argued, as an extension of Jean Piaget's theory of cognitive development, that children and adults move through a sequence of stages in their moral reasoning, each stage growing out of, but superseding, the one that came before. In this view, each stage reflects a meaning system or model, an internally consistent and pervasive set of assumptions about what is right and wrong and how it should be judged in others (Kohlberg, 1981, 1984).

Kohlberg made an important distinction between the form of thinking (what one thinks) and the content of thinking (why one thinks a certain way). The issue is not whether a person thinks, for example, that stealing is wrong, but why he or she thinks it is wrong. Kohlberg searched for developmental changes in the form of thinking about moral questions, just as Piaget searched for developmental changes in broader forms of logic.

The Measurement Procedure. Kohlberg assessed a person's level or stage of moral reasoning by means of a moral judgment interview in which the subject is asked to respond to a series of hypothetical moral dilemmas. In each dilemma, two different principles are in conflict. For example, in the now-famous Heinz dilemma (presented at the top of Table 9.2), the subject must grapple with the question of whether a man named Heinz ought to steal a drug to save his dying wife if the only druggist who can provide it is demanding a higher price than he can pay. In this instance, the conflicting principles are the value of preserving life and the value of respecting property and upholding the law.

The Stages. Based on many subjects' responses to such dilemmas, Kohlberg concluded that there are three basic levels of moral reasoning, each of which can be divided further into two stages, resulting in six stages in all, summarized in Table 9.2.

The *preconventional level* is typical of most children under age 9 but is also found in some adolescents and in some adult criminal offenders. At both stages of this level, one sees rules as something outside oneself. In stage 1, the *punishment-and-obedience orientation,* what is right is what is rewarded or what is not punished; in stage 2, right is defined in terms of what brings pleasure or serves one's own needs. Stage 2 is sometimes described as the *naive hedonism orientation,* a phrase that captures some of the flavor of this stage.

CRITICAL THINKING ●

How might an adult make a moral decision that reflects the preconventional level of reasoning? Hint: Perhaps while driving on an interstate highway.

At the *conventional level,* which is characteristic of most adolescents and most adults in our culture, one internalizes the rules and expectations of one's family or peer group (at stage 3) or of society (at stage 4). Stage 3 is sometimes called the *good-boy or good-girl orientation,* while stage 4 is sometimes labeled as the *social-order-maintaining orientation.*

The *postconventional (or principled) level,* which is found in only a minority of adults, involves a search for the underlying reasons behind society's rules. At stage 5, which Kohlberg calls the *social contract orientation,* laws and regulations are seen as important ways of ensuring fairness, but they are not perceived as immutable, nor do they necessarily perfectly reflect more fundamental moral principles. Since laws and contracts are usually in accord with such underlying principles, obeying society's laws is reasonable nearly all the time. But when the underlying principles or reasons are at variance with some specific

Table 9.2 Kohlberg's Stages of Moral Development

Kohlberg's theory of moral development was based on responses about moral dilemmas. This story of Heinz is the best known of these moral dilemmas:

In Europe a woman was near death from a special kind of cancer. There was one drug that doctors thought might save her. It was a form of radium that a druggist in the same town had recently discovered. The drug was expensive to make, but the druggist was charging $2000, or 10 times the cost of the drug, for a small (possibly lifesaving) dose. Heinz, the sick woman's husband, borrowed all the money he could, about $1000, or half of what he needed. He told the druggist that his wife was dying and asked him to sell the drug cheaper or to let him pay later. The druggist replied, "No, I discovered the drug, and I'm going to make money from it." Heinz then became desperate and broke into the store to steal the drug for his wife. Should Heinz have done that?

The following responses are examples of people operating in different stages of moral development:

Level 1: Preconventional morality

Stage 1: Punishment and obedience orientation

Yes, Heinz should take the drug. *Why?* Because if he lets his wife die, he could be responsible for it and get into trouble.

No, Heinz should not take the drug. *Why?* Because it is stealing. It doesn't belong to him and he can get arrested and punished.

Stage 2: Naive hedonism orientation

Yes, Heinz should take the drug. *Why?* Because he really isn't hurting the druggist and he wants to help his wife. Maybe he can pay him later.

No, Heinz shouldn't take the drug. *Why?* The druggist is in business to make money. That's his job. He needs to make a profit.

Level 2: Conventional morality

Stage 3: Good-boy or good-girl orientation

Yes, Heinz should take the drug. *Why?* Because he is being a good husband and saving his wife's life. He would be wrong if he didn't save her.

No, Heinz should not take the drug. *Why?* Because he tried to buy it and he couldn't, so it's not his fault if his wife dies. He did his best.

Stage 4: Social Order Maintaining orientation

Yes, Heinz should take the drug. *Why?* Because the druggist is wrong to be interested only in profits. But Heinz also must pay for the drug later and maybe confess that he took it. It's still wrong to steal.

No, Heinz should not take the drug. *Why?* Because even though it is natural to want to save your wife, you still need to obey the law. You can't just ignore it because of special circumstances.

Level 3: Postconventional (or principled) morality

Stage 5: Social contract orientation

Yes, Heinz should take the drug. *Why?* Although the law says he shouldn't, if you consider the whole picture, it would be reasonable for anyone in his situation to take the drug.

No, Heinz should not take the drug. *Why?* Although some good would come from him taking the drug, it still wouldn't justify violating the consensus of how people have agreed to live together. The ends don't justify the means.

Stage 6: Individual principles of conscience orientation

Yes, Heinz should take the drug. *Why?* When a person is faced with two conflicting principles, they need to judge which is higher and obey it. Human life is higher than possession.

No, Heinz should not take the drug. *Why?* Heinz needs to decide between his emotion and the law—both are "right" in a way, but he needs to decide what an ideally just person would do, and that would be not to steal the drug.

Source: After Kohlberg, 1976, 1984.

According to Kohlberg's theory, only a few individuals, such as Martin Luther King, Jr. (*left*) and Mahatma Gandhi (*right*), reach the highest level of moral reasoning.

social custom or rule, the stage 5 adult argues on the basis of the fundamental principle, even if it means disobeying or disagreeing with a law. Civil rights protesters in the early 1960s, for example, typically supported their civil disobedience with stage 5 reasoning. Stage 6, known as the *individual principles of conscience orientation,* is simply a further extension of the same pattern, with the person searching for and then living in a way that is consistent with the deepest set of moral principles possible.

Another way to look at the shifts from preconventional, to conventional, to postconventional levels of reasoning is to see them as a process of **decentering,** a term Piaget used to describe cognitive development more generally as a movement outward from the self. At the preconventional level, the children's reference points are themselves—the consequences of their own actions, the rewards they may gain. At the conventional level, the reference point has moved outward away from the center of the self to the family or society. Finally, at the postconventional level, the adult searches for a still broader reference point, some set of underlying principles that lie behind or beyond social systems. Such a movement outward from the self is one of the constant themes in writings on the growth or development of meaning systems in adult life.

The Data. Only longitudinal data can tell us whether Kohlberg's model is valid. If it is, not only should children and adults move from one step to the next in the order he proposes, but they should not show regression to earlier stages. Kohlberg and his colleagues tested these hypotheses in three samples, all interviewed repeatedly, and each time asked to discuss a series of moral dilemmas: (1) 84 boys from the Chicago area first interviewed when they were between 10 and 16 in 1956, and some of whom were reinterviewed up to five more times (the final interview was in 1976–1977, when they were in their 30s) (Colby, Kohlberg, Gibbs, et al., 1983); (2) a group of 23 boys and young men in Turkey (some from a rural village and some from large cities), followed over periods of up to 10 years into early adulthood (Nisan & Kohlberg, 1982); and (3) 64 male and female subjects from kibbutzim (collective communities) in Israel, who were first tested as teenagers and then retested once or twice more over periods of up to 10 years (Snarey, Reimer, & Kohlberg, 1985).

Figure 9.5 gives two kinds of information about the findings from these three studies. In the top half of the figure are total "moral maturity scores" derived from the interview. These scores reflect each subject's stage of moral reasoning and can range from 100 to 500. As you can see, in all three studies the average score went up steadily with age, although there are some interesting cultural differences in speed of movement through the stages. In the bottom half of the figure are the percentages of answers to the moral dilemmas that reflected each stage of moral reasoning for the subjects at each age. These data are for the Chicago sample only, since it has been studied over the longest period of time. As we would expect, the number of stage 1 responses drops out quite early, while conventional morality (stages 3 and 4) rises rapidly in the teenage years and remains high in adult-

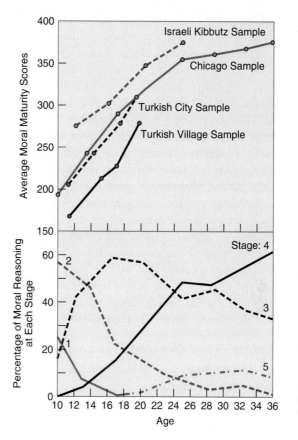

Figure 9.5 The upper panel shows that scores of four diverse samples of boys on a moral reasoning test show a general in- crease from middle childhood through young adulthood. The lower panel shows the percent of responses given that reflect the different stages of moral development. It is clear that Stage 4 re- sponses increase with age and that Stage 2 responses decrease.

Source: Data from Colby, Kohlberg, Gibbs, et al., 1983; Nisan & Kohlberg, 1982; and Snarey Reimer, & Kohlberg, 1985.

hood. Only a very small percentage of answers, even of respondents in their 30s, shows stage 5 reasoning (postconventional reasoning), and none show stage 6 reasoning.

Both analyses show the stages to be strongly sequential. The sequential pattern is sup- ported by the fact that in none of these three studies was there a single subject who skipped a stage, and only about 5 percent showed regressions—a percentage that would be con- sistent with scoring errors. Each subject also showed a good deal of internal consistency at any one testing, using similar logic in analyzing each of several quite different moral problems. The same patterns were found in both shorter-term longitudinal studies (Walker, 1989) and in studies using a questionnaire method of measuring moral judgment rather than the more open-ended interview (Rest & Thoma, 1985).

Unfortunately, no equivalent longitudinal data exist for any adults past midlife. Cross- sectional results show no age differences in overall level of moral judgment between young, middle-aged, and older adults (Lonky, Kaus, & Roodin, 1984; Pratt, Golding, & Hunter, 1983). Such findings might be taken to mean that the level of reasoning achieved in early adulthood remains relatively stable throughout adulthood. But the longitudinal data do not support such an assertion, at least not through the middle 30s. Among Kohlberg's sam- ple were quite a few people who shifted from stage 3 to stage 4 while in their 20s, and a few who moved to stage 5 while in their 30s. At least some adults may thus continue to develop through Kohlberg's stages throughout adulthood. The only way to know this for sure would be to assess moral reasoning longitudinally over the full years of adult life.

Stage 6, and the Possibility of Stage 7. In his early work Kohlberg suggested that a fair number of college students reached stage 6. In his later writings, however, he changed his mind and concluded that this universalistic stage is extremely uncommon (Colby &

Kohlberg, 1987). The longitudinal data suggest that stage 5 may be the typical "endpoint" of the developmental progression. Adults who reach stage 6 (about 15 percent of those in their 30s in Kohlberg's samples) do indeed operate on some broad, general principles. What they lack, however, is "that which is critical for our theoretical notion of Stage 6, namely, the organization of moral judgment around a clearly formulated moral principle of justice and respect for persons that provides a rationale for the primacy of this principle" (Kohlberg, 1984, p. 271). In other words, at stage 5 one develops some broad principles that go beyond (or "behind") the social system; at stage 6, the rare person develops a still broader and more general ethical system in which these basic principles are embedded. Among those Kohlberg lists as apparently stage 6 thinkers are Martin Luther King, Jr., and Mahatma Gandhi.

Kohlberg and his colleagues also speculated about the existence of a still higher stage, Stage 7, a *unity orientation,* which they thought might emerge only toward the end of life, after an adult has spent some years living within a principled moral system. It is the confrontation of one's own death that can bring about this transition. As they ask the fundamental questions "Why live?" and "How do I face death?" some people transcend the type of logical analysis that typifies all the earlier forms of moral reasoning and arrive at a still deeper or broader decentering. It is a sense of unity with being, with life, or with God (Kohlberg, Levine, & Hewer, 1983).

Evaluation and Comment. The body of evidence that has accumulated concerning the development of moral reasoning provides strong support for several aspects of Kohlberg's theory:

- There do appear to be stages that children and adults move through in developing concepts of fairness and morality.

- At least up to stage 5, these stages appear to meet the tests of a hierarchical stage system: they occur in a fixed order, each emerging from and replacing the one that preceded it, and together forming a structural whole.

- The stage sequence appears to be universal. The specific content of moral decisions may differ from one culture to the next, but the overall form of logic seems to move through the same steps in every culture in which this has been studied—a list that includes 27 different countries, Western and non-Western, industrialized and nonindustrialized (Snarey, 1985).

The stages have relevance for real life as well as theory. For example, researchers in one study found that adults who reason at the principled level are more able than are those at the conventional level to deal positively and constructively with significant losses in their lives, such as the death of a family member or the breakup of a relationship (Lonky, Kaus, & Roodin, 1984).

At the same time, a number of critics have pointed out that Kohlberg's theory is relatively narrow, focusing almost exclusively on the development of concepts of justice or fairness. Other aspects of moral/ethical reasoning, other facets of meaning systems, are omitted.

The most eloquent of the critics is psychologist Carol Gilligan (1982). She argues that Kohlberg was interested in concepts of justice and not concepts of care, so his theory and research largely ignore an ethical/moral system based on caring for others, on responsibility, on altruism or compassion. In particular, Gilligan proposes that women more often than men approach moral and ethical dilemmas from the point of view of responsibilities and caring, searching not for the "just" solution, but for the solution that best deals with the social relationships involved. She argues that men, in contrast, use a morality of justice more often than women.

This aspect of Gilligan's argument is not strongly supported by research findings. In studies in which boys and girls have been compared on stage of moral reasoning using Kohlberg's revised scoring system, no gender differences are typically found (Smetana, Killen, & Turiel, 1991), although several studies of adults do show the difference that Gilligan hypothesizes (Lyons, 1983). What is clear from the research to date is that girls and women can and do use moral reasoning based on principles of justice when they are presented with dilemmas in which that is a central issue.

Development of Faith

In talking about stages of faith development, theologian and developmental psychologist James Fowler (1981) goes beyond questions of moral reasoning to search for the emergence of our individual worldview or model of our relationship to others and to the universe. He uses the word *faith* to describe this personal model.

In Fowler's view, each of us has a faith whether or not we belong to a church or religious organization. Moral reasoning is only a part of faith (perhaps quite a small part). Faith is a broader set of assumptions or understandings, often so basic that they are not articulated, about the nature of our connections with others and with the world in which we live. At any point in our lives, he argues, each of us has a "master story" which is "the answer you give to the questions of what life is about, or who's really in charge here, or how do I live to make my life a worthy, good one. It's a stance you take toward life" (Fowler, 1983, p. 60).

> **● CRITICAL THINKING**
>
> Do you have a "master story"? Has it changed in the last 10 years? What do you think caused the change?

Like Kohlberg, Fowler is interested not in the specific content of one's faith, but in its structure or form. A Christian, a Hindu, a Jew, a Muslim, and an atheist may all have faiths that are structurally similar but sharply different in content. And like Kohlberg, Fowler hypothesizes that each of us develops through a shared series of faith structures (or worldviews, broad internal working models, meaning systems, or whatever we choose to call them) over the course of childhood and adulthood. Two of the six stages he proposes occur primarily in childhood, and I won't describe them here; the remaining four can be found among adults.

The Stages of Faith. The first of the adult forms of faith, which Fowler calls *synthetic-conventional faith,* normally appears first in adolescence and then continues well into early adulthood for most of us. Like Kohlberg's level of conventional morality, conventional faith is rooted in the implicit assumption that authority is to be found outside oneself.

Many adults remain within this form of faith throughout their lives, defining themselves and interpreting their experiences within the meaning system of a group or a specific set of beliefs. Let me give you an example from Fowler's own interviews that may make the point clearer. Mrs. H. is a 61-year-old southern woman who grew up on a tenant farm. At the time Fowler interviewed her, she had recently rededicated herself to the Baptist Church after many years away from church activity. At one point she said:

> I feel very sad and ashamed for the way I have wasted my life. I do know that God has forgiven me for every wrong that I've done, and that He loves me. I feel very close to God most of the time, now that I am active in the work of the church again. Of course there are times that I don't feel as close to Him as I'd like to, but I know that I am the one who moves away, not He. I've learned that we all have so much to be thankful for, if we only stop and count our blessings. (Fowler, 1981, p. 172)

It is precisely this reliance on external authority that changes when an adult moves to the next proposed stage, which Fowler calls *individuative-reflective faith.* This move requires an interruption of reliance on an external source of authority—a relocation of authority from external to internal. In making this shift, many adults reject or move away from the faith community to which they belong. Often, there is also a rejection of ritual or myth and an embracing of science or rationality. But the transition can occur without such rejections. The key is that the person not only reexamines old assumptions but takes responsibility in a new way.

It is hard to convey just how profound a change this is. The metaphor I have found most helpful is one I have adapted from mythologist Joseph Campbell's writings (1986). It is as if in the stage of conventional faith we experience ourselves as like the moon, illuminated by reflected light. We are not ourselves the source of light (or knowledge) but are created by outside forces. In the stage of individuative faith, we experience ourselves as like the sun, radiating light of our own. We are no longer defined by the groups to which we belong; rather, we choose the groups, the relationships, based on our self-chosen beliefs or values. Thus, even if the specific beliefs we choose at this point are the same ones with which we have grown up, the underlying meaning system is changed.

Rebecca, a woman in her mid-30s, seems clearly to have made this transition:

> I know I have very defined boundaries and I protect them very carefully. I won't give up the slightest control. In any relationship I decide who gets in, how far, and when. What am I afraid of? I used to think I was afraid people would find out who I really was and then not like me. But I don't think that's it anymore. What I feel now is—"that's me. That's mine. It's what makes me. And I'm powerful. It's my negative side, maybe, but it's also my positive stuff—and there's a lot of that. What it is is me, it's my self—and if I let people in maybe they'll take it, maybe they'll use it—and I'll be gone.". . . This "self," if I had to represent it I think of two things: either a steel rod that runs through everything, a kind of solid fiber, or sort of like a ball at the center that is all together. (Kegan, 1982, pp. 240–241)

The next stage in Fowler's model, *conjunctive faith,* requires an opening outward from the self-preoccupation of the individuative reflective level. There is an openness here to paradox, a moving away from fixed truth toward a search for balance, not only of self and other, but of mind and emotion, of rationality and ritual. The person who lives within this meaning system, which is not typically found before midlife, accepts that there are many truths, that others' beliefs, others' ideas, may be true for them—a point of view that not only brings far greater tolerance toward others but also very commonly brings the person to an interest in service or commitment to the welfare of others.

Here's one illustrative voice, that of Miss T., a 78-year-old woman who had been variously a Unitarian, a Quaker, and a follower of Krishnamurti and other Eastern teachers. When asked if there were beliefs and values everyone should hold, she said:

> If somebody asked me that and gave me just two minutes to answer it, I know what I'd say. It's a line from George Fox, the founder of Quakerism. It's old-fashioned English and it seems to me to have the entire program of anybody's life. It's a revolution, it's an enormous comfort, it's a peace maker. The line is: "There is that of God in every man." Now, you can start thinking about it. You can see that if you really did believe that, how it would change your relationships with people. It's far-reaching. It applies nationally and individually and class-wise; it reaches the whole. To anyone that I loved dearly I would say, "Put that in your little invisible locket and keep it forever." (Fowler, 1981, p. 194)

Other statements by Miss T. make it clear that the content of her faith at this point involves a kind of return to some of the elements of her earlier religious teachings, but she has reframed it, casting it in language that has meaning for her now and that focuses on finding fulfillment in service to others—all of which are significant elements of conjunctive faith.

CRITICAL THINKING

Does Fowler's stage of conjunctive faith remind you of one of Erikson's stages of psychosocial development discussed in Chapter 8?

The final proposed stage in Fowler's system is *universalizing faith*. Like Kohlberg's stage 6, reaching this stage is a relatively rare achievement, but Fowler argues that it is the next logical step. To some extent, it involves a step beyond individuality. In the stage of conjunctive faith, the person may be "open" and "integrated" but is still struggling with the paradox of searching for universality while attempting to preserve individuality. In the stage of universalizing faith, the person lives the principles, the imperatives, of absolute love and justice. Because such people live their lives based on such basic outward-oriented principles, they are heedless of their own self-preservation, much as Mother Theresa continued caring for the dying up until the end of her own life. They may even be seen by others as subversive to the structures of society or traditional religion, since they do not begin with the assumption that society or religion is necessarily correct in its institutions or customs.

Some Basic Points About Fowler's Stages. Some key points need emphasis. First, like Kohlberg, Fowler assumes that these stages occur in a sequence, but that the sequence is only very roughly associated with age, especially in adulthood. Some adults remain within the same meaning system, the same faith structure, their entire lives; others make one or more transitions in their understanding of themselves and their relationships with others.

Second, Fowler nonetheless contends that each stage has its "proper time" of ascendancy in a person's lifetime, a period at which that particular form of faith is most consistent with the demands of life. Most typically, the stage of conventional faith is in its ascendance in adolescence or early adulthood, and the stage of individuative-reflective faith in the years of the late 20s and 30s, while a transition to the stage of conjunctive faith, if it occurs at all, may occur around midlife. Finally, the stage of universalizing faith, if one can reach it, would be the optimal form of faith in old age, when issues of integrity and meaning become still more dominant.

Third, Fowler conceives of each stage as wider or more encompassing than the one that preceded it. And this greater breadth helps to foster both a greater capacity for a sense of sureness and serenity and a greater capacity for intimacy—with the self as well as with others.

Research Findings. No longitudinal data have yet been collected to test the sequential aspect of Fowler's theory. However, Fowler (1981) has reported some cross-sectional data that show the incidence of the stages of faith at each of several ages. He asked over 300 adolescents and adults open-ended questions about their faith and had raters assign a stage to each person based on these interviews. The results fit the theory relatively well, showing that conventional faith is most common in the teenage years, individuative-reflective faith among people in their 20s, and conjunctive faith emerging only in the 30s. Furthermore, only one person fit the category of universalizing faith, a man in his 60s.

Another study that offers consistent evidence comes from psychologist Gary Reker, who has developed a very similar model of the emergence of meaning systems over the years of adulthood. Reker (1991) argues that an adult can find meaning in life through any of a variety of sources, such as leisure activities, personal relationships, personal achievement, traditions and culture, altruism or service to others, or enduring values and ideals. Reker suggests that these various sources of meaning can be organized into four levels: *self-preoccupation,* in which meaning is found primarily through financial security or meeting basic needs; *individualism,* in which meaning is found in personal growth or achievement, or through creative and leisure activities; *collectivism,* which includes meaning from traditions and culture and from societal causes; and *self-transcendence,* in which meaning is found through enduring values and ideals, religious activities, and altruism.

Reker's work does not provide a direct test of Fowler's model, but it is consistent with the basic idea that there may be systematic changes over the years of adulthood in the framework that adults use to define themselves and find meaning in their lives.

A Preliminary Assessment. Theories like Fowler's and research like Reker's supplement our thinking about adulthood in important ways, if only to help us focus on the importance of meaning systems and their possible sequential change with age. But it is still very early in our empirical exploration of this and related theories. The greatest immediate need is for good longitudinal data, perhaps initially covering the years that are thought to be transitional for many adults, but ultimately covering the entire adult age range.

Integrating Meaning and Personality: A Preliminary Theoretical Synthesis

No doubt some of the parallels between these several theories and the ones I discussed in Chapter 8 have already struck you. The surface similarities are obvious, as you can see in Table 9.3.

Loevinger's conformist stage in her theory of ego development certainly sounds like both Kohlberg's conventional morality and Fowler's conventional faith. There seems to be agreement that in adolescence and early adulthood, people tend to be focused on adapting to the demands of the roles and relationships society imposes on them and assume that the source of authority is external.

Loevinger's conscientious and individualistic stages are a great deal like Maslow's layer of esteem needs, Kohlberg's social contract orientation, and Fowler's individuative-reflective faith. All four theorists agree that the next step involves a shift in the central source of meaning or self-definition from external to internal, accompanied by a preoccupation with the self and one's own abilities, skills, and potentials.

Loevinger's autonomous and integrated stages are similar to Fowler's conjunctive faith, possibly related to self-actualization needs as described by Maslow. All speak of a shift

Table 9.3	Review of Stages of Personality, Morality, and Faith Development			
General Stage	**Loevinger's Stages of Ego Development**	**Maslow's Levels of Needs Hierarchy**	**Kohlberg's Stages of Moral Reasoning Development**	**Fowler's Stages of Faith Development**
Conformist; culture-bound self	Conformist; Self-aware Stages	Love and Belongingness Needs	Good-Boy or Good-Girl Orientation; Social Order Maintaining Orientation	Synthetic-Conventional Faith
Individuality	Conscientious; Individualistic Stages	Self-esteem Needs	Social Contract Orientation	Individuative-Reflective Faith
Integration	Autonomous; Integrated Stages	Self-Actualization	Individual Principles of Conscience Orientation	Conjunctive Faith
Self-transcendence		Peak Experiences	Unity Orientation	Universalizing Faith

away from self-preoccupation toward a search for balance, a shift toward greater toler-ance toward both self and others.

Finally, there seems to be agreement about a still higher stage that involves some form of self-transcendence: Kohlberg's unity orientation, Fowler's stage of universalizing faith, Maslow's peak experiences.

Of course, we are not dealing with four independent visions here. These theorists all knew of each other's work and were influenced by each other's ideas. This is particularly true in the case of Fowler and Kohlberg, since Fowler's theory is quite explicitly an extension of Kohlberg's model. So the fact that they all seem to agree does not mean that we have uncovered "truth" here. However, my confidence in the validity of the basic sequence these theorists describe is bolstered by three additional arguments:

First, although they have influenced one another, there are still three quite distinct theoretical heritages involved. Kohlberg's (and Fowler's) work is rooted in Piaget's the-ory and in studies of normal children's thinking; Loevinger's work is rooted in Freud's theory and in clinical assessments of children and adults, including those with emotional disturbances; Maslow's theory, although influenced by psychoanalytic thought, is based primarily on his own observations of a small number of highly unusual "self-actualized" adults. The fact that one can arrive at such similar views of the sequence of emergence of meaning systems from such different roots makes the convergence more impressive.

Second, in the case of both Kohlberg's and Loevinger's models, we have reasonably strong supporting empirical evidence, especially concerning the first step in the com-monly proposed adult sequence, of a move from conforming/conventional to individu-alistic. Transitions beyond that are simply much less well studied, in part because longitudinal studies have not yet followed adults past early midlife, perhaps in part because the later transitions are simply less common. Still, this is not all totally speculative stuff. We can anchor at least part of the commonly proposed basic sequence in hard data.

Finally, this basic model seems plausible to me because the sequence makes sense in terms of a still more encompassing developmental concept proposed by Robert Kegan.

A Synthesizing Model

Psychologist Robert Kegan (1982) proposes that each of us has two enormously power-ful and equal desires or motives built in. On the one hand, we deeply desire connection, the state of being joined or integrated with others. On the other hand, we equally desire independence, the state of being differentiated from others. No accommodation between these two is really in balance, so whatever *evolutionary truce* (as Kegan calls each stage) we arrive at, it will lean further toward one than toward the other. Eventually, the unmet need becomes so strong that we are forced to change the system, to change our under-standing. In the end, what this creates is a fundamental alternation, a moving back and forth of the pendulum, between perspectives or meaning systems centered on inclusion or union and perspectives centered on independence or separateness.

The child begins life in a symbiotic relationship with the mother or mother figure, so the pendulum begins on the side of connection and union. By age 2 the child has pulled away and seeks independence, a separate identity. The con-formist or conventional meaning system that we see in adolescence and early adulthood (if not later) is a move back toward connection, with the group, while the transition to the individualistic meaning system is a return to sep-aration and independence. The term "detribalization" fits nicely with Kegan's basic model (Levinson, 1978). In shifting the source of authority from

● CRITICAL THINKING

Do you identify the competing drives of connection and independence in your own life? Have there been "stages" in your life during which they have alternated?

external sources to one's own resources, there is at least initially a pushing away of the tribe and all its rituals and rules.

If the model is correct, the step after this ought to be another return toward connection, which seems to me to be precisely what is proposed by most of the theorists I have described. As I see it, most of them talk about two substeps in this shift of the pendulum, with Fowler's conjunctive faith or Kohlberg's individual principles of conscience orientation being intermediate steps on the way toward the more complete position of union or community represented by Fowler's universalizing faith or Kohlberg's unity orientation.

Although my explanation here describes the process with the image of a pendulum moving back and forth, clearly Kegan is not proposing that movement is simply back and forth in a single groove. Instead, he sees the process as more like that of a spiral in which each shift to the other "side" of the polarity is at a more integrated level than the one before.

If such a basic alternation, such a spiral movement, really does form the underlying rhythm of development, why should we assume that it stops even at so lofty a point as Kohlberg's unity orientation? When I first understood this aspect of Kegan's theory, I had one of those startling "ah ha!" experiences, for I realized that the stages of the mystical "journey" described in case studies by Evelyn Underhill and by William James could be linked seamlessly with the sequence Kegan was describing.

I am well aware that a discussion of such subjective mystical experiences here will seem to some to be going very far afield, perhaps totally outside the realm of psychology. But to me the risk is worth it, not only because in this way perhaps I can make a case for my own basic assumptions regarding the immense potential of the individual human spirit, but also because the pattern that emerges fits so remarkably well with the research evidence and the theories I have discussed thus far.

Stages of Mystical Experience

The stages I am describing here were suggested by theologian and philosopher Evelyn Underhill in her book *Mysticism* (1911/1961), based on her reading of autobiographies, biographies, and other writings of the lives of hundreds of people from every religious tradition, all of whom described some form of **mysticism,** or self-transcendent experience, in which they know that they are part of a larger whole and that they have an existence beyond their own physical body and personal history. They did not all describe all of the steps or stages listed, but Underhill reported that there was a remarkable degree of unanimity about the basic process, despite huge differences in historical period and religious background.

Step 1 in this process, which Underhill calls *awakening,* seems to me to correspond to the usual endpoint in theories like Kohlberg's or Fowler's. It involves at least a brief self-transcendent experience, such as the peak experiences that Maslow describes. In Kegan's model, this step is clearly represented on the "union" end of the polarity; it is an awakening to the possibility of stepping outside one's own perspective and understanding the world from a point of deep connection.

Step 2, which Underhill calls *purification,* is clearly a move back toward separateness. The person, having "seen" himself or herself from a broader perspective, also sees all his or her own imperfections, fruitless endeavors, and flaws. As St. Teresa of Ávila, one of the great mystics of the Christian tradition, put it, "In a room bathed in sunlight not a cobweb can remain hidden" (1562/1960, p. 181). To understand and eliminate the flaws, the cobwebs, the person must turn inward again. At this stage many people are strongly focused on self-discipline, including special spiritual disciplines such as regular prayer or meditation and fasting.

Step 3 clearly moves us back toward union. Underhill calls this *illumination*. It involves a much deeper, more prolonged awareness of light, or greater reality, or God, and may in fact encompass some of what Kohlberg refers to as stage 7.

But even this illumination is not the end of the journey. Underhill finds two other steps described by many mystics that appear to lie beyond. The first of these, stage 4, often called the *dark night of the soul,* involves a still further turn inward, back toward separateness. At stage 3, illumination, the person still feels some personal satisfaction, some personal pleasure or joy in having achieved illumination. According to mystics who have described these later stages, if one is to achieve ultimate union, even this personal pleasure must be abandoned. And the process of abandonment requires a turning back to the self, to awareness, and exploration, of all the remaining ways in which the separate self has survived. Only then can the person achieve the endpoint, stage 5, which is *unity*—with God, with reality, with beauty, with the ultimate—however this may be described within a particular religious tradition.

I cannot say, of course, whether this sequence, this spiral of inner human progress, reflects the inevitable or ultimate path for us all. I can say only that the developmental analyses of stages of morality, or stages of faith or personality, that have been offered by many psychologists, for which we have at least some preliminary supporting evidence, appear to form a connected whole with the descriptions of stages of mystical illumination. For example, Jung (1917/1966) describes similar stages in his journey to discover his own inner world through psychoanalysis. At the very least, we know that a pathway similar to this has been trod by a long series of remarkable individuals, whose descriptions of their inner journeys bear striking similarities. There may be many other paths or journeys. But the reflections of these remarkable few point the way toward the possibility of a far vaster potential of the human spirit than is apparent to most of us in our daily humdrum lives.

The Process of Transition

Coming down a bit from these lofty heights, but still assuming for the moment that there is some basic rhythm, some developmental sequence, in the forms of meaning we create, let me turn to a question that may be of special personal importance: What is the process by which transitions or transformations from one stage to the next take place? What triggers them? What are the common features of transitions? How are they traversed?

Most developmental psychologists who propose stages of adult development have focused more on the stages than on the transition process. But there are some common themes in the ways transitions are described.

A number of theorists have described transitions in parallel terms, with each shift from one "level" or "stage" to the next seen as a kind of death and rebirth—a death of the earlier sense of self, of the earlier faith, of the earlier equilibrium (James, 1902/1958; Kegan, 1980). The process typically involves first some glimpses or precursors or premonitions of another stage or view, which are then followed by a period (which may be brief or prolonged) in which the person struggles to deal with the two "selves" within. Sometimes the process is aborted and the person returns to the earlier equilibrium. Sometimes the person moves instead toward a new understanding, a new equilibrium.

The middle part of this process, when the old meaning system has been partially given up but a new equilibrium has not yet been reached, is often experienced as profoundly dislocating. Statements such as "I am beside myself" or "I was out of my mind" may be used

(Kegan, 1980). The process of equilibration may be accompanied by an increase in physical or psychological symptoms of various kinds, including depression.

Kegan perhaps best summarizes the potential pain of the process: "Development is costly—for everyone, the developing person and those around him or her. Growth involves a separation from an old system of meaning. In practical terms this can involve both the agony of felt meaninglessness and the repudiation of commitments and investment. . . . Developmental theory gives us a way of thinking about such pain that does not pathologize it" (1980, p. 439). Such transitions may emerge slowly or may occur rapidly; they may be the result of self-chosen activities such as therapy or exercise, the happenstances of ordinary life, or unexpected experiences. In Table 9.4 I have suggested some of the stimuli for such transitions, organized around what appear to be the three most frequent adult transitions: (1) from conformity to individuality, (2) from individuality to integration or conjunctive faith, and (3) from integration to self-transcendence. I offer this list quite tentatively. We clearly lack the longitudinal evidence that might allow us to say more fully what experiences may or may not stimulate a transition.

You can see in the table that I am suggesting that somewhat different experiences may be involved in each of these three transitions. Attending college or moving away from home into a quite different community seem to be particularly influential in promoting aspects of the transition to individuality. For example, in longitudinal studies, both Kohlberg (1973) and Rest and Thoma (1985) have found a correlation between the amount of college education completed and the level of moral reasoning. Principled reasoning was found only in those who had attended at least some college. This transition, then, seems to be precipitated by exposure to other assumptions, other faiths, other perspectives. Such a confrontation can produce disequilibrium, which may be dealt with by searching for a new, independent, self-chosen model.

I have also suggested that therapy may play some role in triggering or assisting with either of the first two transitions. In fact, helping a client to achieve full integration is the highest goal of many humanistically oriented therapies, such as those based on the work of Carl Rogers or Fritz Perls. But my hypothesis is that traditional forms of therapy do little to assist the transition from integrated person to a level of self-transcendence. This transition, I think, requires or is assisted by a different form of active process, such as meditation or other forms of yoga or systematic prayer.

Both painful experiences and transcendent ones can also be the occasion for a new transition. The death of a child or of a parent may reawaken our concern with ultimate questions of life and death. A failed marriage or discouragement at work may lead to questioning or to a loss of the sense of stability of one's present model. Peak experiences, too, by giving glimpses of something not readily comprehensible within a current view, may create a dise-

The transition from college to first job can be a triggering situation for new growth in meaning systems.

Table 9.4	Transitions from One Stage to Another: Some Possible Triggering Situations of Experiences That May Assist in Passing Through a Transition	
Specific Transition	**Intentional Activities That May Foster That Transition**	**Unintentional or Circumstantial Events That May Foster That Transition**
From conformist to individualistic	Therapy; reading about other religions or faiths	Attending college; leaving home for other reasons, such as job or marriage; usual failures or reversals while "following the rules"; development of personal or professional skills
From individualistic to integrated	Therapy; introspection; short-term programs to heighten self-awareness (e.g., Gestalt workshops)	Illness or prolonged pain; death in the family or prolonged crisis; peak experiences
From integrated to self-transcendent	Meditation or prayer; various forms of yoga; self-disciplines	Near-death experience; transcendent experiences such as peak or immediate mystical experiences

quilibrium. Most adults who have had a "near-death experience," for example, report that their lives are never again the same. Many change jobs or devote their lives to service in one way or another. Other forms of peak experiences or religious "rebirth" may have the same effect.

I have been consistently using the word *may* in the last few paragraphs to convey the fact that such life changes do not invariably result in significant reflection or decentering. In an argument reminiscent of the concept of scheduled and unscheduled changes, psychologists Patricia Gurin and Orville Brim (1984) have offered an interesting hypothesis to explain such differences in the impact of major life changes. In essence, they argue that widely shared, age-linked changes are not likely to trigger significant reassessments of the sense of self precisely because expected changes are interpreted differently than unexpected ones. Shared changes are most often attributed to causes outside oneself, for which one is not personally responsible. In contrast, unique or off-time life changes are more likely to lead to significant inner reappraisals precisely because it is difficult to attribute such experiences to outward causes. If everyone at your job has been laid off because the company has gone out of business during a recession, you need not reassess your own sense of self-worth. But if you are the only one fired during a time of expanding economy, it is much more difficult to maintain your sense of worth.

Some shared experiences, such as college, may commonly trigger reappraisals or restructuring of personality, moral judgment, or faith. But most age-graded experiences can be absorbed fairly readily into existing systems. It may then be the unique or mistimed experiences that are particularly significant for changes in meaning systems. This hypothesis remains to be tested but raises some intriguing issues.

Commentary and Conclusions

For me, one of the striking things about the information I have presented in this chapter is that it is possible to find such similar descriptions emerging from such different traditions. But let me say again that the fact that there is a great deal of apparent unanimity in the theoretical (and personal) descriptions of the development of moral judgment, meaning systems, motive hierarchies, and spiritual evolution does not make this shared view true.

It does seem fair to say that most adults are engaged in some process of creating or searching for meaning in their lives. But this is not necessarily—perhaps not commonly—a conscious, deliberate process. Some adults, such as Tenkai, who appeared in the opening of this chapter, appear to engage in a conscious search, and their descriptions of the process are remarkably similar. But as I pointed out earlier, this may or may not mean that such a search, or even a nonconscious, or nonintentional, sequence of faiths, is a "natural" or essential part of adult development. A good number of equally spiritual adults, such as Sister Anne Richard, find meaning in a sudden and quiet moment, and never feel the need to search alternative pathways.

Furthermore, it is important to realize that all of what I have said and all of what these various theorists have said is based on a single metaphor of development, the metaphor of "life as a journey." We imagine the adult trudging up some hill or along some road, passing through steps or stages as he or she moves along. Implicit in this metaphor is the concept of a goal, an endpoint or *telos* (a Greek word from which our word *teleological* comes, meaning "having purpose or moving toward a goal"). This is a journey going somewhere. And if the purpose of the journey is thought of as personal growth, we must have some concept of an endpoint, of some highest level of personal growth.

The linearity and teleology of the journey metaphor may well limit our thinking about changes in adult meaning systems. Philosopher and television producer, Sam Keen (1983) suggests several other ways in which we might think of the process, two of which I find particularly appealing:

- "When we think of this eternal dimension of our being, the circle is more appropriate than the line. If life is a journey, then, it is not a pilgrimage but an odyssey in which one leaves and returns home again" (Keen, 1983, p. 31). Each step may be a circling back, a remembering of the "still point" within (to use poet T. S. Eliot's phrase). Progressively, we understand or "know" ourselves and our world differently with each movement of the circle, but there is no necessary endpoint.

- We can also think of the entire process as "musical themes that weave together to form a symphony; the themes that are central to each stage are anticipated in the previous stage and remain as resonant subthemes in subsequent stages" (Keen, 1983, p. 32). Another metaphor for this is that of life as a tapestry in which one weaves many colors. A person who creates many different meaning systems or faiths is weaving a tapestry with more colors, but it may be no more beautiful or pleasing than a tapestry woven intricately of fewer colors.

The basic point I am trying to make here is a simple one, although often hard to absorb thoroughly: Our theories of the quest for meaning are based in part on metaphors. We begin our search for understanding of adult development with a metaphor, and it colors all of what we choose to examine and all of what we see. The journey metaphor has dominated most of the current thinking, but it is not the only way to think about the process.

If we are to understand this process further, if we are to choose among the several metaphors, what we need is a great deal more empirical information to answer questions like the following. First, is there a longitudinal progression through Fowler's stages of faith or through equivalent sequences proposed by others, such as Loevinger's stages of ego development? A number of cross-sectional studies and several longitudinal studies suggest that some indicators of spiritual growth increase with age. But as we discussed in the first chapter of this book, age alone does not cause much of anything except the number of candles on one's cake. We need to ask: Is it due to the collected wisdom that comes from experience, from some kind of biological change in the nervous system, from facing the adversities of late adulthood, or something else? There has been a very large increase in research in this area, and I am confident that answers to this question are forthcoming.

Second, what are the connections, if any, between movement through the several sequences described by the various theorists? If we measure a given person's moral reasoning, the stage of ego development in Loevinger's model, and the type of faith he or she holds, will that person be at the same stage in all three? And when a person shifts in one area, does the shift occur across the board? Alternatively, might integration occur only at the final steps, at the level of what Loevinger calls the "integrated person"? These questions have been explored for many years in children's stages of cognitive development, and should be explored within the context of the quest for meaning in adulthood.

Third, assuming that longitudinal data confirm that there are stages of meaning making, we need to know what prompts a shift from one to the next. What supports a transition? What delays it? Finally, we need to know more about the possible connection between stages of faith (or models of meaning, or constructions of the self) and a sense of well-being, or greater physical health, or greater peace of mind. My own hypothesis is that one experiences greater happiness or satisfaction with one's life when it exists within a meaning system that lies at the "union" end of the dichotomy than when it is embedded in any of the more self-oriented stages.

Answers to some of these questions may be forthcoming in the next decades, because researchers have begun to devise measuring scales for spirituality and to explore various components of the quest for meaning. The recent evidence of a connection between health and religious practices is a promising start to further investigations that include other forms of spirituality. And the work on genetic coding for spirituality brings its own intrigue to the mix. For now, much of what I have said in this chapter remains tantalizing and intriguing speculation—but speculation that nonetheless points toward the potential for wisdom, compassion, even illumination within each adult.

Summary

1. The quest for meaning, or spirituality, is an integral part of the human experience, with signs of its existence found in archaelogical sites, in all cultures today, and even as a genetic trait in humans.

2. Psychology has long held that it is the meaning we attach to our experiences rather than the experiences themselves that defines reality for us. We filter experience through a set of basic assumptions we have each created, known as internal working models or meaning systems.

3. The idea of gerotranscendence, or the growth of meaning systems as we go through adulthood, is well known in literature, mythology, and psychological theories, although there is no agreement on what experiences in life cause the changes in meaning systems.

4. Empirical study of spirituality has increased dramatically in the last 15 years, and most of the studies address the question of whether this trait changes as we age. Religious participation is greater in older adults than younger adults, but there is a drop-off in late adulthood, possibly due to poor health. More women attend religious services and belong to religious organizations than men, and this gender difference is even greater for African Americans and Mexican Americans.

5. Rates of private religious practices, such as prayer and reading sacred texts, also increase with age, but remain steady into late adulthood, when participation in religious services drops off. It is suggested that people in late adulthood retain their spiritual beliefs and private practices even though they are no longer able to attend services.

6. Two groups that were followed longitudinally show an increase in spirituality during the adult years, but women begin the increase earlier in adulthood than men. Those in a younger cohort showed a different pattern of increase than those in an older cohort, indicating that events we experience during our lifetimes also have an impact on changes in spirituality over time.

7. It is as yet uncertain whether the experience of living for many years causes changes in spirituality, or whether the changes are due to the adversity older adults have to cope with. This will be an important topic of future research.

8. People, especially women, who attend religious services live longer than those who do not. One reason is that spirituality is related to lower levels of cortisol response during stressful situations. Cortisol has been implicated in many of the negative physiological effects of stress reactions, such as lowered immune function. This finding has been replicated in a number of populations and for a number of measures of spirituality, especially forgiveness and frequency of prayer.

9. One theory of the development of meaning systems is Kohlberg's theory of the development of moral reasoning. Based on Piaget's theory of cognitive development, this theory consists of six stages of moral reasoning, evaluating the level of moral reasoning by the explanations people give for their responses to moral dilemmas. At the first level, preconventional, reasoning reflects the punishment and obedience orientation in which what is moral is simply behavior that is rewarded, and the naive hedonism orientation in which the moral choice is the one that brings pleasure. At the second level, conventional, moral decisions are explained by following rules of the family or society. The third level, postconventional, chooses moral responses based on a search for underlying reasons for rules and laws.

10. Kohlberg's theory has been evaluated and refined over the years. For example, Carol Gilligan has pointed out that Kohlberg based his theory on interviews with boys, who use a system of justice, while girls base their moral decisions on a system of caring.

11. A second theory of spiritual development is Fowler's theory of faith development. Like Kohlberg, Fowler was interested in the individual search for meaning, not the specific beliefs. In Fowler's first stage, synthetic-conventional faith, meaning comes from an authority outside oneself. In the second stage, individuative-reflective faith, the individual takes responsibility for his or her own meaning system. In the third stage, conjunctive faith, an individual opens up to others' beliefs and welfare. Finally there is universalizing faith, the full opening of a person to disregard personal concerns.

12. There are similarities between the theories that seek to explain the development of spirituality over the adult years. There are also similarities between the theories of spiritual development and the personality theories discussed in previous chapters. One theory that seems to encompass all of them is Kegan's Synthesizing Model,

which proposes that we move between the need to be part of the group and the need to be individuals.

13.   Autobiographies, biographies, and case histories offer valuable information about individuals' search for meaning and thoughts about spiritualism. Underhill studied the accounts of many diverse individuals who described their quests for meaning, and she found commonalities in these quests that made up five possible stages. The first stage is awakening to a self-transcendence experience. This is followed by purification, in which the person is made aware of his or her faults and imperfections. The third stage is illumination, in which the person is made even more aware of the presence of a higher power. In the fourth stage, the person undergoes the dark night of the soul, turning inward for more critical self-examination. Stage five is unity, in which the individual feels one with the universe.

14.   This process described by Underhill has been described similarly by many people from different eras and fields of interest, for example, American psychologist William James in the early 20th century, Spanish nun St. Teresa of Ávila in the 16th century, and Swiss-born American psychoanalyst Carl Jung in the mid-20th century.

15.   The question of what factors lead to changes in meaning systems over adulthood is a relatively new topic of research. It is known that these changes may be triggered by unique life changes, by adversity, by peak experiences, and by intentionally pursuing self-knowledge and spiritual growth.

Key Terms

quest for meaning, 268

self-transcendence, 268

gero-transcendence, 269

postformal stages, 269

religiosity, 270

moral reasoning, 275

decentering, 278

mysticism, 286

Suggested Reading

Reading for Personal Interest

Birren, J. E., & Feldman, L. (1997). *Where to go from here: Discovering your own life's wisdom in the second half of your life.* New York: Simon & Schuster.

James Birren is a pioneer in the field of successful aging and most familiar for his scholarly writing. But in this book he teams up with journalist Linda Feldman to introduce his technique of guided autobiography to help older adults take stock of their past and find meaning in their future.

Dalai Lama (2005). *The universe in a single atom: The convergence of science and spirituality.* New York: Morgan Road Books.

At a time when science has discovered religion as a topic of interest, it seems that religion has discovered science. The 14th Dalai Lama, leader of the Tibetan people and the incarnation of the Buddha of Compassion, has spent much time during his exile meeting with scientists around the world and exploring how science can better serve humanity. This book is the result of conferences with scientists and Buddhist scholars to exchange ideas about meditation, prayer, awareness, evolution, cloning, and genetic engineering. The fact that science and religion often seem to be on opposite sides of most issues makes this a refreshing book.

Goodall, J. (1999). *Reasons for hope: A spiritual journey.* New York: Warner.

Jane Goodall is best known for her work documenting the natural behavior of chimpanzees in the Gombe forest of Africa. She has inspired a generation of young women (and young men) to follow in her footsteps. In this book she writes of her hope for our planet and its inhabitants, in spite of the destruction of the environment and the cruelty toward animals she has witnessed. At a time when many scientists are experiencing conflict between their work and their religion, Goodall explains how science has deepened and strengthened her faith.

Hamer, D. (2004). *The god gene: How faith is hardwired into our genes.* New York: Doubleday.

Geneticist Gene Hamer gives an interesting and readable explanation of how spirituality may be part of our genetic endowment.

Muggeridge, M. (1986). *Something beautiful for God: Mother Teresa of Calcutta.* San Francisco: Harper.

Malcolm Muggeridge began this book as a religious skeptic and ended up producing an inspired account of the life and work of this Nobel Peace Prize winner. Although this is a biography and not an autobiography, he includes transcripts of his conversations with Mother Teresa, making much of the book her story in her own words.

Classic Work

James, W. (1902/1958). *The varieties of religious experience.* New York: Mentor.

I find this a delightful book, remarkably free of the convoluted style that otherwise seems to be common in this area.

Kohlberg, L. (1984). *Essays on moral development,* (vol. 2). *The psychology of moral development.* San Francisco: Harper & Row.

Lawrence Kohlberg explains his ideas about moral development proceeding in stages.

St. Theresa of Ávila. (1577/1960). *Interior castle.* Garden City, NY: Image Books.

St. Theresa was a Spanish nun. Many experts consider her description of her inner spiritual journey the most complete and comprehensible account of the mystical experience. I found it delightfully written, provocative, and stimulating.

Underhill, E. (1911/1961). *Mysticism.* New York: Dutton.

Philosopher Evelyn Underhill combined and distilled reports of hundreds of mystics and other teachers from all religious traditions into a single coherent account of the human quest for meaning. Her style is clear and straightforward.

Contemporary Scholarly Work

Cartwright, K. B. (2001). Cognitive development theory and spiritual development. *Journal of Adult Development, 8,* 213–220.

A novel approach that compares spiritual development (an individual's relationship with a higher power) with the Piagetian stages of cognitive development, including post-formal thought.

Idler, E. (2006). Religion and aging. In R. H. Binstock & L. K. George (Eds.), *Handbook of aging and the social sciences* (pp. 277–300). San Diego: Academic Press.

Sociologist Ellen Idler explains how religion views aging and how aging affects people's religious beliefs. She also addresses cohort differences in religious beliefs and practices, the impact of religion on health, and how religious communities care for their aging members.

Krause, N. (2006). Religion and health in late life. In J. E. Birren & K. W. Schaie (Eds.), *Handbook of the psychology of aging* (pp. 499–518). San Diego: Academic Press.

In this handbook chapter, sociologist Neal Krause reviews how late-life health is affected by church attendance, religious coping, forgiveness, and social support.

Krebs, D. (2005). *The evolution of morality.* In D. M. Buss (Ed.), *The handbook of evolutionary psychology* (pp. 747–771). Hoboken, NJ: Wiley.

A discussion Kohlberg's stages of moral thought from the viewpoint of evolutionary psychology.

Chapter 10

Stress, Coping, and Resilience

MIGUEL LEFT CUBA for Miami in an unusual way; he took a boat west to Mexico and then bought his way across the border into Texas. He was only 15. The other people in the group were eight pregnant women who were trying to get into the United States to have their babies in American hospitals—not so much for the medical care but so they would have United States citizenship. In spite of being promised a safe journey across the border, Miguel and the women were left on the riverbank to make their own way across. Suddenly gunshots rang out from somewhere. Miguel helped woman after woman cross the river and finally made it to safety himself before realizing he had been shot in the thigh. He ended up in the hospital with two of the women who had gone into labor during the river crossing.

This is an exciting story, and to the best of my knowledge it is true. I heard it from Miguel himself and saw the scar from the bullet wound in his thigh. He showed me photos of the two Mexican American teenagers, now living in Texas, whose mothers he had helped cross the river. They were named Miguel, after him, and he keeps in touch with the families. The amazing part of the story, to me, is that today he is so similar to my younger son, Derek. They are both American citizens, and they work together as civil engineers. They drive their trucks to work, go out in the field together, go home at night to their wives and children, and plan their vacations to Disney World or Las Vegas or the Bahamas. You would not notice any difference between Miguel and Derek except that Miguel has a touch of a

Stress, Stressors, and Stress Reactions

Types of Stress

Effects of Stress
  Physical Disease
  Mental Health Disorders
  Individual Differences
    in Stress-Related Disorders
  Stress-Related Growth

Coping with Stress
  Types of Coping Behaviors
  Social Support
  Personality Traits and Coping

Resilience
  Reactions to Trauma
  Individual Differences
    in Resilience

Summary

Key Terms

Suggested Reading

Cuban accent (and a scar on his thigh). And yet my son grew up in a middle-class home and was riding a skateboard and playing Senior League baseball when he was 15. When I think about Miguel, I look around at the students in my classes, the people who work in my neighborhood grocery store, the woman who delivers my mail, and I wonder what their stories are. The more I get to know my fellow south Floridians, the more stories I hear like Miguel's. We have people who have come to our state on rafts made out of inner tubes and styrofoam coolers, people who have fled their country one step ahead of rebel troops, people who survived concentration camps and people who liberated concentration camps after World War II, people who have seen their family and neighbors killed, people who have survived earthquakes and hurricanes, and people who have been in prison for their political and religious beliefs. Adversity is not just in history books in our part of the country, and I'm sure the same is true of yours.

This chapter is about stress, coping, and resilience. The main theme is how people face the adversities of life, whether these entail helping pregnant women across a river to freedom or being caught in a traffic jam on the interstate highway with a crying baby buckled into the car seat behind you. How does stress affect us? What resources do we have to deal with it on a daily basis? And how do we cope with large-scale adversity and then get on with our lives? I will begin with some of the leading theories and research on the effects of stress. Then I will present some information on social support and other coping mechanisms. Finally, I will turn to an examination of the most common response to stressful events, resilience.

Stress, Stressors, and Stress Reactions

Stress is a set of physical, cognitive, and emotional responses that humans (and other organisms) display in reaction to demands from the environment. These environmental demands are known as **stressors.** The scientific study of stress (and stressors) is a very old field, going back to the early 1900s, and has been "claimed" by medical researchers and social scientists alike (Dougall & Baum, 2001). It seems that every new research tool or technological advance results in more knowledge about stress and its antidote, **coping.**

The best-known explanation of the stress response is that of medical researcher Hans Selye (1936, 1982), who first coined the term "stress" and then developed the concept of the **general adaptation syndrome.** According to Selye, there are three stages to this response. The first is the *alarm reaction,* in which the body quickly responds to a stressor by becoming alert and energized, preparing for "fight or flight." If the stressor continues for a longer time, the body goes into the second stage, *resistance,* in which it attempts to regain its normal state. One notable physical change in this stage is that the thymus gland, which is involved in immune responses, decreases in size and function. Thus, in this phase, the person is able to control the initial alarm reaction to the stressor but does so at the expense of the immune function. If the stressor continues long enough (and many chronic stressors do continue over very long periods of time), the resistance phase cannot be sustained and the person reaches the third stage, *exhaustion,* when some of the alarm-stage responses reappear. If the stressor is severe enough, according to Selye, exhaustion is accompanied by physical illness or even death.

Selye postulates that the "return to rest" after the stressor has stopped and the general adaptation syndrome is terminated is never complete. One almost gets back to one's former state, but not quite, leading some to suggest that the process of aging may thus simply be the accumulation of the effects of many years of stress.

Selye's theory was one of the earliest demonstrations of the link between psychological reactions and physical illnesses. He was careful not to claim that stress itself *caused* physical changes, but that our reaction to stress (which he called "distress") was the culprit, leaving the door open for others to suggest preventative measures, such as coping mechanisms and social support, which will be discussed later in this chapter.

In the 30-some years since Selye's theory was published, over 300 studies have been done on the effects stress reactions have on the human immune system. Selye's idea of stress leading to a general suppression of the immune system has been refined to postulate two separate types of immune responses: a *natural immunity* that is a quick defense against pathogens in general, and a *specific immunity* that is slower and requires more energy because the body needs to identify specific pathogens and form matching lymphocytes to combat them. Ordinarily the two systems work in balance, but a stress reaction results in the natural immune system going quickly into overdrive and the specific immune system being suppressed, to conserve energy. Stressful events of longer duration, such as bereavement, lead to a decline in the natural immune system over time and an increase in the specific immune system. And when stress is chronic, such as caregiving for a relative with dementia, being a refugee, or being unemployed, both immune systems eventually decline in function (Segerstrom & Miller, 2004).

Evolutionary psychologists suggest that the reaction to acute stress (the fight-or-flight response) is an adaptive mechanism that enabled our primitive ancestors to summon optimal levels of energy (increased adrenaline and increased blood supply to the heart and large muscles) while at the same time preparing the body for accelerated healing of wounds and prevention of infection from whatever antigens entered through them (natural immunity). Modern humans seldom need this set of responses because the types of stressors we encounter do not often have physical consequences, nor do they require us to defend ourselves physically. However, as with many other evolved mechanisms, the stress response reflects the demands of more primitive environments, resulting in a mismatch of physical responses to psychological events (Flinn, Ward, & Noone, 2005).

> **● CRITICAL THINKING**
>
> Can you think of situations modern humans deal with in which physical stress responses are helpful? Hint: think of putting on "game faces."

Selye's theory took a **response-oriented viewpoint,** meaning that it was focused on the physiological reactions within the individual that resulted from exposure to stressors. Other researchers have focused on the stressors themselves. In order to do this, it is necessary to evaluate events in the environment to determine whether they are stressors and, if they are, the relative magnitude of the stress they cause. The earliest evaluation method came from psychiatrists Thomas Holmes and Richard Rahe (1967), who devised a checklist that would rate the level of a person's stressors based on **life-change events.** This rating scale consisted of 43 events with points assigned to each event depending on how much stress it caused. For example, death of a spouse was the most stressful at 100 points; being fired was 47 points, and getting a speeding ticket was 11 points. The researchers focused on life changes, not just negative events, and included some positive events, such as pregnancy (40 points), outstanding personal achievement (28 points), and vacation (13 points). Holmes and Rahe hypothesized that the more points a person had accumulated in the recent past, the higher the stress level and the greater the chances of illness in the near future.

> **● CRITICAL THINKING**
>
> What features of a vacation might be stressful?

Holmes and Rahe approached the topic of stress from a **stimulus-oriented viewpoint,** meaning that their focus was on the stressors themselves, the stimuli that trigger the stress reactions, or more specifically, life events. Their rating scale, along with similar measures of life stressors, proved to be a fairly accurate predictor of physical illness and psychological symptoms. Most of the research today on stress reactions uses some form of life-event rating scale. At the same time, serious questions have been raised about this definition of stress and this method of measurement. First of all, it is not so obvious that life changes all produce stress in the same way. Are positive life changes and negative life changes really equally stressful? And even among life changes that may be classed as negative, perhaps some subvarieties are more stress producing or more likely to lead to illness than others. And what about events that can be positive in one situation (pregnancy to a long-married couple who have been trying to conceive for years) and negative in another (pregnancy to an unprepared teenage girl)?

Types of Stress

With these questions in mind, several researchers have suggested subcategories of stressors or life-change events that may help answer some of the preceding questions. For example, sociologist Leonard Pearlin (1980) made a distinction between *short-term life events,* which are stressors that may cause immediate problems but have a definite beginning and end, and *chronic life strains,* which are continuous and ongoing. He explained that chronic life strains were the type of stressors that caused the most health problems and also eroded social relationships (ironically, the very interactions that help alleviate stress).

CRITICAL THINKING

In what types of jobs would workers be more apt to suffer work stress? What about work strain?

Another distinction is made between types of job-related stressors. *Work stress* is what a worker experiences on jobs with high demands but a good amount of control and sense of personal accomplishment. *Work strain* results from situations in which a worker is faced with high demands, but low control, no sense of personal accomplishment, and low reward (Nelson & Burke, 2002).

Life-span developmental psychologist David Almeida (2005) distinguishes between *major life events,* such as divorce and death of a loved one, and *daily stressors,* the routine challenges of day-to-day living, such as work deadlines, malfunctioning computers, and arguments with children. While he acknowledges that major life events may be associated with prolonged physiological reactions, he believes that daily stressors, which occur far more frequently, also have serious effects on one's well-being. Almeida contends that the daily stressors not only have direct and immediate effects on emotional and physical functioning, but accumulate over time to create persistent problems that may result in more serious stress reactions.

Daily stressors are difficult to measure because they are small issues that are not easily recalled over time, but Almeida used a diary method to follow the daily stressors of about 1,500 adults, part of a nationally representative sample of people in the United States participating in the National Study of Daily Experiences (NSDE). Instead of requiring participants to keep their own diaries (and perhaps fail to fill them out on a regular basis), he had telephone interviewers call each person in the study each evening during an 8-day period. And instead of using a checklist, the interviewers asked semi-structured questions that allowed the participants to tell about their daily stressors and their subjective appraisals of the events (Almeida, 2005).

Almeida and his colleagues found that adults in the United States typically experienced at least one stressor on 40 percent of the days studied and more than one on 10 percent of the days. The most common stressors were interpersonal arguments and tensions, which accounted for half of the reported stressful events. The types of stressors are shown in Figure 10.1 along with the frequency with which they were reported. Interestingly, the subjective appraisals of the severity of stressful events overall was "average," while the objective appraisals, given by expert coders, was "low." In other words, we tend to perceive our own stressful events as more severe than they are perceived by a noninvolved rater (Almeida & Horn, 2004).

CRITICAL THINKING

List your top 10 sources of stress. Do they fit the ratios in Figure 10.1?

Almeida's model of the factors involved in the build-up of daily stressors is shown in Figure 10.2. If you look at the box on the left, you will see a number of factors within the individual that may affect the stress/well-being connection, such as age, marital status,

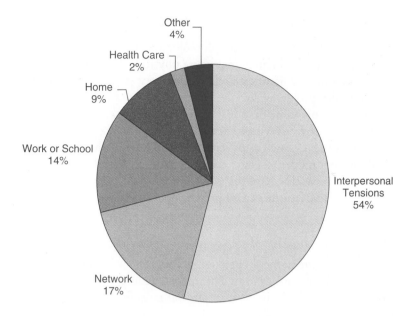

Figure 10.1 U.S. adults from 25–74 years report that the largest proportion of their daily stressors arise from interpersonal tensions, followed by stressful events that happen to other people in their networks and events that happen at work or school.

Source: Data from Almeida (2005).

personality traits, and chronic health problems. The box on the right shows factors of the stressors, such as their frequency and the subjective severity of loss. If you are a young woman in good health, living with your parents and attending school, and you are faced with transportation problems on a regular basis because your car is not dependable, it may be a daily hassle to ask a friend for a ride to class or to take your mother to work and borrow her car, but even if this continues for the whole semester, chances are it won't have a negative effect on your well-being. It's just an inconvenience and a regular hassle. However, if you are a middle-aged man living on disability benefits and need dialysis two days a week, transportation problems may pose a very different set of stressors (such as not getting life-sustaining medical treatment, feeling helpless and hopeless). These drains on daily well-being would feed back to the individual factors and cause them to decline even more. In the case of the young college student, the fact that her friends are there for her and that her mother is so helpful may actually increase her ability to handle stress.

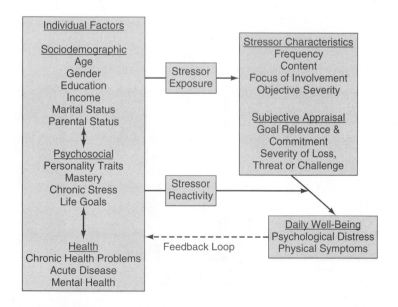

Figure 10.2 Characteristics of the individual determine (1) whether they will be exposed to certain stressors and (2) what their reaction will be, resulting in a potential effect on daily well-being.

Source: Adapted from Almeida (2005).

Effects of Stress

If you recall Selye's theory, stressors cause physiological stress reactions that lead to lowered immune function and ultimately may cause physical disease and mental health disorders. Early studies showed a significant relationship between self-rated life-change events and a number of health problems, but the effects were very small and it was difficult to know whether the stressors came first or the health problems. Also, there is the problem of stress causing unhealthy behaviors, such as tobacco and alcohol use and overeating, and certain common factors, such as poverty, that cause both a high number of stressors and poor health. Recent researchers have controlled for many of these confounds in order to concentrate on the areas that have the most promise for unwrapping the stress/disease package and find effective treatment and prevention measures.

Physical Disease

Stressors seem to contribute to the progression of heart disease and HIV/AIDS, and to be associated with the onset of some cancers. Therapy that reduces stressors and mediates stress reactions has been successful in increasing survival rates for patients with heart disease and cancer, and improving immune status in patients with HIV/AIDS. (Schneiderman, Antoni, Saab, et al., 2001). For example:

- A longitudinal study of over 10,000 women in Finland showed that accumulation of stressful life events (divorce or separation, death of a husband, personal illness or injury, job loss, and death of a close friend or relative) was associated with an increased risk of breast cancer. Women were surveyed in the initial stage of the study and asked to report stressful life events they had experienced over the past 5 years. Fifteen years later, 180 incidents of breast cancer had been reported for women in the study (doctors are required to report all cancer diagnoses to the Finnish Cancer Registry). Grouping the women by how many stressful life events they reported (none, one, two, or three or more), researchers found a linear relationship, as shown in Figure 10.3, between the number of stressful events and the incidence of breast cancer in the subsequent 15 years (Lillberg, Verkasalo, Kaprio, et al., 2003). The greater the number

Figure 10.3 Women who reported one, two, or three or more major life events in the past 5 years were significantly more likely to be diagnosed with breast cancer during the next 15 years than those who reported no major life events. The more events reported, the greater incidence of breast cancer.

Source: Adapted from Lillberg, Verksalo, Kaprio, et al. (2003).

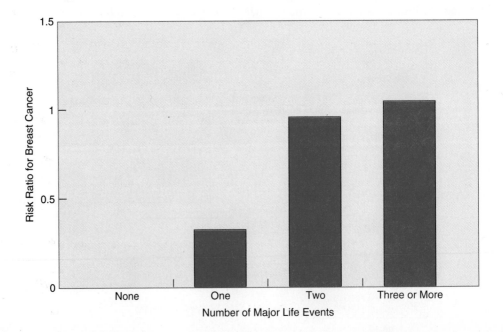

of stressful events they reported, the greater the women's chance of having breast cancer, and since the surveys had been done years before the cancer appeared and not after the fact, this is very strong support that stressors are related to subsequent physical illness.

• Another longitudinal study of almost 13,000 men who were at risk for heart disease showed that work-related stress (such as being fired or laid off, not being able to work because of a disability, failure of a business) was related to an increased risk of death from heart disease. Men were given physical examinations and surveys annually for six years. Nine years after the study was completed, death records were examined along with causes of death. When the men were grouped according to the number of job stressors they had reported during the study, researchers found a linear relationship between the number of stressful events and the incidence of death due to heart disease in the 9 years since the study ended (Matthews & Gump, 2002). These data are illustrated in Figure 10.4. As you can see, the greater the number of stressful events, the higher the risk of death from heart disease. This provides support from another area that life stressors and physical illness are strongly related.

• A third longitudinal study followed 82 homosexual men who were HIV positive but did not have AIDS at the beginning of the study. They were given physical examinations and survey questions about stressful life events every six months for over 7 years. (Disease-related stressors were not included.) At the end of the study, participants' records were divided into two groups based on their average stress scores. The high-stress group had scores above the median and the low-stress group had scores below the median. Based on the data of those participants whose HIV progressed to AIDS during the study, the researchers calculated a week-by-week probability for the high-stress group and the low-stress group. As you can see from Figure 10.5, both groups began as 100 percent AIDS-free during the first six-month period. Then the high-stress group dropped to 90 percent for the next two six-month periods, while the low-stress group remained close to 100 percent AIDS-free. By 42 months into the study, only 50 percent of the high-stress group remained AIDS-free, while 80 to 90 percent of the low-stress group was still healthy. By the end of the study (7 years later), over half the men in the high-stress group had progressed to AIDS, compared with one-third of the men in the low-stress group (Leserman, Petitto, Golden, et al., 2000). These results indicate that

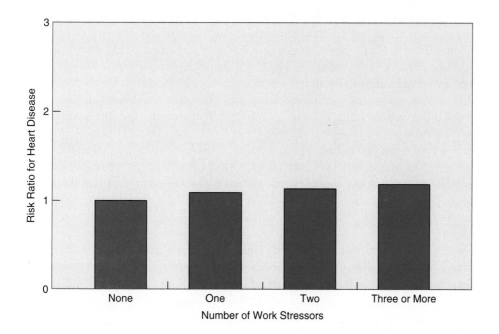

Figure 10.4 Men who are at risk for heart disease and report work-related stressors are at greater risk of death from heart disease in the next 9 years than those who report no work-related stress. The number of stressors increase the risk.

Source: Data from Mathews & Gump (2002).

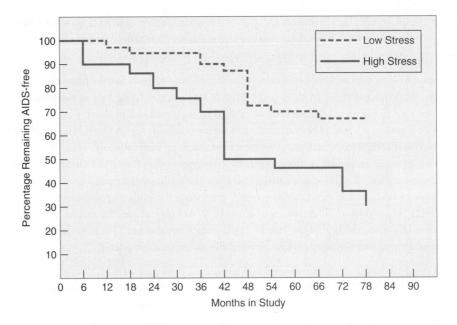

Figure 10.5 HIV-Positive men with a high number of life stressors progress more quickly to AIDS than those with lower numbers.

Source: Adapted from Leserman, Petitto, Golden, et al. (2000).

once men are diagnosed as HIV positive, the amount of stress in their lives is strongly related to the time it takes for their disease to progress to AIDS. Those with more stress make the progression faster.

Mental Health Disorders

High levels of stressors are associated with the onset of various mental disorders, such as depression and anxiety, and this relationship has been demonstrated in a number of studies. There is a significant link, but the effect is relatively small, showing that there are many factors at work, other than stress, in determining which of us will have depression and which will not.

One type of mental disorder that is strongly related to high levels of stressors, though, is **post-traumatic stress disorder (PTSD),** the psychological response to a traumatic experience, such as military combat, rape, terrorist attack, natural disasters, or automobile accidents. This is a fairly new disorder that was only identified by the American Psychiatric Association in 1980, although it has been described throughout history as battle fatigue, shell shock, nervous breakdown, and with other nonscientific terms. Symptoms of PTSD include reexperiencing the event in intrusive thoughts and dreams, numbing of general responses and avoiding stimuli associated with the event, and increased arousal of physiological stress mechanisms. Unlike other stress reactions, PTSD does not decline over time and is not alleviated by social support (American Psychiatric Association, 2000).

Since 1980, researchers have often been with the first wave of rescue personnel after traumatic incidents in the United States, such as the explosion of the space shuttle *Challenger* in 1986, Hurricane Katrina in 2005, the Oklahoma City bombing in 1995, and the terrorist attacks on the World Trade Center and the Pentagon on September 11, 2001, ready to gather data on the effects the events have on those who are traumatized. Around the world, researchers have tagged along with rescuers in war zones, at the sites of genocide and mass rape, areas where famine has occurred, and places where mass exodus has taken place resulting in large groups of refugees. Although it seems cold-hearted to be using victims as research participants during these difficult times, many useful results have come from such projects.

One in three survivors of Hurricane Katrina showed signs of PTSD a month after the tragedy; one in 10 continued to have symptoms a year later.

For example, because of this research, we knew on September 11th, 2001, that about 35 percent of the people who were directly exposed to the terrorist attacks would develop PTSD, and that another large group would reexperience PTSD symptoms from traumatic events they had experienced earlier in their lives. We also knew that the symptoms would appear within a month and that people would most likely contact their primary-care physicians first. A year later, about 10 percent would still have symptoms of PTSD. As a result of this knowledge, healthcare professionals, as well as the victims of the attack, were immediately given information on diagnosing and treating PTSD, and how it differs from other types of anxiety disorders (Gorman, 2005).

Basically, feelings of vulnerability and powerlessness are the psychological effects of traumatic stress. The best remedy is to examine the source of the fear and correct exaggerated beliefs, but when part of the syndrome is to avoid thoughts of the trauma, this is not possible. The feelings of vulnerability and powerlessness may be accompanied by horror, anger, sadness, humiliation, and guilt. The biological effects seem to involve more than just extreme general-anxiety reactions. For example, the physical stress response in patients with PTSD are different from those in a normal person—the hormone levels are different, and different areas of the brain are involved in the responses. In addition, patients with PTSD have structural alterations in two areas of the brain, the amygdala and the hippocampus. All this evidence leads us to believe that extreme trauma causes long-lasting alterations in the brain and nervous system that lead to changes in the stress reaction mechanism causing the intrusive thoughts, the numbing of responses, and the increased reactivity of stress response mechanisms (Yehuda, 2002).

Treatment includes counseling, during which patients are helped to understand that their condition is a normal reaction to trauma and not a sign of weakness or a character flaw. Once a trusting relationship is formed between the patient and the counselor, work can begin on confronting painful memories and rebuilding thoughts of trust and safety. Medication, such as antianxiety and antidepression drugs, is often helpful.

Individual Differences in Stress-Related Disorders

Everyone is exposed to stressors on a daily basis, and everyone meets them with stress reactions, but not everyone suffers from physical disease and mental disorders as a result. In fact the majority of people handle stress very well. Of course the type of stress and the amount of stress can make a difference, but researchers have found that other factors affect an individual's susceptibility to stress-related health problems, such as gender, age, and the experience of racial discrimination.

Gender. When it comes to daily stressors, women report more days with at least one stressor than men do. Women and men also report different sources of stress. Men are more apt than women to report daily stressors related to work or school, while women are more apt than men to report experiencing daily stressors as a result of things that happened to people in their social or family networks. Men are more apt to report stressors that threaten them financially; women are more apt to report stressors that threaten the ways others feel about them (Almeida, 2005).

Some researchers argue that Selye's theory of fight or flight applies only to men, and that women have a totally different reaction to stressors. Social psychologist Shelley Taylor (2002) argues that males and females have evolved different survival and reproductive behaviors, and that females may have developed a response to stress that differs from the one typically seen in studies of males. Instead of fight or flight, Taylor suggests that women have a genetic response to stress that involves "tend and befriend." Instead of being based on either fleeing the dangerous situation or defeating an aggressor, as is the case with males, this response in females is aimed at tending to one's immature offspring and seeking support from others, especially other females. As Taylor and her colleagues explain, "We suggest that females respond to stress by nurturing offspring, exhibiting behaviors that protect them from harm and reduce neuroendocrine responses that may compromise offspring health (the tending pattern), and by befriending, namely affiliating with social groups to reduce risk" (Taylor, Klein, Lewis, et al., 2000, p. 411). These researchers believe that female responses to stress are based on the attachment-caregiving process and may be regulated, in part, by sex hormones.

This research fits well with other findings on gender differences in social behavior. Women have larger social networks, have deeper and more emotional friendships, and are more apt to respond to emotional events by seeking out friends and talking. They are the kinkeepers and caregivers in families. It has been well demonstrated that men and women do not react with the same intensity to stress and the stressors that bring on stress reactions. Why not differences in the role of stressors in their lives?

Women have the role of kin-keeper in almost all cultures. This may cause them to react to stress by "tending and befriending" instead of "fighting or fleeing."

There are also gender differences in PTSD. Men are more exposed to trauma than women during their lifetimes, but women are more likely to experience PTSD as a result of trauma. Figure 10.6 shows the number of traumatic events men and women report (total length of bars), and the incidence of PTSD for both genders (dark areas of bars). However, this does not tell the whole story. Some events are more apt to lead to PTSD for one gender than another. For example, women are much more likely to experience rape than men (9 percent versus 1 percent), but men are more likely to suffer from PTSD as a result (65 percent versus 46 percent). Men have a higher rate of experiencing physical assault than women (11 percent versus 6 per-

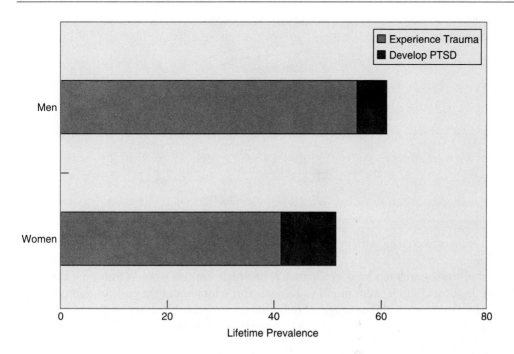

Figure 10.6 Men experience more trauma in their lifetimes, but women are more likely to develop PTSD.

Source: Data from Yehuda (2002).

cent), but women's rates of developing PTSD as a result are higher than men's (21 percent versus 2 percent). Clearly the likelihood of developing PTSD as the result of a traumatic experience depends on more factors than just the objective severity of the event.

Age. In general, stress decreases with age. The highest amount of stress is reported by young adults, and the lowest is reported by older adults (Aldwin & Levenson, 2001). There are several reasons for this. First, younger people have more complex lives than older people, thus more potential sources of stress. Older people have more experience with stressful events and, hopefully, have developed some expertise in coping with situations that might become stressors. Although older people often have more chronic health problems and experience more loss in their lives, they often compare their own situation with others their age and consider themselves to be doing well. As you will recall from Chapter 2, a large number of older adults consider themselves to be in excellent or very good health, but at the same time report chronic health conditions.

In the diary study I described earlier, participants ranged in age from 25 to 74. Approximately half were men and half were women. As seen in Figure 10.7, the proportion of days that people reported experiencing any stressors declined after middle adulthood, and women reported more days with stressors than men at all ages (Almeida & Horn, 2004).

Although the number of stressors is lower for older adults than for younger adults, there is evidence that the physiological reactions to stress are more severe in older adults. In a longitudinal study of older adults who were caregivers for a spouse with Alzheimer's disease, researchers measured levels of certain proteins in the blood of the caregivers for six years and compared them to the blood tests of a matched control group who were not caregivers. One protein, IL-6 (cytokine interleukin-6), is a marker of chronic stress and has been linked to a number of age-related diseases. Over the 6-year period of the study, the levels of IL-6 for the caregiver group showed an average annual rate of increase four times as large as that of the noncaregiver group. Even several years after the death of their spouses, the caregivers continued to show higher rates of IL-6 than the control group, leading

CRITICAL THINKING

What have you learned about gender differences so far that might account for the greater prevalence of traumatic events in men's lives versus women's? What about the differences in PTSD?

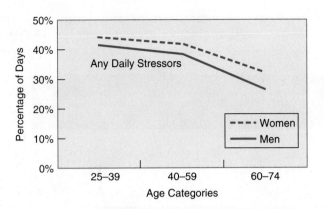

Figure 10.7 Men and women report having fewer days with stressors as they go from middle to older adulthood, and men report fewer days with stressors than women at all ages.

Source: Adapted from Almeida & Horn (2004).

researchers to conclude that chronic stress may contribute to premature aging of the immune system (Keicolt-Glaser, Preacher, MacCallum, et al., 2003). This study may remind you of the research reported in Chapter 2, in which younger women who were caregivers for disabled children were found to have shorter telomeres at the ends of their chromosomes than women the same age who did not have disabled children, suggesting that the chronic stress of caregiving is related to premature aging on a cellular level (Epel, Blackburn, Lin, et al., 2004).

Similar evidence comes from studies of older adults who experienced trauma in their younger years, such as in combat or other war-related events, and who suffer from PTSD. For example psychologist Rachel Yehuda and her colleagues (Yehuda, Golier, Harvey, et al., 2005) examined memory abilities of men and women who were Holocaust survivors, some with symptoms of PTSD and others who had no symptoms. She compared these with a matched group who had not experienced the Holocaust or any other traumatic event. Figure 10.8 shows the scores for the memory tasks performed by the three groups. As you can see, the group of Holocaust survivors who had PTSD remembered significantly fewer of both the highly associated pairs of words (*apple-orange; dog-cat*) and the less associated words (*banana-truck; book-tree*) than those in the other two groups. The researchers concluded that PTSD combines with age to cause more severe memory deficits than what would be caused by age alone. Thus, even if PTSD is less prevalent among older adults, it exacts a toll when it is present.

Racial Discrimination. It has long been known that black adults in the United States have greater incidence of high blood pressure and stroke than other racial/ethnic groups. On the surface, this seems to be an example of a genetic predisposition, but with new evidence of the vast genetic variability among people of African descent (Cavalli-Sforza & Cavalli-Sforza, 1995), some researchers have investigated more plausible factors that might be responsible for this health problem. One recent line of investigation has focused on racial discrimination as a chronic stressor that can elevate blood pressure and increase risk of stroke. For example, in a study of 110 black college women, a relationship was found between perceived racism and changes in blood pressure following a public-speaking task. The higher the women's reports of perceived racism, the more their systolic blood pressure was elevated as a result of giving a short talk before an audience (Clark, 2006).

Other studies that have controlled for age, gender, income, and education show that racial discrimination presents a distinct form of stress for many people and contributes to many of the health problems that affect a dispropor-

CRITICAL THINKING

In the study of Holocaust survivors discussed here, why do you think the researchers included the group of Holocaust survivors without PTSD? What confound did it rule out?

CRITICAL THINKING

How would you design an experiment to show that high blood pressure is not simply a condition related to the amount of pigment in one's skin?

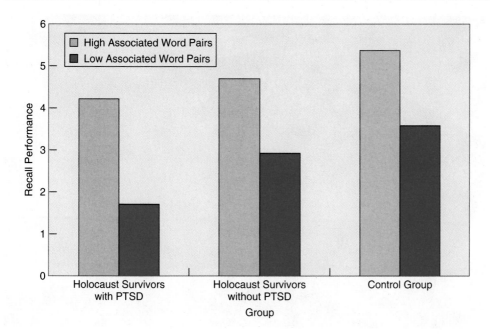

Figure 10.8 Holocaust Survivors with PTSD perform less well on a two memory tasks than either Holocaust survivors without PTSD or a matched control group who did not experience the Holocaust.
Source: Data from Yehuda, Golier, Harvey, et al. (2005).

tionately large number of African American adults (Klonoff, Landrine, & Ullman, 1999). Recent reviews have suggested the possibility that racial discrimination is implicated in the high rates of preterm infants, low-birthweight infants, and infant deaths among black families in the United States (Giscombé & Lobel, 2005).

Stress-Related Growth

In Chinese, the characters that form the word *crisis* mean both "danger" and "opportunity." Other cultures have equivalent words of wisdom to express the idea that "what doesn't kill us makes us stronger." The same idea is what has motivated the recent wave of research examining **stress-related growth**—the positive changes that follow the experience of stressful life events. Indeed, this idea is not a new one. Many theories of development, such as Erikson's, include the concept that crisis, or stress, can make useful changes in the individual, and that personal growth may result from facing difficult life events.

Some earlier studies examining the negative effects of stress also found some positive effects. One study of middle-aged adults whose parents had recently died showed that although the participants reported typical symptoms of emotional distress, many also reported that they had experienced personal growth as a result of the loss, in that they finally felt they were complete adults with increased self-confidence and a sense of maturity. They also reported that they had learned to value personal relationships more (Scharlach & Fredrickson, 1993). Similar results have been noted in studies of divorce (Helson & Roberts, 1994) and widowhood (Lieberman, 1996).

A more recent study of stress-related growth involved surveys of over 600 men who had served in World War II, whose average age was 74. Researchers found that those who had been exposed to moderate levels of stress in combat and believed that there were benefits to serving in the military showed higher levels of wisdom than those who reported otherwise. Researchers concluded that how one appraises and copes with problems may be the key to deriving benefits from stressful experiences (Jennings, Aldwin, Levenson, et al., 2006).

Stress-related growth has also been studied in breast cancer survivors (Bellizzi & Blank, 2006), Turkish college students (Kesimci, Göral, & Gençöz, 2005), heart disease patients

Older people who experienced stressful events in their younger years may show personal growth and wisdom in later years as a result.

(Sheikh, 2004), and families of police officers killed in the line of duty (Bear & Barnes, 2001), among other groups. The findings generally agree that, depending on the stressful event itself, the personal beliefs of the individual, and the support available, people in the most dire circumstances are able to later report personal growth, increased wisdom, growth in relationships with others, a new appreciation for life, a new sense of maturity, a stronger religious belief, or a greater sense of self-efficacy and self-confidence.

Coping with Stress

There has been a shift recently in psychology from the "illness" model of stress, which catalogs symptoms, probabilities, and groups more prone to stress-related disorders, to a "wellness" approach, which involves prevention, preparation, and early intervention immediately after trauma occurs (Friedman, 2005). These priorities emphasize the importance of **resistance resources,** the personal and social resources that may buffer a person from the impact of stress. Central among these are individual coping responses, a sense of personal control, and the availability of social support.

Types of Coping Behaviors

At the top of the list of protections against the effects of stressors in our lives are **coping behaviors,** an all-purpose term that refers to anything you might think, feel, and do to reduce the effects of stressful events. Suppose that you received a rejection letter from a graduate program you had been working hard to get into. Or suppose that your apartment was damaged by a fire and most of your belongings were lost. How would you cope with these stressors? There are a number of behaviors you might employ, and some of them are found in Table 10.1, which lists styles of coping and examples of each from the Brief COPE Inventory (Carver, 1997).

These are not the only ways of coping. Many theorists and investigators have made their own lists and organized them into useful subcategories. One way of doing this is to divide coping mechanisms into four categories: problem focused, emotion focused, meaning focused, and social (Folkman & Moskowitz, 2004).

Table 10.1	Styles of Coping and Examples from the Brief COPE Inventory
Style of Coping	**Example**
Self-distraction	"I've been turning to work or other activities to take my mind off things."
Active coping	"I've been concentrating my efforts on doing something about the situation I'm in."
Denial	"I've been saying to myself, 'This isn't real.' "
Substance use	"I've been using alcohol or other drugs to make myself feel better."
Use of emotional support	"I've been getting comfort and understanding from someone."
Use of instrumental support	"I've been getting help and advice from other people."
Behavioral disengagement	"I've been giving up trying to deal with it."
Venting	"I've been saying things to let my unpleasant feelings escape."
Positive reframing	"I've been looking for something good in what is happening."
Planning	"I've been trying to come up with a strategy about what to do."
Humor	"I've been making jokes about it."
Acceptance	"I've been learning to live with it."
Religion	"I've been praying or meditating."
Self-blame	"I've been criticizing myself."

Source: Adapted from Carver (1997).

Problem-focused coping directly addresses the problem causing distress. If you were not accepted into your first-choice grad school, calling for more information would be an example of problem-focused coping. You might inquire about whether you could reapply for midyear acceptance or ask if it would be helpful to retake your admission exams. For the problem of having a fire in your apartment, calling the insurance company would be an example of a problem-focused coping strategy, as would taking an inventory of the things that were damaged and making plans about how to replace them.

In a study of the aftermath of the Washington, DC, sniper attacks in 2002, psychologists Ari Zivotofsky and Meni Koslowsky surveyed 144 residents of the area to find out about their coping strategies in response to three weeks of random shootings that left 10 residents dead and four injured. Specifically, they asked people about changes in their usual routines, which would be considered problem-focused coping. Figure 10.9 shows the activities that male and female respondents said they had restricted in order to cope with the stress of the situation. The first seven activities were mentioned significantly more often by women than men; the last activity, socializing with friends, showed no gender differences—possibly because it provided social support, which in itself is a buffer against stress (Zivotofsky & Koslowsky, 2004).

The second category of coping mechanisms is **emotion-focused coping,** which includes ways that people try to ameliorate the negative emotions associated with the stressful situation. Dealing with the rejection from graduate school by going out and running for an hour is a good example. Using alcohol or drugs to blunt the stress is also emotion-focused, but is not a good example because it can lead to even more stress in your life.

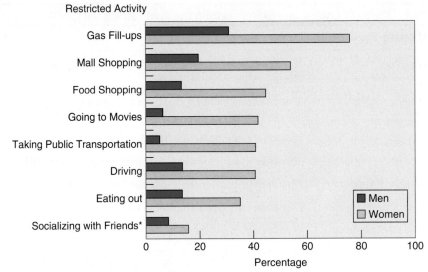

Figure 10.9 Men and women in Washington, D.C., used problem-focused coping with the D.C. sniper attacks by restricting their usual activities in many areas. Women reduced activities significantly more than men for all types of activities except socializing with friends (a source of social support).

Source: Data from Zivotofsky & Koslowsky (2004).

Distancing oneself from the problem emotionally can be helpful in some cases and maladaptive in others.

The use of drugs and alcohol as a coping mechanism may not be an effective one, but for college students, substance abuse of all kinds is related to stress levels. Interestingly, this relationship differs by gender and by race. In a large study of over 1,500 students at a large midwestern university in the United States, general college-life stress (such as problems with professors, grades, relationships) was associated with increased alcohol use for all groups except black males. Traumatic stress (such as being victimized or witnessing violence) was related to alcohol problems for white students only and with binge drinking for white females students only. Although this was only one university and the sample was not a representative one, the authors suggest that university counselors consider the larger finding that substance-abuse problems can be symptoms of underlying stress (Broman, 2005)

In the study described earlier that was done in the aftermath of the DC sniper, a number of emotion-focused coping strategies were reported in addition to the problem-focused strategies shown in Figure 10.9. These included taking medication, disconnecting, watching the news, blaming the government, and blaming the terrorists. Unlike the problem-focused strategies discussed earlier, there were no gender differences in these ways of coping (Zivotofsky & Koslowsky, 2004).

Meaning-focused coping includes ways that people find to manage the meaning of a stressful situation. Telling yourself that you would probably be happier at a different grad school that doesn't have such a rigorous program (or is closer to home, or where you know some of the students) is an example of reframing the stressful situation of being rejected to decrease the stress. Dealing with the fire in your apartment, you could tell yourself that the loss was only material things and it's good no one was hurt, or you could tell yourself that everything happens for a reason—both would be meaning-focused ways to cope. Such coping is especially useful in chronic stress situations like caregiving, where people often report that they are simply following religious teachings or fulfilling their marriage vows.

The fourth category of coping strategies, **social coping,** involves seeking help from others, both instrumental and emotional support. If you call your best friend to share your bad news about the grad school, and he or she offers kind words of support, you are indulging in social coping. And if you ask your parents to help you replace the belongings you lost in the fire (and they do), that's more of the same. In the study discussed before of mechanisms people used to cope with the stress of a sniper at large, one of the more-reported ways of coping was to call or be in touch with relatives or friends. And although women reported using this form of social coping more than men, the numbers were high for both (92 percent of the women and 68 percent of the men). This was also seen after the terrorist attacks on September 11, 2001, when the number of phone calls and Internet messages reached a record high all over the world. When we are stressed, whether as individuals or as a nation, we seek comfort in contacting those in our support networks.

● CRITICAL THINKING

On September 11, 2001, whom did you contact?

Evaluating the Effectiveness of Coping. Which coping mechanisms are the best in a given situation? Sometimes it depends on whether you feel that you are in control of the problem. If you feel in control, then problem-focused coping is usually the most effective. An example would be a student who has an exam coming up and feels stressed. Problem-focused coping would include reviewing notes or meeting with a study group. But in a situation that offers little feeling of control, such as dealing with chronic illness, emotion-focused coping gives greater stress relief. Some examples would be distancing and finding other activities to keep one's mind occupied.

Two abilities are important in dealing with the stressors one encounters in life. First is the ability to use a variety of coping skills, depending on the situation, known as *coping flexibility.* The other is the ability to match the appropriate coping skill with the situation at hand, known as *goodness of fit* (Folkman & Moskowitz, 2004).

New Directions in Coping Research. Most coping research to date has been concerned with how people cope with situations that happened in the past (bereavement) or are happening at present (chronic illness), but a few researchers are now investigating **proactive coping,** the ways people cope in advance to prevent or mute the impact of a stressful event that will happen in the future, such as a scheduled medical procedure or an impending layoff at work (Aspinwall & Taylor, 1997). They consider five interrelated components of proactive coping:

- Building a reserve of resources.
- Recognizing potential stressors.
- Initial appraisal of initial stressors.
- Preliminary coping efforts.
- Seeking feedback about one's success and acting on it.

For example, for the past two years our family has experienced three major hurricanes, and these certainly qualify as stressful events. We are now engaged in proactive coping in anticipation of the next season. We have built a reserve of resources (canned food, batteries, bottled water) and we have recognized potential stressors (putting up shutters, riding out the hurricane itself, losing electricity and water supply to the house, being unable to leave the immediate neighborhood, and being unable to contact others in the family for several days). We have already made preliminary coping efforts by buying a generator and long-range walkie-talkies. We often talk to neighbors and family members about our preparedness and our concerns, getting feedback and acting on their suggestions. At the moment my husband is considering using a different cell phone carrier than I use so that our chances of having communications after a hurricane will be doubled—a suggestion we heard on a local TV program. Although a repeat of the past two seasons will still be stressful, it will be less so because of our proactive coping.

Another area that has attracted research attention is **religious coping,** in which a person relies on religious or spiritual beliefs to reduce stress. This type of coping ranges from finding meaning in suffering, achieving a sense of control by trusting in God, and gaining social solidarity with others who have similar beliefs. One way of viewing religious coping is to categorize it as either positive or negative. Positive religious coping includes people trusting that God will take care of their problems and believing that there is a higher purpose for their suffering. Negative religious coping involves people wondering whether God has abandoned them or questioning whether God loves them. Generally speaking, positive religious coping leads to positive adjustment to stress, and negative religious adjustment is related to negative adjustments (Ano & Vasconcelles, 2005). For example, one study that examined the effect of religious coping on health showed that reporting negative religious thoughts was related to increased risk of death in older hospitalized patients (Pargament, Koenig, Tarakeshwar, et al., 2001).

Social Support

Social support refers to affect, affirmation, and aid received from others. But how should we measure such support? In many early studies, it was measured only by objective criteria like marital status and frequency of contact with friends and relatives. Now we know that subjective measures are often more valuable. A person's *perception* of the quality of his or her social contacts and emotional support is more strongly related to physical and emotional health than are most objective measures (Feld & George, 1994), just as subjective measures of stress have turned out to be more accurate predictors of stress responses than mere listings of life-change events. It is not the actual amount of contact with others that is important, but how that contact is understood or interpreted.

However it is measured, it is clear that adults who have adequate social support have lower risk of disease, death, and depression than adults with weaker social networks or less supportive relationships (Uchino, Cacioppo, & Kiecolt-Glaser, 1996). Similar patterns have been found in other countries, including Sweden (Orth-Gomér, Rosengren, & Wilhelmsen, 1993) and Japan (Sugisawa, Liang, & Liu, 1994), so the link between social contact and physical hardiness is not restricted to the United States, or even to Western cultures.

The Buffering Effect of Social Support. The beneficial effect of social support is even clearer when a person is under high stress. That is, the negative effect of stress on health and happiness is smaller for those who have adequate social support than for those whose social support is weak. This pattern of results is usually described as the **buffering effect** of social support, meaning that it won't keep stressors from entering one's life, but it will provide some protection against the harm they do. It may not be a coincidence that many of the top-rated life changes on the Holmes and Rahe list involve the loss of social support, such as divorce, separation, death of a loved one, and loss of a job.

Research has shown that women who fill multiple roles of parent, wife, worker, and caregiver of elderly parents suffer greater effects of stress when they don't have adequate social support in their own lives (Stephens, Franks, & Townsend, 1994). The buffering effect of social support is not limited to women. For example, in a study of men and women veterans who had been exposed to war-zone stress 10 years earlier (during the Gulf War of 1990–1991), the amount of encouragement and assistance they perceived from other unit members, unit leaders, and the military in general was related to the amount of depression they reported since their return from the war. Figure 10.10 shows the postwar depression scores for men and women, based on the lack of social support they

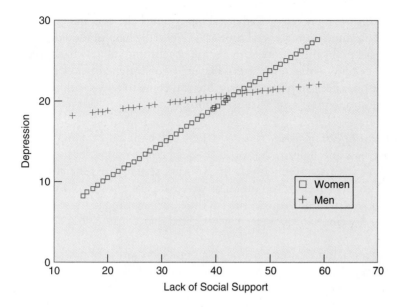

Figure 10.10 For Gulf War veterans, lack of social support in the field is related to post-war depression. The relationship is significantly stronger for women than men.

Source: Vogt, Pless, King, et al. (2005).

felt during their deployment. Although men's depression increases somewhat as their lack of social support increases, women's depression increases more quickly and to a higher level. These findings indicate that social support in a high-stress situation may serve as a buffer against later stress reactions such as depression, and that social support is an important buffer against negative mental health consequences of stress and trauma (Vogt, Pless, King, et al., 2005).

Another interesting gender difference in the giving and receiving of social support comes from a longitudinal study of over 700 adults in Finland. Researchers measured their "intimate reciprocity" at the beginning of the study, finding out how much social support they received from people close to them and how much of this they gave. Then they followed the participants' work records for nine years, taking note of the number of days each participant was absent from work due to sickness. The men who had the best record of attendance on the job were the ones who *received* the most social support from their family and friends; the women with the best records were the ones who *gave* the most social support to those close to them. The authors concluded that men benefit the most from receiving social support and women benefit the most from giving it, presumably because women gain in self-esteem when they are able to give support (Väänänen, Buunk, Kivimäki, et al., 2005).

Social support also reduces the negative impact of stressful experiences among the elderly. Sociologists Neal Krause and Elaine Borawski-Clark (1994) have shown this in studies of a random sample of more than 300 older adults living in Galveston, Texas. In one analysis they showed that chronic financial strain significantly increases the chances that elderly adults will report depressive symptoms, but this effect is considerably weaker among those with adequate social support. The researchers propose that social support has a beneficial effect in part because it bolsters feelings of control and self-worth, and that this is especially true if the stress is occurring in some area of life that threatens an important role. In a later study of some of the same participants, Krause (2005) showed that the effects of social support to buffer financial stress are stronger in the oldest groups (85 years of age or older) than in the younger groups (65 to 74 years).

Social Support and Coping. Social support can also help in times of stress by aiding with active coping. Social network members can help a person define the source of stress and plan a solution. They can give advice about coping behaviors and give feedback about the results. This dimension of social support is especially helpful for older adults, because they often have problems maintaining a sense of meaning in life when faced with stressful events or a buildup of chronic stress. Having a good friend or close relative who helps the older person reflect on his or her past life and come to terms with the distressing circumstances can be a great asset (Krause, 2006).

Some Negative Effects of Social Networks. Lest I give the impression that there is nothing but sweetness and light in the world of social relationships, let me quickly add that there are also costs associated with them. Network systems are generally reciprocal. Not only do you receive support, you give it as well. And as I pointed out in Chapters 5 and 6, there are points in the life course, such as the early parenting years, when the giving side of the equation seems to be more heavily weighted than the receiving side, which may increase stress.

Everyday social interactions can also be a significant source of hassles. Most of us have at least some regular interactions with people we do not like or who irritate us to distraction. When these negative social interactions involve anger, dislike, criticism, or undermining, especially when the negative feelings come from people who are central to our social convoy, they have a substantial negative effect on one's overall feeling of well-being (Antonucci, 1994).

Social support can operate in a negative way even if it is well intentioned—for example, when the support given is not what is needed, or the offer of support is perceived as criticism, or intrusion, or an insult to our independence. When this occurs, instead of buffering, the misdirected social support can result in our losing the desire to cope, reducing our efforts to cope, or making our coping efforts less effective (DeLongis & Holtzman, 2005).

Social support at a time of chronic strain, such as financial problems or long-term caregiving, can also have negative effects, especially in the late years of adulthood. Support providers may not have the resources to sustain their support over the long periods of time required and may begin to feel resentful and frustrated as a result. In addition, the care receivers may not have the wherewithal to reciprocate and may feel as though they are losing what little independence they have left (Krause, 2006).

Personality Traits and Coping

Another major buffer against the impact of stress is a sense of personal control, a concept I talked about at some length in Chapter 3. You'll recall that whether we measure the sense of personal control by assessing internal versus external locus of control or optimism versus pessimism or helplessness, those who have a stronger sense of control are less likely to become physically ill or depressed. A sense of control also serves as a buffer against stress, in much the same way that social support acts as a buffer. That is, among people facing some major life change or chronic stress, those who approach the problem with a strong sense of self-efficacy or optimism are less likely to develop physical or emotional symptoms, or recover more quickly from physical problems.

One example is shown in a study of women who had been diagnosed and treated for breast cancer. Those who were more optimistic after their treatment was completed had higher scores of well-being at the end of the study, some 5 to 13 years later (Carver, Smith, Antoni, et al., 2005). In another study that may hit closer to home, college students who reported higher levels of optimism at the beginning of their first semester of college had

CRITICAL THINKING

What are some of the direct and indirect ways optimism could affect success in college?

smaller increases in stress and depression over the semester, and more perceived social support than those lower in optimism (Brisette, Scheier, & Carver 2002).

Resilience

I have covered various stressors and stress reactions, ways that people can cope with stress once it sets in, and how people may gain personal growth from their stressful experiences, but as you can tell from the statistics for different stress reactions, not everyone who is exposed to stress, even traumatic stress, suffers its effects. Recently, in an effort to emphasize the positive outcomes in psychology, researchers have been investigating **resilience,** the maintenance of healthy functioning following exposure to potential trauma.

Resilience is not the same as recovery, and quite different from chronic and delayed post-traumatic stress reactions (PTSD). Figure 10.11 shows the trajectories of resilience compared to these three other outcomes. As you can see, chronic stress symptoms, which are experienced by 10 to 30 percent of people exposed to trauma, are severe reactions immediately after the traumatic event and remain severe two years afterwards. Delayed-stress reactions, which account for 5 to 10 percent of reactions, begin moderate but have increased to severe two years after the trauma. Recovery, reported by 15 to 35 percent, begins with moderate-to-severe reactions but has become mild two years after trauma. Resilience is a reaction that may increase slightly at the time of the trauma, but never leaves the mild range. According to psychologist George Bonanno, resilience is the most common response to traumatic stress, found in 35 to 55 percent of people who are exposed to a traumatic event (Bonanno, 2005).

Reactions to Trauma

In studies of a variety of traumatic events, resilience is the most common outcome, not recovery or PTSD. Studies that investigate the responses of widows or widowers after the death of their spouses show that reactions of resilience are near 50 percent (Zisoock, Paulus, Shuchter, et al, 1997; Bonanno & Keltner, 1997). Contrary to popular belief, there is no evidence that these individuals will later suffer from "delayed grief," or that they were only superficially attached to their spouses. In a longitudinal study of older married couples, those who became widowed in the course of the study were followed for 18

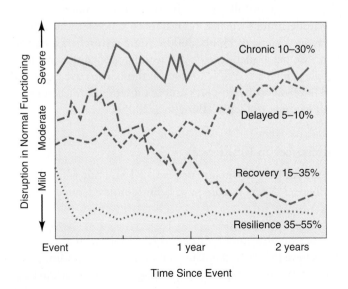

Figure 10.11 Of four outcomes people can have after exposure to trauma, the most prevalent is resilience. Others, such as chronic stress reaction, delayed stress reaction, and recovery, are not as typical as resilience.

Source: Bonanno (2005)

months after the deaths of their spouses, and almost half of the surviving spouses showed only low levels of depression and had relatively few sustained symptoms of grief. When the marital histories of these resilient widowed individuals were examined, there were no signs of marital problems or of cold, distant personalities. They did have high scores on acceptance of death, belief in a just world, and having a strong support network. And they did have moments of intense sadness and yearning for their spouses, but these grief symptoms did not interfere with their ability to continue with their lives, including their ability to feel positive emotions (Bonanno, Wortman, Lehman, et al., 2002).

Researchers are challenging the concept of "grief work," the Freudian-based idea that everyone experiencing traumatic loss must "work through" the negative feelings and "let it all out." This concept labels resilient people (often the majority) as pathological—either in denial or showing abnormal detachment. In light of the research findings on resilience, not only does grief work seem unnecessary, it may be harmful to many individuals (Bonanno & Kaltman, 1999). One study of grief-work therapy showed that 38 percent of people receiving this type of postbereavement help actually got worse when compared to a control group who got no treatment (Neimeyer, 2000). Clearly, for resilient people who have experienced the death of a loved one, therapy that expects you to express emotions that you do not feel, and then questions your mental health or your attachment to the deceased loved one, is a classic example of adding insult to injury, and it is understandable how this type of "help" could result in secondary trauma.

Similar findings have come from research on exposure to violent and life-threatening events. Studies of various violent events show levels of PTSD ranging from 7–10 percent during the Los Angeles riots in 1992 (Hanson, Kilpatrick, Freedy, et al., 1995), to 13 percent for Gulf War veterans (Sutker, Davis, Uddo, et al., 1995), to 17 percent for hospitalized survivors of auto accidents (Ehlers, Mayou, & Bryant, 1998), and 18 percent for victims of physical assault (Resnick, Kilpatrick, Dansky, et al., 1993). A survey of Manhattan residents one month after the September 11th terrorist attacks in 2001 found that about 8 percent met the criteria for PTSD, and another 17 percent had high levels of symptoms. Six months later, the rate for PTSD had dropped to 4 percent, and high levels of stress to 5 percent (Galea, Vlahov, Resnick, et al., 2003). Although these rates are disturbing, they support the findings that resilience is the most common response to trauma of many kinds. While intervention is important for those who will sustain or eventually develop extreme levels of chronic stress, the current practice of giving all exposed individuals psychological treatment may actually undermine their natural resilience processes and impede their recovery (Mayou, Ehlers, & Hobb, 2000). Some researchers are proposing that first-response personnel develop a screening device that would quickly identify people at high risk of PTSD (such as those who have experienced prior trauma and have low social support), and not interfere with anyone who is responding with genuine resilience (Bonanno, 2005).

CRITICAL THINKING ●

If you were in charge of developing a short screening test for first responders to use, based on what you have learned about stress, coping, and resilience, what five questions would you include?

Individual Differences in Resilience

We know a little about people who are prone to PTSD, but what about the people who are prone to resilience? A few factors have been identified, such as hardiness and positive emotion.

Hardiness. This personality construct describes people who are committed to finding meaning in life, believe that they can control their own surroundings and the outcome of events, and believe that all life experiences bring growth and knowledge (Maddi, 2005).

With this way of thinking, hardy individuals approach difficult situations with less fear and with confidence that they will cope and maybe even benefit from the experience. Not surprisingly, hardy individuals use more coping skills and have more social support than those who do not fit this type (Florian, Mikulincer, & Taubman, 1995).

Positive emotion (and even laughter). Although long been thought to be a symptom of unhealthy denial, recent evidence shows that people who respond to aversive events with positive emotion (gratitude, concern for others, love) have better adjustments than those who are more negative. In addition, this behavior brings out more positive responses from family and others in their social support network. For example, bereaved spouses who spoke about their loss with stories that were accompanied with smiles and genuine laughter showed better adjustment over several years after the loss of their loved one (Bonanno & Keltner, 1997).

These findings about resilience are centered on reactions to traumatic events, but it stands to reason that the lessons here can be generalized to reactions most of us have to daily stressors at home or at work. Sure, the number of stressors and their intensity make a difference in our reactions, but not all of us will succumb to health problems and mental disorders as a result. In fact most of us will deal successfully with them, hopefully finding some positive benefits in the experiences. To reiterate, stress is life, and most of us have what it takes to not only deal with it, but to embrace it and grow from our experiences.

Summary

1. The best-known theory of stress response is Selye's general adaptation syndrome, in which we meet stressors with alarm reactions, followed by resistance and exhaustion if the stressor is still present. This sequence of events has an effect on the body's immune system and can lead to an increase in natural immunity at the expense of specific immunity, resulting in a lowered defense against specific diseases.

2. Types of stressors have been studied, and scoring systems have been proposed to rate the number and intensity of stressors in a person's life. Early studies showed that there was a relationship between the number and intensity of stressors and some health outcomes.

3. The most common types of stressors are interpersonal tensions, followed by things that happen to other people in one's family or social network and things that happen at work or school.

4. Longitudinal studies have linked stress with the occurrence of breast cancer, death from heart disease, and faster progression of HIV to AIDS. Stress has also been shown to be one of several factors in the onset of some mental disorders.

5. Post-traumatic stress disorder (PTSD), a long-lasting, extreme reaction to acute stress, is a mental health disorder strongly related to stress. From examining people who have been exposed to a variety of disasters, researchers know that about one-third of people will develop PTSD either immediately after the traumatic event or in the weeks following. About 10 percent will continue to have PTSD a year after the event. PTSD causes alterations in the brain and changes in the brain function. Treatment is counseling and medication.

6. Men and women have different sources of stress and different reactions. Evolutionary psychologists suggest that the response systems of men developed differently from those of women due to the types of threats each gender was exposed to in our primitive

ancestors' time. Men respond with "fight or flight," women with "tend and befriend." Men are exposed to more trauma, but women are more likely to develop PTSD.

7.   Some researchers have suggested that racial discrimination is a form of chronic stress, and that the greater incidence of high blood pressure and stroke among African Americans is a result of this stress.

8.   Along with the negative effects of stress, there is evidence that some people experience personal growth, increased wisdom, new appreciation for life, and a stronger religious belief.

9.   The measures we take to reduce stress are known as coping. Problem-focused coping directly addresses the source of the stress. Emotion-focused coping is an attempt to reduce the emotional reactions. Meaning-focused coping is used to help us make sense of the situation, and social-focused coping is seeking help from others close to you.

10. All categories of coping skills are useful if implemented at the right time. It is important to have a wide repertoire of coping skills and to know when to use which one.

11. New ideas in coping research involve proactive coping, or coping with something before it happens, and religious coping, which is using one's religious or spiritual beliefs to cope.

12. Social support is an important antidote of stress because it serves as a buffer to provide some protection against the negative effects of stress. Social networks can also be a source of stress, if the interactions are difficult or the support offered is not welcome or what is needed. Other protectors against stress are having a sense of personal control and optimism.

13. The most common reaction to stress is resilience, maintaining healthy functioning. Even with extreme trauma such as the September 11th terrorist attacks, most of the people involved did not suffer disruption of their normal functioning.

14. Resilience has been misdiagnosed as "delayed PTSD" in trauma victims and "denial" in bereaved spouses. The popular idea that it is necessary for a person to experience debilitating stress reactions to trauma or the death of a loved one is not supported by research. Engaging these people in "grief work" may undermine their resilience.

15. One feature of resilient people is hardiness. They show commitment, control, and a quest for meaning in their lives. Another feature is positive emotion.

Key Terms

stress, 298

stressors, 298

coping, 298

general adaptation syndrome, 298

response-oriented viewpoint, 299

life-change events, 299

stimulus-oriented viewpoint, 299

post-traumatic stress disorder (PTSD), 304

stress-related growth, 309

resistance resources, 310

coping behaviors, 310

problem-focused coping, 311

emotion-focused coping, 311

meaning-focused coping, 312

social coping, 312

proactive coping, 313

religious coping, 314

social support, 314

buffering effect, 314

resilience, 317

Suggested Reading

Reading for Personal Interest

de Becker, G. (2002). *Fear less: Real truth about risk, safety, and security in a time of terrorism.* New York: Little, Brown.

Gavin de Becker, a security specialist, has served on many government advisory boards and written several books on personal safety. In this book he presents ways to find a sense of safety and peace of mind by learning about fear responses, how to separate real threats from media hype, and how to defeat terror in our lives by putting the threat of terrorism in perspective and taking sensible steps to protect ourselves, our families, and our country.

Dewey, L. (2004). *War and redemption: Treatment and recovery in combat-related traumatic stress disorder.* Aldershot: Ashgate Publishing.

The author, a psychiatrist, has treated combat veterans over the last 20 years. He compiled this book, based on that experience, for everyone who deals with combat veterans—caregivers, family members and friends, coworkers—and anyone interested in learning about the terrors, grief, and spiritual devastation caused by war.

Luskin, F., & Pelletier, K. (2006). *Stress free for good: 10 scientifically proven life skills for health and happiness.* San Francisco: Harper.

Practical suggestions for putting into practice many of the research findings discussed in this chapter. A good resource for you if there is stress of any kind in your life.

Sapolsky, R. M. (2004). *Why zebras don't get ulcers* (3rd ed.). New York: Owl Books.

Sometimes humorous explanation of the stress response in modern humans and how it goes awry. The chapters feature how stress affects sleep, aging, pain, and depression, among other things. Author is a renowned primotologist who studies stress reactions in humans and other mammals.

Taylor, S. E. (2002). *The tending instinct: Women, men, and the biology of nurturing.* New York: Time Books.

Shelley Taylor, whose work on stress is discussed in this chapter, expanded her ideas in this book. Her premise is that science has given too much attention to the aggression side of human nature and not enough to the nurturing side. She believes that nurturing, cooperation, and caregiving are just as important to the survival of the species, and that both men and women have the tending instinct. A very interesting and novel approach to human nature.

Classic Work

Cannon, W. B. (1914). The interrelations of emotions as suggested by recent physiological researches. *American Journal of Physiology, 25,* 256–282.

Cannon, W. B. (1932). *The wisdom of the body.* New York: Norton.

These two works are considered the beginning of modern stress theories. In the first, physiologist Walter Cannon suggested that certain events cause the sympathetic nervous system to react, and that this reaction leads to disequilibrium in the body. This theory was innovative because it stated that stressors had a psychological component—they had to be recognized as threatening before they could elicit a stress response. In the second selection, Cannon reviewed his work and his ideas about physiological reactions to stress, including the "fight-or-flight" concept.

Holmes, T. H., & Rahe, R. H. (1967). The Social Readjustment Rating Scale. *Journal of Psychosomatic Research, 11,* 213–218.

Although the link between stress and illness is well known today, in 1967 it was a radical idea. This was the article that started the ball rolling. Not only was it important in its day, but it is still regularly cited in research. The SRRS remains a favorite measurement instrument in studies of stress.

Selye, H. (1956/1984). *The stress of life* (Rev. ed.). New York: McGraw-Hill.

Hans Selye is considered the major pioneer of stress research, and his focus is on the almost universal physiological response to almost all types of stress. This book summarizes his contribution to the field.

Contemporary Scholarly Work

Lazarus, R. S., & Lazarus, B. N. (2006). *Coping with aging.* New York: Oxford University Press.

The last book by psychologist Richard Lazarus, a pioneer in the study of coping who died at the age of 80 in 2002. In this book, written with his wife, Bernice Lazarus, he reflects on the years of his life and the interplay of stress and coping that contribute to our overall well-being.

Moren-Cross, J. L., & Lin, N. (2006). Social networks and health. In R. H. Binstock & L. K. George (Eds.), *Handbook of aging and the social sciences* (pp. 111–126). San Diego: Academic Press.

These authors, both sociologists, review the literature on the importance of social networks to health, including such factors as the size of the network, the frequency of contact, and whether social contacts via the Internet have the same effects on health.

Chapter 11

Death and Bereavement

DAVID TASMA WAS a young man with inoperable cancer who was dying in a hospital in England, alone with no family. His native language was Polish and he did not fully understand the English conversations that surrounded him. He was a Jew and did not feel comforted by the Anglican priests who visited the ward. Although his medical care was skilled and efficient, he faced death feeling frustrated and distressed. His only consolation was a young woman social worker who visited him and patiently listened as he struggled with English to talk about his childhood, his family, and his thoughts about death. For two months she sat with him daily as he went through the physical and mental process of dying. His greatest fear, he told her, was that he would leave this earth without making a mark on it. He was young and had no children. He had never written a book or built a house or planted a field of corn. Perhaps they fell in love; we don't know. When he died, he left her all that he had, about 500 pounds, and the seed of an idea—that dying involves much more than physical pain; there is also the social pain of leaving loved ones, the mental pain of trying to know the unknowable, the spiritual pain of finding meaning in the life-and-death process, and the emotional pain of fear, disappointment, frustration, and regret. The medical community had nothing to offer the dying.

The young social worker was Cicely Saunders, founder of the modern hospice movement. The event recounted above took place in 1948, and as a tribute to Tasma, Saunders dedicated her life to finding ways for society

Achieving an Understanding of Death
  Meanings of Death
  Death Anxiety
  Accepting the Reality of One's Eventual Death

The Process of Death
  Stages of Death Reactions
  The Importance of Farewells
  Individual Adaptations to Dying
  Choosing Where to Die
  Choosing When to Die

After Death Occurs: Rituals and Grieving
  Ritual Mourning: Funerals and Ceremonies
  The Process of Grieving

Living and Dying: A Final Word

Summary

Key Terms

Suggested Reading

to minister to its members at the end of their lives. She was one of the few women to become a medical doctor in England in the 1950s, and the first medical doctor of either gender to specialize in the treatment of dying patients. Ten years later, she opened St. Christopher's Hospice in London in memory of her young Polish friend, David Tasma, showing that he had indeed made his mark on the world—inspiring over 8,000 hospice centers in more than 100 countries. These centers all give the same message that defined Saunders's long career, "You matter because you are you, and you matter to the last moment of your life." Dame Cicely died at the age of 82 at the hospice she had founded (Field, 2005).

This chapter is about death—how we think about it at different ages, how we cope with the death of loved ones, and how we face the reality of our own death. This has long been a central topic in psychoanalytic theory and clinical psychology, but recently it has become a topic of interest for researchers in many other fields. I will begin by discussing how we think about death, then will explore the process of death, and finally will consider how we cope with the death of a loved one. This is a difficult topic, but one that must be included in a course on adulthood and aging.

Achieving an Understanding of Death

Death has a significant impact on individuals, families, and the community. The meaning of death changes with age and goes well beyond the simple understanding of inevitability and universality. Most broadly, death has important social meaning. The death of any one person changes the roles and relationships of everyone else in a family. When an elder dies, everyone else in that particular lineage moves up one step in the generational system. Beyond the family, death also affects other roles; for instance, it makes opportunities for younger adults to take on significant tasks. Retirement serves some of the same functions because the older adult "steps aside" for the younger, but death brings many permanent changes in social systems.

Meanings of Death

Four meanings that death may have for adults have been identified. Typically, they are all present in any person's meaning system.

- *Death as an organizer of time.* Death defines the endpoint of one's life, so the concept of "time until death" may be an important one for a person trying to organize his or her life. In fact, sociologist Bernice Neugarten suggests that one of the key changes in thinking in middle age is a switch in the way one marks one's own lifetime, from time since birth to time until death. Her interviews with middle-aged adults frequently yielded statements like the following: "Before I was 35, the future just stretched forth. There would be time to do and see and carry out all the plans I had. . . . Now I keep thinking, will I have time enough to finish off some of the things I want to do?" (Neugarten, 1970, p. 78).

- *Death as punishment.* Children are quite likely to think of death as punishment for being bad—a kind of ultimate Stage 1 of Kohlberg's moral reasoning theory. But this view and its reverse (that long life is the reward for being good) are still common in adults. Such a view is strengthened by religious teachings that emphasize a link between sin and death.

- *Death as transition.* Death involves a transition—from life to some sort of life after death, or from life to nothingness. In recent surveys, 72 percent of people in the United States said that they believed in an afterlife, meaning that they would exist after death with some sort of consciousness (Hargrove & Stempel, 2006), and 27 percent believed in reincarnation, meaning that they had lived before and will live again in another body after death (Harris Poll, 2005b).

• *Death as loss.* Perhaps most pervasively, death is seen by most of us as a loss—loss of the ability to complete projects or carry out plans; loss of one's body; loss of experiencing, of taste, smell, and touch; loss of relationships with people. Unlike beliefs in an afterlife, in this domain there are age differences. In particular, the specific losses that adults associate with death appear to change as they move through the adult years. Young adults are more concerned about loss of opportunity to experience things and about the loss of family relationships; older adults may be more concerned with the loss of time to complete some inner work (Kalish, 1985).

> ● **CRITICAL THINKING**
>
> How might you design a study to show age-related differences in the meaning adults attach to death?

Death Anxiety

The most studied aspect of attitudes toward death is **death anxiety,** or fear of death. This fear is strongly linked to the view of death as a loss. If we fear death, it is, in part, because we fear the loss of experience, sensation, and relationships. Fear of death may also include fear of the pain or suffering or indignity often involved in the process of death, fear that one will not be able to cope well with such pain or suffering, fear of whatever punishment may come after death, and a fundamental fear of loss of the self.

Age. Researchers have quite consistently found that middle-aged adults show the greatest fear of death, and older adults the least, with young adults falling somewhere in between (Thorson & Powell, 1992). These results are consistent with the idea that one of the central tasks of midlife is to come to terms with the inevitability of death. The greater awareness of body changes and aging that is part of this period, coupled perhaps with the death of one's parents, breaks down the defenses we have all erected against the knowledge of and fear of death. In particular, the death of one's parents may be especially shocking and disturbing, not only because of the specific loss to be mourned but because you must face the realization that you are now the oldest generation in the family lineage and thus "next in line" for death. So in midlife we become more aware of the fear, more preoccupied with death and its imminence. In these years, many adults grope toward new ways of thinking about death, eventually accepting it in a different way, so that the fear recedes in old age. This does not mean that older adults are unconcerned about death. On the contrary, they are more likely to talk about it and think about it than younger adults. But while death is highly salient to the elderly, it is apparently not as frightening as it was in midlife.

Religiosity. Age is not the only element in fear of death. Several other personal qualities have been nominated as factors. First, a likely factor would be **religiosity,** the degree of one's religious or spiritual belief. Presumably, there would be a negative correlation, the more religiosity one expresses, the less fear of death one should have. However, research has been mixed, and recent findings show that there is no direct relationship between religiosity and fear of death. For example, in a study of older adults (70 to 80 years of age), those who were low in religiosity and those who were high in religiosity feared death less than participants who were moderate in their religious and spiritual beliefs. It was an inverted U-shaped function. The researchers suggest that those who are high in religiosity are not anxious about death because they believe that there is an afterlife and they have earned a place there. Those low in religiosity are not anxious about death because they don't believe there is an afterlife and aren't worried about missing out on any rewards. It's just those in the middle, the moderately religious, who are anxious about death because they believe there may be an afterlife and they may not have earned a place in it (Wink & Scott, 2005).

Religiosity can be divided into two separate factors: *extrinsic religiosity* is practiced by people who use religion for social purposes and as an arena for doing good deeds, and *intrinsic religiosity* is practiced by people who live their lives according to their religious beliefs and seek meaning in life through their religion. In a study of older adults, extrinsic religiosity was positively related to death anxiety—those who scored higher on measures of extrinsic religiosity had higher fears of death. In addition, intrinsic religiosity had a strong positive relationship with anticipation of a better existence after death (Ardelt & Koenig, 2006).

Researchers suggest that extrinsic religiosity might be useful for middle-aged adults whose focus is social support and opportunities for generative activities, such as volunteer work within the religious community. In later years, however, intrinsic religiosity has a purpose because this is a time when actively participating in religious activities becomes difficult and the need is more for finding answers to fundamental questions of life, such as, Where did we come from? Where are we going? Why are we here? (McFadden, 2000).

CRITICAL THINKING

What would you predict about students' fear of death in the United States versus that of students in Israel or in one of the other Middle Eastern countries where suicide bombers are a fact of life? Would that make young adults have higher death anxiety scores or lower?

Gender. Death anxiety is also linked with gender. A number of studies from various cultures show that women have higher levels of death anxiety than men. This gender difference was found for a group of Episcopal parishioners in New York (Harding, Flannelly, Weaver, et al., 2005) as well as young adults in Egypt, Kuwait, and Syria (Abdel-Khalek, 2004). However, this may be an artifact of the higher rates of anxiety disorders of all kinds for women, as you will remember from Chapter 3. In fact in a study of clinical patients with various mental health diagnoses, those with anxiety disorders (male and female) had higher rates of death anxiety than those diagnosed with schizophrenia and those in a nonclinical control group (Abdel-Khalek, 2005).

Personality traits. Certain personality traits seem to be factors in people's attitudes toward death. Self-esteem has been related to death anxiety, with high levels of self-esteem seeming to serve as a buffer against the fear of death (Xiangkui, Juan, & Lumei, 2005). Another study investigated the link between death anxiety and a **sense of purpose in life,** the extent to which individuals feel they have discovered satisfying personal goals and believe that their lives have been worthwhile. Psychologists Monika Ardelt and Cynthia Koenig (2006) studied a group of adults who were 61 years of age and older (some healthy and some hospice patients). Those who had a higher sense of purpose in life had lower death anxiety. This was especially interesting because general religiosity, for this sample, was not related to death anxiety. A sense of purpose in life has also been linked to lower levels of death anxiety in young adults (Rasmussen & Johnson, 1994). Related to this is the finding that regrets are linked to death anxiety. People who feel a great deal of regret, both for things they have done (or not done) in the past and things they may not do in the future, have higher levels of death anxiety (Tomer & Eliason, 2005).

Such findings suggest that adults who have successfully completed the major tasks of adult life, adequately fulfilled the demands of the roles they occupied, and developed inwardly are able to face death with greater equanimity. In contrast, adults who have not been able to resolve the various tasks and dilemmas of adulthood face their late adult years more fearfully, more anxiously, even with what Erikson describes as despair. Fear of death may be merely one facet of such despair.

In some sense, then, all of adult life is a process of moving toward death. Adults' attitudes toward death, and their approaches to it, are influenced by many of the same qualities that affect the way they approach other life changes or dilemmas.

Accepting the Reality of One's Eventual Death

Becoming comfortable with the fact of your own death, no matter how far in the future, occurs on other levels in addition to thought processes. At a practical level, for example, you can make out a will or obtain life insurance. Such preparations become more common with increasing age, especially in late middle age and thereafter. For example, older people are more apt to have life insurance than younger people. They are also more likely to prepare for death by making a will; only about 45 percent of all adults in the United States have done so, but 83 percent of adults who are 65 years of age or older (Harris Poll, 2005).

At a somewhat deeper level, adults may start making preparations for death through some process of **reminiscence,** or reviewing their memories. This is often done by writing a memoir or autobiography, or seeking out old friends and relatives to talk with about the past. We have little evidence that older adults typically or necessarily go through such a review process. But for some, a life review may be an important aspect of "writing the final chapter" or legitimizing one's life in some fashion (Birren & Feldman, 1997).

One type of planning for eventual death that has become increasingly popular recently is the **living will,** a document that takes effect if you are no longer able to express your wishes about end-of-life decisions. These documents (which may differ from state to state) give people the opportunity to decide, while they are still healthy, which specific treatments they would accept or refuse if they had a terminal illness or permanent disability and were not able to communicate their wishes. Living wills can be prepared with the assistance of an attorney or by using forms available on the Internet. For adults of all ages in the United States, 34 percent have a living will, but for adults 65 and over, 60 percent do (Harris Poll, 2005a).

Living wills help alleviate the fear that dying will be a long and painful process. A person writing one can take responsibility for his or her own end-of-life decisions and not burden family members. And they help avoid situations such as the Terry Schaivo case in which family members became divided and confrontive over whether she should be kept alive or allowed to die after 13 years in a vegetative state. This case became the center of public attention in 2005 when her husband was allowed by the courts to have her feeding tube removed over the objections of her parents, and she died shortly therafter. One positive result of this tragedy was a record number of people in the United States and around the world writing living wills. Regardless of what stand one took on the case itself, all agreed that they didn't want this to happen to them or their families (Cerminara, 2006).

Another way people accept the reality of their eventual death is to consider becoming an **organ transplant donor,** agreeing that at the time of death, their usable organs and other tissue can be transplanted to people who have been approved to receive them. Medicine has advanced in organ transplantation faster than the idea of being a donor has been accepted by the public. At the moment there are thousands of people waiting for donated organs. The process varies by area, but in many states it can be done quickly when you renew your driver's license. Who chooses to be an organ transplant donor? One study of young adults in Israel showed that it is typically a person who knows other potential donors, has a lot of information about organ transplantation, and has low levels of

> **CRITICAL THINKING**
>
> Does reading this section about reminiscence make you more tolerant of older relatives who want to tell you their life stories?

> **CRITICAL THINKING**
>
> Could you make the opposite argument, that people with high levels of death anxiety would *more* be likely to be organ transplant donors?

death anxiety (Besser, Amir, & Barkan, 2004). Many people view their potential as an organ donor as a way to give back to others and to gain a little immortality.

The Process of Death

Death and mourning have always been part of the human experience, but the thoughts people have about death and the way mourning is expressed differ from culture to culture and from era to era. For example, 50 years ago, a chapter like this one would not have been included in a textbook about adult development. Science was fixated on life and life-saving treatment. Death was failure of science; dying people were isolated in hospital wards, and every attempt was made to "cure" them. The idea of welcoming death or even accepting it was not discussed. This mindset was changed largely through the writings of physician Elisabeth Kübler-Ross (1969), whose book *On Death and Dying* was acclaimed for having "brought death out of the darkness."

Stages of Death Reactions

Kübler-Ross's book was based on her work with terminally ill adults and children and is probably best known for describing five stages of dying: denial, anger, bargaining, depression, and acceptance. Although she later wrote that these stages are not experienced by all people and do not necessarily occur in this order, her terminology is still used to describe the reactions to impending death of both the person who is dying and those who are bereaved (Kübler-Ross, 1974). I will describe these stages because they are often used to describe the constellation of reactions to impending death:

- *Denial.* When confronted with a terminal diagnosis, the first reaction most patients report is some form of "No, not me!" "It must be a mistake," "The lab reports must have been mixed up," "I don't feel that sick, so it can't be true," "I'll get another doctor's opinion." All these are forms of denial. Kübler-Ross argues that denial is a valuable, constructive first defense. It gives the patient a period of time in which to marshal other strategies of coping with the shock.

- *Anger.* The classic second reaction, so Kübler-Ross argues, is "Why me?" The patient resents those who are healthy and becomes angry at whatever fate put him or her in this position. This may be reflected in angry outbursts at nurses, family members, doctors—anyone within reach.

- *Bargaining.* At some point, Kübler-Ross saw anger being replaced by a new kind of defense. The patient now tries to "make a deal" with doctors, with nurses, with God. "If I do what I'm told and don't yell at everyone, then I'll be able to live till Christmas." She describes one woman with terminal cancer who wanted to live long enough to attend the wedding of her oldest son.

- *Depression.* Bargaining only works for so long, however, and as disease processes continue and the signs of the body's decline become more obvious, patients typically become depressed. This is a kind of mourning—for the loss of relationships as well as of one's own life.

- *Acceptance.* The final step, according to this theory, is a quiet understanding, a readiness for death. The patient is no longer depressed but may be quiet, even serene. In a widely quoted passage, author Stewart Alsop, who was dying of leukemia, described his own acceptance: "A dying man needs to die as a sleepy man needs to sleep, and there comes a time when it is wrong, as well as useless, to resist" (1973, p. 299).

CRITICAL THINKING

Why would it be important for a physician who deals with terminal diseases to be familiar with the various reactions to impending death? Which reactions would they be most likely to witness in their patients?

Since the publication of Kübler-Ross's *On Death and Dying* in 1969, the process of dying has been changed in many ways. Patients with terminal conditions are treated as whole people with wishes and needs, not just failures of medical science. The vast majority do not want to die in a hospital ward, but prefer to be at home in their familiar surroundings. Most reach a point when they choose not to continue with heroic measures that might give them a few more days at the expense of their comfort and dignity. But refusing medical treatment does not mean that they don't need professional care. There is still a need for pain management, spiritual counseling, and accurate information about their condition and the time they have left. From loved ones there is a need for social support, listening, forgiving, and even laughter.

Perhaps more important than her stage theory, Kübler-Ross identified three key issues: The dying are still alive and have unfinished needs they may want to address. We need to listen actively to the dying and identify with their needs in order to provide effectively for them. And we need to learn from the dying in order to know ourselves better and our potential for living (Corr, 1993).

The Importance of Farewells

One aspect of the process of dying that is not reflected in Kübler-Ross's stages or in most research on dying, but which is clearly a significant feature for the dying person and his or her family, is the process of saying farewell. A study in Australia by sociologists Allan Kellehear and Terry Lewin (1988–1989) gave us a first exploration of such goodbyes. They interviewed 90 terminally ill cancer patients, all of whom had been told they were within a year of death, and a smaller group of 10 patients who were in hospice care and thought to be within 3 months of death. Most had known they had cancer for over a year before the interview but had only recently been given a specific short-term prognosis. Subjects were asked whether they had already said some goodbyes or intended future farewells to family or friends and, if so, when and under what circumstances. The minority (19 of the 100) said they did not plan any farewells at all. The rest had either already begun to say goodbye (22 of the 100) or had planned their farewells for the final days of their lives—deathbed goodbyes, if you will.

The early farewells had often been in the form of a letter or a gift, such as giving money to a child or grandchild, or passing on personal treasures to a member of the family who might especially cherish them. One woman made dolls that she gave to friends, relatives, and hospital staff. Another knit a set of baby clothes to give to each of her daughters for the child that neither daughter had yet had.

More commonly, both planned and completed farewells were in the form of conversations. One subject asked her brother to come for a visit so that she could see and talk to him one last time; others arranged with friends for one last get-together, saying goodbye quite explicitly on these occasions. Those who anticipated saying farewell only in the last hours of their conscious life imagined these occasions to be times when loving words would be spoken or a goodbye look would be exchanged.

All such farewells, whether spoken or not, can be thought of as forms of gifts. By saying goodbye to someone, the dying person signals that that person matters enough to warrant a farewell. Saying goodbye also serves to make the death real, to force the imminent death out of the realm of denial into acceptance by others as well as by the dying person. And finally, as Kellehear and Lewin point out, farewells may make the dying itself easier, especially if they are completed before the final moments of life. They may make it easier for the dying person to disengage, to reach a point of acceptance.

Individual Adaptations to Dying

The process of dying varies hugely from one person to the next, not only in the emotions expressed (or not expressed), but also in the physical process. Some experience a long, slow decline; others die instantly, with no "stages" or phases at all. Some experience great pain; others little or none. Similarly, the way each person handles the process also varies. Some fight hard against dying; others appear to accept it early in the process and struggle no further. Some remain calm; others fall into deep depression. The question that researchers have begun to ask is whether such variations in the emotional response to impending or probable death have any effect at all on the physical process of dying.

I should say at the outset that virtually all of the research we have on individual variations or adaptations to dying involves studies of patients with terminal cancer. Not only is cancer a clear diagnosis, but many forms of it progress quite rapidly, and patients not only know that they are terminally ill but roughly how long they have to live. Some other diseases, such as AIDS, have the same features, but most diseases do not. Most particularly, heart disease, the leading cause of death in middle and old age in industrialized countries, may exist for a long period during which the patient may not know that he or she has significant heart disease, and the prognosis is highly variable. We simply do not know whether any of the conclusions drawn from studies of cancer patients can be applied to adults dying less rapidly or less predictably. Still, the research is quite fascinating.

The most influential single study in this area is the work of psychiatrist Steven Greer and his colleagues (Greer, 1991; Pettingale, Morris, Greer, et al., 1985). They followed a group of 62 women diagnosed with early stages of breast cancer. Three months after the original diagnosis, each woman was interviewed at some length, and her reaction to the diagnosis and to her treatment was classed in one of five groups:

- *Positive avoidance (denial):* rejection of evidence about diagnosis; insistence that surgery was just precautionary.

- *Fighting spirit:* an optimistic attitude, accompanied by a search for more information about the disease; they often saw their disease as a challenge and planned to fight it with every method available.

- *Stoic acceptance (fatalism):* acknowledgment of the diagnosis but without seeking any further information; ignoring the diagnosis and carrying on their normal life as much as possible.

- *Helplessness/hopelessness:* overwhelmed by diagnosis; saw themselves as dying or gravely ill; devoid of hope.

- *Anxious preoccupation* (originally included in the helplessness group but separated later): response to the diagnosis was strong, persistent anxiety; if they sought information, they interpreted it pessimistically; they monitored their body sensations carefully, interpreting each ache or pain as a possible recurrence.

Greer checked on the survival rates of these five groups 15 years later. Table 11.1 shows the results. Only 35 percent of those whose initial reaction had been either positive avoidance (denial) or fighting spirit had died of cancer 15 years later, compared to 76 percent of those whose initial reaction had been stoic acceptance, anxious preoccupation, or helplessness/hopelessness. Because the five groups had not differed initially in the stage of their disease or in treatment, these results support the hypothesis that psychological response contributes to disease progress, just as coping strategies more generally affect the likelihood of disease in the first place.

Similar results have emerged from studies of patients with melanoma (a deadly form of skin cancer) as well as other cancers (Temoshok, 1987) and from several studies of AIDS patients (Reed, Kemeny, Taylor, et al., 1994; Solano, Costa, Salvati, et al., 1993). In general, those who report less hostility, more stoic acceptance, and more helplessness and who fail to express negative feelings die sooner (O'Leary, 1990). Those who struggle the most, who fight the hardest, who express their anger and hostility openly, and who find

Table 11.1	Cancer Survival Rates According to Psychological Response to Diagnosis			
	Outcomes 15 Years after Diagnosis			
Psychological Response	Alive and Well	Died of Cancer	Died of Other Causes	Total
Positive avoidance	5	5	0	10
Fighting spirit	4	2	4	10
Stoical acceptance	6	24	3	33
Anxious preoccupation	0	3	0	3
Hopelessness	1	5	0	6
Total	16	39	7	62

Source: Adapted from Greer (1991).

some sources of joy in their lives live longer. In some ways, the data suggest that "good patients"—those who are obedient and not too questioning, who don't yell at their doctors or make life difficult for those around them—are, in fact, likely to die sooner.

Furthermore, there are studies linking these psychological differences to immune-system functioning. A particular subset of immune cells called NK cells, thought to be an important defense against cancer cells, have been found to occur at lower rates among patients who report less distress and seem better adjusted to their illness (O'Leary, 1990). And among AIDS patients, one study shows that T-cell counts declined more rapidly among those who respond to their disease with repression (similar to the stoic acceptance or helplessness groups in the Greer study), while those showing fighting spirit had a slower loss of T cells (Solano, Costa, Salvati, et al., 1993).

Despite the growing body of results of this type, two important cautions are nonetheless in order before we leap to the conclusion that a fighting spirit is the optimum response to any disease. First, there are some careful studies in which no link has been found between depression/stoic acceptance/helplessness and more rapid death from cancer (Richardson, Zarnegar, Bisno, et al., 1990). Second, it is not clear that the same psychological response is necessarily optimum for every form of disease. Consider heart disease, for example. There is a certain irony in the fact that many of the qualities that appear to be optimal for cancer patients could be considered reflections of a type A personality. Because the anger and hostility components of the type A personality are a risk factor for heart disease, it is not so obvious that a fighting-spirit response which includes those components would necessarily be desirable.

One of the major difficulties in all this research is that investigators have used widely differing measures of psychological functioning. Greer and his colleagues have found quite consistent results with their category system; others, using standardized measures of depression or hopelessness, have not necessarily found the same patterns. My own reading of the evidence is that there is indeed some link between psychological responses to stress (including a fatal diagnosis) and prognosis, but that we have not yet zeroed in on just what psychological processes may be critical for which disease. Fortunately, this is an area in which a great deal of research is under way, giving some hope that clearer answers may emerge before long.

Another important ingredient in a person's response to imminent death is the amount of social support that he or she may have available. High levels of social support are linked to lower levels of pain, less depressive symptoms, and longer survival times. For example,

CRITICAL THINKING ◑

When people learn that a friend is dying, they sometimes stay away because they don't know what to do or to say. How can this decision be harmful? What are some helpful things they can do and say?

heart attack patients who live alone are more likely to have a second attack than those who live with someone else (Case, Moss, Case, et al., 1992), and those with significant levels of atherosclerosis live longer if they have a confidant than if they do not (Williams, 1992). The latter study involved a sample of African Americans, suggesting that the connection is not unique to Anglo culture.

Choosing Where to Die

In the United States and other industrialized countries today, the majority of adults report that they would prefer to die in their homes, but the fact is that the great majority die in hospitals and nursing homes. In a large study that surveyed family members of individuals who had died recently of chronic disease, physician Joan Teno and her colleagues (Teno, Clarridge, Casey, et al, 2004) asked about the details of the deaths. The sample, which consisted of over 1,500 families, was selected to be representative of the 1.97 million deaths from chronic illnesses that occurred that year in the United States. Respondents were asked about their deceased family members' last place of care; the results showed that one-third died at home, while two-thirds died in an institution, either a hospital or a nursing home. However, the critical difference in quality of care was not whether they died at home or not, but whether they received home care nursing services or **hospice care,** which is care focused on pain relief, emotional support, and spiritual comfort for the dying person and his or her family. When asked about the quality of care the deceased family member had received at the end of life, the responses indicated that there was little difference between dying at home with nursing services, dying in a nursing home, and dying in a hospital—fewer than half of the respondents reported that their family members who had spent their last days in these situations received "excellent" care. In contrast, over 70 percent of the respondents whose family members had died at home with hospice care evaluated this care as "excellent." Unfortunately, the number of people whose family members died at home with hospice care represented only about 16 percent of the total survey respondents.

Figure 11.1 shows some of the problem areas survey respondents reported in this study, divided by whether their loved ones died at home with home care nursing services, at home with hospice care, in a nursing home, or in a hospital. As you can see, the biggest concern was lack of emotional support for the patient, which was reported by twice as many respondents whose family members had their final care at home with home nursing care (70 percent) than at home with hospice care (35 percent). The same ratio is shown for lack of emotional support for the family, with families of those dying at home with home health nursing reporting this problem twice as often (45 percent) as those at home with hospice care (21 percent).

The authors of the study concluded that although the study only tapped the respondents' perceptions of their family members' care, and, at that, only after some time had passed, it is still appropriate to be alarmed about the problems associated with end-of-life care in the United States. They were especially concerned about the problems reported with nursing homes, which are more apt to be the last places of care for the very old. We will have more and more elderly people requiring end-of-life care in the years to come, at a time when nursing homes are receiving less and less federal support. In addition, hospitals are unable to keep terminally ill patients, so are increasingly transferring them to nursing homes.

What exactly does hospice care consist of? I talked about the beginnings of the hospice movement in the story that opened this chapter, but what exactly is it today, and why is it so successful in providing "excellent" services to dying people and their families?

The hospice movement was given a good deal of impetus by Kübler-Ross's writings because she emphasized the importance of **a good death,** meaning a death with dignity,

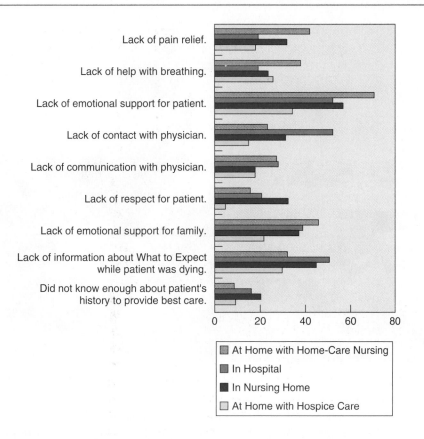

Figure 11.1 After the death of a loved one, family members report concerns about last place of care.

Source: Data from Teno, Clarridge, Casey, et al. (2004).

with maximum consciousness and minimum pain, and with the patient and the patient's family having full information and control over the process. Hospice care began in England in the 1960s. It started in the 1970s in the United States as a grassroots movement to give terminal cancer patients an alternative to continued aggressive treatment. By 1982, the idea had gained so much support that Congress was persuaded to add hospice care to the list of benefits paid for by Medicare. Today there are more than 3,000 hospice programs in the United States, serving about a half million terminally ill patients and their families each year (Wilkinson & Lynn, 2001).

The philosophy that underlies the **hospice approach,** has several aspects:

- Death should be viewed as a normal, inevitable part of life, not to be avoided but to be faced and accepted.

- The patient and the family should prepare for the death by examining their feelings and planning for their later life.

- The family should be involved in the care to as full an extent as possible, so that each family member can come to some resolution of his or her relationship with the dying person.

- Control over the care and the care-receiving setting should belong to the patient and family.

- Medical care provided should be *palliative,* not curative, meaning that pain should be alleviated and comfort maximized, but a minimum of invasive or life-prolonging measures should be undertaken.

In real terms, this philosophy translates into a constellation of services available to the dying person and his or her family and friends. These services are listed and described in Table 11.2. Hospice care is used mostly with patients who have terminal cancer because

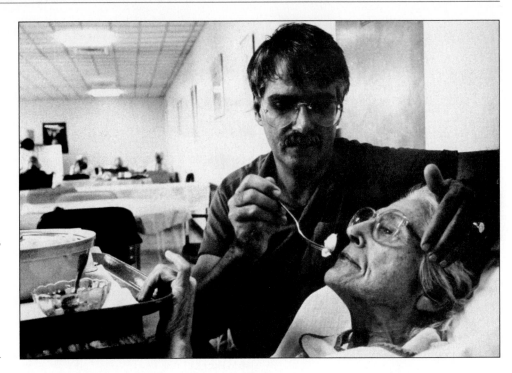

Hospice care is based on the belief that when death is inevitable, professional caregivers should focus on helping the patient and family accept it as a natural part of the life process.

this disease has a more predictable course than other diseases, such as congestive heart failure or dementia. Over half of Medicare cancer patients use hospice services during the year before their deaths. Although hospice is designed to provide care during the last 6 months of a person's life, the average length of care is only around 1 month, primarily due to the difficulty of predicting the course of many terminal illnesses (National Hospice and Palliative Care Association, 2005). Although end-of-life care (medical care dur-

Table 11.2   What Is Hospice Care?
An interdisciplinary team of physicians, nurses, social workers, counselors, home health aides, clergy, therapists, and trained volunteers who care for the patient based on their areas of expertise to relieve symptoms and provide support to the patient and his or her family.
Pain and symptom control that helps the patient be comfortable yet in control of his or her life.
Spiritual care for the patient and his or her family, based on their individual beliefs, to help the patient find meaning, say goodbye, or perform religious rituals.
Home care for those who are able to stay in their own homes, but also inpatient care in hospitals or nursing homes when needed.
Respite care for family caregivers.
Family conferences to enable family members to learn about the patient's condition and to share feelings, talk about expectations, learn about dying, and ask questions.
Bereavement care from counselors and clergy to help family members through the grieving process with visits, phone calls, and support groups.
Coordinated care provided by the interdisciplinary team to communicate with the physicians, home care agency, community professionals such as pharmacists, clergy, and funeral directors.

Source: Adapted from American Cancer Society (2006).

ing the last 12 months of life) accounts for about 25 percent of Medicare's payouts, hospice care accounts for only 4 percent. Among the reasons are the increasing number of patients dying of heart disease and Alzheimer's disease (which are not as predictable), the psychological blocks patients and family have against accepting death as imminent, and the difficulty some physicians (and family members) have in ceasing aggressive treatment. The result is that although hospice care is a positive move toward allowing people to have a "good death," it is still used by only a small number of people and for a short period of time.

Choosing When to Die

Another way of looking at the advances of modern medicine is that instead of extending life, it prolongs death. Today about 90 percent of the people who die each year do so after experiencing prolonged illnesses and steady decline. Many believe that there is a fundamental right to die a good death and to choose when, how, and even where it will occur.

In 1976, California passed the first law in the United States concerning living wills, documents discussed earlier which allow individuals to legally express the wish that if they are in a condition with no hope of recovery, no heroic measures should be taken to extend their lives. Living wills are now valid in all 50 states of the United States and in many other countries. In 1990 the U.S. Supreme Court ruled that Americans have the right to refuse medical treatment, even if refusing it will result in death.

In 2001, the Netherlands passed legislation to permit physicians to prescribe medication to allow patients to end their lives under certain conditions. The only place in the United States with this practice is the state of Oregon, where in 1997 voters passed the Death with Dignity Act, which allows for **physician-assisted suicide,** meaning that under certain circumstances, physicians are allowed to assist patients to obtain medication that will end their lives. Among other requirements, the patient must request the medication voluntarily, be terminally ill, and be mentally competent, and these points must be confirmed by a second physician. There is a waiting period of 15 days, and the prescription must be registered with the state. In spite of the warnings by opponents of this law, not many terminally ill patients have requested physician-assisted deaths. The first year this option was available, 24 people received prescriptions and 16 used them to end their lives. In 2005, 64 people received prescriptions, and 37 used them to end their lives (Oregon Department of Human Services, 2006).

Oregon keeps careful records of requests and prescriptions for physician-assisted suicides. When comparing people who choose to die this way with other deaths that occur in the state, officials found that those who choose physician-assisted suicide are younger than those who die naturally (70 vs. 78 years of age), they are more apt to have at least a bachelor's degree (37 percent vs. 15 percent), and more likely to have cancer (84 percent vs. 24 percent). The reasons most often given for wishing to end their lives are decreasing ability to participate in activities that make life enjoyable, loss of dignity, and loss of autonomy (Oregon Department of Human Services, 2006).

> ● **CRITICAL THINKING**
>
> Why would younger people be more apt to choose physician-assisted suicide than older people? And why would it be an option for more educated people?

Physician and bioethicist Ezekial Emanuel and his colleagues (Emanuel, Fairclough, & Emanuel, 2000) surveyed almost 1,000 terminally ill patients about their attitudes toward physician-assisted suicide. Although a majority (60 percent) of the patients supported it hypothetically, only about 10 percent seriously considered it for themselves. Those who were more likely to consider physician-assisted suicide had depressive symptoms, substantial caregiving needs, and were in pain. Those who were less likely to consider it felt appreciated, were 65 years of age or older, and were African American. Interestingly, about

4 months later, the surviving patients were interviewed again, and about half of each group had changed their minds. Those who now favored physician-assisted suicide were more likely to have developed depressive symptoms or breathing difficulties.

This is an interesting study for several reasons. It is the first study I have seen that actually interviewed terminally ill patients about physician-assisted suicide, making a distinction between the hypothetical construct and the actual application to oneself. It is also interesting because it showed that the key indicators in this decision were more social than medical. It followed up on the patients and showed that the wish to be assisted in suicide was not consistent over time for about half of the patients who were still alive four months later. These findings show the importance of evaluating patients for depression, unrelieved pain and breathing difficulties, and the feeling that they are a burden or unappreciated when considering physician-assisted suicide. And it also reinforces the idea of having a waiting period between requesting the medication and receiving it.

Certainly the advances we have made in medicine and healthcare have given us a whole host of blessings. It is very unusual for a woman to die in childbirth or a toddler not to live to adulthood. Many of us reach middle age with all our siblings and our parents still in our lives. Our children often have four grandparents and probably a few great-grands, too. But there is a downside, and that is our diminished opportunity to die a "good death," as described this way:

> Humans have faced all manner of challenges over time. As things go, the challenge of having the opportunity to grow old and die slowly is not such a bad thing. However, it is a challenge. Society has simply never been in this position before. We have to work on language, categories, framing, meanings, rituals, habits, social organization, service delivery, financing, and community commitment. Much remains to be learned and done. The burgeoning numbers of persons living into old age and coming to the end of life makes the need for that learning and implementing all the more urgent (Wilkinson & Lynn, 2001, p. 457).

After Death Occurs: Rituals and Grieving

Whether a death is sudden or prolonged, anticipated or unexpected, it leaves survivors who must somehow come to terms with the death and eventually pick up the pieces of their lives. I touched briefly on bereavement as trauma when I discussed stress and coping in Chapter 10. Let me turn here to a more general discussion of the process of grieving.

Ritual Mourning: Funerals and Ceremonies

All human cultures have participated in **ritual mourning,** a set of symbolic rites and ceremonies associated with death. Far from being empty gestures, these rituals have clear and important functions. As sociologists Victor Marshall and Judith Levy put it, "Rituals provide a . . . means through which societies simultaneously seek to control the disruptiveness of death and to make it meaningful. . . . The funeral exists as a formal means to accomplish the work of completing a biography, managing grief, and building new social relationships after the death" (1990, pp. 246, 253).

One way in which rituals accomplish these goals is by giving the bereaved a specific role to play. The content of the role differs markedly from one culture to the next, but the clarity of the role in most cases provides a shape to the days or weeks immediately following the death of a loved person. In our culture, the rituals prescribe what one should wear, who should be notified, who should be fed, what demeanor one should show, and far more. Depending on one's religious background, one may need to arrange to sit shiva, or gather friends and family for a wake, or arrange a memorial service. One may be expected to respond stoically or to wail and tear one's hair. But whatever the social rules, there is a role to be filled that provides shape to the first numbing hours and days following the death of someone important to us.

The rituals surrounding death can also give some meaning to the death by emphasizing the meaning of the life of the person who has died. It is not accidental that most death rituals include testimonials, biographies, and witnessing. By telling the story of the person's life, by describing that life's value and meaning, the death can be accepted more readily. And of course, ceremonies can also provide meaning by placing the death in a larger philosophical or religious context.

The United States, which is known as a nation of immigrants, has a very diverse collection of funeral and mourning rituals. There are many subgroups, and Table 11.3 shows the practices of some of the major ones. As you can see, there are very large differences in the ways people express their loss and pay tribute to their loved ones.

Every culture has funeral rituals that help its members mark the passing of one of their own and console those who are bereaved.

The Process of Grieving

When the funeral or memorial service is over, what do you do then? How does a person handle the grief of this kind of loss, whether it be of a spouse, a parent, a child, a friend, or a lover? The topic of grief was dominated for many years by stage theories of various kinds, such as the ones proposed by Kübler-Ross (described earlier in the chapter) and John Bowlby, who is no doubt familiar to you from the discussion of his attachment theory in Chapter 6. Although Kübler-Ross softened the stage-like progression in her theory, Bowlby and others did not. These neoFreudian theories describe the reaction to the death of a loved one as a series of stages and state that everyone must go through all the stages in a fixed order. At any given moment in the process, the bereaved person is either in one stage or another, never in two at once. According to these theories, one cannot skip stages or return to a stage once one has left it. The result of this "grief work" is that at the end of the stages, the bereaved have adjusted to the loss and regained their normal lives.

Bowlby's theory has four stages: numbness, yearning, disorganization, and despair, followed by a time of reorganization (1980). Kübler-Ross's five stages are described earlier in this chapter. Reseach does not support the claim that these stages are experienced in the stated order or even experienced by all bereaved individuals. For example, one critic wrote:

> We are discovering that just as there are multitudinous ways of living, there are numerous ways of dying and grieving. . . . The hard data do not support the existence of any procrustean stages or schedules that characterize terminal illness or mourning. This does not mean that, for example, Kübler-Ross's "stages of dying" and Bowlby's "phases of mourning" cannot provide us with implications and insights into the dynamics and process of dying and grief, but they are very far from being inexorable hoops through

CRITICAL THINKING

Does Table 11.3 describe the experiences you have had with mourning and funeral rites in your community? What are the differences?

Table 11.3   Funeral Rituals and Practices among U.S. Cultural Groups

Cultural Group	Predominant Religious Beliefs	Mourning Traditions	Funeral Traditions
African American (in the south)	Protestant, believe that all will be reunited in heaven and that events in life are in accordance with God's plan.	Open and emotional grief by men and women. Many wear black to signify mourning.	Viewing of the body at home; large gatherings of family and community members; funeral in church with support for mourners from church "nurses." Burial in cemetery, often with deceased's favorite belongings in the casket, such as CDs, sports uniforms, trophies, and photos.
African American (immigrants from Western Africa and Caribbean West Indies)	Mostly Catholic mixed with African folk-medicine beliefs, some Protestants.	Long period of mourning and elaborate ceremonies, including prayers, drumming, and singing. Photographs are taken of the deceased. Children are included in all parts of mourning to instill respect for ancestors.	Traditional, formal funeral ceremonies conducted by males in native dialects passed down from elders. Paid for by the community and extended family. No embalming or cremation. Usually burial, but cremation sometimes allowed if remains are returned to homeland.
U.S. Latinos (Cuban, Puerto Rican, and Dominican descent)	Catholic. Believe that death is entry to heaven and that there is a continued relationship between the living and the dead.	Women express grief openly; men control emotions and remain "strong."	Open-casket wake for two days as family gathers with food, prayers, candles. Funeral is traditional mass and burial is in a Catholic cemetery.
U.S. immigrants from Muslim countries (Caribbean islands, Asian and African countries)	Islam. Believe that the purpose of life is to prepare for eternity. At death the soul is exposed to God for judgment.	Crying is acceptable, but no extreme emotional displays, such as wailing.	Burial must take place within 24 hours. Imam directs funeral. No viewing of remains, no embalming, no cremation. Deceased is buried facing Mecca. Women are not allowed to visit cemeteries.
Asian immigrants from China	Mixture of Taoism, ancestor worship, veneration of local deities, Buddhism.	The more mourners and the more emotion expressed, the more the person was loved. After the funeral, the family observes a 100-day period of mourning during which they wear a piece of colored cloth signifying their relationship to the deceased.	Determined by the age of the deceased. Children and young adults without children do not have full funeral rites. Wake takes place in the home with traditional rules about what colors different family members must wear and where people must sit. Guests donate money to help pay the expenses. Coffin goes from home to cemetery, which is on a hill. The higher the gravesite, the more prestige. The eldest son brings back earth from the grave to be used at home in a shrine to the deceased family member.
Asian immigrants from Thailand, Vietnam, Myanmar, and Cambodia	Buddhism. Believe that death is an opportunity for improvement in the next life.	Deep mourning, sometimes with somatic (bodily) symptoms.	Wake with open casket in home for one to three days. Family wears white clothing or headbands. Funeral includes altar with flowers, fruit, incense, water, and candles. Ceremony begins with one hour of chanting by priests. Mourners place pinch of ashes in a bowl and say personal prayer for the deceased. Private cremation witnessed by a priest.

Table 11.3   Funeral Rituals and Practices among U.S. Cultural Groups (*continued*)

Cultural Group	Predominant Religious Beliefs	Mourning Traditions	Funeral Traditions
Indian	Hindu. Believe that birth and death are part of a cycle. Good actions in life (kharma) lead to final liberation of the soul.	Mourning is done to let the soul know that it should depart and to let the family say goodbye.	Body is bathed and dressed in new clothes, then cremated before the next sunrise to assure the soul's transition to the next world. Family conducts rituals for 10 days, and on the 11th, the soul leaves the earth. No burial, no embalming. Children participate in all parts of the ceremony. Remains are sent to India or scattered over a river in the U.S. along with flowers.
Native American (Navajo and related tribes)	Navajo tradition mixed with Catholic and Protestant beliefs. Belief that the soul is present in the products the person created (pottery, blankets).	Mourners sprinkle dirt on the casket before burial.	Deceased is wrapped in Navajo blankets and placed in the casket. Broken pots or frayed blankets are included to help the release of the soul from these products. Also in the casket are an extra set of clothing, food, water, and personal items. Services are in English and Navajo. Burial is facing east to west. No footprints are left in the dirt around the grave to confuse spirit guide.
European Americans, Christian faith	Belief in afterlife, that friends and family will be reunited in heaven.	Mourners wear black clothing or black armbands. Some put dark wreath on the door of the deceased's home.	Gathering in a funeral home or church in the days before the funeral to console each other and pay final respects to the deceased. Sometimes the casket is open so mourners can view the body. Funeral is at church or funeral home. The clergy conducts a service with prayers and songs. Friends and family members eulogize the deceased. Catholics celebrate mass. Burial takes place after service with a short graveside ceremony. Mourners gather at the home of the deceased or close relative to have a meal and continue consolation. Cremation is more common for Protestants than Catholics.
European Americans, Jewish faith	Belief that one's good works live on in the hearts and minds of others. No specific teachings on the afterlife. Funeral is celebration of the life of the deceased.	Family "sits Shiva" for a week in the home and mourns by sitting on low stools, covering mirrors, not attending to clothing or appearance, and wearing a black ribbon or torn clothes. Friends bring food to the house and attend to the needs of the family.	Funeral and burial take place soon after death. Deceased is buried in plain shroud and simple casket to symbolize that all were created equal by God. Earth from Israel may be sprinkled on casket during burial. Family says traditional prayers for one year, after which a headstone can be put on the grave.

Source: Hazell (1997); Lobar (2006); Santillanes (1997); Techner (1997).

which most terminally ill individuals and mourners inevitably pass. We should beware of promulgating a coercive orthodoxy of how to die or mourn (Feifel, 1990, p. 540).

Some argue that it would be better to think in terms of themes or aspects rather than stages, such as themes of numbness, yearning, anger, disorganization, and despair. In the first few days or weeks after the death of a loved one, the dominant theme is likely to be numbness, with yearning coming later but perhaps not replacing numbness totally. Exhaustion may be a later theme, although yearning could also occur at that time. Like Kübler-Ross's stages of death acceptance, Bowlby's stages of mourning are perhaps best viewed as descriptors of human emotions that many people experience in bereavement, but not in totality and not in this specific order.

However, for many decades Bowlby's theory was the basis for professional understanding of grief by psychologists, counselors, healthcare professionals, and clergy. In fact, as I discussed in Chapter 10, the dominant belief was that failure to experience trauma and the proper stages of grief was a sign that normal, healthy grieving had not taken place and that some pathology was present, such as repression or denial (Rando, 1993). In these cases, clinical intervention was recommended to help the person work through hidden, unresolved grief feelings (Jacobs, 1993). The obvious alternative was that the loved one must not have been truly "loved" (Fraley & Shaver, 1999). More recently, researchers have found that many bereaved people do not follow any particular set of stages. In fact the most common reaction to grief is resilience, the maintenance of healthy functioning after a potentially traumatic event.

In a study of participants who had recently experienced the death of their spouses, almost half failed to show even mild symptoms of depression following the loss (Zisook, Paulus, Shuchter, et al., 1997). Other studies have shown that positive emotions, including genuine smiling and laughter, are not only present when the bereaved discuss their recent losses, but seem to promote well-being (Bonanno & Kaltman, 1999; Bonanno & Keltner, 1997).

In a longitudinal study, gay men who had been caregivers for their partners with AIDS were interviewed shortly after their partners' deaths. The bereaved partners' appraisals of the experience were more positive than negative; many said that they had experienced feelings of personal strength and self-growth, and that their relationship had become stronger. Twelve months later, the individuals who had been the most positive in their appraisals of the caregiving experience were more likely to show high levels of psychological well-being (Moskowitz, Folkman, & Acree, 2003). These studies and others with similar findings show that the experiences of actual bereaved people do not follow traditional theory; the typical reaction to the death of a spouse or partner was not all-encompassing negative thoughts and feelings occurring in predictable stages. Furthermore, the participants who did not follow the theory were not maladjusted or in need of clinical intervention. To the contrary, those who showed the most positive thoughts and affect were the best adjusted a year later. One problem remained—how genuine was their grief? Did they truly have a close and loving relationship with the deceased person, or did the lack of negative grief simply indicate that there wasn't much to mourn? Asking a person about a relationship with a recently deceased partner may not bring forth an honest answer.

To investigate this possibility, psychologist George Bonanno and his colleagues (Bonanno, Wortman, Lehman, et al., 2002) conducted a longitudinal study that covered the time before bereavement. They recruited 1,500 older married couples and interviewed them over the course of several years about their relationships, their attachment styles, their coping mechanisms, and their personal adjustment. During this time 205 participants experienced the death of their spouses. Using the preloss data, researchers were able

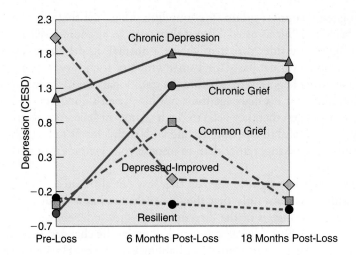

Figure 11.2 Bereaved spouses studied before loss, at the time of loss, and 18 months after loss show five distinct patterns of grief, the most common being resilience.

Source: Bonanno, Wortman, Lehman, et al. (2002).

to evaluate the quality of the marriage before the death occurred along with the adjustment of the widowed spouse for 18 months afterwards. The researchers were able to distinguish five patterns of adjustment and the preloss factors that predicted each pattern.

The results are illustrated in Figure 11.2. The most common pattern of adjustment following the death of a spouse was resilience (46 percent), followed by chronic grief (16 percent), common grief (11 percent), depressed-improved (10 percent), and chronic depression (8 percent). When the quality of the marriage was compared to the grief response, there were no differences between the top three groups (resilience, chronic grief, common grief). The one group that showed significantly low quality-of-marriage scores was the depressed-improved group, which, as you can see in the figure, had high levels of depression before the death of their spouses and improved after the spouse died. This strongly suggests that the popular view that the relative absence of grief shown by bereaved individuals is due to poor relationships before their loss is only appropriate for about 10 percent of cases.

More recently, Bonanno and his colleagues (Bonanno, Moskowitz, Papa, et al., 2005) conducted a similar study with a population of bereaved spouses, bereaved parents, and bereaved gay men, and found similar levels of resilience. They also found no association between the reaction to bereavement and the quality of relationship or the caregiver burden before death. However, there was an association between reaction to bereavement and personal adjustment, with participants who were rated more positively and better adjusted by close friends being more apt to react to the loss of a loved one with resilience.

In summary, recent research has shown that the stage theories of bereavement, such as those proposed by Bowlby and Kübler-Ross, are helpful in defining possible reactions people may have to the death of a loved one, but do not describe the common path that grief takes for the majority of bereaved individuals. Grief is highly personal and individualized. It is also complex. No doubt bereaved individuals run the gamut of reactions described by theorists, but most are not overwhelmed by their grief or unable to function in their usual roles. They have moments of yearning and despair, but they also have moments of positive feelings—of appreciation to those who offer support, words of comfort for others who share their loss, fond memories of their loved one, and even some funny stories and jokes. Grief is not an altered state of consciousness to be feared. The death of a loved one is painful, and a departed loved one will never be forgotten, but for most people, death becomes part of life, and life goes on.

How to help someone cope who has become widowed? Like many other questions in this book, the answer is, "It depends." For those who are deeply distressed or depressed, you could suggest a support group or counseling. Don't tell them to cheer up or push them to get back into "life as usual." But if they seem to be coping well and not showing high levels of grief, consider that it might be a normal, healthy reaction and don't be shocked if they host a dinner party for a small group of friends two months after the funeral. Or if a widower begins to date before the traditional year of mourning is over, don't automatically think that his marriage must not have been a good one. When people are coping well, don't suggest that they need to "let it all out" or "take time to grieve." As usual, the best way to be helpful to a person dealing with such a loss is to be highly attentive to the signals you are receiving, rather than to impose your own ideas of what is normal or expected.

Finally, let us not lose sight of the fact that loss can also lead to growth. Indeed, the majority of widows say not only that they have changed as a result of their husband's death, but that the change is in the direction of greater independence and greater skill (Wortman & Silver, 1990). Like all crises and all major life changes, bereavement can be an opportunity as well as, or instead of, a disabling experience. How we respond is likely to depend very heavily on the patterns we have established from early childhood: our temperament or personality, our internal working models of attachment and self, our intellectual skills, and the social networks we have created.

Living and Dying: A Final Word

Our understanding of death and its meaning, our attitude toward the inevitability of death, and the way we come to terms with that inevitability affect not only the way we die but the way we choose to live our lives throughout adulthood. David Steindl-Rast, a Benedictine monk, makes this point: "Death . . . is an event that puts the whole meaning of life into question. We may be occupied with purposeful activities, with getting tasks accomplished, works completed, and then along comes the phenomenon of death— whether it is our final death or one of those many deaths through which we go day by day. And death confronts us with the fact that purpose is not enough. We live by meaning" (Steindl-Rast, 1977, p. 22).

An awareness of death is thus not something we can put off until one day we hear a diagnosis of our own impending demise. It can, instead, help to define and give meaning to daily life. My grandmother's funeral was ended with the statement: "Let us go forth and celebrate life!" It is a good ending for any discussion of death.

Summary

1. Death is an inevitable fact of life, and the way we think about it, how we cope with the death of loved ones, and how we come to terms with the reality of our own ultimate deaths are topics of interest for those concerned with adult development.

2. Death has various meanings. To some it is an organizer of time, to others it is punishment (and long life is a reward). Most believe that death is a transition either to an afterlife or to a new life through reincarnation. The most pervasive meaning of death is loss—of opportunity, of relationships, of time.

3. Death anxiety has been studied extensively. We know that it occurs most strongly in middle-aged adults and people of mid-level religiosity. Presumably middle age is a time when the effects of aging become noticeable. Older adults think more about death, but have less fear. Those who are mid-level in religious beliefs seem

to fear death more because they believe there may be an afterlife but have not prepared for it. Women express more death anxiety than men, but that might reflect higher rates of anxiety in general. Those who feel a sense of purpose in life and few regrets are less likely to fear death.

4. People accept the reality of their own eventual deaths by purchasing life insurance, making wills, collecting memories, and reminiscing about their lives. In recent years, as medical technology has become able to extend life, many people have come to fear the dying process more than they fear death itself. They also have concerns about leaving family members to make the difficult decisions about such matters. A good number of adults have drawn living wills which express the limits they want in end-of-life care. Another way people prepare for eventual death is by becoming an organ transplant donor.

5. Physician Elisabeth Kübler-Ross was the first to write about the personal acceptance of death some 40 years ago. Before that time, the focus was on extending life, not accepting death. She described five stages of death reactions, and although not everyone goes through these stages, and they do not always occur in the same sequence, her descriptions are accurate and her terminology is used in every field that deals with death. The stages are denial, anger, bargaining, depression, and acceptance.

6. Elisabeth Kübler-Ross identified three key issues about the dying process: those who are dying are still alive and have unfinished needs, we need to listen to them to be able to provide the care they need, and we need to learn from the dying how to live ourselves.

7. Dying people can accept the reality of their deaths by giving farewell messages to their loved ones. These can be conversations, letters, or gifts.

8. Psychological responses to disease seems to have an effect on the course of the illness. Those who react to a diagnosis of a porentially terminal disease with positive avoidance (denial), with a fighting spirit, and even with hostility are more apt to survive than those who show anxiety, depresion, or fatalism. Another factor in a person's response to death is the amount (and quality) of social support they have.

9. Most people express the wish to die at home in familiar surroundings, but the majority die in hospitals and nursing homes. An alternative for those who have predictable terminal conditions, such as cancer, is hospice care. A hospice provides a team of professionals and volunteers who focus on pain relief, emotional support, and spiritual comfort for the patient and family, usually in their own home. The goal of hospice is not to cure the patient but to provide a good death. Families of people who have died in hospice care report significantly fewer concerns about their care than those whose family members died in hospitals, nursing homes, or at home with home nursing care.

10. A good number of people believe that they have the right to control when they die, and several countries, along with the state of Oregon, have enacted laws that allow physicians, under certain conditions, to assist dying patients in ending their lives. In 2005 this option was used by 37 people in Oregon; they tended to be younger, more educated, and more apt to have cancer than other people who died in that state in 2005.

11. A defining characteristic of our species is that we have ritual ways of dealing with the death of a member of our community. The earliest evidence of human

habitations usually consists of ancient graves with decorative objects placed around the remains. Each culture has its own traditions, and in the United States, a nation of immigrants from many cultures, there are many ways of expressing loss and grief. The only common bond is that we feel loss and grief when someone dies who has touched our lives, either directly or as a public figure.

12. There are also many ways of feeling personal grief. There is no set of stages or processes that everyone experiences, and the way one feels grief does not reflect one's bond with the deceased.

13. The most common reaction to the death of a loved one is resilience. Most people are able to function in a healthy way despite their genuine feelings of loss and sorrow. These feelings are accompanied by fond memories, concern for others, appreciation of social support, and even laughter. The pattern of bereavement is not related to the quality of the relationship before death in most cases. It is related to the quality of the bereaved person's overall adjustment.

14. Loss can lead to gains, and bereavement can lead to personal growth.

Key Terms

death anxiety, 325

religiosity, 325

sense of purpose in life, 326

reminiscense, 327

living will, 327

organ transplant donor, 327

hospice care, 332

a good death, 332

hospice approach, 333

physician-assisted suicide, 335

ritual mourning, 336

Suggested Reading

Reading for Personal Interest

Albom, M. (1997) *Tuesdays with Morrie: An old man, a young man, and life's greatest lesson.* New York: Doubleday.

The true story of the relationship between a student (now professional sportswriter Mitch Albom) and his mentor (former Brandeis sociology professor Morrie Schwartz), who has reached the end of his life and uses his impending death to continue teaching his former student. It's a small book but packed full of wisdom, honesty, and even humor.

Didion, J. (2005). *The year of magical thinking.* New York: Knopf.

Award-winning book by writer Joan Didion, who describes the year following the death of her husband, author John Gregory Dunne. This book, which has been declared a classic in grief literature, tells the honest, unflinching, heart-rending story of overwhelming personal pain at the loss of her 40-year partner in life. Although not a spiritually uplifting book, it is a skillfully written account of a year of grief.

Kessler, D. (2000). *The needs of the dying: A guide for bringing hope, comfort, and love to life's final chapter.* New York: Harper.

David Kessler is active in the hospice care field, and he wrote this book as a compassionate guide for caregivers of dying patients. He discusses pain relief, advanced directives, and how to start important end-of-life conversations.

Terkel, S. (2001). *Will the circle be unbroken? Reflections on death, rebirth, and hunger for a faith.* Waterville, ME: Thorndike Press.

Pulitzer Prize–winning writer Studs Terkel has spent a lifetime getting people to talk, and in this book he gets them to talk about death. Each chapter presents a different person, answering Terkel's questions about this topic from his or her particular point of view—bartender, hospice worker, comedian, undertaker, city sanitation worker, and more.

Classic Work

Kübler-Ross, E. (1969). *On death and dying.* New York: Macmillan.

The original major book by Kübler-Ross that significantly changed the way many physicians and other health professionals view the dying process. It is full of case material and reflects Kübler-Ross's great skill as a listener and a clinician.

Contemporary Scholarly Work

Kübler-Ross, E., & Kessler, D. (2001). *Life lessons: Two experts on death and dying teach us about the mysteries of life and living.* New York: Scribner.

Just before her own death, Elisabeth Kübler-Ross asked her friend and leader in the field of hospice care, David Kessler, to write a book with her on what may seem like the unlikely topic of life and living. However, as you will see from this book, the two experts on dying had learned much from their patients about living.

Staudinger, U. M., Freund, A. M., Linden, M., & Maas, I. (1999). Self, personality, and life regulation: Facets of psychological resilience in old age. In P. B. Baltes & K. U. Mayer (Eds.), *The Berlin aging study: Aging from 70 to 100* (pp. 302–328). Cambridge: Cambridge University Press.

Researchers from the Berlin Aging Study write about how late adulthood brings unexpected resilience.

Chapter 12

The Successful Journey

Themes of Adult Development
Young Adulthood (Age 20 to 39)
Middle Adulthood (Age 40 to 64)
Older Adulthood (Age 65 to 74)
Late Adulthood (Age 75 and Older)

Variations in Successful Development
Individual Differences in Quality of Life
Other Measures of Life Success
A Model of Adult Growth and Development: Trajectories and Pathways

Summary

Key Terms

Suggested Readings

HANK WAKES UP every morning and makes himself a glass of fresh-squeezed orange juice, commenting to the world in general, "Ah, this is the life!" He is just short of his 80th birthday and has not had an easy life. He has scars on his chin and upper lip from having an incoming shell blow up in his face as he and his regiment of Marines stormed Peleliu Island in World War II. He has scars on his chest from coronary-bypass surgery, and discolored places on his arms and legs due to the blood thinner he takes to ward off more heart trouble. He has a pacemaker and defibrillator implanted in his chest and needs surgery to have his batteries changed from time to time. He tells his great-grandsons that Grandma B. has a remote control device in her handbag, and if he gets "out of line," she will turn it on and make him behave. They think this is the funniest thing they have ever heard.

Hank raised five kids and supported them by always working at least two jobs. He married after the war and lived in his in-laws' house while he and his father built a house next door for the new family. Two years after they moved in, his father-in-law lost his eyesight (and his job) and the in-laws moved in with the new family, who now had three sons—a 2-year-old and a new pair of twins. Within three years of leaving the Marines, he was 26 and the head of a household of seven people.

When I first met Hank, he was a 60-year-old police officer—a job he did not like, but that had good pay and medical insurance, plus a chance

347

for overtime. On Saturday nights he would turn on the TV a little before 8:00 and wait for the Lotto drawing. He would pat the phone on the table next to him and say, "If I win, the first thing I will do is call the chief and put in my two-weeks notice." Then he would talk about what he would do with the winnings—buy a mansion on the hill for his wife, take a cruise around the world, send all his grandchildren to college, buy a vacation home on the beach in Florida.

Well, Hank never won the lottery, but he did leave his job when he retired a few years later, and he did buy a new house for his wife, smaller and newer than the family homestead. He started a lawn service and gave the college-aged grandkids jobs in the summer to help with their tuition. He bought a condo in Florida. He took a cruise to the Bahamas. He lives on a budget, watches his diet carefully, follows his doctor's orders strictly, and gets plenty of exercise on the small golf course near his condo. He and his wife go to concerts at the community center on Friday nights and out for pizza on Wednesdays (coupon night). He attends church and plays cards with the neighbors. He has a new cellphone with unlimited long-distance calls, so he talks to all his children and grandchildren every Sunday evening, wherever they are.

By most yardsticks, Hank's journey of adulthood has been a good one. He served his country, took care of his family, launched successful children, nurtured grandchildren, sustained a happy marriage for over 50 years, and is loved and respected by everyone who knows him. But by his own yardstick, he is the luckiest guy in the world. Hank happens to be my father-in-law, but over the years I have met many men and women like him. In spite of the headlines in the papers and the lead stories on the nightly news, the vast majority of people in this country and in developed countries all over the world are satisfied with their lives and view themselves as successful adults. This chapter is about the successful journeys of people like Hank and the millions of others of every age who greet the world each morning saying, "Ah, this is the life!"

I plan to start this chapter with a summary of the major themes of development that describe the typical person's experience on the journey of adulthood. In the earlier chapters of this book I have carved up adulthood into different topics to examine them more closely; in this chapter I will put them back together again into a chronological review that readers can relate to a little better. Our lives are not neatly sliced up in separate topics. As you have no doubt sensed throughout the book, the topics merge into each other. I'd like to present whole lives in this chapter, and how we evaluate our progress on the journey of adulthood.

Themes of Adult Development

In many of the earlier chapters I presented a review table to illustrate the major trends and age changes, so I will end the book with a mega-table showing a chronological review that spans adulthood from early adulthood (20 to 39 years) to late adulthood (75 years and over).

As always, these ages are approximate. Also note that the table describes the typical sequence of events for an adult who follows the culturally defined order of role transitions at the appropriate ages. I'll have more to say about individual pathways later in this final chapter. For now, though, it is important to think about the typical or average. The normative pattern is to marry and have one's first child in the 20s. The children then typically leave home by the time one is about 50. Most people make major career changes in their mid-60s when they retire, change to part-time work, or become volunteer workers. Each row of the table represents a highly condensed version of one facet of the change that we might see over the lifetime of a person who follows such a modal pattern.

Of the seven horizontal rows in the table, four seem to me to describe genuinely maturational or developmental sequences. Clearly, the physical and mental changes

	Early Adulthood 20–39	**Middle Adulthood** 40–64	**Older Adulthood** 65–74	**Late Adulthood** 75+
Physical change	Peak functioning in most body systems and physical abilities; optimal reproductive years; health habits established now will create pattern of later well-being.	Beginning signs of physical decline in some areas (e.g., near vision, stamina, muscle and bone mass, cardiovascular functioning). Climacteric ends reproduction for women and diminishes it significantly for men.	Physical decline more noticeable, but rate of decline is still relatively slow; reaction time slows.	Acceleration of rate of physical and health declines.
Cognitive change	Peak period of cognitive skill on most measures, fastest reaction time.	Some signs of loss of cognitive skill on fluid, timed, unexercised skills; little functional loss.	Small declines for virtually all adults on crystallized, exercised skills; larger losses on fluid skills, but rate of loss it still slow for most.	Acceleration in the rate of cognitive decline, particularly in memory.
Family and gender roles	Major family roles are acquired (e.g., spouse, parents). Advances in these areas dominate life. Clear separation of gender roles.	Launch children; postparental phase; for many, added role of caregiver for elderly family members. Grandparent role begins for most.	Grandparent role continues in importance; significantly less dominance of gender roles.	Participation in family roles declines as activities are restricted and resources are limited.
Relationships	Emphasis on forming new friendships, cohabitation, and marriage. Continued relationship with parents, siblings, and often grandparents. When children arrive, the focus turns toward parenting and away from other relationships.	Increased marital satisfaction as focus turns from parenting to other relationships. Adult children remain important. Increased importance of relationships with siblings and friends.	High marital satisfaction for those who have spouses; friendships and sibling relationships may become more intimate. Relationships with adult children frequent but not central to wellbeing.	Majority are widowed; small network of friends and siblings remain important.
Work roles	Emphasis on choosing career, changing jobs, and establishing oneself in a career.	Peak years of career success and income for most, also work satisfaction. Slight physical and cognitive decline is compensated for by increases in job expertise.	Most leave their full-time jobs and take less stressful or part-time jobs, do volunteer work, or retire entirely.	Work roles unimportant for most. Some continue to volunteer.
Personality and meaning	Establish identity and then intimacy in relationships. Increased individuality (self-confidence, independence, autonomy).	Establish generativity within family or workplace. Some sign of a softening of the individuality of the earlier period; fewer immature defenses; possibly autonomous level. Increase in spirituality for some, especially women.	Task of ego integrity; perhaps more interiority; a few may reach integrated level. Increase in spirituality for most.	Continuation of previous pattern. Increase in spirituality for most, even if outward signs decrease.
Major tasks	Renegotiate relationship with parents; form partnerships; begin family, begin career, create individual identity, strive for success in both personal and professional life.	Guide children into adulthood; cope with death of parents; strengthen marriage; redefine life goals; achieve individuality; care for aging family members.	Find alternative to lifelong job; cope with health problems of self and spouse; redefine life goals and sense of self.	Come to terms with one's own life, possibly through reviewing memories or writing a memoir. Cope with the deaths of loved ones and the eventuality of own death. Value remaining family members and friends, and other remaining joys in life.

Table 12.1   **Review of Changes in Eight Different Domains of Adult Functioning**

described in the first two rows are strongly related to highly predictable and widely shared physical processes. While the rate of change is affected by lifestyle and habits, the sequences appear to be maturational. More tentatively, I have argued that the sequences of change in personality and in systems of meaning may also be developmental in the sense in which I have used that term throughout the book. These are not strongly age-linked changes, but there is at least some evidence that they are sequential and not merely a function of particular or culture-specific changes in roles or life experiences. The remaining three rows, describing roles, tasks, and relationships, seem to describe sequences that are common insofar as they are shared by many adults in a given cohort in a given culture. If the timing or the sequence of these roles or tasks changes in any particular culture, however, the pattern described in the table changes as well.

A second way to look at the table is to read down the columns rather than across the rows. This gives some sense of the various patterns that may occur simultaneously.

Young Adulthood (Age 20 to 39)

Anyone who has been this age has probably been told by older people to enjoy it, that it is "the prime of life." This can be a frightening thought for the typical young adult who is struggling to balance school, work, and family obligations. The truth is that although young adulthood may be the time of peak performances in physical and cognitive abilities, it also is the period of adult life with the most changes. Consider that during these years, most young adults:

- Complete the major part of their education, which requires intensive learning and remembering.

- Separate from their parents, establishing an independent existence.

- Move into more major roles than at any other time in their lives: a work role, marriage, and parenthood.

- Change jobs and places of residence more frequently than any other age group.

- Have jobs that are the most physically demanding, least interesting, least challenging, and lowest paying than at any other time in their careers.

- Form romantic partnerships and select long-term partners for marriage or cohabitation relationships.

- Become parents of one or more children, participating in marathon childcare during the early years.

CRITICAL THINKING

Can you think of any other transitions that occur during young adulthood that I have missed?

Fortunately, young adults have a number of striking assets to help them deal with these high levels of demand. Most obviously, these years are the ones in which body and mind are at their peak. Neurological speed is at maximum, so physical and mental reaction time is swift; new information is learned easily and recalled easily; the immune system is at its efficient best, so that one recovers quickly from disease or injury; the cardiovascular system is similarly at its peak, so that sports can be played with speed and endurance. One feels immortal.

Young adults also deal with the changes by creating a network of friendships and other close relationships—part of what Erik Erikson talks about as the task of intimacy. Friendships are not only numerous but particularly important in these years; those who lack friendship networks report more loneliness and depressive symptoms than socially isolated people at other stages of adulthood.

Perhaps because the role demands are so powerful, the young adult's sense of himself or herself, the meaning system with which he or she interprets all these experiences, seems

Young adulthood brings the greatest number of role transitions and highest levels of demands than any other stage, but this is also a time for peak physical and mental abilities and large social networks.

to be dominated by rules, by conformity, by a sense that authority that is external to the self. We think of these years as a time when the young person is becoming independent, but in becoming independent of their parents, most young adults are not becoming individualized in the sense in which I used that term in Chapter 9. Most are still locked into a conformist view, seeing things in black-and-white terms, looking to outside authority to tell them the rules. The years of young adulthood are a time of maximal *tribalization*. We define ourselves by our tribe and our place in the tribe.

> **CRITICAL THINKING**
>
> How do you stand in relationship to your "tribe"?

The early years of young adulthood are typically spent on longer and longer periods of dependence and searching (for the right career, the right major in school, the right girl-friend or boyfriend), but the latter part of this stage is spent in overdrive. Once the course of the journey of adulthood is set, young adults usually waste no time settling into their myriad roles and working at being successful spouses, workers, and parents.

At the same time, the conventional worldview they entered adulthood with begins to give way to a more individualistic outlook. This change comes over time and seems to happen for several reasons. Among other things, we discover that following the rules doesn't always lead to reward, a realization that causes us to question the system itself. Neither marriage nor having children, for example, leads to unmitigated bliss, as evidenced by the well-replicated drop in marital satisfaction after the birth of the first child and during the period when the children are young. For those who married in their early or middle 20s, this drop in satisfaction occurs in their late 20s and 30s, contributing to a kind of disillusionment with the entire role system. A second reason for the change in perspective, I think, is that this is the time in which we develop highly individualized skills. In conforming to the external role demand that we find work and pursuing it, we also discover our own talents and capacities, a discovery that helps to turn our focus inward. We become more aware of our own individuality, more aware of the parts of ourselves that existing roles do not allow us to express.

> **CRITICAL THINKING**
>
> How would you design an experiment to test the hypothesis that workers with greater individual skills would have more individualistic worldviews?

But while the individualization process begins in our 30s, it is nonetheless true that this period of young adulthood, like the period from 18 to 25, is dominated by the social clock. In our 30s we may begin to chafe at the strictures of the roles in which we find our-selves; we may be less and less likely to define ourselves solely or largely in terms of the roles we occupy, but the role demands are still extremely powerful in this period. This fact tends to make the lives of those in young adulthood more like one another than will be true at any later point. To be sure, some adults do not follow the normative pattern, and their lives are less predictable. But the vast majority of adults do enter into the broad river of family and work roles in their 20s and are moved along with the common flow as their children grow older and their work status progresses. One of the key changes as we move into middle adult life is that the power of these roles declines; the social clock begins to be less audible, less compelling.

Middle Adulthood (Age 40 to 64)

Although the change is usually gradual rather than abrupt, the period of middle adulthood is really quite distinctly different from the years that come before. As Elizabeth Barrett Browning said in another context, "Let me count the ways."

Biological and Social Clocks. Most obviously, the biological clock begins to be audible, since it is during these years that the first signs of physical aging become apparent—the changes in the eyes that mean most adults require glasses for reading; loss of elasticity in the skin that makes wrinkles more noticeable; the diminished reproductive capacity, most notice-able for women but present for men as well; the heightened risk for major diseases, such as heart disease or cancer; the slight but measurable slowing in reaction time or foot speed; perhaps some slowing in the speed of bringing names or other specific information out of long-term memory.

The early stages of this physical aging process normally don't involve much functional loss. Mental skills may be a trifle slower but not enough slower that you can't do your job well or learn something new, such as using a palm pilot. In fact, the expertise gained from experience compensates for the physical and cognitive slowing. Achieving and maintain-ing fitness may take more work, but it's still quite possible. If you've been out of shape, you can even improve significantly, running faster or doing more pushups than you could when you were 30. But as you move through these middle years towards older adulthood, the signs of aging become more and more apparent and less and less easy to overcome.

At the same time, the social clock becomes much less significant. If you had your chil-dren in your 20s, then by your late 40s or early 50s they are likely to be on their way to independence. And in your work life you are likely to have reached the highest level that you will achieve. You know the role well, and the drive to achieve may peak and then de-cline. You may find satisfaction in the achievement of young colleagues you have mentored rather than in your own accomplishments.

If young adulthood is a time of *tribalization,* the middle years bring *detribalization,* perhaps part of a deeper shift in personality or meaning systems toward a more individ-ualistic view. The greater openness to self that emerges at this time includes an openness to unexpressed parts of the self, parts that are likely to be outside the pre-scribed roles. The change is thus both external and internal.

CRITICAL THINKING ●

Find your position on the graph shown in Figure 12.1. Can you give examples of how the biological and social clocks are influencing you at your age?

If you think about the relationship of these two clocks over the years of adulthood, you might visualize them as something like the pattern in Figure 12.1. The specific point of crossover of these two chronologies is obviously going to differ from one adult to another, but it is most likely to occur some-time in this middle-adulthood period.

Work and Marriage. One of the ironies is that the decline in the centrality of work and relationship roles in midlife is often accompanied by greater satisfaction with both work

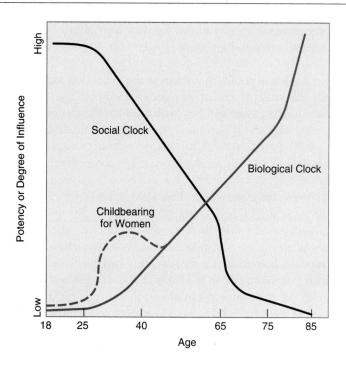

Figure 12.1 One way to think about the different phases or stages of adulthood is in terms of the relative potency or importance of the biological and social clocks. Except for the issue of childbearing for women, the biological clock is relatively unimportant until some time in midlife, after which it becomes increasingly important. The social clock follows an opposite pattern.

and relationships. You'll recall from Chapters 6 and 7 that both marital and work satisfaction rise in the years of middle adulthood. As always, there are undoubtedly many reasons for the rise, including the fact that the actual work one is doing in these years is likely to be less physically demanding, more interesting, and more rewarded than was true in young adulthood, and that once the children are older and require less hands-on parenting, one of the major strains on a marriage declines. But the improvement in satisfaction with both work and relationships may also be a reflection of the inner shift of perspective I have been talking about. Adults who experience the world from a more individualist or

Middle age brings greater career satisfaction than young adulthood, sometimes through major job changes.

conscientious perspective take responsibility for their own actions, so they may find ways to make their work and relationships more pleasant. Or they may choose to change jobs or partners.

It is precisely this sense of choice that seems to me to be a key aspect of this age period. There are certainly still roles to be filled; one does not stop being a parent just because the children have been launched; one still has work roles to fill, relationships with one's own parents, with friends, with the community. But adults in middle life have more choices about how they will fill these roles, both because the roles of this age have more leeway and because we now perceive roles differently, as being less compellingly prescriptive.

Is this picture too rosy? For those who have not been there yet, midlife sounds like the best of all worlds. And as someone who is there already, I tend to agree. In midlife we have more choices; our work and marital satisfaction is likely to rise and there is a likelihood of some inner growth or transformation as well. To be sure, there is also the growing awareness of physical aging, but for most of us such an awareness is not dominant. We still feel fit and capable. It sounds as if these years, when both the biological and the social clocks are ticking away quietly in the background, are the best of all worlds.

But isn't this also the time when the infamous midlife crisis is supposed to hit? In this more negative view of midlife, "midlife men [are seen] as anxious, conflicted, and going through a crisis. The women are menopausal, fretful, and depressed" (Hunter & Sundel, 1989, p. 13). Can these two views be reconciled? I have discussed bits and pieces of this in earlier chapters; now I need to face it more squarely.

Midlife Crisis: Fact or Myth? An interesting part of our popular culture involves the **midlife crisis,** portrayed as a time when the responsible middle-aged person (usually a man who has a lot of responsibilities) makes a 180-degree turn on the road of life and suddenly becomes irresponsible. Movies, novels, and TV shows have entertained us with stories of staid bankers who suddenly trade in their gray sedans for red sportscars and start coloring their hair. Often these crises involve leaving one's long-term spouse and becoming involved with a younger person who has a more carefree lifestyle. We may even know of middle-aged people who have had a "breakdown" of some kind and made drastic lifestyle changes as a result. But is this something that happens to a great number of people in middle age? Is it something that is more apt to happen in middle age than at other times of life? Is the midlife crisis predictable?

CRITICAL THINKING ●

Can you think of a movie or book based on the "midlife crisis"?

Scholars became interested in these questions several decades ago, and perhaps the best-known writing on the subject was presented in journalist Gail Sheehy's 1976 book, *Passages.* Using survey data from a sample of people, Sheehy reported that many middle-aged adults experience a midlife crisis which can result in either damaging or positive changes in their lives. Her book opened the topic up to the public as well as researchers. It was followed by a number of books and articles by clinicians giving accounts of their middle-class, middle-aged patients who experienced problems and unrest at this time of life. But more recently, data-based research has shown that the general population of middle-aged individuals is not more likely to suffer breakdowns and crises than adults of other ages. In fact, middle-aged people, as a group, report an increase in positive moods and a decrease in negative emotions (Mroczek & Kolarz, 1998).

For example, a recent survey of over 700 adults between 28 and 78 years of age showed that 26 percent of the respondents (both male and female in equal numbers) claimed they had experienced a midlife crisis (Wethington, 2000). When questioned more closely, the events they described were not crises, nor had they occurred at midlife. Instead, the term *midlife crisis* seems to have come to mean coping successfully with some threatening situation in one's adult life and making personal changes as a result. People reported that these events had taken place at almost any age during adulthood, though they considered them "midlife crises."

Other research evidence also casts doubt on the notion of midlife crisis. For example, researchers developed a midlife-crisis scale that included items about a sense of inner turmoil, a sense of failing power, marital dissatisfaction, and job dissatisfaction. When this scale was used in a cross-sectional study of over 500 men aged 35 to 70, they could find no age at which scores were particularly high. Some men at each age reported feelings of crisis (McCrae & Costa, 1984).

Of course, all of this is cross-sectional evidence. Studies such as these may tell us that there is no specific age at which some kind of upheaval is common, but they don't tell us whether each person, as he or she passes through the decades of midlife, is likely to have an upheaval at some time. Since the span of years we are calling *midlife* is fairly broad, it might still be that some kind of crisis is common between 40 and 64, but that it happens at different times for different adults, depending on the timing of various life changes, such as the topping out of one's career or the children leaving home.

Longitudinal evidence is obviously the best antidote to this problem. Yet here, too, there is little support for the expectation of widespread midlife crises. For instance, in an analysis of the subjects in the Berkeley and Oakland longitudinal studies, researchers found no indication of a widespread upheaval in midlife. Those who experience a genuine upheaval at this period of life, and perhaps 5 percent of the population do, are likely to be people who have experienced upheavals at other times as well (Haan, 1981). That is, the midlife crisis (along with its cousin, the empty-nest syndrome) is, to some extent, an aspect of individual personality rather than a characteristic of this particular age period.

Older Adulthood (From 65 to 74)

In many ways people in this group are more like middle-aged adults than like those in late adulthood. So why make a division at age 65? From a physical point of view there is nothing notable about age 65 that would suggest that some new stage or phase has begun. Certainly, some adults in this age range experience significant disease or chronic disability. But the norm is rather that small—albeit noticeable—physical changes or declines continue to accumulate at roughly the same rate as was true in one's middle years. Hearing loss is now more likely to become a problem, as is arthritis; one is likely to have an increased sense of being a bit slower. But for most adults (in developed countries at least) the rate of physical or mental change does not appear to accelerate in these years. What makes this 10-year period unique is the rapid drop in role demands that accompanies retirement, a drop that once again changes the balance between what I have been calling the social clock and the biological clock, as I illustrated back in Figure 12.1.

There is certainly little evidence that this change is marked by any kind of crisis. As I pointed out in Chapter 7, research on retirement shows no increase in illness or depression or other distress that can be linked causally to the retirement itself. For those who must retire because of ill health, the picture is rather different; for this subgroup retirement is linked with further declines in health and perhaps depression. But for the majority, and with the notable exception of the continuing rise in suicide among white males, every indication is that mental health is as good—or perhaps better—in this age group than at younger ages.

What does mark this change is the loss of the work role, which is of course accompanied by a continuing decline in the centrality of other roles. Spousal roles continue, of course, for those whose spouse is still living; there is still some parental role, although that too is less demanding and less clearly defined; the

CRITICAL THINKING

Explain why the family role of parent declines in older adulthood while the role of sibling becomes more central?

Older adulthood can be a time of independence and exploration as responsibilities diminish and the rules and norms become more flexible.

roles of friend and of brother or sister to one's aging siblings may actually become more central. But even more than was true in middle life, these roles are full of choices.

Late Adulthood (Age 75 and Older)

The fastest-growing segment of the U.S. population is the group in late adulthood. As life expectancy increases, more and more of us are living well past the fabled "four-score and ten" years. And as health has improved, it is often not until these years that the processes of physical and mental aging begin to accelerate. It is at this point that the functional reserve of many physical systems is likely to fall below the level required for everyday activities (Pendergast, Fisher, & Calkins, 1993), creating a new level of dependence or disability.

I do not want to make too big a deal of the age of 75. The demarcation point between the period of older adulthood and late adulthood is more a function of health than of age. Some adults may be frail at 60; others may still be robust and active at 85. But if you look at the norms, as I have been doing in this chapter, it appears that age 75 is roughly where the shift begins to takes place, at least in today's cohorts in the United States and other developed countries.

Our knowledge of late adulthood is growing. Only in recent years have there been large numbers of adults in this group; only quite recently has the Census Bureau begun to divide some of its statistics for the elderly into decades rather than merely lumping everyone over age 65 into a single category. But we do have some information that points to a qualitative change that takes place at roughly this time.

Go back and look again at Figure 4.1, for example. You'll see that the acceleration in the decline in total mental ability scores starts at about 70 or 75. There is decline before that, but the rate of decline increases in late adulthood. And as one moves into the 80s and beyond, the incidence of physical and mental frailty rises rapidly (Guralnik & Simonsick, 1993). Psychologist Edwin Shneidman (1989), writing about the decade of one's 70s, puts it this way: "Consider that when one is a septuagenarian, one's parents are gone, children are grown, mandatory work is done; health is not too bad, and responsibilities are relatively light, with time, at long last, for focus on the self. These can be sunset years, golden years, an Indian Summer, a period of relatively mild weather for both soma and psyche in the late autumn or early winter of life, a decade of greater independence and increased opportunities for further self-development" (p. 684). But what is it that adults in this period of early old age, of "Indian Summer," choose to do with their lives? Do they remain active and involved, or do they begin to withdraw, to turn inward toward self-development or reminiscence? If there is controversy about this age period, it has centered on some variant of this question. The issue is usually framed in the terms of disengagement in old age.

The term **disengagement** was first proposed by gerontologists Elaine Cumming and William Henry (1961) to describe what they saw as a key psychological process in old age. This process was seen as having three features or aspects: (1) adults' social "life space" shrinks with age, a change especially noticeable in the period from 75 on when we interact with fewer and fewer others and fill fewer and fewer roles as we move through late adulthood; (2) in the roles and relationships that remain, the aging person becomes more individualized, less governed by rules and norms; and (3) the aging person anticipates this set of changes and actively embraces them, disengaging more and more from roles and relationships (Cumming, 1975).

Few would disagree with the first two of these points. In late adulthood, most people do show a decline in the number of social activities they engage in, they occupy fewer roles, and their roles have fewer clear prescriptions. Adults of this age participate in fewer clubs or organizations, go to church less often, have a smaller network of friends. This has been found in both longitudinal studies (Palmore, 1981), and in cross-sectional ones (Morgan, 1988), so the pattern seems well established.

But the third of Cumming and Henry's points about disengagement is in considerable dispute. They argued that disengagement is not only natural but optimally healthy in late adulthood, so that those who show the most disengagement are going to be the happiest and healthiest. And this is simply not supported by the research. There is no indication that those who show the greatest decline in social activity (who "disengage" the most) are happier or healthier. On the contrary, the common finding is that the least disengaged adults report greater satisfaction with themselves and their lives, are healthiest, and have the highest morale (Adelmann, 1994; Bryant & Rakowski, 1992). The effect is not large, but the direction of the effect is consistently positive: More social involvement is linked to better outcomes.

The picture is not totally one-sided. On the other side of the ledger is a significant body of work pointing to the conclusion that solitude is quite a comfortable state for many older adults. Note, for example, that among all age groups loneliness is least common among the elderly. Indeed, some older adults clearly find considerable satisfaction in an independent, socially isolated (highly disengaged) life pattern. Clearly it is possible to choose and to find

Reduced mobility in late adulthood often results in more limited activities and smaller social networks.

contentment in a largely disengaged lifestyle in these older years. But does this mean that disengagement is necessary for mental health? On the contrary, most of the evidence says exactly the opposite. For most older adults, social involvement is both a sign of, and probably a cause of, higher levels of satisfaction. Those who do not have satisfactory contact with others, particularly with friends, are typically less satisfied with their lives. These changes appear to be part of a more general adaptive process.

Reserve Capacity and Adapting to Limitations. Psychologists Paul Baltes and Margaret Baltes (1990) suggested that one of the key features of late adulthood is that the person operates much closer to the edge of reserve capacity than is the case for younger or middle-aged adults. To cope with this fact, and with the fact of various physical declines, one must use a process that they call **selective optimization with compensation.** Older adults *select* the range of activities or arenas in which they will operate, concentrating energy and time on needs or demands that are truly central. They *optimize* their reserves by learning new strategies and keeping old skills well practiced. And when needed, they *compensate* for losses.

CRITICAL THINKING

Select a sport and then tell how an aging athlete would use selective optimization with compensation to continue their participation.

The very fact that such selection, optimization, and compensation are necessary in later adulthood is a crucial point. Reserve capacities are reduced, but it is also crucial to realize that many adults in this age group can and do compensate and adjust their lives to their changing circumstances.

Life Review. Finally, let me say just a word about another process that may be involved in the process of adaptation in late life. If you think back to my description of Erikson's theory in Chapter 8, you'll recall that the stage he proposes for late adulthood is *ego integrity versus despair.* One of Erikson's notions was that to achieve integrity, older adults must think back over their lives and try to come to terms with the person they once were and the one they are now.

Some years ago, professor of geriatric medicine Robert Butler (1993) expanded on Erikson's idea. Butler proposed that in old age, all of us go through a process he called a **life review,** in which there is a "progressive return to consciousness of past experience, and particularly, the resurgence of unresolved conflicts." Butler argued that in this final stage of life, as preparation for our now clearly impending death, we engage in an analytic and evaluative review of our earlier life. According to Butler, such a review is a necessary part of achieving ego integrity at the end of life.

This is an attractive hypothesis. Clinicians who work with the elderly have devised life-review interventions for use with older adults. Gerontologist James Birren recommends that older adults form autobiography groups and discuss various stages and turning points in their lives in order to determine how to best spend their remaining years (Birren & Feldman, 1997). And indeed, several studies show that a process of structured reminiscence may increase life satisfaction or self-esteem among older adults (Haight, 1992). However, at this point we do not know whether reminiscence is actually more common in the elderly than among the middle-aged or any other age group. We are left with many unanswered questions: Is some form of reminiscence really more common among the elderly than at other ages? How much do the elderly vary in the amount of reminiscence they engage in? How much of reminiscence is really integrative or evaluative rather than merely storytelling for amusement or information? Is reminiscence a necessary ingredient in achieving some form of integration in late life?

On the whole, I think there is good reason to doubt the validity of Butler's hypothesis that life review is a necessary part of old old age. At the same time, it is clear that some kind of preparation for death is an inevitable, or even central, part of life in these last years. Although death certainly comes to adults of all ages, most younger adults can continue to push the idea of death away: that's something for later. But in the years past 75, the imminence of death is inescapable and must be faced by each of us. Life review may be one of the ways this is done.

Variations in Successful Development

The study of adult development is based on the means of large groups of people. It gives us information on the *typical* person's life changes and the *average* type of behavior. It is important information and very useful to professionals and to the layperson who wants to learn some general truths about the development of adults in general. But for the individual reflecting on his or her own life, it is less useful. Few of us fit the average; few of us are on the typical journey of adulthood.

I opened this book in Chapter 1 with a description of my own adult journey, and as you could see, I have not practiced what I preach as typical adult development. I married early and had three children before I was 25. I spent my young adulthood as a stay-at-home mom, tending to the children and volunteering at the neighborhood library. Once they were all in school, I enrolled at the local community college, and by the time the kids were in middle school, I was writing magazine articles and teaching part-time at the university where I had received my master's degree in developmental psychology. This is certainly not the typical career path (and not a typical career). As you know from this book, I was *off-time*—younger than the parents of my children's friends and older than my fellow students.

I became a divorced mother when my youngest was still at home, and then within one wonderful year I remarried and became a grandmother for the first time. What a combination of new roles! Fortunately my new husband, a professor of child development, saw instant grandfatherhood as a bonus. At 50, I enrolled in a Ph.D. program and three years later marched down the aisle to Elgar's *Pomp and Circumstance* at the University of Georgia to be hooded in red and black, with four generations of relatives applauding.

My own version of the journey of adulthood has been interesting, but it was not easy. I am tempted to add the warning: *do not try this yourselves!* But few of us have master plans for our lives. Most of us make one small decision at a time, and sometimes we are a bit surprised when we look back and see what the big picture looks like. Today I teach part-time at the university where my husband is a professor. I revise this book every 3 or 4 years, often working on a laptop as I accompany my husband on his travels around the world. I keep involved with my parents, my three sisters, my adult children, and my grandchildren—all eight of them.

In contrast, the author emeritus of this book, Helen Bee, was atypical in her own way as she moved through adulthood. She completed her education and launched her career "on-time," but then, in her 30s, lightened her academic work load and put her energy into more domestic pursuits. She married and became an instant mother by adopting her husband's two young children. At the age that I was raising children full-time, Helen was in graduate school, and when I started my college career, she was a new mother. I used volunteer work in my 20s to keep in touch with the outside world; Helen uses it in her 60s as a tasty dessert after her successful career. At the age that I received my Ph.D., Helen was simplifying her professional life and branching out in a variety of new areas—singing in a choral group, volunteering at a spiritual camp, getting involved in political campaigns. She asked me to help with the fourth edition of her textbook and our separate but atypical paths converged for a time. Beginning with the fifth edition, she was fully retired from writing textbooks and I was in charge (although the spirit of this book will always be Helen's).

Two people on greatly different journeys, but both successful and satisfied with their lives. I'm sure you can describe other people, such as Hank from the opening of this chapter, who have taken yet different roads and are still good examples of "successful aging." And no doubt your own journey of adulthood has aspects that do not fit the typical. Knowing all about the means and the norms of adult development still leaves some questions. To fully understand the process of adult development and change, we also have to understand the ways in which individual's lives are likely to differ, the variations in their reactions to the stresses and challenges they will encounter, and the eventual satisfaction or inner growth they may achieve.

CRITICAL THINKING ●

Think of two people you know of similar ages whose journeys of adulthood have been vastly different so far. How do you think they will compare in the future?

Reaching such understanding is as immense a task as the diversity is great. But let me offer two approaches, beginning with an exploration of the literature explaining individual differences in what has come to be called *quality of life* (Achenbaum, 1995) or its close cousins, *subjective well-being* (Pinquart & Soerensen, 2000) and *successful aging* (Baltes & Baltes, 1990; Rowe & Kahn, 1998), and concluding with my own attempt at a model of both normative and individual aging.

Individual Differences in Quality of Life

- *Health and socioeconomic status.* The strongest predictor of quality of life for adults under 65 is socioeconomic status (income and education). The strongest predictor for adult over 65 is health, with socioeconomic status coming in second. When these factors are considered, quality-of-life differences between other groups become weaker. In this sense, socioeconomic status (SES) and health are *proximal predictors;* they play intervening roles between quality of life and other more *distal predictors,* such as age, gender, race/ethnicity, and marital status (George, 2006). This will be explained in more detail below.

- *Age.* Recent research has shown consistently that the older one is, the higher one's quality of life. This has been found in both cross-sectional studies and longitudinal studies, although longitudinal studies show a peak at age 65 and a slight decline afterwards (Mroczek & Spiro, 2005). However, this can be explained by the increase in chronic health problems after 65 and the decrease in socioeconomic status for people in this age group.

- *Gender.* Women under 65 report higher quality of life than men in this age group, but women 65 and over report lower quality of life than their male counterparts (Pinquart & Soerensen, 2001). This, again, can be partially explained by socioeconomic differences (women have lower incomes than men in older adulthood) and health (women in older adulthood have more chronic illnesses), and also the fact that women in older adulthood are more apt to experience the death of their spouses.

- *Race and ethnicity.* These factors do not relate to quality of life, and when some relationship is shown, it can be accounted for by socioeconomic status (Krause, 1993).

- *Marital status.* Married people have higher quality of life than unmarried people, and this has been found for adults in 45 different countries (Pinquart & Soerensen, 2001; Diener, Gohm, Suh, et al., 2000). This can be partially explained by socio-economic differences (married people have higher incomes than single people). When these data are examined by age, though, this is stronger among young and middle-aged adults than those in older or late adulthood. In fact, researchers report that widows report a 1- to 2-year decline in quality of life following the death of their husbands, with a return to their prewidowhood quality of life afterwards (Lucas, Clark, Georgellis, et al., 2003).

- *Activities.* In a nutshshell, quality of life is related to any kind activity—physical, social, or any combination of the two. And these results are found in cross-sectional (Warr, Butcher, & Robertson, 2004) and longitudinal studies (Menec, 2003). People who do more things enjoy a higher quality of life than those who are more sedentary and isolated.

- *Social integration.* Adults who have multiple roles report higher levels of well-being than those who have few roles, unless their roles bring additional stress, such as becoming a caregiver for a spouse or parent (Pinquart & Soerensen, 2003). And as reported in Chapter 10, attending religious services is a strong predictor of positive well-being and quality of life in adults (Kirby, Coleman, & Daley, 2004). Several longitudinal studies show that volunteering is important for quality of life in adults, especially those 65 and older (George, 2006). And not surprisingly, a meta-analysis of almost 300 studies shows that social support is strongly related to quality of life, both in the quantity of significant others and the quality of the relationships (Pinquart & Soerensen, 2000).

- *Psychosocial factors.* Adults who have a strong *sense of control* over their lives (also expressed as mastery, self-efficacy, and cognitive hardiness) enjoy a higher quality of life at every age than those who do not share this feeling (George, 2006). As discussed in Chapter 10, people who have a strong sense of meaning (also expressed as sense of coherence, a perception of life as predictable and manageable) report higher quality of life than others (Ardelt, 2003).

- *Social comparisons.* It seems to be part of our human character to compare ourselves to others, especially on aspects of ourselves that aren't easily measured, such as quality of life. This may be one of the reasons that older adults consider themselves as enjoying a high level of well-being and good health even though their health is not as good as it was in earlier adulthood and their activities and social circles are limited. The trick seems to be comparing oneself with others in the same age group. "Compared to others my age, I'm doing great!" This was demonstrated in several studies of older adults that showed they were more apt to compare themselves to others who are less advantaged than they are (Gana, Alaphilippe, & Bailey, 2004; Beaumont & Kenealy, 2004). Young and middle-aged adults were more likely to compare themselves to others who are more advantaged (thus deflating their quality-of-life assessments).

- *Cultural differences.* Surveys conducted in the United States over the past 50 years have shown that a stable 85 percent of people rate their lives as "satisfying" or "very satisfying" (Diener & Diener, 1996). This stability has been found for European countries as well, with more affluent countries (such as Germany and Denmark) having larger percentages of satisfied or very satisfied people and less affluent countries (such as Portugal and Greece) having smaller percentages (Fahey & Smyth, 2004).

Psychologist Bruce Kirkcaldy and his colleagues (Kirkcaldy, Furnham, & Siefen, 2004), examined data from 30 developed and developing countries to determine what factors were responsible for the differences in well-being reported by people in those countries. They examined economic factors (e.g., economic growth and gross national product indices), health indicators (e.g., life expectancy and disability rates), and educational attainment (e.g., literacy). The strongest predictor of well-being was literacy. The countries that had the highest scores on tests of reading, science, and math literacy were the ones in which the people reported the highest levels of well-being and happiness. Conversely, the countries that scored the lowest on these three literacy measures were more apt to have the lowest levels of well-being and happiness. (The top-performing countries on the literacy measures were Japan, South Korea, Finland, Canada, and New Zealand; the lowest were Brazil, Mexico, Luxembourg, Latvia, and Greece.) Economic and health factors were not valid predictors of well-being for either developed or developing countries. The researchers concluded that the finding that people living in countries with prosperous economies report greater levels of well-being is due more to the better educational systems and higher literacy rates than the gross national product or health care systems of those countries.

And finally, in a study that examined cross-cultural quality of life for adults of various ages, researchers found that older adults report the same levels of well-being and happiness as younger adults regardless of what political structures they live in and their country's economic resources (Diener & Suh, 1998).

In summary, quality of life in adulthood is determined largely by health, income, education, and the people we choose to compare ourselves with. Another contributing factor is having a sense of control, meaning, or purpose in one's life. It is probably more informative to list the factors that don't matter much: age, race and ethnicity, living in a country with good health care, living in a country with a healthy economy. And factors that matter somewhat (but are probably part of health, income, and education) are gender, marital status, activities, religious participation, and living in an affluent country. I look forward to a comprehensive study that will take all these factors into account and give us a model showing the proximal and distal effects of quality of life in adulthood.

Other Measures of Life Success

The quality of life that individuals report is one of the best measures of success in the adult years. But there are other ways of defining successful adulthood that rely on professional assessments of psychological health or on objective measures of life success. Two approaches, both involving analyses of rich longitudinal data, are particularly interesting.

Researchers working with the Berkeley longitudinal data have developed a measure of ideal adult adjustment that they call *psychological health*. In this research, psychotherapists and theorists agreed that the pattern of qualities of an optimally healthy person includes the capacity for work and satisfying relationships, a sense of moral purpose, and a realistic perception of self and society. According to this view, adults who are psychologically healthy show a great deal of warmth, compassion, dependability and responsibility, insight, productivity, candor, and calmness. They value their independence and autonomy as well as their intellectual skill and behave in a sympathetic and considerate manner, consistent with their personal standards and ethics (Peskin & Livson, 1981).

In one study, the participants received scores evaluating their psychological health. When this measure was correlated with self- reports of satisfaction with work, family life, and marriage, participants who had been rated by the professionals as having higher levels of psychological health were found to have reported themselves as more satisfied with their lives.

Psychiatrist George Vaillant and social worker Caroline Vaillant (1990) approached the definition of successful aging somewhat differently in their studies of the Harvard men included in the Grant study. They searched for a set of reasonably objective criteria reflecting what they call *psychosocial adjustment* and then investigated what factors in the men's childhood or adult lives predict good or poor psychosocial adjustment.

Despite their quite different strategies for measuring successful aging, the findings from the Berkeley and Grant studies are reasonably consistent and lead to some intriguing suggestions about the ingredients of a healthy or successful adult life. Both studies show that the most successful and well-adjusted middle-aged adults had grown up in warm, supportive, intellectually stimulating families. In the Berkeley study, researchers found that those who were higher in psychological health at age 30 or 40 had grown up with parents who were rated as more open-minded and more intellectually competent, with good marital relationships. Their mothers had been warmer, more giving and nondefensive, more pleasant and poised (Peskin & Livson, 1981). Similarly, the men who were rated as having the best adjustment at midlife had come from warmer families and had had better relationships with both their fathers and mothers in childhood than had the least well-adjusted men (Vaillant, 1974).

Both studies also show that well-adjusted or successful middle-aged adults began adulthood with more personal resources, including better-rated psychological and physical health at college age, a practical, well-organized approach in college (Vaillant, 1974), and greater intellectual competence (Livson & Peskin, 1981). Both of these sets of findings are pretty much what we might expect. To put it most directly, those who age well are those who start out well. To be sure, none of the correlations is terribly large, so even among the midlife subjects there were some who began with two strikes against them but nonetheless looked healthy and successful at 45 or 50, and some who started out with many advantages but did not turn out well. But in general, the findings point to a kind of consistency.

Yet when the researchers looked at their subjects again at retirement age, a very different picture appeared. Among these 173 men, no measure of early family environment remained a significant predictor of psychosocial adjustment at 63, nor did any measure of early-adult intellectual competence. Those who turned out to be "successful" 63-year-olds had been rated as slightly more personally integrated when they were in college, and they had had slightly better relationships with their siblings. But other than that, there were simply no childhood or early-adulthood characteristics that differentiated those who had turned out well and those who had turned out less well (Vaillant & Vaillant, 1990).

What does predict health and adjustment at age 63 among these men is health and adjustment at midlife. The least successful 63-year-olds were those who had used mood-altering drugs at midlife (primarily prescribed drugs intended to deal with depression or anxiety), abused alcohol or smoked heavily, and used mostly immature defense mechanisms in their 30s and 40s.

These findings come from only a single study, one that only included men, and only very well-educated professional men at that. So we shouldn't make too many huge theoretical leaps from this empirical platform. Still, the pattern of results suggests one (or both) of two possibilities:

1. It may be that each era in adult life simply calls for different skills and qualities, so that what predicts success or healthy adjustment at one age is simply not the same as what predicts it at another age. As one example, college-aged intellectual competence may be a better predictor of psychosocial health at midlife simply because at midlife adults are still in the midst of their most productive working years, when intellectual skill is more central. By retirement age, this may not be so critical an ingredient.

2. Alternatively, we might think of a successful adult life not as something foreordained by one's childhood or early-adult qualities, but as something created out of the resources and opportunities available over the course of the decades. Those who start out with certain familial and personal advantages have a greater chance of encountering still further advantages, but it is what one does with the experiences—stressful as well as constructive—that determines the long-term success or psychosocial health one achieves. The choices we make in early adulthood help to shape the people we become in midlife; our midlife qualities in turn help to shape the kind of older people we become—a process I might describe as cumulative continuity. Early-childhood environment or personal qualities such as personality or intellectual competence are not unimportant, but by age 65 their influence is indirect rather than direct.

It seems likely that both of these options are at least partially true, but it is the second possibility that I find especially compelling. It helps to make sense out of a series of other facts and findings.

One relevant fragment comes from yet another longitudinal study in which George Vaillant has been involved, in this case of a group of 343 Boston men, all white, and nearly all from lower-class or working-class families. As teenagers, these men had been part of a nondelinquent comparison group in a major study of delinquency originated by criminologists Sheldon Glueck and Eleanor Glueck (1950, 1968). They had been interviewed at length when they were in early adolescence and were then reinterviewed by the Gluecks when they were 25, and 31, and by Vaillant and his colleagues when they were in their late 40s. In one analysis by the Vaillant group (Snarey, Son, Kuehne, et al., 1987), the researchers looked at the outcomes for those men who had not had children at the normative time to see how they had handled their childlessness.

Of the group of childless men, those independently rated at age 47 as clearly generative in Erikson's terms were likely to have responded by finding someone else's child to parent, such as by adopting a child, joining an organization like Big Brothers/Big Sisters, or becoming an active uncle. Those childless men who were rated low in generativity at 47 were much less likely to have adopted a child; if they had chosen a substitute it was more likely a pet. Among the childless men, the generative and the nongenerative had not differed at the beginning of adult life in either social class or level of industry, so the eventual differences in psychosocial maturity do not seem to be the result of differences that existed at age 20. Rather, they seem to be a result of the way the men responded to or coped with an unexpected or nonnormative event in early adult life, namely childlessness.

The central point is that there are many pathways through adulthood. The pathway each of us follows is affected by the departure point, but it is the choices we make as we go along, and our ability to learn from the experiences that confront us, that shapes the people we become 50 or 60 years later. If we are going to understand the journey of adulthood, we need a model that will allow us to make some order out of the diversity of lifetimes that results from such choices and such learning or lack of it. So as a final step in the synthesis I have been attempting in this final chapter, let me try my hand at a more general model.

A Model of Adult Growth and Development: Trajectories and Pathways

Let me offer a set of four propositions. The first takes us back to many of the points I made earlier in this chapter as I summarized the information we have on normative or common pathways:

CRITICAL THINKING ●

Give an example of a shared developmental process that is age-linked. What about processes that are not age linked?

Proposition 1. There are shared, basic sequential physical and psychological developments occurring during adulthood, roughly (but not precisely) age-linked.

Whatever other processes may influence adult life, it is clear that the entire journey occurs along a road that has certain common features. The body and the mind change in predictable ways with age. These changes, in turn, affect the way adults define themselves and the way they experience the world around them. As I said earlier in the chapter, I place the sequence of changes in self-definition or meaning system outlined by Loevinger, Fowler, and others in the same category. The difference is that unlike physical and mental changes, the process of ego development or spiritual change is not an inevitable accompaniment of aging, but a possibility or potentiality.

Within the general confines of these basic processes and sequences of development, however, there are many individual pathways—many possible sequences of roles and relationships, many different levels of growth or life satisfaction or "success." Which brings me to the second major proposition:

Proposition 2: Each adult's development occurs primarily within a specific pathway or trajectory, strongly influenced by the starting conditions of education, family background, ethnicity, intelligence, and personality.

I can best depict this individuality by borrowing biologist Conrad Waddington's image of the epigenetic landscape, a variation of which is shown in Figure 12.2 (Waddington, 1957). Waddington introduced this idea in a discussion of the strongly "canalized" development of embryos, but the same concept can serve for a discussion of adult development. The original Waddington image was of a mountain with a series of gullies running down it. He demonstrated how a marble placed at the top had an almost infinite number of possibilities for its final destination at the bottom of the mountain, due to the many possible intersections of gullies and ravines. However, because some of the gullies are deeper than others, some outcomes have a greater probability than others. In my version of this metaphor, the bottom of the mountain represents late adulthood, while the top of the mountain represents young adulthood. In our adult years, each of us must somehow make our way down the mountain. Since we are all going down the same mountain (following the same basic "rules" of physical, mental, and spiritual development), all journeys will have some features in common. But this metaphor also allows for wide variations in the specific events and outcomes of the journey.

Imagine a marble placed in one of the gullies at the top of the mountain. The pathway it follows to the bottom of the mountain will be heavily influenced by the gully in which it starts. If I also assume that the main pathways are deeper than the side tracks, then shifting from the track in which one starts is less probable than continuing along the same track. Nonetheless, the presence of choice points or junctions makes it possible for marbles starting in the same gully to end up in widely varying places at the bottom of the

CRITICAL THINKING

Give an example of a deep main pathway you have been on and a choice point you reached to change paths? How would you describe the effort involved in moving from a deep gully to an alternative pathway?

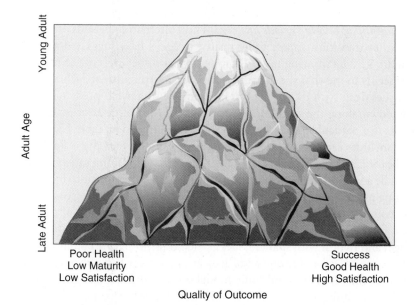

Figure 12.2 One way to illustrate the journey of adulthood is with the image of a mountain landscape. One begins the journey at the top and follows along in the ravines and gullies toward the bottom. There are many options and alternative paths, and the landscape changes as cultural and social changes occur.

Source: Adapted from Waddington, (1957).

mountain. From any given starting point, some pathways and some outcomes are much more likely than others. But many possible pathways diverge from any one gully. In addition, the landscape is constantly shifting in response to environmental changes, such as cultural or historical influences and changes in health.

This model or metaphor certainly fits with the general findings from Vaillant's long-term study of the Grant study men. The gully one starts in certainly does have an effect on where you are likely to be on the mountain at midlife. But the eventual endpoint is much more strongly linked to where you were at midlife than where you started out. One might depict this thought using the mountain-and-gully model by showing the main gullies becoming deeper and deeper (harder to get out of) as you trace them down the mountain.

The model also fits with another finding I mentioned earlier in this chapter, that there is an increase in the variability of scores on various measures of health, mental skill, personality, and attitudes with increasing age. In early adulthood, the various alternative gullies are more like each other (closer together) than is true 40 or 60 years later.

Still another feature implicit in Figure 12.2 as I have drawn it is significant enough to state as a separate proposition:

Proposition 3: Each pathway is made up of a series of alternating episodes of stable life structure and disequilibrium.

In the mountain-and-gully metaphor, the stable life structures are reflected in the long, straight stretches between junction points; the junctions represent the disequilibria. I conceive of each stable life structure as the balance one achieves among the collection of role demands one is then facing, given the skills and temperamental qualities at one's command. This balance is normally reflected in a stable, externally observable life pattern: getting up at a particular time every day to get the kids off to school, going off to your job, doing the grocery shopping on Saturday, having dinner with your mother every Sunday, going out to dinner with your spouse every Valentine's Day. It is also reflected in the quality and specific features of relationships and in the meaning system through which we filter all these experiences. These patterns are not totally fixed, of course. We all make small adjustments regularly, as demands or opportunities change. But there do appear to be times in each adult's life when a temporary balance is achieved.

The Relationship of Stable Periods and Age. These alternating periods of stability and disequilibrium or transition appear to be related to age. I have suggested a rough age linkage in Figure 12.2 by showing more choice points at some levels of the mountain than at others. It seems to me that the content of the stable structures at each approximate age, and the issues dealt with during each transition, are somewhat predictable. After all, we are going down/along the same mountain. There is a set of tasks or issues that confront most adults in a particular sequence as they age, as I outlined in Table 12.1. In early adulthood this includes separating from one's family of origin, creating a stable central partnership, bearing and beginning to rear children, and establishing satisfying work.

In middle adulthood the tasks include launching one's children into independence, caring for aging parents, redefining parental and spousal roles, exploring one's own inner nature, and coming to terms with the body's aging and with the death of one's parents. An adult who follows the modal "social clock" will thus be likely to encounter transitions at certain ages and to deal with shared issues at each transition. But I am not persuaded that there is only one order, or only one set of ages, at which these tasks are or can be confronted. In this respect the mountain-and-gully model is misleading, since it does not convey the variability in the timing of major choice points, such as what happens when an adult does not marry, does not have children until his or her 30s or 40s, or becomes physically disabled or widowed or ill in the early adult years, or the like. But whatever the variations in timing, it still appears to me to be valid to describe adult life as alternating between periods of stability and transition.

Turning Points. The periods of disequilibrium, which we might think of as turning points in individual lives, may be triggered by any one or more of a whole series of events. There is no way to depict these in the mountain-and-gully model, so I have to turn to a more common kind of two-dimensional diagram, the (very complicated!) flowchart or path diagram shown in Figure 12.3. The major sources of disequilibrium, listed on the left-hand side of the figure, are the following:

- *Asynchrony of developmental patterns* in the several different dimensions of adult change or growth. When physical development, or mental development, or role patterns are "out of sync," there is tension or disequilibrium in the system. Being significantly off-time in any one dimension of adulthood automatically creates asynchrony and is thus associated with higher rates of stress. Having a first child in your late 30s is not only a role change but an asynchronous role change, which should increase the likelihood of a major disequilibrium, just as will the failure to have children at all, as among the childless men in the Glueck/Vaillant study of working-class men mentioned earlier. The general rule, as I have indicated, is that on-time role changes seldom trigger major crises or self-reexamination precisely because they are shared with one's peers. You can easily explain both the change and the strain it may cause as originating "outside" yourself. Nonnormative changes, by contrast, are difficult to explain away except with reference to your own choices or failures or successes. These more individual experiences, then, are far more likely than the normative ones to bring about reassessment or redefinition of the self, of values, of systems of meaning.

- *Role transitions,* such as becoming a spouse or a parent, the departure of the last child from home, retirement, and changes in jobs.

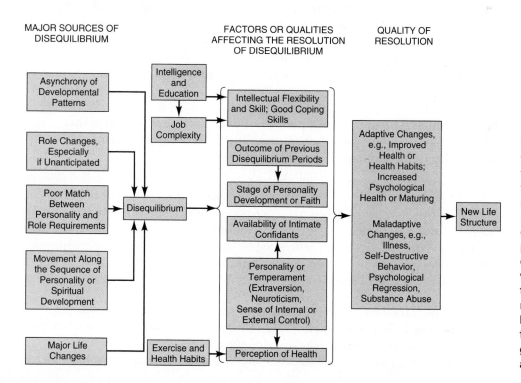

Figure 12.3 I know this is complicated, but take a crack at it anyway. This is a model of disequalibrium and its resolution. I am suggesting that such a process occurs repeatedly during adulthood, with the effects of these transitions accumulating over time. Each such transition affects the pathway (the gully) along which the adult then moves.

- *Poor match between personality and role requirements.* This is, in some sense, another kind of asynchrony. For example, research shows that adults who looked psychologically healthy at 50 but had shown signs of distress or disturbance at 40 were likely to have had qualities as teenagers that didn't match the then-prevalent gender roles. The less social and more intellectual young women in this group tried to fit into a mold of full-time homemaking and found it distressing; the more creative and emotional men tried to fit into the mold of the gray-flannel-suit society and were disturbed at 40. Both groups went through a process in their 40s of freeing themselves of the constraints of those early, ill-fitting roles and emerged at 50 looking very much put together (Livson, 1981).

- *Personality or spiritual development* can trigger disequilibrium, such as any movement along the dimensions described by Erikson or by Fowler's stages of faith. Such inner changes typically occur in response to the disequilibrium-causing agents I have just described. But once begun, a transition, say from conformist to conscientious ego structure, or from individuative to conjunctive faith, carries its own disequilibrium. Any new stable life structure that emerges at the end of the disequilibrium period must be built on the new sense of self, or faith, that has evolved.

- *Major life changes,* particularly losses in relationships, such as the death of a close family member or friend or the loss of a friendship or love relationship. While unanticipated or off-time changes may be the most difficult in most instances, anticipated changes that involve such relationship losses, such as the death of your parents when you are in your 40s or 50s, still call for significant reassessment and reorganization.

Whether a person will experience a disequilibrium period as a crisis or merely as a rather transitory phase seems to depend on at least two things: the number of different sources of disequilibrium and the individual's own personality and coping skills. When there is a pileup of disequilibrium-producing events within a narrow span of years, such as changes in roles, major relationship losses, and asynchronous physical changes, anyone is likely to experience a major transition. But the tendency to respond to this pileup as a crisis may also reflect relatively high levels of neuroticism, low levels of extraversion, or the lack of effective coping skills.

In the model I am proposing here, it is our response to these disequilibrium periods that determines our pathway down the mountain, which leads me to the fourth basic proposition:

Proposition 4: The outcome of periods of disequilibrium may be either positive (psychological growth, maturity, improved health), neutral, or negative (regression or immaturity, ill health).

What kind of outcome occurs at any choice point—which channel one follows—is determined or affected by the wide range of variables sketched in the middle of Figure 12.3. Intellectual flexibility or skill seems to be an especially critical ingredient in leading to the "higher" stages of maturity and growth that Vaillant and Loevinger describe. Our adult intellectual flexibility, in turn, is influenced by the complexity of the environments in which we live, particularly the complexity of job (either a job outside the home or even the complexity of housework). Sociologist Janet Giele (1982) puts it well:

It is the degree of social complexity on the job or in other aspects of everyday life that appears critical. Those who must learn a great deal and adapt to many different roles seem to be the most concerned with trying to evolve an abstract self, conscience, or life structure that can integrate all these discrete events. By contrast, those with a simple job, limited by meager education and narrow contacts, are less apt to experience aging as a process that enhances autonomy or elaborates one's mental powers (p. 8).

And, of course, job complexity is itself partially determined by the level of original education we have attained. Well-educated adults are more likely to find complex jobs and are thus more likely to maintain or increase their intellectual flexibility. Linkages such as these help to create the pattern of predictability between early adulthood and midlife, but since none of these relationships is anywhere near a perfect correlation, there is a good deal of room for shifts from one gully to another. Some blue-collar jobs, for example, are quite complex, while some white-collar jobs are not, and such variations may tend to push people out of the groove in which they started.

Underlying temperamental tendencies are another key ingredient. Adults who are high in what Costa and McCrae call *neuroticism* appear to be more likely to respond to disequilibrium by increases in substance abuse, illness, depression, or regressive patterns of defense. Adults with less neurotic or more extraverted temperaments, in contrast, respond to disequilibrium by reaching out to others, by searching for constructive solutions.

The availability of close supportive confidants is also a significant factor, clearly not independent of temperament. Adults who lack close friends or the supportive intimacy of a good marriage are more likely to have serious physical ailments in midlife, or to have significant emotional disturbances, to drink or use drugs, and to use more immature forms of defense. Friendless or lonely adults more often come from unloving and unsupportive families, but a poor early environment can be overcome more readily if the adult manages to form at least one close, intimate relationship. Vaillant (1977) describes several men in the Grant study who had grown up in unloving or highly stressful families, and were withdrawn or even fairly neurotic as college students, but nonetheless went on to become "successful" and emotionally mature adults. One of the common ingredients in the lives of these men, especially compared to those with similar backgrounds who had poorer outcomes, was the presence of a "healing" relationship with a spouse. Similarly, sociologist David Quinton and his colleagues looked at the adult lives of several groups of young people in England, some of whom had had teenage histories of delinquency (Quinton, Pickles, Maughan, et al., 1993). They found that a continuation of problem behavior (such as criminality) was far less likely when the person had a nondeviant, supportive partner than when the problem teen later joined up with a nonsupportive or problem partner. Thus early maladaptive behavior can be redirected, or "healed," through an appropriately supportive partner relationship. Health may also make some difference in the way an adult responds to a period of disequilibrium. Poor health reduces options; it also reduces your level of energy, which affects the range of coping strategies open to you or the eventual life structures you can create.

Cumulative Effects of Transitions. As a final point, I would argue that the effects of these several disequilibrium periods are cumulative, a process that sociologist Gunhild Hagestad and psychologist Bernice Neugarten (1985) describe as the "transition domino effect." The cumulative effect of earlier stages or transitions is a key element in Erikson's theory of development, as you will recall from Chapter 8. Unresolved conflicts and dilemmas remain as unfinished business—excess emotional baggage that makes each succeeding stage more difficult to resolve successfully. Vaillant and others who have studied adults from childhood through midlife have found some support for this notion. Harvard men in the Grant study who could reasonably be described as having failed to develop trust in their early childhood did have many more difficulties in the first few decades of adulthood. They were more pessimistic, self-doubting, passive, and dependent as adults and showed many more maladaptive or unsuccessful outcomes compared to those with more trusting childhoods.

Other forms of cumulative effect operate as well. One major off-time experience early in life, for example, may trigger a whole series of subsequent off-time or stressful experiences. The most obvious example is the impact of adolescent parenthood, which often leads to early school departure, which in turn affects the complexity of the job one is likely to find, which affects intellectual flexibility, and so on through the years.

Adaptive or Maladaptive Outcomes Versus Happiness. It is important to emphasize that the range of possible outcomes I have labeled adaptive and maladaptive changes are not identical to happiness and unhappiness. Maladaptive changes such as illness, substance abuse, suicide attempts, or depression obviously are correlated with unhappiness. But such adaptive changes as improved health habits, increased social activity, or movement along the sequence of stages of ego or spiritual development are not uniformly associated with increases in happiness. For example, McCrae and Costa (1983) did not find that adults at the conscientious or higher levels of ego development reported any higher life satisfaction than did adults at the conformist stage. Thus profound changes can result from a disequilibrium period without being reflected in alterations of overall happiness or life satisfaction. Instead, a change in ego development stage may alter the criteria of happiness one applies to one's life. As McCrae and Costa say:

> We suggest that the quality and quantity of happiness do not vary with levels of maturity, but that the circumstances that occasion happiness or unhappiness, the criteria of satisfaction or dissatisfaction with life, may vary with ego level. The needs and concerns, aspirations and irritations of more mature individuals will doubtless be different—more subtle, more individualistic, less egocentric. The less psychologically mature person may evaluate his or her life in terms of money, status, and sex; the more mature, in terms of achievement, altruism, and love. (1983, p. 247).

Maturing does not automatically make an adult happy, as demonstrated by (among other things) the lack of correlation between age and happiness. Maturing and other adaptive changes alter the agenda and thus alter the life structures we create and the way we evaluate those life structures.

I am sure it is clear to you already that the model I have sketched in this chapter, complex as it is, is nonetheless too simplistic. It is doubtless also too culture-specific, although I have tried to state the elements of the model broadly enough to encompass patterns in other cultures. It may also be quite wrong in a number of respects. Among other things, I have assumed throughout this discussion that something like Loevinger's sequence of ego development stages actually exists, and that all adults mature in this pattern if they mature at all. But as you know from Chapters 8 and 9, that assumption is based on slim evidence.

Despite these obvious limitations, however, the model may give you some sense of the rules or laws that seem to govern the richness and variety of adult life. In the midst of a bewildering array of adult patterns there does appear to be order, but the order is not so much in fixed, age-related sequences of events as in process. To understand adult development, it is useful to uncover the ways in which all the pathways, all the gullies, are alike. But it is equally important to understand the factors and processes that affect the choices adults will have and the way they will respond to those choices as individuals. Perhaps the most remarkable thing about this journey is that, with all its potential pitfalls and dilemmas, most adults pass through it with reasonable happiness and satisfaction, acquiring a modicum of wisdom on the way to pass along to those who travel behind them.

May your journey be successful!

Summary

1. To understand adult development, it is important to divide it into topics, as is done in the other chapters of this book. But it is also important to put it back together again and view people as wholes.

2. Young adulthood is the time of peak physical and cognitive abilities. Some decline begins as early as 30, but it is not noticeable except for top-performing athletes. This period is the time of peak role transitions, relationship formation, and tribalization (a sense of belonging to a group).

3. Middle adulthood is the time in which the biological clock begins to tick noticeably. The first signs of physical aging appear, and the first signs of cognitive decline, though it is slight. Reproductive ability declines for both men and women, and then ends for women. The social clock becomes less loud. There is more flexibility in family roles and careers. There is time to question the rules and actions of the tribe and to become more of an individual.

4. Although middle adulthood is known as a time of crisis, this myth does not stand up to empirical research.

5. The hallmark of older adulthood is retirement. There is little biological difference between this group and those in middle adulthood, but the social differences can be significant if retirement is considered. The end of one's regular work life can have major financial and social effects, although there is no evidence that retirement has an effect on physical or mental health. Most older adults spend this stage adapting to a new lifestyle and finding new roles to fill now that the role of worker is finished.

6. Late adulthood is the fastest-growing age group in the United States and in all developed countries. As a result, we know more about this age than ever before. The slow decline in physical and cognitive abilities that began back in early adulthood speeds up in late adulthood. This is accompanied by a decrease in social activities and social networks. However, most people this age enjoy fewer but closer relationships. The hypothesis that those who disengage from the world are mentally healthier has not held up to close examination.

7. Late adulthood is a time for reviewing one's life and perhaps coming to grips with one's eventual death. Some adults in this time of life write memoirs or mend fences with former friends and family members.

8. Although this book emphasizes the typical pathways through adulthood, there are many variations that can lead to success and well-being.

9. Quality of life for adulthood in the United States depends highly on socioeconomic status and health. These two factors explain many of the more distal predictors, such as race and gender. Another factor is age, with older adults reporting greater quality of life than middle-aged or young adults. Those who are married, participate in

physical and social activities, feel they have control over their lives, and base their comparisons on others their age, also report higher quality of life.

10. In spite of the variablility in adult development, most of us have similarities in our journeys of adulthood, and these journeys are strongly influenced by our education, family background, intelligence, and personality.

11. The developmental pathways we travel along are made up of alternating stable times and times of disequilibrium. The periods of disequlilibium can result in positive change, negative change, or neutral outcomes.

12. Most adults pass through adulthood with reasonable happiness and satisfaction, picking up some wisdom along the way and passing it along to those who come behind them.

Key Terms

midlife crisis, 354

disengagement, 357

selective optimization
with compensation, 358

life review, 358

Suggested Reading

Reading for Personal Interest

Ellis, N. (2002). *If I live to be 100: Lessons from the centenarians.* New York: Crown.

Neenah Ellis is well known to listeners of National Public Radio. This is a collection of interviews she did over a year while traveling around the United States talking to people who were age 100 or older. The book is also available on audiocassette and CD and is very nice to listen to on car trips (as I did).

Pestalozzi, T. (2004) *Life skills 101: A practical guide to leaving home and living on your own.* New York: Stonewood.

The author offers a helpful guide to living on your own, including how to read contracts, do laundry, keep a car running, open a bank account, and equip a kitchen.

Robbins, A., & Wilner, A. (2001). *Quarterlife crisis: The unique challenges of life in your twenties.* Los Angeles: J. P. Tarcher.

Generation Y members talk about the adjustments they face in job hopping, living with parents, spirituality, romance, and social life. The authors based this book on interviews with hundreds of new adults, and the common problems and concerns should be a comfort to readers who are their peers (or readers who are their parents, teachers, or grandparents).

Sammons, S. D. (1997). *Life after youth: Making sense of one man's journey through the transition at midlife.* Staten Island, NY: Alba House.

As a midife transition, the author faced surgery for a brain tumor, and although we all hope not to follow in the same path, the lessons he learned have been very popular with middle-aged men who have read his book. It deals with common midlife issues, such as awareness of mortality, changes in relationships and sexuality, rethinking faith and the religion of childhood, and creating a legacy by making a difference.

Vaillant, G. E. (2002). *Aging well: Surprising guideposts to a happier life from the landmark Harvard study.* New York: Little, Brown.

George Vaillant uses the findings from the Harvard Medical School Longitudinal Study to give practical advice about how to reach a happy and healthy old age. The combined histories of 824 men and women help to explain why some are more resilient than others, what the long-term effects of marriage and divorce are, and why one's background has less to do with one's eventual happiness than the specific lifestyle choices one makes. It is unusual to find a self-help book that is based on such solid evidence.

Classic Work

Cummings, E., & Henry, W. E. (1961). *Growing old.* New York: Basic Books.

Disengagement theory is formulated and discussed in detail.

Sears, R. R. (1977). Sources of life satisfaction of the Terman gifted men. *American Psychologist, 32,* 119–128.

Pioneer developmentalist Robert Sears interviewed in old age the men who had been child participants in Terman's famous longitudinal study of gifted children.

Sheehy, G. (1976) *Passages.* New York: Dutton.

Journalist Gail Sheehy compiled interviews with a good number of adults and used them to propose a series of set stages that occur in adulthood. Although the book is over three decades old, and although her subjects were mostly white, university-educated professional people, it struck a chord, and "passages" has become a household word.

Waddington, C. H. (1957). *The strategy of the genes.* London: Allen & Son.

Embryologist Conrad Waddington used an epigenetic landscape model to describe the idea that the development of an organism can take many paths on its way to differentiation. His model has since been borrowed by other developmental scientists to describe the transactional properties of the influences people encounter during their lifetimes.

Contemporary Scholarly Work

Dunkle, R. E., Roberts, B., & Haus, M. R. (Eds.). (2001). *The oldest old in everyday life: Self-perception, coping with change, and stress.* New York: Springer.

Researchers involved in the National Institute of Aging longitudinal study report their findings in this book.

George, L. K. (2006). Perceived quality of life. In R. H. Binstock & L. K. George (Eds.), *Handbook of aging and the social sciences* (pp. 320–336). San Diego: Academic Press.

The author reviews research on quality of life and the factors that determine how people of different ages judge the quality of their own lives.

Lachman, M. (Ed.). (2001). *Handbook of midlife development.* New York: Wiley.

A fairly new field of interest, midlife development is explored by a number of researchers in this first handbook on the subject.

References

A

Abdel-Khalek, A. M. (2004). The Arabic Scale of Death Anxiety (ASDA): Its development, validation, and results in three Arab countries. *Death Studies, 28,* 435–457.

Abdel-Khalek, A. M. (2005). Death anxiety in clinical and non-clinical groups. *Death Studies, 29,* 251–259.

Achenbaum, W. A. (1995). *Crossing frontiers. Gerontology emerges as a science.* Cambridge: Cambridge University Press.

Adams, C., Smith, M. C., Pasupathi, M., et al. (2002). Social context effects on story recall in older and younger women: Does the listener make a difference? *Journals of Gerontology: Psychological Sciences, 57B,* P28–P40.

Adelmann, P. K. (1994). Multiple roles and physical health among older adults: Gender and ethnic comparisons. *Research on Aging, 16,* 142–166.

Adler, N. E., Boyce, T., Chesney, M., et al. (1994). Socioeconomic status and health: The challenge of the gradient. *American Psychologist, 49,* 15–24.

Aiken. L. R. (1998). *Human development in adulthood.* New York: Plenum Press.

Ainsworth, M. D. S., Blehar, M., Waters, E., et al. (1978). *Patterns of attachment.* Hillsdale, NJ: Erlbaum.

Alaimo, K., Briefel, R. R., Frongillo, E. A., et al. (1998). Food insufficiency exists in the United States: Results from the 3rd National Health and Nutrition Examination Survey (NHANES III). *American Journal of Public Health, 88,* 419–426.

Aldous, J. (1995). New views of grandparents in intergenerational context. *Journal of Family Issues, 16,* 104–122.

Aldwin, C. M., & Levenson, M. R. (2001). Stress, coping, and health at mid-life: A developmental perspective. In M. E. Lachman (Ed.), *The Handbook of Midlife Development* (pp. 188–214). New York: Wiley.

Alea, N., Diehl, M., & Bluck, S. (2004). Personality and emotion in late life. *Encyclopedia of Applied Psychology, 1–10.* San Diego: Elsevier.

Alesina, A., Glaeser, E., & Sacerdote, B. (2005). *Work and leisure in the U.S. and Europe: Why so different?* Harvard Institute of Economic Research, Discussion paper no. 2068. Retrieved March 20, 2006, from http://post.economics .harvard.edu/hier/2005papers/hier2068.pdf.

Alexander, E. A., & Allison, A. L. (1995). Sexuality in older adults. In W. Reichel (Ed.), *Care of the elderly: Clinical aspects of aging* (4th ed., pp. 540–546). Baltimore: Williams & Wilkins.

Almeida, D. M. (2005). Resilience and vulnerability to daily stressors assessed via diary methods. *Current Directions in Psychological Sciences, 14,* 64–68.

Almeida, D. M., & Horn, M. C. (2004). Is daily life more stressful during middle adulthood? In O. G. Brim, C. D. Ryff, & R. C. Kessler (Eds.), *How healthy are we? A national study of well-being at midlife* (pp. 425–451). Chicago: University of Chicago Press.

Almeida, O. P., Waterreus, A., Spry, N., et al. (2004). One year follow-up study of the association between chemical castration, sex hormones, beta-amyloid, memory and depression in men. *Psychoneuroendocrinology, 29,* 1071–1081.

Alsop, S. (1973). *Stay of execution.* New York: Lippincott.

American Cancer Society (2005). *Cancer facts and figures: 2005.* Retrieved May 25, 2006, from http://www.cancer.org/ downloads/STT/CAFF2005f4PWSecured.pdf.

American Cancer Society (2006). *What is hospice care?* Retrieved March 20, 2006, from http://www.cancer.org/docroot/ ETO/eto_2_4_hospicecare.asp?sitearea=MLT&level=1.

American Psychiatric Association (1980). *Diagnostic and statistical manual of mental disorders,* (3rd ed.). Washington, DC: APA.

American Psychiatric Association (2000). *Diagnostic and statistical manual of mental disorders* (4th ed.). Washington, DC: APA.

American Psychological Association (2004). *Public policy, work, and families: The report of the APA presidential initiative on work and families.* Retrieved March 14, 2006, from http://www.apa.org/work-family/fullreport.pdf.

American Society of Plastic Surgeons (2005). *National plastic surgery statistics: Cosmetic and reconstructive procedure trends.* Arlington Heights, IL: American Society of Plastic Surgeons.

Andreasen, N. C. (2001). *Brave new brain: Conquering mental illness in the era of the genome.* New York: Oxford University Press.

Andresen, E. M., Malmgren, J. A., Carter, W. B., et al. (1994). Screening for depression in well older adults: Evaluation of a short form of the CES-D (Center for Epidemiological Studies Depression Scale). *American Journal of Preventative Medicine, 10,* 77–84.

Ano, G. G., & Vasconcelles, E. B. (2005). Religious coping and psychological adjustment to stress: A meta-analysis. *Journal of Clinical Psychology, 61,* 461–480.

Antonucci, T. C. (1986). Social support networks: A hierarchical mapping technique. *Generations, 3,* 10–12.

Antonucci, T. C. (1990). Social supports and social relationships. In R. H. Binstock & L. K. George (Eds.), *Handbook of aging and the social sciences* (3rd ed., pp. 205–226). San Diego: Academic Press.

Antonucci, T. C., Akiyama, H., & Takahashi, K. (2004). Attachment and close relationships across the life span. *Attachment and Human Development, 6,* 353–370.

Aquilano, W. S. (2005). Impact of family structure on parental attitudes toward the economic support of adult children over the transition to adulthood. *Journal of Family Issues, 26,* 143–167.

Araujo, A. B., Mohr, B. A., & McKinlay, J. B. (2004). Changes in sexual function in middle-aged and older men:

Longitudinal data from the Massachusetts Male Aging Study. *Journal of the American Geriatic Society, 52,* 1502–1509.

Ardelt, M. (2003). Effects of religion and purpose in life on elders' subjective well-being and attitudes toward death. *Journal of Religious Gerontology, 14,* 55–77.

Ardelt, M., & Koenig, C. S. (2006). The role of religion for hospice patients and relatively healthy older adults. *Research on Aging, 28,* 184–215.

Ardila, A., Ostrosky-Solis, F., Roselli, M., et al. (2000). Age related decline during normal aging: The complex effect of education. *Archives of Clinical Neuropsychology, 15,* 495–513.

Arnett, J. J. (2000). Emerging adulthood. *American Psychologist, 55,* 469–480.

Aron, A., Fisher, H., Mashek, D., et al. (2005). Reward, motivation and emotion systems associated with early-stage intense romantic love. *Journal of Neurophysiology, 93,* 327–337.

Arterburn, D. E., Crane, P. K., & Sullivan, S. D. (2004). The coming epidemic of obesity in elderly Americans, *Journal of the American Geriatric Society, 52,* 1907–1912.

Aspinwall, L. G., & Taylor, S. E. (1997). A stitch in time: Self-regulation and proactive coping. *Psychological Bulletin, 121,* 417–436.

Atchley, P., & Dressel, J. (2004). Conversation limits the functional field of view. *Human Factors, 46,* 664–675.

Atchley, R. (1997), Everyday mysticism: Spiritual development in later adulthood. *Journal of Adult Development, 4,* 123–134.

Atkinson, R. C., & Shiffrin, R. M. (1968). Human Memory: A proposed system and its control processes. In K. W. Spence & J. T. Spence (Eds.), *The psychology of learning and motivation* (Vol. 2, pp. 89–195). New York: Academic Press.

Austad, S. N. (2001). Concepts and theories of aging. In E. J. Masoro & S. N. Austad (Eds.), *Handbook of the biology of aging* (5th ed., pp. 3–22). San Diego: Academic Press.

B

Bäckman, L., Hill, R. D., & Forsell, Y. (1996). The influence of depressive symptomatology on episodic memory among clinically nondepressed older adults. *Journal of Abnormal Psychology, 105,* 97–105.

Bäckman, L., & Nilsson, L. G. (1996). Semantic memory functions across the adult life span. *European Psychologist, 1,* 27–33.

Bäckman, L., Small, B. J., Wahlin, Å., et al. (2000). Cognitive functioning in very old age. In F. I. M. Craik & T. A. Salthouse (Eds.), *Handbook of aging and cognition* (pp. 499–558). Hillsdale, NJ: Erlbaum.

Bäckman, L., Small, B. J., & Wahlin, Å. (2001). Aging and memory: Cognitive and biological perspectives. In J. E. Birren & K. W. Schaie (Eds.), *Handbook of the psychology of aging* (5th ed., pp. 349–377). San Diego: Academic Press.

Bacon, C. G., Mittleman, M. A., Kawachi, I., et al (2003). Sexual function in men older than 50 years of age: Results from the health professionals' follow-up study. *Annals of Internal Medicine, 139,* 161–168.

Baddeley, A. D. (1986). *Working memory.* Oxford: Oxford University Press.

Bakker, R. (1999). Elderdesign: Home modifications for enhanced safety and self-care. *Care Management Journals, 1,* 47–54.

Ball, K. K. (1997). Enhancing mobility in the elderly: Attentional interventions for driving. In S. M. Clancy Dollinger & L. F. DiLalla (Eds.), *Assessment and intervention issues across the life span* (pp. 267–292). Mahwah, NJ: Erlbaum.

Balsam, K. F., Rothblum, E. D., & Beauchaine, T. P. (2005). Victimization over the life span: A comparison of lesbian, gay, bisexual, and heterosexual siblings. *Journal of Consulting and Clinical Psychology, 73,* 477–487.

Baltes, P. B. (1987). Theoretical propositions of life-span developmental psychology: On the dynamics between growth and decline. *Developmental Psychology, 23,* 611–626.

Baltes, P. B., & Baltes, M. M. (1990). Psychological perspectives on successful aging: The model of selective optimization with compensation. In P. B. Baltes & M. M. Baltes (Eds.), *Successful aging: Perspective from the behavioral sciences* (pp. 1–34). Cambridge: Cambridge University Press.

Baltes, P. B., & Lindenberger, U. (1997). Emergence of a powerful connection between sensory and cognitive function across the adult life span: A new window to the study of cognitive aging? *Psychology and Aging, 12,* 12–21.

Baltes, P. B., & Mayer, K. U. (Eds.) (1999). *The Berlin aging study: Aging from 70 to 100.* Cambridge: Cambridge University Press.

Baltes, P. B., Reese, H. W., & Lipsitt, L. P. (1980). Life-span developmental psychology. *Annual Review of Psychology, 31,* 65–110.

Baltes, P. B., & Smith, J. (1990). Toward a psychology of wisdom and its ontogenesis. In R. J. Sternberg (Ed.), *Wisdom: Its nature, origins, and development* (pp. 87–120). New York: Cambridge University Press.

Baltes, P. B., & Staudinger, U. M. (1993).The search for a psychology of wisdom. *Current Directions in Psychological Science, 2,* 75–80.

Bandura, A. (1997). *Self-efficacy.* New York: Freeman.

Baranowski, M. C. (1987). The grandfather-grandchild relationship: Meaning and exchange. *Family Perspective, 24,* 201–215.

Barker, D. J. (2004). Developmental origins of adult health and disease. *Journal of Epidemiology and Community Health, 58,* 114–115.

Barker, D. J., Winter, P. D., Osmond, C., et al. (1989). Weight in infancy and death from ischaemic heart disease. *Lancet, 2,* 577–580

Bartholomew, K. (1990). Avoidance of intimacy: An attachment perspective. *Journal of Social and Personal Relationships, 7,* 147–178.

Bartholomew, K., & Horowitz, L. M. (1991). Attachment styles among young adults: A test of a four-category model. *Journal of Personality and Social Psychology, 61,* 226–244.

Bass, D. M., Noelker, L. S., & Rechlin L. R. (1996). The moderating influences of service use on negative caregiving consequences. *Journals of Gerontology: Social Sciences, 51B,* S121–S131.

Bauer, J. J., & McAdams, D. P. (2004). Personal growth in adults' stories of life transitions. *Journal of Personality, 72,* 573–602.

Baulieu E. E., Thomas G., Legrain S., et al, (2000*)*. Dehydroepiandrosterone (DHEA), DHEA sulfate, and aging: Contribution of the DHEAge study to a sociobiomedical issue. *Proceedings of the National Academy Science (USA), 97,* 4279–4284.

Baumeister, R. F., & Leary, M. R. (1995). The need to belong: Desire for interpersonal attachments as a fundamental human motivation. *Psychological Bulletin, 117,* 497–529.

Beal, C. R. (1994). *Boys and girls: The development of gender roles.* New York: McGraw-Hill.

Bear, T. M., & Barnes, L. B. (2001). *Posttraumatic growth in survivors of law enforcement officers killed in the line of duty.* Re-

trieved March 27, 2006, from http://www.nationalcops
.org/forms/OSU%20Study.pdf.

Beaumont, J. G., & Kenealy, P. M. (2004). Quality of life perceptions and social comparisons in healthy old age. *Aging and Society, 24*, 755–769.

Beers, M.H. (2004). *Merck manual of health and aging.* Whitehouse Station, NJ: Merck Research Labs.

Bell, D. C., & Richard, A. J. (2000). Caregiving: The forgotten element in attachment. *Psychological Inquiry, 11*, 69–83.

Bell, R. R. (1981). *Worlds of friendship.* Beverly Hills, CA: Sage.

Bellizzi, K. M., & Blank, T. O. (2006). Predicting posttraumatic growth in breast cancer survivors. *Health Psychology, 25*, 47–56.

Belsky, J. (2001). Emmanuel Miller Lecture: Developmental risks (still) associated with early child care. *Journal of Child Psychology and Psychiatry, 42*, 845–859.

Belsky, J., & Kelly, J. (1994). *The transition to parenthood: How a first child changes marriage.* New York: Dell.

Belsky, J., Spanier, G. B., & Rovine, M. (1983). Stability and change in marriage across the transition to parenthood. *Journal of Marriage and the Family, 45*, 567–577.

Bem, S. L. (1981). Gender schema theory: A cognitive account of sex typing. *Psychological Review, 88*, 354–364.

Bem, S. L. (1993). *The lenses of gender: Transforming the debate on sexual inequality.* New Haven: Yale University Press.

Bengtson, V. L., & Schrader, S. S. (1982). Parent-child relations. In D. Mangen & W. Peterson (Eds.), *Research instruments in social gerontology* (pp. 114–128). Minneapolis: University of Minnesota Press.

Bengtsson, T., & Lindström, M. (2003). Airborne infectious diseases during infancy and mortality in later life in southern Sweden, 1766–1894. *International Journal of Epidemiology, 32*, 286–294.

Benjamins, M. R., Musick, M. A., Gold, D. T., et al. (2003). Age-related declines in activity level: The relationship between chronic illness and religious activities. *Journals of Gerontology: Social Sciences, 58B*, S377–S385.

Berenson, G. S., & Srinivasan, S. R., (2005). Cardiovascular risk factors in youth with implications for aging: The Bogalusa heart study. *Neurobiology of Aging, 26*, 303–307.

Berg, C. A., & Sternberg, R. J. (2003). Multiple perspectives on the development of adult intelligence. In J. Demick & C. Andreoletti (Eds.), *Handbook of adult development* (pp. 103–119). New York: Kluwer.

Berg, S. (1996). Aging, behavior, and terminal decline. In J. E. Birren & K. W. Schaie (Eds.), *Handbook of the psychology of aging* (4th ed., pp. 323–337). San Diego: Academic Press.

Berscheid, E. (1999). The greening of relationship science. *American Psychologist, 54*, 260–266.

Besser, A., Amir, M., & Barkan, S. (2004). Who signs an organ transplant donor card? A study of personality and individual differences in a sample of Israeli university students. *Personality and Individual Differences, 36*, 1709–1723.

Bianchi, S. M., Milkie, M. A., Sayer, L. C., et al. (2000). Is anyone doing the housework? Trends in the gender division of household labor. *Social Forces, 79*, 191–228.

Binstock, R. H., Fishman, J. R., & Johnson, T. E. (2006). Anti-aging medicine and science: Social implications. In R. H. Binstock & L. K. George (Eds.), *Handbook of aging and the social sciences* (pp. 436–455). San Diego: Academic Press.

Birkhill, W. R., & Schaie, K. W. (1975). The effect of differential reinforcement of cautiousness in the intellectual performance of the elderly. *Journal of Gerontology, 30*, 578–583.

Birren, J. E., & Feldman, L. (1997). *Where to go from here.* New York: Simon & Schuster.

Bjerkeset, O., Nordahl, H. M., Mykletun, A., et al. (2005). Anxiety and depression following myocardial infarctions: Gender difference in a 5-year prospective study. *Journal of Psychosomatic Research, 58*, 153–161.

Blieszner, R. (2000). Close relationships in old age. In C. Hendrick & S. S. Hendrick (Eds.), *Close relationships: A sourcebook* (pp. 85–95). Thousand Oaks, CA: Sage.

Bliwise, D. L. (1997). Sleep and aging. In M. R. Pressman & W. C. Orr (Eds.), *Understanding sleep: The evaluation and treatment of sleep disorders.* Washington, DC: American Psychological Association.

Bloom, B. (2005). Public health in transition. *Scientific American, 293*, 92–99.

Bonanno, G. A, & Kaltman, S. (1999). Toward an integrative perspective on bereavement. *Psychological Bulletin, 125*, 760–776.

Bonanno, G. A. (2005). Resilience in the face of potential trauma. *Current Directions in Psychological Sciences, 14*, 135–138.

Bonanno, G. A., & Keltner, D. (1997). Facial expressions of emotion and the course of conjugal bereavement. *Journal of Abnormal Psychology, 106*, 126–137.

Bonanno, G. A., Moskowitz, J. T., Papa, A., et al., (2005). Resilience to loss in bereaved spouses, bereaved parents, and bereaved gay men. *Journal of Personality and Social Psychology, 88*, 827–843.

Bonanno, G. A., Wortman, C. B., Lehman, D. R., et al. (2002). Resilience to loss and chronic grief: A prospective study from pre-loss to 18 months post-loss. *Journal of Personality and Social Psychology, 83*, 1150–1164.

Bond, J., Galinski, E., & Swanberg, J. (1998) *The national study of the changing workforce.* New York: Families and Work Institute.

Bond, J. T., Thompson, C., Galinsky, E., et al. (2002). *The 2002 national study of the changing workforce.* New York: Families and Work Institute.

Bowlby, J. (1969). *Attachment and loss* Vol. 1, *Attachment.* New York: Basic Books.

Bowlby, J. (1980). *Attachment and loss* Vol. 3, *Loss, sadness, and depression.* New York: Basic Books.

Branlett, M. D., & Masher, W. D. (2002). Cohabitation, marriage, divorce, and remarriage in the United States. *National Center for Health Statistics: Vital Health Statistics, 23*, 1–32.

Brébion, G., Smith, M. J., & Ehrlich, M. F. (1997). Working memory and aging: Deficit or strategy differences? *Aging, Neuropsychology, and Cognition, 4*, 58–73.

Bren, L. (2004). Joint replacement: An inside look. *FDA Consumer, 38*, 12–19.

Brennan, K. A., & Shaver, P. R. (1995). Dimensions of adult attachment, affect regulation, and romantic functioning. *Personality and Social Psychological Bulletin, 21*, 267–283.

Bridges, J. S. & Etaugh, C. (1995). College students' perceptions of mothers: Effects of maternal employment-childrearing pattern and motive for employment. *Sex Roles, 32*, 735–751.

Brisette, I., Scheier, M. F., & Carver, C. S. (2002). The role of optimism and social network development, coping, and psychological adjustment during a life transition. *Journal of Personality and Social Psychology, 82*, 102–111.

Brockmann, H., & Klein, T. (2003). Love and death in Germany: The marital biography and its effect on mortality. *Journal of Marriage and Family, 66*, 567–581.

Brody, E. M. (1981).Women in the middle and family help to old people. *Gerontologist, 25,* 19–29.

Brody, E. M., Litvin, S. J., Albert, S. M., et al. (1994). Marital status of daughters and patterns of parent care. *Journals of Gerontology: Social Sciences, 49B,* S95–S103.

Broman, C. L., (2005). Stress, race, and substance abuse in college. *College Student Journal, 38,* 340–352.

Bronfenbrenner, U. (1979). *The ecology of human development.* Cambridge, Harvard University Press.

Brown, L. H., & Roodin, P. A. (2003). Grandparent-grandchild relationships and the life course perspective. In J. Demick & C. Andreoletti (Eds.), *Handbook of adult development* (pp. 459–474). New York: Kluwer.

Brown, K. (2004). A radical proposal. *Scientific American, 14,* 31–35.

Bryant, A. S., & Demian. (1994). Relationship characteristics of American gay and lesbian couples: Findings from a national survey. *Journal of Gay & Lesbian Social Services, 1,* 101–117.

Bryant, S., & Rakowski, W. (1992). Predictors of mortality among elderly African-Americans. *Research on Aging, 14,* 50–67.

Buchner, D. M., Beresford, S. A. A., Larson, E. B., et al. (1992). Effects of physical activity on health status in older adults: II. Intervention studies. *Annual Review of Public Health, 13,* 469–488.

Burack, O. R., & Lachman, M. E. (1996). The effects of list-making on recall in young and elderly adults. *Journals of Gerontology: Psychological Sciences, 51B,* P226–P233.

Burke, D. M., MacKay, D. G., Worthley, J. S., et al. (1991). On the tip of the tongue: What causes word finding failures in young and older adults? *Journal of Memory and Language, 30,* 542–579.

Buss, D. M. (1991). Evolutionary personality psychology. *Annual Review of Psychology, 42,* 459–491.

Buss, D. M. (1997). Evolutionary foundations of personality. In R. Hogan, J. Johnson, & S. Briggs (Eds.), *Handbook of personality psychology* (pp. 317–344). San Diego: Academic Press.

Buss, D. M., & Kenrick, D. T. (1998). Evolutionary social psychology. In D. T. Gilbert, S. T. Fisk, & G. Lindzey (Eds.), *Handbook of social psychology,* (Vol. 2, pp. 982–1026). New York: McGraw-Hill.

Buss, D. M., Shackelford, T. K., Kirkpatrick, L. A., et al. (2001). A half-century of mate preferences: The cultural evolution of values. *Journal of Marriage and Family, 63,* 491–503.

Busse, E. W., & Maddox, G. L. (1985). *The Duke longitudinal studies of normal aging 1955–1980: Overview of history, design, and findings.* New York: Springer.

Butler, R. N. (1993). The importance of basic research in gerontology. *Age and Ageing, 22,* S53–S55.

C

Campbell, J. (1949 /1990). *Hero with a thousand faces.* Princeton, NJ: Princeton University Press.

Campbell, L. D., Connidis, I. A., & Davies, L. (1999). Sibling ties in later life: A social network analysis. *Journal of Family Issues, 20,* 114–148

Campbell, L., & Ellis, B. J. (2005). Commitment, love, and mate retention. In D. M. Buss (Ed.), *Handbook of evolutionary psychology* (pp. 419–442). New York: Wiley.

Caporeal, L. R. (1997). The evolution of truly social cognition: The core configuration model. *Personality and Social Psychology Review, 1,* 276–298.

Carrére, S., & Gottman, J. M. (1999). Predicting divorce among newlyweds from the first three minutes of a marital conflict discussion. *Family Process, 38,* 293–301.

Carstensen, L. L. (1992). Social and emotional patterns in adulthood: Support for socioemotional selectivity theory. *Psychology and Aging, 7,* 331–338.

Carstensen, L. L. (1995). Evidence for a life span theory of socioemotional selectivity. *Current Directions in Psychological Science, 4,* 151–156.

Carstensen, L. L., Fung, H. H., & Charles, S. T. (2003). Socioemotional selectivity theory and the regulation of emotion in the second half of life. *Motivation and Emotion, 27,* 103–123.

Carstensen, L. L., Graff, J., Levenson, R. W., et al. (1996). Affect in intimate relationships. In C. Magai & S. H. McFadden (Eds.), *Handbook of emotion, adult development, and aging* (pp. 227–242). San Diego: Academic Press.

Carstensen, L. L., Mickels, J. A., & Mather, M. (2006). Aging and the intersection of cognition, motivation, and emotion. In R. H. Binstock & L. K. George (Eds.), *Handbook of aging and the social sciences* (pp. 343–362). San Diego: Academic Press.

Carver, C. S. (1997). You want to measure coping but your protocol's too long: Consider the Brief COPE. *International Journal of Behavioral Medicine, 4,* 92–100.

Carver, C. S., Smith, R. G., Antoni, M. H., et al. (2005). Optimistic personality and psychosocial well-being during treatment predict psychosocial well-being among long-term survivors of breast cancer. *Health Psychology, 24,* 508–516.

Case, R. B., Moss, A. J., Case, N., et al. (1992). Living alone after myocardial infarction: Impact on prognosis. *Journal of the American Medical Association, 267,* 515–519.

Caspi, A. (1998). Personality development across the life course. In W. Damon (Series Ed.) and N. Eisenberg (Vol. Ed.), *Handbook of child psychology* Vol. 3, *Social, emotional, and personality development* (pp. 311–388). New York: Wiley.

Caspi, A., & Roberts, B. W. (1999). Personality continuity and change across the life course. In L. A. Pervin & O. P. John (Eds.), *Handbook of personality psychology: Theory and research* (pp. 300–326). New York: Guilford Press.

Caspi, A., Roberts, B. W., & Shiner, R. L. (2004). Personality development: stability and change. *Annual Review of Psychology, 56,* 453–484.

Cate, R. M., & Lloyd, S. A. (1992). *Courtship.* Newbury Park, CA: Sage.

Cattell, R. B. (1963). Theory of fluid and crystallized intelligence: A critical experiment. *Journal of Educational Psychology, 54,* 1–22.

Cattell, R. B., Eber, H. W., & Tatsuoka, M. M. (1970). *Handbook for the Sixteen Personality Factor Questionnaire.* Champaigne, IL: Institute for Personality and Ability Testing.

Cavalli-Sforza, L. L., & Cavalli-Sforza, F. (1995). *The great human diasporas: The history of diversity and evolution.* Reading, MA: Addison-Wesley.

Cejka, M. A., & Eagly, A. H. (1999). Gender-stereotypic images of occupations correspond to the sex segregation of employment. *Personality and Social Psychology Bulletin, 25,* 413–423.

Centofanti, M. (1998). Fear of Alzheimer's undermines health of elderly patients. *APA Monitor, 29,* 1–33.

Cerda-Flores, R. M., Barton, S. A., Marty-Gonzales, L. F., et al. (1999). Estimation of nonpaternity in the Mexican population of Neuvo Leon: A validation study of blood group markers. *American Journal of Physical Anthropology, 109,* 281–293.

Cerminara, K. L. (2006). Theresa Marie Schaivo's long road to peace. *Death Studies, 30,* 101–112.

Chandra, R. K. (1997). Graying of the immune system: Can nutritional supplements improve immunity in the elderly? *Nutrition, 19,* 978.

Charness, N. (1981). Search in chess: Age and skill differences. *Journal of Experimental Psychology: Human Perception and Performance, 7,* 467–476.

Charness, N. (2001). Aging and communication: Human factors issues. In N. Charness, D. C. Park, & B. A. Sabel (Eds.), *Communication, technology, and aging: Opportunities and challenges for the future* (pp 1–29). New York: Springer.

Charness, N., Park, D. C., & Sabel, B. A. (2001). *Communication, technology, and aging: Opportunities and challenges for the future.* New York: Springer.

Chen, Y. Y., Subramanian, S. V., Acevedo-Garcia, D., et al. (2005). Women's status and depressive symptoms: A multilevel analysis. *Social Science and Medicine, 60,* 49–60.

Cheung, A. M. (2005). Medical aspects of perimenopause and menopause. In D. E. Stewart (Ed.), *Menopause: A mental health practitioner's guide* (pp. 105–142*).* Washington, DC: American Psychiatric Publishing.

Christensen, H., & Henderson, A. S. (1991). Is age kinder to the initially more able? A study of eminent scientists and academics. *Psychological Medicine, 21,* 95–946.

Chrousos, G. P., Torpy, D. J., & Gold, P. W. (1998). Interaction between the hypothalamic-pituitary-adrenal axis and the female reproductive system. *Annals of Internal Medicine, 129,* 229–240.

Cicirelli, V. G. (1989). Feelings of attachment to siblings and well-being in later life. *Psychology and Aging, 4,* 211–216.

Cicirelli, V. G. (1991). Attachment theory in old age: Protection of the attached figure. In K. Pillemer & K. McCartney (Eds.), *Parent-child relations throughout life* (pp. 2–42). Hillsdale, NJ: Erlbaum.

Cicirelli, V. G. (1998). A frame of reference for guiding research for the relationship between adult attachment and mental health in aging families (pp. 341–353). In J. Lomranz (Ed.), *Handbook of aging and mental health: An integrative approach.* New York: Plenum.

Clancy, S. M., & Hoyer, W. J. (1994). Age and skill in visual search. *Developmental Psychology, 30,* 545–552.

Clark, A. E., Oswald, A. J., & Warr, P. B. (1996). Is job satisfaction U-shaped in age? *Journal of Occupational Psychology, 69,* 57–81.

Clark, L., & Stephens, M. A. P. (1996). Stroke patients' well-being as a function of caregiving spouses' helpful and unhelpful actions. *Personal Relationships, 3,* 171–184.

Clark, R. (2006). Perceived racism and vascular reactivity in black college women, moderating effects of seeking social support. *Health Psychology, 25,* 20–25.

Clark, R. L., Burkhauser, R. V., Moon, M., et al. (2004). *The economics of an aging society.* Malden, MA: Blackwell.

Clarkson-Smith, L., & Hartley, A. A. (1990). The game of bridge as an exercise in working memory and reasoning. *Journals of Gerontology: Psychological Sciences, 45B,* P233–P238.

Cleary, P. D., Zaborski, L. B., & Ayanian, J. Z. (2004). Sex differences in health over the life course. In O. G. Brim, C. D. Ryff, & R. C. Kessler (Eds.), *How healthy are we? A national study of well-being at midlife* (pp. 37–63). Chicago: University of Chicago Press.

Clunis, D. M., Fredriksen-Goldsen, K. I., Freeman, P. A., et al. (2005). *Lives of lesbian elders: Looking back, looking forward.* New York: Hayworth.

Cohan, C., & Kleinbaum, S. (2002). Toward a greater understanding of the cohabitation effect: Premarital cohabitation and marital communication. *Journal of Marriage and the Family, 64,* 77–84.

Cohen, L. H. (1998). Measurement of life events. In L. H. Cohen (Ed.), *Life events and psychological functioning: Theoretical and methodological issues* (pp. 11–30). Newbury Park, CA: Sage.

Cohen, P., Kasen, S., Chen, H., et al. (2003). Variations in patterns of developmental transmissions in the emerging adulthood period. *Developmental Psychology, 39,* 657–669.

Cohen-Mansfield, J., Creedon, M. A., Malone, M. A., et al. (2005). Electronic memory aids for community dwelling elderly persons: Attitudes, preferences, and potential utilization. *Journal of Applied Gerontology, 24,* 3–20.

Colby, A., & Kohlberg, L. (1987). *The measurement of moral judgment* Vol. 1, *Theoretical foundations and research validation.* Cambridge: Cambridge University Press.

Colby, A., Kohlberg, L., Gibbs, J., et al. (1983). A longitudinal study of moral judgment. *Monographs of the Society for Research in Child Development, 48* (1–2, Serial No. 200).

Colcombe, S., & Kramer, A. F. (2003). Fitness effects on the cognitive function of older adults: A meta-analytic study. *Psychological Science, 14,* 125–130.

Colcombe, S., Erickson, K. I., Raz, N., et al. (2003). Aerobic fitness reduces brain tissue loss in aging humans. *Journals of Gerontology: Medical Sciences, 58A,* M176–M180.

Cole, E. R., & Stewart, A. J. (1996). Meanings of political participation among black and white women: Political identity and social responsibility. *Journal of Personality and Social Psychology, 71,* 130–140.

Coltrane, S. (2000). Research on household labor: Modeling and measuring the social embeddedness of routine family work. *Journal of Marriage and the Family, 62,* 1208–1233.

Compton, D. M., Bachman, L. D., Brand, D., et al. (2000). Age associated changes in cognitive function in highly educated adults: Emerging myths and realities. *International Journal of Geriatric Psychiatry, 15,* 75–85.

Conger, R. D., Cui, M., Bryant, C. M., et al. (2000). Competence in early adult romantic relationships: Developmental perspective on family influences. *Journal of Personality and Social Psychology, 79,* 224–237.

Connidis, I. A., & McMullin, J. A. (1993). To have or have not: Parent status and the subjective well-being of older men and women. *Gerontologist, 33,* 630–636.

Cooney, T. M., Hutchinson, M. K., & Leather, D. M. (1995). Surviving the breakup? Predictors of parent-adult child relations after parental divorce. *Family Relations, 44,* 53–61.

Corr, C. A. (1993). Coping with dying: Lessons we should and should not learn from the work of Elisabeth Kübler-Ross. *Death Studies, 17,* 69–83.

Costa, P. T., Jr., & McCrae, R. R. (1992). *NEO-PI-R professional manual.* Odessa, FL: Psychological Assessment Resources.

Costa, P. T., Jr., & McCrae, R. R. (1997). Longitudinal stability of adult personality. In R. Hogan, J. Johnson, & S. Briggs

(Eds.), *Handbook of personality psychology* (pp. 269–290). San Diego: Academic Press.

Costello, C. B., & Stone, A. J. (2001). *The American woman 2001–2002: Getting to the top.* New York: Norton

Costello, C. B., Wight, V. R., & Stone, A. J., (2003). *The American woman 2003–2004.* New York: Palgrave Macmillan.

Couzin, J. (2005). To what extent are genetic variation and personal health linked? *Science, 309,* 81.

Cowan, C. P., & Cowan, P. A. (1992). *When partners become parents.* New York: Basic Books.

Cowan, C. P., & Cowan, P. A. (1995). Interventions to ease the transition to parenthood: Why they are needed and what they can do. *Family Relations, 44,* 412–423.

Cowan, C. P., Cowan, P. A., Herning, G., et al., (1991). Becoming a family: Marriage, parenting, and child development. In P. A. Cowan & E. M. Hetheringon (Eds.), *Family transitions: Advances in family research series* (pp. 79–109). Hillsdale, NJ: Erlbaum.

Craik, F. I. M. (2000). Age related changes in human memory. In D. Park & N. Schwarz (Eds.), *Cognitive aging: A primer* (pp. 75–92). Philadelphia: Taylor & Francis.

Craik, F. I. M. & Byrd, M. (1982). Aging and cognitive deficits: The role of attentional resources. In F. I. M. Craik & S. Trehub (Eds.), *Aging and cognitive processes* (pp. 191–211). New York: Plenum.

Crawford, D. W., & Huston, T. L. (1993). The impact of the transition to parenthood on marital leisure. *Personality and Social Psychology Bulletin, 19,* 39–46.

Cromwell, R. L., & Newton, R. A. (2004). Relationship between balance and gait stability in health older adults. *Journal of Aging and Physical Activity, 12,* 90–100.

Crooks, R., & Baur, K. (1990). *Our sexuality.* Redwood City, CA: Cummings.

Crystal, S., & Beck, P. (1992). A room of one's own: The SRO and the single elderly. *Gerontologist, 32,* 684–692.

Cullum, S., Huppert, F. A., McGee, M., et al. (2000). Decline across different domains of cognitive function in normal ageing: Results of a longitudinal population-based study using CAMCOG. *International Journal of Geriatric Psychiatry, 15,* 853–862.

Cumming, E. (1975). Engagement with an old theory. *International Journal of Aging and Human Development, 6,* 187–191.

Cumming, E., & Henry, W. E. (1961). *Growing old.* New York: Basic Books.

Cutrona, C. E. , Russell, D.W., Brown, P.A., et al. (2005). Neighborhood context, personality, and stressful life events as predictors of depression among African-American women. *Journal of Abnormal Psychology, 114,* 3–15.

Czaja, S. J. (2001). Technological change and the older worker. In J. E. Birren and K.W. Schaie (Eds.) *Handbook of the Psychology of Aging* (pp. 547–555). San Diego: Academic Press.

Czaja, S. J. & Lee, C. C. (2001). The Internet and older adults: Design challenges and opportunities. In N. Charness, D. C. Parks, & B. A. Sabel (Eds.), *Communication, technology, and aging: Opportunities and challenges for the future* (pp 60–78). New York: Springer.

D

Dalby, P. (2006). Is there a process of spiritual change or development associated with ageing? A critical review of research. *Aging and Mental Health, 10,* 4–12.

Damush, T. M., Stump, T. E., & Clark, D. O. (2002). Body-mass index and 4-year change in health-related quality of life. *Journal of Aging and Health, 14,* 195–210.

Danner, D. D., Snowdon, D. A., & Friesen, W. V. (2001). Positive emotions in early life and longevity: Findings from the nun study. *Journal of Personality and Social Psychology, 80,* 804–813.

Daviglus, M. L., Liu, K., Yan, L. L., et al. (2004). Relation of body mass index in young adulthood and middle age to Medicare expenditures in older age. *Journal of the American Medical Association, 292,* 2743–2749.

Deci, E. L., & Ryan, R. M. (1985). The general causality orientations scale: Self-determination in personality. *Journal of Research in Personality, 19,* 109–134.

Deeg, D. H. J., Kardaun, J. W. P. F., & Fozard, J. L. (1996). Health, behavior, and aging. In J. E. Birren & K. W. Schaie (Eds.), *Handbook of the psychology of aging* (pp. 129–149). San Diego: Academic Press.

DeKay, W. T. (2000). Evolutionary psychology. In W. C. Nicholas, N. A. Pace-Nichols, D.S. Becvar, et al. (Eds.), *Handbook of family development and intervention* (pp. 23–40). New York: Wiley.

DeLongis. A., & Holtzman, S., (2005). Coping in context: The role of stress, social support, and personality in coping. *Journal of Personality, 73,* 1633–1656.

DeMaris, A., & Longmore, M. A. (1996). Ideology, power, and equity: Testing competing explanations for the perception of fairness in household labor. *Social Forces, 74,* 1043–1072.

Denney, N. W. (1982). Aging and cognitive changes. In B. B. Wolman (Ed.), *Handbook of developmental psychology* (pp. 807–827). Englewood Cliffs, NJ: Prentice Hall.

de Waal, F. (1996). *Good natured: The origins of right and wrong in humans and other animals.* Cambridge, MA: Harvard University Press.

Diekman, A. B., Eagly, A. H., Mladinic, A., et al. (2005). Dynamic stereotypes about women and men in Latin America and the United States. *Journal of Cross-Cultural Psychology, 36,* 209–226.

Diener, E., & Diener, C. (1996). Most people are happy. *Psychological Science, 7,* 181–183.

Diener, E., Gohm, C. L., Suh, E., et al. (2000). Similarity of the relations between marital status and subjective well-being across cultures. *Cultural Psychology, 31,* 419–436.

Diener, E., & Suh, E. (1998). Measuring quality of life: Economic, social, and subjective indicators. *Social Indicators Research, 40,* 189–216.

Dixon, R. A. (2000). Concepts and mechanisms of gains in cognitive aging. In D. Park & N. Schwarz (Eds.), *Cognitive aging: A primer* (pp. 23–42). Philadelphia: Taylor & Francis.

Dixon, R.A., de Frias, C.M., & Maitland, S.B. (2001). Memory in midlife. In M. E. Lachman (Ed.), *Handbook of midlife development* (pp. 248–278). New York: Wiley.

Doty, R. L. (2001). Olfaction. *Annual Review of Psychology, 52,* 423–452.

Dougall, A. L., & Baum, A. (2001). Stress, health and illness. In A. Baum, T. A. Revenson, & J. E. Singer (Eds.) *Handbook of health psychology* (pp. 321–337). Mahweh, NJ: Erlbaum.

Dunham, C. C. (1995). A link between generations: Intergenerational relations and depression in aging parents. *Journal of Family Issues, 16,* 50–465.

Dye, J. L. (2005). Fertility of American women: June 2004. *Current Population Reports, P20–555.* Washington, DC: U.S. Census Bureau.

E

Eagly, A. H. (1987). *Sex differences in social behavior: A social role interpretation.* Hillsdale, NJ: Erlbaum.

Eagly, A. H. (1995). The science and politics of comparing men and women. *American Psychologist, 50,* 145–158.

Eagly, A. H., & Wood, W. (1999). The origins of sex differences in human behavior: Evolved dispositions versus social roles. *American Psychologist, 54,* 408–423.

Echt, K. V. (2002). Designing Web-based health information for older adults: Visual considerations and design directives. In R. W. Morrell (Ed.), *Older adults, health information, and the World Wide Web* (pp. 61–87). Mahwah, NJ: Erlbaum.

Edwards, B. K., Brown, M., Wingo, P. A., et al. (2005). Annual report to the nation on the status of cancer. *Journal of the American Cancer Institute, 97,* 1407–1427.

Ehlers, A., Mayou, R. A., & Bryant, B. (1998). Psychological predictors of chronic posttraumatic stress disorder after motor vehicle accidents. *Journal of Abnormal Psychology, 107,* 508–519.

Ehrensaft, M., Moffitt, T. E., & Caspi, A. (2004). Clinically abusive relationships in an unselected birth cohort: Men's and women's participation and developmental antecedents. *Journal of Abnormal Psychology, 113,* 258–270.

Ekerdt, D. J., Kosloski, K., & DeViney, S. (2000). The normative anticipation of retirement by older workers. *Research on Aging, 22,* 3–22

Elder, G. H., Jr. (1979). Historical change in life patterns and personality. In P. B. Baltes & O. G. Brim, Jr. (Eds.). *Lifespan development and behavior* (Vol. 2, pp. 117–159) New York: Academic Press.

Elder, G. H., Jr. (1995). The life course paradigm: Social change and individual development. In P. Moen, G. H. Elder, Jr., & K. Luscher (Eds.), *Examining lives in context: Perspectives on the ecology of human development* (pp. 101–139). Washington DC: American Psychological Association.

Elder, G. H., Jr. (2001). Life course: Sociological aspects. In N. J. Smelser & P. B. Baltes (Eds.), *International encyclopedia of the social and behavioral sciences* (Vol. 13, pp. 8817–8821). Oxford: Elsevier.

Eliason, S. R. (1995). An extension of the Sorensen-Kalleberg theory of the labor market matching and attainment process. *American Sociological Review, 60,* 247–271.

Ellis, B. J., & Ketelaar, T. (2000). On the natural selection of alternative models: Evaluation of explanations in evolutionary psychology. *Psychological Inquiry, 11,* 56–68.

Ellis, R. D., & Kurniawan, S. H. (2000). Increasing the usability of on-line information for older users: A case study in participatory design. *International Journal of Human-Computer Interaction, 12,* 263–276.

Emanuel, E. J., Fairclough, D. L., & Emanuel, L. L. (2000). Attitudes and desires related to euthanasia and physician-assisted suicide among terminally ill patients and their caregivers. *Journal of the American Medical Association, 284,* 2460–2468.

Emery, C. F., & Gatz, M. (1990). Psychological and cognitive effects of an exercise program for community-residing older adults. *Gerontologist, 30,* 184–192.

Eserink, M. (2005). Let's talk about sex—and drugs. *Science, 308,* 1578–1580.

Epel, E. S., Blackburn, E. H., Lin, J., et al., (2004). Accelerated telomere shortening in response to life stress. *Proceedings of the National Academy of Sciences U.S.A., 101,* 17312–17315.

Erikson, E. H. (1950). *Childhood and society.* New York: Norton.

Erikson, E. H. (1959). *Identity and the life cycle.* New York: Norton. (Reissued 1980).

Erikson, E. H. (1982). *The life cycle completed.* New York: Norton.

Eriksson, P. S., Perfilieva, E., Bjork-Eriksson, T., et al. (1998). Neurogenesis in the adult human hippocampus. *Nature Medicine, 4,* 1313–1317.

Essen, K. M., & Leeder, S. R. (2004). *The millennium development goals and tobacco control: An opportunity for global partnership.* Geneva: World Health Organization.

Evans, D. A., Hebert, L. E., Beckett, L. A., et al. (1997). Education and other measures of socioeconomic status and risk of incident Alzheimer disease in a defined population of older persons. *Archives of Neurology, 54,* 1399–1405.

Evans, R. I. (1969). *Dialogue with Erik Erikson.* New York: Dutton.

F

Fahey, T., & Smyth, E. (2004). Do subjective indicators measure welfare? Evidence from 33 European countries. *European Societies, 6,* 5–27.

Fahlander, K., Wahlin, Å., Fastbom, J., et al. (2000). The relationship between signs of cardiovascular deficiency and cognitive performance in old age: A population-based study. *Journals of Gerontology: Series B: Psychological Sciences, 55B,* P259–P265.

Federal Interagency Forum on Aging Related Statistics (2004). *Older Americans 2004: Key indicators of well-being.* Washington, DC: U.S. Government Printing Office.

Feeney, J., & Noller, P. (1996). *Adult attachment.* Thousand Oaks, CA: Sage.

Feifel, H. (1990). Psychology and death: Meaningful rediscovery. *American Psychologist, 45,* 537–543.

Feinberg, L. F., Horvath, J., Hunt, G., et al., (2003). *Family caregiving and public policy: Principles for change.* Retrieved March 22, 2006, from http://www.thefamilycaregiver.org/pdfs/Principles.pdf.

Feinsilver, S. H. (2003). Sleep in the elderly: What is normal? *Clinics in Geriatric Medicine, 19,* 177–188.

Feld, S., & George, L. K. (1994). Moderating effects of prior social resources on the hospitalizations of elders who become widowed. *Aging and Health, 6,* 275–295.

Feldman, H. (1971). The effects of children on the family. In A. Michel (Ed.), *Family issues of employed women in Europe and America.* Leiden: E. J. Brill.

Ferraro, K. F. (2001). Aging and role transitions. In R. H. Binstock & L. K. George (Eds.), *Handbook of aging and the social sciences,* (pp. 313–330). San Diego: Academic Press.

Fetzer Institute, National Institute on Aging Working Group (1999). *Multidimensional measurement of religiousness, spirituality for use in health research.* Kalamazoo, MI: Fetzer Institute.

Field, B. (2005). *Science hero: Dame Cicely Saunders.* Retrieved May 16, 2006, from http://myhero.com/myhero.asp?hero=Cicely_Saunders>06.

Field. D. (1999). Continuity and change in friendships in advanced old age: Findings from the Berkeley older generation study. *International Journal of Aging and Human Development, 48,* 325–346.

Field, D., & Millsap, R. E. (1991). Personality in advanced old age: Continuity or change? *Journals of Gerontology: Psychological Sciences, 46B,* P299–P308.

Fields, J. (2003a). America's families and living arrangements, 2002. *Current Population Reports P20–553*. Washington, DC: U.S. Census Bureau.

Fields, J. (2003b). Children's living arrangements and characteristics, 2002. *Current Population Reports P20–547*. Washington, DC: U.S. Census Bureau.

Fields, J., & Casper, L. M. (2001). America's families and living arrangements, 2000. *Current Population Reports*. Washington, DC: U.S. Census Bureau.

Finch, C. E., & Crimmins, E. M. (2004). Inflammatory exposure and historical changes in human life-spans. *Science, 305*, 1736–1736.

Fincham, F. D., & Beach, S. R. (1999). Conflict in marriage: Implications for working with couples. *Annual Review of Psychology, 50*, 47–77.

Fisher, H. L. (2000). Lust, attraction, attachment: Biology and evolution of the three primary emotion systems for mating, reproduction, and parenting. *Journal of Sex Education and Therapy, 25*, 96–104.

Fisher, H. L. (2004). *Why we love: The nature and chemistry of romantic love.* New York: Holt.

Fleeson, W. (2004). The quality of American life at the end of the century. In O. G. Brim, C. D. Ryff, & R. C. Kessler (Eds.), *How healthy are we? A national study of well-being at midlife* (pp. 252–272). Chicago: University of Chicago Press.

Flinn, M. V., Ward, C. V., & Noone, R. J. (2005). Hormones and the human family. In D. M. Buss (Ed.), *The handbook of evolutionary psychology* (pp. 552–580). New York: Wiley.

Florian, V., Mikulincer, M., & Taubman, O. (1995). Does hardiness contribute to mental health during a stressful real-life situation? The roles of appraisal and coping. *Journal of Personality and Social Psychology, 68*, 687–695.

Floyd, K., & Morman, M. T. (2005). Fathers' and sons' reports of fathers' affectionate communication: Implications of a naïve theory of affection. *Journal of Social and Personal Relationships, 22*, 99–109.

Folkman, S., & Moskowitz, J. T. (2004). Coping: Pitfalls and promises. *Annual Review of Psychology, 55*, 745–774.

Fontaine, K. R., Redden, D. T., Wang, C., et al. (2003). Years of life lost to obesity, *Journal of the American Medical Association, 289*, 187–193.

Fowler, J. (1981). *Stages of faith.* New York: Harper & Row.

Fowler, J. (1983). Stages of faith: PT conversation with James Fowler. *Psychology Today, 17*, 55–62.

Fraley, R. C., & Shaver, P. R. (1999). Loss and bereavement: Attachment theory and recent controversies concerning "grief work" and the nature of detachment. In J. Cassidy & P. R. Shaver (Eds.), *Handbook of attachment: Theory, research, and clinical approaches* (pp. 239–260). New York: Guilford Press.

Frankl, V. E. (1984). *Man's search for meaning* (3rd ed.). New York: Simon & Schuster.

Fraser, J., Maticka-Tyndale, E., & Smylie, L. (2004). Sexuality of Canadian women at midlife. *Canadian Journal of Human Sexuality, 13*, 171–187.

Freedman, V. A., Crimmins, E., Schoeni, R. F., et al. (2004). Resolving inconsistencies in trends in old-age disability: Report from a technical working group. *Demography, 41*, 417–441.

Friedman, B. X., Blesky, A. L., & Sheyd, G. J. (2000). Incompatible with evolutionary theorizing. *American Psychologist, 55*, 1069–1060.

Friedman, D. S., Wolfs, R. C., O'Colmain, B. J., et al., (2004). Prevalence of open-angle glaucoma among adults in the U. S. *Archives of Opthamology, 122*, 532–538.

Friedman, M., & Rosenman, R. H. (1959). Association of a specific overt behavior pattern with increases in blood cholesterol, blood clotting time, incidence of arcussenilis and clinical coronary artery disease. *Journal of the American Medical Association, 169*, 1286–1296.

Friedman, M. J. (2005). Introduction: Every crisis is an opportunity. *CNS Spectrum, 10*, 96–98.

Fromm, E. (1956) *The art of loving.* New York: Harper & Row.

Fukunaga, A., Uematsu, H., & Sugimoto, K. (2005). Influences of aging on taste perception and oral somatic sensation. *Journals of Gerontology: Medical Sciences, 60A*, M109–M113.

Fung, H. H., & Carstensen, L. L. (2003). Sending memorable messages to the old: Age differences in preferences and memory for advertisements. *Journal of Personality and Social Psychology, 85*, 163–178.

Fung, H. H., Carstensen, L. L. & Lang, F. (2001). Age-related patterns in social networks among European-Americans and African-Americans: Implications for socioemotional selectivity across the life span. *International Journal of Aging and Human Development, 52*, 185–206.

G

Galambos, N. L., Barker, E. T., & Krahn, H. J. (2006). Depression, self-esteem, and anger in emerging adulthood: Seven year trajectories. *Developmental Psychology, 42*, 350–365.

Galea, S., Vlahov, D., Resnick, H., et al. (2003). Trends of probable post-traumatic stress disorder in New York City after the September 11th terrorist attacks. *American Journal of Epidemiology, 158*, 514–524.

Gana, K., Alaphilippe, D., & Bailey, N. (2004). Positive illusions and mental and physical health in later life. *Aging and Mental Health, 8*, 58–64.

Ganong, L., & Coleman, M. (1998). Attitudes regarding filial responsibilities to help elderly divorced parents and stepparents. *Journal of Aging Studies, 12*, 271–290.

Gatz, M. (2005). Educating the brain to avoid dementia: Can mental exercise prevent Alzheimer's disease? *Public Library of Medicine, 2*, 38–40.

Gatz, M., Fratiglioni, L., Johansson, B., et al. (2005). Complete ascertainment of dementia in the Swedish Twin Registry: The HARMONY study, *Neurobiology of Aging, 26*, 439–447.

Geary, D. C. (2005). Evolution of paternal investment. In D. M. Buss (Ed.), *The handbook of evolutionary psychology* (pp. 483–505). New York: Wiley.

Genevay, B. (2000). There is life after work: Re-creating oneself in the later years. In N. Peterson & R. C. González (Eds.), *Career counseling models for diverse populations Hands-on applications by practitioners* (pp. 258–269). Pacific Grove, CA: Wadsworth/Brooks–Cole.

George, L. K. (2006). Perceived quality of life. In R. H. Binstock & L. K. George (Eds.), *Handbook of aging and the social sciences* (pp. 320–336). San Diego: Academic Press.

Gerdes, E. (1995). Women preparing for traditionally male professions: Physical and psychological symptoms associated with work and stress. *Sex Roles, 32*, 787–807.

Gibbs, W. W. (2004), Untangling the roots of cancer. *Scientific American, 14*, 60–69.

Gidron, Y., Davidson, K., & Bata, I. (1999). The short-term effects of a hostility-reduction intervention on male coronary heart disease patients. *Health Psychology, 18*, 416–420.

Giele, J. Z. (1982). Women in adulthood: Unanswered questions. In J. Z. Giele (Ed.), *Women in the middle years* (pp. 1–36). New York: Wiley.

Gilligan, C. (1982). *In a different voice: Psychological theory and women's development.* Cambridge, MA: Harvard University Press.

Giscombé, C. L., & Lobel, M. (2005). Explaining disproportionately high rates of adverse birth outcomes among African Americans: The impact of stress, racism, and related factors in pregnancy. *Psychological Bulletin, 131,* 662–683.

Gist, Y. J., & Hetzel, L. I. (2004). *We the people: Aging in the United States.* Washington, DC: U.S. Census Bureau.

Gluckman, P. D., & Hanson, M. A. (2004). Living with the past: Evolution, development, and pattern of disease. *Science, 305,* 1733–1739.

Glueck, S., & Glueck, E. (1950). *Unraveling juvenile delinquency.* New York: Commonwealth Fund.

Glueck, S., & Glueck, E., (1968). *Delinquents and nondelinquents in perspective.* Cambridge, MA: Harvard University Press.

Gohdes, D. M., Appathurai, B., Larsen, B. A., et al. (2005). Age-related eye diseases: An emerging challenge for public health professionals. *Preventing Chronic Disease, 2,* 1–5.

Gold, C. H., Malmberg, B., McClearn, G. E., et al. (2002). Gender and health: A study of older, unlike-sex twins. *Journals of Gerontology: Social Sciences, 57B,* S168–S176.

Gold, D. T. (1996). Continuities and discontinuities in sibling relationships across the life span. In V. L. Bengtson (Ed.), *Adulthood and aging: Research on continuities and discontinuities.* New York: Springer.

Goldberg, A. E., & Perry-Jenkins, M. (2004). Division of labor and working-class women's well-being across the transition to parenthood. *Journal of Family Psychology, 18,* 225–236

Goldman, M. B., & Hatch, M. C. (2000). An overview of women's health. In M. B. Hatch & M. C. Goldman (Eds.), *Women and health* (pp. 5–14). San Diego: Academic Press.

Gonsiorek, J.C. (1991). The empirical basis for the demise of the illness model of homosexuality. In J. Gonsiorek & J. Weinrich (Eds.), *Homosexuality: Research implications for public policy* (pp. 115–136). Thousand Oaks, CA: Sage.

Gonyea, J. G., & Hooyman, N. R. (2005). Reducing poverty among older women: Social security reform and gender equality. *Families in Society, 86,* 338–346.

Goode, W. J., (1960). A theory of role strain. *American Sociological Review, 5,* 483–496.

Gorman, E. H. (2000). Marriage and money: The effect of marital status on attitudes toward pay and finance. *Work and Occupations, 27,* 64–88.

Gorman, J. M. (2005). In the wake of trauma. *CNS Spectrums, 10,* 81–85.

Gottfried, A. E. (2005). Maternal and dual-earner employment and children's development: Redefining the research agenda. In D. Halpern & S. E. Murphy (Eds.), *From work-family balance to work-family interaction: Changing the metaphor* (pp. 197–217). Mahwah, NJ: Erlbaum.

Gottman, J. M. (1994a). *What predicts divorce? The relationship between marital processes and marital outcomes.* Hillsdale, NJ: Erlbaum.

Gottman, J. M. (1994b). *Why marriages succeed or fail.* New York: Simon & Schuster.

Gottman, J. M., & Levenson, R. W. (2002). A two-factor model for predicting when a couple will divorce: Exploratory analyses using 14-year longitudinal data. *Family Process, 41,* 83–96.

Gottman, J. M., & Notarius, C. I. (2000). Marital research in the 20th century and a research agenda for the 21st century. *Family Process, 41,* 159–197.

Gottman, J. M., & Silver, N. (1999). *The seven principles for making marriage work.* New York: Three Rivers Press.

Gottman, J. M., Katz, L. F., & Hooven, C. (1997). *Meta-emotion: How families communicate emotionally.* Mahwah, NJ: Erlbaum.

Gough, H. G. (1957/1987). *Manual for the California Psychological Inventory.* Palo Alto, CA: Cousulting Psychologists Press.

Gould, D. C., Petty, R., & Jacobs, H. S. (2000). The male menopause—does it exist? *British Medical Journal, 320,* 858.

Gray, J. S. (1997). The fall in men's returning to marriage: Declining productivity effects or changing selection? *Journal of Human Resources, 32,* 481–504.

Green, R. J. (2004). Risk and resilience in lesbian and gay couples: Comment on Solomon, Rothblum, & Balsam (2004). *Journal of Family Psychology, 18,* 290–292.

Greendale, G. A., Kritz-Silverstein, D., Seeman, T., et al. (2000). Higher basal cortisol predicts verbal memory loss in postmenopausal women: Rancho Bernardo study. *Journal of the American Geriatric Society, 48,* 1655–1658.

Greene, S. M., & Griffith, W. A. (1998). Symptom study in context: Effects of marital quality on signs of Parkinson's disease during patient-spouse interaction. *Psychiatry, 61,* 35–45.

Greenstein, T. N. (1995). Gender ideology, marital disruption, and the employment of married women. *Journal of Marriage and the Family, 57,* 31–42.

Greer, S. (1991). Psychological response to cancer and survival. *Psychological Medicine, 21,* 43–49.

Gregoire, J., & Van der Linden, M. (1997). Effects of age on forward and backward digit span. *Aging, Neuropsychology, and Cognition, 4,* 140–149.

Gruber-Baldini, A. L., Schaie, K. W., & Willis, S. L. (1995). Similarity in married couples: A longitudinal study of mental abilities and flexible-rigidity. *Journal of Personality and Social Psychology: Personality Processes and Individual Differences, 69,* 191–203.

Grunberg, L., Moore, S. Y., & Greenberg, E. (2001). Differences in psychological and physical health among layoff survivors: The effect of layoff contact. *Journal of Occupational Health Psychology, 6,* 15–25.

Guallar-Castillón, P., López, G. E., Lozano, P. L., et al. (2002), The relationship of overweight and obesity with subjective health and use of health-care services among Spanish women. *International Journal of Obesity and Related Metabolic Disorders, 26,* 247–252.

Gupta, S. (2006). The consequences of maternal employment during men's childhood for their adult housework performance. *Gender and Society, 20,* 60–86.

Guralnik, J. M., & Simonsick, E. M. (1993). Physical disability in older Americans [Special issue]. *Journals of Gerontology, 48,* 3–10.

Gurin, P., & Brim, O. G., Jr. (1984). Change in self in adulthood: The example of a sense of control. In P. B. Baltes & O. G. Brim, Jr. (Eds.), *Life-span development and behavior* (pp. 282–334). Orlando, FL: Academic Press.

Gustafson, S. B., & Magnusson, D. (1991). *Female life careers: A pattern approach.* Hillsdale, NJ: Erlbaum.

Gutmann, D. (1975). Parenthood: A key to the comparative study of the life cycle. In N. Datan & L. H. Ginsberg (Eds.),

Life-span developmental psychology: Normative life crises (pp. 167–184). New York: Academic Press.

Gutmann, D. (1987). *Reclaimed powers: Toward a new psychology of men and women in later life.* New York: Basic Books.

H

Haan, N. (1981). Common dimensions of personality development: Early adolescence to middle life. In D. H. Eichorn, J. A. Clausen, N. Haan, et al. (Eds.) *Present and past in middle life* (pp. 117–153). New York: Academic Press.

Hagestad, G. O., & Neugarten, B. L. (1985). Age and the life course. In R. H. Binstock & E. Shana (Eds.), *Handbook of aging and the social sciences* (pp. 35–61). New York: Van Nostrand Reinhold.

Haight, B. K. (1992). Long-term effects of a structured life review process. *Journals of Gerontology: Psychological Sciences, 47B,* P312–P315.

Halpern, D. F. (2005). Psychology at the intersection of work and family: Recommendations for employers, working families, and policymakers. *American Psychologist, 60,* 397–409.

Hamer, D. (2004). *The God gene: How faith is hardwired into our genes.* New York: Doubleday.

Hamilton, B. E., Ventura, S. J., Martin, J. A., et al. (2005). *Preliminary births for 2004.* Washington, DC: National Center for Health Statistics.

Handy, B. (1998). The Viagra craze. *Time, 151,* 50–57.

Hanson, R. F., Kilpatrick, D. G., Freedy, J. R., et al. (1995). Los Angeles county after the 1992 civil disturbance: Degree of exposure and impact on mental health. *Journal of Consulting and Clinical Psychology, 63,* 987–996.

Harding, S. R., Flannelly, K. J., Weaver, A. J., et al. (2005). The influence of religion on death anxiety and death acceptance. *Mental Health, Religion, & Culture, 8,* 253–261.

Hardy, D. J., & Parasuraman, R. (1997). Cognition and flight performance in older pilots. *Journal of Experimental Psychology: Applied, 3,* 313–348.

Hardy, M. A., & Shuey, K. (2000). Retirement. In E. F. Borgatta & M. L. Borgatta (Eds.), *Encyclopedia of Sociology.* New York: Macmillan.

Hareven, T. K. (2001. Historical perspectives on aging and family relations. In R. H. Binstock & L. K. George (Eds.), *Handbook of aging and the social sciences* (pp. 141–159). San Diego: Academic Press.

Hargrove, T., & Stempel, G. H., III (2006). *Poll: Most don't believe in body's resurrection.* Scripps-Howard/Ohio University Poll. Retrieved May 16, 2006, from http://www/shns.com/shns/g_index2.cfm?action=detail&pk=RESURRECTION-04-05-06.

Harris Poll (2005a). *Majorities of U.S. adults favor euthanasia and physician assisted suicide by more than two-to-one.* Retrieved May 16, 2006, from http://www.harrisinteractive.com/harris_poll/index.asp?PID=561.

Harris Poll (2005b). *The religions and other beliefs of Americans 2005.* Retrieved May 16, 2006, from http://www.harrisinteractive.com/harris_poll/index.asp?PID=618.

Hartley, J. (1994). *Designing instructional text.* East Brunswick, NJ: Nicholas.

Hartley, J., & Harris, J. L. (2001). Reading the typography of text. In J. L. Harris, A. G. Kamhi, & K. E. Pollack (Eds.), *Literacy in African-American communities* (pp. 109–125). Mahwah, NJ: Erlbaum.

Hartung, P. J., & Niles, S. G. (2000). Using traditional career theories with college students. In D. Luzzo (Ed.), *Career development of college students: Translating theory and research into practice* (pp. 3–22). Washington, DC: American Psychological Association.

Hasher, L., & Zacks, R. T. (1988). Working memory, comprehension, and aging: A review and a new view. In G. H. Bower (Ed.), *The psychology of learning and motivation* (Vol. 2, pp. 193–225). San Diego: Academic Press.

Hatfield, E. (1988). Passionate and compassionate love. In R. J. Sternberg & M. L. Barnes (Eds.), *The psychology of love* (pp. 191–217). New Haven: Yale University Press.

Hawkins, H. L., Kramer, A. F., & Capaldi, D. (1992). Aging, exercise, and attention. *Psychology and Aging, 7,* 643–653.

Hayflick, L. (1977). The cellular basis for biological aging. In C. E. Finch & L. Hayflick (Eds.), *Handbook of the biology of aging* (pp. 159–186). New York: Van Nostrand Reinhold.

Hayflick, L. (1994). *How and why we age.* New York: Ballantine Books.

Hazan, C., & Shaver, P. (1987). Romantic love conceptualized as an attachment process. *Journal of Personality and Social Psychology, 52,* 511–524.

Hazan, C., & Shaver, P. (1991). Love and work: An attachment-theoretical perspective. *Journal of Personality and Social Psychology, 59,* 270–280.

Hazell, L. V. (1997). Cross-cultural funeral rites. *Director, 69,* 53–55.

He, W., & Schachter, J. P. (2003). *Internal migration of the older population: 1995 to 2000.* U.S. Census Bureau Census 2000 Special Reports. Retrieved March 18, 2006, from www.census.gov/prod/2003pubs/censr-10.pdf.

Heath, A. C., Berg, K., Eaves, L. J., et al. (1985). Education policy and the heritability of educational attainment. *Nature, 314,* 734–736.

Heath, C. W. (1945). *What people are.* Cambridge, MA: Harvard University Press.

Heckhausen, J. (2001). Adaptation and resilience in midlife. In M. E. Lachman (Ed.), *Handbook of midlife development* (pp. 345–394). New York: Wiley.

Heflin, C. M., Siefert, K., & Williams, D. R. (2005). Food insufficiency and women's mental health: Findings from a 3-year panel of welfare recipients. *Social Science and Medicine, 61,* 1971–1982.

Helms, S. T. (1996). Some experimental tests of Holland's congruity hypothesis: The reactions of high school students to occupational simulations. *Journal of Career Assessment, 4,* 253–268.

Helson, R., & Kwan, V. S. Y. (2000). Personality development in adulthood: The broad picture and processes in one longitudinal sample. In S. Hampson (Ed.), *Advances in personality psychology* (Vol. 1, pp. 77–106). London: Routledge.

Helson, R., Kwan, V. S. Y., John, O. P., et al. (2002). The growing evidence for personality change in adulthood: Findings from research with personality inventories. *Journal of Research in Personality, 36,* 287–306.

Helson, R., Pals, J., & Solomon, M. (1997). Is there adult development distinctive to women? In R. Hogan, J. Johnson, & S. Briggs (Eds.), *Handbook of personality psychology* (pp. 291–314). San Diego: Academic Press.

Helson, R., & Roberts, B. W. (1994). Ego development and personality change in adulthood. *Journal of Personality and Social Psychology, 66,* 911–920.

Helson, R., & Wink, P. (1992). Personality change in women from the early 40s to the early 50s. *Psychology and Aging, 7,* 46–55.

Henretta, J. C. (2001). Work and retirement. In R. Binstock & L. George (Eds.), *Handbook of aging and the social sciences* (pp. 255–271). San Diego: Academic Press.

Henretta, J. C., O'Rand, A. M., & Chan, C. G. (1993). Joint role investments and synchronization of retirement: A sequential approach to couples' retirement timing. *Social Forces, 71,* 981–1000.

Hequembourg, A., & Brallier, S. (2005). Gendered stories of parental caregiving among siblings. *Journal of Aging Studies, 19,* 53–71.

Hershey, D. A., & Wilson, J. A. (1997). Age differences in performance awareness on a complex financial decision-making task. *Experimental Aging Research, 23,* 257–273.

Hertzog, C., Park, D. C., Morrell, R. W., et al. (2000). Ask and ye shall receive: Behavioural specificity in the accuracy of subjective memory complaints. *Applied Cognitive Psychology, 14,* 257–275.

Hess, T. M. (2005). Memory and aging in context. *Psychological Bulletin, 131,* 383–406.

Hess, T. M., Auman, C., Colcombe, S. J., et al. (2003). The impact of stereotype threat on age differences in memory performance. *Journals of Gerontology: Psychological Sciences, 58B,* P3–P11.

Hess, T. M., Hinson, J. T., & Statham, J. A. (2004). Implicit and explicit stereotype activation effects on memory: Do age and awareness moderate the impact of priming? *Psychology and Aging, 19,* 495–505.

Heuveline, P., & Timberlake, J. M. (2004). The role of cohabitation in family formation: The U.S. in comparative perspective. *Journal of Marriage and Family, 66,* 1214–1230.

Hill, R. D., Storandt, M., & Malley, M. (1993). The impact of long-term exercise training on psychological function in older adults. *Journals of Gerontology: Psychological Sciences, 48B,* P12–P17.

Hipple, S. (1999). Worker displacement in the mid 1900s. *Monthly Labor Review, 122,* No. 7. Retrieved May 21, 2006, from http://www.bls.gov/opub/mlr/1999/07/art2full.pdf.

Hodgson, L. G., (1992). Adult grandchildren and their grandparents: The enduring bond. *International Journal of Aging and Human Development, 34,* 20–225.

Hoffman, L., Atchley, P., McDowd, J. M., et al. (2005). The role of visual attention in predicting driving impairment in older adults. *Psychology and Aging, 20,* 610–622.

Holden, C. (2005). Sex and the suffering brain. *Science, 308,* 1574–1577.

Holland, J. L. (1958). A personality inventory employing occupational titles. *Journal of Applied Psychology, 42,* 336–342.

Holland, J. L. (1992). *Making vocatinal choices: A theory of vocational personalities and work environments,* Odessa, FL: Psychyological Assessment Resources. (page 29).

Holland, J. L. (1996). Integrating career theory and practice. In M. L. Savickas & W. B. Walsh (Eds.), *Handbook of career counseling theory and practice* (pp. 1–11). Palo-Alto: Davies-Black.

Holland, J. L. (1997). *Making vocational choices* (3rd ed.). Odessa, FL: Psychological Assessment Resources.

Holmes, T. H., & Rahe, R. H. (1967). The Social Readjustment Rating Scale. *Journal of Psychosomatic Research, 11,* 213–218.

Holt, B. J., & Morrell, R. W. (2002). Guidelines for Web site design for older adults: The ultimate influence of cognitive factors. In R. W. Morrell (Ed.), *Older adults, health information, and the World Wide Web* (pp. 109–132). Mahwah, NJ: Erlbaum.

Horn, J. L., & Cattell, R. B. (1966). Refinement and test of the theory of fluid and crystallized intelligence. *Journal of Educational Psychology, 57,* 253–270

Horn, J. L., & Donaldson, G. (1980). Cognitive development in adulthood. In O. G. Brim, Jr., & J. Kagan (Eds.), *Constancy and change in human development* (pp. 415–529). Cambridge, MA: Harvard University Press.

Horn, J. L., & Hofer, S. M. (1992). Major abilities and development in the adult period. In R. J. Sternberg & C. A. Berg (Eds.), *Intellectual development* (pp. 44–99). Cambridge: Cambridge University Press.

Hornsby, P. J. (2001). Cell proliferation in mammalian aging. In E. J. Masoro & S. N. Austad (Eds.), *Handbook of the biology of aging* (pp. 207–245), San Diego: Academic Press.

House, J. S., Kessler, R. C., & Herzog, A. R. (1990). Age, socioeconomic status, and health. *Milbank Quarterly, 68,* 383–411.

House, J. S., Kessler, R. C., Herzog, A. R., et al. (1992). Social stratification, age, and health. In K. W. Schaie, D. Blazer, & J. House (Eds.), *Aging, health behaviors, and health outcomes* (pp. 1–37), Hillsdale, NJ: Erlbaum.

Howard, A. (1998). New careers and older workers. In K. W. Schaie & C. Schooler (Eds.), *Commentary: Impact of work on older adults* (pp. 235–245). New York: Springer.

Hoyert, D. K., Kung, H. C., & Smith, B. L. (2005). *Deaths: Preliminary data for 2003.* Hyattsville, MD: National Center for Health Statistics.

Huang, T. T.-K., Harris K. J., Lee, R. E., et al. (2003). Assessing overweight, obesity, diet, and physical activity in college students. *Journal of American College Health, 52,* 83–86.

Hultsch, D. F., Hertzog, C., Dixon, R. A., et al. (1998). *Memory change in the aged.* Cambridge: Cambridge University Press.

Hunter, S., & Sundel, M. (Eds.). (1989). *Midlife myths: Issues, findings, and practice implications.* Newbury Park, CA: Sage.

Hurwicz, M., Dunham, C. C., Boyd-Davis, S. L., et al. (1992). Salient life events in three-generation families. *Journals of Gerontology: Psychological Sciences, 47B,* P11–P13.

Hy, L. X., & Loevinger, J. (1996). *Measuring ego development.* Mahwah, NJ: Erlbaum

Hyde, J. S., Essex, M. J., & Horton, F. (1993). Fathers and parental leave: Attitudes and experiences. *Journal of Family Issues, 14,* 616–638.

Hyde, V., & Gibbs, I. (1993). A very special relationship: Granddaughters' perceptions of grandmothers. *Ageing and Society, 13,* 83–96.

I

Idler, E. L., (2006). Religion and aging. In R. H. Binstock & L. K. George (Eds.), *Handbook of aging and the social sciences* (pp. 277–300). San Diego: Academic Press.

Idler, E. L., Kasl, S. V., & Hays, J. C. (2001). Patterns of religions practice and belief in the last years of life. *Journals of Gerontology: Social Sciences, 56B,* S326–S334.

Idler, E. L., Musick, M. A., Ellison, C. G., et al. (2003). Measuring multiple dimensions of religion and spirituality for health research. *Research on Aging, 25,* 327–365.

Ingram, V. (2003). Alzheimer's disease. *American Scientist, 91,* 312–321.

Ironson. G., Solomon, G. F., Balbin, E. G., et al. (2002). The Ironson-Woods Spirituality/Religiousness Index is associated with long survival, health behaviors, less distress, and low cortisol in people with HIV/AIDS. *Annals of Behavioral Medicine, 28,* 189–213.

J

Jackson, D. N., & Paunonen, S. V. (1980). Personality structure assessment. *Annual Review of Psychology, 31,* 503–582.

Jacobs, S. (1993). *Pathologic grief: Maladaption to loss.* Washington, DC: American Psychiatric Press.

James, W. (1902/1958). *The varieties of religious experience.* New York: Mentor.

Jankowiak W. R., & Fischer, H. L. (1992). A cross-cultural perspective on romantic love. *Ethnology, 31,* 149.

Janus, S. S., & Janus, C. L. (1993). *The Janus report on sexual behavior.* New York: Wiley.

Jennings, P. A., Aldwin, C. M., Levenson, M. R., et al. (2006). Combat exposure, perceived benefits of military service, and wisdom in later life: Findings from the Normative Aging Study. *Research on Aging, 28,* 115–1334

Jensen, A. R. (1998). *The g factor: The science of mental ability.* Westport, CT: Praeger.

Johnson, C. A., Stanley, S. M., Glenn, N. D., et al. (2002). *Marriage in Oklahoma: 2001 baseline statewide survey on marriage and divorce.* Oklahoma City: Oklahoma Department of Human Services.

Johnson, C. L. (1985). Grandparenting options in divorcing families: An anthropological perspective. In V. L. Bengtson & J. F. Robertson (Eds.), *Grandparenthood* (pp. 81–96). Beverly Hills, CA: Sage.

Johnson, F. (1996). Friendships among women: Closeness in dialogue. In J. T. Wood (Ed.), *Gendered relationships,* (pp. 79–94). Mountain View, CA: Mayfield.

Johnson, M. K., Reeder, J. A., Raye, C. L., et al. (2002). Second thoughts versus second looks: An age-related deficit in reflectively refreshing just-active information. *Psychological Science, 13,* 63–66.

Johnson, M. M. S. (1993). Thinking about strategies during, before, and after making a decision. *Psychology and Aging, 8,* 231–141.

Johnson, N. J., Backlund, E., Sorlie, P. D., et al. (2000). Marital status and mortality. *Annals of Epidemiology, 10,* 224–238.

Jones, C. J., & Meredith, W. (1996). Patterns of personality change across the life span. *Psychology and Aging, 11,* 57–65.

Jones, E. (1981). *The life and work of Sigmund Freud.* New York: Basic Books.

Jones, M. G. (1995). Visuals for information access: A new philosophy for screen and interface design. In A. C. Eric (Ed.), *Imagery and visual literacy: Selected readings from the Annual Conference of the International Visual Literacy Association* (pp. 264–272). Tempe, AZ.

Joseph, J. A., Shukitt-Hale, B., Denisova, N. A., et al. (1999). Reversal of age-related declines in neuronal signal transduction, cognitive, and motor behavioral deficits with blueberry, spinach, or strawberry dietary supplementation. *Journal of Neuroscience, 19,* 8114–8121.

Judge, T. A., Higgins, C. A., Thoreson, C. J., et al. (1999). The Big Five personality traits, general mental ability, and career success across the life span. *Personnel Psychology, 52,* 621–652.

Jung, C. G. (1917/1966). *Two Essays on Analytical Psychology.* London: Routledge.

Jung, C. G. (1933). *Modern man in search of a soul.* New York: Harcourt, Brace, & World.

Jung, C. G. (1964). *Man and his symbols.* New York: Laurel.

K

Kahn, R. L., & Antonucci, T. C. (1980). Convoys over the life course: Attachment, roles, and social support. In P. B. Baltes & O. Brim (Eds.), *Life-span development and behavior* (Vol. 3, pp. 253–268), New York: Academic Press.

Kaiser, F. E., Wilson, M. M., & Morley, J. E. (1997). Menopause and beyond. In C. K. Cassel, H. J. Cohen, E. D. Larson, et al. (Eds.), *Geriatric medicine (*3rd ed. pp. 527–540) New York: Springer Verlag.

Kalish, R. A. (1985). The social context of death and dying. In R. H. Binstock & E. Shanas (Eds.), *Handbook of aging and the social sciences* (pp. 149–170). New York: Van Nostrand Reinhold.

Kalleberg, A. L. (1998). Commentary: The institution of gradual retirement in Japan. In K. W. Schaie & C. Schooler (Eds.), *Commentary: Impact of work on older adults* (pp. 92–100). New York: Springer.

Kaplan, M. S., Huguet, N., Newsom, J. T., et al. (2004). The association between length of residence and obesity among Hispanic immigrants, *American Journal of Preventive Medicine, 27,* 323–326.

Karney, B. R., & Bradbury, T. N. (1995). The longitudinal course of marital quality and stability: A review of theory, method, and research. *Psychological Bulletin, 118,* 3–34.

Kasser, V. M., & Ryan, R. M. (1999). The relation of psychological needs for autonomy and relatedness to health, vitality, well-being, and mortality in a nursing home. *Journal of Applied Social Psychology, 29,* 935–954.

Kaufman, G., & Uhlenberg, P. (2000). The influence of parenthood on the work effort of married men and women. *Social Forces, 78,* 931–949.

Keen, S. (1983). *The passionate life: Stages of loving.* New York: Harper & Row.

Kegan, R. (1980). There the dance is: Religious dimensions of developmental theory. In J. W. Fowler & A. Vergote (Eds.), *Toward moral and religious maturity* (pp. 403–440). Morristown, NJ: Silver Burdette.

Kegan, R. (1982). *The evolving self.* Cambridge, MA: Harvard University Press.

Kellehear, A., & Lewin, T. (1988–89). Farewells by the dying: A sociological study. *Omega, 19,* 275–292.

Keller, R. T. (1983). Predicting absenteeism from prior absenteeism, attitudinal factors, and nonattitudinal factors. *Journal of Applied Psychology, 68,* 536–540.

Kelley, C., & Charness, N. (1995). Issues in training older adults to use computers. *Behaviour and Information Technology, 14,* 107–120.

Kemp, C. L. (2005). Dimensions of grandparent-adult grandchild relationships: From family ties to intergenerational friendships. *Canadian Journal on Aging, 24,* 161–178.

Kemperman, G., Wiskott, L., & Gage, F. H. (2004). Functional significance of adult neurogenesis. *Current Opinion in Neurobiology, 14,* 186–191.

Kennedy, G. E. (1992). Shared activities of grandparents and grandchildren. *Psychological Reports, 70,* 211–227.

Kesimci, A., Göral, F. S., & Gençöz, T. (2005). Determinants of stress-related growth: Gender, stressfulness of the event, and coping strategies. *Current Psychology, 24,* 68–75.

Kessler, R. C., Berglund, P., Demler, O., et al. (2005). Lifetime prevalence and age-of-onset distributions of *DSM-IV* disorders in the National Comorbidity Survey replication. *Archives of General Psychiatry, 62,* 593–602.

Kessler, R. C., Chiu, W. T., Demler, O., et al. (2005). Prevalence, severity, and comorbidity of 12-month *DSM-IV* disorders in the National Comorbidity Survey Replication. *Archives of General Psychiatry, 62,* 617–627.

Kessler, R. C., Mickelson, K. D., Walters, E. E., et al. (2004). Age and depression in the MIDUS Survey. In O. G. Brim, C. D. Ryff, & R. C. Kessler (Eds.). *How healthy are we? A national study of well-being at midlife* (pp. 227–251). Chicago: University of Chicago Press.

Kiecolt-Glaser, J. K., Glaser, R., Gravenstein, S., et al. (1996). Chronic stress alters the immune response to influenza virus vaccine in older adults. *Proceedings of the National Academy of Sciences, 93,* 3043–3047.

Kiecolt-Glaser, J. K., & Newton, T. L. (2001). Marriage and health: His and hers, *Psychological Bulletin, 127,* 472–503.

Kiecolt-Glaser, J. K., Preacher, K. J., MacCallum, R. C., et al. (2003). Chronic stress and age-related increases in the proinflammatory cytokine interleukin-6. *Proceedings of the National Academy of Sciences, USA, 100,* 9090–9095.

Kieran, K., (2002). Cohabitation in western Europe: Trends, issues, and implications. In A. Booth & A. Crouter (Eds.), *Just living together: Implications of cohabitation on families, children, and social policy* (pp. 3–32). Mahwah, NJ: Erlbaum.

Kinderman, S. S., & Brown, G. G. (1997). Depression and memory in the elderly: A meta-analysis. *Journal of Clinical and Experimental Neuropsychology, 19,* 625–642.

Kirby, S. E., Coleman, P. G., & Daley, D. (2004). Spirituality and well-being in frail and non-frail older adults. *Journals of Gerontology: Psychological Sciences, 59B,* P123–P129.

Kirkcaldy, B., Furnham, A., & Siefen, G. (2004). The relationship between health efficacy, educational attainment, and well-being among 30 nations. *European Psychologist, 9,* 107–119.

Kirkpatrick, L. A., & Davis, K. E. (1994). Attachment style, gender and relationship stability: A longitudinal analysis. *Journal of Personality and Social Psychology, 66,* 501–512.

Kleyman, E. (2000). From allies to adversaries? *American Psychologist, 55,* 1061–1062.

Kliegl, R., Smith, J., & Baltes, P. B. (1990). On the locus and process of magnification of age differences during mnemonic training. *Developmental Psychology, 26,* 894–904.

Kline, G. H., Stanley, S. M., Markman, H. J., et al. (2004). Timing is everything: Pre-engagement cohabitation and increased risk for poor marital outcomes. *Journal of Family Psychology, 18,* 311–318.

Klonoff, E. A., Landrine, H., & Ullman, J. B. (1999). Racial discrimination and psychiatric symptoms among blacks. *Cultural Diversity and Ethnic Minority Psychology, 5,* 329–339.

Koenig, H. G. (2006). Religion, spirituality and aging. *Aging and Mental Health, 10,* 1–3.

Koenig, H. G., George, L. K., Hays, J. C., et al. (1998). The relationship between religious activities and blood pressure in older adults. *International Journal of Psychiatric Medicine, 28,* 189–213.

Kohlberg, L. (1973). Continuities in childhood and adult moral development revisited. In P. B. Baltes & K. W. Schaie (Eds.), *Life-span developmental psychology: Personality and socialization* (pp. 180–204). New York: Academic Press.

Kohlberg, L. (1976). Moral stages and moralization: The cognitive-developmental approach. In T. Likona (Ed.), *Moral development and behavior: Theory, research, and social issues* (pp. 31–53). New York: Holt.

Kohlberg, L. (1981). *Essays on moral development* (Vol. 1), *The philosophy of moral development.* New York: Harper & Row.

Kohlberg, L. (1984). *Essays on moral development* (Vol. 2), *The psychology of moral development.* San Francisco: Harper & Row.

Kohlberg, L., Levine, C., & Hewer, A. (1983). *Moral stages: A current formulation and a response to critics.* New York: Karger.

Kolomer, S., & McCallion, P. (2005). Depression and caregiver mastery in grandfathers caring for their grandchildren. *International Journal of Aging and Human Development, 60,* 283–294.

Korenman, S., & Neumark, D. (1991). Does marriage really make men more productive? *Journal of Human Resources, 26,* 282–307.

Korhonen, M. T., Mero, A., & Suominen, H. (2003). Age related differences in 10-m sprint performance in male and female master runners. *Medicine and Science in Sports and Exercise, 35,* 1419–1428.

Koski, L. R., & Shaver, P. R. (1997). Attachment and relationship satisfaction across the lifespan. In R. J. Sternberg & M. Hojjat, (Eds.), *Satisfaction in close relationships* (pp. 26–55). New York: Guilford Press.

Krampe, R. T., & Ericsson, K. A. (1996). Maintaining excellence: Deliberate practice and elite performance in young and old pianists. *Journal of Experimental Psychology: General, 125,* 331–359.

Krause, N. (1993). Race differences in life satisfaction among aged men and women. *Journals of Gerontology: Social Sciences, 48B,* S235–S244.

Krause, N. (1995). Assessing stress-buffering effects: A cautionary note. *Psychology and Aging, 10,* 518–526.

Krause, N. (2005). Negative interaction and heart disease in late life: Exploring variations by socioeconomic status. *Journal of Aging and Health, 17,* 28–55.

Krause, N. (2006). Social relationships in late life. In R. H. Binstock & L. K. George (Eds.), *Handbook of aging and the social sciences* (pp. 181–200). San Diego: Academic Press.

Krause, N., & Borawski-Clark, E. (1994). Clarifying the functions of social support in later life. *Research on Aging, 16,* 251–279.

Kreider, R. M. (2005). Number, timing, and duration of marriages and divorces: 2001. *Current Population Reports P70–97.* Washington, DC: U.S. Census Bureau.

Krettenauer, T., Urlich, M., Hofmann, V., et al. (2003). Behavioral problems in childhood and adolescence as predictors of ego-level attainment in early adulthood. *Merrill-Palmer Quarterly, 49,* 125–153.

Krothe, J. S. (1997). Giving voice to elderly people: Community based long-term care. *Public Health Nursing, 14,* 217–226.

Krueger, R. F., Hicks, B. M., & McGue, M. (2001). Altruism and antisocial behavior: Independent tendencies, unique personality correlates, distinct etiologies. *Psychological Science, 12,* 397–402.

Kübler-Ross, E. (1969). *On death and dying.* New York: Macmillan.

Kübler-Ross, E. (1974). *Questions and answers on death and dying.* New York: Macmillan.

Kuehn, B. M. (2005). Better osteoporosis management a priority: Impact predicted to soar with aging population. *Journal of the American Medical Association, 23,* 2453–2458.

Kulkarni, J. (2005). Psychotic illness in women at perimenopause and menopause. In D. E. Stewart (Ed.), *Menopause: A mental health practitioner's guide* (pp. 85–133). Washington, DC: American Psychiatric Publishing.

Kurdek, L. A. (1998). Relationship outcomes and their predictors: Longitudinal evidence from heterosexual married, gay cohabiting, and lesbian cohabiting couples. *Journal of Marriage and the Family, 60,* 553–568.

Kurdek, L. A. (2004). Are gay and lesbian cohabiting couples really different from heterosexual married couples? *Journal of Marriage and Family, 66,* 880–900.

L

Labouvie-Vief, G., & Diehl, M. (1998). The role of ego development in the adult self. In P. M. Westenberg, A. Blasi, & L. D. Cohn (Eds.), *Personality development: Theoretical, empirical, and clinical investigations of Loevinger's conception of ego development* (pp. 219–235). London: Erlbaum.

Labouvie-Vief, G., & Gonda, J. N. (1976) Cognitive strategy training and intellectual performance in the elderly. *Journals of Gerontology, 31,* 327–332.

Lamberts, S. W. J., van den Beld, A. W., & van der Lely, A. J. (1997). The endocrinology of aging. *Science, 278,* 419–424.

Lane, M. A., Ingram, D. K., & Roth, G. S. (2004). The serious search for an antiaging pill. *Scientific American, 14,* 36–41.

Lauman, E. O., Gagnon, J. H., Michael, R. T., et al. (1994). *The social organization of sexuality: Sexual practices in the United States.* Chicago: University of Chicago Press.

Launer, L. J. (2005). The epidemiologic study of dementia: A lifelong quest? *Neurobiology of Aging, 26,* 335–340.

Laursen, P. (1997). The impact of aging on cognitive function. *Acta Neurologica Scandinavica Supplementum, 96,* 3–86.

Lawton, L., Silverstein, M., & Bengtson, V. L. (1994). Affection, social contact and geographic distance between adult children and their parents. *Journal of Marriage and the Family. 57,* 465–476.

Lazarus, R. S. (1993). Coping theory and research: Past, present, and future. *Psychosomatic Medicine, 55,* 234–247.

Lemasters, E. E. (1957). Parenthood as a crisis. *Marriage and Family Living, 19,* 352–355.

Lerman, R., & Sorensen, E. (2000). Father involvement with their nonmarital children: Patterns, determinants, and effects on their earnings. *Marriage and Family Review, 29,* 137–158.

Lerner, R. M. (2006). Developmental science, developmental systems, and contemporary theories of human development. In W. Damon & R. M. Lerner (Gen. Eds.), *Handbook of Child Psychology,* R. M. Lerner (Vol. Ed.), Vol. 1, *Theoretical models of human development,* (pp. 1–17). New York: Wiley.

Leserman, J., Petitto, J. M., Golden, R. N., et al. (2000). Impact of stressful life events, depression, social support, coping, and cortisol on progression to AIDS. *American Journal of Psychiatry, 157,* 1221–1228.

Lethbridge-Çejku, M., & Vickerie, J. (2005). *Summary health statistics for U.S. adults: National Health Interview Survey.* Hyattsville, MD: National Center for Health Statistics.

Levinson, D. J. (1978). *The seasons of a man's life.* New York: Knopf.

Levitt, M. J., Weber, R. A., & Guacci, N. (1993). Convoys of social support: An intergenerational analysis. *Psychology and Aging, 7,* 323–326.

Li, L. W., Seltzer, M. M., & Greenberg, J. S. (1997). Social support and depressive symptoms: Differential pattern in wife and daughter caregivers. *Journals of Gerontology: Social Sciences, 52B,* S200–S211.

Libby. P. (2004). Atherosclerosis: The new view. *Scientific American, 14,* 50–57.

Lichtenstein, P., Hershberger, S. L., & Pedersen, N. L. (1995). Dimensions of occupations: Genetic and environmental influences. *Journal of Biosocial Science, 27,* 193–206.

Lieberman, M. (1996). *Doors close, doors open: Widows, grieving and growing.* New York: Putnam.

Lillberg, K., Verkasalo, P. K., Kaprio, J., et al. (2003). Stressful life events and risk of breast cancer in 10,808 women: A cohort study. *American Journal of Epidemiology, 157,* 415–423.

Lin, G., & Rogerson, P. A. (1995). Elderly parents and geographic availability of their children. *Research on Aging, 17,* 303–331.

Lindahl, K., Clements, M., & Markman, H. (1998). The development of marriage: A 9-year perspective. In T. N. Bradbury (Ed.), *The developmental course of marital dysfunction* (pp. 205–236). New York: Cambridge University Press.

Lindahl, K. M., Malik, N. M., and Bradbury, T. N. (1997). The developmental course of couples' relationships. In W.K. Halford, & H.J. Markman (Eds.), *Clinical Handbook of Marriage and Couples Interventions.* Chichester: Wiley.

Lindenberger, U., & Baltes, P. B. (1994). Sensory functioning and intelligence in old age: A strong connection. *Psychology and Aging, 9,* 339–355.

Lindenberger, U., & Baltes, P. B. (1997). Intellectual functioning in old and very old age: Cross-sectional results from the Berlin Aging Study. *Psychology and Aging, 12,* 410–432.

Littman, A. J., Kristal, A. R., & White, E. (2005). Effects of physical activity intensity, frequency, and activity type on 10-year weight change in middle-aged men and women. *International Journal of Obesity, 29,* 523–533.

Liu, L. L., & Park, D. C. (2003). Technology and the promise of independent living for adults: A cognitive perspective. In N. Charness & K. W. Schaie (Eds.), *Impact of technology on successful aging* (pp. 262–289). New York: Springer.

Livson, F. B. (1981). Paths to psychological health in the middle years: Sex differences. In D. H. Eichorn, J. A. Clausen, N. Haan, et al. (Eds.), *Present and past in middle life* (pp. 195–221). New York: Academic Press.

Livson, N., & Peskin, H. (1981). Psychological health at 40: Prediction from adolescent personality. In D. H. Eichorn, J. A. Clausen, N. Haan, et al. (Eds.), *Present and past in middle life* (pp. 184–194). New York: Academic Press.

Lobar, S. L. (2006). Cross-cultural beliefs, ceremonies, and rituals surrounding death of a loved one. *Pediatric Nursing, 32,* 44–50.

Loevinger, J. (1976). *Ego development.* San Francisco: Jossey-Bass.

Loevinger, J. (1997). Stages of personality development. In R. Hogan, J. Johnson, & S. Briggs (Eds.), *Handbook of personality psychology* (pp. 199–208). San Diego: Academic Press.

Longino, C. F., Jr. (2001). Geographical distribution and migration. In R. H. Binstock & L. K. George (Eds.), *Handbook of Aging and the Social Sciences* (pp. 103–124). San Diego: Academic Press.

Longino, C. F., Jr., & Bradley, D. E. (2006). Internal and international migration. In R. H. Binstock & L. K. George (Eds.), *Handbook of aging and the social sciences* (pp. 76–93). San Diego: Elsevier Academic Press.

Lonky, E., Kaus, C. R., & Roodin, P. A. (1984). Life experience and mode of coping: Relation to moral judgment in adulthood. *Developmental Psychology, 20,* 1159–1167.

Low, K. S. D., Yoon, M., Roberts, B. W., et al. (2005). The stability of vocational interests from early adolescence to middle adulthood: A quantitative review of longitudinal studies. *Psychological Bulletin, 131,* 713–737.

Lucas, R. E., Clark, A. E., Georgellis, Y., et al. (2003). Re-examining adaptation and the set-point model of happiness: Reactions to changes in marital status. *Journal of Personality and Social Psychology, 84,* 527–539.

Luff, J. A., Khine, K., Schmidt, P. J., et al. (2005). Mood disorders, midlife, and reproductive aging. In D. E. Stewart (Ed.), *Menopause: A mental health practitioner's guide* (pp. 57–84). Washington, DC: American Psychiatric Publishing.

Lupien, S. J., DeLeon, M., DeSanti, S., et al. (1998). Cortisol levels during human aging predict hippocampal atrophy and memory deficits. *Nature Neurosciences, 1,* 69–73.

Luzzo, D. A. (2000). Career development of returning-adult and graduate students. In D. A. Luzzo (Ed.), *Career counseling of college students: An empirical guide to strategies that work* (pp. 191–200). Washington, DC: American Psychological Association.

Lynch. L. M. (1992). *Differential effects of post-school training on early career mobility.* Retrieved on May 13, 2006, from http://www.nber.org/papers/w4034.pdf

Lynn, J., Wilkinson, A., & Etheredge, L. (2001). Financing care for those coming to the end of life. In L. Snyder & T. Quill (Eds.), *Physician's guide to end-of-life care* (pp. 214–233). Philadelphia: American College of Physicians.

Lyons, N. P. (1983). Two perspectives: on self, relationships, and morality. *Harvard Educational Review, 53,* 125–145.

M

Mackey, R. A., & O'Brien, B. A. (1999). Adaptation in lasting marriages. *Families in Society: The Journal of Contemporary Human Services, 80,* 587–596.

Madden, D. J., Blementhal, J. A., Allen, P. A., et al. (1989). Improving aerobic capacity in healthy older adults does not necessarily lead to improved cognitive performance. *Psychology and Aging, 4,* 307–320.

Maddi, S. R. (2005). On hardiness and other pathways to resilience. *American Psychologist, 60,* 261–262.

Magdol, L., Moffitt, T. E., Caspi, A., et al. (1998). Developmental antecedents of partner abuse: A prospective-longitudinal study. *Journal of Abnormal Psychology, 107,* 375–389.

Main, M., & Hesse, E. (1990). Parents' unresolved traumatic experiences are related to infant disorganized attachment status: Is frightened and/or frightening parental behavior the linking mechanism? In M. T. Greenberg, D. Cicchetti, & E. M. Cummings (Eds.), *Attachment in the preschool years:*

Theory, research, and intervention (pp. 161–182). Chicago: University of Chicago, Press.

Main, M., Kaplan, N., & Cassidy, J. (1985). Security in infancy, childhood, and adulthood: A move to the level of representation. *Monographs of the Society for Research in Child Development, 50* (Serial No. 209), 66–104.

Manly, J. J., Jacobs, D. M., Sano, M., et al. (1999). Effect of literacy on neuropsychological test performance in nondemented, education-matched elders. *Journal of the International Neuropsychological Society, 5,* 191–202.

Marcenes, W., & Sheihan, A. (1996). The relationship between marital quality and oral health status. *Psychology and Health, 11,* 357–369.

Marion, F. (2006). An unconventional life: Sister Anne Richard Baker reflects on 60 years in the sisterhood. *Palm Beach Post,* June 3, 2006, pp. 1D & 6D.

Markides, K. S., & Black, S. A. (1996). Race, ethnicity, and aging: The impact of inequality. In R. H. Binstock & L. K. George (Eds.), *Handbook of aging and the social sciences* (pp. 153–170). San Diego: Academic press.

Marks, G., & Houston, D. M. (2002). The determinants of young women's intentions about education, career development, and family life. *Journal of Education and Work, 15,* 321–336.

Marks, N. F. (1996). Social demographic diversity among American midlife parents. In C. D. Ryff & M. M. Seltzer (Eds.), *The parental experience in midlife* (pp. 29–75). Chicago: University of Chicago Press.

Marks, N. F., Bumpass, L. L., & Jun, H. (2004). Family roles and well-being during the middle life course. In O. G. Brim, C. D. Ryff, and R. C. Kessler (Eds.), *How healthy are we? A national study of well-being at midlife* (pp. 514–549), Chicago: University of Chicago Press.

Marshall, V. W., & Levy, J. A. (1990). Aging and dying. In R. H. Binstock & L. K. George (Eds.), *Handbook of aging and the social sciences* (pp. 245–260). San Diego: Academic Press.

Martire, L. M., & Schulz, R. (2001). Informal caregiving to older adults: Health effects of providing and receiving care. In A. Baum, T. A. Revenson, & J. E. Singer (Eds.), *Handbook of health psychology* (pp. 477–493). Mahwah, NJ: Erlbaum.

Maslach, C., Schaufeli, W. B., & Leiter, M. P. (2001). Job burnout. *Annual Review of Psychology, 52,* 397–422.

Maslow, A. H. (1968/1998). *Toward a psychology of being.* (3rd ed.). New York: Wiley.

Maslow, A. H. (1970a). *Motivation and personality* (2nd ed.). New York: Harper & Row.

Maslow, A. H. (1970b). *Religions, values, and peak-experiences.* New York: Viking.

Masunaga, H., & Horn, J. (2001). Expertise and age-related changes in the components of intelligence. *Psychology and Aging, 16,* 293–311.

Mathers, C. D., Stein, C., Fat, D. M., et al. (2002). *Global burden of disease 2000: Version 2 methods and results.* Brussels: World Health Organization.

Matthews, K. A. & Gump, B. B. (2002). Chronic work stress and marital dissolution increase risk of posttrial mortality in men from the multiple risk intervention trial. *Archives of Internal Medicine, 162,* 309–315.

Matthews, T. J., & Hamilton, B. E. (2002). Mean age of mother, 1970–2000. *National Vital Statistics Reports, 51,* 1–12.

Mattson, M. P. (2003). Will caloric restriction and folate protect against AD and PD? *Neurology, 60,* 690–695.

Maylor, E. A. (1990). Age and prospective memory. *Quarterly Journal of Experimental Psychology, 42A,* 471–493.

Mayou, R. A., Ehlers, A., & Hobbs, M. (2000). Psychological debriefing for road traffic accident victims. *British Journal of Psychiatry, 176,* 589–593.

McAdams, D. P. (2000). Attachment, intimacy, and generativity. *Psychological Inquiry, 11,* 117–120.

McAdams, D. P. (2001). Generativity in midlife. In M. E. Lachman (Ed.), *Handbook of midlife development* (pp. 395–443). New York: Wiley.

McAdams, D. P., & Azarow, J. (1996). *Generativity in black and white: Relations among generativity, race, and well-being.* Paper presented at the convention of the American Psychological Association, Toronto.

McAdams, D. P., de St. Aubin, E., & Logan, R. L. (1993). Generativity among young, midlife, and older adults. *Psychology and Aging, 8,* 221–230.

McAdams, D. P., Hart, H. M., & Maruna, S. (1998). The anatomy of generativity. In D. P. McAdams & E. de St. Aubin (Eds.), *Generativity and adult development: How and why we care for the next generation* (pp.7–43). Washington, DC: American Psychological Association.

McAvay, G. J., Seeman, T. E., & Rodin, J. (1996). A longitudinal study of change in domain-specific self-efficacy among older adults. *Journals of Gerontology: Psychological Sciences, 51B,* P243–P253.

McCay, C., Crowell, M., & Maynard, L. (1935). The effect of retarded growth upon the length of life and upon ultimate size. *Journal of Nutrition, 10,* 63–79.

McClearn, G. E., & Heller, D. A. (2000). Genetics and aging. In S. B. Manuck, R. Jennings, B. S. Rabin, et al. (Eds.), *Behavior, health, and aging* (pp. 1–25). Mahwah, NJ: Erlbaum.

McClearn, G. E., Johansson, B., Berg, S., et al. (1997). Substantial genetic influence on cognitive abilities in twins 80 or more years old. *Science, 276,* 1560–1563.

McClearn, G. E., Vogler, G. P., & Hofer, S. M. (2001). Environment-gene and gene-gene interactions. In E. J. Masaro & S. N. Austad (Eds.), *Handbook of the biology of aging,* (pp. 423–444), San Diego: Academic Press.

McConnell, E. S., & Murphy, A. T. (1997). Nursing diagnoses related to physiological alterations In M. A. Matteson, E. S. McConnell, & A. D. Linton (Eds.), *Gerontological Nursing: Concepts and Practices* (pp. 406–551). Philadelphia: Saunders.

McCrae, R. R., & Costa, P. T., Jr. (1983). Psychological maturity and subjective well-being: Toward a new synthesis. *Developmental Psychology, 19,* 243–248.

McCrae, R. R., & Costa, P. T., Jr. (1984). *Emerging lives, enduring dispositions: Personality in adulthood.* Boston: Little, Brown.

McCrae, R. R., & Costa, P. T. (1990). *Personality in adulthood.* New York: Guilford Press.

McCrae, R. E., & Costa, P. T. Jr. (1987). Validation of the five-factor model of personality across instruments and observers. *Journal of Personality and Social Psychology, 52,* 81–90.

McCrae, R. R., Costa, P. T., Jr., Pedroso de Lima, M., et al. (1999). Age differences in personality across the adult life span: Parallels in five cultures. *Developmental Psychology, 35,* 466–477.

McCullough, M. E., Hoyt, W. T., Larson, D. B., et al. (2000). Religious involvement and mortality: A meta-analytic review. *Health Psychology, 19,* 211–222.

McFadden, S. H. (1999). Religion, personality, and aging: A life span perspective. *Journal of Personality, 67,* 1081–1104.

McFadden, S. H. (2000). Religion and meaning in late life. In G. T. Reker & K. Chamberlain (Eds.), *Exploring existential meaning: Optimizing human development across the life span* (pp. 171–183). Thousand Oaks, CA: Sage.

McGue, M., Bouchard, T. J., Iacono, W. G., et al. (1993). Behavioral genetics of cognitive ability: A life-span perspective. In R. Plomin & G. E. McClearn (Eds.), *Nature, nurture, and psychology* (pp. 59–76). Washington, DC: American Psychological Association.

McKee-Ryan, F. M., Song, A., Wanberg, C. R., et al. (2005). Psychological and physical well-being during unemployment: A meta-analytic study. *Journal of Applied Psychology, 90,* 53–76.

McKinley, S. M. (1996). The normal menopause transition: An overview. *Maturitas, 23,* 137–145.

McLay, R. N., & Lyketsos, C. G. (2000). Veterans have less age-related cognitive decline. *Military Medicine, 165,* 622–625.

Medina, J. J. (1996). *The clock of ages: Why we age, how we age, winding back the clock.* Cambridge: Cambridge University Press.

Melamed, T. (1995). Career success: The moderating effect of gender. *Journal of Vocational Behavior, 47,* 35–60.

Menaghan, E. G., & Parcel, T. L. (1991). Determining children's home environments: The impact of maternal characteristics and current occupational and family condition. *Journal of Marriage and the Family, 53,* 417–431.

Menec, V. H. (2003). The relations between everyday activities and successful aging: A 6-year longitudinal study. *Journals of Gerontology: Social Sciences, 58B,* S74–S82.

Meyer, B. J. F., Russo, C., & Talbot, A. (1995). Diverse comprehension and problem solving: Decisions about the treatment of breast cancer by women across the life span. *Psychology and Aging, 10,* 84–103.

Michelson, K. D., Kessler, R. C., & Shaver, P. R. (1997). Adult attachment in a nationally representative sample. *Journal of Personality and Social Psychology, 73,* 1092–1106.

Mikulincer, M., & Orbach, I. (1995). Attachment styles and repressive defensiveness: The accessibility and architecture of affective memories. *Journal of Personality and Social Psychology, 5,* 917–925.

Milevsky, A. (2005). Compensatory patterns of sibling support in emerging adulthood: Variations in loneliness, self-esteem, depression, and life satisfaction. *Journal of Social and Personal Relationships, 22,* 743–755.

Milkie, M. A. & Peltola, P. (1999). Playing all the roles: Gender and the work-family balancing act. *Journal of Marriage and the Family, 61,* 476–490.

Miller, A. S., & Stark, R. (2002). Gender and religiousness: Can socialization explanations be saved? *American Journal of Sociology, 197,* 1399–1423.

Miller, T. Q., Smith, T. W., Turner, C. W., et al. (1996). A meta-analytic review of research on hostility and physical health. *Psychological Bulletin, 119,* 322–348.

Moffat, S. D., Zonderman, A. B., Metter, E. J., et al (2004). Free testosterone and risk for Alzheimer disease in older men. *Neurology, 27,* 188–193.

Morgan, D. L. (1988). Age differences in social network participation. *Journals of Gerontology: Social Sciences, 43B,* S129–S1137.

Morrell, R. W., & Dailey, S. R. (2001). *The process of applying scientific research findings in the construction of a Web site for older adults.* Pre-conference workshop presented at the Annual Meeting of the Gerontological Society of America, Chicago.

Morrell, R. W., Dailey, S. R., & Rousseau, G. K. (2003). Applying research: The NIHSeniorHealth.gov project. In N. Charness & K. W. Schaie (Eds.), *Impact of technology on successful aging* (pp. 134–161). New York: Springer.

Moskowitz, J. T., Folkman, S., & Acree, M. (2003). Do positive psychological states shed light on recovery from bereavement? Findings from a 3-year longitudinal study. *Death Studies, 27,* 471–500.

MRC Human Nutrition Research (2006). *Bone health: Peak bone mass.* Retrieved on May 16, 2006 from http://www.mrc-hnr.cam.ac.uk/research/bone_health/pbm.html.

Mroczek, D. K., & Kolarz, C. M. (1998). The effect of age on positive and negative affect: A developmental perspective on happiness. *Journal of Personality and Social Psychology, 75,* 1333–1349.

Mroczek, D. K., & Spiro, A., (2003). Personality structure, process, variance between and within: Integration by means of a developmental framework. *Journals of Gerontology: Psychological Sciences, 58B,* P305–P306.

Mroczek, D. K., & Spiro, A. (2005). Change in life satisfaction during adulthood: Findings from the Veterans Affairs Normative Aging Study. *Journal of Personality and Social Psychology, 88,* 189–202.

Mykityshyn, A. L., Fisk, A. D., & Rogers, W. A. (2002). Learning how to use a home medical device: Mediating age-related differences with training. *Human Factors, 44,* 354–364.

N

National Alliance for Caregiving and AARP (2004). *Caregiving in the U.S.* Retrieved March 14, 2006, from http://www.caregiving.org/data/04finalreport.pdf.

National Center for Health Statistics (2004). *Health United States 2004.* Hyattsville, MD: National Center for Health Statistics.

National Center for Statistics and Analysis (2001). *Traffic safety facts.* Washington, DC: U.S Department of Transportation.

National Council on the Aging (2002). *American perceptions of aging in the 21st century.* Retrieved March 28, 2006, from http://www.ncoa.org/Downloads/study_aging.pdf.pdf.

National Hospice and Palliative Care Organization (2005). *Blueprint for quality and access: Update 2005.* Retrieved May 16, 2006, from http://www.nhpco.org/files/public/2005_update.pdf.

National Institute of Arthritis and Musculoskeletal Diseases (2005). *Health topics: Osteoporosis overview.* Bethseda, MD: National Institutes of Health.

National Marriage Project (2005). *The state of our unions 2005.* Retrieved on May 16, 2006, from http://marriage.rutgers.edu/Publications/SOOU/SOOU2005/pdf.

National Senior Services Corps (2004). *The state performance report: Program year 2002–2003.* Retrieved March 22, 2006, from http://www.seniorcorps.org/pdf/2004_PERF_Seniorcorps.pdf.

Neimeyer, R. A. (2000). Searching for the meaning of meaning: Grief therapy and the process of reconstruction. *Death Studies, 24,* 541–558.

Nelson, D. L., & Burke, R. J. (2002). *Gender, work stress, and health.* Washington, DC: APA.

Nelson, D. L., Quick, J. C., & Simmons, B. L. (2001). Preventive management of work stress: Current themes and future challenges. In A. Baum, T. A. Revenson, & J. E. Singer (Eds.), *Handbook of health psychology* (pp. 349–363). Mahwah, NJ: Erlbaum.

Neugarten, B. L. (1970). Dynamics of transition of middle age to old age. *Journal of Geriatric Psychiatry, 4,* 71–87.

Neugarten, B. L. (1979). Time, age, and the life cycle. *American Journal of Psychiatry, 136,* 887–894.

Neugarten, B. L. (1996). *The meanings of age: Selected papers of Bernice L. Neugarten.* Chicago: University of Chicago Press.

Neugarten, B. L., Moore, J. W., & Lowe, J. C. (1965). Age norms, age constraints, and adult socialization. *American Journal of Sociology, 70,* 710–717.

Newsom, J. T., & Schulz, R. (1998). Caregiving from the recipient's perspective: Negative reactions to being helped. *Health Psychology, 17,* 172–181.

Newtson, R. L., & Keith, P. M. (1997). Single women in later life. In J. M. Coyle (Ed.), *Handbook on women and aging* (pp. 385–399). Westport, CT: Greenwood Press.

Nielson, H., Lolk, A., Andersen, K., et al. (1999). Characteristics of elderly who develop Alzheimer's disease during the next two years—a neurological study using CAMCOG: The Odense Study. *International Journal of Geriatric Psychiatry, 14,* 957–963.

Nisan, M., & Kohlberg, L. (1982). Universality and variation in moral judgment: A longitudinal and cross-sectional study in Turkey. *Child Development, 53,* 865–876.

Nock, S. (1998). *Marriage in men's lives.* New York: Oxford University Press.

Norburn, J. E. K., Bernard, S. L., Konrad, T. R., et al. (1995). Self-care and assistance from others in coping with functional status limitations among a national sample of older adults. *Journals of Gerontology: Social Sciences, 50B,* S101–S109.

O

O'Brien, K. M., Friedman, S. M., Tipton, L. C., et al. (2000). Attachment, separation, and women's vocational development: A longitudinal analysis. *Journal of Counseling Psychology, 47,* 301–315

O'Bryant, S. L. (1988). Sibling support and older widows' well-being. *Journal of Marriage and the Family, 50,* 173–183.

O'Farrell, B. (1995). Women in blue collar occupations: Traditional and nontraditional. In J. Freeman (Ed.), *Women: A feminist perspective* (pp. 238–261). Mountain View, CA: Mayfield.

O'Leary, A. (1990). Stress, emotion, and human immune function. *Psychological Bulletin, 108,* 363–382.

Olshansky, J. S., Hayflick, L., & Carnes, B. A. (2002). No truth to the fountain of youth. *Scientific American, 14,* 98–102.

O'Rand, A. M., & Henretta, J. C. (1999). *Age and inequality: Diverse pathways through later life.* Boulder, CO: Westview Press.

Orbuch, T. L., & Eyster, S. L. (1997). Division of household labor among black couples and white couples. *Social Forces, 76,* 301–332.

Orchard, A., & Solberg, K. (1999). Expectations of the stepmother's role. *Journal of Divorce and Remarriage, 31,* 107–123.

Oregon Department of Human Services (2006). Eighth annual report on Oregon's death with dignity act. Retrieved May 16, 2006, from http://egov.oregon.gov/DHS/ph/pas/docs/year8.pdf.

Orth-Gomér, K., Rosengren, A., Wedel, H., et al. (1993). Stressful life events, social support, and mortality in men born in 1933. *British Medical Journal, 307,* 1102–1105.

Owsley, C., Ball, K., McGwin, G., et al. (1998). Visual impairment and risk of motor vehicle crash among older adults. *Journal of the American Medical Association, 279,* 1083–1088.

P

Palmore, E. B. (1981). *Social patterns in normal aging: Findings from the Duke Longitudinal Study.* Durham, NC: Duke University Press.

Pargement, K. I. (1997). *The psychology of religion and coping: Theory, research, and practice.* New York: Guilford Press.

Pargament, K. I., Koenig, H. G., Tarakeshwar, N., et al. (2001). Religious struggle as predictor of mortality among medically ill elderly patients. *Archives of Internal Medicine, 161,* 1881–1885.

Park, D. C. (1992). Applied cognitive aging research. In F. I. M. Craik & T. A. Salthouse (Eds.), *Handbook of cognition and aging* (pp. 449–493). Mahwah, NJ: Erlbaum.

Park, D. C., & Jones, T. R. (1997). Medication adherence and aging. In A. D. Fisk & W. A. Rogers (Eds.), *Handbook of human factors and the older adult* (pp. 257–287). San Diego: Academic Press.

Park, D. C., Lautenschlager, G., Hedden, T., et al. (2002), Models of visuospatial and verbal memory across the adult life span, *Psychology and Aging, 17,* 299–320.

Park, D. C., & Mayhorn, C.B. (1996). Remembering to take medications: The importance of nonmemory variables. In D. Herrmann, M. Johnson, C. McEvoy, et al. (Eds.), *Research on practical aspects of memory* (Vol. 2, pp. 95–110). Mahweh, NJ: Erlbaum.

Parmet, S. (2004). Coronary artery disease. *Journal of the American Medical Association, 292,* 2540.

Parnes, H. S., & Sommers, D. G. (1994). Shunning retirement: Work experiences of men in their seventies and early eighties. *Journals of Gerontology: Social Sciences, 49B,* S117–S124.

Patel, N. V., Gordon, M. N., Connor, K. E. et al. (2005). Caloric restriction attenuates A β-deposition in Alzheimer transgenic models. *Neurobiology and Aging, 26,* 995–1000.

Patterson, C. J. (2000). Family relationships of lesbians and gay men. *Journal of Marriage and the Family, 62,* 10052–1069.

Patterson, R. E., Frank, L. L., Kristal, A. R., et al. (2004). A comprehensive examination of health conditions associated with obesity in older adults. *American Journal of Preventive Medicine, 27,* 385–390.

Pearlin, L. I. (1980). Life strains and psychological distress among adults. In N. J. Smelser & E. H. Erikson (Eds.), *Themes of work and love in adulthood* (pp. 174–192). Cambridge, MA: Harvard University Press.

Pendergast, D. R., Fisher, N. M., & Calkins, E. (1993). Cardiovascular, neuromuscular, and metabolic alterations with age leading to frailty [Special issue]. *Journal of Gerontology, 48,* 61–67.

Perls, T. T. (2004). Anti-aging quackery: Human growth hormone and tricks of the trade—more dangerous than ever. *Journals of Gerontology: Biological Sciences, 59A,* B682–B691.

Perry-Jenkins, M. & Folk, K. (1994). Class, couples, and conflict: Effects of the division of labor on assessment of marriage in dual-earner families. *Journal of Marriage and the Family, 56,* 165–180.

Peskin, H., & Livson, N. (1981). Uses of the past in adult psychological health. In D. H. Eichorn, J. A. Clausen, N. Haan, et al. (Eds.), *Present and past in middle life* (pp. 158–194). New York: Academic Press.

Peterson, N., & González, R. C. (2000). *The role of work in people's lives.* Pacific Grove, CA: Brooks-Cole.

Pettingale, K. W., Morris, T., Greer, S., et al. (1985). Mental attitudes to cancer: An additional prognostic factor. *Lancet, 1,* 750.

Pillemer, K., & Suitor, J. J. (1992). Violence and violent feelings: What causes them among family caregivers? *Journal of Gerontology, 47,* 165–172.

Piña, D. L., & Bengtson, V. L. (1995). Division of household labor and the well-being of retirement-aged workers. *Gerontologist, 35,* 308–317.

Pinquart, M. (2003). Loneliness in married, widowed, divorced, and never-married adults. *Journal of Social and Personal Relationships, 20,* 31–53.

Pinquart, M., & Soerensen, S. (2000). Influences of socioeconomic status, social network, and competence on subjective well-being in later life: A meta-analysis. *Psychology and Aging, 15,* 187–224.

Pinquart, M., & Soerensen, S. (2001). Gender differences in self-concept and psychological well-being in old age: A meta-analysis. *Journals of Gerontology: Psychological Sciences, 56B,* P195–P213.

Pinquart, M., & Soerensen, S. (2003). Differences between caregivers and non-caregivers in psychological health and physical health: A meta-analysis. *Psychology and Aging, 18,* 250–267.

Pirkola, S. P., Isometsä, E., Suvisaari, J., et al. (2005). DSM-IV mood, anxiety, and alcohol use disorders and their comorbidity in the Finnish subpopulation: Results from the Health 2000 Study. *Social Psychiatry and Psychiatric Epidemiology, 40,* 1–10.

Plomin, R. (1990). The role of inheritance in behavior, *Science, 248,* 183–188.

Plomin, R. (2004). Genetics and developmental psychology. *Merrill-Palmer Quarterly, 50,* 341–352.

Plomin, R., & Nesselroade, J. R. (1997). Behavioral genetics and personality change. *Journal of Personality, 58,* 191–220.

Ponds, R. W. H. M., van Boxtel, M. P. J., & Jolles, J. (2000). Age-related changes in subjective cognitive functioning. *Educational Gerontology, 26,* 67–81.

Poortman, A.-R., & van Tilburg, T. G. (2005). Past experiences and older adults' attitudes: A lifecourse perspective. *Ageing and Society, 25,* 19–30.

Popenoe, D., & Whitehead, B. D. (2005). *The state of our union: 2005.* Piscataway, NJ: Rutgers University National Marriage Project.

Powell, R. R. (1974). Psychological effects of exercise therapy upon institutionalized geriatric mental patients. *Journals of Gerontology, 29,* 157–161.

Pratt, M. W., Golding, G., & Hunter, W. J. (1983). Aging as ripening: Character and consistency of moral judgment in young, mature, and older adults. *Human Development, 36,* 277–288.

Presser, H. B. (2000). Nonstandard work schedules and marital instability. *Journal of Marriage and the Family, 62,* 93–110.

Proctor, B. D., & Dalaker, J. (2003). *U.S. Census Bureau, Current population reports, P60-222, Poverty in the United States: 2002.* Washington, DC: U.S. Government Printing Office.

Pruchno, R. (1999). Raising grandchildren: The experiences of black and white grandmothers. *Gerontologist, 39,* 209–221.

Pryor, J. (1999). Waiting until they leave home: The experiences of young adults whose parents separate. *Journal of Divorce and Remarriage, 32,* 47–61.

Purcell, P. J. (2000). Older workers: Employment and retirement trends. *Monthly Labor Review, 123,* No. 10. Retrieved May 25, 2006, from http://www.bls.gov.ezproxy.fau.edu/opub/mlr/2000/10/art3full.pdf.

Putney, N. M., & Bengtson, V. L. (2001). Families, intergenerational relationships, and kinkeeping in midlife. In M. E. Lachman (Ed.), *Handbook of midlife development* (pp. 528–570). New York: Wiley.

Q

Quick, H., & Moen, P. (1998). Gender, employment, and retirement quality: A life course approach to the different experiences of men and women. *Journal of Occupational Health Psychology, 3,* 44–64.

Quinton, D., Pickles, A., Maughan, B., et al. (1993). Partners, peers, & pathways: Assortive pairing and continuities in conduct disorder. *Development and Psychopathology, 5,* 763–783.

R

Radloff, L. S. (1977). The CES-D scale: A self-report depression scale for research in the general population. *Applied Psychological Measurement, 1,* 385–401.

Rando, T. A. (1993). *Treatment of complicated mourning.* Champaign, IL: Research Press.

Rasmussen, C. H., & Johnson, M. E. (1994). Spirituality and religiosity: Relative relationships to death anxiety. *Omega: Journal of Death and Dying, 29,* 313–318.

Reed, D., & Yano, K. (1997). Cardiovascular disease among elderly Asian Americans. In L. G. Martin & B. J. Soldo (Eds.), *Racial and ethnic differences in the health of older Americans* (pp. 270–284). Washington, DC: National Academy Press.

Reed, G. M., Kemeny, M. E., Taylor, S. E., et al. (1994). Realistic acceptance as a predictor of decreased survival time in gay men with AIDS. *Health Psychology, 13,* 299–307.

Reitzes, D. C., & Mutran, E. J. (2002). Grandparenthood: Factors influencing frequency of grandparent-grandchildren contact and grandparent role satisfaction. *Journals of Gerontology: Social Sciences, 59B,* S9–S16.

Reker, G. T. (1991). *Contextual and thematic analyses of sources of provisional meaning: A life-span perspective.* Paper presented at the biennial meeting of the International Society for the Study of Behavioral Development, Minneapolis.

Resnick, H. S., Kilpatrick, D. G., Dansky, B. S., et al. (1993). Prevalence of civilian trauma and posttraumatic stress disorder in a representative national sample of women. *Journal of Consulting and Clinical Psychology, 61,* 984–991.

Rest, J. R., & Thoma, S. J. (1985). Relation of moral judgment development to formal education. *Developmental Psychology, 21,* 709–714.

Rhoden , E. L., & Morgentaler, A. (2004). Medical progress: Risks of testosterone replacement therapy and recommendations for monitoring. *New England Journal of Medicine, 350,* 482–492.

Richardson, J. L., Zarnegar, Z., Bisno, B., et al. (1990). Psychosocial status at initiation of cancer treatment and survival. *Journal of Psychosomatic Research, 34,* 189–201.

Riegel, K. (1973). Dialectic operations: The final period of cognitive development. *Human Development, 16,* 346–370.

Riemann, R., Angleitner, A., & Strelau, J. (1997). Genetic and environmental influences on personality: A study of twins reared together using the self- and peer-report NEO-FFI scales. *Journal of Personality, 65,* 449–475.

Riggio, H. R., & Desrochers, S. (2005). Maternal employment and the work and family expectations of young adults. In D. Halpern & S. E. Murphy (Eds.), *From work-family balance to work-family interaction: Changing the metaphor* (pp. 177–196), Mahwah, NJ: Erlbaum.

Riley, K. P., Snowdon, D. A., Desrosiers, M. F., et al. (2005). Early life linguistic ability, late life cognitive function, and neuropathology: Findings from the Nun Study. *Neurobiology of Aging, 26,* 341–347.

Roberts B. W., & DelVecchio, W. F. (2000). The rank-order consistency of personality traits from childhood to old age: A quantitative review of longitudinal studies. *Psychological Bulletin, 126,* 3–25.

Roberts, B. W., Walton, K. E., & Bogg, T. (2005). Conscientiousness and health across the life course. *Review of General Psychology, 9,* 156–168.

Roberts, B. W., Walton, K. E., & Viechtbauer, W. (2006). Patterns of mean-level change in personality traits across the life course: A meta-analysis of longitudinal studies. *Psychological Bulletin, 132,* 1–25.

Roberts, R. E., Deleger, S., Strawbridge, W. J., et al. (2004). Prospective association between obesity and depression: Evidence from the Almeda County Study, *International Journal of Obesity and Related Metabolic Disorders, 27,* 514–521.

Robinson, J., & Godbey, G. (1997). *Time for life.* University Park: Pennsylvania State University Press.

Robles, T. F., & Kiecolt-Glaser, J. K. (2003). The physiology of marriage: Pathways to health. *Physiology and Behavior, 79,* 409–416.

Rodrigue, K. M., Kennedy, K. M., & Raz, N. (2005). Aging and longitudinal change in perceptual-motor skill acquisition in healthy adults. *Journals of Gerontology: Psychological Sciences, 60B,* P174–P181.

Roenker, D. L., Cissell, G. M., Ball, K. K., et al. (2003). Speed-of-processing and driving simulator training result in improved driving performance. *Human Factors, 39,* 438–444.

Rogers, R. G. (1991). Health related lifestyles among Mexican-Americans, Puerto Ricans, and Cubans in the United States. In I. Rosenwaike (Ed.), *Mortality of Hispanic populations* (pp. 145–167). New York: Greenwood Press.

Rogers, R. L., Meyer, J. S., & Mortel, K. F. (1990). After reaching retirement age physical activity sustains cerebral perfusion and cognition. *Journal of the American Geriatric Society, 38,* 123–128.

Rogers, W. A., & Fisk, A. D. (2000). Human factors, applied cognition, and aging. In F. I. M. Craik, and T. A. Salthouse (Eds.), *The handbook of aging and cognition* (pp. 559–591). Mahwah, NJ: Erlbaum.

Rojas, G., Araya, R., & Lewis, G. (2005). Comparing sex inequities in common affective disorders across countries: Great Britain and Chile. *Social Science and Medicine, 60,* 1693–1703.

Romano, J. M., Turner, J. A., Friedman, L. S., et al. (1992). Differences in the perceived well-being of wives and husbands caring for persons with Alzheimer's disease. *Gerontologist, 38,* 224–230.

Roof, W. C. (1999). *Spiritual marketplace: Baby boomers and the remaking of American religion.* Princeton, NJ: Princeton University Press.

Rosenfield, I. (2005). *Breakthrough health*. Emmaus, PA: Rodale Press.

Rosenkrantz Aronson, S., & Huston, A. C. (2004). The mother-infant relationship in single, cohabiting, and married families: A case for marriage? *Journal of Family Psychology, 18,* 5–18.

Rose-Rego, S. K., Strauss, M. E., & Smyth, K. A. (1998). Differences in the perceived well-being of wives and husbands caring for persons with Alzheimer's disease. *Gerontologist, 38,* 224–230.

Ross, C. E., Mirowsky, J., & Goldsteen, K. (1990). The impact of the family on health: The decade in review. *Journal of Marriage and the Family, 52,* 1059–1078.

Rossi, A. S. (2004). The menopause transition and aging processes. In O. G. Brim, C. D. Ryff, & R. C. Kessler (Eds.), *How healthy are we? A national study of well-being at midlife* (pp. 153–201). Chicago: University of Chicago Press.

Rowe, J. W., & Kahn, R. L. (1998). *Successful aging.* New York: Pantheon Books.

Russek, L. G., & Schwartz, G. E. (1997). Perceptions of parental caring predict health status in midlife: A 35-year follow-up of the Harvard Mastery of Stress Study. *Psychosomatic Medicine, 59,* 144–149.

Ryan, R. M., & Deci, E. L. (2000). Self-determination theory and facilitation of intrinsic motivation, social development, and well-being. *American Psychologist, 55,* 68–78.

Ryan, R. M., & La Guardia, J. G. (2000). What is being optimized? Self-determination theory and basic psychological needs. In S. H. Qualls & N. Abeles (Eds.), *Psychology and the aging revolution: How we adapt to longer life* (pp. 145–172). Washington, DC: American Psychological Association.

S

Salkind, N. (2003). *Exploring research,* 5th ed. Upper Saddle River, NJ: Prentice-Hall.

Salthouse, T. A. (1984). Effects of age and skill in typing. *Journal of Experimental Psychology: General, 113,* 345–371.

Salthouse, T. A. (1991). *Theoretical perspectives on cognitive aging.* Hillsdale, NJ: Erlbaum.

Salthouse, T. A. (1996). The processing-speed theory of adult age differences in cognition. *Psychological Review, 103,* 401–428.

Salthouse, T. A. (1998). Independence of age-related influences on cognitive activities across the life-span. *Developmental Psychology, 34,* 851–864.

Salthouse, T. A. (2004). What and when of cognitive aging. *Current Directions in Psychological Sciences, 13,* 140–144.

Salthouse, T. A., Babcock, R. L., Skovronek, E., et al. (1990). Age and experience effects in spatial visualization. *Developmental Psychology, 26,* 128–136.

Salthouse, T. A., Hancock, H. E., Meinz, E. J., et al. (1996). Interrelations of age, visual acuity, and cognitive functioning. *Journals of Gerontology: Psychological Sciences, 51B,* P317–P330.

Salthouse, T. A., & Maurer, T. J. (1996). Aging, job performance, and career development. In J. E. Birren & K. W. Schaie (Eds.), *Handbook of the psychology of aging* (pp. 353–364). San Diego: Academic Press.

Sanchez, L., & Thomson, E. (1997). Becoming mothers and fathers: Parenthood, gender, and the division of labor. *Gender and Society, 11,* 747–772.

Sands, R. G., & Goldberg-Glen, R. S. (2000). Grandparent caregivers' perception of the stress of surrogate parenting. *Journal of Social Services Research, 26,* 77–95.

Sanfey, A. C., & Hastie, R. (2000). Judgment and decision making across the adult life span: A tutorial review of psychological research. In D. Park & N. Schwarz (Eds.), *Cognitive aging: A primer.* Philadelphia: Taylor & Francis.

Santillanes, G. (1997). Releasing the spirit: A lesson in Native American funeral rituals. *Director, 69,* 32–34.

Santoro, N. (2004). What a SWAN can teach us about menopause. *Contemporary Obstetrics and Gynecology, 49,* 69–79.

Scarr, S. (1992). Developmental theories for the 1990s: Development and individual differences. *Child Development, 63,* 1–19.

Schacter, D. L. (1997). False recognition and the brain. *Current Directions in Psychological Science, 6,* 65–70.

Schacter, D. L., & Tulving, E. (1996). What are the memory systems of 1994? In D. L. Schacter & E. Tulving (Eds.), *Memory systems 1994* (pp 1–38). Cambridge, MA: MIT Press.

Schaie, K. W. (1983). The Seattle longitudinal study: A 21-year exploration of psychometric intelligence in adulthood. In K. W. Schaie (Ed.), *Longitudinal studies of adult development* (pp. 64–135). New York: Guilford.

Schaie, K. W. (1994). The course of adult intellectual development. *American Psychologist, 49,* 304–313.

Schaie, K. W. (1996). Intellectual development in adulthood. In J. E. Birren & W. K. Schaie (Eds.), *Handbook of the psychology of aging* (pp. 265–286). San Diego: Academic Press.

Schaie, K. W., & Willis, S. L. (1986). Can decline in adult intellectual functioning be reversed? *Developmental Psychology, 22,* 223–232.

Scharlach, A. E., & Fredrickson, K. I. (1993). Reactions to the death of a parent during midlife. *Omega, 27,* 307–319.

Scheier, M. F., & Carver, C. S. (1993). On the power of positive thinking. *Current Directions in Psychological Science, 2,* 26–30.

Schmidt, R., Schmidt, H., Curb, J. D., et al. (2002). Early inflammation and dementia: A 25-year follow-up of the Honolulu-Asia aging study. *Annals of Neurology, (53),* 168–174.

Schmiedeskamp, M. (2004). Preventing good brains from going bad. *Scientific American, 14,* 84–91.

Schneider, E. C., Zaslavsky, A. M., & Epstein, A. M. (2002). Racial disparities in the quality of care for enrollees in Medicare managed care. *Journal of the American Medical Association, 287,* 1288–1294.

Schneiderman, N., Antoni, M. H., Saab, P. G., (2001). Health psychology: Psychosocial and biobehavioral aspects of chronic disease management. *Annual Review of Psychology, 52,* 555–580.

Schoen, R., & Wooldredge, J. (1989). Marriage choices in North Carolina and Virginia, 1969–71 and 1979–81. *Journal of Marriage and the Family, 51,* 465–481.

Schoenborn, C. A. (2004). Marital status and health: United States, 1999–2002. *Advance data from vital and health statistics, 351.* Hyattsville, MD: National Center for Health Statistics

Schooler, C., Caplan, L., & Oates, G. (1998). Aging and work: An overview. In K. W. Schaie & C. Schooler (Eds.), *Impact of work on older adults* (pp. 1–10). New York: Springer.

Schousboe, K., Willemsen, G., Kyvic, K. O., et al. (2003). Sex differences in heritability of BMI: A comparative study of results from twin studies in eight countries. *Twin Research, 6,* 409–421.

Schover, L. R., Fouladi, R. T., Warneke, C. L., et al. (2002). The use of treatments for erectile dysfunction among survivors of prostate cancer carcinoma. *Cancer, 95,* 2397–2407.

Schroeder, K. A., Blood, L. L., & Maluso, D. (1992). An intergenerational analysis of expectations for women's career and family roles. *Sex Roles, 26,* 273–291.

Schulenberg, J. E., Sameroff, A. J., & Cicchetti, D. (2004). The transition to adulthood as a critical juncture in the course of psychopathology and mental health. *Development and Psychopathology, 16,* 799–806.

Schulz, R., O'Brien, A. T., Bookwala, J., et al. (1995). Psychiatric and physical morbidity effects of dementia caregiving: Prevalence, correlates, and causes. *Gerontologist, 35,* 771–791.

Schwartz, R. (1992). Is Holland's theory worthy of so much attention, or should vocational psychology move on? *Journal of Vocational Behavior, 40,* 170–187.

Seeman, T. E., Bruce, M. L., & McAvay, G. J. (1996). Social network characteristics and onset of ADL disability: MacArthur studies of successful aging. *Journals of Gerontology: Social Sciences, 51B,* S191–S200.

Seeman, T. E., Dubin, L., & Seeman, M. (2003). Religiosity/spirituality and health: A critical review of the evidence for biological pathways. *American Psychologist, 58,* 53–63.

Segerstrom, S. C., & Miller, G. E. (2004). Psychological stress and the human immune system: A meta-analytic study of 30 years of inquiry. *Psychological Bulletin, 130,* 601–630.

Seligman, M. E. P. (1991). *Learned optimism.* New York: Knopf.

Seligman, M. E. P., & Csikszentmihalyi, M. (2000). Positive psychology: An introduction. *American Psychologist, 55,* 5–14.

Selye, H. (1936). A syndrome produced by diverse nocuous agents. *Nature, 138,* 32.

Selye, H. (1982). History and present status of the stress concept. In L. Goldberger & S. Breznitz (Eds.), *Handbook of stress: Theoretical and clinical aspects* (pp. 7–20). New York: Free Press.

Semmer, N. (1996). Individual differences, work, stress, and health. In M. J. Schabracq, J. A. M. Winnubst, & C. L. Cooper (Eds.), *Handbook of work and health psychology* (pp. 51–86). Chichester: Wiley.

Shackelford, T. K., Schmitt, D. P., & Buss, D. M. (2005). Universal dimensions of human mate preferences. *Personality and Individual Differences, 39,* 447–458.

Shanahan, M. J. (2000). Pathways to adulthood in changing societies: Variability and mechanisms in life course perspective. *Annual Review of Sociology, 26,* 667–692.

Shapiro, A. F., Gottman, J. M., & Carrère, S. (2000). The baby and marriage: Identifying factors that buffer against decline in marital satisfaction after the first baby arrives, *Journal of Family Psychology, 14,* 59–70.

Sheehy, G. (1976). *Passages.* New York: Dutton.

Sheehy, G. (2006). *Sex and the seasoned woman: Pursuing the passionate life.* New York: Workman.

Sheikh, A. I. (2004). Posttraumatic growth in the context of heart disease. *Journal of Clinical Psychology in Medical Settings, 11,* 265–273.

Sheldon, K. M., & Kasser, T. (2001). Getting older, getting better? Personal strivings and psychological maturity across the life span. *Developmental Psychology, 37,* 491–501.

Sherwood, P., Given, C.W., Given, B., et al. (2005). Caregiver burden and depressive symptoms: Analysis of common outcomes in caregivers of elderly patients. *Journal of Aging Health, 17,* 125–147.

Shneidman, E. S. (1989). The Indian summer of life: A preliminary study of septuagenarians. *American Psychologist, 44,* 684–694.

Siegler, I. C. (1994). Hostility and risk: Demographic and lifestyle variables. In A. W. Siegman & T. W. Smith (Eds.), *Anger, hostility, and the heart* (pp. 199–214). Hillsdale, NJ: Erlbaum.

Silver, C. B. (1998). Cross-cultural perspective on attitudes toward family responsibility and well-being in later years. In J. Lomranz (Ed.), *Handbook of aging and mental health: An integrative approach* (pp. 383–412). New York: Plenum.

Silverstein, M., Giarrusso, R., & Bengtson, V. L. (1998). Intergenerational solidarity and the grandparent role. In M. Szinovacz (Ed.), *Handbook on grandparenting* (pp. 144–170). Westport, CT: Greenwood Press.

Silverstein, M., & Long, J. D. (1998). Trajectories of grandparents' perceived solidarity with adult grandchildren: A growth curve analysis over 23 years. *Journal of Marriage and the Family, 60,* 912–923.

Silverstein, M. & Marenco, A. (2001). How Americans enact the grandparent role over the life course. *Journal of Family Issues, 22,* 493–522.

Simmons, T., & Dye, J. L. (2003). *Grandparents living with grandchildren: 2000.* Washington, DC: U.S. Census Bureau.

Simmons, T., & O'Connell, M. (2003). *Married-couple and unmarried partner households: 2000.* Washington, DC: U.S. Bureau of the Census.

Simon, V. (2005). Wanted: Women in clinical trials. *Science, 308,* 1517.

Simpson, R. (2005). Men in nontraditional occupations: Career entry, career orientation, and experience of role strain. *Gender, Work, and Organization, 12,* 363–375.

Simpson, J. A., Rholes, W. S., & Nelligan, J. S. (1992). Support seeking and support giving within couples in an anxiety-provoking situation: The role of attachment styles. *Journal of Personality and Social Psychology, 62,* 434–446.

Sims, R. V., McGwin, G., Jr., & Allman, R. M., et al. (2000). Exploratory study of incident vehicle crashes among older drivers. *Journals of Gerontology: Medical Sciences, 55A,* M22–M27.

Sinnott, J. (1994). Development and yearning: Cognitive aspects of spiritual development. *Journal of Adult Development, 1,* 91–99.

Sinnott, J. D. (1996). The development of complex reasoning: Postformal thought. In F. Blanchard-Fields & T. Hess (Eds.), *Perspectives on cognitive change in adulthood and aging* (pp. 358–383). New York: McGraw-Hill.

Small, B. J., & Bäckman, L. (1999). Time to death and cognitive performance. *Current Directions in Psychological Science, 8,* 168–172.

Smetana, J. G., Killen, M., & Turiel, E. (1991). Children's reasoning about interpersonal and moral conflicts. *Child Development, 62,* 629–644.

Smith, C. D., Walton, A., Loveland, A. D., et al. (2005). Memories that last in old age: Motor skill learning and memory preservation. *Neurobiology of Aging, 26,* 883–890.

Smith, J., & Baltes, P. B. (1999). Trends and profiles of psychological functioning in very old age. In P. B. Baltes & K. U. Mayer (Eds), *The Berlin Aging Study: Aging from*

70 to 100 (pp. 197–226). Cambridge: Cambridge University Press.

Smith, J., Staudinger, U. M., & Baltes, P. B. (1994). Occupational settings facilitating wisdom-related knowledge: The sample case of clinical psychologists. *Journal of Consulting and Clinical Psychology, 62*, 989–999.

Smith, J. P., & Kington, R. S. (1997). Race, socioeconomic status, and health in late life. In L. G. Martin & B. J. Soldo (Eds.), *Racial and ethnic differences in the health of older Americans* (pp. 105–162). Washington, DC: National Academy Press.

Smith, S. K., & House, M. (2005). *Snowbirds, sunbirds, and stayers: Seasonal migration of the elderly in Florida.* Paper presented at the annual meeting of the Population Association of America, Philadelphia, March 31–April 2.

Smith, T. W., & Gallo, L. C. (2001). Personality traits as risk factors for physical illness. In A. Baum, T. A. Revenson, & J. E. Singer (Eds.), *Handbook of health psychology* (pp. 139–173). Mahwah, NJ: Erlbaum.

Smock, P. J., Manning, W. D., & Gupta, S. (1999). The effect of marriage and divorce on women's economic well-being. *American Sociological Review, 64*, 794–812.

Snarey, J. R. (1985). Cross-cultural universality of social-moral development: A critical review of the Kohlbergian research. *Psychological Bulletin, 97*, 202–232.

Snarey, J. R., Reimer, J., & Kohlberg, L. (1985). Development of social-moral reasoning among kibbutz adolescents: A longitudinal cross-sectional study. *Developmental Psychology, 21*, 3–17.

Snarey, J. R., Son, L., Kuehne, V. S., et al. (1987). The role of parenting in men's psychosocial development: A longitudinal study of early adulthood infertility and midlife generativity. *Developmental Psychology, 23*, 593–603.

Snowdon, D, (2001). *Aging with grace: What the Nun Study teaches us about leading longer healthier, more meaningful lives.* New York: Bantam Books.

Soares, C. N., Steiner, M., & Prouty, J. (2005), Effects of reproductive hormones and selective estrogen receptor modulators on the central nervous system during menopause. In D. E. Stewart (Ed.), *Menopause: A mental health practitioner's guide* (pp. 33–56). Washington, DC: American Psychiatric Publishing.

Solano, L., Costa, M., Salvati, S., et al. (1993). Psychosocial factors and clinical evolution in HIV-1 infection: A longitudinal study. *Journal of Psychosomatic Research, 37*, 39–51.

Soldz, S., & Vaillant, G. E. (1999). The big five personality traits and the life course: A 45-year longitudinal study. *Journal of Research in Personality, 33*, 208–232.

Solomon, S. E., Rothblum, E. D., & Balsam, K. F. (2004). Pioneers in partnership: Lesbian and gay male couples compared with those not in civil unions, and married heterosexual siblings. *Journal of Family Psychology, 18*, 275–286.

Somary, K., & Stricker, G. (1998). Becoming a grandparent: A longitudinal study of expectations and early experiences as a function of sex and lineage. *Gerontologist, 38*, 53–61.

Somers, M. D. (1993). A comparison of voluntarily child-free adults and parents. *Journal of Marriage and the Family, 55*, 643–650.

Spearman, C. (1904). General intelligence, objectively determined and measured. *American Journal of Psychology, 15*, 201–203.

Spies, R. A., & Plake, B. S. (2005). *The sixteenth mental measures yearbook.* Lincoln: University of Nebraska Press.

Spinks, R., Gilmore, G. C., & Thomas, C. (1996). *Age simulation of a sensory deficit does impair cognitive test performance.* Poster session presented at the Cognitive Aging Conference, Atlanta, GA.

Spotts, E. L., Neiderhiser, J. M., Towers, H., et al. (2004) Genetic and environmental influences on marital relationships. *Journal of Family Psychology, 18*, 107–119.

Stanley, S. M., Whitton, S. W., & Markman, H. J. (2004). Maybe I do: Interpersonal commitment and premarital or nonmarital cohabitation. *Journal of Family Issues, 25*, 496–519.

Steindl-Rast, B. D. (1977). Learning to die. *Parabola, 2*, 22–31.

Stephens, M. A. P., Franks, M. M., & Townsend, A. L. (1994). Stress and rewards in women's multiple roles: The case of women in the middle. *Psychology and Aging, 9*, 45–52.

Stephens, M. A. P., & Townsend, A. L. (1997). Stress of parent care: Positive and negative effects of women's other roles. *Psychology of Aging, 12*, 376–386.

Stern, Y., Tang, M.-X., Albert, M., et al. (1997). Predicting time to nursing home care and death in individuals with Alzheimer disease. *Journal of the American Medical Association, 277*, 806–812.

Sternberg, R. J. (1986). A triangular theory of love. *Psychological Review, 93*, 119–135.

Sternberg, R. J., Grigorenko, E. L., & Oh, S. (2001). The development of intelligence at midlife. In M. Lachman (Ed.), *Handbook of midlife development.* New York: Wiley.

Stigsdotter, A., & Bäckman, L. (1989). Comparison of different forms of memory training in old age. In M. A. Luszca & T. Nettelbeck (Eds.) *Psychological development: Perspectives across the life span.* Amsterdam: Elsevier.

Stigsdotter, A., & Bäckman, L. (1993). Long-term maintenance of gains from memory training in older adults: Two 3-1/2 year follow-up studies. *Journals of Gerontology: Psychological Sciences, 48B*, P233–P237.

Stratton, T. D., McLaughlin, M. A., Witte, F. M., et al. (2005). Does students' exposure to gender discrimination and sexual harassment in medical school affect specialty choice and residency program selection? *Academic Medicine, 80*, 400–408.

Strothers, H. S., Rust, G., Minor, P., et al. (2005). Disparities in anti-depressant treatment in Medicaid elderly diagnosed with depression. *Journal of the American Geriatrics Society, 53*, 456–461.

Sugisawa, H., Liang, J., & Liu, X. (1994). Social networks, social support, and mortality among older people in Japan. *Journals of Gerontology: Social Sciences, 49B*, S3–S13.

Super, C. M., & Harkness, S. (1994). Temperament and the developmental niche. In W. B. Carey & S. C. McDevitt (Eds.), *Prevention and early intervention: Individual differences as risk factors for the mental health of children* (pp. 115–125). New York: Brenner/Mazel.

Super, D. E. (1957). *The psychology of careers.* New York: Harper & Row.

Super, D. E. (1990). A lifespan/lifespace approach to career development. In D. Brown, L. Brooks, et al. (Eds.), *Career choice and development: Applying contemporary theories to practice* (2nd ed., pp. 197–261). San Francisco: Jossey-Bass.

Super, D. E., Savickas, M. L., & Super, C. M. (1996). The lifespan, life-space approach to careers. In D. Brown, L. Brooks, et al. (Eds.), *Career choice and development: Ap-*

plying contemporary theories to practice (pp. 121–178) San Francisco: Jossey-Bass.

Super, D. E., Starishevsky, R., Matlin, N., et al. (1963). *Career development: A self-concept theory.* New York: College Entrance Examination Board.

Sutker, P. B., Davis, J. M., Uddo, M., et al. (1995). War zone stress, personal resources, and PTSD in Persian Gulf War returnees. *Journal of Abnormal Psychology, 104,* 444–452.

Swensen, M. M. (1998). The meaning of home to five elderly women. *Health Care for Women International, 19,* 381–393.

Szinovacz, M. E., & DeViney, S. (2000). Marital characteristics and retirement decisions. *Research on Aging, 22,* 470–498.

T

Tartaro, J., Luecken, L. J., & Gunn, H. E. (2005). Exploring heart and soul: Effects of religiosity/spirituality and gender on blood pressure and cortisol stress response. *Journal of Health Psychology, 10,* 753–766.

Taylor, R. J., Chatters, L. M., & Levin, J. (2004). *Religion in the lives of African Americans.* Thousand Oaks, CA: Sage.

Taylor, S. E. (2002). *The tending instinct: How nurturing is essential to who we are and how we live.* New York: Holt.

Taylor, S. E., Klein, L. C., Lewis B. P., et al. (2000). Biobehavioral responses to stress in females: Tend-and-befriend, not fight-or-flight. *Psychological Review, 107,* 411–429.

Techner, D. (1997). The Jewish funeral—A celebration of life. *Director, 69,* 18–20.

Temoshok, L. (1987). Personality, coping style, emotion and cancer: Towards an integrative model. *Cancer Surveys, 6,* 545–567.

Tennov, D. (1979). *Love and limerance.* New York: Stein & Day.

Teno, J. M., Clarridge, B. R., Casey, V., et al. (2004). Family perspectives on end-of-life care at the last place of care. *Journal of the American Medical Association, 291,* 88–93.

Teresa of Ávila, St. (1562/1960). *Interior castle.* Garden City, NJ: Image Books.

Terkel, S. (1995). *Coming of age: The story of our century by those who've lived it.* New York: St. Martin's Press.

Thoits, P. A. (1983). Multiple identities and psychological well-being: A reformulation of the social isolation hypothesis. *American Sociological Review, 48,* 174–187

Thorslund, M., & Lundberg, O. (1994). Health and inequalities among the oldest old. *Journal of Aging and Health, 6,* 51–69.

Thorson, J. A., & Powell, F. C. (1992). Meanings of death and intrinsic religiosity. *Journal of Clinical Psychology, 46,* 379–391.

Thurstone, L. L. (1938). *Primary mental abilities.* Chicago: University of Chicago Press.

Todosijevic, J., Rothblum, E. D., & Solomon, S. E. (2005). Relationship satisfaction, affectivity, and gay-specific stressors in same-sex couples joined in civil unions. *Psychology of Women Quarterly, 29,* 158–166.

Tomer, A., & Eliason, G. (2005). Life regrets and death attitudes in college students. *Omega: Journal of Death and Dying, 51,* 173–195.

Tomic, D., Gallicchio, L., Whiteman, M. K., et al. (2006). Factors associated with determinants of sexual functioning in midlife women. *Maturitas, 53,* 144–157.

Tornstam, L. (1996). Gerotranscendence—a theory about maturing into old age. *Journal of Aging and Identity, 1,* 37–50.

Torpy, J. M. (2002). Heart disease and women. *Journal of the American Medical Association, 288,* 3230.

Torpy, J. M. (2003). Risk factors for heart disease. *Journal of the American Medical Association, 290,* 980.

Torpy, J. M. (2004). Preventing cancer. *Journal of the American Medical Association, 291,* 2510.

Truluck, J. E., & Courtenay, B. C. (2002). Ego development and the influence of gender, age, and educational levels among older adults. *Educational Gerontology, 28,* 325–336.

Tulving, E. (1985). How many memory systems are there? *American Psychologist, 40.* 385–398.

Turk, D. C., Kerns, R. D., & Rosenberg, R. (1992). Effects of marital interaction on chronic pain and disability: Examining the down side of social support. *Rehabilitation Psychology, 37,* 259–273.

Turner, B. F., & Turner, C. B. (1994). Social cognition and gender stereotypes for women varying in age and race. In B. F. Turner & L. E. Troll (Eds.), *Women growing older: Psychological perspectives* (pp. 94–139). Thousand Oaks, CA: Sage.

Tworoger, S. S., Yasui, Y., Vitiello, M. V., et al. (2003). Effects of a yearlong moderate-intensity exercise and stretching intervention on sleep quality in postmenopausal women. *Sleep: Journal of Sleep and Sleep Disorders Research, 26,* 830–836.

U

Uccello, C. E. (1998). *Factors influencing retirement: Their implications for raising retirement age.* Report to the AARP. Retrieved March 28, 2006, from http://www.urban.org/url.cfm?ID=1000207.

Uchino, B. N., Cacioppo, J. T., & Kiecolt-Glaser, J. K. (1996). The relationship between social support and physiological processes: A review with emphasis on underlying mechanisms and implications for health. *Psychological Bulletin, 119,* 488–531.

Umberson, D. (1992). Gender, marital status and the social control of health behavior. *Social Science and Medicine, 24,* 907–917.

Underhill, E. (1911/1961). *Mysticism.* New York: Dutton.

United Nations Statistics Division (2005). *Statistics and indicators on women and men.* Retrieved March 24, 2006, from http://unstats.un.org/unsd/demographic/products/indw/ww2005/tab5c/htm.

U.S. Bureau of Labor Statistics (2003). *National Longitudinal Survey of Youth.* Retrieved on May 23, 2006 from http://www.bls.gov/news.release/pdf/n/soy.pdf

U.S. Bureau of Labor Statistics (2004). *National Longitudinal Survey of Youth: Results from more than two decades of a longitudinal survey.* Retrieved March 28, 2006, from http://www.bls.gov/news.release/pdf/nlsoy.pdf.

U.S. Bureau of Labor Statistics (2005). *Women in the labor force: A databook.* Washington, DC: Government Printing Office.

U.S. Center for Disease Control and Prevention (2004). *National Health and Nutrition Examination Survey.* Washington, DC: National Center for Health Statistics.

U.S. Department of Health and Human Services (2004). *Statistics related to overweight and obesity.* Bethesda, MD: National Institutes of Health.

Usui, C. (1998). Gradual retirement: Japanese strategies for older workers. In K. W. Schaie & C. Schooler (Eds.), *Commentary: Impact of work on older adults* (pp. 45–84) New York: Springer.

Uttl, B., & Van Alstine, C. L. (2003). Rising verbal intelligence scores: Implications for research and clinical practice. *Psychology and Aging, 18,* 616–621.

V

Väänänen, A., Buunk, B.P., Kivimäki, M., et al. (2005). When it is better to give than to receive: Long-term health effects of perceived reciprocity in support exchange. *Journal of Personality and Social Psychology, 89,* 176–193.

Vaillant, G. E. (1974). Natural history of male psychological health: XII. Some antecedents of healthy adult adjustment. *Archives of General Psychiatry, 31,* 15–22.

Vaillant, G. E. (1977). *Adaptation to life: How the best and brightest come of age.* Boston: Little, Brown.

Vaillant, G. E. (1993). *Wisdom of the ego.* Cambridge, MA: Harvard University Press.

Vaillant, G. E. (2002). *Aging well: Surprising guideposts to a happier life from the landmark Harvard study.* Boston: Little, Brown.

Vaillant, G. E., & Mukamal, K. (2001). Successful aging. *American Journal of Psychiatry, 158,* 839–847.

Vaillant, G. E., & Vaillant, C. O. (1990). Natural history of male psychological health: XII. A 45-year study of predictors of successful aging at 65. *American Journal of Psychiatry, 147,* 31–37.

van Ijzendoorn, M. (1995). Adult attachment representations, parental responsiveness, and infant attachment: A meta-analysis on the predictive validity of the Adult Attachment Interview. *Psychological Bulletin, 117,* 387–403.

Van Manen, K. & Whitbourne, S. (1997). Psychosocial development and life experiences in adulthood: A 22 year sequential study. *Psychology and Aging, 12,* 239–246.

Van Ranst, N., Verschueren, K., & Marcoen, A. (1995). The meaning of grandparents as viewed by adolescent grandchildren: An empirical study in Belgium. *International Journal of Aging and Human Development, 41,* 311–324.

van Reekum, R., Binns, M., Clarke, D., et al. (2005). Is late life depression a predictor of Alzheimer's disease? Results from a historical cohort study. *International Journal of Psychiatry, 20,* 80–82.

Ventura, S. J., & Bachrach, C. A. (2000). Nonmarital childbearing in the United States, 1940–1999. *National vital statistics reports* (Vol. 48). Hyattsville, MD: National Center for Health Statistics.

Vierck, E. (2004). *Growing old in America.* Detroit: Thomson Gale.

Vitaliano, P. P., Russo, J., Scanlan, J., et al. (1996). Weight changes in caregivers of Alzheimer's care recipients: Psycho-behavioral predictors. *Psychology and Aging, 11,* 155–163.

Vitaliano, P. P., Young, H., Russo, J., et al. (1993). Psychosocial factors associated with cardiovascular reactivity in older adults. *Psychosomatic Medicine, 55,* 164–177.

Vogt, D. S., Pless, A. P., King, L. A., et al. (2005). Deployment stressors, gender, and mental health outcomes among Gulf War I veterans. *Journal of Traumatic Stress, 18,* 115–127.

W

Wachs, T. D. (1994). Fit, context, and the transition between temperament and personality. In C. F. Halverson, Jr., G. A. Kohnstamm, & R. P. Martin (Eds.), *The developing structure of temperament and personality from infancy to adulthood* (pp. 209–220). Hillsdale, NJ: Erlbaum.

Waddington, C. H. (1957). *The strategy of the genes.* London: Allen & Son.

Wahl, H-W., & Tesch-Römer, C. (2001). Aging, sensory loss, and social functioning. In N. Charness, D. C. Parks, & B. A. Sabel (Eds.), *Communication, technology, and aging: Opportunities and challenges for the future.* New York: Springer.

Walaskay, M., Whitbourne, S. K., & Nehrke, M. F. (1983–84). Construction and validation of an ego-integrity status interview. *International Journal of Aging and Human Development, 18,* 61–72.

Waldfogel, J. (1997). Working mothers then and now: A cross-cohort analysis of the effects of maternity leave on women's pay. In F. Blau & R. G. Ehrenberg (Eds.), *Gender and family issues in the workplace* (pp. 92–126). New York: Sage.

Waldstein, S. R . & Katzel, L. I. (2006). Interactive relations of central versus total obesity and blood pressure in cognitive function. *International Journal of Obesity, 30,* 201–207.

Walker, L. J. (1989). A longitudinal study of moral reasoning. *Child Development, 60,* 157–160.

Wallace, S. P., Villa, V. M., Enriquez-Haass, V., et al. (2001). *Access is better for racial/ethnic elderly in Medicare HMOs—but disparities persist.* Los Angeles: UCLA Center for Health Policy Research.

Wang, P. S., Berglund, P., Olfson, M., et al. (2005). Failure and delay in initial treatment contact after first onset of mental disorders in the National Comorbidity Survey Replication. *Archives of General Psychiatry, 62,* 603–613.

Wang, P. S., Lane, M., Olfson, M., et al. (2005). Twelve-month use of mental health services in the United States. *Archives of General Psychiatry, 62,* 629–640.

Warr, P. (1994). Age and employment. In M. Dunnette, L. Hough, & J. Triandis (Eds.), *Handbook of industrial and organizational psychology* (Vol. 4, pp. 487–550). Palo Alto, CA: Consulting Psychologists Press.

Warr, P., Butcher, V., & Robertson, J. (2004). Activity and psychological well-being in older people. *Aging and Mental Health, 8,* 172–183.

Waters, E., Merrick, S. K., Albersheim, L. J., et al. (1995). *Attachment security from infancy to early adulthood: A 20-year longitudinal study.* Poster presented at the biennial meeting of the Society for Research in Child Development, Indianapolis.

Weaver, S. E., & Coleman, M. (2005). A mothering but not a mother role: A grounded theory study of the nonresidential stepmother role. *Journal of Social and Personal Relationships, 22,* 477–497.

Webster, J. D. (1997). Attachment style and well-being in elderly adults: A preliminary investigation. *Canadian Journal on Aging, 16,* 101–111.

Wechsler, D. (1939). *The measurement of adult intelligence.* Baltimore: Williams & Wilkins.

Weiss, R. S. (1982). Attachment in adult life. In C. M. Parkes & J. Stevenson-Hinde (Eds.), *The place of attachment in human behavior* (pp. 171–184). New York: Basic Books.

Weiss, R. S. (1986). Continuities and transformation in social relationships from childhood to adulthood. In W. W. Hartup & Z. Rubin (Eds.), *On relationships and development* (pp. 95–110). Hillsdale, NJ: Erlbaum.

Wethington, E. (2000). Expecting stress: Americans and the "midlife crisis." *Motivation and Emotion, 24,* 85–103.

Whitbourne, S. K., Zuschlag, M. K., Elliot, L. B., et al. (1992). Psychosocial development n adulthood: A 22-year sequential study. *Journal of Personality and Social Psychology, 63,* 260–271.

Whitson, S. C., & Keller, B. K. (2004). The influence of the family of origin on career development: A review and analysis. *Counseling Psychologist, 32,* 493–568.

Wickrama, K. A. S., Lorenz, F. O., & Conger, R. D. (1997). Marital quality and physical illness: A latent growth curve analysis. *Journal of Marriage and the Family, 59,* 143–155.

Wilkinson, A. M., & Lynn, J. (2001). The end of life. In R. H. Binstock & Linda K. George (Eds.), *Handbook of aging and the social sciences* (pp. 444–461). San Diego: Academic Press.

Williams, A., & Nussbaum, J. E. (2001). *Intergenerational communication across the life span.* Mahwah, NJ: Erlbaum.

Williams, D. R. (1992). Social structure and the health behaviors of blacks. In K. W. Schaie, D. Blazer, & J. S. House (Eds.), *Aging, health behaviors, and health outcomes* (pp. 59–64). Hillsdale, NJ: Erlbaum.

Williams, J. E., & Best, D. L. (1990). *Measuring sex stereotypes. A multination study* (Rev. ed.). Newbury Park, CA: Sage.

Willis, S. L., & Schaie, K. W. (1994). Cognitive training in the normal elderly. In F. Forette, Y. Christen, & F. Boller (Eds.), *Plasticité cérébrale et stimulation cognitive,* (pp. 91–113). Paris: Foundational National de Gérontologie.

Wilson, R. S., Bennett, D. A., Beckett, L. A., et al. (1999). Cognitive activity in older persons from a geographically defined population. *Journals of Gerontology: Psychological Sciences, 54B,* P155–P160.

Wilson, R. S., Bennett D. A., & Swartzendruber, A. (1997). Age related change in cognitive function. In P. D. Nussbaum (Ed.), *Handbook of neuropsychology and aging* (pp. 7–14). New York: Plenum Press.

Wink, P., & Dillon, M. (2002). Spiritual development across the adult life course: Findings from a longitudinal study. *Journal of Adult Development, 9,* 79–94.

Wink, P., & Scott, J. (2005). Does religiousness buffer against the fear of death and dying in late adulthood? Findings from a longitudinal study. *Journals of Gerontology: Psychological Sciences, 60B,* P207–P214.

Winstead, B., Derlaga, V. J., & Rose, S. (1997). *Gender and close relationships.* Thousand Oaks, CA: Sage.

Wood, W., & Eagly, A. H. (2002). A cross-cultural analysis of the behavior of women and men: Implications for the origins of sex differences. *Psychological Bulletin, 128,* 699–727.

Woodruff-Pak, D. S. (1997). *Neuropsychology of aging.* Malden, MA: Blackwell.

Woods, L. N., & Emery, R. E. (2002). The cohabitation effect on divorce: Causation or selection? *Journal of Divorce and Remarriage, 37,* 101–122.

Woollett, S., & Marshall, H. (2001). Motherhood and mothering. In R. K. Unger (Ed.), *Handbook of the psychology of women and gender* (pp. 170–182). New York: Wiley.

World Health Organization (2001). *The world health report 2001. Mental health: New understanding, new hope.* Geneva: World Health Organization.

Wortman, C. B., & Silver, R. C. (1989). The myths of coping with loss. *Journal of Consulting and Clinical Psychology, 57,* 349–357.

X

Xiangkui, Z., Juan, G., & Lumei, T. (2005). Can self-esteem buffer death anxiety? The effect of self-esteem on death anxiety caused by mortality salience. *Psychological Science (China), 28,* 602–605.

Y

Yan, L. L., Daviglus, M. L., Liu, K., et al. (2004). BMI and health-related quality of life in adults 65 years and older. *Obesity Research, 12,* 69–76.

Yehuda, R. (2002). Current concepts: Post-traumatic stress disorder. *New England Journal of Medicine, 346,* 108–114.

Yehuda, R., Golier, J. A., Harvey, P. D., et al. (2005). Relationship between cortisol and age-related memory impairments in Holocaust survivors with PTSD. *Psychoneuroendocrinology, 30,* 678–687.

Yesavage, J., Lapp, D., & Sheikh, J. A. (1989). Mnemonics as modified for use by the elderly. In L. W. Poon, D. Rubin, & B. Wilson (Eds.), *Everyday cognition in adulthood and late life.* Cambridge: Cambridge University Press.

Z

Zelinski, E. M., & Burnight, K. P. (1997). Sixteen year longitudinal and time lag changes in memory and cognition in older adults. *Psychology and Aging, 12,* 503–513.

Zhang, Z., & Hayward, M. D. (2001). Childlessness and the psychological well-being of older persons. *Journals of Gerontology: Social Sciences, 56B,* S311–S320.

Zisook, S., Paulus, M., Shuchter, S. R., et al. (1997). The many faces of depression following spousal bereavement. *Journal of Affective Disorders, 45,* 85–94.

Zivotofsky, A. Z., & Koslowsky, M. (2004). Short communication: Gender differences in coping with the major external stress of the Washington, DC sniper. *Stress and Health, 21,* 27–31.

Glossary

a good death a death with dignity, with maximum consciousness and minimum pain.

ability/expertise tradeoff observation that as general ability declines with age, job expertise increases.

accommodate the ability of the lens of the eye to change shape to focus on near objects or small print.

acute conditions short-term health disorders.

adaptive nature of cognition how cognitive abilities adapt to life changes across a lifetime.

ADLs (activities of daily living) basic self-care activities.

adult development changes that take place within individuals as they progress from emerging adulthood to the end of life.

ageism discrimination against those who are in a later period of adulthood.

aging in place remaining in one's own home in later adulthood, often with the assistance of relatives or other caregivers.

alternative medicine providers health care providers whose treatments are not supported by scientific data.

Alzheimer's disease progressive, incurable deterioration of key areas of the brain.

antibodies proteins that react to foreign organisms such as viruses and other infectious agents.

antioxidants substances that protect against oxidative damage from free radicals.

anxiety disorders category of mental health disorders that involves feelings of fear, threat, and dread when no obvious danger is present

assisted-living facilities housing option in which older adults are able to be fairly independent while receiving some assistance.

assistive technology mechanical and electronic devices designed to help with the activities of daily living.

atherosclerosis process by which fat-laden deposits called plaques form in the artery walls.

attachment the strong affectional bond an infant forms with his or her caregivers.

attachment behaviors outward expressions of attachment.

attachment theory Bowlby's theory that infants form a strong affectional bond with their caregivers that provides basic security and understanding of the world and serves as a foundation for later relationships.

attrition dropout rate of participants during a study.

atypical unique to the individual.

B cells cells of the immune system produced in the bone marrow that manufacture antibodies.

balance ability to adapt body position to change.

behavior genetics study of the contributions genes make to individual behavior.

biological age measure an individual's physical condition.

biological clock patterns of change over adulthood in health and physical functioning.

biosocial perspective viewpoint that gender-role bias is based on both biological differences and current social and cultural influences.

body mass index (BMI) number derived from a person's weight and height; a standard indicator of body composition.

bone mass density (BMD) measurement of bone density used to diagnose osteoporosis.

bridge job part-time job or a less stressful full-time job usually taken after retirement.

buffering effect pattern of results that cushion the outcomes of a distressing situation.

caloric restriction (CR) diet in which calories are severely reduced, but contain essential nutrients; found to slow down aging in animal studies.

cancer disease in which abnormal cells undergo rapidly accelerated, uncontrolled division and later move into adjacent normal tissues.

cardiovascular disease disorder of the heart and blood vessels that occurs more frequently with age.

career patterns and sequences of occupations or related roles held by people across their working lives and into retirement.

career recycling in vocational psychology, the notion that people may go back and revisit earlier stages of career development.

caregiver burden common symptoms of decline in mental and physical health among caregivers.

cataracts visual disorder characterized by gradual clouding of the lens.

change slow and gradual movement in a predictable direction.

chronic conditions long-term health disorders.

chronological age number of years that have passed since birth.

climacteric time of life for men and women that involves the reduction of sex hormone production resulting in the loss of reproductive ability.

clinical depression mood disorder that involves long-term, pervasive sense of sadness and hopelessness; major depression.

cochlea small shell-shaped structure in the inner ear containing auditory receptor cells.

cochlear implant surgical procedure that restores hearing by allowing sound waves to bypass auditory receptor cells and go directly to the acoustic nerve.

cohabitation living together in an intimate partnership without marriage.

cohort group of people who shared a common historical experience at the same stage of life.

commonalities aspects that are typical of adult life.

communal qualities personal characteristics that nurture and bring people together, such as being expressive and affectionate; stereotypical female qualitites.

community dwelling living in one's own home either with a spouse or alone.

comorbid relationship of two or more conditions that occur in an individual at the same time.

comparison of means statistical analysis that allows researchers to determine whether the difference in measurements taken on two groups are large enough to be considered statistically significant.

complementary medicine providers healthcare providers whose treatments are not supported by scientific data.

congregate living facilities housing option in which older adults have private living quarters but communal meals, housekeeping, and transportation.

contextual perspective approach to cognition that considers the context within which thought processes take place.

convoy ever-changing network of social relationships that surrounds each of us throughout our adult life.

coping ways to reduce the effects of stress reactions.

coping behaviors thoughts, feelings, and actions that serve to reduce the effects of stressful events

correlational analysis statistical analysis that tells us the extent to which two sets of scores on the same individuals vary together.

CR mimetic substance that would mimic the effects of caloric restriction (CR) and slow down aging.

crossover of gender roles hypothesized change in gender roles at midlife causing women to become masculine and men to become feminine; research has shown that this is not really a "crossover," but more of an expansion of gender roles.

cross-sectional study in the study of development, research method in which data is gathered at one time from groups of participants who represent different age groups.

crystallized intelligence learned abilities based on education and experience, measured by vocabulary and by verbal comprehension.

cultures large social environment in which development takes place.

cyclic GMP substance released by the brain during sexual arousal.

dark adaptation the ability of the pupil of the eye to adjust to changes in the amount of available light.

death anxiety fear of death.

decentering cognitive movement outward from the self.

defense mechanism in Vaillant's theory of mature adaptation, the set of normal, unconscious strategies used for dealing with anxiety.

dementia category of various types of brain damage and disease that involve significant impairment of memory, judgment, social functioning, and control of emotions.

dendrites projections from the cell body of neurons that form connections with other neurons.

depressive symptoms feelings of sadness or hopelessness that are not as severe or long-lasting as major depression; subclinical depression.

descriptive research defines the current state of participants on some measure on interest.

developmental-origins hypothesis the idea that events during the fetal period, infancy, and the early years of childhood are significant factors in subsequent adult health.

developmental psychology field of study that deals with changes that take place in behavior, thoughts, and emotions of individuals as they go from conception to the end of life.

dexterity skill and grace in physical movement, especially in the use of the hands.

DHEA (dehydroepiandrosterone) hormone involved in the production of sex hormones for both males and females; available as nutritional supplement.

differential continuity stability of individuals' rank order within a group over time.

disability the extent to which an individual is unable to perform certain activities of daily living.

disengagement early hypothesis which held that late adulthood is a time when people withdraw from activities and relationships in preparation for the end of life.

distal causes factors that were present in the distant past.

domestic migration moving one's residence from one county to another or to a different state within the United States.

ecological systems approach method of studying the developing person within the context of multiple environments.

egalitarian roles roles based on equality between genders.

ego integrity in Erikson's theory of psychosocial development, the tendency older adults develop to review their life for meaning and integration.

emotion-focused coping stress-reducing technique that directly addresses the emotions causing stress.

empirical research scientific studies of observable events that are measured and evaluated statistically.

episodic memory in information processing, the segment of the long-term store that contains information about sequences of events.

estrogen female sex hormone.

evolutionary psychology field of psychology that explains human behavior in terms of genetic patterns that were useful in our primitive ancestors for survival and reproduction success.

exchange theory theory that we select mates by evaluating the assets we have to offer in a relationship and the assets the potential mates have to offer, and try to make the best deal.

expansion of gender roles change in gender roles at midlife causing men and women to broaden their gender roles to include more attributes of the opposite gender.

extended families grandparents, aunts and uncles, cousins and other relatives.

feminization of poverty the fact that in the last few decades, more and more people who live in poverty are women.

filter theory theory that we select mates by using finer and finer filtering mechanisms.

Five-Factor Model inventory of five basic personality factors first demonstrated by Costa and McCrae.

fluid intelligence basic adaptive abilities, measured by tests of digit span, response speed, and abstract reasoning.

food insufficiency not having enough food for yourself and your family.

free radicals molecules or atoms that possess an unpaired electron; by-products of cell metabolism.

friendship voluntary interpersonal relationship carried out within a social context.

full-scale IQ combined verbal IQ and performance IQ.

functional age measure of how well an individual is functioning in various aspects of adulthood.

g central, general intellectual capacity which influences the way we approach many different tasks

gait stability movement measurement; length of time both feet are on the floor at once.

gender crossover relaxation of gender roles that is hypothesized to occurs in men and women when the parenting years are over.

gender roles actual behaviors and attitudes of men and women in a given culture during a given historical era.

gender stereotypes sets of shared beliefs or generalizations about how men and women in a society ought to behave.

general adaptation syndrome in Selye's theory, three stages of symptoms that occur in response to stress: alarm reaction, resistance, and exhaustion.

generational squeeze situation in which middle-aged adults are sandwiched between the needs of their elderly parents and their adult children.

generativity in Erikson's theory of psychosocial development, the tendency middle-aged adults develop to help establish and guide the next generation.

genotype an individual's complement of genes.

gerotranscendence idea that meaning systems increase in quality as we age.

glaucoma visual disorder characterized by a buildup of pressure inside the eye which can lead to blindness if not treated.

Hayflick limit the maximum number of times cells are programmed to divide for a species.

hGH (human growth hormone) hormone involved in childhood physical growth; widely (and illegally) used as anti-aging remedy.

hormone replacement therapy (HRT) therapy in which women take estrogen and progestin at menopause to replace hormones once produced by the ovaries; relieves menopause symptoms.

hospice care end-of-life care focused on pain relief, emotional support, and spiritual comfort for dying people and their families.

hostility negative cognitive set against others.

hot flash physical symptom of menopausal transition involving a sudden sensation of heat spreading over the body, especially the chest, face, and head.

household labor unpaid work done in the home for oneself and family that includes meal preparation and cleanup, grocery shopping, laundry, and housecleaning.

human factors research field of research that combines psychology with engineering to uncover real-world problems people have and to locate or create devices that will solve them.

IADLs (instrumental activities of daily living) complex everyday tasks.

identity in Erikson's theory of psychosocial development, the set of personal values and goals a young adult develops pertaining to gender, occupation, and religious beliefs.

impulse-control disorders mental health disorders that affect a person's judgment or ability to control strong and often harmful impulses.

individual differences aspects that are unique to the individual.

information-processing perspective approach to the study of cognition that emphasizes processes, representations, and strategies individuals use to perform intellectual tasks.

inner changes internal alterations not apparent to the casual observer.

insomnia inability to have normal sleep patterns.

instrumental qualities personal characteristics that have an active impact, such as being competitive, adventurous, and physically strong; stereotypical male qualities.

intelligence visible indicator of the efficiency of various cognitive processes that work together behind the scenes to process information.

interactionist view idea that genetics influence how one interacts with the environment and the environment one chooses.

intergenerational effects prenatal experiences that affect the female fetus as an adult and also her subsequent offspring.

intergenerational solidarity the extent to which family members of different generations are close to each other.

internal working model in Bolwby's attachment theory, the set of beliefs and assumptions a person has about the nature of all relationships based on specific experiences in childhood.

intimacy in Erikson's theory of psychosocial development, the ability young adults develop that allows them to enter into intimate relationships without losing their own sense of self.

intra-individual variability stability or instability of personality traits within an individual over time.

IQ (intelligence quotient) score on an intelligence test that reflects general intellectual capacity.

job burnout job-related condition that is a combination of exhaustion, depersonalization, and reduced effectiveness.

job expertise high level of skill that results from years of experience at a certain job.

job loss having paid employment taken away from an individual.

labor force those who are officially working at paid jobs.

learning-schema theory explanation of gender roles stating that children are taught to view the world and themselves through gender-polarized lenses that make artificial or exaggerated distinctions between what is masculine and what is feminine.

lens transparent structure in the eye that focuses light rays on receptors in the retina.

libido sexual desire.

life-change events in Holmes and Rahe's theory, events that alter the status quo of an individual's life; when accumulated can lead to stress reactions.

life review process described by Butler in which older people seem to enjoy and benefit from taking stock of their personal histories and often write their memoirs as a way to put closure on their lives.

life-span developmental psychology approach idea that development is lifelong, multidimensional, plastic, contextual, and has multiple causes.

life-span/life-space theory in vocational psychology, Super's theory that careers develop in stages and cannot be studied in isolation from other aspects of a person's life.

living will legal document that states a person's end-of-life decisions.

long-term store in information processing, the third step of memory processing, in which information is stored—both facts (in the semantic memory) and events (in episodic memory).

longitudinal study research method in which data is gathered over a period of time from the same group of people as they age.

macular degeneration visual disorder of the retina, causing central vision loss.

major depression mood disorder that involves long-term, pervasive sense of sadness and hopelessness; clinical depression.

marital protection the greater financial resources, social support, and heathier lifestyle married people enjoy compared to unmarried people; researchers believe this leads to longer lives and better health.

marital selection statistical effect in which healthier people are more apt to marry and stay married, producing the appearance that marriage benefits health.

masters' events athletic competitions for those age 30 and older.

mate selection process of choosing a long-term partner for an intimate relationship.

meaning-focused coping stress-reducing technique that refers to anything you might think, feel, and do to give a positive meaning to a stressful situation.

mean-level change changes in a group's average scores over time.

memory ability to retain or store information and retrieve it when needed.

menopause cessation of women's menstrual periods, occurring 12 months after the final menstrual period; climacteric.

meta-analysis comparison of data from a large number of studies that deal with the same research question.

midlife crisis popular myth that portrays middle age as a time of unstable and unpredictable behavior.

mood disorders category of mental health disorders that involves loss in the sense of control over emotions, resulting in feelings of distress.

moral reasoning analyzing what is right and wrong, judging the rightness or wrongness of an act.

morbidity rate illness rate.

mortality rate probability of dying in any one year.

mysticism self-transcendent experience.

name-finding failures failure to recall a name that is known but momentarily absent.

neurogenesis the formation of new neurons

neurons brain cells

non-normative life events aspects that influence one's life that are unique to the individual.

nontraditional student in college, a student who is older than the traditional age, or over 25.

normative age-graded influences common effects of age that are experienced by most adults.

normative history-graded influences effects connected to historical events and conditions that are experienced by everyone within a culture at that time.

nuclear families parents and their children.

nursing home skilled-care facility.

obsessive-compulsive disorder anxiety disorder that involves guilt and anxiety over certain thoughts or impulses

occupational gender segregation separation of jobs into stereotypical male and female categories.

olfactory membrane specialized part of the nasal membrane that contains olfactory receptor cells.

onset first occurrence.

optimism positive outlook on life.

organ transplant donor individual who agrees to the transplantation, at the time of death, of his or her usable organs and other tissue to approved recipients.

osteoarthritis condition caused by loss of cartilage that protects the bones at joints; can involve pain, swelling, and loss of motion.

osteopenia moderate loss of bone mass; not as severe as osteoporosis.

osteoporosis severe loss of bone mass.

outer changes external alterations visible and apparent to those we encounter.

parental imperative genetically programmed tendency for new parents to become more traditional in their gender roles.

peak experiences in Maslow's theory of positive well-being, the feeling of perfection and momentary separation from the self when one feels in unity with the universe.

performance IQ intellectual capacity for performance (nonverbal) tasks.

personal interview research method in which the experimenter meets with the participant and gathers data directly, often through open ended and follow-up questions.

personality enduring set of characteristics that define our individuality and affect our interactions with the environment and other people.

personality factors groups of traits that occur together in an individual.

personality states short-term patterns of thoughts, feelings, and behaviors.

personality traits stable patterns of thoughts, feelings, and behaviors.

person-environment transactions combinations of genetic endowment and environmental factors that maintain the stability of personality traits over time.

phased retirement situation in which an older person continues to work for an employer part-time as a transition to retirement.

phobias anxiety disorders that involve fears and avoidance out of proportion to the danger presented

physician-assisted suicide situation in which physicians are legally allowed to assist patients, under certain circumstances, to obtain medication that will end their lives.

plaques fat-laden deposits formed in the coronary artery walls as a result of inflammation.

plasticity in neurons, the ability to form new connections or grow new extensions.

positive psychology recent emphasis of psychology research to turn away from negative outcomes, such as mental illness and crime, and toward positive outcomes, such as well-being, optimism, and spiritual growth.

postformal stages adult stage of cognitive development that involves thinking beyond the linear and logical ways.

post-traumatic stress disorder (PTSD) psychological response to a traumatic experience.

Symptoms include re-experiencing the event in intrusive thoughts and dreams, numbing of general responses, avoiding stimuli associated with the event, and increased arousal of the physiological stress mechanisms.

presbyopia visual condition caused by loss of elasticity in the lens, resulting in the inability to focus sharply on nearby objects.

prevalence proportion of people experiencing a certain disorder at a given time.

primary aging physical changes that are gradual, shared, and largely inevitable as people grow older.

primary memory in information processing, the segment of the short-term store that holds information in place for immediate recall.

proactive coping stress-reducing techniques done in advance of a potentially stressful event.

problem-focused coping stress-reducing techniques that directly address the problem causing stress.

procedural memory in information processing, the long-term memory system responsible for skill learning and retention.

progesterone female sex hormone.

proximal causes factors present in the immediate environment.

pruning the ability to shut down neurons that are not needed in order to "fine-tune" the system and improve functioning of the remaining neurons.

psychological age measure of an individual's ability to deal effectively with the environment.

psychometrics field of psychology that studies the measurement of human abilities.

pupil opening in the eye that changes in diameter in response to available light.

qualitative research research without numerical data, such as case studies, interviews, participant observations, direct observations, and exploring documents, artifacts, and archival records.

quantitative research research with numerical data.

quest for meaning the self's search for ultimate knowledge of life through an individualized understanding of the sacred.

redundancy in neurons, the tendency for some cells to be present in duplicate.

reliability the extent to which a test instrument gives the same results repeatedly under the same conditions.

religiosity the outward expression of spiritual beliefs.

religious coping stress-reducing techniques that involve relying on religious or spiritual beliefs.

reminiscense review of one's personal memories.

replicative senescence state in which older cells stop dividing.

resilience the ability to maintain healthy functioning following exposure to potential trauma.

resistance resources personal and social resources that may buffer a person from the impact of stress.

response-oriented viewpoint explanations of stress that focus on the physiological reactions within the individual.

retina structure at the back of the eye that contains receptor cells.

retirement career stage in which an older worker leaves the full-time work force to pursue other interests, such as part-time work, volunteer work, or leisure interests.

retirement-related value in retirement decisions, the amount of personal wealth one has, plus social security and pension benefits, salary from part-time jobs, and health insurance benefits available if one retires; can be weighed against work-related value.

ritual mourning set of symbolic rites and ceremonies associated with death and bereavement.

role-enhancement theory states that multiple roles are beneficial because some roles serve as buffers against stress from other roles.

role-strain theory states that there is a limit to the number of roles a person can take on before physical and psychological well-being decline.

role transitions changes in roles due to changes in the individual or in his or her life circumstances.

seasonal migration moving one's residence to another location temporarily, usually to spend the winter in a warmer climate, and then returning home in the spring,

secondary aging physical changes that are sudden, not shared, and often caused by disease, poor health habits, and environmental events as people grow older.

selective optimization with compensation process described by Baltes and Baltes in which older people cope with limitations by selecting their activities, optimizing their strategies, and compensating for their losses.

self-actualization in Maslow's theory, the drive to become everything that one is capable of being. It is reached when more basic needs are met.

self-determination theory explanation of personality based on individuals' evolved inner resources for growth and integration.

self-trancendence knowing the self as part of a larger whole that exists beyond the physical body and personal history.

semantic memory in information processing, the segment of the long-term store that contains factual information.

sense of purpose in life discovery of satisfying personal goals and the belief that one's life has been worthwhile.

sensorineural hearing loss loss in the ability to discriminate between loud and soft sounds caused by damage to receptors in the inner ear.

sensory store in information processing, the first step of memory processing, in which information is detected by the senses and processed briefly by the perceptual system.

sequential study series of several longitudinal studies begun at different points in time.

shift work jobs with nonstandard work schedules, including evening shifts, night shifts, and rotating shifts.

short-term store in information processing, the second step of memory processing, in which information is held "in mind" for immediate recall (primary memory) or for active processing (working memory).

social age measure of the number and type of roles an individual has taken on at a specific point in his or her life.

social clock patterns of change over adulthood in social roles.

social clock time schedule of the normal sequence of adult life experiences.

social coping stress-reducing technique that involves seeking both instrumental and emotional support from others.

social relationships dynamic, recurrent patterns of interactions with other individuals.

social role theory explanation of gender roles based on children viewing the gender divisions around them and then modeling their behavior on those divisions.

social roles expected behaviors and attitudes that come with one's position in society.

social support positive affect, affirmation, and aid received from others at stressful times.

social timing pattern of when we occupy certain roles, how long we occupy them, and the order in which we move from one to another.

sociobiographical history level of professional prestige, social position, and income that one experiences throughout one's life.

socioemotional selectivity theory according to Carstensen, the explanation that people emphasize more meaningful, emotionally satisfying social relationships as they become older because they are then more aware of the end of life than younger people.

stability having little or no change for significant periods of time.

stages parts of the lifespan where there seems to be no progress for some time, followed by an abrupt change.

stamina ability to sustain moderate or strenuous activity.

standardized tests established instruments that measure a specific trait or behavior.

stem cells immature undifferentiated cells that can multiply easily and mature into many different kinds of cells

stereotype threats anxiety that arises when members of a group (such as older adults) are put in positions that might confirm widely held, negative stereotypes about them (such as taking a memory test).

stimulus-oriented viewpoint explanations of stress that are focused on the stressors themselves, the stimuli or life events, that trigger the stress reactions.

stress set of physical, cognitive, and emotional responses that humans (and other organisms) display in reaction to demands from the environment.

stressors environmental demands that lead to stress reactions.

stress-related growth positive changes that follow the experience of stressful life events.

subclinical depression feelings of sadness or hopelessness that are not as severe or long-lasting as major depression; depressive symptoms.

substance abuse disorders mental health disorders that involve abuse or dependence on drugs or alcohol.

surrogate parenting role assumed by grandparents when the parents are not able to raise their children.

survey questionnaire written form that participants can fill out on their own consisting of structured and focused questions.

T cells cells of the immune system produced in the thymus gland that reject and consume harmful or foreign cells.

taste buds receptors cells for taste found on the tongue, mouth, and throat.

telomeres lengths of repeating DNA that chromosomes have at their tips.

testosterone major male sex hormone.

transition to adulthood period during which young people take on the social roles of early adulthood.

twin studies studies that compare similarities of monozygotic twin pairs with dizygotic twin pairs on some behavior or trait of interest.

type A behavior pattern state of being achievement-striving, competitive, and involved in one's job to excess.

typical common to most people.

unemployment state of being without a paid job when you are willing to work.

useful field of view (UFOV) area of the visual field that can be processed in one glance.

validity the extent to which a test instrument measures what it claims to measure

verbal IQ intellectual capacity for verbal tasks.

visual acuity ability to perceive detail in a visual pattern

vocational interests in vocational psychology, personal attitudes, competencies, and values a person has relating to his or her career; basis of Holland's theory of career selection.

word-finding failures failure to recall a word that is known but momentarily absent.

working memory in information processing, the segment of the short-term store that peforms cognitive operations on information.

work-related value in retirement decisions, the amount of salary, pension, and social security benefits a worker will receive later if he or she continues working; can be weighed against retirement-related value.

Credits

Photographs

Cover Image Simon Krzic/Shutterstock

Title Page Karl Weatherly, Getty Images, Inc./PhotoDisc.

Chapter 1 p. 2 N. Frank, The Viesti Collection, Inc; p. 5 Barbara Bjorklund; p. 11 Robert Clark, Aurora & Quanta Productions, Inc.; p. 14 Comstock Royalty Free Division.

Chapter 2 p. 32 Photos.com.; p. 42 D. Degnan/Robertstock, Getty Images/Retrofile; p. 55 Blend Images, Alamy Images; p. 57 Timothy Heally, Joel Gordon Photography/Design Conceptions.

Chapter 3 p. 68 Photos.com; p. 72 Joel Gordon Photography/Design Conceptions; p. 83 BSIP, Phototake NYC.

Chapter 4 p. 100 Ablestock/Photos.com; p. 111 Michael Heron, Woodfin Camp & Associates; p. 125 Bill Bachmann, Stock Boston.

Chapter 5 p. 132 Photos.com; p. 138 David Young-Wolff, PhotoEdit, Inc.; p. 147 David Young-Wolff, PhotoEdit, Inc.; p. 149 © Stefan Schuetz/Zefa, CORBIS-NY, all rights reserved.

Chapter 6 p. 164 Ablestock/Photos.com; p. 171 Comstock Royalty Free Division; p. 181 Tom & Dee Ann McCarthy, CORBIS/Bettmann; p. 182 Deborah Davis, PhotoEdit, Inc.

Chapter 7 p. 200 Photos.com; p. 207 Aurora & Quanta Productions, Inc.; p. 210 Charles Coffey; p. 216 Joel Gordon Photography; p. 218 Steven Peters, Getty Images, Inc./Stone Allstock; p. 228 Charles Gupton, CORBIS/Bettmann.

Chapter 8 p. 236 Photos.com; p. 250 Jon Feingersh, CORBIS/Bettmann; p. 261 Comstock Royalty Free Division.

Chapter 9 p. 266 Photos.com; p. 270 Norbert Schaefer, CORBIS/Bettmann; p. 275 Mark Thiessen, CORBIS/Bettmann; p. 278 (left) SuperStock, Inc.; p. 278 (right) CORBIS/Bettmann; p. 288 John Madere, CORBIS/Bettmann.

Chapter 10 p. 296 Photos.com; p. 305 Alex Brandon/Newhouse News Service, Landov LLC; p. 306 David Young-Wolff, PhotoEdit, Inc.; p. 310 Winn McNamee/Getty Images, Inc.

Chapter 11 p. 322 Photos.com; p. 334 Holmes/Omni-Photo Communications, Inc.; p. 337 Joel Gordon Photography/Design Conceptions.

Chapter 12 p. 346 Photos.com; p. 351 CORBIS Royalty Free; p. 353 Chuck Savage/CORBIS–NY; p. 356 PhotoEdit, Inc.; p. 357 Mark Scott/Getty Images, Inc./Taxi.

Figures and Tables

Chapter 1 Table 1-2—From Baltes, P. B. (1987). "Theoretical propositions of life-span developmental psychology: On the dynamics between growth and decline." Developmental Psychology, 23, 611–626. Adapted with permission of the American Psychological Association. Figure 1-2—Adapted from Cleary, P. D., Zaborski, L. B., & Ayanian, J. Z (2004). "Sex differences in health over the life course." In O. G. Brim, C. D. Ryff, & R. C. Kessler (Eds.), How healthy are we? A national study of well-being at midlife (pp. 37–63). Chicago: University of Chicago Press. Figure 1-6—From Whitbourne, S. K., Zuschlag, M. K., Elliott, L. B., et al. (1992). "Psychosocial development in adulthood: A 22-year sequential study." Journal of Personality and Social Psychology, 63, 260–271. Adapted with permission of the American Psychological Association. Figure 1-8—Adapted from Colcombe, S., & Kramer, A. F. (2003). "Fitness effects on the cognitive function of older adults: A meta-analytic study." Psychological Science, 14, 125–130. Table 1-3—Adapted from Salkind, N. (2003). Exploring research, 5th ed. (Table 11.1, page 225). Upper Saddle River, NJ: Prentice-Hall.

Chapter 2 Table 2-3—American Society of Plastic Surgeons, reprinted by permission. Figure 2-4—Journal of American Medical Association, reprinted by permission of the American Medical Association. Figure 2-5—Medical Research Council, Human Nutrition Research, Cambridge,

United Kingdom. Figure 2-6—Adapted from Cleary, P. D., Zaborski, L. B., & Ayanian, J. Z. (2004). "Sex differences in health over the life course." In O. G. Brim, C. D. Ryff, & R. C. Kessler (Eds.), How healthy are we? A national study of well-being at midlife (pp. 37–63). Chicago: University of Chicago Press. Figure 2-7—Adapted from Korhonen, M. T., Mero, A., & Suominen, H. (2003). "Age related differences in 100 m sprint performance in male and female master runners." Medicine and Science in Sports and Exercise, 35, 1419–1428.

Chapter 3 Figure 3-4—"Structural changes in the aging brain," Handbook of Mental Health and Aging, ed by J. E. Birren, R. B. Sloane, & G. D. Cohen. Used with permission of Academic/Elsevier Publishers; Figure 3-5—Adapted from Gatz, M., Fratiglioni, L., Johansson, B., et al. (2005). Neurobiology of Aging, 26, 439–447. Table 3-6—Reprinted with permission from Diagnostic and Statistical Manual of Mental Disorders, Fourth Edition, text revision, (Copyright 2000). American Psychiatric Association. Table 3-7—Test for Depressive Symptoms, by L. S. Radloff in Applied Psychological Measurement, 1, 1977, pp. 385–401. Copyright © 1977. Reprinted by permission of Sage Publications, Inc. Figure 3-6—Reprinted by permission of the American Medical Association. Figure 3-7—Adapted from Gluckman, P. D., & Hanson, M. A. (2004). "Living with the past: Evolution, development, and pattern of disease." Science, 305, 1733–1739.

Chapter 4 Figure 4-1—"The Seattle longitudinal study: A 21-year exploration of psychometric intelligence in adulthood," by D. Terri Heath in Families in Multicultural Perspective, ed. by Bron B. Ingoldsby and Suzanna Smith, pp. 161–186. Copyright 1983 by Guilford Press. Reprinted with permission. Figure 4-2—From Lindenberger, U., & Baltes, P. B. (1994). "Sensory functioning and intelligence in old age: A strong connection." Psychology and Aging, 9, 339–355. Adapted with permission of the American Psychological Association. Figure 4-3—From Schaie, K. W. (1994). "The course of adult intellectual development." American Psychologist, 49, 304–313. Reprinted by permission. Figure 4-5—From Park, D. C., Hedden, T., Davidson, N. S., et al., (2002). "Models of visuospatial and verbal memory across the adult life span." Psychology and Aging, 17, 299–320. (Page 305, panels B & D). Adapted with permission of the American Psychological Association. Figure 4-6—From Fung, H. H., & Carstensen, L. L. (2003). "Sending memorable messages to the old: Age differences in preferences and memory for advertisements." Journal of Personality and Social Psychology, 85, 163–178. Adapted with permission of the American Psychological Association. Figure 4-11—McClearn, G. E., Johansson, B., Berg, S., et al. (1997). "Substantial genetic influence on cognitive abilities in twins 80 or more years old." Science 5318, 1560–1563. Reprinted by permission of Science Magazine.

Chapter 5 Table 5-1—"Examples of Gender Role Stereotypes," adapted from A. B. Diekman, A. H. Eagly, A. Mladinic, et al., in Journal of Cross Cultural Psychology, 36, 2005, pp. 209–226. Copyright © 2005. Reprinted by permission of Sage Publications, Inc. Figure 5-2—From Cohen, P., Kasen, S., Chen, H., et al. (2003). "Variations in patterns of developmental transmissions in the emerging adulthood period." Developmental Psychology, 39, 657–669. Adapted with permission of the American Psychological Association. Figure 5-3—Adapted from National Marriage Project (2005). The State of Our Unions 2005. Figure 5-4—Adapted from Heuveline, P., & Timberlake, J. M. (2004). "The role of cohabitation in family formation: The U.S. in comparative perspective." Journal of Marriage and Family, 66, 1214–1230.

Chapter 6 Table 6-1 From M. T. Greenberg, D. Cicchetti, & E. M. Cummings (eds.). "Attachment in the preschool years: Theory, research, and intervention." University of Chicago Press. Reprinted with permission of The University of Chicago Press. Figure 6-1—Adapted from Antonucci, T. C., Akiyama, H., & Takahashi, K. (2004). "Attachment and close relationships across the life span." Attachment and Human Development, 6, 353–370. Table 6-2—Copyrighted 2001 by the National Council on Family Relations, 3989 Central Ave. NE, Suite 550, Minneapolis, MN 55421. Reprinted by permission. Table 6-3—From Bartholomew, K., & Horowitz, L. M. (1991). "Attachment styles among young adults: A test of a four-category model." Journal of Personality and Social Psychology, 61, 226–244. Adapted with permission of the American Psychological Association. Figure 6-2—From Karney, B. R., & Bradbury, T. N. (1995). "The longitudinal course of marital quality and stability: A review of theory, method, and research." Psychological Bulletin, 118, 3–34. Adapted by permission of The American Psychological Association. Table 6-4—From "The seven principles for making marriage work" by J. M. Gottman and N. Silver. Reprinted by permission of Three Rivers Press, a division of Random House, Inc. Figure 6-3—Adapted from DeKay, W. T. (2000). "Evolutionary psychology." In W. C. Nichola, et al. (Eds.), Handbook of family development and intervention (pp. 23–40). New York: John Wiley & Sons, Inc. Figure 6-6—Adapted from Webster, J. D. (1997). "Attachment style and well-being in elderly adults: A preliminary investigation." Canadian Journal on Aging, 16, 101–111.

Chapter 7 Table 7-1—From Hartung, P. J., & Niles, S. G. (2000). "Using traditional career theories with college students." In D. Luzzo (Ed.). Career development of college students: Translating theory and research into practice (pp. 3–22). Washington, DC: American Psychological Association. Adapted with permission from The American Psychological Association. Figure 7-2—Copyright © 1992 by PAR, Inc. Reprinted by permission. All rights reserved. Figure 7-8—Harvard Institute of Economic Research.

Chapter 8   Table 8-1—Copyright © 2005 by PAR, Inc. Reprinted by permission. All rights reserved. Figure 8-1—From Roberts B. W., & DelVecchio, W. F., (2000). "The rank-order consistency of personality traits from childhood to old age: A quantitative review of longitudinal studies." Psychological Bulletin, 126, 3–25. Reprinted by permission of The American Psychological Association. Figure 8-2—From Roberts, B. W., Walton, K. E., Viechtbauer, W. (2006). "Patterns of mean-level change in personality traits across the life course: A meta-analysis of longitudinal studies." Psychological Bulletin, 132, 1-25. Reprinted by permission of The American Psychological Association. Figure 8-3—From Roberts, B. W., Walton, K. E., Bogg, T. (2006). "Patterns of mean-level change in personality traits across the life course: A meta-analysis of longitudinal studies." Psychological Bulletin, 132, 1–25. Adapted by permission of The American Psychological Association. Figure 8-4—Adapted from Riemann, R., Angleitner, A., & Strelau, J. (1997). "Genetic and environmental influences on personality: A study of twins reared together using the self- and peer-report NEO-FFI scales." Journal of Personality, 65, 449–475. Figure 8-5—From Whitbourne, S. K., Zuschlag, M. K., Elliot, L. B., et al., (1992). "Psychosocial development in adulthood: A 22-year sequential study." Journal of Personality and Social Psychology, 63, 260–271. Adapted with permission of the American Psychological Association. Figure 8-6—From Whitbourne, S. K., Zuschlag, M. K., Elliot, L. B., et al., (1992). "Psychosocial development in adulthood: A 22-year sequential study." Journal of Personality and Social Psychology, 63, 260–271. Adapted with permission of the American Psychological Association. Table 8-3—Adapted from D. N. Jackson and S. V. Paunonen, "Personality Structure Assessment," Annual Review of Psychology, 31, pp. 503–582. Reprinted by permission of Wolters Kluwer Health. All rights reserved. Figure 8-7—From McAdams, D. P., Hart, H. M., & Maruna, S. (1998). "The anatomy of generativity." In D. P. McAdams & E. de St. Aubin (Eds.), "Generativity and adult development: How and why we care for the next generation" (pp.7–43). Washington, DC: American Psychological Association. Reprinted by permission of The American Psychological Association. Table 8-4—Academic Press; Used with the permission of Dr. Jane Loevinger. Figure 8-9—Reprinted with permission of John Wiley & Sons, Inc.

Chapter 9   Figure 9-2—Reprinted by permission of Journal of Adult Development. Figure 9-3—Reprinted by permission of Journal of Adult Development. Figure 9-4—"Explorign Heart and Soul: Effects of Religiosity/Spirituality and Gender on Blood Pressure and Cortisol Stress Response," from J. Tartaro, L. J. Leucken & H. E. Gunn, in Journal of Cross Cultural Psychology, 36, 2005, pp. 209–226. Copyright © 2005. Reprinted by permission of Sage Publications, Inc. Table 9-2—Adapted from L. Kohlberg, "Continuities in childhood and adult moral development revisited," in P. B. Baltes & K. W. Schaie (Eds.), Life-span developmental psychology: Personality and socialization, pp. 180–204. Copyright © 1973, with permission from Elsevier Ltd.

Chapter 10   Figure 10-2—Adapted from Almeida, D. M. (2005). "Resilience and vulnerability to daily stressors assessed via diary methods." Current Directions in Psychological Sciences, 14, 64–68. Table 10-1—International Journal of Behavioral Medicine (pending credit line). Figure 10-5—Adapted from Leserman, J., Petitto, J. M., Golden, R. N., et al. (2000). "Impact of stressful life events, depression, social support, coping, and cortisol on progression to AIDS." American Journal of Psychiatry, 157, 1221–1228. Figure 10-7—Adapted from Almeida, D. M., & Horn, M. C. (2004). "Is daily life more stressful during middle adulthood?" In O. G. Brim, C. D. Ryff, & R. C. Kessler (Eds.), How healthy are we" A national study of well-being at midlife (pp. 425–451). Chicago: University of Chicago Press. Table 10-1—International Journal of Behavioral Medicine, reprinted with permission of the Lawrence Erlbaum Associates, Inc. Figure 10-10—Adapted from Vogt, D. S., Pless, A. P., King, L. A., et al. (2005) "Development stressors, gender, and mental health outcomes among Gulf War I veterans." Journal of Traumatic Stress, 18, 115–127. Figure 10-11—From Bonanno, G. A., Moskowitz, J. T., Papa, A., et al. (2005). "Resilience to loss in bereaved spouses, bereaved parents, and bereaved gay men." Journal of Personality and Social Psychology, 88, 827–843. Adapted with permission of the American Psychological Association.

Chapter 11   Table 11-1—Adapted from S. Greer, "Cancer survival rates by adaptation Greer 1991," in Psychological Medicine, 21, 1991, pp. 43–44. Reprinted with the permission of Cambridge University Press. Table 11-2—Journal of the American Medical Association, reprinted by permission of the American Medical Association. Figure 11-2—From Bonanno, G. A., Wortman, C. B., Lehman, et al. (2002). "Resilience to loss and chronic grief: A prospective study from pre-loss to 18 months post-loss." Journal of Personality and Social Psychology, 83, 1150–1164. Adapted with permission of the American Psychological Association.

Author Index

A

Abdel-Khalek, A. M., 326
Acevedo-Garcia, D., 87, 88
Acree, M., 340
Adams, C., 113
Adelmann, P. K., 357
Adler, N. E., 89
Aiken, L. R., 215
Ainsworth, M. D. S., 166
Akiyama, H., 168, 169, 170
Alaimo, K., 89
Alaphilippe, D., 361
Albersheim, L. J.,167
Albert, M., 77
Albert, S. M., 151
Aldous, J., 188
Aldwin, C. M., 307, 309
Alea, N., 238
Alesina, A., 224
Alexander, E. A., 60
Allen, P. A., 126
Allison, A. L., 60
Allman, R. M., 118
Almeida, D. M., 300, 301, 306, 307, 308
Almeida, O. P., 52
Alsop, S., 328
American Cancer Society, 80, 89, 334
American Psychiatric Associa-
    tion, 1, 84, 257, 304
American Psychological Associa-
    tion, 219
American Society of Plastic Sur-
    geons, 41, 42, 43
Amir, M., 328
Andersen, K., 89
Andreasen, N. C., 80
Andresen, E. M., 85
Angleitner, A., 245
Antoni, M. H., 302, 316
Antonucci, T. C., 168, 169, 170, 316
Appathurai, B., 44, 45
Aquilino, W. S., 210
Araujo, A. B., 57, 59
Araya, R., 88
Ardelt, M., 326, 361
Ardila, A., 125
Aron, A., 172
Arterburn, D. E., 38
Aryanian, J. Z., 17, 18, 23
Aspinwall, L. G., 313
Atchley, P., 119

Atchley, R., 269
Atkinson, R. C., 108
Auman, C., 114
Austad, S. N., 34
Ayanian, J. Z., 49, 50, 87
Azarow, J., 253

B

Babcock, R. L., 124
Bachman, L. D., 124
Bachrach, C. A., 144, 145
Backlund, E., 142
Bäckman, L., 109, 111, 112, 122, 124
Bacon, C. G., 59
Baddeley, A. D., 109
Bailey, N., 361
Bakker, R., 117
Balbin, E. G., 275
Ball, K., 119
Balsam, K. F., 183, 184
Baltes, M. M., 358, 360
Baltes, P. B., 14, 15, 20, 104, 105, 106, 108, 111, 112, 122, 124, 127, 212, 358, 360
Bandura, A., 155
Baranowski, M. C., 188
Barkan, S., 328
Barker, D. J., 94
Barker, E. T., 18, 19, 20
Barnes, L. B., 310
Bartholomew, K., 174, 175, 193
Barton, S. A., 189
Bass, D. M., 154
Bata, I., 93
Bauer, J. J., 255
Baulieu, E. E., 54
Baum, A., 298
Baumeister, R. F., 171
Baur, K., 60
Beach, S. R., 143
Beal, C. R., 210
Bear, T. M., 310
Beaumont, J. G., 361
Beck, P., 73
Beckett, L. A., 89, 125
Beers, M. H., 49, 50, 51, 57
Bell, D. C., 175
Bell, R. R., 194
Belsky, J., 147, 218
Bem, S. L., 135
Bengtson, D. L., 221
Bengtson, V. L., 150, 153, 185
Bengtsson, T., 94

Benjamins, M. R., 271
Bennett, D. A., 107, 125
Berensen, G. S., 75
Beresford, S. A. A., 126
Berg, C. A., 105, 108, 109
Berg, K., 211
Berg, S., 122, 123, 124
Berglund, P., 81, 82, 83, 85, 90, 91
Bernard, S. L., 155
Berscheid, E., 171
Besser, A., 328
Best, D. L., 135
Beuchaine, T. P., 184
Bianchi, S. M., 221
Binns, M., 83
Binstock, R. H., 36
Birkhill, W. R., 107
Birren, J. E., 327, 358
Bisno, B., 331
Bjerkeset, O., 83
Bjork-Eriksson, T. 50
Blackburn, E. H., 35, 308
Blehar, M., 166
Blementhal, J. A., 126
Bleske, A. L., 135
Bliesner, R., 184
Bliwise, D. L., 56
Blood, L. L., 204
Bloom, B., 83
Bluck, S., 238
Bogg, T., 244, 245
Bonanno, G. A., 317, 318, 318, 319, 340, 341
Bond, J. T., 218
Bond, T., 146
Bookwala, J., 153
Borawski-Clark, E., 315
Bouchard, T. J., 123
Bowlby, J., 166, 185, 337
Boyce, T., 89
Boyd-Davis, S. L., 161
Bradbury, T. N., 176, 177, 243
Bradley, D. E., 229
Brallier, S., 27, 152
Bramlett, M. D., 141, 180
Brand, D., 124
Brébion, G., 110
Bren, L., 48
Brennan, K. A., 174
Bridges, J. S., 204
Briefel, R. R., 89
Brim, O. G. Jr., 289
Brisette, I., 317
Brockman, H., 143

Brody, E. M., 151, 153
Broman, C. L., 312
Bronfenbrenner, U., 16
Brown, G. G., 122
Brown, K., 35
Brown, L. H., 188, 190
Brown, M., 76, 77, 90, 91
Brown, P. A., 89
Bruce, M. L., 155
Bryant, A. S., 183
Bryant, B., 318
Bryant, C. M., 176
Bryant, S., 357
Buchner, D. M., 126
Bumpass, L. L., 151, 152
Burack, O. R., 112
Burke, D. M., 111
Burke, R. J., 300
Burkhauser, R. V., 223, 224, 225
Burnight, K. P., 110
Buss, D. M., 170, 173, 174, 247
Busse, E. W., 104
Butcher, V., 360
Butler, R. N., 3, 58
Buunk, B. P., 315
Byrd, M., 109

C

Cacioppo, J. T., 314
Calkins, E., 356
Campbell, J., 268, 282
Campbell, L., 171,174
Campbell, L. D., 193
Capaldi, D., 126
Caplan, L., 125, 213
Caporeal, L. R., 170
Carnes, B. A., 35, 62
Carrère, S., 147, 179
Carstensen, L. L., 113, 149, 170, 193, 194
Carter, W. B., 85
Carver, C. S., 244, 310, 311, 316, 317
Case, N., 332
Case, R. B., 332
Casey, V., 332, 333
Casper, L. M., 141
Caspi, A., 180, 240, 243, 244, 246
Cassidy, J., 167
Cate, R. M., 173
Cattell, R. B., 104, 239
Cavalli-Sforza, F., 308
Cavalli-Sforza, L. L., 308

Cejka, M. A., 207
Centofanti, M., 107
Cerda-Flores, R. M., 189
Cerminara, K. L., 327
Chan, C. G., 225
Chandra, R. K., 51
Charles, S. T., 170
Charness, N., 115, 120, 125, 213
Chatters, L. M., 271
Chen, H., 139, 140
Chen, Y. Y., 87, 88
Chesney, M., 89
Cheung, A. M., 54
Chiu, W. T., 82, 84, 89
Christensen, H., 124
Chrousos, G. P., 87
Cicchetti, D., 137
Cicirelli, V. G., 167, 186, 193
Cissell, G. M., 119
Clancy, S. M., 212
Clark, A. E., 213, 360
Clark, D. O., 38
Clark, L., 155
Clark, R., 308
Clark, R. L., 223, 224, 225
Clarke, D., 83
Clarkson-Smith, L., 125
Clarridge, B. R., 332, 333
Cleary, P. D., 17, 18, 23, 49, 50, 87
Clements, M., 176
Clunis, D. M., 60
Cohan, C., 180
Cohen, L. H., 221
Cohen, P., 139, 140
Cohn-Mansfield, J., 117
Colby, A., 278, 279
Colcombe, S. J., 26, 114, 126
Cole, E. R., 253
Coleman, M., 159, 210
Coleman, P. G., 361
Coltrane, S., 221
Compton, D. M., 124
Conger, R. D., 143, 176
Connidis, I . A., 158, 193
Connor, K. E., 36
Cooney, T. M., 187
Corr, C. A., 329
Costa, M., 330, 331
Costa, P. T., Jr., 238, 239, 240, 355, 370
Costello, C. B., 208, 209, 227, 228
Courtenay, B. C., 255, 256
Couzin, J., 93
Cowan, C. P., 146, 147
Cowan, P. A., 146, 147
Craik, F. M., 109, 111
Crane, P. K., 38
Crawford, D. W., 147
Creedon, M. A., 117
Crimmins, E. M., 95, 116
Cromwell, R. L., 56
Crooks, R., 60
Crowell, M., 36

Crystal, S., 73
Csikszentmihalyi, M., 260
Cui, M., 176
Cullum, S., 124
Cumming, E., 134, 357
Curb, J. D., 79
Cutrona, C. E., 89
Czaja, S. J., 212

D

Dailey, S. R., 120, 121
Dalaker, J., 227
Dalby, P., 273
Daley, D., 361
Damush, T. M., 38
Danner, D. D., 93, 244
Dansky, B. S., 318
Davidson, K., 93
Davies, L., 193
Daviglus, M. L., 38, 40
Davis, J. M., 318
Davis, K. E., 175
de Frias, C. M., 111
de St. Aubin, E., 252
Deci, E., 260, 261
DeKay, N. T., 189
Deleger, S., 38
DeLeon, M., 123
DeLongis, A., 316
DelVecchio, W. F., 240, 241
DeMaris, A., 222
Demian, 183
Demler, O., 81, 82, 83, 84, 85, 89, 90, 91
Denisova, N. A., 34
Denney, N. W., 104
Derlga, V. J., 142
DeSanti, S., 123
Desrocher, S., 218
Desrosiers, M. F., 28, 79
DeViney, S., 222, 225
deWaal, F., 171
Dickman, A. B., 135, 136
Diehl, M., 238, 256
Diener, C., 361
Diener, E., 142, 360, 361, 362
Dillon, M., 268, 272, 273
Dixon, R. A., 109, 111, 127
Donaldson, G., 105
Doty, R. L., 46
Dougall, A. L., 298
Dressel, J., 119
Dubin, L., 275
Dunham, C. C., 161, 188
Dye, J. L., 150, 157

E

Eagly, A. H., 135, 136, 207
Eaves, L. J., 211
Eber, H. W., 239
Echt, K. V., 121
Edwards, B. K., 76, 77, 90, 91
Ehlers, A., 318
Ehrensaft, M., 243
Ehrlich, M. F., 110

Ekerdt, D. J., 222
Elder, G. H., Jr., 9, 137, 159
Eliason, G., 326
Eliason, S. R., 204
Elliot, L. B., 20, 21, 250, 251
Ellis, B. J., 135, 171, 174
Ellis, R. D., 120
Ellison, C. G., 271, 272
Emanuel, E. J., 335
Emanuel, L. L., 335
Emery, C. F., 126
Emery, R. E., 180
Enriquez-Haass, V., 62
Enserink, M., 59
Epel, E. S., 35, 308
Epstein, A. M., 91, 92
Ericsson, K. A., 212
Erikson, E. H., 248, 249
Erikson, K. I., 126
Eriksson, P. S., 50
Essen, K. M., 80
Essex, M. J., 217
Etaugh, C., 204
Evans, D. A., 89
Evans, R. I., 248
Eyster, S. L., 221, 222

F

Fahey, T., 361
Fahlander, K., 122
Fairclough, D. L., 335
Fastbom, J., 122
Fat, D. M., 70, 74
Federal Interagency Forum on Aging Related Statistics, 71, 155, 226
Feeney, J., 174
Feifel, H., 340
Feinberg, L. F., 220
Feinsilver, S. H., 56
Feld, S., 314
Feldman, H., 147
Feldman, L., 327, 358
Ferraro, K. F., 134, 154
Fetzer Institute, 274
Field, B., 324
Field, D., 193, 241
Fields, J., 138, 141, 145, 156
Finch, C. E., 95
Fincham, F. D., 143
Fischer, H. L., 172
Fisher, N. M., 356
Fishman, J. R., 36
Fisk, A. D., 117, 120, 121
Flannelly, K. J., 326
Fleeson, W., 148
Flinn, M. V., 299
Florian, V., 319
Floyd, K., 186
Folk, K., 147
Folkman, S., 310, 313, 340
Fontaine, K. R., 38
Forsell, Y., 122
Fouladi, R. T., 58, 59
Fowler, J. W., 269, 281, 282, 283

Fozard, J. L., 89
Fraley, R. C., 340
Frank, L. L., 38
Frankl, V. E., 269
Franks, M. M., 90, 314
Fraser, J., 58
Fratiglioni, L., 78, 79
Fredrickson, K. I., 309
Fredriksen-Goldsen, K. L. 60
Freedman, V. A., 116
Freedy, J. R., 318
Freeman, P. A., 60
Friedman, B. X., 135
Friedman, D. S., 45
Friedman, L. S., 156
Friedman, M., 92
Friedman, M. J., 310
Friedman, S. M., 208
Friesen, W. V., 93, 244
Fromm, E., 269
Frongillo, E. A., 89
Fukunaga, A., 46
Fung, H. H., 113, 170
Furnham, A., 361

G

Gage, F. H., 50
Gagnon, J. H., 57, 190
Galambos, N. L., 18, 19, 20
Galea, S., 318
Galinsky, E., 146, 218
Gallicchio, L., 59
Gallo, L. C., 92
Gana, K., 361
Ganong, L., 210
Gatz, M., 78, 79, 126
Geary, D. C., 135
Gençöz, T., 309
Genevay, B., 225
George, L. K., 275, 314, 360, 361
Georgellis, Y., 360
Gerdes, E., 208
Giarrusso, R., 150
Gibbs, I., 189
Gibbs, J., 278, 279
Gibbs, W. W., 76
Gidron, Y., 93
Giele, J. Z., 368
Gilligan, C., 280
Gilmore, G. C., 109
Giscombé, C. L., 309
Gist, Y. J., 150
Given, B., 153
Given, C. W., 153
Glaeser, E., 224
Glaser, R., 153
Glenn, N. D., 180
Gluckman, P. D., 94
Glueck, E., 364
Glueck, S., 364
Godbey, G., 221
Gohdes, D. M., 44, 45
Gohm, C. L., 142, 360
Gold, C. H., 87
Gold, D. T., 191, 192, 193, 271

Gold, P. W., 87
Goldberg, A. E., 146, 147
Goldberg-Glen, R. S., 150
Golden, R. N., 303, 304
Golding, G., 279
Goldman, M. B., 47, 48
Goldsteen, K., 144
Golier, J. A., 308, 309
Gonda, J. N., 107
Gonsiorek, J. C., 182
Gonyea, J. G., 228
González, R. C., 213
Goode, W. J., 153
Göral, F. S., 309
Gordon, M. N., 36
Gorman, E. H., 215
Gorman, J. M., 305
Gottfried, A. E., 218
Gottman, J. M., 147, 178, 179,
    180, 243
Gough, H. G., 239
Gould, D. C., 54
Graff, J., 149
Gravenstein, S., 153
Gray, J. S., 215
Green, R. J., 184
Greenberg, E., 215
Greenberg, J. S., 153
Greendale, G. A., 123
Greene, S. M., 143
Greenstein, T. N., 216
Greer, S., 330, 331
Gregoire, J., 109
Griffith, W. A., 143
Grigorenko, E. L., 105
Gruber-Baldini, A. L., 125
Grunberg, L., 215
Guacci, N., 193
Guallar-Castillón, P., 38
Gump, B. B., 303
Gunhild, G. O., 369
Gunn, H. E., 273, 275
Gupta, S., 159, 218, 221
Guralnik, J. M., 89, 356
Gurin, P., 289
Gustafson, S. B., 210
Gutmann, D., 145, 149, 258

H
Haan, N., 355
Hagestad, G. O., 369
Haight, B. K., 358
Halpern, D. F., 218, 219
Hamer, D., 268
Hamilton, B. E., 144, 145
Hancock, H. E., 122
Handy, B., 59
Hanson, M. A., 94
Hanson, R. F., 318
Harding, S. R., 326
Hardy, D. J., 212
Hardy, M. A., 223
Hareven, T. K., 149
Hargrove, T., 325
Harris Poll, 268, 325, 327
Harris, J. L., 121

Harris, K. J., 40
Hart, H. M., 252, 253
Hartley, A. A., 125
Hartley, J., 121
Hartung, P. J., 202, 203, 205
Harvey, P. D., 308, 309
Hasher, L., 110
Hastie, R., 114
Hatch, M. C., 47, 48
Hatfield, E., 172
Hawkins, H. L., 126
Hayflick, L., 35, 53, 62
Hays, J. C., 272, 275
Hayward, M. D., 158
Hazan, C., 174
Hazell, L. V., 339
He, W., 229
Heath, A. C., 211
Heath, C. W., 257
Heckhausen, J., 160
Hedden, T., 109, 110
Heflin, C. M., 89
Heller, D. A., 34
Helms, S. T., 205
Helson, R., 149, 240, 246, 258,
    309
Henderson, A. S., 124
Henretta, J. C., 204, 211, 213,
    225, 230
Henry, W. E., 134, 357
Hequembourg, A., 27, 152
Herbert, L. E., 89
Herning, G., 146
Hershberger, S. N., 211
Hershey, D. A., 115
Hertzog, C., 109, 117
Herzog, A. R., 89
Hess, T. M., 112, 113, 114, 123
Hesse, E., 167
Hetzel, L. I., 150
Heuveline, P., 141
Hewer, A., 280
Hicks, B. M., 246
Higgins, C. A., 243, 244
Hill, R. D., 122, 126
Hinson, J. T., 114
Hipple, S., 214
Hobb, M., 318
Hodgson, L. G., 190
Hofer, S. M., 61, 105
Hoffman, L., 119
Hofmann, V., 255
Holden, C., 87
Holland, J. L., 205, 206
Holmes, T. H., 299
Holt, B. J., 121
Holtzman, S., 316
Hooven, C., 179
Hooyman, N. R., 228
Horn, J. L., 104, 125
Horn, M. C., 300, 307, 308
Hornsby, P. J., 35
Horowitz, L. M., 175, 193
Horton, F., 217
Horvath, J., 220
House, J. S., 89

House, M., 230
Houston, D. M., 205
Howard, A., 225, 226
Hoyer, W. J., 212
Hoyert, D. K., 70, 71
Hoyt, W. T., 273, 274
Huang, T. T. -K., 40
Huguet, N., 40
Hultsch, D. F., 109
Hunt, G., 220
Hunter, S., 354
Hunter, W. J., 279
Huppert, F. A., 124
Huston, A. C., 181
Huston, T. L., 147
Hutchinson, M. K., 187
Hy, L. X., 255
Hyde, J. S., 217
Hyde, V., 189

I
Iacono, W. G., 123
Idler, E. L., 271, 272
Ingram, D. K., 36
Ingram, V., 77
Ironson, G., 275
Isometsä, E., 89

J
Jackson, D. N., 252
Jacobs, D. M., 125
Jacobs, H. S., 54
Jacobs, S., 340
James, W., 270, 287
Jankowiak, W. R., 172
Janus, C. L., 60
Janus, S. S., 60
Jennings, P. A., 309
Jensen, A. R., 102
Johansson, B., 78, 79, 123, 124
John, O. P., 246
Johnson, C. A., 180
Johnson, C. L., 188
Johnson, F., 194
Johnson, M. E., 326
Johnson, M. K., 110
Johnson, M. M. S., 115
Johnson, N. J., 142
Johnson, T. E., 36
Jolles, J., 127
Jones, C. J., 241
Jones, E., 172
Jones, M. G., 121
Jones, T. R., 116
Joseph, J. A., 34
Juan, G., 326
Judge, T. A., 243, 244
Jun, H., 151, 152
Jung, C. G., 258, 269, 287

K
Kahn, R. L., 168, 360
Kaiser, F. E., 60
Kalish, R. A., 325
Kalleberg, A. L., 231

Kaltman, S., 318, 340
Kaplan, M. S., 40
Kaplan, N., 167
Kaprio, J., 302
Kardaun, J. W. P. F., 89
Karney, B. R., 177, 243
Kasen, S., 139, 140
Kasl, S. V., 272
Kasser, T., 251
Kasser, V. M., 261
Katz, L. F., 179
Katzel, L. I., 122
Kaufman, G., 217
Kaus, C. R., 279, 280
Kawachi, I., 59
Keen, S., 290
Kegan, R., 282, 285, 287, 288
Keith, P. M., 156, 157
Kellehear, A., 329
Keller, B. K., 208
Keller, R. T., 215
Kelley, C., 213
Kelly, J., 147
Keltner, D., 317, 319, 340
Kemeny, M. E., 330
Kemp, C. L., 190
Kempermann, G., 50
Kenealy, P. M., 361
Kennedy, G. E., 189
Kennedy, K. M., 107
Kenrick, D. T., 170
Kerns, R. D., 156
Kesimci, A., 309
Kessler, R. C., 81, 82, 83, 84,
    85, 89, 90, 91, 174
Ketelaar, T., 135
Khine, K., 53
Kiecolt-Glaser, J. K., 143, 153,
    308, 314
Killen, M., 281
Kilpatrick, D. G., 318
Kinderman, S. S., 122
King, L. A., 315
Kington, R. S., 91
Kirby, S. E., 361
Kirkcaldy, B., 361
Kirkpatrick, L. A., 173, 174,
    175
Kivimäki, M., 315
Klein, L. C., 306
Klein, T., 143
Kleinbaum, S., 180
Kleyman, E., 135
Kliegl, R., 112
Kline, G. H., 180
Koenig, C. S., 326
Koenig, H. G., 271, 275,
    314
Kohlberg, L., 276, 277, 278,
    279, 280, 288
Kolarz, C. M., 354
Kolomer, S., 151
Konrad, T. R., 155
Korenman, S., 215
Korhonen, M. T., 55, 56
Koski, L. R., 175

Kosloski, K., 222
Koslowsky, M., 311, 312
Krahn, H. J., 18, 19, 20
Kramer, A. F., 26, 126
Krampe, R. T., 212
Krause, N., 155, 315, 316, 360
Kreider, R. M., 141, 142, 156, 158
Krettenauer, T., 255
Kristal, A. R., 38
Kritz-Silverstein, D., 123
Krothe, J. S., 73
Krueger, R. F., 246
Kübler-Ross, E., 328
Kuehn, B. M., 47, 48
Kuehne, V. S., 364
Kulkarni, J., 53
Kung, H. C., 70, 71
Kurdek, L. A., 183
Kurniawan, S. H., 120
Kwan, V. S. Y., 240, 246
Kyvik, K. O., 40

L

Labouvie-Vief, G., 107, 256
Lachman, M. E., 112
LaGuardia, J. G., 261
Lamberts, S. W. J., 54
Lane, M., 85, 86, 89
Lane, M. A., 36
Lang, F., 170
Lapp, D., 112
Larsen, B. A., 44, 45
Larson, D. B., 273, 274
Larson, E. B., 126
Laumann, E. O., 57, 190
Launer, L. J., 77, 78, 79
Laursen, P., 124
Lautenschlager, G., 109, 110
Lawton, L., 185
Leary, M. R., 171
Leather, D. M., 187
Lee, R. E., 40
Leeder, S. R., 80
Legrain, S., 54
Lehman, D. R., 318, 340, 341
Leiter, M. P., 214
Lemasters, E. E., 147
Lerman, R., 217
Lerner, R. M., 13
Leserman, J., 303, 304
Lethbridge-Çejku, M., 73, 74
Levenson, M. R., 307, 309
Levenson, R. W., 149, 179
Levin, J., 271
Levine, C., 280
Levinson, D. J., 285
Levitt, M. J., 193
Levy, J. A., 336
Lewin, T., 329
Lewis, B. P., 306
Lewis, G., 88
Li, L. W., 153
Liang, J., 314
Libby, P., 74
Lichtenstein, P., 211

Lieberman, M., 309
Lillberg, K., 302
Lin, G., 185
Lin, J., 35, 308
Lindahl, K. M., 176
Lindenberger, U., 104, 105, 106, 108, 111, 122, 124
Lindström, M., 94
Lipsitt, L. P., 14
Littman, A. J., 38
Litvin, S. J., 151
Liu, L. L., 117, 120
Liu, X., 314
Livson, F. B., 368
Livson, N., 362, 363
Lloyd, S. A., 173
Lobar, S. L., 339
Lobel, M., 309
Loevinger, J., 253, 254, 255
Logan, R. L., 252
Lolk, A., 89
Long, J. D., 188, 190
Longino, C. F., Jr., 229
Longmore, M. A., 222
Lonky, E., 279, 280
López, G. E., 38
Lorenz, F. O., 143
Loveland, A. D., 107
Low, K. S. D., 206
Lowe, J. C., 160
Lozano, P. L., 38
Lucas, R. E., 360
Lueken, L. J., 273, 275
Luff, J. A., 53
Lui, K., 38, 40
Lumei, T., 326
Lundberg, 0., 89
Lupien, S. J., 123
Luzzo, D. A., 212
Lyketsos, C. G., 124
Lynch, L. M., 215
Lynn, J., 333, 336
Lyons, N. P., 281

M

MacCallum, R. C., 308
MacKay, D. G., 111
Mackey, R. A., 177
Madden, D. J., 126
Maddi, S. R., 275, 318
Maddox, G. L., 104
Magdol, L., 180
Magnusson, D., 210
Main, M., 167
Maitland, S. B., 111
Malmgren, J. A., 85
Malik, N. M., 176
Malley, M., 126
Malmberg, B., 87
Malone, M. A., 117
Maluso, D., 204
Manly, J. J., 125
Manning, W. D., 159
Marcenes, W., 143
Marcoen, A., 188
Marenco, A., 150

Marion, F., 268
Markman, H. J., 176, 180
Marks, G., 205
Marks, N. F., 149, 151, 152, 157
Marshall, H., 157
Marshall, V., 336
Martin, J. A., 144
Martire, L. M., 153, 155
Marty-Gonzales, L. F., 189
Maruna, S., 252, 253
Mashek, D., 172
Masher, W. D., 141, 180
Maslach, C., 214
Maslow, A. H., 259
Masunaga, H., 125
Mather, M., 170
Mathers, C. D., 70, 74
Mathews, T. J., 145
Matlin, N., 202
Matthews, K. A., 303
Mattson, M. P., 36
Maughan, B., 369
Maurer, T. J., 212
Mayer, K. U., 20
Mayhorn, C. B., 116
Maylor, E. A., 111
Maynard, L., 36
Mayou, R. A., 318
McAdams, D. P., 160, 175, 252, 253, 255
McAvay, G. J., 155
McCallion, P., 151
McCay, C., 36
McClearn, G. E., 34, 61, 87, 123, 124
McConnell, E. S., 60
McCrae, R. R., 238, 239, 240, 355, 370
McCullough, M. E., 273, 274
McDowd, J. M., 119
McFadden, S. H., 269, 326
McGee, M., 124
McGue, M., 123, 246
McGwin, G., 118, 119
McKee-Ryan, F. M., 214, 215
McKinlay, J. B., 57, 59
McKinley, S. M., 52
McLaughlin, M. A., 208
McLay, R. N., 124
McMullin, J. A., 158
Medina, J. J., 58
Meinz, E. J., 122
Melamed, T., 204
Menaghan, E. G., 218
Menee, V. H., 361
Meredith, W., 241
Mero, A., 55, 56
Merrick, S. K., 167
Metter, E. J., 54
Meyer, B. F. J., 115
Michael, R. T., 57, 190
Michelson, K. D., 174
Mickels, J. A., 170
Mickelson, K. D., 83
Mikulincer, M., 174, 319
Milevsky, A., 191

Milkie, M. A., 221
Miller, A. S., 271
Miller, G. E., 299
Miller, T. Q., 92, 244
Millsap, R. E., 241
Minor, P., 91
Mirowsky, J., 144
Mittleman, M. A., 59
Mladinic, A., 135, 136
Moen, P., 232
Moffat, S. D., 54
Moffitt, T. E., 180, 243
Mohr, B. A., 57, 59
Moon, M., 223, 224, 225
Moore, J. W., 160
Moore, S. Y., 215
Morgan, D. L., 357
Morgentaler, A., 51, 54
Morley, J. E., 60
Morman, M. T., 186
Morrell, R. W., 117, 120, 121
Morris, T., 330
Moskowitz, J. T., 310, 313, 340, 341
Moss, A. J., 332
MRC Human Nutrition Research 47
Mroczek, D. K., 242, 354, 360
Mukamal, K., 61
Murphy, A. T., 60
Musick, M. A., 271, 272
Mutran, E. J., 149
Mykityshyn, A. L., 117
Mykletun, A., 83

N

National Alliance for Caregiving and AARP, 220, 225
National Center for Health Statistics, 70, 73, 74, 90, 91
National Center for Statistics and Analysis, 118
National Council on the Aging, 225
National Highway Traffic Safety Administration, 118
National Hospice and Palliative Care Association, 334
National Institute on Aging, 121
National Institutes of Arthritis and Musculoskeletal Disease, 48
National Marriage Project, 140, 144
National Senior Services Corps, 231
Nehrke, M. F., 250
Neiderhauser, J. M., 25
Neimeyer, K. A., 318
Nelligan, J. S., 175
Nelson, D. L., 214, 300
Nesselroade, J. R., 246
Neugarten, B. L., 10, 134, 160, 324, 369
Neumark, D., 215
Newsom, J. T., 40, 155

Newton, R. A., 56
Newton, T. L., 143
Newtson, R. L., 156, 157
Nielson, H., 89
Niles, S. G., 202, 203, 205
Nilsson, L. G., 111
Nisan, M., 278, 279
Nock, S., 217, 222
Noelker, L. S., 154
Noller, P., 174
Noone, R. J., 299
Norburn, J. E. K., 155
Nordahl, H. M., 83
Notarius, C. L., 178
Nussbaum, J. E., 185, 188

O

Oates, G., 125, 213
O'Brien, A. T., 153
O'Brien, B. A., 177
O'Brien, K. M., 208
O'Bryant, S. L., 193
O'Colmain, B. J., 45
O'Connell, M., 182
O'Farrell, B., 208
Oh, S., 105
O'Leary, A., 330, 331
Olfson, M., 81, 82, 85, 86, 89
Olshansky, J. S., 35, 62
O'Rand, A. M., 204, 213, 225, 230
Orbach, I., 174
Orbuch, T. L., 221, 222
Orchard, A., 159
Oregon Department of Human Services, 335
Orth-Gomér, K., 314
Osmond, C., 94
Ostrosky-Solis, F., 125
Oswald, A. J., 213
Owsley, C., 119

P

Palmore, E. B., 357
Pals, J., 258
Papa, A., 341
Parasuraman, R., 212
Parcel, T. L., 218
Pargament, K. I., 274, 314
Park, D. C., 109, 110, 115, 116, 117, 120, 121
Parmer, S., 75
Parnes, H. S., 230
Pasupathi, M., 113
Patel, N. V., 36
Patterson, C. J., 182
Patterson, R. E., 38
Paulus, M., 317, 340
Paunonen, S. V., 252
Pearlin, L. I., 300
Pedersen, N. L., 211
Pedroso de Lima, M., 240
Peltola, P., 221
Pendergast, D. R., 356
Perfilieva, E., 50
Perls, T. T., 55, 96
Perry-Jenkins, M., 146, 147

Peskin, H., 362, 363
Peterson, N., 213
Petitto, J. M., 303, 304
Pettingale, K. W., 330
Petty, R., 54
Pickles, A., 369
Pillemer, K., 155
Piña, D. L., 221
Pinquart, M., 73, 157, 360, 361
Pirkola, S. P., 89
Plake, B. S., 23
Pless, A. S., 315
Plomin, R., 12, 123, 246
Ponds, R. W. H. M., 127
Poortman, A. -R., 187
Powell, F. C., 325
Powell, R. R., 107
Pratt, M. W., 279
Preacher, K. J., 308
Presser, H. B., 216, 217
Proctor, B. D., 227
Prouty, J., 53
Pruchno, R., 190
Pryor, J., 187
Purcell, P. J., 231
Putney, N. M., 153

Q

Quick, H., 232
Quick, J. C., 214
Quinton, D., 369

R

Radloff, L. S., 85
Rahe, R. H., 299
Rakowski, N., 357
Rando, T. A., 340
Rasmussen, C. H., 326
Raye, C. L., 110
Raz, N., 107, 126
Rechlin, L. R., 154
Redden, D. T., 38
Reed, D., 90
Reed, G. M., 330
Reeder, J. A., 110
Reese, H. W., 14
Reimer, J., 278, 279
Reitzes, D. C., 149
Reker, G. T., 283
Resnick, H. S., 318
Rest, J. R., 279, 288
Rhoden, E. L., 51, 54
Rholes, W. S., 175
Richard, A. J., 175
Richardson, J. L., 331
Riegel, K., 269
Riemann, R., 245
Riggio, H. R., 218
Riley, K. P., 28, 79
Roberts, B. W., 206, 240, 241, 242, 243, 244, 245, 246, 309
Roberts, R. E., 38
Robertson, J., 361
Robinson, J., 221
Rodin, J., 155
Rodrigue, K. M., 107

Roenker, D. L., 119
Rogers, R. G., 91
Rogers, W. A., 117, 120, 121
Rogerson, P. A., 185
Rojas, G., 88
Romano, J. M., 156
Roodin, P. A., 188, 190, 279, 280
Roof, W. C., 270
Rose, S., 142
Roselli, M., 125
Rosenberg, R., 156
Rosenfeld, I., 41, 42, 46, 51
Rosengren, A., 314
Rosenkrantz Aronson, S., 181
Rosenman, R. H., 92
Rose-Rego, S. K., 153
Ross, C. E., 144
Rossi, A. S., 37
Roth, G. S., 36
Rothblum, E. D., 183, 184
Rousseau, G. K., 120
Rovine, M., 147
Rowe, J. W., 360
Russek, L. G., 93
Russell, D. W., 89
Russo, C., 115
Russo, J., 143, 153
Rust, G., 91
Ryan, R. M., 260, 261

S

Saab, P. G., 302
Sabel, B. A., 115
Sacerdote, B., 224
Salberg, K., 159
Salkind, N., 28
Salthouse, T. A., 106, 110, 111, 122, 124, 125, 212
Salvati, S., 330, 331
Sameroff, A. J., 137
Sanchez, L., 221
Sands, R. G., 150
Sanfey, A. C., 114
Santillanes, G., 339
Santoro, N., 52
Savickas, M. L., 202, 203
Sayer, L. C., 221
Scarr, S., 207
Schachter, J. P., 229
Schacter, D. L., 108, 112
Schaie, K. W., 103, 105, 106, 107, 124, 125, 127
Scharlach, A. E., 309
Schaufeli, W. B., 214
Scheier, M. F., 244, 317
Schmidt, H., 79
Schmidt, P. J., 53
Schmidt, R., 79
Schmiedeskamp, M., 77
Schmitt, D. P., 173
Schneider, E. C., 91, 92
Schneiderman, N., 302
Schoen, R., 173
Schoenborn, C. A., 142, 143
Schoeni, R. F., 116

Schooler, C., 125, 213
Schousboe, K., 40
Schover, L. R., 58, 59
Schrader, S. S., 185
Schroeder, K. A., 204
Schulenberg, J. E., 137
Schulz, R., 153, 155
Schwartz, G. E., 93
Schwartz, R., 205
Scott, J., 326
Seeman, M., 275
Seeman, T. E., 123, 155, 275
Segerstrom, S. C., 299
Seligman, M. E. P., 93, 260
Seltzer, M. M., 153
Selye, H., 298
Semmer, N., 214
Shackelford, T. K., 173, 174, 189
Shanahan, M. J., 137
Shapiro, A. F., 147
Shaver, P. R., 174, 175, 340
Sheehy, G., 149, 354
Sheikh, A. I., 310
Sheikh, J. A., 112
Sheiman, A., 143
Sheldon, K. M., 251
Sherwood, P., 153
Sheyd, G. L., 135
Shiffron, R. M., 108
Shiner, R. L., 240, 243, 244, 246
Shneidman, E. S., 356
Shuchter, S. R., 317, 340
Shuey, K., 223
Shukitt-Hale, B., 34
Siefen, G., 361
Siefert, K., 90
Siegler, I. C., 93
Silver, C. B., 154
Silver, K. C., 342
Silver, N., 179, 180
Silverstein, M., 150, 185, 188, 190
Simmons, B. L., 214
Simmons, T., 150, 182
Simon, V., 89
Simonsick, E. M., 89, 356
Simpson, J. A., 175
Simpson, R., 209
Sims, R. V., 118
Sinnott, J. D., 127, 269
Skovronek, E., 124
Small, B. J., 109, 122, 124
Smetana, J. G., 280
Smith, B. L., 70, 71
Smith, C. D., 107
Smith, J., 112, 127, 212
Smith, J. P., 91
Smith, M. C., 113
Smith, M. J., 110
Smith, R. G., 316
Smith, S. K., 230
Smith, T. W., 92, 244
Smith, U., 124
Smock, P. J., 159
Smylie, L., 58

Smyth, E., 361
Smyth, K. A., 153
Snarey, J. R., 278, 279, 364
Snowdon, D. A., 28, 79, 93, 244
Soares, C. N., 53
Soerensen, S., 360, 361
Solano, L., 330, 331
Soldz, S., 258
Solomon, G. F., 275
Solomon, M., 258
Solomon, S. E., 183
Somary, K., 150
Somers, M. D., 157
Sommers, D. G., 230
Son, L., 364
Song, A., 214, 215
Sorensen, E., 217
Sorensen, S., 73
Sorlie, P. D., 142
Spanier, G. B., 147
Spearman, C., 102
Spies, R. A., 23
Spinks, R., 109
Spiro, A., 242, 360
Spotts, E. L., 25
Spry, N., 52
Srinivasan, S. R., 75
Stanley, S. M., 180
Starishevsky, R., 202
Stark, R., 271
Statham, J. A., 114
Staudinger, U. M., 127, 212
Stein, C., 70, 74
Steindl-Rast, B. D., 342
Steiner, M., 53
Stempel, G. H., III, 325
Stephens, M. A. P., 90, 153, 154, 155
Stern, Y. 77
Sternberg, R. J., 105, 108, 109, 172
Stewart, A. J., 253
Stigsdotter, A., 112
Stone, A. J., 208, 209, 227, 228
Storandt, M., 126
Stratton, T. D., 208
Strauss, M. E., 153
Strawbridge, N. J., 38
Strelau, J., 245
Stricker, G., 150
Strothers, H. S., 91
Stump, T. E., 38
Subramanian, S. V., 87, 88
Sugimoto, K., 46
Sugisawa, H., 314
Suh, E., 142, 360, 362
Suitor, J. J., 155
Sullivan, S. D., 38
Sundel, M., 354
Suominen, H., 55, 56
Super, C. M., 202, 203
Super, D. E., 202, 203
Sutker, P. B., 318
Suvisaari, J., 89

Swanberg, J., 146, 218
Swartzendruber, A., 107
Swensen, M. M., 73
Szinovacz, M. E., 225

T
Takahashi, K., 168, 169, 170
Talbot, A., 115
Tang, M. -X., 77
Tarakeshwar, N., 314
Tartaro, J., 273, 275
Tatsuoka, M. M., 239
Taubman, O., 319
Taylor, R. J., 271
Taylor, S. E., 306, 313, 330
Techner, D., 339
Temoshok, L., 330
Tennov, D., 172
Teno, J. M., 332, 333
Teresa of Ávila, St., 286
Terkel, S., 201, 202
Tesch-Römer, C., 45
Thoits, P. A., 153
Thoma, S. J., 279, 288
Thomas, C., 109
Thomas, G., 54
Thompson, C., 218
Thomson, E., 221
Thoreson, C. J., 243, 244
Thorslund, M., 89
Thorson, J. A., 325
Thurstone, L. L., 105
Timberlake, J. M., 141
Tipton, L. C., 208
Todosijevic, J., 183
Tomer, A., 326
Tomic, D., 59
Tornstam, L., 269
Torpy, D. J., 87
Torpy, J. M., 75, 76
Towers, H., 25
Townsend, A. L., 90, 153, 154, 314
Truluck, J. E., 255, 256
Tulving, E., 108, 111
Turiel, E., 281
Turk, D. C., 156
Turner, B. F., 135
Turner, C. B., 135
Turner, C. W., 92, 244
Turner, J. A., 156
Tworoger, S. S., 57
Tyndale, E., 58

U
U.S. Bureau of Labor Statistics, 203, 204, 205, 214, 217, 218, 223, 230
U.S. Center for Disease Control and Prevention, 116, 145
U.S. Department of Heath and Human Services, 38, 39, 40
Uccello, C. E., 225

Uchino, B., 314
Uddo, M., 318
Uematsu, H., 46
Uhlenberg, P., 217
Umberson, D., 144
Underhill, E., 270, 286
United Nations Statistics Division, 218
Urlich, M., 255
Usui, C., 231
Uttl, B., 103

V
Väänänen, A., 315
Vaillant, C. O., 362, 363
Vaillant, G. E., 61, 256, 257, 258, 362, 363
Van Alstine, C. L., 103
van Boxtel, M. P. J., 127
van den Beld, A. W., 54
van der Lely, A. J., 54
Van der Linden, M., 109
van Ijzendoorn, M., 167
Van Manen, K., 207
Van Ranst, N., 188
van Reekum, R., 83
van Tilburg, T. G., 187
Ventura, S. J., 144, 145
Verkasalo, P. K., 302
Verschueren, K., 188
Vickerie, J., 73
Viechtbauer, W., 241, 242, 246
Vierck, E., 72
Villa, V. M., 62
Vitaliano, P. P., 143, 153
Vitiello, M. V., 57
Vlahov, D., 318
Vogler, G. P., 61
Vogt, D. S., 315

W
Wachs, T. D., 247
Waddington, C. H., 365
Wahl, H- W., 45
Wahlin, Å., 109, 122, 124
Walaskay, M., 250
Waldfogel, S., 215
Waldstein, S. R., 122
Wallace, S. P., 62
Walters, E. E., 83
Walton, A., 107
Walton, K. E., 241, 242, 244, 245, 246
Wanberg, C. R., 214, 215
Wang, C., 38
Wang, P. S., 81, 82, 85, 86, 89
Ward, C. V., 299
Warneke, C. L., 58, 59
Warr, P. B., 212, 213, 360
Waterreus, A., 52
Waters, E., 166, 167
Weaver, A. J., 326
Weaver, S. E., 159
Weber, R. A., 193
Webster, J. D., 193, 194

Wechsler, D., 102
Weiss, R. S., 166, 167, 185
Wethington, E., 354
Whitbourne, S. K., 20, 21, 250, 251, 207
White, E., 38
Whiteman, M. K., 59
Whitson, S. C., 208
Whitton, S. W., 180
Wickrama, K. A. S., 143
Wight, V. R., 227, 228
Wilhelmsen, L., 314
Wilkinson, A. M., 333, 336
Willemsen, G., 40
Williams, A., 185, 188
Williams, D. R., 90
Williams, J. E., 135
Willis, S. L., 107, 125
Wilson, J. A., 115
Wilson, M. M., 60
Wilson, R. S., 107, 125
Wingo, P. A., 76, 77, 90, 91
Wink, P., 149, 268, 272, 273, 326
Winstead, B., 142
Winter, P. D., 94
Wiskott, L., 50
Witte, F. M., 208
Wolfs, R. C., 45
Wood, W., 135
Woodruff-Pak, D. S., 43, 50
Woods, L. N., 180
Wooldredge, J., 173
Woollett, S., 157
World Health Organization, 83
Worthley, J. S., 111
Wortman, C. B., 318, 340, 341, 342

X
Xiangkui, Z., 326

Y
Yan, L. L., 38, 40
Yano, K., 90
Yasui, Y., 57
Yehuda, R., 305, 307, 308, 309
Yesavage, J., 112
Yoon, M., 206
Young, H., 143, 153

Z
Zaborski, L. B., 17, 18, 23, 49, 50, 87
Zacks, R. T., 110
Zarnegar, Z., 331
Zaslavsky, A. M., 91, 92
Zelinski, E. M., 110
Zhang, Z., 158
Zisook, S., 317, 340
Zivotofsky, A. Z., 311, 312
Zonderman, A. B., 54
Zuschlag, M. K., 20, 21, 250, 251

Subject Index

A

Ability/expertise tradeoff, 212
Accommodation, in vision, 43
Activities of daily living (ADLs), 72
Acute health conditions, 71
Adaptive nature of cognition, 113
ADHD (Attention deficit/hyperactivity disorder) in adulthood, 84
ADLs (see Activities of daily living)
Adult attachment styles, 175–176
Adult children
    as caregivers for aging parents, 155
    as cause of values change in parents, 186–187
    leaving home, 137–140, 148–149
    problems of, 188
Adult development, 4
    authors' model of, 364–371
    basic concepts of, 4
    themes of, 348–349
    variations in, 359–360
Aerobic exercise
    and cognitive functioning, 26
Adult siblings
    as caregivers to parents, 27
African American adults
    and discrimination in health care, 91–92
    and health, 90–91
    and poverty in late adulthood, 227
    raising grandchildren, 150
Age
    and causes of death, 70–71
    and stability/disequilibrium of life structures, 366–368
    biological, 13
    chronological, 13
    functional, 14
    psychological, 13
    social, 13
Ageism, 17
Age differences
    in mood disorder rates, 83–84
    in prescription drug use, 116–117
    in proportion living in poverty, 227
    in quality of life, 360
    in timing of retirement, 223–224
Age-related changes
    in death anxiety, 325
    in intelligence, components of, 104–106
    in intelligence, overall, 102–104
    in stress reactions, 307–308
Age-related macular degeneration (see macular degeneration, age related)
Age spots, 41

Aging in place, 72
A good death, 332–335
Alcohol abuse, 84–85
Aldosterone production, in aging, 51
Alternative medicine providers, 86
Alzheimer, Alois, 77
Alzheimer's disease, 77–80
    dementia, 77, 80
    diagnosis of, 77–80
    genes for, 77–79
    prevention of, 79
    risk factors 78–80
    twin studies of, 78–79
American Indians and Alaskan Natives and health, 91
American Psychological Association
    recommendations for family/work intersection, 219–220
Androgen
    and intimate partnerships, 172
Antibodies, in immune system, 51
Anxiety disorders, 82–83
    in caregivers, 153–154
Antioxidants, 34–35
Arthritis (see osteoarthritis)
Asian American adults, and health, 90–91
Asset income
    in retirement, 226–227
Assisted living facilities, 73
Assistive technology, 115–121
Atherosclerosis, in cardiovascular disease 74–75
Athletic Abilities, and primary aging, 55
    masters events, 55
Attachment behaviors, 166
Attachment theory
    and friendship in late adulthood, 193–194
    in adulthood 167–168
    in infancy, 166–167
    in intimate partnerships, 173–176
Attention deficit/hyperactivity disorder (ADHD) in adulthood, 84
Attraction, in establishing intimate partnership, 172–173
Atypical development, 6
Atypical families
    social roles in, 156–159

B

Balance
    and primary aging, 56
Baltes' life-span developmental psychology approach 14–16

B cells, in immune system, 51
Bereavement
    and insomnia, 57
    and resilience, 340–342
    process of grieving, 337–342
    recovery from, 317–319
    ritual mourning, 336–339
Berlin Study of Aging, 20
Beta-amyloid
    deposits in Alzheimer's disease, 77–78
Biological age, 13
Biological clock, 7
    and social roles, 134
    in middle adulthood, 352–353
Biosocial perspective of gender roles, 135
Birth weight
    and adult health outcomes, 94–95
Black adults (see African American adults)
BMD (bone mass density), 47
BMI (Body Mass Index), 38–40
Bogalusa Heart Study, 74–75
Bone mass, peak, 47
Bone mass density (BMD), 47
Bones and muscles, 46–49
Botox, 41–42
Bowlby's theory of grief, 337, 340
Bowlby's theory of attachment
    in infancy, 166–167
    in intimate partnerships, 173–174
Brain and nervous system
    primary aging of, 50–51
Breast cancer survivors
    and stress-related growth, 309–310
Breast augmentation, 41–42
Bridge job, 230
Brief Multidimensional Measure of Religiousness/Spirituality (BMMRS), 273–274
Bronfenbrenner's ecological systems approach, 16–17
Buffering effect
    of social support, 314–315
Burnout, job, 214

C

Calcium
    and bone loss 47
California Psychological Inventory (CPI), 239
Caloric Restriction (CR), 36
Cancer, 75–77
    early detection, 76–77
    risk factors 76
Cardiovascular disease, 74–75

Cardiovascular system
    primary aging of, 49–50
Career, 202
    and personal life, 213–222
    development, 202–203
    family influences, 209–211
    gender differences in patterns, 203–205
    genetic influences, 211
    nontraditional, 297–209
    recycling, 212
    selection, 205
    stages of, 203
    theories of, 202–203, 205–207
Career commitment
    and timing of retirement, 225–226
Caregiver burden, 153–154
Caregiving for family members
    and career adjustments, 220
    and divorce, 187–188
    and gender roles, 151–153
    and stress reactions, 307–308
    impact of, 153–154
    with Alzheimer's disease, 80
Care receiving role, 154–155
Cataracts, 44
Cell phone use
    and driving, 119
Center for Epidemiologic Studies Short De-
        pression Scale (CES-D 10), 23,
        83–85
Change
    in development, 5
    inner versus outer, 6
    in personality traits, 245–248
Childless adults, 157–158
China's one-child policy, 8
Chronic health conditions, 71
    and cognitive decline, 122–123
Chronic stress as reaction to trauma,
        317–319
Chronological age, 13
Climacteric
    in men, 51–52
        testosterone, 51–52
    in women, 52–54
        menopause, 52–54
    hormone replacement, 53–55, 59–60
Cochlea, in hearing, 45
Cochlear implants, 45
Cognition
    individual differences in age-related
        change, 127
    intelligence, 102–107
    judgment and decision making, 114–115
    memory, 107–114
Cohabitation
    and gender roles 142
    and household labor division, 222
    by same-sex couples, 182–184
    mother-infant relationships in, 181
    number of couples in U.S., 141
    proportion of women by country,
        141–142
    vs marriage, 179–182
    types of, 141–142, 180–181

Cohort, 8–9
Collagen, 41–42
Comorbid mental disorders, 82
Commonalities in development, 5
Communal qualities, 135–136
Community dwelling older adults, 72
Comparison of means analysis, 23–24
Complementary medicine providers, 86
Congregate living facilities, 73
Contextual perspective, 112
Continuity
    in personality traits, 245–248
Continuous development, 6
Control, sense of
    and coping, 316
    and quality of life, 360–361
Convoy model of social relationships,
        168–170
Coping behavior, 310–317
    effectiveness of, 313
    personality and, 316–317
    social support, 314–316
    types of, 310–313
Correlational analysis, 24–25
Cortisol levels and religiousness/spirituality,
        273–274
CR memetic, 36
Crossover of gender roles, 149, 258–259
Cross-sectional study, 17–18
    compared to longitudinal study, 18–20
Crystallized intelligence, 104–106
Cuban-American cohort, 9
Cuckold rate, 189
Cultural differences
    and quality of life, 360–361
Cultures, 8
Cyclic GMP, 58–59

D

Dark adaptation, in vision, 44
Death
    anxiety, 325–327
    causes by age, 70–71
    location of, 332–335
    meanings of, 324–325
    stages of acceptance, 328–329, 337,
        340
    timing of, 335–336
Death With Dignity Act (Oregon), 335–336
Decentering, in cognition, 278
Decision making, 114–115
Defense mechanisms, in personality develop-
        ment, 256–258
Delayed stress as reaction to trauma,
        317–319
Dementia, 77
    prevalence of, 71
    (see also Alzheimer's disease)
Denver Family Project
    and long-term marriages, 176
Depression (see also Mood disorders)
    depressive symptoms, 83–84
        and food insufficiency, 90
        in caregivers of aging parents
            153–154

    in care receivers, 155
    major depression, 83–84
Descriptive research, 27
Developed countries
    birthrates to single mothers, 144–145
    cohabitation rates, 141–142
    mental health rates, 81
    timing of retirement, 224
Development in adulthood
    atypical, 6
    basic concepts of, 4
    change, 5
        outer, 6
        inner, 6
    continuity, 6
    commonalities, 5
    individual differences, 4
    stability, 5
    stages of, 6
    typical, 6
Developing countries
    effects of childhood infectious diseases, 95
    gender inequalities in health, 88
    HIV/AIDS rates, 88
    mortality rates, 70
    tobacco use, 80
Developmental origins
    and health, 94
Developmental psychology, 4
Dexterity, and primary aging, 56
DHEA (dehydroepiandrosterone), 54–55
Differential continuity
    of personality traits, 239–240, 242–243
Disability, 72–74
Disengagement, 357
Disequilibrium (see stability/disequilibrium)
Distal causes, 135
Divorce
    and social roles, 158–159
    effect on children's career, 210
    effect on grandparents' roles, 188–189
    effect in late life, 187–188
Domestic migration, 229
Dopamine
    and intimate partnership, 172
Driving
    and age related changes in, 117–120
Disability, 72–74
Drug abuse 84–85
Dual career families, 216–220
    gender roles, 145–146
DXA scan (dual-energy x-ray absorptiometry
        scan), 47

E

Earnings
    in retirement, 226–227
Ecological systems approach to development,
        16
Economics
    and aging, 62
    and divorce, 159
ED (erectile dysfunction), 58–59
Education
    and cognitive change, 124–125

Egalitarian roles, 142
Ego development, 253–256
    and education level, 255–256
    and personal growth 255–256
    Loevinger's stages of, 254–255
Ego integrity
    in personality development, 249
Elder abuse
    by caregivers, 155
Emotional content in memory, 113–114
Emotion focused coping, 311
Empirical research, 4
Empty nest, 148–149
Environment
    and stability in development 12
Epigenetic landscape, 365–366
Episodic memory, 110–111
Equilibrium
    in spiritual development, 287–288
Erectile dysfunction (ED)
    cyclic GMP, 58–59
    Viagra (sildenafil citrate), 58–59
Erikson's theory of psychosocial develop-
    ment, 248–253
    and death anxiety, 326
Estrogen, 52
    and depression, 87
    and health protection in young adult-
        hood, 87
    creams and patches, 59
    (see also Hormone replacement therapy)
Ethnic differences (see Racial/ethnic
    differences)
Evolutionary psychology theory
    and gender roles
    and personality traits, 247
    and preference for maternal grandparents,
        189
    and social relationships, 170–171
    and stress reactions, 299
Exchange theory
    in intimate partnership, 173
Exercise
    and age-related change in bone, 47
    and age-related changes in cardiovascular
        system, 50
    and age-related change in muscles, 49
    and Alzheimers disease risk, 79
    and cancer risk, 76
    and cardiovascular disease risk, 75
    and insomnia, 57
    and osteoporosis, 47
    and primary aging, 61
    and sexual dysfunction, 59
Expansion of gender roles, 149
Experimental designs, 27
Expertise/ability tradeoff, 212
Extended families, 185
Eyelid surgery, 41–42

F
Face lifts, 41–42
Faith, development of, 281–284
Family 184
    interaction, 184–193

Family and work intersection, 219–220
Family influences
    in career selection, 209–211
    in timing of retirement, 225
Family leave policy, 218–219, 220, 229
Family relationships, 184–194
    general patterns of, 184–185
    grandparent-grandchild relationships,
        188–191
    parent-child relationships in adulthood,
        185–188
    sibling relationship in adulthood,
        191–193
Feminizaton of poverty, 227–229
Filter theory
    in intimate partnerships, 173
Finances
    and timing of retirement, 224–225
Five-Factor Model (FFM) of personality,
    239–240
    and mature adaptation, 257–258
Fluid intelligence, 105–106
Food insufficiency
    and depression, 90
Fosomax (biosophosphonates), 47–48
Fowler's theory of faith development
    and the quest for meaning, 284–285,
        290
Free radicals, 34
Freud, Sigmund, 213
    and concept of libido, 172
Friendship
    age-related changes, 193
Functional age, 14
Farewells, before death, 329
Funeral practices in the U. S., 336–339

G
g, 102
Gandhi, Mahatma, 278
Gay and lesbian retirement homes and as-
        sisted living facilities, 60
Gay and lesbian partnerships
    and fear of violence, 184
    and relationship with parents, 184
    civil unions, 183–184
    long-term partnerships, 182–183
    vs heterosexual couples, 183
Gender crossover
    and personality development, 149,
        258–259
Gender differences
    in age of leaving home, 138–139
    in cardiovascular disease, 75
    in career patterns 203–205
    in career selections, 207–209
    in chronic health conditions, 71
    in death anxiety, 326
    in depression, worldwide, 83
    in development of private belief systems
        272–273
    in friendship patterns, 194
    in health, 86–88
    in health benefits of marriage, 144
    in household labor division, 220–222

    in impulse control disorders, 84
    in mate selection preferences, 173–174
    in mood disorders 83
    in quality of life, 130
    in retirement income, 227–229
    in timing of retirement, 225
    in sources of retirement income,
        228–229
    in stress reactions, 306–307
    in time spent with children 218
Gender inequality
    and health in U. S., 87–89
    and health in developing countries, 88
    in health research, 88–89
    in retirement income, 227–229
Gender roles, 134–137
    and role strain theory, 153
    and role enhancement theory, 153
    crossover, 149, 258–259
    expansion at midlife, 149
    in early partnerships, 142
Gender stereotypes, 134–137
General adaptation syndrome, 298
General Causality Orientation Scale,
    261–262
Generational squeeze, 153–154
Generativity
    in personality development, 248–249,
        251–253
Genetic limits
    Hayflick limit, 35
    replicative senescence, 35
    telomeres, 35–36
    theory of, 35–36
Genetic influences
    and behavior genetics, 11
    and twin studies, 12
    in career selection, 211
    on age-related cognitive changes, 123
    on health, 93–94
    on personality traits, 245–248
    on stability in development, 11–12
Gerotranscendence, 269
Gilligan's proposals on moral development,
    280–281
Glaucoma, 44–45
Good death, a, 332–335
Gradual retirement, 230–231
Grandparent-grandchild relationships,
    188–191
Grandparenting, 149–151
Grandparents raising grandchildren
    150–151
Grant Study of Harvard men, 12
    and life success, 257–258, 362–364. 366,
        369
    and successful aging, 61
Great Depression, children of the, 9
Grief, 337–342
"Grief work," 337, 340
Gulf War Veterans
    and depression, 314–315
    and lack of social support, 314–315
Gutmann's theory of gender crossover, 149,
    258–259

H

Hair loss and thinning, 42
Hair transplant, 42
Hardiness
    and quality of life, 360–361
    in resilience, 318–319
Harvard men, study of
    see Grant Study of Harvard Men
Hayflick limit, 35
Health
    and age-related cognitive change,
        122–123
    and life-long singles, 156–157
    and marriage, 142–144
    and personality traits, 244–245
    and quality of life, 360
    and timing of retirement, 225
    health and religion, 273–275
Health conditions, mental
    (See mental disorders)
Health conditions, physical, 71–81
    acute conditions, 71
    and aging, 80
    and tobacco use, 80
    chronic conditions, 71
    gender differences, 71, 86–88
    morbidity rate, 71
    self-ratings of, 73
Health and Retirement Study, 38
Hearing
    and primary aging, 45
Heart disease
    and stress reactions, 303
    prevalence by gender, 71
hGH (human growth hormone), 54–55
Hierarchy of needs, 259–260
Hispanic American adults
    and health, 90–91
    and obesity, 40
HIV/AIDS
    and spirituality, 275
    and stress, 309–310
    in developing countries, 88
Holland, John, 205–206
Holocaust survivors
    and long-term stress, 308–309
Home care nursing
    and end-of-life care, 332–335
Honolulu Asian Aging Study
    of Alzheimer's disease 79
Hormonal system, 51–55
Hormone replacement therapy, 53–55
Hospice
    approach 333
    care, 332–335
    history of, 323–324
Hostility
    and health, 92–93
Hot flash, 52
Household labor, 220–222
HRT (hormone replacement therapy), 53–55
Human factors research, 115–121
Human growth hormone (HGH), 54–55
Humanistic psychology, 259–262, 288–289
Hyaluronic acid, 41–42

I

IADLs (Instrumental activities of daily
        living), 72
Identity
    in personality development, 248,
        250–251
Immune system, 51
    primary aging of, 51
Impulse control disorders, 84
Income
    in retirement, 226
Individual differences
    in cognitive decline, 122–127
    in death acceptance, 329–332
    in death anxiety, 325–327
    in development, 4
    in health conditions, 86–95
    in primary aging, 60–62
    in quality of life, 360
    in resilience to trauma, 318–319
    in stress-related disorders, 305–309
Inflammation, role of
    in Alzheimer's disease, 79
    in cardiovascular disease, 74
Information processing perspective, 108
Influences on development
    normative age-graded, 7–8
    normative history graded, 8–9
    nonnormative life events, 9–11
Insomnia, 56
Institute for Human Development
    and development of private belief systems,
        272–273
Instrumental activities of daily living
        (IADLs), 72
Instrumental qualities, 135–136
Integrated personality 271
Intellectual activity
    and age-related cognitive change,
        125–126
Intelligence, 102
    age-related changes, 102
    reversing declines in, 107
Intelligence quotient (see IQ)
Interactionist view
    of stability in development, 12–13
Intergenerational effects
    and health, 94
Intergenerational solidarity, 185, 186
Internal change processes, 8
Instrumental activities of daily living
        (IADLs), 115–116
Internal working model
    of attachments, 166
International comparisons
    and quality of life, 360–361
Internet use
    and older adults, 120–121
Intimacy
    in personality development 248, 251–252
Intra-individual variability
    in personality traits, 241–243
Intimate partnerships, 171–185
Inventory of Psychosocial Development
        (IPD), 250–252

IQ, 102–103
    verbal IQ, 102
    performance IQ, 102
    full-scale IQ, 102

J

Japanese social relationships (vs U.S.),
        168–178
Job
    achievement and personality traits
        243–244
    burnout, 214
    expertise, 212
    loss 214–205
    performance and age, 212
    satisfaction and age 213
    training and age 212–213
Judgment and decision making, 114–115

K

Kegan's model of evolutionary truce,
        285–286
King, Jr., Martin Luther, 278
Kohlberg's theory of moral reasoning,
        275–281
    and the quest for meaning, 284–285
Kübler-Ross, Elizabeth, 328–329, 337, 340

L

Labor force, 223
Late adulthood (75 Years and Older)
    age-related cognitive change, 103,
        105–107, 109
    age-related changes in taste and smell,
        46
    causes of death, 70–71
    changing values due to adult children's
        lifestyles, 186–187
    childlessness, 157–158
    effects of earlier divorce, 187–188,
        227–229
    mortality rates, 70
    overall view, 356–358
    personality change, 241
    poverty, 227–229
    social roles, 154–156
Laughter
    in resilience, 319
Learning schema theory, 135
Leaving home (and returning), 137–140
Leisure time interests
    and timing of retirement, 226
Lens, in vision, 43
Lesbian partnerships
    and fear of violence, 184
    and relationship with parents, 184
    civil unions, 183–184
    long-term partnerships, 182–183
    vs heterosexual couples, 183
Libido, 172
Life changes
    and turning points, 368
Life change events, 299
Lifelong singles, 156–157
Life review, 358

Life-span developmental psychology approach, 14
Life-span/life space theory of career development, 202–203
Living alone, in late adulthood, 154
Living arrangements for older adults, 155
Living wills, 327, 335
Loevinger's theory of ego development, 271
 and the quest for meaning, 284–285, 290, 291
 (see also Ego development)
Longitudinal study, 18–19
 compared to cross-sectional study 18–20
 attrition, 20
Long term marriages, 176–178
Long-term store (of memory) 108, 110–112
 episodic memory, 110–111
 procedural memory, 111
 semantic memory, 110–111
Loyola Generativity Scale (LGS), 252–253
Lust, in establishing intimate partnership, 172

M

Macular degeneration, age related, 44–45
 risk factors, 44
Major depression, 83
Marital protection effect, 142
Marital selection effect, 142
Marital status
 and quality of life, 360
Marriage
 age of first, 140–141
 and health, 142–144, 156–157
 and loneliness, 157
 and parenthood, 147–148
 and work, 215–216
 establishing a partnership, 171–176
 "Four Horsemen of the Apocalypse" 179
 "Good" and "Bad" marriages, 178–179
 in middle adulthood, 352–354
 long-term marriages, 176–178
 predictions of success, 178–179
 types of, 179
 vs cohabitation, 179–182
 vs gay and lesbian long term partnerships, 182–184
Maslow's theory of positive well-being, 259–260, 271
 and the quest for meaning, 284–285
Massachusetts Male Aging Study
 and sexual activity, 58–59
Massachusetts Women's Health Study
 and menopause symptoms, 52–53
Masters events
 and aging of athletic abilities, 55
Mastery, sense of
 and quality of life, 360–361
Maternal employment, 216–220
Maternity leave, 218–219
Mate selection, 172–174
Mature adaptation, 256–258
Meaning focused coping, 312–313
Meaning, quest for, 268–270, 275–281

Mean-level change
 in personality traits, 240–241, 242–243
Medical instructions
 adherence to, 116–117
Medication adherence, 116–117
Medication use
 role in cognitive decline, 123
Memory, 107–114
 age-related changes, 107–114
 components of, 108–112
 emotional content 113–114
 in context, 112–114
 long-term store (of memory), 108, 110–112
 primary memory, 109
 reversing declines in, 112
 sensory store (of memory), 108–109
 short-term story (of memory), 108, 109–110
 working memory, 109–110
Mental disorders, 81–86
 onset of, 81–82
 prevalence of, 81–82
 treatment of 85–86
Mental Measures Yearbook, 23
Meta-analysis, 25–26
Microdermabrasion, 41
Middle adulthood (40–64 years)
 age-related cognitive change, 103, 104, 106–107, 111
 caring for aging parents, 151–153
 causes of death, 70–71
 gender roles, 149
 grandparenting, 149–151
 generativity, 252–253
 long-term marriage quality, 177–178
 obesity and quality of life, 38
 overall view of, 352–355
 personal effort toward health, 17–18
 retirement, 222–232
 social roles in, 148–154
Midlife crisis, 354–355
Midlife in the U. S. Study (MIDUS), 17–18
 and blood pressure treatment, 49
 weight and body composition, 37–38
MMPI (Minnesota Multiphasic Personality Inventory), 239
Mood disorders, 83–84
Morality of justice, 280–281
Morality of care, 280–281
Moral reasoning
 development of, 275–281
Morbidity rate, 71
 and marital status, 143–144
Mortality rate, 70–71
 and marital status, 144
 by age in U. S., 70
Mourning, ritual, 336–339
Muscles (see bones and muscles)
Mysticism, 271, 286–287

N

Name-finding failures, 111
National Comorbidity Survey, 81–86

National Institute on Aging
 website design, 120–121
Native American adults
 and health, 90–91
Natural disasters
 and stress reactions, 304–305
NEO Personality Inventory, 239
Nervous system (see Brain and nervous system)
Neurofibrillary tangles
 in Alzheimer's disease 77–78
Neurogenesis, 50
Neurons
 neurogenesis, 50
 plasticity, 50
 pruning, 50
 redundancy, 50
 stem cells, 50
Never-married adults, 156–157
Non-hispanic black adults (see African American adults)
Non-hispanic white adults
 and health 90–91
Nonnormative life events, 9–11
Nontraditional students, 212
Normative age-graded influences, 7–8
Normative history-graded influences, 8–9
Nose reshaping, 41–42
Nuclear families, 185
Nun Study of the School Sisters of Notre Dame, 27–28, 89
 and Alzheimer's disease, 79
 and longevity, 93
Nursing homes
 and end-of-life care, 332–335
 proportion of older adults living in, 72

O

Obesity, 38–40
 among Hispanic immigrants, 40
 and health, 61
Obsessive-compulsive disorder, 82
Occupational gender segregation, 207–209
"Off-time," 359
 in role transitions, 159–160
Older adulthood (65–74 years)
 aerobic exercise, 26
 and job performance, 212
 and job satisfaction, 212–213
 and job training and retraining, 213
 assisted-living facilities, 73
 causes of death, 70–71
 congregate living facilities, 73
 ego development, 255–256
 friendship patterns, 93–94
 mortality rates, 70
 overall review, 355–3356
 preference for aging in place, 72–73
 proportion in nursing homes, 72–73
 proportion community dwelling, 72–73
 sibling relations, 191–194
 treatment for mental disorders, 85
Olfactory membrane, 46
On Death and Dying, 328–329

Onset
    of mental disorders, 81–82
"On time"
    in role transitions, 159–160
Optimism
    and coping, 316
    and health, 93
Oregon's Death With Dignity Act, 335–336
Organ transplant donors, 327–328
Osteoarthritis, 48–49
Osteoarthritis
    exercise, 48–49
    hyaluronic acid, 48
    joint replacement, 48
    prevalence, 71
    treatment for, 48–49
Osteopenia, 47
Osteoporosis, 47–48
Outward appearances
    and primary aging, 37–43
Oxidative damage, theory of, 34
    free radicals, 34
    antioxidants, 34–35

P

Parental imperative, 145
Parent-child relationships in adulthood,
    185–188
Parenting
    and effects on marriage, 147–148
    and gender roles, 146–147
    and work, 216–220
    in young adulthood, 144–148
Patient adherence
    to bone loss treatment, 47–48
Peak experiences, in Maslow's theory,
    259–260
Peak bone mass, 47
Pensions
    as source of income in retirement,
    226–227
Personal computer use
    and older adults, 120–121
Personal interview, 22
Personality development, 248–262
    and turning points, 368
Personality factors, 238–248
Personality states, 239
Personality traits
    and death anxiety, 326–327
    and health, 92–93, 244–245
    and job achievement, 243–244
    and relationships, 243
Person-environment transactions, 246–247
Phased retirement, 231–232
Physical behavior
    and primary aging, 55–60
Physical changes (see Primary aging)
Physician assisted suicide, 335–336
Plaques
    in Alzheimer's disease, 77–78
    in cardiovascular disease, 74–75
Plasticity, of neurons, 50
Plastic surgery, 41–42
Positive emotion
    in resilience 319

Positive psychology, 260
Positive well-being
    and personality development, 259–262
Postformal stages of cognitive development,
    269
Post-traumatic stress syndrome (PTSD)
    and gender, 306–307
    and resilience, 317–319
    and stress reactions 304–305
Poverty
    in retirement, 227–229
Presbyopia, and age, 43
    risk factors, 44
Prescription drug use
    age related changes in, 116–117
Preparation for retirement, 222–223
Prevalence
    of chronic health conditions, 71–72
    of mental disorders, 81–82
Primary aging
    individual differences in, 60–62
    of bones and muscles, 46–49
    of outward appearance, 37–43
    of physical behavior, 55–60
    of the brain and nervous system, 50–51
    of the cardiovascular and Respiratory sys-
    tem, 49–50
    of the hormonal system, 51–55
    of the immune system, 51.
    overview, review table, 62–63
    theories of, 34–37
    turning back the clock, 62
Primary memory, 109
Principles for a successful marriage, 181
Private belief system
    changes in adulthood, 271–273
Pro-active coping, 313
Problem focused coping, 310
Procedural memory, 111
Progesterone, 52
Propecia (finasteride), 42
Proximal causes, 135
Pruning, of neurons, 50
Psychological age, 13
Psychological health, 362
Psychometrics, 102
Psychosocial adjustment,
    predicting from childhood, 362–364
Psychosocial development, 248–253
Psychosocial factors
    and quality of life, 360–361
PTSD (see Post-traumatic stress syndrome)
Pupil, in vision, 43

Q

Qualitative research, 27
Quality of life, 360
Quantitative research, 27
Quest for meaning, 268–270
    theories of, 275–281

R

Racial and ethnic differences
    and living arrangements in late adult-
    hood, 154
    and poverty in retirement, 227

    in cohabitation rates, 141
    in grandparenting practices, 190
    in health, 90–91
    in quality of life, 360
    in spiritual development, 271
Racial discrimination
    and health care, 91–92
    and stress reactions, 308–309
Real-world cognition, 114–115
    judgment, 114–115
    decision making, 114–115
Recovery from trauma, 317–319
Redundancy
    of neurons, 50
Relationships
    and personality traits, 243
Reliability, 23
Religion and health, 273–275
Religiosity, 270–271
    and death anxiety, 325–326
    theories of, 275–281
Religious coping, 314
Remarriage, 158–159
Reminiscence, 327
Replicative senescence, 35
Research in developmental psychology,
    16–28
Research analyses, 23–26
    comparison of means, 23–24
    correlational analysis, 24–25
    meta-analysis, 25–26
Research designs, 26–28
    experimental designs, 27
    descriptive research, 27
    qualitative research, 27
    quantitative research, 27
Research measures, 22–23
    personal interview, 22
    survey questionnaire, 22
    standardized tests, 22–23
    validity, 23
    reliability, 23
Research methods, 17–22
Reserve capacity, 358
Residence
    changes at retirement, 229–230
Resilience
    as outcome of trauma, 317–318
    as reaction to death, 340–342
    individual differences, 318–319
Resistance resources, 310
Respiratory system
    primary aging of, 49–50
Response-oriented viewpoint, of stress,
    299
Restylane, 41–42
Retina, in vision, 43
Retin-A (tretinoin), 41
Retirement, 222–232
    effects of, 226–230
    nonstandard types of, 230–232
    preparation for, 222–223
    reasons for, 224–226
    timing of, 223–224
Retirement related value
    in retirement decisions, 225

Return to work after retirement, 230
Review
    of career changes over adulthood, 232
    of cognitive changes over adulthood,
        127–128
    of health and illness over adulthood, 95
    of overall adult development, 349
    of relationships over adulthood, 195
    of social roles in adulthood 160
Risk factors
    for Alzheimer's disease, 79
    for cancer, 76
    for cardiovascular disease, 74–75
    for hearing loss, 45
    for osteoarthritis, 48
    for osteoporosis, 47–48
    for taste and smell loss, 46
    for vision loss, 44–45
Ritual mourning, 336–339
Rogaine (monoxidil), 42
Roles
    social, 134
    gender 134–137
Role transitions, 134, 367–368

S
"Sandwich generation", 153–154
Saunders, Dame Cicely, 323–324
Schaivo, Terry, 327
Schooling
    and age-related cognitive change,
        124–125
    and ego development, 255–256
Seasonal migration, 229–230
Seattle Longitudinal Study, 103
Secondary aging, 34
Selective optimization with compensation,
    358
Self-actualization, in Maslow's theory,
    259–260, 271
Self-determination theory, 260–262
Self-ratings of health, 73
Self-transcendence, 268–269, 286, 288
Semantic memory, 110–111
Senescence, replicative, 35
Sense of purpose in life, 326
Sensorineural hearing loss, 45
Sensory store (of memory), 108–109
September 11th, 2001 terrorist attack,
    9–11
Sequential research design, 20–22
Sexual activity, and primary aging, 57–60
    desire, lack of, 59–60
    frequency of intercourse, 57
    physical ability, lack of, 58–59
    privacy, lack of, 60
    sexual Partner, lack of, 60
Shared experiences, 7
Shift work
    and marriage, 216
Short-term store (of memory) 108, 109–110
    primary memory, 109
    working memory, 109–110
Shunning retirement, 230
Sibling relationship in adulthood, 191–193
Sibling rivalry in adulthood, 186

Siblings
    as caregivers for aging parents, 151–153
Single fathers, living arrangements, 145–146
Single mothers, birthrates, 144–145
Singles, lifelong, 156–157
Sixteen Personality Factor Questionnaire,
    239
Skin and Hair
    primary aging of, 41–43
Sleep, 56–57
"Snowbirds," 229–230
Social age, 13
Social clock, 7, 134, 352–253
    and childless adults, 157–158
Social comparisons
    and quality of life, 360–361
Social coping, 312
Social integration
    and quality of life, 360–361
Social relationships
    age-related changes in, 166
    theories of, 166–171
Social roles, 134
Social role theory, 135
Social security
    as source of retirement income, 226–227
Social support
    as aid to coping, 314–316
    negative effects of, 316
Social timing of role transitions, 159–160
Sociobiographical history
    and age-related cognitive change, 124
Socioeconomic level
    and health, 89–92
    and quality of life, 360
Socioemotional selectivity theory of social re-
    lationships, 170
Spirituality
    and turning points, 368
    changes in adulthood, 271–273
    theories of, 275–281
Stability/disequilibrium, 5
    in life structures, 366–368
    sources of, 11–13
Stages, in development, 6
Stamina, and primary aging, 56
Standardized tests, 22–23
Steindl-Rast, David, 342
Stepmother role, 159
Stem cells, 50
Stereotypes
    gender, 134–137
Stereotype threat, 113–114
Stimulus-oriented viewpoint, of stress, 299
Stress
    and marital conflict, 143–144
    and mental disorders 304–305
    and physical disease, 302–304
    and resilience, 317–319
    and the immune system, 298–300
    coping with, 310–317
    effects of, 302–310
    theories of, 298–299
    types of, 300–302
Stress reactions, 298
Stress related growth, 309–310

Stressors, 298
Study of Women's Health Across the Nation
    (SWAN), 89
    and menopause symptoms, 52
Subjective evaluation
    of age-related cognitive change, 127
Subjective well-being, 360
Substance abuse disorders, 84–85
Successful aging, 360
Super, Donald, 202–203
Surrogate parenting, by grandparents,
    150–151
Survey questionnaire, 22
Swedish Twins Registry, 25
    and cognitive decline, 123–124
    and gender differences in health, 87
    and career choice, 211
    and Alzheimer's disease, 78

T
Tasma, David, 323–324
Taste and smell, changes with age, 46
Taste buds, 46
T cells, 51
Telomeres
    age related changes in, 35–36
    in stressed caregivers, 35–36
Testosterone, 51–52
    and depression, 87
    and impulse control, 87
    treatment for women, 59
Theories
    attachment theory of social relationships,
        166–168
    Baltes' life-span developmental psychol-
        ogy approach, 14–16
    biosocial perspective of gender roles, 135
    Bowlby's theory of grief, 337, 340
    Bowlby's theory of attachment, 166–168
    Bronfenbrenner's ecological systems ap-
        proach, 16–17
    convoy model of social relationships,
        168–170
    developmental origins hypothesis, 94
    Erikson's theory of psychosocial develop-
        ment 248–253
    evolutionary psychology theory and social
        relationships, 170–171
    evolutionary psychology theory of gender
        roles, 135
    exchange theory of intimate partnerships,
        173
    filter theory of intimate partnerships, 173
    Fowler's theory of faith development,
        281–285
    gender crossover, 258–259
    Gilligan's proposal on moral development,
        280–281
    Holland's theory of career selection
        205–207
    Kohlberg's theory of moral reasoning,
        275–281
    learning schema theory of gender roles,
        135
    Loevinger's theory of ego development,
        253–256

Theories (*continued*)
    Maslow's theory of positive well-being, 259–260, 271, 284–285
    of primary aging, 34–37
    of reactions to stress, 298–299
    self-determination, 260–262
    social role theory of gender roles, 135
    socioemotional selectivity theory of social relationships, 170
    Super's theory of career development 202–203
    Vaillant's theory of mature adaptation, 256–258
Timing of retirement, 223–224
    in European countries, 224
Timing of role transitions, 159–160
Tobacco use, 80
Traits, personality, 238–248
Transition
    in social roles, 134, 367–368
    in spiritual development, 287–289
    to adulthood, 137
    to parenthood, 144–148
Trauma
    reactions to, 317
Truth About Human Aging (The), 62
Turning back the clock, 62
Turning points, 367–368
Twin studies, 12
    of body weight and body composition, 40
    of cognitive decline, 123–124
    of marital happiness, 25
    of personality structures, 245–246
Type A behavior pattern
    and health, 92
Typical development, 6

U

Underhill's descriptions of mysticism, 286–287
Unemployment, 214–215
Useful field of view (UFOV),
    age related changes, 118
    reversing declines, 119–120
U. S. Food and Drug Administration
    and hGH therapy, 54–55
    and testosterone treatment for women, 59

U. S. National Health Interview Study, 73

V

Vaillant's theory of mature adaptation, 256–258
Viagra (sildenafil citrate), 58–59
Vaginal dryness
    and decline of sexual activity, 58–59
    and estrogen creams and patches, 59
Validity, 23
Varieties of Religious Experience (The), 270
Vision and hearing, role of in cognitive decline, 122
Vision, and primary aging, 43–45
Visual acuity, and age, 43
Vitamin D
    and bone loss, 47
Vitamins and nutritional supplements, 51
Vocational interest
    types, 205–207
    stability of, 205–206
Volunteer work after retirement, 231

W

Waddington's epigenetic landscape, 365–366
Website designs
    and older adults, 120–121
Weight and body composition
    in primary aging, 37–40
White adults (see Non-Hispanic white adults)
Widows
    and positive emotion, 319
    and retirement income, 227–229
    living alone, 319
    resilience of, 317–318
Wisdom, 260
Women
    and cardiovascular disease, 75
    and depression worldwide, 83
    and osteoporosis, 46–47
    career patterns, 203–205
    career choices, 207–209
    effects of food insufficiency, 90–91
    equality and depression, 87–88
    hormone replacement therapy, 53–54

    lack of medical research about, 88–89
    menopause, 52–53
    poverty in late adulthood
    professional degrees, 208–209
Women's Health Initiative (WHI), 89
Word-finding failures, 111
Work
    and personal life, 213–222
    family influences, 209–211
    gender differences 203–205, 207–209
    genetic influences, 211
    importance of, 202
    in middle adulthood, 352–354
    nontraditional careers, 207–209
    older workers, 211–213
    theories of, 202–203
Working memory, 109–110
Working model of attachment, 167
Work-related value
    in retirement decisions, 224–225
World Health Organization (WHO)
    report on tobacco use, 80
    report on depression in women, 83
    report on world mortality rates, 70
Wrinkles, 41–42
WWII Veterans
    and stress-related growth, 309

Y

Young adulthood (20–39 years)
    birthrates for single mothers, 144–145
    career choices, 144–145
    causes of death, 70
    cohabitation, 179–182
    death rates, 70
    identity stage, 248, 250–251
    industry (work ethic), 20–22
    intimacy stage, 248, 251–252
    leaving (and returning) home, 137–140
    marriage stability, 176
    mate selections, 172–175
    overall view of, 350–352
    relationships with grandparents, 189
    relationship with siblings, 191
    self-esteem, 19–20
    transition to adulthood, 137
    transition to marriage, 140–142